ien and
fascism
pain. It
efs they
fascism
minant
nation"
" could
We also
nation
iolence
ll social
uggests
ope and
ts of its
though

ngeles,

Advance praise for *Fascists:*

"Michael Mann is the outstanding historical sociologist of his generation. He invariably asks penetrating questions and his rigorous comparative method enables him to reach novel and striking conclusions. He has now produced one of the most original studies of Fascism ever written, a brilliant and disturbing analysis which constitutes a seminal work on the most destructive political phenomenon of the modern era."

> – Sir Ian Kershaw, Professor of Modern History, University of Sheffield

"Fascism was one of the characteristic political movements that affected Europe in the epoch following the First World War. Although the Fascists attained power and their greatest notoriety in Italy and Germany, several other countries had fascist parties. All such movements shared certain obvious features, even though they exhibited important differences. Recently, however, the comparative study of fascism has been pushed to the margins, and for more than a decade the approach largely fell out of fashion in favor of investigations of particular cases and specific themes. Professor Mann reverses the trend. He deals not only with the movements inspired and led by Mussolini and Hitler, but with events in Austria, Spain, Hungary and Romania. His social-science-oriented and comparative account focuses on the rise to power of the various fascist parties. This incisively written and boldly argued book is full of insights and offers many challenges to the specialists. Mann breathes fresh life into this complex topic, and this study is bound to stimulate renewed discussion across the disciplines."

> – Robert Gellately, Earl Ray Beck Professor of History,
> Florida State University

"Michael Mann here applies his legendary combination of historical sweep, synthetic verve, and common sense to a major unsolved problem: what and why was European fascism? We leave his company much the wiser."

> – Charles Tilly, Joseph L. Buttenwieser Professor of Social Science,
> Columbia University

"Mann's newest book provides fascinating insights into the sources of European fascism. Erudite and theoretical, yet plain-speaking, Mann analyzes the beliefs and actions of fascists themselves, coming to the conclusion that youth culture and society across class played a critical part in this ultimately self-destructive movement."

> – Norman Naimark, Robert and Florence McDonnell Professor
> of History, Stanford University

Fascists

MICHAEL MANN

University of California, Los Angeles

CAMBRIDGE
UNIVERSITY PRESS

PUBLISHED BY THE PRESS SYNDICATE OF THE UNIVERSITY OF CAMBRIDGE
The Pitt Building, Trumpington Street, Cambridge, United Kingdom

CAMBRIDGE UNIVERSITY PRESS
The Edinburgh Building, Cambridge CB2 2RU, UK
40 West 20th Street, New York, NY 10011-4211, USA
477 Williamstown Road, Port Melbourne, VIC 3207, Australia
Ruiz de Alarcón 13, 28014 Madrid, Spain
Dock House, The Waterfront, Cape Town 8001, South Africa

http://www.cambridge.org

First published 2004

Printed in the United States of America

Typeface Bembo 11/13 pt.   *System* LATEX 2$_\varepsilon$ [TB]

A catalog record for this book is available from the British Library.

Library of Congress Cataloging in Publication Data

Mann, Michael, 1942–
Fascists / Michael Mann.
p. cm.
Includes bibliographical references and index.
ISBN 0-521-83131-8 (HB) – ISBN 0-521-53855-6 (pbk.)
1. Fascism – Europe – History. 2. Radicalism – Europe – History – 20th century.
3. Nationalism. 4. Paramilitary forces. 5. State, The. I. Title.
D726.5.M34   2004
335.6′094′0904–dc22   2003063966

ISBN 0 521 83131 8 hardback
ISBN 0 521 53855 6 paperback

Contents

Preface

I originally designed this study of fascism as a single chapter in a general book about the twentieth century, the third volume of my *The Sources of Social Power*. But my third volume still remains to be written, since fascism grew and grew to absorb my entire attention span over seven years. My "fascist chapter" was to be written first, since I was at that time spending a year in a Madrid institute with a fine library collection on the interwar struggle between democracy and authoritarianism. But then my research on fascism grew to the size of a whole book. I realized with a sinking heart (since this is not a pleasant subject on which to work for years) that it had to grow yet further. Since the deeds of fascists and their fellow-travelers culminated in mass murder, I had to engage with a second large body of literature, on the events centering on "The Final Solution" or "Holocaust." I soon realized that these two bodies of literature – on fascists and their genocides – had little in common. Fascism and the mass murders committed during World War II have been mostly kept in separate scholarly and popular compartments inhabited by different theories, different data, different methods. These compartments have mostly kept them segregated from other rather similar phenomena of murderous cleansing that have been regularly recurring across the modern period – from seventeenth-century America to the mid-twentieth-century Soviet Union, to Rwanda-Burundi and Yugoslavia at the very end of the twentieth century.

All these three main forms of deeply depressing human behavior – fascism, "the Holocaust," and ethnic and political cleansing more generally – share a family resemblance. This resemblance has been given by three main ingredients most openly revealed in fascism: *organic nationalism, radical statism,* and *paramilitarism.* Ideally, the entire family should be discussed together. But being of an empiricist bent, I felt I had to discuss them in some detail.

This would have generated a book of near 1,000 pages, which perhaps few would read – and which no publisher would publish.

So I have broken my overall study into two. This volume concerns fascists, centering on their rise to power in interwar Europe. My forthcoming volume, *The Dark Side of Democracy: Explaining Ethnic Cleansing*, concerns the whole swath of modern ethnic and political cleansing, from colonial times through Armenia and Nazi genocides to the present day. The weakness of this particular division between the two volumes is that the "careers" of the worst types of fascists, especially Nazis, but also their collaborators, are broken up between two volumes. Their rise is traced in this volume, their final deeds in my other volume. The advantage of this division is that the final deeds of these fascists appear alongside others with whom they share a genuine family resemblance – colonial militias, the Turkish Special Forces of 1915, the Cambodian Angka, the Red Guards, Hutu Interahamwe, Arkan's Tigers, and so on. Indeed, popular speech, especially among their enemies and victims, recognizes this kinship by denouncing them all as "Fascists!" – a rather imprecise but nonetheless justifiable term of abuse. For these are brutal men and women using murderous paramilitary means to attain, albeit rather crudely voiced, goals of organic nationalism and/or radical statism (all qualities of fascism proper). Scholars tend to reject this broad label of "Fascist!" – preferring to reserve the term (without exclamation mark) for those adhering to a rather more tightly structured doctrine. Since I also have pretensions to scholarship, I suppose I must ultimately share this preference for conceptual precision. But deeds can share commonality as well as doctrine. This volume concerns fascists as scholars understand the term; my other volume concerns perpetrators and "Fascists!" in the more popular, looser sense of the word.

I have greatly benefited from the advice and criticism of colleagues in writing this book. I wish to especially thank Ivan Berend, Ronald Fraser, Bernt Hagtvet, John Hall, Ian Kershaw, Stanley Payne, and Dylan Riley. I thank the Instituto Juan March in Madrid for its hospitality during the first year of research for this book, and the Sociology Department of the University of California at Los Angeles for providing a very congenial home throughout.

1

A Sociology of Fascist Movements

This book seeks to explain fascism by understanding fascists – who they were, where they came from, what their motivations were, how they rose to power. I focus here on the rise of fascist movements rather than on established fascist regimes. I investigate fascists at their flood tide, in their major redoubts in interwar Europe, that is, in Austria, Germany, Hungary, Italy, Romania, and Spain. To understand fascists will require understanding fascist movements. We can understand little of individual fascists and their deeds unless we appreciate that they were joined together into distinctive power organizations. We must also understand them amid their broader twentieth-century context, in relation to general aspirations for more effective states and greater national solidarity. For fascism is neither an oddity nor merely of historical interest. Fascism has been an essential if predominantly undesirable part of modernity. At the beginning of the twenty-first century there are seven reasons still to take fascists very seriously.

(1) Fascism was not a mere sideshow in the development of modern society. Fascism spread through much of the European heartland of modernity. Alongside environmentalism, it was the major political doctrine of world-historical significance created during the twentieth century. There is a chance that something quite like it, though almost certainly under another name, will play an important role in the twenty-first century. Fascists have been at the heart of modernity.

(2) Fascism was not a movement set quite apart from other modern movements. Fascists only embraced more fervently than anyone else the central political icon of our time, the nation-state, together with its ideologies and pathologies. We are thankful that today much of the world lives under rather mild nation-states, with modest, useful powers, embodying only

a fairly harmless nationalism. National government bureaucracies annoy us but they do not terrorize us – indeed, they predominantly serve our needs. Nationalism usually also appears in comforting domesticated forms. Though French people often proclaim themselves as culturally superior, Americans assert they are the freest people on Earth, and the Japanese claim a unique racial homogeneity, these highly suspect beliefs comfort themselves, amuse foreigners, and rarely harm anyone else.

Fascism represents a kind of second-level escalation beyond such "mild nation-statism." The first escalation came in two parallel forms, one concerning the nation, the other the state. Regarding the nation, aspirations for democracy became entwined with the notion of the "integral" or "organic" nation. "The people" must rule, but this people was considered as one and indivisible and so might violently exclude from itself minority ethnic groups and political "enemies" (see my forthcoming volume, *The Darkside of Democracy*, chap. 1, for more analysis of this). Regarding the state, the early twentieth century saw the rise of a more powerful state, seen as "the bearer of a moral project," capable of achieving economic, social, and moral development.[1] In certain contexts this involved the rise of more authoritarian states. The combination of modern nationalism and statism was to turn democratic aspirations on their head, into authoritarian regimes seeking to "cleanse" minorities and opponents from the nation. Fascism, the second-level escalation, added to this combination mainly a distinctively "bottom-up" and "radical" paramilitary movement. This would overcome all opposition to the organic nation-state with violence from below, at whatever the cost. Such glorification of actual violence had emerged as a consequence of the modern "democratization" of war into one between "citizen armies." Fascism thus presented a distinctively paramilitary extreme version of nation-statism (my actual definition of fascism is given below in this chapter). It was only the most extreme version of the dominant political ideology of our era.

(3) Fascist ideology must be taken seriously, in its own terms. It must not be dismissed as crazy, contradictory, or vague. Nowadays, this is quite widely accepted. Zeev Sternhell (1986: x) has remarked that fascism had "a body of doctrine no less solid or logically indefensible than that of any other political movement." Consequently, said George Mosse (1999: x), "only . . . when we have grasped fascism from the inside out, can we truly judge its appeal and its power." Since fascists did offer plausible solutions to modern social problems, they got mass electoral support and intense emotional commitment from militants. Of course, like most political activists, fascists were diverse and opportunistic. The importance of leadership and

power in fascism enhanced opportunism. Fascist leaders were empowered to do almost anything to seize power, and this could subvert other fascist values. Yet most fascists, leaders or led, believed in certain things. They were not people of peculiar character, sadists or psychopaths, or people with a "rag-bag" of half-understood dogmas and slogans flitting through their heads (or no more so than the rest of us). Fascism was a movement of high ideals, able to persuade a substantial part of two generations of young people (especially the highly educated) that it could bring about a more harmonious social order. To understand fascism, I adopt a methodology of taking fascists' values seriously. Thus each of my case-study chapters begins by explaining local fascist doctrine, followed, if possible, by an account of what ordinary fascists seem to have believed.

(4) We must take seriously the social constituency of fascist movements and ask what sorts of people were drawn to them. Few fascists were marginals or misfits. Nor were they confined to classes or other interest groups who found in fascism a "cover" for their narrow material interests. Yet there were "core fascist constituencies" among which fascist values most resonated. This is perhaps the most original part of this book, yielding a new view of fascism, and it derives from a methodology of taking fascist values seriously. For the core fascist constituency enjoyed particularly close relations to the sacred icon of fascism, the nation-state. We must reconstruct that nation-state–loving constituency in order to see what kinds of people might be tempted toward fascism.

(5) We must also take seriously fascist movements. They were hierarchical yet comradely, embodying both the leadership principle and a constraining "social cage," both of which heightened commitment, especially by single young men for whom the movement was almost a "total institution." We must also appreciate its paramilitarism, since "popular violence" was crucial to its success. Fascist movements also changed as they were tempted by two different prospects. One was to use power in more and more radical and violent ways. The other was to enjoy the fruits of power by compromising under the table with powerful traditional elites. These led toward either a hardening of fascism (as in Germany) or a softening (as in Italy, at least until the late 1930s). Fascists also experienced "careers" in the movement, which might lead them down either path. We must observe fascists in action: committing violence, trimming, pursuing careers.

(6) We must take "hardened" fascists seriously in a far more sinister sense, as the eventual perpetrators of great evil. We must not excuse or relativize this but seek to understand it. The capacity for evil is an essential human attribute, and so is our capacity to commit evil for what we believe to be

moral purposes. Fascists were especially self-deluded. We need to know more of the circumstances in which we humans do this. Though we prefer to write history and sociology as a happy, progressive, moral tale, this grotesquely distorts the reality of human experience. The twentieth century saw massive evil, not as an accident or as the resurgence of the primitive in us, but as willed, purposive, and essentially "modern" behavior. To understand fascism is to understand how people of apparently high modernizing ideals could then act to produce evil that was eventually unmitigated. However, I leave the very worst for my forthcoming book, *The Dark Side of Democracy*.

(7) We must take seriously the chance that fascists might return. If we understand the conditions that generated fascists, we can better understand whether they might return and how we might avoid this. Some of the conditions that generated fascism are still present. Organic nationalism and the adoption of paramilitary forms, committed to ethnic and political cleansing, at present moves many thousands of people across the world to commit supposedly "idealistic" yet in reality murderous acts against neighbours and political opponents whom they call "enemies." This may horrify us, but it is not dismissible as a return to the "primitive" in us. Ethnic and political cleansing has been one of European civilization's main contributions to modernity; while violent paramilitarism has been distinctively twentieth-century. We must comprehend these aspects of modernity. It is rather fortunate nowadays that "statism" (the third main component of fascism after organic nationalism and paramilitarism) is greatly out of fashion, since both its historic carriers, fascism and communism, collapsed disastrously. Current cleansing regimes tend to be paramilitary and authoritarian, but pretend they are democratic; the words "fascist" and "communist" have largely become terms of imprecise abuse. Given time for a supposedly stateless neoliberalism to do similar damage to parts of the world, this rejection of the powerful state will probably fade. Then extreme statist values might be harnessed again to extreme paramilitary nationalism in movements resembling fascism – unless we can learn from the history I record here. I doubt new movements will call themselves fascist, since the word is now so abhorred. Yet some of the substance of fascism lives on.

There are two main schools of thought on fascism. A more idealist "nationalist school," which I discuss first, has focused on fascists' beliefs and doctrines, while a more materialist "class school," discussed second, has focused on its class basis and its relationship to capitalism. The debates between them constitute yet another replay of the traditional polemic between idealism and materialism in the social sciences. But since the two approaches often appear to be discussing different levels of phenomena – beliefs versus social base/functions – they frequently talk past each other. Thus we lack an acceptable general theory of fascism. Such a theory would have to build on top of both approaches, taking from each what is useful and adding what both neglect.

I have chosen not to here give the reader a heavy dose of sociological theory. But my own approach to fascism derives from a more general model of human societies that rejects the idealism-versus-materialism dualism. My earlier work identified four primary "sources of social power" in human societies: ideological, economic, military, and political.[2] Class theorists of fascism have tended to elevate economic power relations in their explanations, while nationalist theorists have emphasized ideology. Yet all four sources of social power are needed to explain most important social and historical outcomes. To attain their goals, social movements wield combinations of control over ultimate meaning systems (ideological), control over means of production and exchange (economic), control over organized physical violence (military), and control over centralized and territorial institutions of regulation (political). All four are necessary to explain fascism. Mass fascism was a response to the post–World War I ideological, economic, military, and political crises. Fascists proposed solutions to all four. Fascist organization also combined substantial ideological innovations (generally called "propaganda"), mass political electoralism, and paramilitary violence. All became highly ritualized so as to intensify emotional commitment. In attempting to seize power, fascist leaders also sought to neutralize economic, military, political, and ideological (especially church) elites. Thus any explanation of fascism must rest on the entwining of all four sources of social power, as my empirical case-study chapters demonstrate. My final chapter presents the pay-off from this model: a general explanation of fascism.

TOWARD A DEFINITION OF FASCISM

Obviously, we must define our terms, though this is no easy matter. Some scholars have refused to define fascism at all in any "generic" sense, believing that "true" fascism was found only in Italy, its original home. Along with many others, I disagree. However, I do not initially seek a generic definition that might apply across many times and places. I merely seek one offering heuristic utility across the interwar period in Europe – until my last chapter, when I raise the issue of whether fascist movements have existed in more recent times and in other places.

Let us first get a general sense of fascism through the views of its prominent intellectuals, with the commentaries of Sternhell (1976, 1986, 1994)
and Mosse (1999), plus Griffin's compilation of fascist texts (1995), as my
main guides. Most of them were initially nonmaterialist leftists who then
embraced organic nationalism. In 1898 the Frenchman Barrès called his fusion "Socialist Nationalism," though it was the Italian Corradini's inversion
of these words, as "National Socialism," which caught on, though by socialism he really meant syndicalism: "Syndicalism and nationalism together,
these are the doctrines that represent solidarity," he emphasized. Class and
sectoral conflict could be harmonized with the help of syndicalist (labor
union) organizations coordinated by a "corporate state." So national socialism would be confined within national boundaries, with class struggle
transformed into struggle between nations. "Bourgeois nations" (such as
Britain and France) exploited "proletarian nations" (such as Italy). To resist,
the proletarian nation must fight, with economic weapons and through "the
sacred mission of imperialism." Except for the last phrase, this resembles the
"third world socialism" of recent years. These were not uncommon ideas
in the twentieth century.

As leftists but not materialists, these men also lauded "resistance,"
"will," "movement," "collective action," "the masses," and the dialectic of
"progress" through "struggle," "force," and "violence." These Nietzschean
values made fascism "radical." Fascists were determined to overcome all
opposition ruthlessly, by will, force, whatever was necessary, without compromise or scruples. This meant in practice forming paramilitaries as well
as parties. As collectivists they despised the "amoral individualism" of free
market liberalism and "bourgeois democracy," which neglected the interests of "living communities" and of "the nation as an organic whole." The
nation was essentially one and indivisible, a living and breathing entity, defined as either "integral" or "organic." To be German, Italian, or French,
fascists asserted, meant much more than just living in a geographical space; it
meant something outsiders could not experience, involving a basic identity
and emotion, beyond reason. As Mosse emphasizes, the Germanic version
of the nation differed from the Southern European, being racial as well
as cultural. It drew more on social Darwinism, anti-Semitism, and other
nineteenth-century racialist strands of theory to generate a *Volk*, a singular ethnic-cultural unity transcending all possible conflicts within it, but
erecting higher boundaries against other peoples.

Nonetheless, the nation had both a moral and a rational structure. Building on Rousseau and Durkheim, the theorists said that competitive institutions such as markets, parties, elections, or classes could not generate

morality. This must come from the community, the nation. The Frenchman Berth railed against liberalism: "Society is brought to the point where it is only a market made up of free-trading atoms, in contact with which every-thing dissolves.... dustlike particles of individuals, shut up within the nar-row confines of their consciousness and their money boxes." Panunzio and Bottai followed Durkheim in praising the virtues of "civil society," believing that voluntary communal associations were the foundations of liberty. Yet they must be integrated into an overall corporate state that would then rep-resent the interests of the nation as a whole. Without this linkage between state and communal associations, they said, the state would be "empty," with "a deficiency of sociological content," as was the case in the liberal state (Riley 2002: chap. 1). In contrast, the fascist state would be "corpo-rate" and "sociological," based on strong bonds of association. Again, this sounds quite modern. Berth and Panunzio might have been targeting the neo-liberalism dominant a hundred years later.

Fascist intellectuals also attacked a left trapped within passive "bourgeois materialism." Its revolutionary pretensions had been exposed, they argued, by the superior mobilizing power of modern warfare between entire na-tions. Nations, not classes, were the true masses of modernity. Class conflict between capitalists and workers was not the core of the problem, they in-sisted. Instead, the real struggle was between "workers of all classes," "the productive classes," ranged against "unproductive" enemies, usually iden-tified as finance or foreign or Jewish capitalists. They would defend the productive workers of all classes. The Frenchman Valois wrote that "na-tionalism + socialism = fascism," and the Englishman Oswald Mosley said, "If you love our country, you are national, and if you love our people you are socialist." These were attractive ideas in the early twentieth century, the "age of the masses," since fascists promised to "transcend" a class struggle then seemingly tearing apart the social fabric. Indeed, milder versions of such claims to transcendence have been adopted by most of the successful political movements of the twentieth century.

The nation should be represented through a corporatist, syndicalist state. It could "transcend" the moral decay and class conflict of bourgeois so-ciety with a "total plan" offering a statist "third way" between capitalism and socialism. The Italian Gentile (a late convert to fascism) claimed that fascism resolved the "paradox of liberty and authority. The authority of the state is absolute." Mussolini agreed: "[E]verything in the State, nothing against the State, nothing outside the State." "Ours will be a totalitarian state in the service of the fatherland's integrity," proclaimed the Spaniard José Antonio Primo de Rivera. The Belgian Henri de Man applauded "authoritarian democracy." The "fascist revolution" would produce "the total man in the total society, with no clashes, no prostration, no anarchy." said the Frenchman Déat.

But this was the future. Right now, the nation must struggle against its enemies for self-realization. It would be led by a paramilitary elite. The more radical fascists endorsed "moral murder." They claimed that paramilitary violence could "cleanse," "purify," "regenerate" the elite who committed it, then the nation as a whole. Valois expressed this brutally:

> to the bourgeois brandishing his contracts and statistics:
> – two plus three makes. . . .
> – Nought, the Barbarian replies, smashing his head in.

For Valois the "barbarian" fascist represented morality since he alone represented the organic community of the nation, from which all moral values flow. Of course, for these intellectuals, inhabiting the same post-Nietzschean world that generated vitalism, surrealism, and Dadaism, much of this was just literary metaphor. Yet rank-and-file fascists were later to use these justifications of their activities.

O'Sullivan (1983: 33–69) notes that fascists hated the "limited" nature of liberal democracy, its imperfect, indirect, and only "representative" (rather than "direct") form of rule. Liberal democracy tolerates conflicts of interest, "smoke-filled rooms," "wheeler-dealing," and "dirty" and "unprincipled" compromises. Acceptance of imperfections and compromise is actually the essence of both liberal democracy and social democracy. This reduces the stature of potential "enemies" into mere "opponents" with whom deals might be struck. Liberal and social democracies recognize no monopoly of virtue, no absolute truth. They are antiheroic. I have learned from writing these two books not to expect our democratic politicians to be too principled. We need their instrumentalism, their dirty deals. But fascists differed. They saw politics as unlimited activism to achieve moral absolutes. In Max Weber's terms, this was "value rationality," conduct oriented toward the achievement of absolute values, not merely instrumental interests.

This brought a higher emotional content. Fascism saw itself as a *crusade*. Fascists did not view evil as a universal tendency of human nature. Fascists, like some Marxists, believed that evil was embedded in particular social institutions and so could be shed. The nation was perfectible if organic and cleansed. As O'Sullivan notes, the Romanian fascist leader Codreanu was an extreme example of this. He saw his "Legion of the Archangel Michael" as a moral force: "All [other] political organizations . . . believe that the country was dying because of lack of good programs; consequently they put together a perfectly jelled program with which they start to assemble supporters." In contrast, said Codreanu, "This country is dying of lack of men, not of programs." "We must have men, new men." Thus the Legion would free Romania from "the power of evil." It would contain "heroes," "[t]he finest souls that our minds can conceive, the proudest, tallest, straightest, strongest, cleverest, bravest and most hardworking that our race can produce." They must fight against the "enemies" polluting the nation (Codreanu 1990: 219–21). He believed that in defense of good against evil, violence was morally legitimate.

Obviously, however, to understand fascists we must move beyond the intellectuals. How could the ideas quoted above stir millions of Europeans into action? What conditions of real life made such extraordinary sentiments seem plausible? Sternhell tends to see fascism as complete before World War I, neglecting the war's conversion of the blustering rhetoric of the few into mass movements. Fascism would have probably amounted only to a historical footnote without the Great War. But to investigate the values and emotions of later subaltern fascists is not easy. Most left little record of their views. If they did, many lied (since at the time they were on trial for their lives). My empirical chapters assemble what evidence I have found.

Sternhell's account is also somewhat biased toward early Italian, Spanish, and French intellectuals and glaringly omits Germans. Mosse and others say that "fascism" is not the same as "Nazism." They say that the racist and anti-Semitic Nazis focused more on the people, the *Volk*, and less on the state and that the Nazis altogether lacked a model of a utopian state. The Nazi movement, not the state, represented the nation, just as the Führer personified it. In contrast, few Southern European fascists were racists or anti-Semites, and they developed corporatist, syndicalist blueprints of their desired state. Whereas Nazism was *völkisch*, fascism was statist (Mosse 1964, 1966, 1999; Bracher 1973: 605–9; and Nolte 1965, among others). And only Nazi racism perpetrated genocide, they say. Thus Nazism was not fascism.

Though there is some truth in this, I join those who believe that Nazis *were* fascists and that fascism can be treated as a more general phenomenon. Hitler and Mussolini thought they belonged to the same movement. "Fascism" was an Italian term, which Nazis, being German nationalists, did not want to borrow (nor did some Spanish writers whom everyone calls fascists). But, as we see below, the two movements shared similar core values, had similar social bases, and developed similar movements. Nationalism was more emphasized in Nazism, statism in Italian fascism. But these were variations on common themes.

The tendency to dichotomize Nazism and Italian fascism also reveals an obsession with Germany and Italy. Yet fascism spread more broadly, against a backdrop of wider political ferment, especially on the political right. I focus on five cases of mass fascist movements: Italy, Germany, Austria, Hungary, and Romania. While each was unique, they all shared some features. They were a family of fascists, differing mainly in their abilities to seize power. Only the first three achieved stable (if short-lived) fascist regimes. This was mainly because the different timing of their forward surges led to different strategies of containment by their political rivals, especially those on the right. In fact, Austria, Hungary, and Romania are all cases in which we can analyze a dialectic between fascism and more conservative forms of authoritarianism, a dialectic that helps us better to understand the nature of fascism more generally. I finally analyze Spain, an example of countries that contained relatively few fascists but many fellow-travelers, and where more conservative nationalists and statists managed to keep firm hold over their fascist allies. My forthcoming book also includes a swath of fascist-leaning nationalist movements – Slovakian, Croatian, Ukrainian, Lithuanian, and so on – adapting varying blends of Italian fascism and German Nazism to their own purposes. There was not a dichotomy but a *range* of fascist doctrines and practices – as there has been in movements such as conservatism, socialism, or liberalism.

But unlike socialism (which has Marxism), fascism contains no systematic theory. The men I have quoted above say a variety of things within only a looser *Weltanschauung* ("world view"), a number of views that broadly "hang together" and from which different fascist movements made different selections. Various scholars have sought to identify this core. Nolte (1965) identified a "fascist minimum" combining three ideological "anti's" – anti-Marxism, antiliberalism, and anticonservatism – plus two movement characteristics, the leadership principle and the party-army, all oriented toward a final goal: "totalitarianism." This is not very clear on what the fascists wanted positively, while his stress on the anti's makes him reach the dubious conclusion that fascism was essentially a reactionary form of antimodernism.

Stanley Payne is now the preeminent comparative historian of fascism. He says the fascist core comprises Nolte's three anti's, plus a list of other items: nationalism, authoritarian statism, corporatism and syndicalism, imperialism, idealism, voluntarism, romanticism, mysticism, militarism, and violence. Quite a list! He narrows this down into three categories of style, negations, and programs, though these are more abstract than substantive qualities. And he ends by saying that fascism was "the most revolutionary form of nationalism" and that it centered on philosophical idealism and moralistic violence (1980: 7; 1995: 7–14). The conclusion does not seem quite focused enough, and when he seeks to categorize subtypes of fascism, they turn out to be essentially nationalities (German, Italian, Spanish, Romanian, Hungarian, and a residual "underdeveloped" bunch of others), which seems halfway to denying any theoretical core to fascism.

Juan Linz is the preeminent sociologist of fascism. His definition is even lengthier:

> a hypernationalist, often pan-nationalist, anti-parliamentary, anti-liberal, anti-communist, populist and therefore anti-proletarian, partly anti-capitalist and anti-bourgeois, anti-clerical or at least, non-clerical movement, with the aim of national social integration through a single party and corporative representation not always equally emphasized; with a distinctive style and rhetoric, it relied on activist cadres ready for violent action combined with electoral participation to gain power with totalitarian goals by a combination of legal and violent tactics.

He also approvingly quotes Ramiro Ledesma Ramos, a leading Spanish fascist, who defined fascism at only slightly lesser length, in a series of terse sentences:

> Deep national idea. Opposition to demo-bourgeois institutions, to the liberal parliamentary state. Unmasking of the true feudalistic powers of present society. National economy and people's economy against the great financial and monopolistic capitalism. Sense of authority, discipline and violence. Hostility to the anti-national and anti-human solution that proletarian classism appears to solve the obvious problems and injustices of the capitalist system. (Linz 1976: 12–15)

These writers effectively convey the fascist *Weltanschauung* and suggest that its core is "hyper" nationalism. But a proper generic definition would seem to require more precise yet concise detail.

Recent scholars have attempted to supply this. Roger Eatwell gives a concise definition. Fascism, he says, "strives to forge social rebirth based on a holistic-national radical third way." He adds that in practice, fascism has tended to stress style, especially action and the charismatic leader, more than detailed program, and to engage in a "manichean demonisation of its enemies" (2001: 33; cf. 1995: 11; and 1996). He then amplifies this by elaborating four key characteristics: nationalism, holism (i.e., collectivism), radicalism, and "the third way." The third way lies between capital and labor, right and left, drawing from the best of both of them. Since this means that fascism has something practical to offer modern society, he sees fascism not as antimodern but as an alternative vision of modernity. Eatwell's definition is the closest to my own, given below.

Roger Griffin seeks a generic definition focusing more exclusively on values. In this respect he follows in the footsteps of Sternhell and Mosse. He sees fascism as a "mythic core" of "populist ultra-nationalism" inspired by the idea of a rebirth of the nation, race, or culture and seeking to create a "new man." Fascism is a "palingenetic myth" of populist ultra-nationalism, seeking a nation rising Phoenix-like from the ashes of an old decadent social order. It is "a genus of modern politics which aspires to bring about a total revolution in the political and social culture of a particular national or ethnic community. . . . [G]eneric fascism draws its internal cohesion and affective driving-force from a core myth that a period of perceived decadence and degeneracy is imminently or eventually to give way to one of rebirth and rejuvenation in a post-liberal new order." He agrees with Eatwell that fascism is an alternative modernization. He says that his is becoming the "consensus" view of fascism, opposed only by materialists, whom he ridicules. It reveals "the primacy of culture" in fascism. He also describes fascism as a "political religion" (1991: 44; 2001: 48; 2002: 24).

Yet Griffin's idealism is nothing to be proud of. It is a major defect. How can a "myth" generate "internal cohesion" or "driving force"? A myth cannot be an agent driving or integrating anything, since ideas are not free-floating. Without power organizations, ideas cannot actually *do* anything. What is lacking here is any sense of *power*. Indeed, even a sense of practicality seems to be lacking in such a definition. Surely, fascists must have offered something more useful than the mythical rebirth of the nation. Who would vote for this? Though fascism did have an irrationalist side, it was also rather hard-headed, offering both economic programs and political strategies (as Eatwell 2001 also observes). It was also resolutely this-worldly, unconcerned with the sacred, religious side of human experience, though prepared to bend that to its purposes.

But idealism actually seems to lurk in most of these definitions. Primacy is generally given to fascist ideas. Nationalism seems rather disembodied, divorced from its actual main bearer in the real world, the nation-state. All fascists desired both a very cohesive nation and a very strong state, entwined together. Griffin also sanitizes fascism, remaining silent on its distinctively brutal violence and paramilitarism; while even Eatwell says that fascism only "sometimes" wields violence (Linz, Nolte, and Payne did not neglect violence).

The solution to such omissions, however, is not to embrace the traditional "materialist" alternative to idealism, adding fascism's relationship to capitalism and class. We must define fascism in its own terms, but to its values we must add its programs, actions, and organizations. Fascism was not just a collection of individuals with certain beliefs. Fascism had a great impact on the world *only* because of its collective actions and its organizational forms. Fascists became committed to the elitism, hierarchy, comradeship, populism, and violence contained in a rather loose and paramilitary form of "statism." If fascism had concerned only "palingenetic myths of rebirth," what would be the harm in that? If fascism had been only extreme nationalism, it would have been only unpleasantly xenophobic. But by embracing paramilitarism, fascists coerced each other into extreme action, they destroyed their opponents, and they convinced many bystanders that they could finally bring "order" to modern society. Their authoritarian state then forced compliance from their peoples, quashing opposition and perpetrating mass killings. So our definition of fascism should include both the key values and the key organizational forms of fascism.

A DEFINITION OF FASCISM

I define fascism in terms of the key values, actions, and power organizations of fascists. Most concisely, *fascism is the pursuit of a transcendent and cleansing nation-statism through paramilitarism.* This definition contains five key terms requiring further explanation. Each also contained internal tensions.

(1) *Nationalism.* As everyone recognizes, fascists had a deep and populist commitment to an "organic" or "integral" nation, and this involved an unusually strong sense of its "enemies," both abroad and (especially) at home. Fascists had a very low tolerance of ethnic or cultural diversity, since this would subvert the organic, integral unity of the nation. Aggression against enemies supposedly threatening that organic unity is the original source of fascism's extremism. Racially tinged nationalism proved even more extreme, since race is an ascribed characteristic. We are born with it, and only our death or removal can eliminate it. Thus Nazi racial nationalism proved more obsessed with "purity" and proved more deadly than Italian cultural nationalism, which generally allowed those who showed the right values and conduct to join the nation.

I view the notion of "rebirth," which Griffin saw as the key characteristic of fascism, as characteristic of nationalism more generally, including much milder nationalisms – as, for example, in Irish, Lithuanian, or Zimbabwean nationalism. Since nations are actually modern (with one or two exceptions) but nationalists claim that they are ancient, nationalists solve this paradox with a vision of a revival or rebirth of a supposedly ancient nation, but one now adapted to modern times.[3] In these cases the myth is of continuity back to the former greatness of the High Kings, the Grand

Duchy, and Greater Zimbabwe – but no one supposes they would work today.

(2) *Statism*. This involved both goal and organizational form. Fascists worshiped state power. The authoritarian corporate state could supposedly solve crises and bring about social, economic, and moral development, as Gregor (1979) emphasizes. Since the state represented a nation that was viewed as being essentially organic, it needed to be authoritarian, embodying a singular, cohesive will expressed by a party elite adhering to the "leadership principle." Scholars used to emphasize the "totalitarian" quality of fascist goals and states; Burleigh (2000) and Gregor (2000) still do. Others agree that the fascist goal was "total transformation" of society, but they emphasize backsliding along the way. They see the desired fascist state as vague or contradictory, containing rival party, corporatist, and syndicalist elements, and they often note that fascism in power had a surprisingly weak state. They have detailed the factionalism and horse trading of Mussolini's regime (Lyttleton 1987) and the "polycracy" or even "chaos" of the Nazi regime (Broszat 1981; Kershaw 2000). So they rightly hesitate over the label "totalitarian." Fascist regimes, like communist ones, contained a dialectic between "movement" and "bureaucracy," between "permanent revolution" and "totalitarianism" (Mann 1997). We can also detect a tension between a more organized Italian-style syndicalism/corporatism and Nazi preference for a more "polycratic," fluid dictatorship. And in all regimes tendencies toward a singular, bureaucratic state were undercut by party and paramilitary activism and by deals with rival elites. Fascism was more totalitarian in its transformational aims than in its actual regime form.

(3) *Transcendence*. Fascists rejected conservative notions that the existing social order is essentially harmonious. They rejected liberal and social democratic notions that the conflict of interest groups is a normal feature of society. And they rejected leftist notions that harmony could be attained only by overthrowing capitalism. Fascists originated from the political right, center, and left alike and drew support from all classes (Weber 1976: 503). They attacked both capital and labor as well as the liberal democratic institutions supposedly exacerbating their strife. Fascist nation-statism would be able to "transcend" social conflict, first repressing those who fomented strife by "knocking both their heads together" and then incorporating classes and other interest groups into state corporatist institutions. The term "third way," preferred by Eatwell, seems too weak for this goal of revolutionary transformation, too capable of being appropriated by centrist politicians such as Tony Blair. It was definitely not a compromise or a mere drawing

together of the best of both of them (as Eatwell says). For it did involve the supposed creation of a new man.

Fascism was partly a response to the crisis of capitalism (as materialists say), but it offered a revolutionary and supposedly achievable solution. We see below that the "core constituency" of fascist support can be understood only by taking seriously their aspirations to transcendence, for they were perfectly genuine about it. It was also the most ideologically powerful part of their appeal, for it offered a plausible, practicable vision of movement toward a better society. Transcendence was actually the central plank of fascism's electoral program. In my previous work I have argued that ideologies are at their most powerful when they offer plausible yet transcendent visions of a better world. They combine the rational with the beyond-rational.

Nonetheless, transcendence was the most problematic and the most variable of fascism's five key terms. It was never actually accomplished. In practice most fascist regimes leaned toward the established order and toward capitalism. Fascists lacked a general critique of capitalism (unlike socialists), since they ultimately lacked interest in capitalism and class. Nation and state comprised their center of gravity, not class. This alone brought them into conflict with the left rather than the right since Marxists and anarchists, not conservatives, tended to be committed to internationalism. But fascists, unlike the political left and right, could be rather pragmatic about classes – unless they saw them as enemies of the nation. Thus they attacked not capitalism per se but only particular types of profit-taking, usually by finance, or foreign or Jewish capitalists. In Romania and Hungary, where these types of capitalist dominated, this gave fascism a distinctly proletarian tone. Elsewhere fascist movements were more procapitalist. When they neared power, they encountered a special problem. Though they hoped to subordinate capitalists to their own goals, as authoritarians they believed in managerial powers yet recognized that they themselves lacked the technocratic skills to run industry. Thus they compromised with capitalists. Moreover, the German and especially the Italian fascist coups were aided by upper-class support. In power Mussolini never seemed to be correcting this pro–ruling-class bias, though Hitler was different. Had his regime lasted much longer, I doubt the Reich economy could still have been called "capitalist."

But in the short space of time allowed them, fascists did tend to backtrack from their original project of transcending class conflict. This "betrayal" is stressed by class interpretations of fascism and by others doubting the sincerity or consistency of fascist values (e.g., Paxton 1994, 1996). Yet fascists could not simply "settle down" into betrayal. All fascist movements remained riven between "radicals" and "opportunists," and this imparted an unresolvable dynamic to the movement. One form of this was especially revealed during the Nazi regime. This dynamic displaced rather than abandoned the goal of transcendence. They would transcend ethnic and class strife, but remove only ethnic enemies – since compromise proved necessary with the capitalist class enemy. This displacement of transcendent goals actually increased fascist murderousness – eventually in Italy as well as in Germany, as shown in my forthcoming book.

(4) *Cleansing*. Because opponents were seen as "enemies," they were to be removed, and the nation cleansed of them. This was fascist aggression in action. It is distressing that we have recently become familiar again with "ethnic cleansing," though cleansing of political enemies has been less publicized in the late twentieth century. Organic nationalists usually consider ethnic enemies the more difficult to cope with, since political identities may be changed more easily. Communists may be repressed, some killed, but if they recant, most can be admitted into the nation. Political cleansing thus often starts murderously, but eases off once the "enemy" gives in and is assimilated into the nation. Ethnic cleansing more often escalates, since the "enemy" may not be permitted to assimilate. Most fascisms entwined both ethnic and political cleansing, though to differing degrees. Even the Nazis' supposed "enemies" appeared in mixed political-ethnic garb, as in the dreaded "Judeo-Bolshevik." Movements such as Italian fascism or Spanish Nationalism identified most of their enemies in predominantly political terms. Thus the more ethnic Nazi end of the range was more murderous than the Italian.

(5) *Paramilitarism* was both a key value and the key organizational form of fascism. It was seen as "popular," welling up spontaneously from below, but it was also elitist, supposedly representing the vanguard of the nation. Brooker (1991) homes in on the comradeship of fascist movements as their defining characteristic, and they certainly viewed their battle-hardened comradeship as an exemplar of the organic nation and the new man. Violence was the key to the "radicalism" of fascism. They overturned legal forms by killings. Through it, the people would effect class transcendence, "knocking heads together." Its elitism and hierarchy would then dominate the authoritarian state that it would bring into being. In no case was a fascist movement merely a "party." Indeed, the Italian fascists were organized only into paramilitaries for many years. Fascism was always uniformed, marching, armed, dangerous, and radically destabilizing of the existing order.

What essentially distinguishes fascists from the many military and monarchical dictatorships of the world is this "bottom-up" and violent quality of its paramilitarism. It could bring popularity, both electorally and among elites.

Fascists always portrayed their violence as "defensive" yet "successful" – it could roll over enemies who were the real source of violence. Not everyone believed them, but many did, and this increased their popularity, their votes, and their attractiveness to elites. Paramilitarism thus offered them a distinctive approach to electoral democracy and existing elites, both of which they actually despised. Paramilitarism must always be viewed as entwined with other two main fascist power resources: in electoral struggle and in the undermining of elites. It was paramilitarism – caging the fascists, coercing their opponents, winning the support or respect of bystanders – that enabled fascists to do far more than their mere numbers could. Thus paramilitarism was violence, but it was always a great deal more than violence. It certainly did not confer enough effective violence for fascists to stage coups if that meant taking on the state's army. Paramilitary was not the equivalent of military power. Only if fascists could neutralize military power by appealing to the soldiers themselves could fascist coups occur.

This combination of qualities obviously made fascists "revolutionary," though not in conventional left-right terms. It would be inexact to call them "revolutionaries of the right," as some have done. The combination also means that movements can be more or less fascist. We could in principle plot fascist movements (each one obviously unique) amid a five-dimensional space, though I confess that this is beyond my representational skills. It is also beyond my range here to compare fascist with communist movements in these respects, though there are some obvious similarities as well as some differences. They have been alternative, if failed, visions of modernity.

THE APPEAL OF FASCISM: CLASS THEORY

To whom did these key characteristics appeal? What kinds of people became fascists, and what did they want fascism to accomplish? Curiously – since these are movements denying the importance of classes – class theorists dominate the answers. They see fascism as the product of class conflict and economic crisis, its main accomplishment being to solve the crisis by repressing the working class. Thus it was supported by other social classes. There have been two variants, one seeing fascism as essentially middle or lower middle class, the other as essentially an ally or tool of the capitalist class. Renton (2000) calls these the "right" and the "left" Marxist theories, respectively. Marxists have understood the significance of violence and paramilitarism in fascism. Otto Bauer said that fascism was "the dictatorship of the armed gang." But Marxists tend to discount fascist beliefs, reducing them to their supposed socio-economic base. They have no problem in

·

seeing fascism as a single generic type. Since class and capitalism are universal features of modern societies, fascism is also a universal potentiality. Yet
since other social structures were just as universal across the early twentieth
century, these might also imprint themselves on a single generic fascism –
as I argue was the case with the nation–state and citizen warfare.

Anyone writing about the middle classes has first to cope with the plethora
of labels used of those occupying the middle reaches of the class hierarchy.
Different language groups cope differently. One includes everyone who is
neither proletarian nor upper class in a cognate of the term "petty bourgeoisie." This is so in Italian and Spanish, while the German *Mittelstand*
("middle estate") can be similarly broad. Yet "petty bourgeoisie" is not in
everyday English usage. Those who deploy it indicate only a subset of the
middle strata – artisans, small shopkeepers, and small traders – small independent proprietors who may employ family but very little free-wage labor.
I call this group "the classic petty bourgeoisie." Germans often call them,
together with state employees, the "old" *Mittelstand*. Though the classic
petty bourgeoisie is often falsely believed to be prone to fascism, its small
numbers could not have sustained such a large mass movement. Thus most
"middle class" or "petty bourgeois" theories of fascism have been broader-
based, seeing fascism as a combined movement of (in English usage) the
"lower middle class" and the "middle class." This combination I here label simply as "the middle class," in contradistinction to two other broadly
labeled "classes": the working class and the upper class. These terms are obviously not precision instruments, but since my empirical chapters explore
occupational classifications in considerable detail – and show that classes by
any definition make only a limited contribution to understanding fascists –
this book does not need more precise class definitions.

As early as 1923 Salvatorelli was arguing that fascism was an independent
movement of disgruntled middle-class people (I quote him in Chapter 3)
and the Jewish Comintern leader Karl Radek was labeling fascism as "the
socialism of the petty bourgeoisie." Such interpretations strengthened after
World War II, as research piled up seeming to confirm that fascists came
disproportionately from nonelite, nonproletarian groups – and especially
from the lower middle class (e.g., Lipset 1963: chap. 5; Bracher 1973: 145
Kater 1983: 236; Stachura 1983b: 28). The usual explanation offered for
this was economic:

a malaise, a maladjustment of capitalist society . . . [affected those who were] . . .
uprooted and threatened by social and economic change, whose position in society
was being undermined, who had lost their traditional place, and were frightened of

the future. These were, above all, the lower middle classes – or rather certain groups within them: the artisans and independent tradesmen, the small farmers, the lower grade government employees and white-collar workers. (Carsten 1980: 232–3)

These theorists accept that some fascists were anticapitalist but believe that far more were antisocialist. Under fascism, capitalism would be controlled, but socialism destroyed. For – it is said – the middle class feared the threat from below more than that from above.

Middle-class theory has sometimes come in even broader forms. Fascism has been seen as the failure of an entire "middle class society" founded on liberalism and capitalism (Eley 1986: chaps. 9 and 10). It is difficult to see any precise meaning in this. Neither an entire society nor a whole epoch can be defined only in terms of a single class. Nor did liberalism or capitalism in general fail. Others have stretched the theory by yoking the middle class to other, more marginal groups. Carsten (1976) summarizes a tradition stretching back into the 1920s to Togliatti, Tasca, Fromm, Reich, and Nolte by identifying the backbone of fascism as students, ex-soldiers, "jobless intellectuals," *déclassés*, and the "lumpen proletariat," joining together with small shopkeepers, artisans, and white-collar workers. This is a motley crew, perhaps reflecting more the author's dislike of fascists than any principle of unity among these groups. Carsten suggests that such diverse people became fascists because they shared an experience of economic and status deprivation. Indeed, some writers emphasize economic deprivation more than middle-class identity. Zetkin, Thalheimer, Löwenthal, Sauer, and Germani saw the deprived, the losers, the marginal, the uprooted as flocking to fascism – "a true community of bankruptcy," declared Löwenthal. Whenever such writers believe an occupational group (be it soldiers, students, lawyers, or construction workers) was particularly fascist, they tend to attribute this to economic deprivation, unemployment, or declining wage levels. Rather curiously, most psychological theories of fascism have also been based on the middle class. The Frankfurt School reinterpreted Freudian theory to view "repression," "the authoritarian personality," "status insecurity," and "irrationality" as being distinctively "bourgeois," resulting especially from the decay of the bourgeois family. None of these psychological theories of fascism is empirically well supported (as Payne 1995: 454, notes). And even if some of these groups were predisposed toward fascism, it may not have been for class reasons. Ex-officers might become fascists more because of their military values, students more because of their age and the ideological climate of universities. People do not simply have a single social identity, conferred by class.

In fact none of these middle-class theories now stand up very well. Like most political movements, fascism began among sections of the middle class. But once fascism became an established political movement, this changed, as Chapters 3 to 8 show. Most fascists in the larger movements were neither economically deprived nor particularly middle-class.[4] After 1930 neither Nazis nor Nazi voters were especially bourgeois or petty bourgeois. They drew support from all classes. Italian fascists are still often seen as bourgeois, though the data are poor. Yet the Hungarian and Romanian rank-and-file were more proletarian (as Berend 1998: 342–3, has recently recognized). Payne's comprehensive review accepts most of this, yet still tries to save something of middle-class theory. He concludes: "[M]iddle class radicalism" remains "one of the most important strands of fascism but is inadequate to provide a general theory" (1995: 445). Though this is a sensible conclusion, it does not take us very far. If persons from all classes became fascists, it seems unlikely that class consciousness or class conflict would directly explain much of fascism.

The second class theory sees fascists as essentially the allies or tools of the capitalist class. In its "imperialist" or "monopolist" or "crisis" phase in the early twentieth-century capitalism needed an authoritarian state in order to preserve itself against the rising proletariat. Though this theory may allow fascists a measure of "Bonapartist" "relative autonomy" from capitalism, they were ultimately accountable to capitalists. Thus Poulantzas actually defined fascism as an "exceptional capitalist state," functionally necessary amid crisis to protect the capitalist class from the proletariat (1974: 11). Two crises supposedly threatened capitalism: the post-1918 surge in revolutionary socialism (causing the Italian seizure of power) and the mass unemployment and pressure on state budgets produced by the Great Depression (causing the Hitler seizure of power). Some see capitalists embracing fascism early and enthusiastically, but most have see the embrace as tardy, reluctant, and distrustful.

This theory has lost some of its popularity as Marxism has declined more generally. But Hobsbawm has endorsed it, saying that "faced with insoluble economic problems and/or an increasingly revolutionary working class, the bourgeoisie now had to fall back on force and coercion, that is to say, on something like fascism" (1994: 136).

Disregarding the dangerously functionalist expression "had to," even a casual glance at the five major fascist countries reveals great variation in the extent to which capitalists might plausibly regard the proletariat as a dangerous threat. If they feared a nonexistent threat from below, perhaps we should enter into psychological rather than sociological analysis. Though

I do not quite do this, I puzzle over why the propertied classes appeared to overreact to a rather small level of threat from below. My solution is given in the final chapter. Empirically, while the degree of capitalist support for fascist movements remains controversial, it has varied considerably between the different countries. As in middle-class theory, the evidence is sometimes padded out by rather stronger evidence of support from adjacent social groups, in this case from the "old regime" of the preceding period: monarchs, aristocrats, top civil servants, army high commands, churches, and higher professionals. Though these people also tended to be substantial property owners, their motives for supporting fascism might have derived from their military, religious, or old regime needs rather than from capitalist ones. Capitalist class theory is supported by the tendency of fascist leaders to backtrack on their claim to transcend class conflict. If such "sellouts" always occurred and dominated the subsequent trajectory of fascism, then the social background of the fascist rank-and-file would be largely irrelevant: Fascism would be indeed the handmaiden or stooge of capitalism. Sometimes it has been, more often not. In general I show that capitalist class theory – like middle-class theory – explains something, but not all that much, of fascism.

Some have sought to fuse these two class theories. Renton (2000: 101) says that though fascism is in origin "the socialism of the middle class," it is ultimately reactionary, antiworker, and supportive of capitalism. Kitchen also believes the "social basis" of fascism was middle-class, but its essential "function" was capitalist. He says that "fascist parties were largely organizations of the petit bourgeoisie" who comprised "the overwhelming majority." Yet their role was to operate "in close conjunction with the capitalist elite" (1976: 59, 65). This dual approach can get a handle on some of the dynamics of fascist movements – on the tension between a "radical" petty bourgeois rank-and-file and more conservative and opportunistic leaders. The conflict ranging "radicals" such as Gregor Strasser and the SA rank-and-file against the more conservative-opportunist Hitler and Göring, or between "radical" Ras (local fascist bosses) and Mussolini, are often viewed in this way, with the leaders defeating the radicals. Again, all this has some truth content.

But by centering on "social base" and "objective functions," most class theorists obviously ignore fascists' own beliefs. They view fascism "from outside," from a perspective that made little sense to fascists, who rebutted class theories as they did all "materialism." Fascists focused elsewhere. At the beginning of Chapter 3 I present a class theory of Italian fascism (derived from Salvatorelli), and then Mussolini's own account of why he embraced fascism. They appear to be discussing quite different things. Perhaps others knew better than Mussolini what he was up to, or perhaps he was distort-ing the truth (indeed, he partly was). But the disjunction is disconcerting, especially to a sociologist. Most sociologists subscribe to the maxim: "If people define things as real, they are real in their consequences." If fascists believed they were pursuing certain goals, this belief had consequences for their actions and cannot be merely dismissed.

There is one final difficulty for a class interest–driven approach to fascism. Fascists were motivated by a highly emotional struggle to cleanse their nation of "enemies," and so they indulged in reckless aggression and terrible evil. That aggression and evil usually did not benefit them materially. Fascists were too aggressive for their own good – especially in their keenness for war. They were chronically overconfident about what the new man could achieve. And though material interests drove forward some of the atrocities against Jews and other "enemies" (looting was ubiquitous), genocide is another matter. It did only material harm to Germany (and both army generals and SS officers entrusted with economic planning knew it). The fascist combination of morality, aggression, and murder ultimately confounds material interest theories. Fascists were driven by both value and instrumental rationality. Eventually, the former predominated and destroyed them.

The failure of nationalist interpreters of fascism in this regard is a different one. They fail to explore the core constituencies of fascism, unlike class theorists. They focus on the content of its ideology and ignore its social base. Occasionally, they just borrow the class interpretation. Curiously, values such as nationalism, racism, or militarism are said to be essentially "bourgeois" or "petty bourgeois" (Mosse 1964, 1966; Carsten 1980: 232). I am at a loss to understand why these values should be thought distinctively middle-class. Many scholars don't seem to like the petty bourgeoisie. Maybe it is the class background from which they themselves are trying to escape. Even some nonclass theorists seem obsessed by class. Books with subtitles claiming to be "social profiles" of Nazi members and voters turn out to be 90 percent about occupation and classes (e.g., Kater 1983; Manstein 1988) – as if our social identities were 90 percent conferred by our occupational class!

Payne (1995) provides the most comprehensive review of fascists' back-grounds. He explores their class backgrounds at great length. He also notes more briefly other relevant social characteristics, such as youthfulness and masculinity, the preponderance of military backgrounds, higher education, religion, and (occasionally) region. But he attempts to relate only the class data to general theories of fascism. The rest is treated as complicating detail and is not theorized. Linz (1976) had provided an excellent earlier analy-sis of fascists' backgrounds – their occupations, sectors, regions, religions, age, gender, and so on. But, puzzlingly (since he is a fine sociologist), he failed to find patterns underlying such apparently diverse identities. Though these scholars see fascism as extreme nationalism, they have not attempted to identify "core nationalist constituencies." There is a gaping hole between ideology and social base. We can fill it by recognizing nation-statist and paramilitary constituencies of support, alongside class constituencies. Class theories do have considerable truth content. Fascism borrowed heavily from class ideologies and organizations, was obsessed with the threat of "Bolshevism," and was sensitive to class interests. Kitchen is correct: We should understand fascism's social base and functions. Yet "social" should not be equated with "class." Let us briefly examine the social settings in which fascism resonated.

THE SOCIAL RESONANCE OF FASCISM

Very large numbers of fascists have so far appeared only amid five social settings. I start with the very broadest.

The Macro-Period: Interwar Crises of European Modernity

The interwar period in Europe was the setting that threw up most of the self-avowed fascists and saw them at their high tide. My definition is intended firstly as "European-epochal," to use Eatwell's (2001) term (cf. Kallis 2000: 96), applying primarily to that period and place – though perhaps with some resonance elsewhere. The period and the continent contained four major crises: the consequences of a devastating "world," but in fact largely European, war between mass citizen armies, severe class conflict exacerbated by the Great Depression, a political crisis arising from an attempted rapid transition by many countries toward a democratic nation-state, and a cultural sense of civilizational contradiction and decay. Fascism itself recognized the importance of all four sources of social power by explicitly claiming to offer solutions to all four crises. And all four played a more specific role in weakening the capacity of elites to continue ruling in old ways.

It is nonetheless possible that fascism had different causes in each country – here generated by defeat in war, there by the Great Depression. Yet fascism was strongest where we find distinctive combinations of all four. The problem is one of degree: To what extent did each crisis – economic, military, political, and ideological – contribute to the rise of fascism? The problem is discussed more thoroughly in Chapter 2. These crises seem to have been necessary causes of fascism. Without them, no fascism. But none seems to have been an individually sufficient cause. Most countries coped with crisis without turning to organic nation-statism, let alone fascism. So this leads to a second level of analysis, and specifically to the question: Which places made these turns?

The Macro-Place: One-Half of Europe

In the interwar period, as Map 2.1 will reveal below, virtually all of Central, Eastern, and Southern Europe embraced a family of rightist authoritarian governments, one of whose members was fascism. Only tiny minorities in the northwest of the continent sought such government. There were also fascist-leaning movements in the more economically developed countries of other continents, especially Japan, South Africa, Bolivia, Brazil, and Argentina. Here fascism had some resonance, though just how much is a matter of debate (Payne 1995: chap 10; Larsen 2001). My general view of these non-European cases is that none combined all the essential values of fascism listed above. Japan, for example, did have a highly developed nation-statism that produced the most sophisticated quasifascist economic theory in the world (Gao 1997: chaps. 2 and 3). Yet it lacked a bottom-up mass movement or paramilitary (see Brooker 1991 for comparisons between Japan and Europe). Militarism, not paramilitarism, dominated what many call Japanese "fascism." In contrast, Argentina and Brazil generated mass populist and somewhat authoritarian movements with some "radical" and statist tendencies, but these lacked cleansing nationalism. We can find theorists all over the interwar world reading Barrès, Mussolini, Hitler, and so on, adapting them to local conditions and then arriving at their own quasifascist doctrines. In India, for example, Golwalkar adapted Hitler's racial theories to his demand for a pure and organic Hindu theocratic state. Infuse the RSS Hindu paramilitary movement with such theories and the blend is quite close to Nazism (Jaffrelot 1996). But in the 1930s this movement was tiny, like almost all the other quasifascist militias and parties of the time. Only one continent came anywhere near being dominated by fascism: Europe.

Why did authoritarian nation-statism dominate one-half of Europe, liberal democracy the other half? It cannot have been some general crisis of modern society, such as the Great Depression or the defects of liberalism, for then it would have affected all of Europe, not just half of it. The difference is one that turns crucially on the behavior of political conservatives, "old regimes," and the property-owning classes. For here class does matter, profoundly, if in a rather peculiar way. Right across one-half of Europe, the upper classes turned toward more repressive regimes, believing these could protect themselves against the twin threats of social disorder and the political left. But this does not seem to have been very "rational" behavior. For they greatly exaggerated the threats and neglected safer means of avoiding them that were prevalent across the northwest. They overreacted, reaching for the gun too abruptly, too early. Explaining this puzzle – of class behavior that seems somewhat irrational – is one of the principal tasks of this book. Such an explanation is essential to understanding the macro-regional environment of authoritarian nation-statism in which fascism could flourish. But this cannot also explain the specific emergence of fascism, since only a few countries in this zone actually generated mass fascism, and they did not usually do so at the initiative of the upper classes.

Meso-Places: The Five Fascist Countries

Why did Italians, Germans, Austrians, Hungarians, and Romanians embrace fascism in such large numbers when most of their neighbors stopped at milder movements? It is true that quite large quasi-fascist movements later emerged in a few regions of other countries, as in the Sudetenland, Slovakia, the Ukraine, or Croatia. I examine these, but in my forthcoming book. Yet few fascists emerged in other countries and regions. Fascists did not surge only in the more economically advanced countries or in the Greater Powers of the center, east, and south (as is often argued). This argument stems from obsession with Germany and Italy. But Hungary and Romania were rather backward countries and minor powers – and so some writers argue that it is backwardness that generates fascism (e.g., Berend 1998). Yet fascism had sufficiently broad appeal – like socialism – that it could be interpreted in the light of either an advanced or a backward economy. To explain this, we must look for the commonality between these cases – and this can hardly be level of development. But this will not provide a sufficient answer. For even in these countries, only some people (minorities at that) became fascists. Who were they and why did they become fascists?

Meso-Places: Core Fascist Constituencies

Which particular social groups within these countries were most attracted to fascism? I spend many pages over several chapters examining the social backgrounds of fascist leaders, militants, members, fellow-travelers, coconspirators and voters – compared (wherever possible) with their counterparts in other political movements. How old were fascists, were they men or women, military or civilian, urban or rural, religious or secular, economic winners or losers, and from which regions, economic sectors, and social classes did they come? I have gratefully pillaged the work of the scholars of many countries to assemble the broadest collection of data yet presented on fascists. These data suggest three core "fascist constituencies" among which the fascist values and organizations identified earlier resonated most strongly, and which therefore came to organize actual fascist movements. Of course, fascist constituencies did not come ready-made. Fascists had to discover them and then they had to work on them, organizing, persuading, bribing, coercing. Some fascists were more agile than others. Some fascist movements misperceived their constituencies, some stumbled on them almost by accident (as the Nazis stumbled on German Protestantism). Since not all fascist movements were the same, their constituencies also differed somewhat. Yet amid the variations and the accidents we can perceive the following three broad patterns of mass support. This support came from the millions who voted fascist and the thousands who joined fascist organizations. Both were critical to fascist success, though in very different ways. For the moment, however, I am not distinguishing them

(1) *Constituencies Favoring Paramilitarism*. The fascist core consisted everywhere of two successive generations of young men, coming of age between World War I and the late 1930s. Their youth and idealism meant that fascist values were proclaimed as being distinctively "modern" and "moral." They were especially transmitted through two institutions socializing young men: secondary and higher education, encouraging notions of moral progress, and the armed forces, encouraging militarism. Since the appeal was mainly to young men, it was also distinctly macho, encouraging an ethos of braggart, semi-disciplined violence, in peacetime encouraging militarism to mutate into paramilitarism. The character of fascism was set by young men socialized in institutions favorable to moralizing violence and eventually to murder. Yet the similarity of values between paramilitarism and militarism always gave fascism a capacity to appeal to armed forces themselves, not to the extent of inducing military rebellions but to the extent of generating sympathy there that at its most extreme could immobilize the army.

(2) *Constituencies Favoring Transcendence*. Fascism was usually neither particularly bourgeois nor particularly petty bourgeois. True, there were some class biases in Italy and perhaps also in Austria. But after 1930 there were none in Germany (if we add the SA and SS paramilitaries to the Nazi Party). These fascist coups also received some support from upper classes. But Romanian and Hungarian fascists were recruited more from proletarian than bourgeois backgrounds and received less upper-class support. Class composition was thus complex and variable. Yet there were more constant tendencies

of *economic sector*. Fascists tended to come from sectors that were not in the front line of organized struggle between capital and labor. They were less likely to be workers in urban, manufacturing settings (though they were around Budapest and Bucharest because industry there was more part of the "statist" constituency). They were less likely to be small or large business-men or their managers. Yet they were not "marginal" or "rootless." Their social location was (for the interwar period) relatively secure. But from their slightly removed vantage point they viewed class struggle with distaste, fa-voring a movement claiming to transcend class struggle. Of course, in most cases transcendence was not achieved, and we find tension (noted by many writers) between a more "radical" fascist base and a more "opportunist" leadership faction seeking compromise with elites. Similarly, capitalists and old regimes might also provide a more opportunistic constituency for such flawed transcendence. But if we do take fascists' beliefs seriously, then it would follow that fascism would appeal to those viewing class struggle from "outside," declaring "a plague on both your houses!"

(3) *Constituencies Favoring Nation-Statism.* Fascists' backgrounds appeared rather heterogeneous. They tended to have had military experience, be highly educated, work in the public or service sectors and come from par-ticular regional and religious backgrounds. For many observers, this has confirmed that fascism was a "ragbag" movement (a particularly prevalent view of the Nazis, as we see in Chapter 4). But there was a principle of unity amid these varied attributes: Fascists were at the heart of either the nation or the state. Some "nation-statist" locations were similar across countries: Sol-diers and veterans above all, but also civil servants, teachers, and public sector manual workers were all disproportionately fascist in almost all the countries of mass fascism. Other characteristics varied by country. Rather distinc-tively, industrial development around the capitals of Hungary and especially Romania was state-assisted, which gave some private-sector workers a more statist orientation. Religion was almost everywhere important, reinforcing organic nation-statism (except in Italy, where the Church was transnational). Evangelicals in Germany between 1925 and 1935, the Orthodox faithful and clergy in Romania, and Catholics in "Austro-Fascism" were drawn toward fascism since these religions were central to the identity of their desired nation-state. Among Germans the role of religion varied as Nazism itself changed: The perpetrators of genocide, unlike earlier Nazi voters, were disproportionately ex-Catholics (I demonstrate and seek to explain this in my forthcoming volume). In some countries fascists came more from re-gions that had been at the heart of the historic state or nation, but more often they came from "threatened" border territories or from refugees from

"lost territories." We see below that these were all distinctively nation–statist constituencies.

Obviously, not all fascists were from these three core constituencies, nor were all inhabitants of such constituencies fascists. Nor did fascism remain unchanged in its values or characteristics. Nor were vaguely sympathetic persons taking ten minutes to register their votes the same as elites scheming for a year to do a deal with fascists. Neither were these the same as the fascist member or militant devoting enormous time and energy to the movement – perhaps even risking life. Let us consider them.

The Micro-Cage: Fascist Movements

"Fascists" were not fully formed at the moment they entered the movement. People may formally sign up for a movement and yet possess only a rudimentary knowledge of it – sympathy for a few slogans, respect for a charismatic Führer or Duce, or simply following friends who have joined. Most recruits joined the movement young, unmarried, unformed, with little adult civilian experience. On them, fascist parties and paramilitaries were especially powerful socialization agencies. These movements were proudly elitist and authoritarian, enshrining a pronounced hierarchy of rank and an extreme cult of the leader. Orders were to be obeyed, discipline to be imposed. Above all, they imposed a requirement of activism. Thus militants experienced intense emotional comradeship. Where the movement was proscribed, clandestinity tightened it. Many activists lost their jobs or went into prison or exile. Though this deterred many of the more faint-hearted, among those remaining active such constraints further tightened the movement.

So did paramilitarism. In some fascist movements (such as the early Italian or the Romanian) the paramilitary *was* the movement; in others (such as the Nazi) the paramilitaries existed alongside party institutions. The paramilitaries were time-consuming, enjoining discipline tempered by comradeship in pursuit of small group violence. Members felt strong pressures on them that were simultaneously coercive and pleasurable, since they involved physical hardship and danger, abusive discipline, intense comradeship, and a very active collective social life amounting in some cases to a cage, a virtual "total institution," in Goffman's sense of the term. Obviously, some were put off by this and many left. But for those who stayed, paramilitarism provided distinctive fascist socialization. For example, Austrian Nazis were persecuted by their government during the years 1934 to 1938. Many fled to Germany, where in the SS and its Austrian Legion they became full-time revolutionaries, "working" together, drinking together in Nazi bars, sleeping together in Nazi barracks.[5] It was from such socially caged groups that fascist leaders liked to recruit "reliable," "toughened" cadres for especially murderous tasks.

They became well prepared for violence. The one adult experience of many of the early young recruits was war. The first, or "front," generation of fascists had almost all fought in World War I; the second, or "home," generation had only been schoolboys during the war, though many had been longing to fight and now did so in the many paramilitary border skirmishing campaigns occurring around Europe in the immediate aftermath of the war. The third generation of recruits received only distorted remembrances of war from their elders, but they were plunged into extralegal street violence. By this time the longer-term members might be inured to "peacetime" violence, and they were commanding the new recruits. Moreover, successful and unpunished violence may have both a cathartic and a liberating effect on the perpetrators. It can take them beyond conventional morality and into technically illegal behavior, past points of no return, reinforcing their collective sense of being a segregated, hardened elite, beyond conventional standards of behaviour. For these young men, this was reinforced by two more conventional qualities of "gangs": the resonance of violence amid macho assertions of masculinity and the excessive consumption of inhibition-releasing alcohol. It is difficult to think of fascist paramilitaries without barroom violence. All these qualities make violence easier to repeat, once embarked on.

Careers within the fascist movement also brought material and status rewards. As the movement expanded, so did the promotion prospects and the power, the pickings, and the status. But promotion required character qualities beyond mere opportunism. Fascist elites became staffed disproportionately by experienced, "reliable," "toughened" members. Educated reliables became the "officers" of fascism, less-educated "old fighters" became the "NCOs." At most levels experienced, inured, "toughened" fascists provided an order-giving elite, able to discipline and socialize the newcomers into "normal" fascist behavior. Fascist movements had differing trajectories. The smaller movements of Northwestern Europe often rose and then declined quite quickly. When their members got the worse of street fighting, many sensibly decided to quit. But in the five major fascist countries it is impossible to understand the success of only thousands of fascists, amid the opposition/indifference of millions, without appreciating the contribution made by their extraordinary and violent activism.

OVERVIEW OF THE BOOK

The above conceptual framework helps to explain fascists. I examine the
social crises and the responses of elites, of the thousands who joined fascist
movements, and of the millions who sympathized. The next chapter exam-
ines interwar crises, explaining the macro-level: why one half of Europe was
receptive, the other half hostile. Since I believe I can answer this question, it
is not necessary to examine variations among the hostile cases of Northwestern Europe. Instead, the following seven chapters deal with the other
half of the continent in order to explain why some went more for fascism,
others for other types of authoritarian rightist movements. This is the basis
of my choice of six case-study countries. In Italy, Germany (which gets two
chapters), and Austria, fascism dominated and rose into power unassisted. In
two – Hungary and Romania – fascists became almost equal players in a kind
of dialectic of death within the authoritarian family. The final country –
Spain – was the most riven by struggles between democrats and authoritarians and illuminates those cases where fascism remained a subordinate
member of the authoritarian family. My methodology in these case studies
is almost entirely secondary analysis of other scholars' primary research – to
whom I therefore owe an enormous debt of gratitude. The case studies then
permit me to develop a more general explanation of fascists' rise, which is
presented in my concluding chapter.

2

Explaining the Rise of Interwar Authoritarianism and Fascism

To explain fascism we must place it in its context. For three decades it was just one variant of a broader political ideal: "authoritarian nation-statism." In turn, this was just one version of the dominant political ideal of modernity, the strong nation-state. But fascism dominated only in Europe, where it was set inside a single large geographical bloc of authoritarian regimes. Since Europe elsewhere remained liberal democratic, there were "two Europes." The period of fascism's explosive growth was also rent by economic, military, political, and ideological crises. So this chapter discusses the rise of nation-states across the map of Europe, amid four social crises.

State strength has two dimensions, infrastructural and despotic (see Mann 1988). Infrastructural power indicates the capacity of the state to enforce rules and laws by effective infrastructures covering its territories and peoples. An infrastructurally strong state may be democratic or authoritarian. The democratic United States has more infrastructural state power than did the authoritarian Soviet Union. This type of power is power "through" people, not power "over" them. But despotic power refers to the ability of state elites to take their own decisions "over" their subjects/citizens. Virtually all modern states have come to possess greater infrastructural powers than their historical predecessors, while some have also wielded formidable despotic powers. The combination of a substantial amount of both powers is distinctive to authoritarian states of the twentieth century, which I am here seeking to explain. How did the combination arise? The answer is by exaggerating ordinary modern political ideals.

By the twentieth century, Europe already contained "sovereign nation-states." That is, each of these states was claiming political sovereignty over certain territories, deriving legitimacy from the "people" or "nation"

74173

inhabiting them (many were still multiethnic, of course). Yet nation-states are young. From the sixteenth and seventeenth centuries, monarchs were claiming state sovereignty in foreign policy, "upper-class nations" were emerging, and religious wars might produce "nations of the soul." But the mass of the population became real members of the "nation" more recently. States up to the eighteenth century actually did rather little. They conducted diplomacy and small foreign wars, they wielded the highest level of justice and repression. They formally regulated foreign trade and possessed economic monopolies normally subcontracted out to others. Some controlled the price of grain in order to avoid rioting near the capital. Only if buttressed by established and pliant churches did states penetrate much of social life outside their capitals and "home counties." Yet eighteenth-century states did monopolize the function of military violence, and this now surged. Around 1700, states absorbed perhaps 5 percent of GNP in peacetime, 10 percent in wartime. By 1760, the wartime extraction rate had risen to the range 15 to 25 percent. By 1810, they took 25 to 35 percent and conscripted about 5 percent of the population. These rates (calculated in Mann 1993: chap. 11) are similar to those of the world wars of the twentieth century and to the highest rates in the world today, those of Israel and North Korea. Such comparisons enable us to appreciate the scale of the eighteenth century transformation. From being fairly insignificant, states loomed large in the lives of their subjects through tax gatherers and recruiting sergeants. They aroused subjects out of their historic political indifference to demand representative rights. Thus did membership in the nation, "citizenship," first become the modern political ideal.

Yet even in the nineteenth century, few saw states as the route to achieve many important social purposes. Freedom was mostly seen as freedom from, not through, the state. Only with the Jacobins during the French Revolution was the notion expressed that a stronger state and a more activist conception of citizenship might be socially and morally desirable. Jacobinism was defeated, but state expansion then took a more surreptitious route, fueled by the development of industrial capitalism. States sponsored road and canal building and took over poor relief. France continued to favor more state coordination of economic activity than either Britain or the United States did, while in Germany came a challenge to laissez-faire through the protectionist theories of Friedrich List. By the late century some economic theory had become a little more statist, with the state beginning to coordinate banking and industrial investment. In the late nineteenth century came further state organization of railroads, mass education, public health, and finally the first stirrings of welfare programs. These were all growths in infrastructural power. Since these were all desirable goods, to be paid for by undesirable taxes, more and more of the population became interested in representative government and in citizenship – that is, in reducing despotic powers.

These state activities also had the unintended consequence of consolidating networks of social interaction, "civil societies," substantially bounded by the territories of each state. This fueled an implicit sense of nationhood – less an ideology of nationalism than a recognition that one actually lived in the same society under the same state as one's fellow-subjects/citizens. But explicit nationalism also strengthened during the same period. In the north-western countries of Europe and in European colonies in which "rule by the people" had first been secured, "the people" had been limited to propertied males, recognized as having diverse "interests," as gentlemen, merchants, manufacturers, artisans, and so on. The citizen body was internally stratified and existed above lower classes, who were entitled to some but not all the rights of citizenship. The people or nation was counterposed to reactionary old regimes, yet it was internally diverse, and it was not usually hostile to other nations.

Yet a more aggressive nationalism grew during the nineteenth century (Mommsen 1990). To some extent it grew because aspirations for representative government became dominated by the notion that the *whole* people must rule, since it shared certain virtues and qualities needed for citizenship. It especially grew across the more easterly regions dominated by "multiethnic" dynastic Empires – Habsburg, Romanov, and Ottoman. Here conflicts between the imperial rulers and the locals were transformed by demands for democracy into conflicts between supposed ethnic/national communities. Local disprivileged elites claiming representative rights for themselves, faced with pressures from below, sought to mobilize the "whole" people against the imperial ethnicity and its local ethnic clients. This fostered acceptance of Corradini's notion that "the proletarian nation" might rise up against oppressors. Croats, Slovenes, and others might resent Turkish or Serb domination; Romanians might resent Hungarians; Slovaks might resent Czechs; and almost everyone might resent the dominant Germans, Russians, and Turks. The imperialist Germans, Russians, and Turks (and later the Hungarians) then responded with their own counternationalisms. Jews suffered because they were cosmopolitan and therefore considered antinational. But anti-Semitism was also entwined with other nationalist conflicts: Czech anti-Semitism was propelled by anti-German sentiment, Slovak by anti-Magyar, while Magyar and Austrian anti-Semitism was propelled by yearnings for imperial revisionism. In all these cases Jews were hated partly because of their supposed alliance with some other national enemy. Nationalism, at first an idealistic alliance directed internally against "feudal" rulers, turned aggressive inside and out against other "nations."

Thus emerged the ideal of the organic as opposed to the liberal, stratified nation-state (or "ethnic nationalism," as opposed to "civic nationalism"). Consider Austria (analyzed by Schmidt-Hartmann 1988, and discussed further in my forthcoming volume). In 1882 three young Austrian politicians propounded the "Linz Program," which was intended to found a new German People's Party. The program combined German nationalism, universal suffrage, and progressive social legislation. It denounced equally liberalism, laissez-faire capitalism, and Marxian socialism. The three men declared that whereas liberals advocated a constitution enshrining the conflict of interests, they upheld the "substance" of democracy. Their legitimacy, they said, was grounded in the unity of the people, "the good of all," "the interests of the people." The projected party never materialized. The three split and went off to found their own parties. Adler became a leader of the Social Democrats, Lueger founded the Christian Socials, and Schönerer founded what became the Pan-German Party – these were the three mass parties of interwar Austria, generating rather totalizing social movements, and two of them generating fascist movements (to be encountered in Chapter 6).

These young Austrians were endorsing an *organic* conception of the people and state. The people, they said, was one and indivisible, united, integral. Thus its state need not be grounded on the institutionalization of conflict between contending interests. One national movement could represent the *whole* people, ultimately transcending any conflict of interests among social groups within it. Class conflict and sectional interests were to be not compromised but *transcended*. This seemed a fine ideal, but it had its dark side (discussed at much greater length in my forthcoming volume). All states actually contained minorities who had their own distinct cultural traits. Some had cultural links to another foreign state, which their own ethnicity dominated and which they considered to be their "homeland." Organic nationalists looked suspiciously at these people. They were considered to have divided loyalties and so should be excluded from full membership in the nation. So organic nationalists came to believe in (1) an enduring national character, soul, or spirit, distinguishable from that of other nations, (2) their right to a state that would ultimately express this, and (3) their right to exclude minorities with different characters, who would only weaken the nation.

This is the familiar story of "the rise and rise" of nations and modern states – to which I have contributed myself (Mann 1986, 1993: esp. chaps. 10

and 11). Yet the expansion of these national networks of interaction proceeded *alongside* expanding "transnational" power relations – industrial capitalism and attendant ideologies such as liberalism and socialism, plus the broader cultural networks provided by European/Christian/"white" senses of collective identity. Property was everywhere overwhelmingly "private." No state intervened much in the economy, except to levy tariffs on imports for economic protection, to coordinate communications networks (especially railways), and to regulate banking. Around the European semi-periphery arose further notions of state-aided "late development" policies, but these were not very important before 1914. Thus much of social life remained outside the sphere of competence of the nation-state, even during its great period of expansion. Few expected much more from the state.

Nor did most politicians. Before 1914, most leftists were committed to decentralized versions of democracy and were ambivalent about the state. On the far left, residual Jacobinism was outweighed by profound distrust of all existing states and of the nationalism that supported them. Socialist ideology recognized only transnational classes (though practices often differed). Marx's notorious silence on the postrevolutionary state, his glib statements on how the state would "wither away" and on how the working class had no nation, were examples of the left's indifference toward the emerging nation-state. Marxists hoped to sweep states away, after using them briefly to change property forms. Anarcho-syndicalists felt it was safer for the left to bypass states altogether. True, leftists wanted the state to relieve poverty and to expand free education. Nonetheless, prewar welfare reformism was usually led not by socialists but by "bourgeois" left-liberals who felt more at home in a state that had long enfranchised them. Thus it tended to be German "Socialists of the [Professor's] Chair," British "New Liberals," French Republican Radicals, and Russian liberal *zemstvo* intelligentsia, more than the Marxian or syndicalist left, who looked to an expanded state to sponsor economic, cultural, and moral development. But they all saw this as helping to bring greater democracy. They wanted a reduction in despotic powers.

Things were a little different on the right, since extreme nationalists had emerged before 1914. They were already urging old regimes to mobilize the nation to defeat the corrosive forces of liberalism and socialism. As Sternhell emphasizes, many fascist ideas were already circulating before 1914. But though they excited some intellectuals, they had been harnessed to mass movements, which had been first developed by leftist parties and then copied by just a few nationalist parties. They were held in check by old regimes and churches who still controlled most states and most votes and who still looked askance at mass mobilization. The nation, the masses, were to be spoken for by elites, not activated. As Eley (1980) emphasizes, rightist nationalist pressure groups were beginning to alarm German conservatives and destabilize German foreign policy, but their role in domestic policy was much smaller. Austria probably saw the most developed mass movements of nationalism (Schorske 1981: chap 3). Though state functions were widening, most conservatives saw the state as little more than the preserver of order and the aggrandizer of territory. As on the left, the state was not generally seen as "the bearer of a moral project" (to repeat Perez-Diaz's resonant phrase). Nationalists were beginning to oppress minorities, while a moderate increase in the "infrastructural power" of the state was considered desirable. But these had definite limits and there was no real drive toward increasing the despotic power of the state. Despotism and authoritarianism were generally seen as characteristics of "old regimes" that would eventually wither away in the face of modernity. In 1914 few could have envisaged a fascist or even a milder authoritarian future.

Had Europe remained at peace, state expansion would doubtless have gradually continued and states would have acquired more infrastructural powers. Industrial capitalism would have continued to require state assistance. The enfranchisement of workers and women would have fostered the development of the welfare state. A "moderate nation-statism" would have emerged anyway, amended by state-led "late development" theory on the semi-periphery. But the Great War intervened. It militarized the nation-state and provided an economic model of how state intervention and planning might achieve economic development. It provided a "paramilitary" model of collective social action, weakened traditional conservatism, destroyed the multinational empires that were the main rivals to the nation-state, and strengthened aggressive nationalism against the enemy. With the coming to power of Lloyd George, Clemenceau, and Ludendorff in 1916 came the signal that war was now to be "total" – to be conducted not by a gentlemanly old regime but by a nation mobilized for military and economic service. Businessmen, labor leaders, civil servants, generals, and politicians served alongside each other in a single state-coordinated administration. This did not happen as effectively in Russia, Austria-Hungary, and Italy, and this was blamed on the strength of their old regimes (and on the "unpatriotic" stance of their socialists). Even noncombatant states in Northern Europe were compelled by blockade and submarine warfare to intervene in major ways (especially to introduce rationing, a radical extension of state powers). In Europe only neutral Spain and Portugal continued as before, their old regimes and weak states still legitimate. Yet most states had substituted effectively for private and market actions in achieving massive collective purposes on behalf of the nation. Modern statism had arrived, alongside modern nationalism.

Though wartime apparatuses of intervention were dismantled afterward, the infrastructurally powerful state was here to stay. The franchise was extended and governments were expected to alleviate postwar unemployment and housing shortages. Social citizenship was added to political citizenship. More ambitious schemes of social reconstruction and economic development began to circulate among technocrats, including economists. On the left socialists now vanquished their anarcho-syndicalist rivals (except in neutral Spain) and began to see revolution and reform alike as accomplished through more state action. Prewar visions of a democracy largely bypassing the state seemed obsolete. In Russia, war and civil war made the Bolsheviks more ardent statists. Elsewhere liberalism mutated into social democracy and moderate statism crept forward.

But most of the drama occurred on the right. Mainly under the banner of increasing statism, it swept into power over one-half of interwar Europe. Its eruption was a surprise, for the peace settlements of 1918 had been dominated by liberals. President Woodrow Wilson had proclaimed the coming of the "democratic world revolution." The Versailles delegates replaced the Austro-Hungarian and parts of the Russian and Ottoman Empires with a dozen putative democracies. Though these tended to enshrine the rule of a single dominant nation, their constitutions guaranteed the rights of minorities. Some liberals and socialists even hoped the rest of the world – colonies and dependent states – might soon follow suit. A new world order of mild and democratic nation-states seemed inaugurated.

Indeed, after brief postwar turbulence, Europe did seem headed that way. In late 1920 all but one of its twenty-eight states states had constitutions enshrining parliamentary elections, competing political parties, and guarantees for minorities. Most suffrages still excluded women (some excluded many men), some executives had powers rivaling legislatures, and political practices were often at odds with constitutional norms. But liberal democracy seemed the coming, modern ideal. The sole deviant case, the Soviet Union, actually claimed to be more genuinely democratic. The omens for tolerant nationalism were not so good. Millions of minority refugees were fleeing back to their national homelands under pressure from their former states (this is dealt with in my forthcoming volume). But, overall, the Great Powers believed the liberal democratic nation-state *was* the twentieth century.

By the end of the twentieth century, in Europe as in the west as a whole, it was. The northwest of Europe has been firmly liberal or social democratic

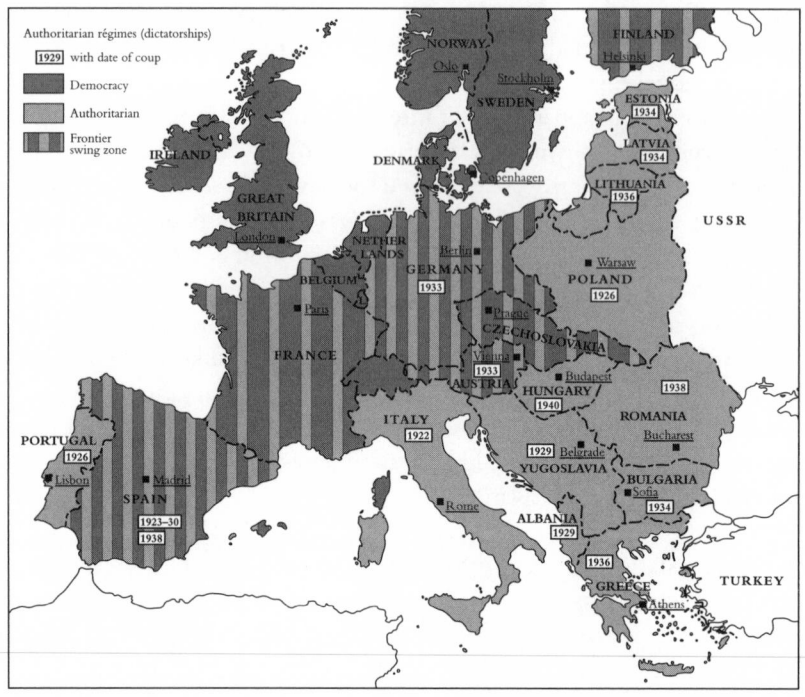

Map 2.1. The two interwar Europes.

for many decades, as have been the political institutions (at first for whites only) of their major settler ex-colonies. Southern European authoritarian regimes were gone by 1975. The communist regimes of the east collapsed suddenly in 1989–91. At the end of the millennium, *all* of Europe's states were formally committed to multiparty democracy, though some regimes in former communist countries had dubious credentials and ethnic tensions surfaced in a few. But Yugoslavia seems an alien exception to most Europeans. Though democracy proves hard to export to other parts of the world, it dominates the west.

But between 1920 and 1945 the liberal democratic nation-state retreated, battered by authoritarians. By 1938, fifteen of Europe's twenty-seven parliamentary regimes were rightist dictatorships, most claiming to embody a single organic nation, curtailing minority rights. Map 2.1 specifies the date each had its main coup. In other continents the four white-majority former British colonies – the United States, Canada, Australia, and New Zealand – had democracies for whites only (only New Zealand then allowed free representation of most nonwhites; South Africa and Rhodesia also had impeccable parliamentary institutions for whites only). But the two major Asian states, Japan and China, had succumbed to authoritarianism; while in Latin America only Uruguay, Colombia, and Costa Rica stayed consistently democratic, with most regimes fluctuating. So the interwar period saw two fairly evenly matched global and European blocs, one liberal democratic, the other organic-authoritarian. Both sought infrastructurally stronger states; only the latter sought greater despotic powers as well. The period then culminated in total warfare between the two. How do we explain the rise of interwar authoritarianism over half, but not all, of the relatively advanced part of the world and of Europe? Answering this question is a necessary preliminary to understanding a second question: Why did fascism arise? The map of Europe gives us our first clues.

Map 2.1, the political map of interwar Europe, reveals two subcontinents, "two Europes," one liberal democratic, the other authoritarian. The two Europes were geographically distinct, one occupying the northwest of the continent, the other its center, east, and south. Except for Czechoslovakia (which slightly curtailed the rights of its German and Slovak minorities), liberal democracy comprised a single bloc of eleven countries across the northwest: Finland, Sweden, Norway, Denmark, Iceland, Ireland, Britain, the Netherlands, Belgium, Switzerland, and France. Almost all the other liberal democracies of the world were former British colonies. Thus the liberal democratic bloc comprised three socio-cultural zones – "Nordic," "Anglo-Saxon," and "Low Country" – linked through a sea-trading economy and political and ideological similarities. They had embraced constitutional rule well before 1900. The Anglo-Saxon world spoke English; the Nordic countries (except for Finland) spoke mutually intelligible dialects of the same language group; and across the whole region, except for France, Belgium, and Czechoslovakia, elites might often converse in English.

Apart from Ireland they also had rather depoliticized religions. Ten of the sixteen were majority Protestant. Belgium, Czechoslovakia, France, and Ireland were majority Catholic, while the Netherlands and Switzerland were divided between the two religions. They included all the majority Protestant countries of Europe except for Germany, Estonia, and Latvia. But they included *all* the Protestant countries where church-state links had weakened significantly over the past century. Dutch and Swiss Catholicism were also independent of the state, while Belgium, Czechoslovakia, and France were rather secular Catholic countries (and the Czech church was in conflict with the Vatican). The northwest shared a great deal besides just the liberal democratic nation-state, and its geographical cohesion permitted the flow of common ideological messages. As we see below, its cultural solidarity was to matter considerably.

Most of the organic-authoritarian family also formed a single geographic bloc, though it was formed of two rather distinct historic socio-cultural zones: "Latin/Mediterranean" and "Slav/East and Central European." Their languages were more diverse and they were not a trading bloc. But (apart from most of Germany, Estonia, and Latvia) they had remained with the two early Christian churches: They comprised most of the Catholic countries and all the Eastern Orthodox countries in Europe. And they comprised all the European countries except for Ireland retaining intense church-state links. Again, these cultural solidarities – and the cultural fault lines within this zone – will prove important in the generation of authoritarianism and fascism.

Around this "continental divide" between the two Europes we can even detect a "frontier zone," indicated on the map. Most of it was comprised by two large countries, France and Germany. These were the swing countries that might have gone the other way. France might have gone authoritarian and Germany might have remained parliamentary, since both saw prolonged struggle between democratic and authoritarian forces, as they had during the previous period. The main prewar proto-fascist theorists (Maurras, Barrès, Sorel) were French, and France had the largest interwar authoritarian parties of both right and left in the northwest. As the power of Nazi Germany rose, the realization of French weakness grew and conservatives began to split over possible solutions. Fascist voices became louder. Had the election due in 1940 been held (and in peacetime), the quasi-fascist PSF might have won over 100 parliamentary seats, suggests Soucy (1991). Later, the Vichy collaborating regime had considerable domestic support. Conversely, the Weimar Republic contained an advanced democracy that might have survived. And the eventual outcome of the struggle in France and Germany might also be explicable in terms of geography, for their political "heartlands" lay close to the "other" geographic bloc. Paris and the surrounding Ile de France lie in the north, while France's advanced economic regions were mostly in the northwest. France was as integrated into the northwestern British/Low Countries free trade/democratic/Protestant sphere as into the more authoritarian Catholic south. Conversely, the core of the German state was in Berlin and Prussia, in the east of the country. German history is often described as the hijacking by Prussia of its liberal southwest and its free-trading northern ports.

The "frontier zone" is also represented in this book by the country that saw the most prolonged struggle between democracy and authoritarianism, Spain. Chapter 9 shows just how enduring and closely contested this was. There are also three politically borderline countries − for there were somewhat imperfect democracies to be found in Finland, Czechoslovakia, and Austria before 1934. Moreover, authoritarian movements in the northwest thrived only in divided settings inside and adjacent to this frontier zone. In ethnically divided Czechoslovakia, the German Sudeten Party enveloped the German minority to reach 15 percent of the national vote in 1935; in Slovakia a further 10 percent went to the Hlinka Party. In linguistically divided Belgium Christus Rex polled 11.5 percent in 1936 (mostly among French-speakers), while the Flemish VNV achieved 7.1 percent. But when the Rexist leaders embraced fascism, their vote fell in 1939 to 4.4 percent, and when the VNV accepted Nazi subsidies their support ebbed. The Finnish Lapua Movement/IKL could exploit the right's victory in the civil war and anti-Soviet irredentism to achieve 8.3 percent in 1936, though this fell to 6.6 percent in 1939. In the religiously divided Netherlands, the NSB polled 7.9 percent in 1935, but dropped to insignificance by 1939 as it drew close to Hitler. These authoritarian movements were not nearly as popular as those further to the east and south, but they were of some significance.

Yet authoritarians situated further inside the northwest bloc received few votes. Fascists and fellow-travelers languished, hovering around 2 percent of the vote in Norway, 1.5 percent in Switzerland, and well under 1 percent in Britain, Ireland, Iceland, Sweden, Denmark, the United States, Canada, Australia, and New Zealand (Lindstrom 1985: 115; Linz 1976: 89–91; Payne 1980: 126–35; 1995: 290–312). Though some intellectuals and elites played with authoritarian and fascist ideas (I quoted some of them in Chapter 1), and though there was intermittent grumbling about the "weakness" and divisions of parliamentary democracy, the decisive factor was that conservatives went populist but remained democratic, content to mobilize the masses on mild nationalism, religion, deference, and a claim to greater expertise at managing a capitalist economy (Mann 1993) Conservatives resisted authoritarian rightists, but social democrats also resisted revolutionaries. Thus both were able to process and to compromise their conflicts through democratic institutions, which deepened as a result.

Yet authoritarians prospered in the center, east, and south of the continent. In Austrian, German, and Spanish free elections they reached near 40 percent of the votes. Across the half-free elections of Eastern Europe they won convincingly. Had fascists been freer to organize, they would have garnered more votes (as we see in Chapters 7 and 8 in Hungary and Romania).

We cannot say that the authoritarians regimes had majority support, since they manipulated executive powers and some used coercive powers during elections. But they had a much more powerful appeal than in the northwest. There were indeed two Europes, one firmly liberal democratic, the other attracted by organic-authoritarian visions of the nation-state – with a politically divided and oscillating frontier zone between them.

The strength of such geographic blocs makes me doubt three common explanations of authoritarianism and fascism. One treats countries as unique and provides what is in effect a "nationalist" explanation. The power of the nation-state has turned many scholars inward, to study one country, usually their own. They favor explanations in terms of "national peculiarities," such as the *Sonderweg*, Germany's "special path" toward Nazism. Historians of Spain emphasize memories of the glorious Siglo de Oro, followed by imperial decline, resulting in a cankered church, an inflated officer corps, unique regionalisms, a violent south, and so on. If I could read Albanian, I could doubtless learn of unique Albanian predispositions for authoritarianism. True, local factors explain the *details* of each national outcome. Nazism was distinctively German and Francoism was Spanish. I can't imagine them in any other country. Yet Map 2.1 reveals very powerful macro-regional effects cutting right across national boundaries. These meant that Spain might go authoritarian, Albania was likely to, and Ireland was not. Ireland had a powerful, reactionary Catholic Church and experienced an actual civil war in the 1920s. Yet Ireland was in the northwest, inheriting some democratic British institutions and sharing a language and population exchanges with democratic Britain and the United States. Albanians did not live amid a democratic civilization; the Irish did. Thus the rival armies of the Irish civil war actually turned into two rival electoral parties – and these two still dominate Irish elections today. We need local details – and they proliferate in my case-study chapters – but we also need a more macro approach.

A second approach is also implicitly nationalist. It divides the continent into nation-states and treats each as a single case in a multivariate comparative analysis. It mobilizes national statistics to test hypotheses suggesting, for example, that fascism emerged in backward countries or in those with rapidly expanding universities. I utilize such statistics later. Yet the method is limited by the brute geography we have just glimpsed. Are all the more backward countries or those with expanding universities so clumped together on the map? Almost certainly not. More likely, geography also provides distinct communication networks of contiguity, so that distinct ideologies are diffused to different degrees across different regions of Europe, somewhat independently of level of development or university structure.

The third approach is therefore a regional one, identifying macro-regional cultures – "the Mediterranean," "Eastern Europe," "Central Europe," and so on – as causally decisive. For example, this approach correctly notes that the kind of organicism that centered on racist anti-Semitism was largely confined to Central and Eastern Europe, failing to much penetrate the south. Yet authoritarianism as a whole was diffused much more broadly than this. It filled half of Europe. It did not reflect "the Special Case of Central Europe," as Newman proclaims (1970: 29–34), nor "East European late development," as Janos (1989) and Berend (1998: 201, 343–5) argue, or even "partial or backward development" in general, as Gregor suggests (1969: xii–xiv).[1] Though all these macro-regional theories contain some truth, fascism was more general, yet also more spotty, than these regional theories. For the five major fascist movements (in Germany, Austria, Hungary, Romania, and Italy) were scattered right across Europe and its levels of development. We need a more general explanation for authoritarianism and perhaps a more particular explanation for fascism. I first examine the dependent variable of regime type.

TYPES OF AUTHORITARIANISM

Our explanatory problem lies on the political right. Across the whole of "Greater Europe" the Soviet Union was the only leftist authoritarian regime. All other authoritarian regimes were viewed as being of the political right – though we see below that fascism was only ambiguously so. So they had certain common features. All these regimes worshiped order and protected private property; all embraced an authoritarian statism, rejecting federalism, democracy, and their supposed "vices": disorderly class conflict, political corruption, and moral decline.[2] They also came to embrace organic nationalism. The nation must be "one and indivisible," cleansed of subverters of national unity. Thus the regimes repressed socialists and liberals committed to internationalism, and they repressed ethnic, regional, and religious minorities who supposedly had loyalties to other countries. Most authoritarians relied on the military and police powers of the old regime; fascists preferred their own paramilitaries. But once they had rejected peaceful compromise of differences, they had all chosen the path of violence – military or paramilitary power – to solve political problems.

Yet the family members were varied (for general surveys, see Polonsky 1975; Payne 1980; Lee 1987 and Berend 1998). Some scholars divide them into two groups: "fascists" and a much larger group labeled either "authoritarian conservatives" or just "authoritarians" (e.g., Linz 1976; Blinkhorn

1990). This is insufficient. First, though it accepts that with fascism comes a change of direction, to a distinctive combination of rightism with radicalism, it does not recognize that this comes as the final stage of a broader problem faced by rightists: the need to cope with organized political pressure from the masses. Modern authoritarianism departed from despotic regimes of the past in trying to absorb the mass pressures from below characterizing all twentieth-century politics. Second, it yields an "authoritarian" group that is too big and diverse. The Franco regime, often blandly labeled "author-itarian conservative," probably killed over 100,000 people in cold blood. The similarly labeled Metaxas regime in Greece killed perhaps a hundred.[3] Third, regimes became nastier through this period. We need more dis-tinctions to cope with variations between countries and through time. I distinguish four ascending degrees of authoritarianism within the family. Of course, since this is a continuum, any boundaries between types are a little arbitrary, and each type includes rather diverse regimes. Remember also that these are regimes, not movements. As Kallis (2000) notes, regimes do not simply express ideologies. They also embody processes that he calls politi-cal consolidation, policy formation, and scope of change sought. These all involve questions of political practicability as well as ideology (cf. Paxton 1998).[4]

Semi-authoritarian Regimes

These regimes were the mildest and most conservative. They tried to hold on to late nineteenth-century methods of rule. They were essentially "dual states" in which an elected legislature and a nonelected executive both wielded considerable powers – hence the "semi-authoritarian" label. Pres-sure from below was deflected by manipulating elections and parliaments. The executive fixed elections, bought deputies, appointed cabinets, and re-pressed "extremists" under emergency powers. Yet parliaments, law courts, and the press retained some freedoms. Monarchies dominated here, aided by traditional clientelist conservative and liberal parties. "Statism" here meant loyalty to the existing "old regime." Nationalism was kept on a tight leash, hardly organic. Where political enemies were cleansed, this was more by intimidation and imprisonment than by murder, except during the short postwar period of revolutionary turbulence. Once the regimes felt basically secure, they did not rely on much murder and they restrained tendencies to pogroms against Jews – Jews were too useful. Though some manipulated popular prejudice against minorities, they were usually only discriminatory, not seeking to expel them. Though they had strong militaries, foreign policy remained cautious. Fiscal and social policies were also conservative and procapitalist. These were resisting modernity as well as democracy.

Examples are most of the early interwar regimes: Greece up to the Metaxas coup, Romanian regimes of the 1920s and early '30s, the Spanish regime of Alfonso XIII up to 1923, the Admiral Horthy/Count Bethlen regimes in Hungary in the 1920s, Chancellor Seipel's Austrian Christian Social government in the late 1920s (covertly subverting freedoms), the pre-fascist Italian governments of Salandra and Sonnino, the pre-Nazi regimes of Brüning, von Schleicher, and von Papen. Fascist ideology had little influence on them, and they were mostly quite mild and pragmatic – compared with what followed. Yet none lasted for long.

Semi-reactionary Authoritarian Regimes

Here the old regime (centered on monarchy, military, and church) coped with popular pressure by upping the level of repression. It overthrew or emasculated the legislature, ending the dualism noted above. Repression alternated with scapegoating discriminatory measures aimed at leftists, minorities, or Jews. These regimes still feared the masses. Nonetheless, they were also making limited modernist moves – hence they were only semi-reactionary. They advocated organic nationalism, though they remained wary of mobilizing the people behind it. Fascist ideology had some influence here. Some (e.g., Salazar, Pilsudski, Primo de Rivera) cultivated one-party rule, mostly imitating Mussolini, but the party was controlled from above, its role being to domesticate rather than to excite the masses. Paramilitaries might be organized, but more to parade than to fight, and so the army retained its effective monopoly over the means of military violence. Foreign policy remained cautious, economic policy remained procapitalist and decidedly developmentalist. Primo and Pilsudski even sought social reform, though their conservative supporters resisted, inducing Primo's fall (see Chapter 9) and Pilsudski's move rightward.

This was the most widespread type of interwar regime. Examples are the Hungarian governments of Admiral Horthy and others through most of the 1930s (see Chapter 7), King Carol's "directed democracy" in Romania in the late 1930s (Chapter 8), General Primo de Rivera in Spain in 1923–30 (though he also introduced many corporatist elements; see Chapter 9), General Pilsudski in Poland in 1926–35 followed by other officers until 1939, the three army-based Baltic regimes (Smetona in Lithuania in 1926–39, Ulmanis in Latvia in 1934–9, and Pats in Estonia in 1934–9),[5] King Zog in Albania in 1928–39, King Alexander and the Regent Paul in Yugoslavia during the 1930s, the regime of King Boris in Bulgaria from 1935, Metaxas's rule in Greece in 1936–8, Dolfuss's rule in Austria from 1932 to early 1934 (Chapter 6), and the Portuguese military rule of 1928–32.

Corporatist Regimes

About a third of the regimes then drifted further. They sought to increase statism, mobilize organic nationalism, and intensify scapegoating of minorities and leftists. Most fundamentally, they began to borrow substantially from fascist organization and ideology, often under pressure from actual fascist movements. The borrowings were more of "top-down" statism than "bottom-up" paramilitarism. "Corporatism" conveys this sense of an integrated, hierarchical organization, though it is not a perfect label since it tends to smooth over the tensions often appearing between its two main constituencies, old regime authoritarians and more "radical" nationalists. Though procapitalist, some corporatist regimes developed patriarchal welfare policies and intervened in the economy to sponsor growth (though others preferred order and stability to capitalist dynamism). The army remained the regime's bedrock, retaining most of its monopoly of military power, yielding only a little to paramilitarism. Foreign policy combined bellicose nationalist rhetoric with diplomacy that was in reality rather cautious.

Examples are the "hyphenated fascist" regimes, in which fascist tendencies are undercut by another tendency: for example, the Metaxas "monarcho-fascism" in Greece after 1938, Dolfuss's "clerico-fascism" or "Austro-fascism" from 1934 (see Chapter 6), King Carol's "monarcho-fascism" in Romania from 1938, followed between 1940 and 1944 by General Antonescu's "military fascism" (Chapter 8). There was also the French Vichy regime, Hungarian "radical rightist" cabinets in World War II (Chapter 7), Salazar's combination of fascism and *deus, patria et familia*, and the Franco dictatorship up to the early 1960s. The Metaxas dictatorship was the most moderate: a paramilitary youth movement and corporatist trappings, mass arrests but few killings, and little pressure on minorities. He purged monarchists but not the monarch himself, and his foreign policy steered carefully between Germany and Britain (Kofas 1983). Elsewhere, the Japanese Imperial government was of this type after 1931 (though it also contained fascist elements); Chiang Kai-shek aspired to this but lacked the infrastructural power over China to implement it.

Of course, these are ideal types and the real-world distinctions between regimes were often rather blurry. Some parliamentary forms were maintained even when the balance of power had shifted firmly to the executive – as, for example, in Hungary and Romania in the late 1930s. Indeed, Hungary not only retained a parliament. Until 1944 this actually contained socialist deputies, uniquely among all the Axis countries. The division between reactionary and organic corporatist regimes was also sometimes blurred – as it was between the latter and fascism. Primo de Rivera might be considered corporatist rather than reactionary. In the Franco and, to a lesser extent, the Salazar regimes, fascists often did the dirty work; whereas Carol, Antonescu, and Horthy all discovered that parts of their own governments had been captured by fascists. Here was vigorous rivalry between corporatists and fascists.

Fascist Regimes

Fascism provided a discontinuity, reversing the flow of power by adding to corporatism a "bottom–up" mass movement centered on paramilitarism and electoralism, while also increasing coercive powers from the top. Paramilitarism flourished amid an obvious decay in the loyalty and cohesion of the state's armed forces. The army became split, with many soldiers' fascist and paramilitary sympathies eroding discipline, threatening the state's monopoly of military power. This also created a basic tension between "bottom–up" paramilitarism and electioneering and a "top-down" statism centered on the "leadership principle." This tension prevented fascist regimes, coming into power with help from old regime elites, from settling down into being simply extreme rightist, giving them their "radical" character. In fact, fascist leaders came from all parts of the political spectrum, many being former socialists (such as Mussolini, Déat, or Mosley). Fascism embraced paramilitarism at home and militarism abroad. It also intervened massively in the economy, with definite fascist theories of economic development. Yet fascists' relations with conservatives and capitalists remained ambiguous, each seeming to need the other.

We do not have many cases of fascist regimes. The Nazis and the Italian fascists were the only two regimes seizing power and holding on to it for some years. Though Austria had proportionately more fascists than either, they were divided into two opposed movements and could not seize power until 1938, on the backs of Hitler's troops. Hungarian and Romanian fascists were equally well supported, but they were also heavily persecuted. They did succeed in infiltrating the ruling regimes and they came to power briefly in 1944 at the end of the war. We see here (as also in the case of Spain) the importance of relations between fascists and other authoritarian rightists: fascist coups depended on the balance of power between them. But the influence of fascism was also much broader. Corporatist regimes were stealing fascist ideas in order to be able to repress real fascists, and so survive. Then amid wartime conditions other organic nationalists flirted with fascism and joined the Axis Powers – the Slovakian Hlinkas, the Croatian Ustasha, and nationalists in the Baltic states, Belarus, and the Ukraine. But the Italians and the Nazis were easily the most important. Their successes influenced others. Mussolini's 1922 March on Rome came so early that all authoritarian regimes had Italian models to copy and adapt. Hitler's geopolitical power carried Nazi influence, though not for long. He brought a world war that destroyed them all. Since fascist regimes never became securely institutionalized, we don't really know what enduring fascism would have looked like. Would it have continued to embody the factionalism and zig-zagging of the Mussolini regime or Hitler's persistent if slightly chaotic radicalization? Or would stable corporatist/syndicalist structures have emerged? And so in discussing fascism, the most extreme of the authoritarian family, I am discussing less actual regimes than the future regimes envisaged by the larger fascist movements. The fascist problem I seek to explain, therefore, is how these future ideals arose and became powerful, against the backdrop of the authoritarian regimes distinguished above.

My typology generates three basic questions: Why did one-half of Europe continue to move further along this authoritarian scale? Why did only a few movements reach as far as fascism for their ideals? and Why did only two of them succeed in seizing power unaided? Not many writers clearly distinguish these three questions. Most explanations link all three to serious social crises erupting in the early twentieth century: ideological, economic, military, and political. These correspond to the four sources of social power I have analyzed in the two volumes of *The Sources of Social Power* (1986, 1993). We see below that notions of general crisis do best at explaining the general authoritarian surge, less well at explaining the rise of fascist movements, and least well at explaining fascist coups.

ECONOMIC POWER, ECONOMIC CRISIS

Economic power relations derive from the human need to extract, transform, distribute, and consume the resources of nature for subsistence. This generates economic institutions and social classes arising out of production and market relations, cooperating yet simultaneously conflicting with one another. Those who control the means of production and exchange possess crucial power resources that allow them a measure of more general social power. Yet severe class conflict may challenge their power. The time and place discussed here was dominated by the capitalist mode of production in its industrial phase. So I discuss the development and crises of industrial capitalism, its class conflicts, and their degree of responsibility for the rise of authoritarianism and fascism.

Though economic power relations have always been important in human affairs, social theory in our materialist age has often seemed obsessed by them. Economic explanations of fascism have been the most popular ones, and I discuss them at greatest length. Long-term causes of authoritarianism and fascism are traced to capitalist "backwardness" or "late development," short-term causes to economic recessions and surges in class conflict. All are believed to have helped undermine the legitimacy of existing governments and increased strife to the point where authoritarian solutions seemed plausible – especially to those with ready access to the means of coercion. I begin with long-term causes.

(1) *Late development theory* suggests that economically backward countries were lured into authoritarian politics by statist theories of "late development." A variant form of the argument links this to nationalism. Backward countries feel exploited by developed ones, and so nationalists urge their countries to "stand by ourselves alone" with economic policies embodying autarchy and protection – which also increased statism.

These theories require that the authoritarian countries are the economic laggards, and this is indeed so. Scholars have mobilized batteries of socio-economic statistics to show that the higher the GNP, urbanization, literacy, and so on, the more democratic the regime. Correlations between indices of development and liberal democracy usually range between $r = .60$ and $r = .85$. By squaring this we find that level of development explains between one-third and two-thirds of the variance found in levels of liberal democracy – quite a robust finding in macro-sociology, where most cross-national statistical comparisons contain considerable error and "noise" (Rueschemeyer, Stephens, and Stephens 1992: 13–20; Maravall 1997). Comparisons among interwar European countries come to the same conclusion (Janos 1989; Stephens 1989; Gomez-Navarro 1991). Does this argument also hold for the two interwar geographic blocs identified above?

In Table 2.1, I have used four indices of socio-economic development: GNP per capita, proportion of the economically active population in agriculture, forestry, or fisheries, the infant mortality rate, and the per capita number of items sent annually through the mail. GNP per capita measures economic development, while agricultural employment measures lack of it. Neither measure is perfect, since data quality and categorization vary

Table 2.1. *Statistics of Authoritarian and Democratic Countries*

Country	Agricultural labor force (%)[a]	GNP per capita[b]	Infant mortality rate[c]	Mailed items per capita[d]	Severity of slump (%)[e]	Peak unemployment rate (%)[f]
1. Democratic						
Australia	25.4	567	53	161	13.4	19.1
Belgium	17.3	1,098	94	179	7.9	19.0
Canada	36.8	1,203	90	96	30.1	19.3
Czechoslovakia	36.9	586	146	76	18.2	17.4
Denmark	35.3	945	81	78	2.9	31.7
Finland	64.6	590	84	29	6.5	(6.2)[g]
France	35.6	982	97	153	11.0	15.4
Ireland	52.1	662	68	67	16.7	
Netherlands	20.6	1,008	52	137	9.1	11.9
New Zealand	33.4		36	215		(10.2)
Norway	35.5	1,033	49	55	8.3	11.3
Sweden	36.0	897	59	88	9.2	23.3
Switzerland	21.3	1,265	54	161	8.0	(4.7)
U.K.	6.0	1,038	69	146	8.1	15.6
U.S.	22.0	1,658	67	227	29.5	22.9
Democratic average	**31.9**	**967**	**73**	**125**	**12.8**	**18.8**
2. Authoritarian						
Austria	29.3	720	120	147	22.5	16.3
Bulgaria	79.8	306	149		8.6	
Estonia	59.0	(95)		51		
Germany	29.0	770	89	94	16.1	30.1
Greece	53.7	390	94	20	8.2	
Hungary	53.0	424	177	41	9.4	30.0[h]
Italy	46.8	517	120	59	6.1	(15.5)
Japan	43.0	(208)	138	60	4.5	(6.8)
Latvia	66.2	(115)		47		
Lithuania	76.7	(69)				
Poland	65.9	350	145	32	22.3	16.7
Portugal	55.0	320	142	23		
Romania	77.2	331	184	21	6.2	
Spain	56.1	445	126	33	20.4	
Yugoslavia	78.1	341	147	35	11.9	
Authoritarian average	**57.9**	**352**	**159**	**48**	**12.4**	

[a] Percent of labor force in agriculture, c. 1930. Czech figure is for 1930 but refers to territory of 1945; Portuguese figure is corrected; Spanish figure is for 1920.

[b] 1929 GNP per capita, expressed in 1960 US$. *Source:* Bairoch 1976: 297; Mitchell 1993; for Estonia, Latvia, and Lithuania from *Latvian Economist,* 1933, estimates for national income, adjusted upward by 15 percent (these figures still seem rather low).

[c] c. 1928 infant mortality rate per 1,000. Note U.S. mortality for black infants alone was 106. *Source:* Mitchell 1993, 1998.

[d] No. of items per inhabitant sent through the mail, c. 1930. *Source:* Mitchell 1993, 1998.

[e] Maximum peak–trough percent fall in GDP during period 1922–35, at constant prices. *Source:* Mitchell 1993, 1995, 1998; Lethbridge 1985: 538, 571, 592. Polish figure estimated.

[f] Highest annual interwar unemployment rate. *Source:* Maddison 1982: 206; Newell and Symons 1988: 70; Toniolo and Piva 1988: 230; Garside 1990: 5; Mitchell 1993, 1995, 1998. These figures are notoriously unreliable. More backward national accounting systems typically produce severely understated unemployment figures. Those I consider too low I have placed in parentheses.

[g] Figures in parentheses are probably unreliable and much too low. They have not been included in calculations of averages.

[h] Industrial work force only.

between countries. Infant mortality is a simpler measure of well-being, collected fairly similarly by governments, though it is very affected by the very poor (who provide most of the mortality).[6] Items sent through the mail measures genuine "discursive" literacy, though it is affected by urbanization, since townspeople write more letters. All these indices have their particularities. It is their combination that matters. More developed countries have higher GNP per capita and more mail, but lower agricultural employment and infant mortality. Were these also the liberal democratic countries?

The table broadly answers "yes": The democracies were more developed by a factor of two or three on these indices.[7] Most democratic countries do better than most authoritarian ones on all four measures, because the northwest of the continent was much more developed than the southeast. There were a few deviant cases, however. All four German and three Austrian statistics reveal that they were developed countries. Czechoslovakia, Finland, and Ireland were economically marginal cases between the two Europes, and they were also somewhat politically marginal. Overall, with the major Germanic exceptions, this is a strong relationship. Whatever qualifications I make later, the rise of authoritarianism was mainly a problem for the less-developed countries of interwar Europe.

Yet the table shows that this cannot be so of fascism. Indeed, some have argued that fascism is not important in very backward countries, since it requires an economy and civil society sufficiently advanced to allow effective mobilization of the masses. The most backward countries, they say, had to rely on old regime organization, such as the monarchy or the military, and so at most could reach only corporatism (Gomez-Navarro 1991). Riley (2002) argues that fascist mass-mobilization presupposed a denser "civil society" – inverting the usual liberal theory of civil society, which sees such density as a precondition for democracy. These writers suggest that fascism developed best in the more developed countries that contained denser networks of markets and voluntary associations. Yet Table 2.1 shows that the largest fascist movements were found at *all* levels of development, including advanced Austria and Germany, middling Italy, and backward Romania and Hungary. Fascism seems unrelated to level of economic development.

"Modernization" and Marxian schools of theory both say that economic development *causes* democratization, with modern social classes as its agents. Drawing on a tradition stretching back to Aristotle, modernization theorists such as Lipset (1960) and Huntington (1991: 66–8) argue that economic development expands the size of the middle class, and this favors democracy. One Marxian writer, Barrington Moore (1966), agreed, arguing that the bourgeoisie (along with a free peasantry) had pressed for liberal constitutions in early modern Europe. Other Marxian writers, especially Rueschemeyer et al. (1992), have questioned this in more recent times. They show that the middle classes have tended to follow rather than lead democratization, being sometimes pro-, sometimes antidemocratic. They say the working class was the main force for democracy, with large agrarian landlords being the main antidemocrats. Capitalist industrialization thus favored democracy by increasing the size of the working class and reducing the power of agrarian landlords. Stephens (1989) explains interwar authoritarianism mainly in terms of conflict between a democratic working class and capitalists, especially agrarian ones, eventually resorting to authoritarian repression. There is a banal argument involved here: The larger the social group capable of mobilization, the more likely it is to favor enfranchising large numbers. First the middle class demanded the suffrage, then the working class – and this caused some outweighted middle-class groups to backtrack on democracy, as during the 1848 Revolution.

Let me add one point. The political legacies of former times may modify later class behavior. Consider agrarian landlords. In premodern Europe they were politically decisive (as Barrington Moore says), since they ran society. But only in backward regions such as Hungary or Andalucia did they retain much economic power in the interwar period, after industrialization and land reform took their toll. Agrarian landlords played a lesser economic role in Weimar Germany and even less in Romania. Nonetheless, landlords often retained control of state executives, especially officer corps and ministries of the interior. This was because landowners had long ago entrenched their rule amid a broader "old regime": kin-connected monarchies, landowning nobilities, and the elites of bureaucracies, armed forces, and established churches. Mayer has emphasized that old regimes survived into the interwar period, maintaining entrenched political, military, and ideological power while their economic power was fading. We see below that authoritarian rightism and even fascism were more closely related to the decisions made by old regimes than to narrowly defined propertied classes.

Luebbert (1991) emphasizes two other important legacies from the prewar period: the degree to which liberal political parties were already powerful and the degree to which agricultural laborers were already mobilized. He notes that strong liberal political traditions helped wavering classes to maintain a prodemocratic stance, while their absence pushed them into the authoritarian camp. And if agricultural laborers were not already organized, interwar socialist attempts to organize them alienated small peasant proprietors and shifted them rightward (as Heberle 1964 showed in his classic study of Schleswig-Holstein). I support his first argument and modify his second.

Classes are useful theoretical constructs that we operationalize with empirical indicators. In historical research our indicators are often poor. In the late nineteenth and early twentieth centuries we acquire information on organizations such as trade unions and political parties, plus gross voting trends. Until after 1945 we have virtually no opinion or exit polls, nor have any of the authors cited above attempted ecological studies of voting. They present only gross voting patterns and examine organizations that they assume represent classes: Socialist parties or labor unions tell us about the working class, conservative parties or employers' organizations about the bourgeoisie or landowners, and so on. Yet to equate classes with particular organizations is risky. Few interwar union movements managed to recruit more than a quarter of manual workers, whereas successful conservative parties must often have derived more votes from workers than from any other class (since workers were so numerous). There are many social influences that might cross-cut class – such as economic sector, region, religion, gender, and generation. Through ecological analysis of voting in my case-study chapters, we see that core "proletarian ghettos" – worker families living amid dense worker urban neighbourhoods containing manufacturing industry or mining – usually did support leftist visions of democracy. But most interwar workers lived and worked in other kinds of communities and were drawn toward liberal or conservative visions of democracy and also to nondemocratic authoritarian and especially fascist views. Small peasants also espoused varied politics, some pro-, others antidemocratic, according to complex economic circumstances (not just fear of their laborers, as Luebbert suggests) and tugged also by regional, ethnic, religious, and gender sentiments. In the interwar period capitalist (especially agrarian capitalist) organizations tended to be antidemocratic, while socialist organizations were relatively prodemocratic, but this concerns minorities, not majorities.

Class theory also has difficulty with fascism. Whereas the other forms of authoritarian regime were staffed by conservatives trying to mobilize and control mass movements, fascism was a populist and "radical" movement, with a strong "bottom-up" thrust. Traditional class explanations work better for the most conservative forms of authoritarianism and less well for fascism. Not that class was irrelevant to fascist support. Fascists received disproportionate support from economic sectors liking the message of class transcendence, people from all classes who were working and living outside the main sites of severe class conflict in modern society.

The interwar period also saw the rise of statism. Authoritarian rule had now acquired plausible claims to sponsor social development – for example, to cure unemployment – that earlier absolutism had not aspired to. This might make it more attractive to workers. Thus the rival attractions of liberal democracy or authoritarianism have varied through time, perhaps for sizable groups in all classes, independently of level of development. Interwar Europe distinctively favored authoritarianism, as earlier or later Europe did not. This means that the gross differences that Table 2.1 revealed may have partially reflected the *past* association of capitalist development with democracy. This possibility seems most evident in terms of the changing nature of the middle class, referred to earlier. In the French revolutionary period, capitalism was highly decentralized, its industrial development mainly the work of small entrepreneurs. Its markets were relatively "free" – helping to develop free politics also. By 1918 "organized capitalism" had arrived (to use Hilferding's contemporary term), and much of the middle class was employed and subordinated within authoritative organizations. Perhaps it might be less attracted by "free politics."

This is speculation. But the statistics do show that the *absolute* level of economic development reached in the interwar period cannot explain the rise of authoritarianism. Take the cases of Italy and Spain. Their per capita incomes around 1930 were close to the median level of countries then plunging into authoritarianism. Such an absolute level had been attained only quite recently in the world: by the United States and Britain in the 1850s, Belgium, the Netherlands, and Switzerland in the 1860s, France and Norway in the 1880s, Denmark in the 1890s, and Sweden in the 1900s (Bairoch 1976: 286, 297).[8] They were the economic equivalents of Italy and Spain in 1930 (though obviously only in gross economic terms). In the late nineteenth century the advance had been toward democracy, not authoritarianism. Yet now Italy and Spain were marching the other way. The same level of economic development accompanied democratization before World War I, but an authoritarian surge after it. The problem remains today, for most countries in the world have reached the level of economic development achieved by Britain in the 1850s or Denmark in the 1890s, yet only a few are genuinely democratic. Through the twentieth century a higher and higher level of per capita income seem "required" in each decade for countries making transitions to democracy (see the statistics presented by Huntington 1991 and Maravall 1997). Other processes of world-historical development must have blocked liberal democracy in the twentieth century. Its economy did not prove particularly favorable to democracy – unlike its wars, which tended to be won by democracies.

"Late development" theory supplies an economic theory of the twentieth century blockage, claiming that the early developers – Britain, Belgium, the Netherlands, and Switzerland, perhaps France and the United States – had experienced uniquely favorable economic conditions for liberal democracy. Their economies had grown gradually, with decentralized markets and weak states. The first "late developers," especially Germany, nurtured more protectionist and statist models of development. As subsequent economic development became more rapid and dislocating, it generated more class confrontation amid more interventionist states. Peasants dislocated by world markets and laborers flocking into much larger factories and cities were exposed to the new viruses of socialism and anarcho-syndicalism. They confronted a more centralized capitalist class, aided by a more dependent middle class. Class conflict became more destabilizing. Two great "armed camps" confronted one another, in the words of the contemporary writer Carl Schmitt (who is referred to at length below). States now also sought to promote economic growth, seeing themselves as the bearers of a desired developmental project (Janos 1982; Gomez-Navarro 1991). Pressed by proletarians below, bourgeois classes could lean on a stronger state. There was also an international dimension, for the global economy was also more tightly integrated. Latecomers said they were "proletarian nations" exploited by the advanced countries, generating nationalism among the lower and middling classes. Because of these macro-economic tendencies, late economic development might generate extreme nation-statism in an attempt to repress "class enemies" at home and abroad.

This argument appears plausible in the Eastern European periphery. Late development policies figure in Hungarian and Romanian authoritarianism, as detailed in Chapters 7 and 8. Yet neither Germany nor Austria were by now "late" developers: Germany had the most advanced economy in Europe, while Austria, though enormously disrupted by the loss of its Empire, had a fairly open economy. So did Spain and Portugal before Salazar and Franco. And though these two near-corporatist dictators brought more autarchic economies, this was for purposes of not economic development but political control. Indeed, both their corporatist economies stagnated badly. Conversely, late development without much state intervention characterized the democratic Nordic periphery (Bairoch 1976). Nordic growth and industrialization rates, factory sizes, and socialist strength were now higher than those of almost all authoritarian countries. Yet the Nordic countries were deepening their democracies in the interwar period. Pressures that in the center, south, and east seemed to overwhelm their fragile democracies deepened democracy in the northwest. Late economic development alone cannot explain authoritarianism, though it figured in some places.

One problem is that this scholarly tradition has been fixated on statism, ignoring nationalism. Yet authoritarian movements – and their economic theorists – were mobilizing nationalism as well as statism. As Berend (1998) has argued, protectionism, import-substitution, covert devaluations, and the like, which were prevalent in Central and Eastern Europe in the interwar period, were not just technical economics. They were also importantly nationalist, presupposing certain nationalist beliefs. Rather similar organic nationalist ideologies and movements were becoming important just about everywhere across the east and south of the continent. This was rarer across the older countries of the northwest, even in the late-developing Nordic countries. But it was ubiquitous across former Habsburg, Romanov, and Ottoman lands. And herein obviously lies the main difference. Most of the democratic countries of the northwest had been independent states for far longer. Whatever sense of "exploitation" they may have had, this could not rest on foreign political domination by Habsburg- or Romanov-type states. Of course, Ireland and Norway differed in this respect. But such differences and exceptions point us to the importance of political and geopolitical power relations, discussed below in the chapter. In contrast to their common political experience the countries of the east and the south experienced far more diverse class conflicts, since these depended far more on the particular economic structure of the country. Moreover, ethnic tensions were also still growing in the early twentieth century, whereas class conflict was older and more institutionalized (though briefly destabilized at the end of World War I). Though both class and national conflict helped generate authoritarianism, we see below that national conflicts were usually more relevant to the projects of fascists. German and Romanian fascists shared more national than class sentiments, as we also see below. Thus long-term economic development and its attendant conflicts were indeed significant causes of the major political conflicts of the period, but they were mediated by nationalism. This is why the most self-conscious development strategies were espoused most enthusiastically by fascists, who combined both.

So relative economic backwardness may help more to explain authoritarianism, but late development strategies may help more to explain fascism. We have not yet fully explained why.

(2) *Economic slump.* Authoritarianism might be a response to short-term economic fluctuations, especially recessions. This seems an obvious explanation, but the data are equivocal. The last two columns of Table 2.1 detail the maximum peak-trough falls in GNP between any two years during

1927 to 1935 and the highest recorded unemployment rate. They reveal no overall difference between liberal democratic and authoritarian countries. The most severely affected by recession were democratic Canada and the United States, followed by authoritarian Austria, Poland, and Spain, then by democratic Czechoslovakia and Ireland, then by authoritarian Germany and democratic Australia. Unemployment rates provide less reliable data. Unfortunately, we cannot calculate real unemployment rates of most of the more backward and authoritarian countries. However, two of the fascist countries, Germany and Austria, did have the highest rates, along with democratic Denmark. But these are hardly convincing evidence of any clear relationship. The problem is that all of the west suffered a slump, but only half of it went authoritarian.

Were authoritarian coups immediately preceded by slumps? Five coups during 1932–34 followed the onset of the Great Depression: in Germany, Austria, Estonia, Latvia, and Bulgaria. It is highly plausible that the Depression precipitated them. I examine in more detail the cases of Germany and Austria in Chapters 4–6. Yet even if they confirmed the hypothesis, this would still leave ten or eleven countries whose coups were not a response to the Great Depression, plus the sixteen northwestern countries that did not experience coups at all, yet experienced the Depression. A few coups at other times also directly followed a recession. The Italian recession from 1918 was reversed only in 1922, the year of the fascist coup. Spain and Romania experienced two main authoritarian surges. Spain had Primo de Rivera's coup in 1926 and the military rising of 1936. Yet there had been a modest Spanish boom between 1922 and 1925, a decline in 1932–3, followed by recovery in 1934 and a leveling-off in 1935 – somewhat ambiguous results. In Romania, King Carol took full powers in 1938, after six years of mild economic growth. The main fascist surge in Hungary occurred in the same year, amid slightly improving economic conditions. Poland, Portugal, and Lithuania all had their main coups in 1926, following several years of mild economic growth. Finally, the 1928–9 Yugoslav crisis and the 1935–6 Greek crisis came after several years of economic growth. These are very mixed results, pointing in no single explanatory direction.

There were three distinct surges of authoritarianism, each including at least one fascist coup: in the mid-1920s, during 1932–4, and from the mid-1930s. Though the second surge was at the tail end of the Great Depression and included the most important fascist coup – in Germany – the first and third surges mostly occurred amid stuttering economic growth. All three affected countries big and small and they were scattered through the

center, east, and south of the continent. There was thus no overall relationship between economic cycles and authoritarian surges in the interwar
period.

Nowhere was economic growth very vibrant in the interwar period. Industrial economies suffered bankruptcies and mass unemployment, agrarian
ones suffered overproduction, falling prices, and indebtedness. Depressed
economies generated political crises. Regimes were shaky amid such economic crisis. But the vital policy question was, how to solve economic
crisis? The traditional "solution" had been do little, since free markets will
recover spontaneously. Thus few conservative, liberal, or labor parties possessed genuine macro-economic policies. Yet "nation-statist" policies were
now stirring. Keynesian policies of demand management proposed mildly
nation-statist solutions. More universally, tariffs were imposed against foreign imports, coupled with currency devaluations to make one's own exports
cheaper. This was economic nationalism. From such policies fascists developed their own autarchic economics. This was not mere technical economics
(as if such a beast had ever lived!). Scandinavian economic policy became
the most Keynesian yet stayed democratic, while most countries, democratic and authoritarian, slapped on the tariffs. Something more is needed
to explain why only some political economies acquired an authoritarian
slant. Economic difficulties weakened regimes in *all* interwar countries. In
the northwestern countries cabinets and parties split, coalition governments
formed and reformed; in the center, south, and east there were coups, surging authoritarianism, and mass fascism. Why the regional difference? We
cannot explain it from the performance of the interwar economy alone.
Though economic difficulties caused crises and political coups, they do not
seem to have been decisive in producing an authoritarian, still less a fascist
outcome, rather than a democratic one.

Of course, this discussion might seem too narrow. Why should we expect last year's trade or unemployment figures to generate this year's coup?
Political movements take a few years to build up steam. Maybe the general
aura of economic crisis in the period is what matters more in weakening
regimes and giving authoritarians, including fascists, the chance to air their
solutions and get organized. But if the economic crisis and solutions matter
most, political elites and voters should say so – another task for my case-study
chapters.

(3) *Class conflict.* Did authoritarianism and fascism result from rising class
conflict? The two class theories I discuss say yes. "Middle-class theorists"
argue that the middle class was worst affected by the period's economic crisis
and sought violent means to restore the balance. Little hard evidence has

been presented to support this argument, though periods of inflation tend to hurt the middle class on fixed incomes and salaries more than others. In some countries (e.g., Germany in the late 1920s) this appears to have been a factor in the decline of bourgeois liberalism. Yet it is not clearly connected to the rise of fascism. Nor did many coups occur after periods of rising inflation. No one has empirically demonstrated that labor did relatively better than the middle class in the vital years – though big business did. More detailed future research might accomplish this, though my case studies more often suggest the reverse. And if fascism was not middle-class, then the whole argument would be shot down.

"Capitalist class theorists" say that economic crisis intensified conflict between capital and labor, inducing capital to rely on repression. This is more plausible. Today we suspect from knowledge of the whole twentieth century that the destiny of labor movements was not to destroy capitalism but to reform it. But this was not so clear in the 1920s and 1930s. The Bolshevik Revolution had an immense impact, and many expected further revolutions in advanced countries. Large socialist, communist, and anarcho-syndicalist movements proclaimed allegiance to "revolution." The stronger the left, perhaps the stronger the authoritarian backlash. Is this so? Usually, though not always. In the 1930s liberal democratic France actually had the largest Communist Party, liberal democratic Norway proportionately the largest left-socialist one. But only central, eastern, and southern leftists sometimes assassinated their enemies and hatched real revolutionary plots. If we placed ourselves in the shoes of Spanish latifundistas, threatened by anarcho-syndicalist and socialist land occupations, bombings, and ostensibly "revolutionary" uprisings, we might also reach for the gun.

Yet if we analyze the class violence more closely, reactions become more puzzling. There was far more violence between 1917 and 1919 than later, and more was committed by the political right than by the left. During 1917 and 1918 various insurrections were launched against governments collapsing under the strains of war. Some had prospects of success. However, except for the civil war in Russia, most of the dead were leftists. Hungary had the only other (short-lived) "successful" revolution. There a communist-socialist coup led by Bela Kun seized the government and held it for just over a year, in the process killing 350 to 600 civilians (three-quarters of them peasants engaged in resisting government requisitioning of their produce). In subsequent reprisals a rightist "White Terror" then killed between 1,000 and 5,000 leftists and imprisoned a massive 60,000 (Rothschild 1974: 153; Janos 1982: 202; Mócsy 1983: 157; Vago 1987: 297). Rightist violence was not a mere response to leftist violence; it vastly exceeded it.

A more routine indicator of class conflict and leftist "threat" might be the strike rate or the socialist-communist vote. The strike rate rocketed at war's end but then declined before the main authoritarian upsurge. Italy was different. Italian strikes peaked in 1919–20, clearly helping to fuel the growth of fascism. They then declined greatly, substantially due to fascist pressure. Italy thus offers some support to the theory. Austrian strikes peaked in 1924 and then declined fairly continuously, well before the rightist surge. German strikes peaked in 1920, with a smaller peak in 1924 and a yet smaller one in 1928, but the secular trend remained downward – again, without any authoritarian surge until 1932–3. Portuguese strikes peaked in 1920, though there was a lower peak in 1924, two years before the first military coup. Polish strikes peaked during 1922–3, well before any coup. Estonian strikes did peak again in 1935 (back to the level of 1921–2) but had little apparent impact on the coup the following year. Here the main leftist threat had come in 1924, with a Soviet-backed insurrection. Its crushing, followed by Stalin's purge of its fleeing leaders, removed any internal "Bolshevik" threat to Estonia (Parming 1975). Strikes actually loomed larger in democracies. Britain's great General Strike was in 1926; the French peak was reached under the Popular Front government from 1936. The problem is that strikes are usually a fairly institutionalized form of expressing grievance, geared at extracting concessions from within the system. They rarely aim at revolution. It is perhaps for the same reason that trade union membership levels do not correlate with rightist coups. Except for Spain, unionization peaked in 1918–21 and then declined. Similarly with the communist/socialist vote. This was in fairly general decline from the mid-1920s (though the Austrian socialist vote held up to the end and the German leftist vote did not decline much and some of it switched from socialism to communism in 1932 and 1933). Eastern European unionization and leftist voting was far too low to explain much. There was little threat in the east from the left. Thus the strength of the left might seem relevant only to the early coups – and especially to the fascist coup in Italy. Workers were not threatening enough to provoke a rightist backlash in many places.

Finally, we have one decisive measure of the strength of left and right – their ability to seize power. During 1917–20 the left might reasonably worry conservatives: Russian and Hungarian revolutionaries did seize power, and there were scattered risings elsewhere. But after 1920 the score reads differently: successful rightist coups in sixteen countries and not a single leftist one. The nearest leftists came to success was probably in 1934 when Spanish leftists seized part of the Asturias region, though not its capital, and they held out for only two weeks (see Chapter 9). If communists, socialists, and anarchists constituted such a serious threat, we would expect at least *one* success, of a month or so. Most rightist coups occurred in the 1930s, simply too *late* to be a realistic response to the threat from the extreme left, then fading rapidly across almost all of Europe (as Eley 1983: 79 has also noted). Of course, some Red scares might have been tactical ploys. Did Hitler believe more in the "Bolshevik threat" or in its electoral utility? Mussolini only pretended to believe in a "communist threat" (see Chapter 3). Metaxas used the "communist threat" as a pretext for his coup in Greece. But the Greek communist party was small and split, and the British Embassy reported home that Metaxas's claim was a smokescreen for a coup that in reality was the result of faction fighting on the right (Kofas 1983: 31–50, 129–45). But someone must have been frightened of a "Red Peril," otherwise Mussolini and Metaxas would not have bothered trying to scare them. It is not clear why, on rational grounds, they would be.

It might alternatively be argued that authoritarians were able to strike precisely *because* of the left's weakness. But if the left was weak, why would the right bother? Why should class interests dictate that the center, east, and south keep moving toward more extreme regimes rather than staying with semi-authoritarian or reactionary ones? We should perhaps not underestimate the role that sheer vindictiveness can play in human conflict. If the left had in the past severely scared the upper classes, then the latter might actually enjoy a chance to crush them cruelly later, when the scare had actually gone. But a question still arises. Why should upper and middle classes increase the level of repression, abolish parliaments and civil liberties, and mobilize mass parties – still less call in dangerous fascists – if tried and tested milder forms were available at lower cost and risk? In fact the best solution to class struggle was visible in the northwest. Its unions, socialist parties, and strikes were larger than in most of the center, east, and south but were implicated in class compromise, posing little threat to capitalist property relations. All its socialist parties first came to power as minority governments or in coalition with center parties, a perfect setting in which to learn the arts of compromise. The center, east, and south's neglect of all this experience appears puzzling.

Nonetheless, worker activity was often perversely described by conservatives as "insurrectionary" or "revolutionary." They were overreacting, fearing revolutions that were not there, reaching for the gun too soon, as Mayer (1981) suggests. Most of the so-called Bolsheviks in Germany denounced by Hitler were actually respectable Social Democrats, ruling with moderation the largest province, Prussia, for over a decade. In Eastern Europe the actual strength of socialists (and the interest shown by Stalin in aiding them) was pitiful compared with the right's anti-Marxist hysteria. Some class theorists acknowledge this. Corner (1975: 83) says of the Italian bourgeoisie: "Convinced that social revolution was on the way, they became incapable of distinguishing between the real and the imagined situation." If so, we need an explanation that goes beyond "objective" class interest. Explaining such hysterical class overreaction is one of the main puzzles of the period.

Some conclude that authoritarianism, especially fascism, had an irrational strain. Faced with the Nazi Final Solution, this is tempting. But I prefer not to separate quite so clearly the rational from the irrational, for "rational" human calculation always comes entwined with ideology. The problem that the bourgeoisie faced has also bedeviled social theory as well. We still do not have a good explanation of the ferocity of class struggle. Marx himself is partly to blame. Ultimately an economist rather than a sociologist, his masterwork *Das Kapital* is stuffed full not with analyses of class conflict but with rational economic calculations of profit and loss, of shares of the surplus going to capital and labor, and so on. Marx appears to have shared the common illusion that capitalism is driven by the rational pursuit of profit, though he believed it was ultimately nonrational for humanity as a whole.

There are two problems with this. First, much of the behavior discussed in this book is difficult to understand by this purely instrumental criterion. Consider, for example, Spanish capitalists between 1939 and the late 1960s, loyal supporters of General Franco and running a stagnant, inefficient economy, producing little profit. Why did they help General Franco into power, and then loyally support him? They would have been much better off with the Second Republic (as they are now with the third one). They seemed driven by a more basic capitalist motive – or rather a motive shared by all the possessing classes of history – to keep their property and privileges. To hell with profit, if property itself seems threatened. Profit is inherently quantitative, divisible, and compromisable, and indeed cooperation between the classes usually increases profits. Yet property rights are finite and zero-sum. If I give you any rights to my property, I lose them. Resistance to potential loss of property will be much more intense and emotional than resistance to potential loss of profit. We can figure out a compromise solution to share profits, but we will fight near to the death to protect our property. Marxists would do better if they did not actually take bourgeois economics so seriously. In this book it is less profit than property defense that dominates capitalist class motivations.

Yet neither of these motives comes on its own, as a rational calculation disembodied from ideology. The pursuit of individual profit is accompanied by a theory of an efficient economy and by a morality of individual freedom and rationality. These theories and morals are not static, and they have changed during our century. But in the nineteenth and early twentieth centuries they were usually accompanied by two notions: that collective organization was an infringement of liberty and that only the educated and refined man (i.e., not a woman) was capable of such rational calculation. Thus capitalists hated trade unions as an infringement on their fundamental freedoms and as irrational blockages to an efficient economy. They also believed that unions would reduce their profits, but this was often not the driving force of their resistance, since the belief was incorrect and was shown to be incorrect where unions were recognized as legitimate. However, this is not the primary source of capitalist hatred and resistance in the countries studied here. It dominated in the United States, not Germany, inspiring the most ferocious and malignant persecution of labor unions of any turn-of-the-century country (see Mann 1993: 638–59). It is still not dead in the United States, inspiring genuine hatred of "Reds" supposedly lurking in any left-of-center organization.

But it was the ideological substratum of the second motive, defense of property rights, that mattered more in the rise of authoritarian regimes. For property was associated in the ideology of the time with two fundamental desirable social values: order and security. The triad of property, order, and security, divinely ordained, was the ideological soul of the old regime. The new authoritarianism began to lay more stress on the order and security part of the formula, and fascism took this even further. There were now two alternative threats that the modern left and the Bolshevik Revolution had supposedly brought. One was the traditional threat to the upper class of having its property and privileges seized. The second was the threat to all classes not of a "successful" revolution but of disorder, class conflict without end. The first was a fundamental threat at the jugular vein of the capitalist class, but the second was a threat to civilized order itself, threatening everyone's security. Genuine hatred and malignity may result from the perception of such threatening enemies.

I have not yet solved the problem of "hysterical overreaction." I have suggested that some fairly basic human sentiments of fear, hatred, and violence might be invoked at the class level in the period immediately after World War I. But why were they not then allayed as the objective threat receded? This was perhaps because of other basic human sentiments, not to forgive but to kick our enemy when he or she is down, especially after he or she has scared us. But it may also be because of the role that ideology plays in defining "interests" more broadly than rational-choice theory suggests. If property is equated with order and security, then they – in the form perhaps of increasing militarism or paramilitarism – might become positive values for classes fearing a threat to property. And if disorder is feared, then possible antidotes – nationalism, statism, and class transcendence – might also become positive values. Indeed, this is exactly what we shall find. The right in one-half of Europe also became attracted to nationalism, statism, and militarism as values in themselves, and these often prevented those on the right who were propertied from accurately calculating their rate of profit or even their likelihood of retaining their property. These values led them to a more enthusiastic embrace of authoritarianism and often of fascism than mere class interest could explain. But to fully appreciate this will involve us in also considering the military, political, and ideological crises of the period.

In view of all this, the most ambitious type of economic explanation could be only a partial, not a total, explanation, and it would have to be a compound drawn from all these approaches. Economic backwardness might favor semi-authoritarian regimes. Late development might destabilize class relations and provide more statist models. Conservative fears of destabilization coupled with more statist ideals might push them further right, toward repression. But neither Germany nor Scandinavia would fit well, and we still have no good explanation of fascism. Though economic and class theories take us part of the way, we need also to investigate the other sources of social power.

MILITARY POWER, MILITARY CRISIS

Military power is the social organization of physical violence. It is universal in human societies because of the need of human groups for organized defense and the ubiquitous utility of aggression. Those who command military resources may acquire social power more generally. Conversely, when dominant military institutions decay, this opens up new opportunities for others, including other armed groups, to seize power. However, either eventuality also presupposes that "militarism" enjoys some positive ideological valuation in society, and specifically that military organization seems to offer legitimate models for power acquisition and rule. In principle, all well-organized militaries could seize power, but only a few actually do so.

Military power has been neglected by social science. Though the early twentieth century produced a flurry of social theories of military power relations, they tended to vanish after 1945 – ironically, with the defeat of fascism. Since then we have had the curious spectacle of a modern age dominated by wars, conquest, and genocide interpreted by pacific, economistic

theories. Even when theorists have turned to consider military power relations, they have tended to focus exclusively on the highly institutionalized
force mobilized by states, in domestic repression and interstate wars. As
we see below, an exclusive focus on violence organized by states could not
explain the rise of fascism.

Yet recent historical sociology has unearthed a set of long-term military
and geopolitical causes of the division of Europe into constitutional and
absolutist regimes that parallel the economic causes identified by Barrington
Moore. Myself (Mann 1986, 1993) Tilly (1990), and Downing (1992) have
argued that (1) struggles over political representation resulted from the state's
need to tax more in order to fight more expensive foreign wars, (2) those
wars became increasingly fought by professional armies under the control of
the state, who could potentially be used for domestic repression to extract
more taxes, but (3) states that could raise funds either from foreign trade
or from taxing conquered foreigners did not need to turn up the repressive
screws in order to get higher taxes, and (4) naval powers could not turn
up the repression as much as land powers, since navies cannot sail on dry
land. To explain Europe's division into constitutional and absolutist regimes
through the sixteenth to the eighteenth centuries would require blending
economic, military, and geopolitical causes – and perhaps other causes, too.
It is also probable that military and geopolitical causes would continue to
play a part in the further development of the "two Europes."

Moreover, explanations of fascism do generally recognize that military
power relations had just been revolutionized. World War I had deepened citizen warfare into "total war." Most writers accept that fascism would never
have triumphed without the emergence of such a catastrophic form of warfare. The capacity to mobilize millions of men to fight and many more millions of men and women to provide economic and logistical support to the
armed forces brought many social changes. In the short term it enormously
increased the infrastructural, and to a lesser extent the despotic, powers of
most states. It is also a truism that victory in war brings more regime legitimacy, while defeat brings the reverse. Total war might seem to strengthen
this argument – especially for defeat, which now becomes a social catastrophe. But modern total war had also introduced a series of tensions between
state power and mass military citizenship that in the circumstances of possible
or actual defeat could radically destabilize states. The initial conflicts erupted
in 1917 and 1918 with a series of soldiers' and sailors' mutinies and insurrections in most of the combatant armies. These peaked in the February
and October Revolutions in Russia. Here soldiers formed many of the revolutionary councils (soviets), and their hastily assembled Red Army then

successfully defended the Revolution through a full-scale civil war. Austria, Germany, and Hungary also saw insurrectionary soldiers' soviets, though these were soon repressed. But the repression was less often by the state's official armed forces than by the doppelganger of the soldiers' soviets, rightist paramilitaries. Such "popular" militarism from below was to provide the core of fascist movements everywhere.

Fascism became a mass movement only at the end of the Great War. Most European states were participants, but even the neutrals were deeply affected. The war obviously intensified nationalism and statism. But there were also three direct military links to fascism. First, the war tended to delegitimate defeated regimes, which had tended to be only semi-authoritarian. Many have thus argued that defeat in World War I was quite likely to produce more authoritarian and fascist outcomes – though the immediate impact was actually the reverse, to increase democratic pressures. This might be plausible for Germany, Austria, and Hungary, the main losers (apart from Russia), all falling to reactionary authoritarians, then corporatists and fascists. The war cost Germany 10 percent of its territories and enormous reparations payments; Hungary lost over half its territories; and Austria lost its entire empire. Rightists in these countries claimed that defeat resulted from a "stab in the back" by civilian politicians, leftists, and sinister "Judeo-Bolsheviks." Spearheaded by refugees flooding in from the lost territories, they demanded the restoration of those territories. Bulgaria was a loser on a lesser scale. Italy is sometimes added to the list of the defeated. Though actually on the winning side, her armies had taken a battering and her territorial gains were fewer than nationalists desired. A "mutilated victory" was blamed on "decadent" liberal governments and "unpatriotic" leftists (De Grand, 1978: 102–14). Since these countries included the main fascist cases (though not Romania), to link military defeat, revisionism, and fascism seems plausible.

Timing remains a problem. Only Italian fascists (1922) and Bulgarian reactionary authoritarians (1923) took power soon after the war, and these countries had suffered the fewest losses. Germany had time to recover. Reparations were settled in 1930, and the Allied occupation of the Rhineland was known to be temporary. Hitler's coup in 1933 was surely too late to be directly attributed to defeat in the First World War. Hungarian politicians knew their revisionism was rhetorical not practical; Austrians knew they could not restore the empire. Defeat could not easily explain enduring authoritarianism or the fascist surge during the 1930s. War defeat did not directly produce fascism. Yet it might have contributed to the first postwar rightist surge, undermining the immediate prospects for democracy, and this might have provided militants for later.

Authoritarianism also triumphed in countries with different war records. Serbia and Romania were victors. Serbia had been rewarded with dominion over Yugoslavia. Romania had its territories and population doubled by the war. These two victors turned authoritarian, and Romania generated mass fascism. Two neutrals – Portugal and Spain – also turned authoritarian. Portugal was not involved in serious warfare in the period. The Spanish Empire had been destroyed by the United States in 1898–9 and a Spanish army was routed by Moroccans in 1921. Yet the blame for these disasters was traded equally between left and right politicians, the monarch and the army itself. Few Spaniards supported imperial revisionism. Nor did many Greeks, after their defeat by Turkey in 1922. Not until 1936 did General Metaxas stage his coup, and foreign policy issues were marginal to it. Finally, the new "successor states" owed their very existence to World War I. Poland, the Baltic states, and Albania also went authoritarian, but most of their postwar leaders were considered heroes of national liberation. Authoritarianism and, to a lesser extent, fascism were thus associated with varied war experiences, not just defeat.

Yet war had a second big impact on a broader area of Europe. Through-out the center, east, and south victors, vanquished and successor states had experienced severe war *dislocation*. Vanquished regimes lost legitimacy, terri-tories, and resources, and some were pressured by refugees. Greece (neutral during 1914–18) experienced much of this after 1922. Italy had only a little dislocation, over Trieste and the South Tyrol. The two clear-cut victors, Romania and Serbia, had to cope with a different yet parallel problem: in-corporating extensive new territories that transformed country and state. Serbs had to institutionalize politics that would ensure their own domi-nance yet leave the other ethnicities in the new Yugoslavia not too unhappy. Romanians now had an enlarged, overwhelmingly rural country, and were no longer quite the oppressed "proletarian nation" of the region. Old states in Germany, Austria, Hungary, Bulgaria, Romania, Serbia, and Italy were suddenly required to deepen parliamentarism. The brand-new "successor states" had to be started almost from scratch – none shared the opportunity of Finns and Czechs to build on past regional administrations and parliaments. This amounted to considerable war-induced political dislocation over vir-tually the entire center, east, and southeast. Only neutral Spain and Portugal escaped this.

The northwest had the opposite experience. All but three northwestern countries were victors or neutrals. The two most marginal liberal democ-racies, Finland and Czechoslovakia, were also the only new successor states. Belgium was the only quasi-defeated state (it was occupied by the German army), but Belgians sensibly blamed geography, not their politicians. Belgium also received small territorial gains and reparations in the Peace Treaties. Amid the victors (France, Britain, the United States, Canada, Australia, and New Zealand), only France received territorial gains, and Alsace-Lorraine had been French before 1871. Nor were their constitutions meddled with. Most were old states. Even the Czechs and Finns had possessed old, hitherto "regional" political institutions, though the Czechs had no tried institutions for ruling Slovaks or Sudeten Germans (this is where their state was later to break down). But virtually none of the northwest had to cope with defeat, incorporate new territories, or devise new constitutions. Thus the center, east, and southeast but almost none of the northwest was witnessing a war-induced dislocation of *political* institutions. But why would destabilization come from the right and lead to authoritarianism and fascism? I turn to the third legacy of the war, paramilitarism.

Prewar fascist theory was influenced by the realization that warfare could now mobilize the whole nation. World War I made this reality. "The nation in arms" proved to be disciplined yet comradely, elitist yet peculiarly egalitarian – since officers and men now fought alongside each other and officers actually suffered the higher casualties. "Total" war conscripted between 25 percent and 80 percent of young and early middle-aged males. But since mass citizen warfare produced mostly horror for the troops, by 1918 most wanted only to get out as quickly as possible, back to jobs and families. A leftist minority took disillusion further, to demand a juster and more pacific society. After a spurt of "workers and soldiers" movements, they became absorbed into civilian left movements. Though some of these did develop uniformed, marching, demonstrating formations conventionally called "paramilitaries," they were much less violent than fascist ones, and they generally lost street battles with them. Leftist veterans had no veneration of militarism and soon lost their distinctive identity as veterans. It was different for a rightist veteran minority. They idealized the disciplined cross-class comradeship of the front and became disenchanted with postwar strife-torn civilian democracy. By extolling military virtues and by continuing certain military practices in peacetime, they devised a distinctive social movement: the citizen paramilitary.

Rightist paramilitaries and organized veterans' leagues assumed significance in most countries. They won a civil war in Finland, repressed the leftist government of Hungary in 1919–20, repressed leftist and foreign opponents in early postwar Germany, Austria, and Poland, overthrew civilian government in Bulgaria in 1923, and almost overthrew the Estonian government in 1934. They were the core of the first wave of all fascist movements. All fascist and some corporatist and reactionary authoritarian movements maintained substantial paramilitaries in which veterans played the core leadership role. Most theories of the modern state follow Max Weber in defining it as possessing the monopoly of the means of violence in society. Yet this has by no means always been true. That is why we must analytically separate military from political power relations even in the modern state. Military power is not only mobilized by states. Though all interwar regimes possessed quite imposing armies, well trained, well armed, experienced in war, some of these armies were largely immobilized by ideological divisions within. Ideologies, especially rightist ones, were sweeping through all ranks, often sponsored by respected military veterans – even the Supreme Commander, General Ludendorff. Armies were losing much of their caste-like professional autonomy. Some states now had arms of clay and divided hearts.

One view of the link between war veterans and fascism focuses on the link between military and economic power, that is, on veterans' resentment at their material deprivation. The second view focuses on the link between military and ideological power, that is, on the rise of paramilitary values. The economic argument suggests that a veteran cohort centering on the lower middle class (including small peasants) was pushed toward extremism by postwar unemployment and economic deprivation. The paramilitary values argument suggests it was their wartime experience of the front, of classless comradeship and hierarchical subordination. Paramilitary organization, veterans believed, could now achieve great social and political purposes, as military organization had in the war. Though rightist veterans were probably no more numerous than leftist veterans, they maintained a distinctive postwar presence, encouraging them toward the violent cleansing of "enemies" of the nation and toward "knocking heads together" to cure social conflict. My case-study chapters evaluate these two rival explanations. The ideological argument will do better.

Wartime dislocation, and defeat in some of the major cases, provided much of the initial political crisis for the new regimes and could have been vital in stemming the initial surge toward democracy. A particular cohort's exposure to military organization and values then provided a core of militants and a plausible paramilitary solution to this crisis. But this is not a sufficient explanation. Once again, it was only in one-half of Europe that significant paramilitarism surfaced, while both halves of Europe (and other countries, too) had experienced the war. It is true that some stirrings of paramilitarism and even protofascist activity among veterans appeared in almost all the combatant countries. They were quite pronounced in democratic France. They were small in Britain yet influential in Mosley's British Union of Fascists. In the United States, Campbell (1998) has shown that the newly formed American Legion was used by rightists as a strike- and "Red"-busting organization in the 1920s. Yet compared with veteran fascism in Germany, Italy, Hungary, or Romania, these were minor skirmishes. Perhaps victory versus defeat offers part of the explanation for the difference (though not for Romania). But it does also seem that other circumstances beyond war and its effects must also have contributed to the interwar dominance of authoritarianism and fascism.

POLITICAL POWER, POLITICAL CRISIS

Political power derives from control of the state, and ultimately from the usefulness to human groups of territorial and centralized regulation of social relations. Clearly, those who control the state can exercise more general power. The interwar period saw many political crises and coups as factions jockeyed for control of states. This is the stuff of "elite theories" of political power, which contend with two reductionist theories of state, class theory and pluralism. But regardless of the degree of autonomous power wielded by state elites, the institutions and the crises of states may have an autonomous influence over political outcomes. The fact that the French state is highly centralized and the American one decentralized has a continuing legacy on contemporary politics, an example of what I have called "institutional statist theory" (Mann 1993: chap. 3). The "new institutionalism" has also emphasized the enduring impact of existing institutions in structuring social life. In the interwar period we find semi-authoritarian states, long institutionalized but now supposedly making a transition toward democracy experiencing their own crises, with important consequences for fascism.

The main problem of explaining authoritarianism in terms only of the effects of World War I and interwar economic crises is that politics in "the two Europes" had already differed over a much longer period of time. Most of the northwest had made their transition to the liberal democratic nation-state through the eighteenth and nineteenth centuries. In contrast, the whole of the center, east, and south was only now embarking, more suddenly, on this transition amid a rising tide of nationalism and statism. Economic backwardness was important in bringing about this difference, and so were military and geopolitical contexts. But there were also specifically political problems in the center, east, and south. These were states in transition, and they had difficulty coping with interwar crises.

I distinguish two main facets of liberal democracy, what Dahl (1977) terms "participation" and "contestation." "Participation" means the extent of participation in government, centering on who could vote. This has dominated discussion of democratic development (Rokkan 1970: part II; Therborn 1977; Rueschemeyer et al. 1992: 83–98). But "contestation" (or competition) is equally necessary for liberal democracy. Contestation means that sovereign power is contested between parties in free elections, and the executive power cannot override elections.

"Participation" does not clearly distinguish between "the two Europes" in the immediate prewar period. Among the early cases of manhood suffrage were Portugal in 1822, Bulgaria in 1879, and Serbia in 1889, and it had been introduced in France and Germany to bolster the rule of semi-authoritarian Napoleon III and the Kaiser. Late nineteenth-century men might often have the vote, but they were still often controlled by local notables, *caciques*, whose powers as employers, magistrates, charity-dispensers, and tax-gatherers could not be lightly challenged (though the new secret ballot helped). Though by 1914 most franchises were broader in the northwest, both regions contained variation, and this grew greater after 1918. In the 1920s all adult women could vote in Germany and Austria yet none could in France, while single British women aged between twenty-one and thirty could vote only in 1929. The breadth of suffrage could not predict whether liberal democracy survived, though sudden jumps in the suffrage in countries such as Italy and Spain did alarm conservatives, leading some to embrace authoritarianism. Again, political dislocation seems important.

"Contestation" (or competition) predicts better. By the 1880s, mostly decades before, countries in the entire northwest (including their white colonial offshoots) had competitive party systems, largely free elections, and parties that alternated in government with little executive interference. In the Nordic countries, estate assemblies had survived even through absolutist periods. Even in northwestern "colonies," in Ireland and Norway, locals had sent elected representatives to the colonial power's assembly in London and Copenhagen. Even the two marginal cases, Finland and Czechoslovakia, had been permitted provincial assemblies by their Russian and Austrian overlords. Northwestern parliaments also enjoyed powers distinct from those of the majority party, so that a ruling party could not easily remain in government by manipulating office patronage or repression. The paradigm cases were the United States (free party contest among most white males from the 1790s) and Britain (free party contest among 15 to 20 percent of men from 1832). Most of the northwest followed suit during the nineteenth century.

True, royal prerogatives in the choice of ministers survived in Sweden and Denmark, though they were rarely exercised and were finally laid to rest in 1917 and 1920.

This criterion does seem to distinguish virtually perfectly between the two Europes. Obviously, this had much to do with level of development, with the class politics of an earlier age, but also with fiscal-military differences (Mann 1986; Downing 1992). Whatever the exact mix of original causes, their legacy was considerable differences between the nature and stability of political regimes in the early twentieth century, and these now emerged to have their own causal impact on outcomes.

Thus by World War I sovereign parliaments were institutionalized across the northwest.[9] When the suffrage was extended across classes and religions and to women, parties adapted entrenched liberal practices (Luebbert 1991). Interwar discontents were expressed through these representative institutions (see the articles in Schmitt 1988). Only Finland and Czechoslovakia had to find new institutions – and so both struggled. The northwestern state was *unitary*, dominated by institutionalized parliamentary sovereignty, experienced in handling conflict between classes, religious communities, and regions. Belgium and Switzerland were uniquely experienced in coping with ethnic differences. What mattered was less liberal ideology than institutions whose everyday practices embodied liberalism.

Consider late nineteenth-century British miners. Probably few believed in "liberalism." They were as radical (and as well organized) as miners in most countries. But enough of them possessed the vote under the property franchise, and they were sufficiently concentrated in certain parliamentary constituencies, to constitute a voting bloc that the existing parties could not ignore. The Liberal Party responded and represented their grievances in parliament, so miners voted Liberal. This arrangements contained tensions, and miners' MPs acquired some autonomy as "Lib-Labs." In the early twentieth century they joined the Labour Party. Their trajectory was dominated by opportunities created by the essential pragmatism of everyday electoral and parliamentary politics much more than by ideology. In comparable ways the new class and other tensions of the interwar period could be filtered through institutionalized parliamentary states, in the process deepening and strengthening them. Such democratic political traditions were simply too institutionalized to allow fascist, Bolshevist, or any other ideology to develop far. In these countries it may even be inappropriate to refer to liberalism as an ideology. It was only so in the residual sense of an "institutionalized ideology," that is, one embedded in mundane ritual practices. It saw values and norms instrumentally, relevant to winning the next election or keeping party factions moderately contented.

As Linz (1976: 4–8) noted, fascist parties were latecomers to parliamentary institutions. If party competition already dominated the state, there was little space left for them. Whatever World War I or capitalism might throw at Norway, Sweden, or Denmark, for example, their democratic parties would cope (Hagtvet 1980: 715, 735–8; Myklebust and Hagtvet 1980: 639–44). If their electoral antennae detect rising nationalism, then conservative parties might offer a bit more of it. If they detect statist sentiments, center-left parties will oblige. So later, when some of these countries were occupied by the Nazis and their party systems were destroyed, things might rapidly change. The Nazis found plenty of willing ideological collaborators once they emasculated parliaments and elections. In Norway, for example, they received the support of 55,000 local national socialist collaborators.

In the center, east, and south of Europe, things differed. Parliaments had either barely existed before 1914 (as in the Russian or Ottoman Empires) or shared political power with a nonelected executive, a monarch, military commanders, or a ministerial regime commanding substantial office patronage. The state was *dual*, its "two states" (parliament and executive) each enjoying partial sovereignty (Newman 1970: 225–6). That is the meaning of the term "semi-authoritarian." A legacy of the earlier absolutist period was that the armed forces were more specifically under the control of the executive than they were in the other half of Europe. The monarch could manipulate elections and parliaments by selective repression plus office patronage in the German and Habsburg Empires, Serbia, Romania, Greece, and Bulgaria. In Restoration Spain and (to a lesser extent) in "liberal" Italy up to 1919, the Ministry of the Interior or Prime Minister helped fix elections to produce compliant oligarchical governments (*el turno* in Spain, *trasformismo* in Italy). In 1901 half of the Italian deputies were actually government officeholders, hardly "independent" men. "Place holders" had been eliminated in Britain in 1832. But in this half of Europe democratic constitutions were partially undermined by executive powers. Here miners were essentially outside political institutions. Notables might continue to "represent" them rather indirectly through political clientelism. But if this faltered, the notables could have recourse to much greater powers of repression than had their counterparts in the northwest. They had authoritarian, despotic options.

In 1918 the center, east, and south was thus confronted by what we might call "*political* late development." Larsen (1998; cf. Griffin 2001: 49) says that the Axis states were "late nationbuilders, late liberalizers and introduced democratic rule only a short period before they broke down," but this was also more generally true right across their half of the continent. Germany and Austria moved suddenly to advanced parliamentary sovereignty and full adult suffrage, as Spain did in 1931. Italy had made its first dramatic suffrage extension just before the war, in 1912, and its second in 1918. These major shifts in the parliamentary side of the state were not accompanied by comparable changes within the executive, which (as we see below in the case-study chapters) remained dominated by "old regime" elements that controlled most of the repressive apparatuses of the state. Dual states, supposedly in the process of liberalizing, were found just about everywhere else. But many central, eastern, and southern countries were confronted by a further transitional problem, for they were also founding nation-states. Here the problems were novel and unlike those earlier experienced in the northwest. Northwestern "ethnic blindness"[10] would not do for those inhabiting the former territories or neighborhood of the multinational Russian, Austrian, or Ottoman Empires – now representation was not just of class but also of nationality. Political movements seeking to mobilize national identities and interests appeared alongside movements mobilizing classes. There were old imperial nations (Russian, German, and Ottoman), more recent imperialists (Magyar), "proletarian" nations (Ukrainian, Romanian), newer subimperial nations (Serb, Czech), and minorities of all these in the majority states of other nations. Where nationalities also differed in their religions, this reinforced their sense of mutual unease.

National conflicts were also more directly linked to international conflicts than were class conflicts. The Versailles and Trianon Treaties involved much redrawing of boundaries according to two conflicting principles. One was to punish the losers and reward the winners. The other was to establish "national self-determination," redrawing boundaries according to patterns of ethnic settlement, so that each new state would be predominantly mono-ethnic. The result was to leave some dissatisfied states with "irredentist" demands for the restoration of "lost territories" coming especially from refugees fleeing from the boundary drawing. We see how demanding and complex were the claims now being made on the dual nation-states of the center, east, and south, and how untried were the political practices for coping with them. Actors were faced with considerable uncertainty and risk, largely absent in the northwest. It was safer perhaps for those who controlled the executive part of the state to repress if faced with crisis. Remember also that this criterion puts the formerly absolutist states of Germany and

Austria in the same position as the less developed states to the east and south.

Let us look at this political crisis of transition through the eyes of the most sophisticated conservative state theorist of the time.[11] Carl Schmitt was a famous German jurist who ended up as an apologist for Nazism after Hitler's accession to power. But in the 1920s he was just a conservative, not wholly committed to any particular type of regime, admiring Mussolini but not Hitler, searching desperately to ground a theory of contemporary constitutional order on a juridical bedrock of absolute legal principle. He wanted certainty, not risk. He believed that certainty was now lacking across continental Europe because the decline of the old semi-authoritarian regime had undermined two essential attributes of constitutional law. First, old regime parliaments had expressed the Enlightenment principle of reason in the form of free debate between rational, independent, educated men. That the best laws were the product of rational discourse between educated men was the essence of nineteenth-century continental liberalism. Now, Schmitt argued, the mass suffrage ("participation" in Dahl's sense) produced the rise of mass parties, and these threatened the independence of these men. Deputies were transformed into mere "representatives" of entrenched interests in society, instructed by their organizations and ideologies how to vote. Free, rational debate was at an end. In fact, he painted an even gloomier scenario of bureaucratically organized, corporatist, "mass armies" (thinking primarily of organized labor, but also occasionally mentioning economic concentration and big business) "invading" and subordinating the state to highly moralistic ideologies of hatred that ultimately failed to conceal their basis in narrow class interests. Perhaps compromise between these interests remained possible, but it would now have to be effected through these organizations themselves, not through parliament. For this, Schmitt correctly noted, was how the Weimar Republic had actually been founded – through an explicit, somewhat insecure "class truce" negotiated between the socialist unions and big businessmen. The participants were not bound together by the normative solidarity of parliament as an assembly of gentlemen. Nor, I would add, were they bound into long-hallowed everyday practices of parties and parliaments. Could they be trusted? Could they trust each other? Schmitt doubted it.

Second, Schmitt argued, domination by political parties (i.e., full "contestation") ended all possibility that the traditional state might continue as the ultimate, neutral guarantor of order and compromise, as it had been in the past. Though we tend to view old regime executives as having been class-biased, favoring the propertied classes, this is not how conservatives themselves viewed them. The monarch and state had been "above" society, Schmitt argued, providing the ultimate constitutional guarantee against encroaching private interests. A party could represent only a "part" of the nation. It could not replace the state as a "universal" power. Schmitt believed, with some justification, that German state elites were now paralyzed. Yet the pluralism of party competition that replaced them was only one step away from a condition of civil war where there would be no judge to determine what is "mine and thine." The unravelling of competition into "war" was a definite risk. If neither the debating chamber nor the old regime executive could provide order, perhaps a new state executive could provide this. And so through the 1920s Schmitt began to formulate the idea that a new type of ruling elite, above society, was necessary to occupy the "vacated" centers of state power and avoid the risk of disorder. This led him through support for the semi-authoritarianism of Bruning and von Papen to Hitler and Nazism.

Schmitt was articulating very widespread fears. His first argument appealed especially to old regime liberals, his second to conservatives. Of course, there was a great deal of class consciousness lying behind these fears. One particular "mass army" loomed largest for Schmitt, as for other conservatives and liberals – workers' unions and their attendant socialist parties. The shadow of the Bolshevik Revolution loomed behind their worst fears. Yet Schmitt based his theory not on property rights but on a broader notion of order and security. He embodies perfectly what I noted earlier when dealing with the fears of the propertied classes: Property fears are displaced onto a positive concern with order and security. His stress on the threat posed by large bureaucratic and corporate organizations to free rational discourse had and still has broader appeal. It is, for example, quite similar to Habermas's more recent theory of distorted communication, a theory that has a decidedly leftist pedigree. Schmitt even looked favorably on welfare benefits, unless they involved society's "encroachment" on the state. His primary worries were about the state and social order, not class and material interests. Nor did he or his circle have much to do with capitalism. His own family origins were poor, his father being a menial railway employee. The family was strongly Catholic and Schmitt's early conservatism took Catholic forms (i.e., until he broke with the church over his own divorce). He then spent his life in German universities as a professor with secure civil servant status. He mixed in cafe and salon society, meeting artists, writers, and other academics. His writings made him famous among jurists and civil servants, and his connections to power elites were primarily with top civil servants.

He was central to the "humanistic bourgeoisie" and to German statism, but not to capitalism. Though his own nationalism was not extreme, and he was no militarist, his geopolitical writings exposed a contemporary international order biased toward the interests of the victors of World War I. Thus he helped legitimate German imperial revisionism. As we see below, fascism's appeal to the upper classes was not merely based on property interests. It was mediated by concerns with order and security to arrive at a transcendent nation-statism.

And so the fears of many conservatives and some liberals were brought into the same ideological ballpark as that of fascists. A crisis of political transition amid a mass society had disrupted prior sources of constitutional order and security. Things were getting risky, and they might unravel further – amid rising nationalism, statism, and militarism. It was better to be safe than sorry. Since conservatives had ready access to repression in the dual state, they could – to use a football expression – "get their retaliation in first" (while shouting "foul"). This was the rationality lying behind apparent paranoia about the Red Peril. They did not realize that the Black Peril of fascism might be even more threatening.

Thus authoritarianism resulted directly from a political crisis, making it more difficult for some states to cope with the crises emanating from capitalism and militarism. Dual states in the south, east, and center (for I have included the German states) could not be guaranteed to handle crisis safely, except by repression. Whatever crises world war and capitalism threw at the northwest, its liberal states survived. Eugen Weber says, "Twentieth-century fascism is a byproduct of disintegrating liberal democracy" (1964: 139). But this is not quite correct. Institutionalized liberal states successfully rode out the crisis. We should rephrase his statement: Fascism reflected a crisis of the dual state, the "semi-authoritarian, semi-liberal" state found across one-half of Europe, faced with simultaneous transitions to liberal democracy and the nation-state just as these countries were beset by economic and military crises. This produced uncertainty, a downward spiral, and a reaction within the state itself against liberalism: a revolt by one-half of the state against the other, each mobilizing core constituencies of support. We must analyze state elites and parties as carefully as social classes. The lightning rod of this crisis was not liberalism but conservatism. It was the success of northwestern conservatives in moving from notable to mass representative parties that ensured the survival there of liberal states. Elsewhere it was the failure of conservatives to effect this transition that produced authoritarianism and opened the door to fascism. Though the political crisis owed much to long-term processes of economic and geopolitical/military development, and something to short-term economic and military crises, it also had more specifically political causes. And in turn the political crisis generated a need for real ideologies.

IDEOLOGICAL POWER, IDEOLOGICAL CRISIS

Ideological power derives from the human need to find ultimate meaning, to share norms, values, and rituals that seem to make sense of the world and that reinforce social cooperation. An ideology mobilizing plausible norms, values, and rituals may also confer power on its initiators. Human existence does not "make its own sense." We draw on more general meaning systems that are not directly "testable" either by science or by our own practical experience. Meaning systems "surpass experience" and so help to define interests. Yet socialization plus the institutionalized routines of education, employment, politics, and so on normally insulate us from needing frequent recourse to general ideologies. Institutions in which we are implicated generate everyday routines that "work" and seem "normal," and they generate minimal "institutionalized ideologies" in which values are routinely undercut by pragmatism. In times of crisis, however, traditional routines and pragmatism may no longer seem to work and we are thrown onto more general ideas in order to find new workable practices. Then intellectuals may offer new meaning systems and so acquire a more general social power. We may then find them plausible, and follow them. This was how I interpreted the rise of the world salvation religions in the first volume of *The Sources of Social Power* (Mann 1986: chap. 10), and how I interpreted the influence of the Enlightenment movement on the French Revolution in volume 2 (Mann 1993: chaps. 6 and 7). Was fascism similar? I investigate fascist communications networks. Geographically, I identify three main networks: transnational networks, macro-regional networks that might help construct or reinforce "the two Europes," and networks confined within nation-states. Socially, I identify core ideological constituencies of fascism.

Fascism was obviously very ideological. Other authoritarian rightists did not live much at the ideological level. They would pragmatically steal as much fascist clothing as was compatible with staying in power, while seeking to defuse fascism's radical, bottom-up thrust. But the prewar progenitors of fascism had been intellectuals, and intellectuals always remained important in fascism. In the prewar period Maurras, Barrès, Sorel, and race theorists such as Chamberlain and Gobineau, plus a host of middlebrow journalists, popularizers, and pamphleteers – right down to the infamous anti-Semitic forgery *Protocols of the Elders of Zion* – had far more readers than prewar fascist or racist political organizations had members. All fascist movements continued to appeal disproportionately to the well educated – to students in high schools and universities and to the most highly educated middle-class strata. Salvatorelli (1923) described this core constituency as the "humanistic bourgeoisie." Though fascism attracted really major intellectuals only in Italy and Romania, everywhere it attracted minor ones, especially communications specialists in newspapers, radio, film, and graphic design. Fascism was a movement of the lesser intelligentsia.

And so fascist programs were formed amid a broader ideology. I quoted Codreanu's contemptuous dismissal of the typical "shopping list" of party programs. Fascists situated interest-based economics or politics amid a *Weltanschauung* (a general orientation to the world). They claimed a higher moral purpose, transcendent of class conflict, capable of "resacralizing" a modern society grown materialistic and decadent. They identified a "civilizational crisis" encompassing government, morality, science, social science, the arts, and "style." They denounced their enemies in moralistic and highly emotional terms. Socialists brought "Asiatic barbarism," liberals were "decadent" and "corrupt." Science was "materialistic." A "degenerate," "elderly" culture needing recasting, rejuvenating. They promoted their own art, architecture, science, and social science, their own youth movements, and a cult of "the new man," enveloping all with an intense interest in style and ritual. Of course, Mussolini and Hitler also recognized the emotional power of art forms – music, marching, rhetoric, painting, graphic design, sculpture, architecture. They found a willing pool of artists who saw their own artistic creativity as being at one with fascist ideology. During the 1920s and 1930s the concatenation of crises listed above produced a severe loss of ultimate meaning. If a country had suffered wars of massive destruction and dislocation, had lost or gained great swaths of territory, saw its own people as refugees (or as displacing refugees), encountered severe recession and class conflict, and was embarked on a fraught political transition, then not merely the "old regime" but also many old ways and beliefs in general seemed inadequate. Social and political ideologies do not require and cannot obtain scientific validation. New ideologies require not truth but plausibility, a seeming ability to "make some sense" of current events at a time when established ideologies are obviously in difficulty. In the interwar period traditional ideologies could not easily interpret contemporary reality, at least across one-half of Europe. Conservatism distrusted the masses who were now on stage, liberalism seemed corrupt and insufficiently statist and nationalist. Socialism distrusted the nation and brought class conflict but not its solution. Christian churches had been in retreat from the secular sphere and were divided. There was an opening for new ideologies and ideologists, capable of what Lucien Goldman called "maximum possible consciousness," the first to experience the inadequacies of conventional ideologies and the first to generate new ones.

Writers such as Hughes (1967), Sternhell (1976: 320–5), and Mosse (1999) have identified a more general and thoroughly transnational ideological crisis permeating Europe. They see a contradiction between "Enlightenment Reason" and a post-Romantic concern with the emotions, passions, the will, and the unconscious – some borne by "mass" phenomena such as crowds, strikes, war, and nationalism. Some have sought to trace a link through "the history of ideas" between fascism and revolutions of "high modernism" that reflected and reinforced a general crisis of the early twentieth century: "disturbing revolutions" in psychoanalysis, abstract painting, atonal music, the decline of the omniscient narrator of the realist novel, a fascination with the bizarre, the fantastic, the decadent, and the irrational, all subversive to the Enlightenment program of calm, confident reason. But if a transnational crisis of high culture helped cause authoritarianism, it should have caused it everywhere. Can we tone down the argument to a macroregional one? In this case we would expect the cultural crisis to be greater in the east and south of the continent. Though it was somewhat weaker in the Anglo-Saxon and Scandinavian countries, democratic Paris dominated the avant-garde, while leftist Vienna led its music and psychoanalysis. Nor was the more backward east or southeast into high modernism. In fact, high culture is generated by small coteries of cosmopolitan elites, not much tied to locality. This is especially true of music and art, largely unhindered by linguistic barriers. But it is difficult to connect the "revolutions" introduced by Freud, Schönberg, Picasso, Joyce, and so on to political revolutions. Since many "radical" artists were rejecting art forms embedded in mass human experience (hummable tunes, beautiful landscapes, and so on), they had little connection to the masses. Schorske (1981) says the cultured elites of Vienna saw that liberalism had failed to reform the Austro-Hungarian Empire and were horrified by its emerging violent mass politics. So they retreated into aesthetic romanticism and the occult and rejected the values of the existing social order, foreshadowing the political horrors to come.

But fascists rejected much of this high modernism as "degenerate." So some say fascism was "antimodern." I prefer Gentile's (1996) notion of resacralized modernity, or Herf's (1984) "reactionary modernism," coined to describe the world view of the Nazi engineers he studied. There was nostalgia, romanticism, medievalism, and even primitivism in Nazism. Yet, as Allen (2002) also notes of SS technocrats, Nazi professionals viewed themselves as modernists. In areas as diverse as engineering, management theory, biology, propaganda, and graphic design, fascists were enthusiastic modernists. They were innovative in mass communication, disseminating their ideology through posters, parades, art shows, movies, and architecture. In architecture and music they were quite conservative; in graphic design, film, and theatrical demonstrations they were radicals. But it does not seem that a crisis of high culture played much role in the power of fascist ideology. Rather, fascists offered plausible general solutions to economic, military, and political crises of the time, which their powers of communication made more resonant.

Indeed, this was the age of rising nation-states, and communication was becoming less transnational, more bounded by states. Eighteenth-century literate communication had been dominated by multilingual churches and aristocratic elites. The Enlightenment had been transnational, diffusing across literate Europeans and beyond. This remained true of its nineteenth-century liberal and socialist heirs, the "enemies" of twentieth-century authoritarianism. Socialist transnationalism was aided by the transnational diffusion of capitalism, the old regimes' habit of punishing dissidents with exile, and the leftward turn of young Jews, pressured by new political anti-Semitism (discussed in my forthcoming book). Cosmopolitan networks of exiles and Jews were the core of the Internationals, easing speedy translation of socialist texts. There were macro-regional subcultures of Marxism, syndicalism, and reformism, but most labor movements felt all these influences. Indeed, authoritarians and especially fascists attacked socialists as cosmopolitan, foreign, treasonous. The late nineteenth-century rise of sociology was implicitly nationalist. Weber, Durkheim, Pareto, and Mosca barely ever referred to each other. They were insulated behind their own national boundaries, all mounting independent critiques of transnational socialism.

The message of liberalism was also transnational, though it had two main homes, Britain and France. Liberalism embodied parliamentary compromise and open debate between independent gentlemen. It began to encounter difficulties in the age of the masses. The gradual extension of the suffrage in Britain had masked this, since mass parties were gradually incorporated into the gentlemanly ways of Westminster. The Third French Republic also masked it for a time, since Republican parties were united by their common need to defend the Republic against the right. But in the view of conservative notables elsewhere (such as Carl Schmitt), the more sudden entry of the masses brought disciplined parties adhering to preset ideologies. Free parliamentary debate was being swamped by ideological armies. "Liberal" notables might cling to power by manipulating emerging mass parties, as in *caciquismo* and *trasformismo*, but these became corrupt and developed authoritarian leanings. British ideological influence on the continent declined in the late nineteenth century as Britain became more absorbed in its empire. British, and to a lesser extent French, liberal influence on Europe declined.

Continental debates with liberalism were often challenges to "Anglo-Saxon" (sometimes to Anglo-French) orthodoxy. In philosophy the utilitarianism of Bentham, the positivism of Comte, and American pragmatism – all carrying the pragmatic wing of the Enlightenment tradition – were countered with neo-idealist intentionality, the emotions, vitalism, and *Lebensphilosophie* associated especially with Schopenhauer, Brentano, Bergson, and Nietzsche. Freud's unconscious was paralleled by LeBon's crowd psychology, Sorel's mass strike, and the primordial role of myth. Tönnies and Durkheim challenged the liberalism of Spencer and Comte: Society, they said, was not formed merely by contracts between individuals but required community and collective conscience. Gumplowicz and Ratzenhofer developed a sociology of ethnic conflict and militaristic "superstratification" to challenge the more pacific Marxian and liberal theories of class and interest group conflict. These new sociologies remained little known in Britain and the United States. Though Social Darwinism encouraged eugenicism everywhere, the northwest saw the reproduction of the lower classes rather than of "lower races" as the main problem. In Germany and Austria racial Social Darwinism permeated best-selling novels, popular sociology, and new political parties. Though few of these writers were rightists, their vulgarization at "the hands of a thousand minor intellectuals" (says Sternhell) encouraged romantic and populist expressions of nationalism and statism.

France and Germany continued to act as ideological intermediaries to the east and south of the continent. Weber saw the duality of instrumental and value rationality. Ortega y Gasset said Bismarck and Kant personified within Germany the entire European political dilemma: Bismarck offered order, stability, community, and authority, Kant freedom, enlightenment, equality, individualism. Liberals turned from Westminster toward the more embattled, nationalist French Republic. Spanish liberals declared that though England had been the cradle of public liberties, France had universalized them (Marco 1988: 37–42). Germany dominated socialism, from Marx to Bernstein, Kautsky, and Rosa Luxemburg, leaders of the world's biggest socialist party, the SPD. Around 1900, as liberalism faded, French and German socialists and authoritarian conservatives both dominated European political thought. The new radical right diffused eastward and southward from the two major players of the "frontier zone," the French and the Germans.

French and German concerns differed. French rightists focused on statism, Germans on nationalism. This was because France had settled territories and few ethnic disputes (Alsace-Lorraine was disputed but contained little ethnic tension). The French disputed instead what kind of state would fill this territory. Its turn-of-the-century protofascist intellectuals were spurred by the Republic's defeat of the monarchical, military, and ultramontane right and advanced new forms of statism embracing modernity, "integral nationalism," and mass mobilization. French rightism thus had more appeal in countries with clear boundaries, where the nation was not problematic but the state was. Maurras, Barrès, and Action Française were cited most in Spain, Portugal, and Italy. Italy was distinctive in that liberals as well as conservatives gravitated toward such protofascism. But these were liberals who had failed to institutionalize liberal practices in their countries.

In contrast, Germans lacked a single state. They argued about the merits of a Klein (little) and a Gross Deutschland (including Austria and other areas where ethnic Germans lived), whereas the major German states, Prussia/Germany and Austria, shared similar constitutions. So Germans debated ethnicity more than state constitutions. Rightists generated *völkisch* ("folkish," "popular") organic nationalism. This resonated more in areas of Europe where the relationship of ethnicity to state was disputed, across most of the east and in the Balkans. Ethno-nationalism was initially spearheaded by Austrian Germans, since only Austria possessed a European empire embroiled in disputes between "imperial" and "proletarian" nations. Though Social Darwinism diffused right through the continent, the more easterly German lands adapted it to intra-European ethnic differences – the product of anti-Semitism and the disassociation between nation and state found there.

The Great War reduced the geopolitical influence of both countries but increased nationalism. The Romanian Eliade denounced "Transylvanian traitors . . . who believe in democracy and have learned French" (Ioanid 1990: 155). Germanic *volkisch* nationalism spread eastward, especially amid resentment at the war's outcome. Nationalism also drew more generally on the Germanic philosophic stress on "will" and "struggle" by heroes or elites against decadence, corruption, and the banal, popularized by Nietzsche, Wagner, Spengler, and Sombart's distinction between Germanic "heroes" and Anglo-Saxon "traders." Nietzsche and Spengler were popular authors everywhere; Maurras, Barrès, and others were read sporadically in the northwest. But they resonated far less in the everyday practices of liberal democracies or amid depoliticized Protestantism or Catholicism.

A third German influence was felt through the nineteenth-century dominance of the German university system, and with it the systematization of knowledge more generally (Collins 1998: chap. 13). German universities especially dominated philosophy. But German philology, ethnography, and archeology greatly influenced nationalism. Nationalists formally reject foreign influences, insisting on their own "cosmic singularity." Nationalist visions of *Hispanidad*, Hungarism, "the Aryan *Volk*," "The Third Greek Civilization," and "the Second Rome" claimed to be rooted in a unique national history, civilization, and soil. A Romanian fascist proclaimed, "[O]ur nationalism will accept nothing but the superman and the supernation elected by the grace of God" (Ioanid 1990: 114). Yet nationalism was actually a comparative doctrine in which each nation's genealogy was inserted within a wider civilizational story, influenced by German-dominated scholarship on the Indo-Europeans, Aryans, Orientalism, the Old Testament, the Barbarians, and early Christianity. From the popularization of scholarly writings Romania was proclaimed "the only Orthodox Latin and the only Latin Orthodox" nation. Hungarian nationalists identified three chosen peoples of the world: Germans, Japanese, and Magyars. Magyars, the only "Turanian" people of Occidental culture, could uniquely mediate east and west to found a "third, middle empire." Turks provided an alternative vision of a Turanian Middle Empire. These were world-historical myths influenced by European, especially German, scholarship of the prewar period.

In the interwar period traditional Germanic statism and militarism blended with *volkisch* nationalism and anti-Semitism to produce Nazism. Its influence spread more eastward than southward, where state borders were firmer and racism and anti-Semitism weaker. French statism fused with Italian authoritarian-leaning liberalism and syndicalism to generate Italian fascism. Pareto and Mosca were adapted to suggest that elites pursuing absolute moral values, whatever the means, were superior to the "corrupt" parliamentarism of the "legal Italy." Spann's corporatism drew on Austrian notions of organization by "estates," Manoilescu's Romanian corporatism pioneered peripheral dependency theory. Like Gentile in Italy, their corporatist schemes of social reorganization blended economic efficiency with the integral nation and "the new man." The corporatist one-party trappings of Italian fascism were imitated, from Poland and the Baltic states to Spain and Portugal. Aided by Mussolini's theatrical style and rhetoric, Italy became the center of the new right during the 1920s. As fascism grew it absorbed more Catholic influence. Mussolini's compromise with the Pope was imitated elsewhere, and Catholic France, Spain, and Portugal adapted Austrian clerico-fascism.

Churches provided key infrastructures of ideological communication. They had been the "soul" of the old regimes and remained powerful mass forces, through school systems providing about half the literate Europeans, and through sermons and pastoral letters reaching every parish, reproduced in newspapers and periodicals. Religious messages flowed through three distinct macro-regions, Protestant, Orthodox, and Catholic. But they were also embedded inside each individual state.

Most of the big Protestant denominations were "established" state churches. In the northwest their education systems had been merged into the state or existed in harmonious tandem with the state system. They tended to reinforce the northwestern state, conservative, procapitalist, and prodemocracy, only mildly statist and nationalist. Protestant respect for individual and the local community also generated dissident sects across Scandinavia and Britain that reinforced liberal and social democracy. Northwestern Protestant churches rarely encouraged radical rightism. Germany was different, the only established Protestant church that remained the soul of a semi-authoritarian regime right up until 1918. It was now wary of the secular and Catholic parties of the Weimar Republic, and many churchmen were searching for an alternative state with a sense of the sacred. They found Nazism.

The Eastern Orthodox churches had originally resembled Protestantism in being "established" in their own local states. But most were then subordinated to foreign rulers – Austrians, Russians, or Turks. The monarchs of new nineteenth-century Orthodox states such as Bulgaria, Romania, and Greece were also drawn from foreign dynasties. Thus the Orthodox churches tended to represent not the soul of the state but the soul of the people – often of the peasantry. Orthodox seminaries and schools helped emerging national liberation movements and organic nationalism. The combination of a mild statism (stemming from their political quietism and their liking for hierarchy) and more pronounced nationalism produced varied political outcomes. Yet important factions in several Orthodox churches bent toward the radical right and even to fascism – especially in Romania (see Chapter 8).

The Catholic Church is transnational except that its base lies within Italy. In some countries its array of teaching orders and schools towered over state schools. Catholic hierarchies had long ago come to terms with the states in which they formed the dominant religion. By the nineteenth century they provided the soul of the old regimes. But they were then beset by liberals and socialists seeking to secularize the state. The Italian state was secular from the first. By 1900 the church was also losing the battle in France and the Low Countries. Thus some Catholics in the hierarchy and the teaching orders were attracted by "social" and "corporatist" concerns. These parallelled fascism in being ambiguously of both the left and the right (Fogarty 1957; Mayeur 1980). Encouraged by the papal encyclical *Rerum novarum* of 1891, "Social Catholicism" first penetrated economically advanced areas such as Belgium, France, South Germany, and Austria. Catholic labor unions and mass parties were founded. The movement then spread eastward and southward, generating parties such as the German Zentrum, the Austrian Christian Socials, the Italian Populari, and the Spanish Mauristas around the time of World War I. Fascism was to build on the social and hierarchical spirit of "Social Catholicism." But in France and Belgium the social and hierarchical factions split. Social Catholics generated leftist movements, while some of those emphasizing hierarchy went into small fascist movements. Portuguese Integralismo Lusitano absorbed Action Française texts and then transmitted them to Spain in the early 1920s. Catholic mysticism blended with organic nationalism. Maurras's call for a populist nationalism based on order, hierarchy, and community as a defense against individualism, secularization, liberalism, and socialism resonated through Catholicover countries – and also had some influence in Orthodox Greece and the Balkans (Augustinos 1977; Morodo 1985: 92–100, 107–14; Lyttleton 1987: 16–20; Close 1990: 205–11; Gallagher 1990: 157–8).

Thus religious ideological powers were exercised variously. Religion reinforced the macro-regional solidity of the northwestern bloc of countries, favoring a liberal democratic compromise between center-right and center-left. Religion had no single general effect elsewhere. Churches tended to see the godless left as the main enemy, but whom would they support against the left? The nationalism of Orthodox churches might turn conservative or radical. But where old regimes and an attendant church remained strong, churches might move a little rightward yet be wary of fascism (e.g., Spain). But weaker, more vulnerable old regimes had lost some of the sacred aura that Weber called "traditional legitimacy." This loss produced moral panic in which some churchmen began to eye corporatism or even fascism sympathetically – as in Germany, Austria, Italy, and Romania. Amid weakening old regimes, all three religions might be tempted by fascism's moral and transcendent claims not to reject modernism but to resacralize it. Fascism emerged in countries in which churches had played an important though now declining role in political power relations, and fascists exploited this by managing to transfer some of the sense of the sacred from God to the nation-state.

We are now closer to explaining distinctively fascist outcomes, since these are four out of the five major fascist movements. As others have noted, successful fascist movements tried to modernize and nationalize the sense of the sacred. The religious spirit of Romanian fascism and (to a lesser extent) Austro-fascism was obvious. Italian fascism specialized in its own non-Christian sacred rituals. Gentile (1990, 1996) says it resacralized an Italian state that had been previously desacralized – and the Pope regarded this with sympathy. Nuremberg rallies and the like were also designed to impart the sacred, and many German Protestant churchmen became Nazis. It is going too far to describe fascism as a religion (as Burleigh 2000 and Griffin 2001 do), since fascism saw men alone as bringing progress and rebirth and it had no conception of the divine. But fascism was usually aided by established religions and borrowed many of their techniques, just as it borrowed techniques from socialist movements.

Secular educational institutions were also crucial to the transmission of values. Between 1900 and 1930, university student numbers increased four-fold across the more developed world, a greater rate of expansion than even that of the late 1950s and 1960s. In both periods the surge caused an explosion in student politics. In the 1960s it went to the left; after World War I it went sharply to the right. Table 2.2 shows that expansion was greater in the authoritarian countries. If we remove the two outlier cases, Bulgaria and Denmark, from the calculation, university expansion was 50 to 100 percent greater in the authoritarian than in the liberal countries in the period immediately before the authoritarians came to power there. The difference declined in the late 1920s, since fascists and authoritarians reaching power in Italy and Hungary deliberately reduced the numbers of turbulent students. Expanded student cohorts meant "more raw" young intellectuals experiencing discontinuity between the university and their family backgrounds. We should remember that this expansion was occurring under German university domination. A German *Problemmatik* was being exported at a time of massive economic, military, and political crisis, not a recipe for socializing European youth into pacific liberalism. There was also a generational contribution, New rightist ideologies were also suffused with the moralizing characteristic of youthful idealism. The exploits of D'Annunzio, the first to exploit theatrical publicity and to glorify youth, diffused rapidly among students. Mussolini quickly imitated. Extreme nation-statists promulgated the cult of youth, fascists above all. Since fascism was youthful, it was therefore modern, the society of the future – so fascists persuasively proclaimed to

Table 2.2. *Expansion in University Student Numbers 1900–1930, Authoritarian and Democratic Countries*

	Ratio 1900 = 1.00			Ratio 1920 = 1.00
	1910	1920	1930	1930
Austria	1.63	–	–	0.97
Bulgaria	4.90	19.31	22.45	1.16
Germany	1.58	2.56	2.90	1.13
Hungary	1.33			0.98
Italy	1.03	2.05	1.78	0.87
Japan	1.92	3.20	7.28	2.28
Poland				1.86
Portugal	1.07	2.53	4.78	1.89
Romania				1.98
Spain				1.52
Yugoslavia				1.31
Authoritarian average	**1.92**	**5.93**	**7.84**	**1.45**
Belgium	1.47	1.73	2.01	1.16
Czechoslovakia				1.15
Denmark	2.00	2.64	12.78	4.84
Finland	1.19	1.25	2.57	2.06
France	1.38	1.67	2.63	1.58
Ireland				1.18
Netherlands	1.32	1.81	3.85	2.12
Norway	1.10	1.31	2.48	1.90
Sweden				1.11
Switzerland	1.62	1.65	1.63	0.99
U.K.	1.48	1.93	2.09	1.08
U.S.	1.45	2.52	4.90	1.94
Democratic average	**1.45**	**1.83**	**3.88**	**1.76**

Source: Mitchell 1993, 1995, 1998.

new cohorts of youth. Young men always provided their main bastion of support.

As we see, below, in every country highly educated professionals and high school, university, seminary, and military academy students contributed disproportionately to fascism across the authoritarian half of Europe. In contrast, northwestern fascist movements were more variably composed. Students were prominent in France and Finland but not in Scandinavia or Britain. Military veterans were always overrepresented in the immediate aftermath of the Great War, but northwestern military academies continued turning out younger fascist-leaning men only in France. In the authoritarian half of Europe, most education was state-run and was often a bastion of conservative statism, while church education produced more varied graduates. In some countries professors were also nationalists.[12] Students were everywhere in the fascist vanguard.

Why did fascism attract the massed lesser intelligentsia? To some extent it reflected the dominance of the German universities and of the German and French military academies in continental education systems. But the power and status of intellectuals who were "notables" in the old regime might also be threatened by the rise of mass movements. The economic explanation would be that highly educated professionals and students became unemployable, receptive to radical politics, and more likely to be rightist since they were middle-class. A more "ideal" explanation would be that intellectuals are entrusted with ideological power in society. It is their job to explore matters of ultimate meaning. If there is a crisis of meaning (produced by the concatenation of contemporary crises), they will experience it most severely and pioneer plausible new answers to the crisis. In fact, highly educated people turning fascist were not those suffering the greatest economic hardship. They seem to have turned to fascism because they were attracted to the message of transcendent nation-statism. Of course, ideology never comes disembodied. These people were inhabiting social milieux in which this message seemed more plausible. Their everyday lives gave resonance to it.

Since most fascists were young males, some have suggested that this was "the generation of 1914," whose first adult experience was of World War I (e.g., Wohl 1979). My case studies reveal that not only the trenches, but also the military academies, universities, and high schools germinated extreme nation-statist and paramilitary values – and among at least two and sometimes three generations of young men. This had started before World War I. Much of the officer corps of Eastern Europe had attended prewar Prussian or Habsburg academies. Metaxas, Codreanu, and Szalasi attested to their importance in forming their ideas. The expansion of reserve systems had brought most young men into contact with militaristic nationalism. World War I cemented this. A cohort of young men left in its wake was armed, uniformed, and committed to paramilitarism as the means of effecting political change. Military academies continued to diffuse military nationalism.

I have tentatively delineated ideological networks communicating authoritarian and fascist ideas. Some were transnational, most derived from the frontier zone states of Germany and France, but they diffused mostly across the center, east, and south of Europe, to be reinterpreted within each national tradition. The core carriers – young educated and military or religious males – developed fascism as an entire meaning system. Their networks of ideological communication also seem to have added the distinctively youthful fascist blend of moralizing and violence that is usually considered to be its "nonrational" side. However, the center, east, and south was not a monolithic bloc, and I have identified some of the infrastructures, especially religious ones, that contributed different types of authoritarianism across the region. But this is only a beginning to identifying ideological causes. It is hoped that the case studies will reveal more.

CONCLUSION

The interwar surge of nationalism and statism was probably unstoppable. Stronger, more insulated nation-states were emerging everywhere. Yet the surge might have culminated in more moderate forms of nation-statism. The major divide – both conceptually and geographically – was between liberal democracy and forms of rightist authoritarianism. The winners of World War I almost all favored the former. Yet it was not easy to establish liberal democratic nation-states by fiat, as attempted among the losers in 1918. In the center, east, and south of Europe, without the reinforcement of traditions and of the culture of one's entire region, parliamentary democracy seemed fragile and risky. Risk aversion amid an ideological concern with order and security could lead to preemptive repressive strikes. Ceding sovereign powers to the opponent if electorally defeated was routine in the northwest but problematic elsewhere, where "we" increasingly represented morality, civilization, and the organic nation, "they" the threatening "foreign" traitors. Parties were often more committed to substantive value goals than to the rules of the democratic game (Linz 1978). Where a movement believes its ends justifies the means, it will more readily turn to violence.

Conversely, parliamentary sovereignty was routinized across the northwest and so resilient. Here socialists withstood communists, conservatives withstood organic nationalists, all subscribing to an instrumental rationality of means not ends – of swing voters and the middle ground – deriving from their long-term historical implication in the liberal institutions of compromise. The northwest withstood crises until Hitler's armies marched on them. Though buffeted by the Great Depression, by strike waves, and by fluctuating party alliances, it was not in serious danger from its own authoritarian right. The rise of fascism was not here viewed as the dawn of a brave new age but as a distant distasteful threat to civilization. The northwest responded to crisis by moving hesitantly toward the center, to widen the suffrage and deepen welfare states. That bit of the explanation seems obvious. Entrenched relations of political power kept authoritarians at bay, even in a period of severe economic crisis and some class tension. There is thus no need to proliferate case studies of the entrenched liberal democracies, since they varied so little.

But we cannot yet explain authoritarianism, especially its fascist variant. We have a problem of "overdetermination." The times favored more nation-statism, but all four sources of social power and all four crises of modernity helped to explain the rise of authoritarianism and fascism. Class conflict boosted by late development and capitalist crises fueled authoritarianism and fascism. So did military crisis, through defeat, disruption, and emerging paramilitarism and rearmament. So did the dual semi-authoritarian/semi-liberal state of the center, east, and south of Europe. So did networks of ideological communication, patterned by the regional divide, conveying messages to educated and armed youth that increasingly verged on fascism. We would ideally establish the relative weights of these four broad causes of authoritarianism and fascism by multivariate analysis. But there are only a limited number of countries as cases and only two Europes. On both sides of the divide we have a number of highly intercorrelated possible causes.

Perhaps the five fascist movements all had different causes. After all, Italy went fascist uniquely early, Germany was a revisionist Great Power, Austria was a shriveled country with two different fascist movements, Hungary was shriveled, Romania swollen, both with authoritarians stealing fascist clothes. All might be very different cases. An explanation of fascist regimes would be largely confined to two cases. Comparative analysis cannot cope with such small numbers. I turn instead to the detail of the case-study method, returning to general explanations in my final chapter.

3

Italy

Pristine Fascists

Fascism was made in Italy. Though the prewar intellectuals subsequently labeled as "fascist" came from various countries, as a mass movement Italian fascism was the pristine case. The very word is Italian, from *fascio*, a tied bundle of sticks, used then to describe any small, tight-knit political group – the sense being that sticks would have more force if bound tightly together, as human groups would if bound by strong comradeship. Note that this indicates organization, not values. Mussolini additionally emphasized its derivation from the Latin *fasces*, the ancient Roman Republic's symbol of popular authority, an axe bound with rods, which he used as the movement's icon.

Though ideas later called "fascist" were aired in prewar Italy, fascism proper emerged only at the end of World War I. After declaring for neutrality in 1914, the Italian government joined the Entente in 1915, lured by promises of territories to be won from the Habsburg Empire. But there was serious conflict over entry into the war. The years 1915 and 1916 saw mass demonstrations, rioting, and street-fighting between pro- and antiwar movements. This had followed hard on two further disruptions: a large extension of the male suffrage suddenly introduced (for tactical reasons) by prime minister Giolitti in 1912 and a period of industrial unrest that had increased the power of the left "maximalist" wing of the Socialist Party. Many conservatives and liberals feared that liberal parliamentarism was being threatened from the streets. Divisions over the war weakened the state and split all the main parties, including the ruling liberal and conservative parties. In the Socialist Party, the leadership opposed the war, making the PSI unique among major socialist parties. This led "patriotic" socialists – including Benito Mussolini – to break with the party and join with radical nationalists, futurist intellectuals, and syndicalists to create the fascist movement. Some of the Italian left was strongly drawn toward nationalism.

Though working-class movements in other countries were to demonstrate patriotic enthusiasm, only Italian leftists joined with nationalists to form a major new party.

This union had three important preconditions. First, many Italians distinguished sharply between the Italian nation and the Italian state. There was a strong popular sense that the Italian state had been created in the 1860s by diplomatic maneuvers among the upper class and foreign governments, in the course of which Garibaldi's popular redshirt movement had been sidelined. Nationalists had repeatedly attempted to rekindle populist national fervor, and many sympathized with the leftist view of the state as a sham, its conservative and liberal parliamentarians representing only the rich. Since the Catholic Church was also hostile to this secularizing state and stood aside from politics, the state lacked sacred authority on the right. There was no diffuse "old regime" controlling this state. The contemporary terms were that the "legal" was not the same as the "real" Italy, that is, that the state did not represent the nation.

Second, the Italian labor movement contained an important syndicalist element. Syndicalists rejected the Marxian stress on party and state, arguing that "syndicates" (unions and professional associations) could achieve the revolution. Parties represented only "electoral masses," whereas syndicates represented the material basis of life and so could become genuine communities. The syndicate of each specialized occupation could force up the price of its labor through a skill monopoly, but the oversupply of unskilled labor meant that its strikes must be general and violent. Laborers must be compelled to share work and privations in order to force up their price. Eventually violent, insurrectionary strikes might unite all occupations into a single revolutionary proletariat. After the revolution, society would be structured into "a state of syndicates," largely decentralized and self-governing, though embodying a technocratic "aristocracy of producers." Though syndicalists were formally antistatist, they shared with fascists antisocialism and a liking for violence. By incorporating *all* productive occupations into the proletariat, some syndicalists moved away from the Marxian preoccupation with class to extol the power of the whole "people" or "nation." For syndicalists, the proletariat *was* the nation, embattled.

Third, Italian nationalism also had many leftist elements. It did not endorse the existing state, though nationalists hoped that populism might revitalize the state. Italy was "the last (or the weakest) of the Great Powers," the only one "deprived of Empire." As Corradini said in 1911, Italy was a "proletarian nation" exploited by the bourgeois Great Powers. Such rhetoric struck a nerve, and there was considerable popular support for Italy to achieve "liberation" from Austrian pressure on her borders and to strike out across the Mediterranean for colonies in Libya. For leftist nationalists, the nation *was* the proletariat embattled. The bridge between syndicalism and nationalism was built by the futurists. Originally a cultural and artistic group, they developed just before the Great War a political program combining aggressive nationalism with a vision of a future technocratic-industrial society. Their contempt for liberal parliamentarianism moved them toward a program of "action rather than words" (De Felice 1995: 738–41).

The splits occasioned by the Great War then produced among these disparate forces a leftist nationalist interventionism that then turned into fascism. Without the war, there would have been no fascism, rightly says Saladino (1966). One of the four crises of modernity identified in Chapter 2 – total citizen war – had precipitated fascism, in its first pristine form. Yet it also presupposed a political crisis and an economic crisis: a weak and only half-legitimate state attempting a rapid transition into full male suffrage amid a postwar recession and class warfare between a relatively weak capitalist class and a divided labor movement. Mussolini and 190 others founded the *fasci di combattimento* ("groups of combatants") in March 1919 at San Sepulchro in Milan. Former soldiers predominated, followed by revolutionary syndicalists, patriotic socialists, and futurists. The model was the futurist *fasci*, of which thirty had been formed over the previous three months (De Felice 1995: 476). Of the 85 with known occupations, 21 were writers and journalists, 20 were white-collar workers, 12 were workers, five were manufacturers, and four were teachers. Almost all were under 40, and 15 percent were under 20. Five were Jews (Gentile 1989: 35).

Renamed as the Partito Nationale Fascista (PNF), the movement had 20,000 members by late 1920, almost 100,000 by April 1921, and 320,000 by November 1921 – very rapid growth. It was less of a party than a paramilitary, and in October 1922 it marched on Rome. The government might have resisted this less-than-overwhelming show of force by the lightly armed fascists, but instead capitulated, asking Mussolini to lead a coalition government. Three years later he had become dictator. Fascism had surged to a share in power in three years, to full power in six. Why was it so rapidly successful? Who supported it, and why?

TWO THEORIES OF ITALIAN FASCISM

One theory has come from the scholars, the other from the fascists. Though citizen warfare first generated and nourished fascism, most scholars argue that a capitalist crisis caused its great expansion. Fascism, they say, became essentially bourgeois or petty bourgeois, its "radical rightism" fueled by these classes' economic discontents, then made use of by the capitalist class to suppress labor and socialism. The distinctive contribution of Italian fascism, they say, was to still class conflict by incorporating labor into corporatist state organizations. Though this has been a popular interpretation of all fascist movements, only in Italy has the view remained dominant ever since (Salvemini 1973: 129; Tasca 1976: 340; De Felice 1980; Abse 1986, 1996; Revelli 1987; Lyttleton 1987: 49–50; Brustein 1991; Luebbert 1991: 274; Elazar 1993). These writers mention other causes of fascism – a frail and suddenly enlarged liberal democracy, nationalism, militarism, youth – but subordinate them to class. Some emphasize the discontent of rural classes, others urban classes; and opinions differ over the relative contributions of capitalists, the middle class, and the lower middle class. Did fascism protect capitalists from proletarian revolution, or was it petty bourgeois radicalism? But even the most nuanced accounts (Roberts 1980; Lyttleton 1996) remain variations on a bourgeois theme. A few dissenters (e.g., Saladino 1966; Gentile, 1996) have seen fascism less as a class movement than as extreme nationalism, a "civic religion" of the nation. But class theory predominates, especially when it comes to identifying who the fascists were and why they had become fascists.

The most interesting class theory is Salvatorelli's (1923: 130–6), added to by De Felice (1977: 128–31, 175–92; 1980). Salvatorelli believed the war had intensified the squeezing of the middle and lower middle classes between the more organized proletarian and capitalist classes. Fascist ideology centered on a "typically petty bourgeois" nationalism. Though unemployed and handicrafts workers also gave support, "the petty bourgeois element not only predominates numerically, but . . . is the characteristic and directing element. . . . [F]ascism represents the class struggle of the lower middle class that was wedged between capitalism and the proletariat, as the third between two combatants." Its core lay amid state employees, bureaucrats, and professionals – called by Salvatorelli "the humanistic petty bourgeoisie" – who constituted not "a true social class with its own strength and functions, but a conglomerate living at the margin of the capitalist process of production." Thus, he argued, fascism had no genuine vision of social and economic development and so could not transcend class conflict. Fascists would have either to bring about the ruin of capitalist civilization or to sell out to the capitalists. He expected them to do the latter. De Felice divided this middle class slightly differently, into a traditional middle class (farmers, merchants, professionals, small businessmen), with some autonomy and homogeneity, and a new middle class (white-collar employees and salaried intellectuals), with less. In the postwar period the new middle class suffered more and so provided the main fascist thrust. Ideological, military, or political causes tend to enter into both men's explanation only insofar as they produce economic and class consequences. Thus World War I exacerbated the discontent of the middle class; Italian democracy proved frail because of its class biases; nationalism was essentially "petty bourgeois" (cf. Tasca 1976: 323, 358).

But this class-centered view was not that of the fascists themselves. It is part of my methodology of "taking fascists seriously" to let them speak for themselves. Mussolini's own account is *The Political and Social Doctrine of Fascism*, written in 1932 from material compiled by Gentile. By then Mussolini was a dictator wishing to legitimate his regime, so we must correct the propaganda element in the document with some of his precoup statements. Mussolini begins by saying that he had been first attracted to politics by the socialist "doctrine of action." This was true (as it was for other fascist intellectuals quoted in Chapter 1). The youthful Mussolini had repeatedly urged his socialist comrades "to make history, not endure it" through an "organization of warriors" preparing for "the greatest bloodbath of all." But he declares that by 1918 "Socialism was already dead as a doctrine: it existed only as a hatred." Fascism then emerged, he says, from the ashes of socialism as a "third force" leading "the working class to real and effectual leadership" under "strict military discipline." From the nationalist D'Annunzio, Mussolini then borrowed a cult of paramilitarism and youth, an elitist cult of leadership and a confidence that he could manipulate mass crowds through myth, symbols, and ritual. This means that ritual became a vital reinforcement for formal ideology in the practice of the movement, as Berezin (1997) and Gentile (1996) have argued. It also fueled fascism's contempt for democracy, expressed here by Mussolini:

Democracy has deprived the life of the people of "style": that is, a line of conduct, the color, the strength, the picturesque, the unexpected, the mystical: in sum, all that counts in the life of the masses. We play the lyre on all its strings: from violence to religion, from art to politics.

Note the union of politics, art, and style, so typical of fascism.

Mussolini neglects to mention that in 1919 fascism had been leftist, committed to an eight-hour day and workers' control. The leftist syndicalists Panunzio, Gentile, Rossoni, and Olivetti provided much of the rhetoric of the movement, adding in their different ways more "integral" syndicalism or corporatism. They declared that "the entire working class movement must be orchestrated to the higher aspirations of the nation" and that "statism and syndicalism are in the process of fusion." Mussolini had been a little wary of them. Between 1922 and 1924 he still nurtured hopes of leading a fascist/socialist parliamentary coalition against conservatism and bourgeois liberal democracy. This apparent adoption of the parliamentary road alienated the futurists, who left the movement. But Mussolini soon abandoned parliamentarianism and then moved to domesticate his syndicalists by bringing them into a more top-down corporatist state. He was proclaiming a "totalitarian ethical state," with workers' control forgotten and the leftists quietened (Nolte 1965: 202–8, 258; Gregor 1979: 106–14; De Felice 1995; Dahl 1999: 46–70; Riley 2002: chap. 2).

Paramilitarism, the legacy of idealist theories of "action" concretized by experience of the war, had been a more constant refrain. At the beginning of 1919 Mussolini joined the futurists in embracing "action" rather than "words" (associated with stifling parliamentarianism), successfully silencing democratic nationalists and socialists. The first *fasci* were founded in March and the first deaths came the following month. Then the first big PNF congress, in 1921, proclaimed its "action squads," the *squadristi*, "a revolutionary militia placed at the service of the nation . . . following three principles: order, discipline, hierarchy" (Gentile 1989: 398). As Dahl (1999: 145–6) says, strikes, action, and violence directed by good against evil were crucial to the Italian blending of syndicalism and statism. In 1932 Mussolini was still declaiming paramilitary virtues:

War alone brings up to its highest tension all human energy and puts its stamp of nobility upon the peoples who have the courage to meet it. . . . [T]he proud motto of the *Squadrista, Me ne frego* ["I don't give a damn," or in the trenches, the obscene expression "I jack off on it"], written on the bandage of the wound is an act of philosophy . . . the education to combat, the acceptance of the risks which combat implies, and a new way of life for Italy . . . holiness and heroism . . . influenced by no economic motive.

Paramilitary virtues were linked to the cult of youth and martyrdom, for the soldiers were young men risking death. Italy itself was a "youthful" nation, united only since the 1860s, "proletarian," exploited by older "plutocratic" nations. A movement that mobilized the forceful energies of its youth could end this exploitation. Gentile (1996: 23–7) says that paramilitarism was a "holy crusade," united by rituals of the holy communion. Its blood, he says (with some exaggeration), was like that of Christ and the Christian martyrs. As the Lucca *squadristi* leader proclaimed at a funeral for local fascists in 1921: "O Holy Trinity, born of blood: your blood, our blood. The veins are emptied of their most vital flow to create a new baptismal font: the chalice full of its scarlet gift." Of course, unlike Christ, these fascists were killed while trying to kill others, for this was the ideology of moral murder. Fascism was too this-worldly and too instrumental really to be a religion.

After seizing power, Mussolini subordinated the paramilitaries to the state, as he subordinated real violence to its ritual commemoration. To use Nazi terms, "order" had to take over from "wildness." By 1932 he claimed his state was a unitary "organized, centralized and authoritative democracy" that was able to represent the nation "organically":

The foundation of Fascism is . . . the State as an absolute, in comparison with which all individuals or groups are relative, only to be conceived of in their relation to the State. . . . [T]he Fascist state is itself conscious, and has itself a will and a personality . . . it represents the immanent spirit of the nation. . . . It is the force which alone can provide a solution to the dramatic contradictions of capitalism. . . . It is not reactionary but revolutionary.

This state makes obsolete "the rivalry of parties . . . and the irresponsibility of political assemblies. . . . Fascism denies that class-war can be the preponderant force in the transformation of society." It was supposedly a transcendent state.

The state is also imperialist: "The expansion of the nation is an essential manifestation of vitality. . . . Empire demands discipline, the co-ordination of all forces and a deeply-felt sense of duty and sacrifice. . . . [N]ever before has the nation stood more in need of authority, of direction and of order."

By 1932 Mussolini's focus was on war, organic nationalism, and the state. Paramilitarism was seen as uncomfortable to the state, but it remained rhetorically and organizationally important, for fascism continued to attempt mass mobilization. And though the party had expounded a full range of economic and social policies, it had seen these as flowing from the primacy of the nation, militarism, and the state (Delzell 1970: 27–37). Even corporatism was defended in terms less of economic efficiency than of its ability to transcend class and interest group conflict and mobilize the masses (Berezin 1997: 60–3). Italian fascism had surged in the immediate postwar period. Thus the economic problem was less one of recession than of the postwar class conflict.

This became the standard fascist agenda across Europe, revealing the core fascist values distinguished in Chapter 1: an organic, paramilitary nation-statism, claiming to transcend social conflict. The main Italian peculiarities were in being first, and so early exhibiting much ideological variety, and then in taming its "radical" paramilitarism into a less dynamic, though mobilized, statism. This also weakened calls to cleanse the nation from its enemies – the paramilitaries had already accomplished the task of cleansing Italy of its political opponents, while there was little sense of ethnic enemies, except later in Africa.

Any short statement of fascist doctrine must simplify. Italian fascism was a developing, pluralistic, decentralized, even disorderly movement. Its paramilitaries valued action over ideology, while Mussolini was an opportunist leader. Nonetheless, most Italian fascists thought they were espousing not a class ideology but a doctrine of transcendent, organic nation-statism cloaked in antimaterialist moral fervor – a total transformation of society. Some say that fascism was "the religion of Italy," "the religion of the nation," "the militia of the nation"; its enemies were "traitors to the nation." They say that the movement stressed faith, symbols, rituals, the cult of martyrs dying to purify the nation. Every party branch office contained a shrine to the nation and its martyrs (Gentile 1990, 1996). But the fascist leaders were well aware that a true religion – miracle-working, commanding a sense of awe, reverence of things set apart from the material realm – existed in Italy. It was not fascism but Catholicism. So they tried to weave fascist rituals into its sacred mantle.

These two views of fascism – emphasizing class and nation-state – are very different. The class theories involve denying the significance and sincerity of fascist ideology. They are part of the tradition of not taking fascists seriously. Was Mussolini sincere, deceiving, or deluded in emphasizing the latter? Was he fronting a class movement or was he leading a movement genuinely committed to paramilitary nation-statist ideas? We see below that he was doing both.

WHO WERE THE FASCISTS?

Gender, Age, Militarism

As in all my case studies I examine in some detail the social backgrounds of the fascists. They offer the best evidence regarding ordinary fascists. Yet social movements are not mere aggregations of individuals, each of whom can be counted equally and statically. Movements contain particular social structures and processes. This fascist movement greatly respected order and hierarchy, and the attainment of substantial power within the movement was an important part of the "career" of fascists. Moreover, paramilitary violence conferred distinctive powers on a "mass" (though less than "majority") movement committed to violence. As in all fascist movements, violence was key to their success. We must observe these fascists in action as well as count their individual attributes.

But I start with the known attributes of the mass of fascists. Unfortunately, the Italian data are not plentiful. The PNF made only one calculation of the social background of its members, based on the records of half its 320,000 members of November 1921. We hope it was a representative half, since we have few other sources of information. Scholars have concentrated on its class composition. Yet its gender, age, and military composition are more striking.

The movement had started with some feminist input. Nine women had been at the founding meeting at San Sepulchro, 5 percent of those present, and early fascist/syndicalist ideas included some freethinking about gender and sexuality. But the movement's violence rapidly made it masculinist. By 1922 only 1 to 2 percent of full members were women, and there were no women leaders. Of course, other parties were probably similar since Italian women could not vote. Indeed, the ancillary fascist women's organizations soon became larger and more active than those of any rival movement save for the Catholic Church. Fascism recruited many women skeptical of the employment-centered feminism that came to dominate most western liberal and socialist feminist movements. But the most important cause of the growth of fascist women's organizations was probably fascism's pretensions to be a "totalitarian" movement. The movement had to organize women in order to control them. It had no desire to do this coercively, so it accomplished it primarily through social and ritual activities. Fascism honored women as mothers, "reproducers of the nation," "angels of the hearth." It gave them a role in the nation not only in principle but in ritual ceremonies comparable to those of religion. The Concordat with the Pope enabled the movement to stage quasi-religious ceremonies honoring mothers or widows of fascist martyrs and women donating their wedding rings to provide gold for the African War (Berezin 1997). De Grazia (1992: 35) considers that fascism now "nationalized" women, just as men had been nationalized in the later nineteenth century. Social policies borrowed from Social Catholicism helped women through protective legislation at work and welfare assistance to mothers and large families. Though comparable policies were emerging in some other Catholic countries, fascist Italy was in the lead – though their effect on working women may have been outweighed by fascism's other labor policies that tended to harm men and women workers alike (Caldwell 1986; Willson 1996). Fascism also enabled women to march, to demonstrate, to join in sporting and dramatic pageants, and to wear fine uniforms. Many felt liberated by the novelty of these public roles (Passerini

1987: 193). As Willson (1996: 81) remarks, fascism was the first movement to bring women onto the national stage – though their lines were mainly written by men. The early movement and the seizure of power had been also decidedly "macho." But Italian women certainly came to offer as much passive support to the established fascist regime as men did.

Fascists were also young. In the national list 25 percent of members were under twenty-one. Probably most of the rest were not much older. The average age of members in both Reggio Emilia and the province of Bologna in 1922 was twenty-five, and of squadristi in both Bologna and Florence it was twenty-three (Cavandoli 1972: 135; Suzzi Valli 2000: 135; Reichardt 2002: 347). Their parliamentary deputies were mostly in their thirties (younger than in other parties) and so were their regional secretaries (Gentile 2000: 411, 491). Unlike other parties, virtually no leader was over fifty. Young men especially dominated fascist violence. Among 400 fascist "martyrs" honored by the party, a quarter have their ages mentioned and they averaged twenty-one. Most precoup fascists belonged to a single generation, born between about 1890 and 1905. I assume that this was easily the youngest, least married of the Italian parties (though I have no actual membership data on other parties). Even fascist deputies (picked for their respectability) were on average thirteen years younger than other deputies.

Youthfulness, entwined with paramilitarism, was probably responsible for the fascist combination (found in all countries) of morality, modernism, and murder. The militants were violent yet seen as "idealistic," "modern," and "the wave of the future." Since Italy was considered in public rhetoric to be a "young nation," fascist youthfulness was claimed to exemplify it. And when we consider class, we must remember that fascism was especially mobilizing young, unmarried men, whose experience can hardly be regarded as typical of the classes to which we assign them. And when combined with gender, youth made an enormous difference: Fascism resembled a violent male teenage gang, though an unusually "idealistic" one, with its primary ties cementing strong and violent comradeship (Lyttleton 1987: 244). It is easy to see the appeal to young males of the motto *me ne frego*. And it is easy to see the power that such disciplined, ideologically legitimated violence might confer on fascism over political parties that debated, demonstrated, but did not lay lives on the line. Mussolini himself declared that his *squadristi* would rule through *trincerocrazia* ("trench power"). This was the generation of 1916, mobilized by militarism.

Indeed, most of them were already trained in military violence. Some 57 percent of the 1921 members had fought in the war (DeFelice 1966: 7; Revelli 1987: 18). Yet virtually none of the quarter who in 1921 were under twenty-one (and none of the few women) could have fought in the war. Thus about 80 percent of those fascists who were eligible for military service (males aged twenty to forty-four during 1916–18) must have fought. Even more of the leaders had fought – between 68 and 81 percent of the cohorts of regional secretaries up to 1931 were veterans (Gentile 2000: 495). The highest Italian wartime recruitment rate among this age group had been about 23 percent – a ratio of overrepresentation of 3.5. Indeed, the very first fascist militants are usually said to have been mostly drawn from the elite volunteer soldiers known as the *arditi*. It seems that some *arditi* units came over wholesale to the fascists, mostly led by futurist officers. They were supplemented mainly by students, too young to have fought, but seemingly fired with similar extreme nationalism The early *squadristi* seem to have been highly educated young men (Gentile 1989: 74; Snowden 1989: 158–60; Riley 2002: chap. 2). Probably about a quarter of *arditi* became fascists, with others joining other nationalist movements. Since most industrial workers had been exempted from military service, most *arditi* were former peasants, serving under middle-class officers. Some contemporaries believed that junior officers were overrepresented among the fascists. Gramsci (1971: 212–13) believed that ordinary career officers were disproportionately drawn from the "medium and small rural bourgeoisie," their training conferring on them the values and power to defend their class interests by force. They were drawn to fascism by both economic goals and military means.

Since the army had comprised three million men, only a small proportion became fascists. Most soldiers just wanted rapid demobilization into civilian life and were concerned more with employment or education than with ideology. Did material discontents lead some into fascism, as is often asserted? Little research has been done on the issue. More soldiers joined the more mainstream veteran association, loosely connected to the Catholic *popolari* but confining itself to lobbying for jobs and welfare benefits and actually opposing fascism. A small leftist paramilitary, the Arditi del Populo, formed but was rebuffed by the socialist and communist parties, who (as we see below) preferred rhetorical to real action. Others joined d'Annunzio's nationalist Legion (Ledeen 1977). Fascism provided a more "radical" destination for a small minority of veterans, keeping alive their organization and their comradeship. Their experience provided them with enduring militarist values and organization. They claimed that the comradeship, discipline, and egalitarian nationalism of the trenches could solve the ills of Italy. Just as "there were no class differences at the front," paramilitarism could now "transcend" class differences. The socialist leader Turati emphasized the inurement to violence such "careers" involved:

The war . . . accustomed the youngsters as well as the grown ups to the daily use of usual and unusual weapons. . . . [I]t praised individual and collective murder, black-mail, arrest, the macabre joke, the torturing of prisoners, the "punitive expeditions," the summary executions. . . . [I]t created in general the atmosphere in which alone the fascist bacillus could grow and spread (quoted in Nolte 1965: 144)

For these fascists disciplined paramilitary violence was viewed positively, as moral. Gentile (1996) quotes many of the official ideologists declaiming the spirituality of paramilitarism. One wonders how the young thugs standing to attention in front of the speech makers understood it! Balbo, the leader of the *squadristi*, was a little more down to earth. He had served with distinction at the front during the war, and he there confided to his diary: "To fight, to struggle, to come home to the land of Giolitti [the arch-fixer prime minister], who transformed every ideal into a business proposition? No, better to deny everything, to destroy everything, in order to renew from the ground up." Violence, he wrote, was "the quickest and most defini-tive way of reaching the revolutionary goal. . . . No bourgeois hypocrisy, no sentimentalism: action, direct and sharp, carried out to the end, at whatever cost" (Segrè 1987: 34). But he did have the sense of commanding thugs to a higher purpose. He described his *squadristi* as the heirs of "the holy rabble of Garibaldi," the redshirts who had liberated Italy from foreign oppression – an analogy often made by fascists.

Paramilitarism also conferred a concrete and enveloping social iden-tity. The returning soldiers were young, mostly unmarried with little labor market experience, poorly integrated into local communities centered on family, occupation, and religion, prone to identify with the nation as a whole – which the mass army had claimed to "represent" (Linz 1976: 37). Where fascist members are described in party records as *arditi*, they are given no other class or occupational label – as if this were a total social identity (Misefari and Marzotti 1980). They may never have been in an employ-ment or family situation that could provide other adult identities. Their military skills would have been their main skills, militarism was among their main values, the *squadristi* unit their social life and provider of an emotional sense of belonging, of comradeship. Unlike the Nazis, party and paramili-tary were usually not even separate: Local party activists were often simply termed "*squadristi*." Tasca (1976: 345; cf. Lyttleton 1987: 46–9, Snowden 1989: 157) concluded that fascism *was* paramilitarism, its edge over its op-ponents being disciplined paramilitary ferocity. But under (somewhat loose) discipline, often permanently living in barracks, with ruthless treatment of "traitors," the hierarchical paramilitary was also coercively socializing fascists themselves into a life of collective violence. The *squadristi* were a substitute for employment, community, and church. They caged and coerced their members into an enjoyable life of violence. In their rhetoric, fascist speech makers endorsed the philosophy of action. But that is also what the paramilitaries actually practiced. In so doing, they coerced others into compliance with fascist dictates. As with all the bigger fascist paramilitaries, we must understand this double coercion, of comrades and enemies, as crucial to fascists' success.

Yet the violent careers of Italian fascists differed from that of other fascisms. As elsewhere, the first cohort of recruits came straight from the war, but the Italian fascist cohort was unique in proceeding straight through violence to the quick seizure of power, without going through a period of prolonged electoral activity. Once in power, the paramilitaries were tamed by Mussolini through their integration into a well-paid state paramilitary, the MSVN. A second burst of violence, now state-sponsored, came in the late 1930s in Africa, and a third burst came near the end of the war in Europe. Italian fascists thus had uneven careers in violence. The first phase was short-lived, supposedly legitimated by military values and a "civil war" situation. The second and third phases (discussed in my forthcoming volume), though murderous, were short-lived and hidden somewhat from the gaze of most Italians.

Thus most early Italian fascists were young males organized into a paramilitary gang. Most had fought as young men in the war, others were even younger. All these were introduced to militarism and/or paramilitarism between the ages of eighteen and twenty-one, either in the war or in the *squadristi*. What better motto for them than *me ne frego*? So far they might seem closer to Mussolini's than Salvatorelli's and De Felice's conception of fascism. Indeed, they delighted in parodying class theorists, taunting their Marxist opponents with the hurtful epithet "bourgeois." Since the Italian *borghese* also means "civilian," the taunt meant to hell with the "respectable," psychologically "repressed," and "feeble" "bourgeoisie." As we shall see, "youth," "action," and even "violence" came to have broader ideological resonance as well.

Region

Fascism was strongest of all in Italy's two smallish "threatened border" regions, the northern Alto Adige (South Tyrol), disputed with Austria, and the northeast, disputed with Yugoslavia. In March 1921, Trieste alone provided almost 15,000 of the movement's 80,000 members, more than twice the contribution of any other province. Trieste and the neighboring province of Udine provided 20 percent of fascist members (there were seventy-one provinces). In the immediate aftermath of war, with the revised borders still disputed, many saw the north and northeast as "threatened," and many of its locals turned to extreme nation-statism to protect them from rising Austro-German and Slovene nationalism (De Felice 1966: 8–11; Linz 1976: 82–4, 92; Steinberg 1986). But fascism was also strong in the modern cities of northern Italy, from where it spread into the more advanced agrarian regions in the northeast and center-north – that is, in Venezia Giulia, of the Veneto, the whole Po Valley, Tuscany, and Umbria. Then the major cities of the northwest were also captured. Riley (2002: chap 2) notes that these were the most modern parts of Italy. The agrarian areas had very varied relations of production – some with large landowners, others with small peasant holdings. But what all these fascist areas had in common were relatively strong "civil societies" – measured by dense networks of voluntary associations such as cooperatives and chambers of labor. He concludes that fascism spread most where civil society was strongest and where it could mobilize existing voluntary associations. Finally, after the March on Rome, fascism was able to spread across most of the country. By 1923, some 40 percent of members were in central Italy, 37 percent in the north, and even 23 percent were to be found in the south – though really backward southern districts remained largely untouched. By 1922 the relative contribution of Trieste and Udine had fallen to 5 percent, while that of the seven biggest Italian cities had fallen from 39 to 25 percent (Revelli 1987: 22).

Northeastern fascists remained distinctive. Members for Udine as of 1922 are detailed in row 2 of Appendix Table 3.1. Though mildly middle-class, they spread across most of the local labor force.[1] I calculate a ratio between the percentage contribution of a group to the fascist movement compared with its percentage in the whole labor force. This generates an index of fascist over- or underrepresentation. Values of over 1.0 indicate overrepresentation of fascists, under 1.0 indicate underrepresentation. I calculate such ratios throughout my case-study chapters.[2] In Udine those in public or private administration were the most overrepresented group (having a ratio of 3.1), followed by large property owners and professionals (ratios of 1.5). Commercial workers were roughly at parity (having a ratio of 1.1). Those in industry were very underrepresented (a ratio of 0.5). The ratio for agriculture was also only 0.4, but remember that this was a city. Yet the "administration" category contained public sector manual workers. Subtracting them would yield a "white-collar" ratio of about 2.0. They and not the "classic (i.e., the independent) petty bourgeoisie" were probably the most over-represented group. Workers made up more than a quarter of the Udine party, but somewhat underrepresented (ratio of about 0.75). In Trieste, contemporaries described fascists as multiclass. Their violent attacks on local socialists and Slovenes brought control of the streets earlier than elsewhere. Newspapers said local fascism was strongest among workers and public officials, combining aggressive nationalism and syndicalism conjoined in provocative demonstrations and parades. Some fascists attacked Jews, but more attacked the socialist "enemy," here also identified as "Slav" or Slovene and so "alien." Alto Adige fascism was also strong, and this was the earliest regional administration taken over by fascists (Silvestri 1969; Payne 1995: 108; Abse 1996). In these two areas we find fascists endorsing ethnic politics, including discrimination against other ethnic groups that at its worst was accompanied by violence aimed at ethnic cleansing, the violence being intended to pressure minorities into flight. However, murder was rare and formal deportation schemes were not aired. Coercive emigration pressures were common across virtually all the disputed borders of Europe after World War I (as my forthcoming companion volume shows), and Italy was no exception. Here it clearly encouraged fascism.

This pattern proves to be common. Fascism appealed most broadly across the classes in supposedly "threatened" border areas. Because Italy was a peninsula with good relations and no border disputes with its main neighbors France and Switzerland, there were only two smallish "threatened" border regions, Trieste and the South Tyrol. Had there been more, Italian fascism might have had a broader class base – and its cleansing tendencies might have become more ethnic, less political.

Class

As in all countries, easily the most attention has been paid to the class backgrounds of the fascists. And as usual, most scholars see these fascists as predominantly middle- or lower middle-class. Yet the best source, the national membership list, does not unequivocally support this view (Payne 1995: 104, also notices this). Appendix Table 3.1, row 1, shows that workers constituted 41 percent of PNF members. They formed 46 percent of the national labor force (Sylos Labini 1978), a ratio of 0.86, which indicates only rather slight underrepresentation. However, the ratio for workers outside agriculture was only 0.64,[3] while agricultural workers were slightly overrepresented (a ratio of 1.10). Fascism may have been broader based in the countryside, though the towns partially conform to the orthodox class view that fascism did not attract all that many workers.

Yet there are problems with these data. First, being young, most fascists might be expected to have had lower occupational attainments than had the adult population as a whole. The members might thus have been potentially more middle-class than these figures indicate – though there is no way of testing this suspicion. Second, labor force data include working women, yet there were few female fascists. The proportion of women in the labor force was a little higher in agriculture than in industry or most service sectors. So if we were able to exclude women from our calculations, the working-class ratio among agrarian fascists might rise to perhaps 1.15–1.20, while the nonagricultural ratio would go down slightly. Third, the boundaries between agricultural laborers and small farm proprietors were fuzzy, since many laborers and sharecroppers often had very small plots of land, which meant that they were both laborers and tenants or owners. There were also many gradations of tenant rights. It is difficult to assign people clear class identities in the countryside. As we see below, this fuzzy class zone was at the heart of the fascist-socialist struggle in the countryside. Fourth, the 1921 figures might be affected by fascist "coercive persuasion" among workers. By then many socialist organizations were already being repressed by fascist violence, and workers were joining the fascist unions – a few being coerced – mostly because these seemed to be the only effective unions left (Tasca 1976). Fascism may thus have been rather more middle-class than the figures reveal, especially in the cities, but much less so in the countryside. Yet the data are not good.

What kind of middle class overrepresentation was there? In the national list artisans and small traders – "the classic petty bourgeoisie" – had a ratio of only 0.77, and so were underrepresented. Their rural counterparts, peasant farmers and tenants, had an even lower ratio (0.39). Is this real? Were small peasants being labeled as laborers? Bigger businessmen were overrepresented (a ratio of 2.5), though their numbers are small. Those in the tertiary sector were clearly the most fascist, especially the most educationally qualified. Students provided no less than 13 percent of all members, yielding a massive ratio of 9.3 (cf. row 4 in Appendix Table 3.1). Some 4 to 5 percent of all teachers and 12 to 13 percent of all students were estimated to be fascists in 1920–21 – making the PNF the largest movement in schools and universities. Most university students in this period were of middle-class origin (Petersen 1975: 660). The kinds of occupations that students went into were also very overrepresented. The ratio for the professions was 8.3, for white-collar workers 10.9, and for public employees and teachers 3.0. Salvatorelli's theory begins to seem apposite (as Linz 1976 and Weiss 1988: 32–5 note) – if to the *youthful* middle class. The youthful "humanistic" or educated bourgeoisie was the main part of the middle class drawn to fascism. But its high level of education would not suggest it was particularly *petty* bourgeois.

These figures would suggest that fascism had more working-class members in the countryside than their "petty bourgeois" reputation would suggest. But this tag – qualified by big sectoral differences – may apply better in the towns. We must therefore distinguish urban from rural fascism.

Class in the Cities. We have estimates available for class backgrounds of fascists in several towns and cities. Rows 4 and 5 of Appendix Table 3.1 detail fascist members or *squadristi* in the stronghold cities of Bologna, Florence, and Reggio Emilia. Bologna and Florence are major university cities, and students alone contributed virtually half their *squadristi*. These were in fact decidedly bourgeois squads, with workers and the petty bourgeoisie underrepresented and professionals and public employees especially overrepresented. Since Suzzi Valli (2000) found that the students tended to be students of the sciences rather than the arts, this was not the "humanistic bourgeoisie" in the strictest sense! In Reggio Emilia workers were also underrepresented, as they were also in the city's hinterland (we see below that this was not the case around Bologna). Cavandoli (1972: 133) notes that this was partly because many workers had just left the local party, unhappy about its rightward drift. He also seems to assign "artisans" to the middle class, a classification that is problematic in most countries in this period.[4] The few job titles he provides – such as "cheese makers" and "street performers" – seem to evoke a back-street casual economy more than secure independent artisans. White-collar employees were the most overrepresented in these samples, probably followed by the gray area where artisanal activity meets the informal and casual labor market.

Appendix Table 3.1, rows 5 and 6, detail two predominantly urban national samples of fascist "martyrs" (who died for the cause) and the MVSN paramilitary. It does seem that fascist violence was largely perpetrated by men from the cities. The dominant groups were students, workers, and public sector workers – who in Italy were mainly police and soldiers, often covert fascists before the seizure of power, open afterward. Note, however, that workers were still somewhat underrepresented. As Reichardt (2002: 344) notes, the Italian martyrs differed from Nazi (SA) martyrs, who were overwhelmingly workers or artisans, with few students or public officials. Fascists in the industrial seaport of Livorno (where socialism was strong) were mainly middle-class. Some 19 percent are described as "liberal professionals, industrialists or students," 30 percent as white-collar, 18 percent as "petty bourgeois" (which included artisans and public sector teachers), and only 9 percent as workers (a local ratio of only 0.20). One ex-member wrote bitterly that "fascism here is hated by all the workers." More workers were in the local MVSN: Students formed 28 percent of the paramilitary, white-collar workers 22 percent, the rest of the middle class 20 percent, and workers 29 percent – a ratio of 0.71 (Abse 1986: 68–9). The figures in the small town of Arezzo are given in suspiciously rounded percentages: 50 percent shopkeepers, traders, and white-collar workers, 25 percent professionals and students, and 25 percent workers (Lyttleton 1987: 68). Snowden (1989: 165–77) believes that most Tuscan parties were petty bourgeois until 1922, when industrial workers began to join from the beaten socialist unions. Yet when he gives earlier figures (for five small Tuscan towns without heavy industry), workers comprised between a quarter and a half of members in each. Most were employed in fairly small workshops, rather than fully fledged factories.

Lyttleton (1987: 49–71) says that the early student and veteran fascist core was broadened by "yellow" and Catholic unions active in less concentrated industries and in smaller workshops involving struggling artisans, traders, and the lumpen proletariat. Francini (1976: 82–4) says the Pistoia *fascio* centered on laborers and traders of the streets and the cattle market. It thus seems that fascism could not easily penetrate the *organized* working class in urban manufacturing industry, the working-class ghettos. Yet the towns also had a large casual, street, and informal economy, putting most workers and "not-quite-artisans" outside the normal reach of the socialist movement, and so recruitable by fascism. This would account for the quite broad social base of the 1921 membership list.

A fascist journalist claimed that big-city fascists were

employees, small rentiers and lesser middling professional men...the new men. They formed the crowd which before the war watched political events with indifference and apathy and which has now entered the contest. Fascism has mobilized its forces from the twilight zones of political life, and from this derives the unruly violence and the juvenile exuberance of its conduct. (Lyttleton 1987: 67)

But this seems more of a description of the fascist leadership cadre than of ordinary city members. Urban fascism seemed to recruit militants from *all* groups left outside the prewar political organizations, the "notable" liberal and conservative parties and the socialists. In the bigger cities they probably first centered on the "new middle class," before sweeping up many others employed in smaller workshops, in more casual and street employment and in the public sector. In small towns, where socialism was weak, a higher proportion of workers might be exposed to fascism. "The unruly violence" referred to by our fascist journalist may have derived less from class than from veterans, while "juvenile exuberance" may have been more an attribute of youth than of class.

So most fascists seem not to have been at the urban capitalist core of either the industrial proletariat or the middle class. Indeed, the fascist claim to transcend class conflict may have found most support among persons of all classes who were situated at the margins of that conflict. In the towns, the PNF was more a middle-class than a working-class party. Yet though it was certainly not a proletarian party, it was "radical" and populist, it was led by ex-syndicalists and ex-socialists, and it had a moderately diverse social base. Indeed, its "radical" base became unhappy with Mussolini's opportunistic alliances with the parliamentary parties and the propertied classes. This is rather a mixed urban picture.

In the past, some writers portrayed the fascists as marginal, even malignant members of the bourgeoisie. *Squadristi* leaders were described as "uprooted," "marginal" men from "the dark criminal underworld" or "shiftless dissipaters of small family inheritances" – "displaced men of ambition who found in their willingness to use violence the key to upward mobility and influence that was denied through conventional channels" (Snowden 1989: 163). More recent work (Suzzi Valli 2000; Reichardt 2002) has tended to refute these stereotypes. True, some fascists were criminals and corruption was common. The Florence *fascio* was dissolved by an investigating party committee piously declaring, "Fascism must remain a movement of ideals for the economic and moral rebirth of our nation; it must not be a band of mercenaries and praetorian guards who, for love of lucre, assassinate, rob and plunder." Keeping morality and violence harnessed together was fascism's perennial problem. Yet Snowden's examples of downwardly mobile leaders do not always convince. For example, Compagni was indeed downwardly mobile until he served with distinction in the army during the war. Afterward he was able to reacquire wealth and patronage as a Veterans Association official. Only then did he become a fascist. Giacomelli seems geographically more than socially mobile, beginning as a crane operator, migrating to America without much success, returning to Italy, and petitioning his friend Pasella for work in the Milan party (because he was a convinced fascist or from economic desperation? It is not clear). Nor is a political renegade necessarily socially marginal. Pasella denounced his former socialist friends to the authorities during the war because of nationalist convictions. If fascism allowed him to "escape from the ruins of his political career," "ruin" resulted from his fascist beliefs, not fascism from ruin.

The creators of a radical movement rarely have conventional work careers. But what is cause and what is effect? Were family fortunes, educational advantages, and occupational opportunities dissipated in the pursuit of extreme political convictions? As we see later, many highly respectable persons came to rather admire the reckless "idealism" of the *squadristi*. Would they have admired shiftless, marginal, and criminal elements? I am skeptical. This may have been an example of scholarly desires to denigrate fascists rather than to take them seriously.

Italian fascists (like those in other countries) are often portrayed as marginal people suffering economic and social frustrations. Did more deprived occupations supply more fascists? Were fascists disproportionately unemployed? Did fascist students have worse job prospects than other students? We lack the data to answer these questions. Barbagli's (1982: 110–28) figures do suggest that higher education was producing far more qualified persons than the professions could handle. The situation was bad for teachers but worse for engineers. He suggests that many turned to extremist politics but acknowledges that the evidence is lacking. In any case many were absorbed by the public sector, growing rapidly, especially in its higher grades. Was the "humanistic bourgeoisie" more affected by inflation, unemployment, or low wages than other middle-class groups? Zamagni's data (1979–80: 41–2) suggest the opposite. Maier (1975: 313) attempts to summarize fascism's social base: "Thus a decaying small-town bourgeoisie and a rising rural one reinforced each other. Both were defensive, either about newly acquired or newly threatened status and property." This is having it both ways! Note that all these assertions correspond to the views of early scholars of German Nazis, before serious research was done on them. Subsequent German research refutes the stereotype, as the next chapter shows.

There is an alternative view. The overrepresented "humanistic bourgeoisie" may not have been the "lower" or "marginal" or "deprived" part of the middle class but persons attracted to nation-statist values and paramilitary means. This fascist movement, more than any other, had captured the sympathy of many intellectuals. Their youthful wing, the students, were also captivated. Most learned professions seem overrepresented, while there were many sympathizers among civil servants. The military and police officers of all ranks evinced such fascist sympathies that ministers and prefects could not get them to enforce public order bans against the fascists (Dunnage 1997: chap. 6). Yet these people had secure jobs. Civil servants were wary of revealing party membership and activism before the seizure of power (as in other countries). They were only slightly overrepresented in membership lists until there was no need for caution, after the coup. By 1927 civil servants were the largest group in the Verona and Rome parties, with ratios of 3.0–5.0 (Revelli 1987). Rome, the capital, became the main fascist stronghold, as it is the neo-fascist stronghold today. Probably, support came less from the "lower" or "marginal" middle class, more from an entire sector of the middle class – from its highest, most privileged levels to its lowest, least privileged. This sector would be defined by its masculinity, youth, military experience, high level of education, experience of the state, and relatively indirect relation to class conflict.

All this would support a more ambiguous class and a rather more "nation-statist" version of Salvatorelli's argument. There might in fact be at least *two* core "fascist constituencies": (1) a bourgeois bias, greatest among those at the margins of Italian class struggle, attracted by the fascist claim to transcend it, and (2) those whose social situation favored paramilitary nation-statism. Given the present paucity of data, these are plausible conjectures, not demonstrable truths.

Class in the Countryside. Rural fascism became larger than urban fascism. The PNF seriously ran in only one free election, in 1921, in alliance with other rightist nationalists. The alliance received 15 percent of the vote, rising to over 25 percent in agricultural areas of the center and north in Tuscany and the Po Valley. Only there might fascism be described as having demonstrated genuinely mass support. Rural fascism also differed socially, though again the data are spotty. Reichardt's (2002: 306) study of *squadristi* in the province of Bologna, summarized in row 7 of Appendix Table 3.1, reveals quite a broad-based party, broader than squadristi in the city of Bologna (evidenced by Suzzi Valli 2000). Half the provincial *squadristi* were laborers, about the same proportion as in the provincial labor force (unfortunately, we cannot exactly determine the relative numbers of agricultural versus industrial workers). Students, property-owners, white-collar workers, and public sector workers were overrepresented, while sharecroppers and the petty bourgeoisie were greatly underrepresented. One large local party near Bologna was predominantly lower class: 7 percent were landowners or lease-holders, 13 percent professionals, 3 percent merchants or manufacturers, 5 percent white-collar workers, 4 percent public service workers, and 11 percent factory workers, leaving 58 percent who were agricultural day laborers or sharecroppers. Cardoza (1982: 320) believes that this was typical of the region. Corner (1975: 151–7) believes that Ferrara recruits came from all classes except poor laborers. Yet Kelikian (1986: 205) says that the Brescia party was staffed by younger, less respectable members of the educated middle class, supported by prosperous lease-holding peasants. This would not correspond to the social composition indicated by the national party list. In the southern towns and villages of Calabria (where fascism was weak), of those persons identified (by Misefari and Marzotti 1980) as fascists, about half were *arditi* war veterans, and most of the rest were middle-class, mainly professionals and civil servants, plus a few landowners and peasants. Thus rural overrepresentation may have been due to the war. A predominantly peasant army had nourished early fascism, as militarism transmuted into paramilitarism.

Indeed, Italian fascism triumphed more through violence than the ballot box. Paramilitary thousands, not voting millions, mattered. Thus fascist violence may reveal something about who the fascists were, while its targets reveal who they were against. Here we have evidence on incidents of violence involving fascists, recorded by the PNF for each province and published by Tasca (1976: 120) and De Felice (1966: 35–9). Tasca expressed reservations about these data, calling them inconsistent and partial. Most were originally drawn from a Socialist Party count of attacks on its own militants, neglecting attacks on nonsocialist "enemies" – only two such incidents are mentioned, in a footnote. The "white" peasant leagues organized by the Catholic *popolari*, the communists, the anarchists, the Slovenes of the northeast, and the Germans of the Tyrol were all suppressed by the fascists, but do not figure in these statistics. There are no figures given for Trieste at all, and those for Udine contain no attacks on Slovenes. These data also suited fascist propaganda. They could be used to justify their own violence as mere self-defense against attacks from socialists. Tasca's data may thus be a little biased. Yet Franzosi's (1996) alternative data source reveals only a little more variety of opponent. In national Italian newspaper reports, "communists" figured in 65 percent of the 1921 clashes and 53 percent of 1922 clashes, socialists in 15 percent and 17 percent, respectively, and the *popolari* and "constitutionalist" parties in only 7 percent and 5 percent, respectively. But the northeast is again omitted.

Whatever their defects, Tasca's figures have been used for "ecological analysis," comparing variations in fascist violence between provinces with variations in economic and political factors. Szymanski (1973) showed there was violence involving fascists in industrial more than in agricultural areas, and much more violence in areas of socialist strength (as measured by the socialist vote in 1919; cf. Tilly 1975: 177). Elazar (1993) uses the figures more thoroughly. She also shows that incidents of fascist violence were much higher in provinces voting socialist in 1920 – and highest of all in provinces ruled by socialist administrations. This relationship was strongest in central and northern areas with a large agricultural proletariat. She also brings more reliable evidence to bear to reveal that the fascists seized power in twelve out of the fourteen provinces with a socialist electoral majority and in only one out of fifteen with a liberal or conservative majority. Thus she deduces that fascism was fundamentally antisocialist. Adding evidence showing army, government, and upper-class support for *squadristi* violence, Elazar concludes that it was essentially class struggle that generated and nourished fascism. Indeed, she says that fascists did not really seize power, they were given it by men of property and state officials to protect them from the working class and socialism. She rejects the Salvatorelli–De Felice theory of an independent middle-class fascism. Rather, she says, fascism was the tool of the capitalist class, and especially of large landowners. Tasca – a socialist leader, of course – had earlier concluded along similar lines, though in more qualified fashion.

Ecological analysis of voting and membership data can also help here. Since fascists seriously contested only one election, in 1921, on a joint list with nationalist candidates, it is not easy to say who supported them. Linz (1976: 82–4) showed that fascist membership was inversely related to the vote for the Catholic *popolari* party, being stronger in relatively de-Christianized areas (the Po Valley and Romagna). Nationalism in Italy tended to be rather secular, opposed to the transnational power of the Catholic Church – and fascism inherited this anticlerical mantle, while distinctively attempting to resacralize the state. Brustein (1991) separates out the vote for the fascist and nationalist candidates in 1921 (though he does not say how he has done this). He supports Linz in finding a high correlation between PNF voting in 1921 and socialist voting in 1919 and 1920. The relationship for 1921 was much weaker, especially in agrarian areas. He thus concludes (contrary to Szymanski and Elazar) that many socialists defected to fascism. This provides an alternative explanation of why fascists seized power in former socialist strongholds: They weakened the socialists by splitting them. Brustein also finds a strong relationship between the fascist vote and profitable commercial farming, whether large- or small-scale. Controlling for urbanization, new voters, region, and the vote for the Catholic *popolari* does not reduce these two correlations. Brustein argues that by 1921 the fascists offered the agrarian program most attractive to commercial farmers and to laborers and sharecroppers who believed they could buy or lease land in the future. Even quite poor peasants might aspire to this goal, however unrealistically. Thus the attractions of fascism might extend far down rural social structure, especially in the more prosperous regions. Indeed, these were the areas of greatest fascist strength and also the most secular areas. Rural fascists, Brustein says, were not economically declining but prospering, modern. They responded positively to the fascist agrarian program, negatively to socialist collectivist policies. Thus Brustein makes apparent sense of not only the class but also some of the regional composition of rural fascism.

Local studies tend to support Brustein, suggesting that modernizing commercially minded farmers were turning against the parliamentary regime that they saw as caving in to the demands of peasant leagues representing the landless and poor sharecroppers (Cardoza 1982; Kelikian 1986; Dunnage 1997). The wartime boom plus peasant league pressure had enabled many laborers and sharecroppers to achieve some financial independence. Land sales had accelerated. Now many peasants defected to the fascists, preferring fascist support for private property ("Land to the peasants" was the slogan, subsidies for purchase were the bribe) to socialist collectivization (Snowden 1972; Corner 1975: 144–67; Maier 1975: 310–11).

It is difficult to be exact about rural fascists. The categories "landowner," "peasant," "sharecropper," "leaseholder," and "day laborer" found in the sources covered a diversity of local conditions, of crops, of wealth, of organizational resources. Yet one thing is sure: Dense communities of roughly equal landless laborers or sharecroppers were rarely fascist. Instead, they provided the core of the socialist or occasionally the "white" peasant leagues organized by the Catholics. The organized proletariat in its proletarian ghettos, just like its urban counterpart, resisted fascism.

Yet violence and organizational turbulence were endemic because of the fundamental problem of the rural economy: a large oversupply of landless labor. This often undercut any attempt to mobilize discontent, but it also meant that collective mobilization tended to be violent and often transitory. Laborers and peasants had to be coerced into solidarity, to accept work only through union hiring-halls, to share work through short working weeks and through mass withdrawals of labor always threatened by "scabs" (or "black-legs") crossing the picket lines (often protected by employers' armed gangs). The revolutionary syndicalists had developed and publicized these tactics. The socialists often applied them, and so now did some of the *popolari*. But most strikes did not work, causing the rapid collapse of the organization and the subsequent rise of new ones. The peasant leagues had grown very recently (membership more than doubled in 1920), and they were fragile, with many enemies. Their "labor exchanges" attempted to distribute jobs, thus creating perceived inequities. They administered rough justice to laborers driven by dire need to break strikes or boycotts and to small proprietors unable to afford the labor terms of the leagues. The more powerful socialist leagues cowed the large but poorly organized white leagues. There were many unwilling members of the socialist leagues, and these provided many fascists (Maier 1975: 174–5; Cardoza 1982: 337–8; Segrè 1987: 36, 59). "Scabs" have been very important in modern labor relations. Remember that the "working class" is not the same as the "organized working class." In the first half of the twentieth century, two-thirds of the labor force generally remained nonunion. In rural areas, this two-thirds tended to be found in localities where unions had not appeared, among workers who were in debt or isolated from worker support networks. Or they were merely timorous, religious, or conservative workers, some kin to foremen or bailiffs, who hoped for such positions themselves, or whose family members (especially wives and daughters) were the servants of the owners and feared or empathized with them. For them guaranteed work was more important than risky protest. They might "scab" if protected. Fascists understood all this. Leading *squadristi* had begun as revolutionary syndicalists, and the *squadristi* offered *better* violence than anyone else, since they were proper paramilitaries. Sometimes their violence was in support of strikers, sometimes of scabs. But fascist violence got results and was positively valued by many rural Italians.

They were also tiring of socialist rhetoric. Socialists' main problem in a party led by "Maximalists" was that they preached revolution but could not achieve it. Mussolini's statement that socialism remained only as ineffectual hatred was a constant fascist theme. "Marxism" and "Bolshevism" brought strife, but not triumph. Since this seemed true in the early 1920s, defections were to the movement that claimed to be able to transcend class struggle. In 1921 socialists wrote candidly of "the daily enthusiastic adhesion of large masses of laborers to the program of the *fascio*"; "the present defections are the work of those who came last to the proletarian organization because they are unhappy with the regime of working-class justice" – a reference to the coercion used to achieve class solidarity. Collectivization was "felt to be an ever-increasing violation of individual liberty." They admitted the popularity of fascist slogans such as "The land to him who works it!" and "To every peasant the entire fruit of his sacred labor!" (Corner 1975: 144, 159; Snowden 1972: 279). Nor did fascism simply betray these people. The mushrooming fascist unions quickly settled disputes over contracts, often with force, perhaps on more proemployer terms than socialist unions demanded. But they did settle them, and this provided work, quickly, to fascist members.

Yet any claim to actually transcend class was specious. Indeed, rural fascism became increasingly conservative, an alliance of the rural propertied classes, that is, between large, commercial farmers and "middling- to lower-middling" peasants – those believing themselves capable of independent economic activity, even many with tiny plots. Balbo said "the strength of our army" came "from the small leaseholders and small proprietors of the countryside" (Corner 1975: 102). The large landowners came to dominate this alliance, as they did the later agrarian policy of the fascist regime. They had the resources to fund rural *fascios* (thus financing the full-time *squadristi*) and to provide their own collective associations to organize the struggle (Maier 1975; Elazar 1993). A discontented radical fascist noted: "Whereas in the cities and the industrial zones it appears as a romantic movement . . . in the agrarian zones . . . it is the party of a class, and it acts as such" (Snowden 1972: 283). A class model – not static but emergent, dynamic – works better in the countryside. Rural fascism was substantially taken over by the landowning classes, though it had not originated among them and they remained among the most conservative and the least ideological fascists. For them, fascism was useful, not the revealed truth.

Yet we must not embrace a one-dimensional model. Even in the countryside, we still need to also explain militants' youth, masculinity, and military experience and their enthusiastic embrace of extreme nationalism. Mussolini himself argued:

The unity of Italy is the work of the intellectual bourgeoisie and of some of the artisan classes of the cities. But the great war of 1915–1918 recruited the *rurali* in their millions. However, their participation in events was on the whole passive. They were once again dragged forward by the cities. Now Fascism has transformed their rural passivity . . . into active support for the reality and sanctity of the nation. (Lyttleton 1987: 70)

He is saying that first the war, then paramilitary fascism, gave peasants collective organization.

But among rural fascists nation-statism seems weaker than class discontent. Fascists did appear to many agriculturalists (including many socialists) to be able to transcend class struggle, but this was to prove somewhat illusory. To a degree, fascism did put Italy back to work again, but on terms that contained a substantial procapitalist bias.

THE SOCIAL COMPOSITION OF OTHER MOVEMENTS

Ideally, we would wish to compare fascists with persons in other movements. I can do this for Germany, in the next chapter. Yet we know little of the ordinary members of other Italian parties. Appendix Table 3.1, rows 5 and 6, compare fascist with Catholic deputies. They seem similar. Data collected by Gentile (2000: 413, 493) on all parties' deputies show that professionals dominated them, especially lawyers. The socialists also had numerous workers, while the fascists had a wider variety of middle-class occupations. Together with the socialists, they also had more journalists (and this was also true of the fascist regional secretaries). We also lack much ecological voting data on the other parties. We must resort to contemporary journalistic assessment of electoral support and party composition.

Most scholars believe the left parties drew mainly northern worker support, with few votes in the south (apart from Apulia). The socialist PSI party had only two-thirds the membership of the PNF, but drew over four times the electoral support, especially in the cities. In 1919 it got 40 percent of urban and 30 percent of rural votes. The Catholic PPI had more nominal members but three times the electoral support of the fascists. This was concentrated in the countryside and the nonindustrial cities of the north. Of the 1.2 million Catholic union members in autumn 1920 (half the number in the socialist unions), 80 percent were in agriculture (compared with only 33 percent of socialist union members). "Whites" rivaled "reds" in the countryside. But the recently founded PPI remained a fragile union of priests, clerical conservatives, and radical populists (Salvemini 1973: 137–51; Molony 1977: 55–6, 88; Mayeur 1980: 109–17).

The "constitutionalist" or "liberal" parties are generally considered bourgeois in their composition (though we lack membership data). Yet their large vote – four times the fascist – must have spread through most classes. These were notable parties, relying on traditional patron-client networks, at risk from the new mass membership parties – socialists, fascists, and *popolari*. From what we know of conservative, liberal, and Catholic parties in other countries, we can guess that while their leaders and members were far more bourgeois than were socialists or fascists, they still managed to pick up the votes of almost as many workers as the socialists did. This was because they still held onto the more backward areas and the most religious areas of Italy as well as the most bourgeois.

The big question is why these three much larger rival movements collapsed so rapidly before fascism. The answer is twofold. First, fascist paramilitarism was the most effective form of power mobilization in the arena that turned out to be most critical, violence. Second, some of these rivals, led by their elites, defected and supported the fascist coup. I now ask why.

ELITE SUPPORT FOR FASCISM

Class Motivations

Fascists did not gain power unaided. They were helped there by elites. I begin with capitalists. Did they finance fascism? PNF records show that the party was mostly financed by small contributions from members and sympathizers. Yet at the local and provincial level and in the financing of fellow-traveling newspapers and strike-breaking organizations, more big money went to fascist front associations. Some industrialists had panicked during the factory occupations of 1920, but they had asked for the cara-binieri, not *squadristi*. Most wanted the socialists repressed by the govern-ment just sufficiently for the restoration of "liberal" managed parliamen-tarism. In 1922 the Italian Confederation of Industry did not support the March on Rome, preferring a "semi-authoritarian" option under Giolitti or Salandra. This option was widely canvassed again during 1924 when the killing of the respected socialist deputy Matteotti by fascists shook the new regime. When fascism revealed its true level of violence, industrialists revealed more moderate preferences. Unlike landowners, few industrial-ists invited in the *squadristi*, though from October 1922 some gave subsi-dies and a few became members. This was later and lesser support than that of landowners, and it was spearheaded by businesses with agricultural interests and in commercialized agricultural provinces (Melograni 1965, 1972; Seton-Watson 1967: 598; Kelikian 1986: 144; Lyttleton 1987: 210–11; 1996: 19; Snowden 1989: 121–56; Elazar 1993: 161–2, 181–9).

All this was important assistance, decisive in some rural areas. But only after the coup did the whole capitalist class swing around. Most upper-class groupings distrusted a fascist violence that was wielded by "radicals," and this seemed especially so in the cities. To assuage their fears and so to reach power, Mussolini began to make clear in late 1921 and 1922 that he was offering a deal. For their support he would damp down the revolutionary violence of true, radical fascists. This brought results, but it had been immediately preceded by other elite defections. As we see below, many among the church and political and military elites also swung around to ally with the fascists. Let us first consider the extent they did so – along with many capitalists – for straightforwardly class reasons. Three propertied class motives might be relevant. The first two concern the supposed need for "property defense," the third concerns the need for "capitalist profit."

(1) The propertied classes might fear the pervasive and growing violence gripping the country and associate it with the need to defend property and order. Unlike the violence of the strike movement of 1911–12, unlike the mob conflicts over entry to the war, unlike even the industrial disputes of 1918–19, hundreds of people were now being killed. Most officials com-piling reports on the violence blamed the left. One wrote hysterically of its "intoxication with violence," of soldiers and police "massacred by anar-chists and socialists." A few officials argued the reverse: The *squadristi* were encouraged by the "mad and above all intransigent spirit of the commercial

and industrial classes" (Maier 1975: 317, 319). Most scholars believe the right was considerably exaggerating. Cardoza (1982: 293) says elites were motivated by violent sentiments of revenge. De Grand (1978: 120) says they showed "frightening," "hysterical" verbal violence. The facts of the fatalities reveal that most violence was by the right. The period of leftist insurgence during 1919–20 had seen few casualties, but the fascist-instigated "civil war" of 1921–2 saw many. Estimates of the total dead vary around 2,000. Around 300 of these were definitely fascists, over 700 definitely leftists. Local estimates also average just above a 2 to 1, leftist to fascist, ratio among both dead and wounded. Serious violence was not primarily the work of the left. And on top of that, more people were still being killed in the traditional "social wars" and Mafiosi struggles of the south – more in Western Sicily alone – than in the main area of socialist-fascist confrontation, Tuscany and the Po Valley (Molony 1977: 99; Lyttleton 1982; Petersen 1982: 280–294; Payne 1995: 105–6). Violence was mostly traditional, then fascist, with the left puffing along in the rear.

But there was an important difference between fascist and other violence. It was not aimed at the state. Whatever the fascist theory of an eventual coup, in practice fascists did not challenge or even much bad-mouth the state. In fact, they attacked those who said that they were attacking the state – leftists. Thus many provincial and local government officials covertly abetted the fascist violence. A few moderate officials complained of the "sympathy", "excessive tolerance," and "collusion" toward the fascists shown by magistrates, police, and troops who were asserting that "the fascists are the defenders of order." Socialists were twice as likely as fascists to get killed, but they were also between two and four times more likely to get arrested. During 1921–2 some police and army units also supplied the fascists with sidearms and supplies, and once with trucks, cannon, and tanks (Lyttleton 1987; Elazar 1993: 227–32). Indeed, much of the executive part of the state rather liked fascist paramilitarism – it was "patriotic," in the service of "order" (De Felice 1966: 35–7; Petersen 1982: 280–1; Segrè 1987: 55–7; Snowden 1989: 194–204; Dunnage 1997: 120–5).

Leftist words, however, contrasted with fascist deeds. Socialists talked of revolution and attacking the state but they actually viewed paramilitarism as a weapon of the class enemy. Moderate socialists repeatedly denounced violence. Turati, ousted from the PSI leadership, denounced the victorious Maximalists at the party congress of 1918:

Violence is nothing other than the suicide of the proletariat; it serves the interests of our adversaries. . . . [O]ur appeal to violence will be taken up by our enemies,

one hundred times better armed than we, and then . . . goodbye Socialist Party.
To speak . . . of violence continually and then always postpone it until tomorrow
is . . . the most absurd thing in the world. It only serves to arm, to rouse, to justify
rather the violence of the adversary, a thousand times stronger than ours. . . . This
is the ultimate stupidity to which a party can come, and involves the renunciation
of any revolution. (quoted by Elazar 1993: 135–6)

But even the Maximalists were offering little more than mass strikes and
demonstrations – with more broken windows and beatings than Turati could
stomach. The War Office sent a colonel to report on the threat. He wrote
that only the Maximalists endorsed revolution and they

. . . are not capable of organization. They act in heterogeneous masses under the im-
pulse of passing emotion. The arms in their possession are scarce and unevenly distributed. They have no organized bodies capable of making use of them. . . . [T]hey
all have a very limited grasp of tactics, the use of arms, discipline, cooperation
and even action itself. . . . [A]ny attempt at co-ordinated preparation remains local,
or at best extends to the district. . . . [L]ong and far-sighted preparation is impossible for them. . . . Hypnotized by noise and crowds they delude themselves as to
their strength and prospects. Their first reverse will be followed by disillusion and
disorder. (Salvemini 1973: 269)

The colonel was right. When the *squadristi* attacked, socialists tried only to
defend themselves. They failed. They rarely attacked local fascist headquarters. At their most aggressive, they would ambush advancing fascist units.
Each socialist local tended to act on its own, whereas fascists regionally co-
ordinated "trucks and telephone." Socialists defended their own turf; the
arditi moved and slept wherever fascism wanted them. There was, the socialist leader Tasca later ruefully concluded, no socialist stomach for war
(1976: 126–7). Not votes or debates decided the issue, but paramilitarism.
Socialist, communist, and anarchist militants were defeated in brief battle,
for which their near-pacifism had ill-prepared them.

   Thus fascist violence did not need to be horrendous. Balbo's glorification of violence, quoted earlier, was not tested. In fact, they claimed their
violence was defensive – it was the socialists who were attacking social order
in general and themselves in particular. We do not know how far the fac-
scists would have gone. They broke bones, poured castor oil down throats,
burned and looted buildings. They usually killed only when encountering
resistance. The dead mounted, but only to the quite early point when the
enemy capitulated. Some leftists were punished with prison, others expelled
from their home area into informal internal exile. Cleansing was almost exclusively political, its violence broadly pragmatic. And it worked. Socialism
was rolled over in a matter of weeks in some areas, and in a year, mid-1921 to

mid-1922, across the whole of Italy. This enabled Italian fascism to relax and to become more benign until the Ethiopian venture. The rollover impressed many Italians, especially those without a ringside seat. From a distance the fascist victory seemed like transcendence of conflict, not the brutal violence it actually was. And this was popular among elites and others who valued social order. Just how widespread was this popularity we do not know, since there were now no fully free elections. But fascist paramilitarism was not just about violence, it also concerned building up the internal solidarity of the movement and its popularity among Italians.

Fears of violence were thus reasonable but focused on the wrong enemy. Leftist violence was dwarfed by the traditional violence of the south and by fascist and state violence. But the upper classes quite liked these last two types of "orderly" violence.

(2) The propertied classes might fear political revolution. Unlike other countries, Italy's turbulent quasi-revolutionary postwar period immediately preceded the fascist coup. The strikes of 1918–19 did seem to combine wage and price grievances with Bolshevik-influenced politics. Several towns were briefly taken over by self-styled "soviets," though projected general strikes all fizzled out. Most strikes were more limited, however. In March 1920 most concerned the joint worker-management "internal commissions" surviving from the war that employers now wished to abolish. The employers won the strikes, but sporadic protests and violence (exaggerated by the press) continued. Some 1.3 million Tuscan industrial workers staged short strikes in late summer over wage claims and internal commissions. The employers refused to concede, locked out the workers, and started disciplinary proceedings against their leaders. The strikes spread and led to factory occupations.

These occupations later acquired mythic status, hailed as a microcosm of the future socialist order and as "a necessary moment of the revolutionary development and of the class war." The police claimed to have seized arms caches, but many observers remained skeptical, since the government failed to produce them. The workers did not try to seize government buildings and few strikes had advance planning. Skirmishes occurred only outside union headquarters or occupied factories, some of which workers attempted to run. Workers "defended their own spaces" – the characteristic activity of interwar socialists (Mann 1995). The slogan *controllo*, Salvemini (1973: 274) cautions us, means not "worker control" but merely the ability to check company accounts, a privilege that the unions had enjoyed during the war. Splits soon appeared among militants, unions, and the socialist party: Did they want higher wages, accountability, or revolution?

Prime Minister Giolitti, now eighty, had two decades of experience as prime minister in dealing with the left. Despite conservative calls for the army, he did not intervene. He said his tactic was "to let the experiment continue up to a certain point, so that the workers might convince themselves of the impracticability of their conceptions and also in order to prevent the ring-leaders from throwing on others the blame of their failure." To use troops "would have been playing into the hands of the revolutionaries, who asked for nothing better" (Giolitti 1923: 437–8). Instead, he brokered a deal on joint councils between moderate industrialists and unionists. The occupations fizzled out, as he had predicted. Thus Giolitti had already called the revolutionary bluff in November 1920 – *before* fascist violence developed (Salvemini 1973: 296–315; Tasca 1976: 83, 122–3).

Thus class motivation theorists have retreated to a secondary "revolutionary" argument: Fascism was not a response to revolution, it was a "preventive counterrevolution," to forestall a revolution happening sometime in the future. Socialist membership had quadrupled between 1914 and 1919, to 200,000, while the socialist union federation, the CGL, increased seven-fold to 2.2 million (including a million agricultural workers) by 1920. Maximalists also defeated reformists in the party, though not in the unions. The party now advocated "the setting up of the Italian Socialist Republic under the dictatorship of the proletariat." In 1921 some leftists split off to form a small Communist Party. "Maximalists" and Communists spouted revolutionary rhetoric. In the national election of 1919, splits among the "constitutional" conservative and liberal parties enabled socialists to capture 156 of the 535 seats, the PPI 100. The "constitutionalists" were reduced from 410 to 239 seats and remained divided. The local elections of 1920 then gave the socialists control of 2,162 local councils, enabling them to take over one-quarter of the local administrations. "The bosses felt they were no longer bosses," remembered one militant. Yet these socialist councils were not revolutionary. Some raised red flags on town hall roofs – often sparking fascist violence. Most raised taxes, especially on landowners, and gave more public contracts to local cooperatives, fewer to big businessmen. They declared they would not use troops to quell strikes and land occupations. This was the Italian variant of interwar "municipal socialism."

True, at the national level the Maximalist-led socialists rejected Giolitti's offer of seats in his cabinet. Yet Giolitti believed they would soon have to accept his offer, since the country was clearly moving rightward. Employers were showing greater solidarity, and the hitherto-divided "constitutional" parties formed common lists and recaptured all the major cities except Milan and Bologna in the local elections in late 1921. Union and socialist membership, the socialist vote, and the strike rate all declined, while leftist faction fighting increased. Maximalist rhetoric and minimalist achievements, militant anticlericalism and alienation from the small farmer all trapped them within their ghettos. As in the rest of Europe, the revolutionary tide had been turned back before the fascists struck. Mussolini himself actually agreed with this analysis, writing in July 1921, "To say that a 'Bolshevik' danger still exists in Italy is to confuse certain vague fears with reality. Bolshevism is conquered. More than that: it has been abjured by the leaders and the masses" (Nolte 1965: 206; cf. Maier 1975: 182–92). Thus fascist help to conquer "Bolshevism" was not actually required.

So this second fear was real but exaggerated. Not even a preventive coun-terrevolution was necessary. But Giolitti got no thanks for his noninterven-tionist victory. He was reviled by the right. It is understandable that a violent surge from one political wing produces panic on the other. If the tide turns, a desire for vengeance, not conciliation, may ensue. But did vengeance need such bloodletting as fascism provided? Was something else also contributing?

The agrarian propertied classes provided most of the conspirators. Perhaps they were terrified by rural agitation and land occupations – especially when the Giolitti government, the PPI Minister of Agriculture, and local priests seemed to treat occupations as acceptable ad hoc land redistribution. The issue was primarily one of property defense. Yet the problem is that most of these occupations occurred in areas of little fascist activity, in the central region of Latium and in the south. Even there they affected only 2.3 percent of the land area – the national proportion was a minuscule 0.33 percent. Few were organized by socialists, most were part of a local tradition of rural insurrection (Salvemini 1973: 227; Tilly 1975: 170–1). And fascist activity aimed less at land occupations than at the labor contracts of the peasant leagues. The point can also be applied to industry. Fascist violence aimed mainly against reformist, not revolutionary projects. This might invoke the third motive.

(3) Capitalists might seek to repress labor in order to protect their profits. In 1936 (with the aid of hindsight) the Austro-Marxist leader Otto Bauer offered such an explanation, of European fascism in general and Italian fascism in particular:

Fascism did not triumph at a moment when the bourgeoisie was threatened by the proletarian revolution, but rather when the proletariat had for long been weakened and forced on to the defensive, and the revolutionary flood had already subsided. The capitalists and large landowners did not surrender state power to the violent hordes of fascism in order to protect themselves from the threat of proletarian revolution but with the aim of driving down wage levels, reversing the social achievements of the working class, and destroying their unions and their political power. Their aim . . . was not so much to suppress revolutionary socialism as to smash the achieve-ments of reformist socialism. "The verbal revolutionism of the maximalists," writes Silone, "endangers only the street lamps and occasionally the bones of a few police agents. But reformism with its co-operatives, its pay increases in times of crisis, and its unemployment insurance threatens something much more sacred: capitalist profit." (Forgacs 1986: 31)

Bauer has here invoked what I have identified as the second great motive of the propertied classes: the pursuit of capitalist profit. But did capitalist profit really require Mussolini? What was wrong with Giolitti's recipe of Northwest European class compromise, perhaps with a mild additional dose of semi-authoritarianism? This was now surely a winning strategy (Giolitti believed so) because labor had peaked. Why did Italian capitalists, especially landlords, oppose reformism so strongly that they would import fascists to kill their opponents and thus threaten themselves? Their support still remains puzzling. We must turn also to other sources of social power besides the economic.

Ideological, Political, and Military Motivations

At first, the Catholic Church had looked askance at fascism. It favored semi-authoritarian, nonnationalist conservatism, yet so far it had played lit-tle role in politics. After the war, leading Catholics persuaded the hierarchy of the need for a mass Catholic party. They founded the PPI. But by 1922 a "clerical-fascist" faction had appeared within the PPI. It now favored ac-commodation with Mussolini and persuaded the Vatican to its view. The party leader, the priest Dom Sturzo, was a democrat, but his vows compelled him to obey. The party abstained on the vital 1922 parliamentary vote con-demning fascist violence. Then it joined Mussolini's coalition government and helped achieve the Concordat between fascism and the church. The church's aim was to preserve its own institutional interests and autonomy. Yet it clearly also preferred a Mussolini regime to a democratic alliance be-tween the PPI and the center-left (Salvemini 1973: 345–56; Molony 1977; Mayeur 1980: 109–17). Fascism and the church were more rivals than en-emies. As Pius XI said, "if a totalitarian regime exists – totalitarian in fact and by right – it is the regime of the Church" (Gaillard 1990: 208). Once fascists recognized the church's legitimate institutional interests, the Vatican preferred them to democracy if that included socialists. Pius seemed satisfied with his deal, thanking Mussolini for implementing the "Social Catholi-cism" of *Rerum novarum*.

One major rival movement and almost the whole of Italy's most powerful ideological institution had defected from democracy. It played a considerable part in "sacralizing" and mobilizing local communities into the ceremonies of the new fascist regime (Gentile 1996; Berezin 1997). This had been primarily engineered by Catholic elites, especially the Vatican – probably against the majority sentiment of the PPI. It is difficult to be sure, since the party was rather amorphous. Only the church hierarchy could steer it in a single direction. Unfortunately, that direction was toward fascism.

Much of the executive hierarchy of the state also defected. This was of crucial military significance, since only the police forces and the army possessed the coercive power to repress the *squadristi* once they had rolled over the socialists. Yet the state's monopoly of armed force proved hollow. Neither the police nor the army resisted fascism. Indeed, they were subverted within by widespread sympathy for fascism. Many members of the higher civil service (especially the interior ministry), regional prefects, magistrates, and the army command effectively became fascist fellow-travelers between 1920 and 1922. In the executive the king's court and some ministries with "softer" functions held out longer. The executive branch of government had enjoyed some autonomy in military and law and order before and during the war. The declaration of war itself in 1916 had been engineered against the wishes of parliament. Though parliamentary control increased in 1918, the magistrates, prefects, and police continued to exercise autonomy. This had always favored the political right, and now it increasingly favored fascism. Some prefects and police and military authorities showed bias toward the "patriotic" fascists, but the main problem lay with lower officials not implementing public order directives against fascists. This fueled disorder, and in turn this persuaded more higher officials to favor incorporating the fascists into the regime, so as to "tame" them and end the violence (Dunnage 1977: 138–45). Thus fascist paramilitarism not only killed, it also persuaded the authorities to legitimate the killing.

Public officials were thus overrepresented among the fascists. During the months surrounding the coup, many more officials came out of the closet. During 1922 newspapers reported "hundreds" of army officers joining the party. At least twelve generals joined between July and September. The March on Rome was commanded by former generals, and it took place only once Mussolini was assured the army would stand aside. This was decisive. With only a few scattered skirmishes, the march was no revolution, perhaps not even a real coup (concludes Salvemini 1973: 316–86). Many officials and soldiers would have preferred only semi-authoritarian government, but this option was failing, and in any case some admired the ideals and "dash" of the fascists – who were often their own children. Extreme nation-statism could also tug at their sentiments. The executive half of the dual state connived at the overthrowal of the parliamentary half.

But even the parliamentary side became divided. *Popolari* elites made the switch noted above. Many "constitutional" politicians also switched. They had hoped to mobilize popular nationalism themselves, but fascism had out-flanked them among the young. They came to terms with Mussolini once he was willing to curb his radicals. But they did not favor fascist revolution, corporatism, or syndicalism (except where it subsidized their own economic activities). Their reasons for switching were typically mixed, entwining class with more nation-statist sentiments. Here is *Nazione*, a Florentine newspaper, exemplifying a conservative nationalism that was also class-conscious:

> Fascism is inevitably a reaction that is often bitter and violent – sometimes exagger-atedly so – but always against an emotional background of maximalist [i.e., socialist] violence. It is the sharp weapon with which the middle class arms itself when it rises up against the forces of destruction. . . . Its youth does not save it from mistakes, but it does deliver it from the boredom in which many venerable parties doze. In any event, it is another phenomenon . . . of that restoration of national values which is the most comforting sign of the end of the year just past. (Snowden 1989: 151)

But there was a political crisis. Full manhood suffrage had suddenly been introduced – though some residual powers were possessed by the executive. A stable parliamentary government could have been based on coalitions, ei-ther a center-left coalition of moderate socialists, the PPI, and the Giolittian liberals or a centrist coalition of liberal and conservative "constitutional-ists" and the PPI. Neither proved possible. Maximalist socialists refused to participate, so did the PPI (which might have split had its leaders chosen either coalition), and the constitutionalists remained fractious. The leaders of both mass parties, socialist and *popolari*, were unaccustomed to the com-promises necessary to discipline their own party within a coalition. The notable party leaders were good at deals behind closed doors, but not at defending them before a mass public. The responsibility for failure to arrive at liberal democratic compromise lay not just with the socialists but across the whole political spectrum. Liberal democracy was in transition, not yet institutionalized (as Maier 1975: 322–50 emphasizes). Thus a class crisis got entwined with a distinctively political crisis.

As fascist violence increased, the "constitutional" parties became less interested in protecting the victims than in an authoritarian government. This brought them toward an order-enforcing alliance between the existing state and the fascist movement. Giolitti hoped to forestall this, but even he convinced himself that the fascists were just youthful, overzealous nationalists – the attitude "of a father for a scapegrace son." He hoped the son's violence would bring moderate socialists to the bargaining table – and in June 1921 most socialist deputies (though not the leadership) declared they would support any government coalition resisting fascism. This panicked Mussolini into his march – though the Vatican was also instructing the PPI against a coalition. Giolitti was typical of semi-authoritarian politicians of the 1920s, unaware that fascist paramilitarism would be of an order different from his own occasional selective repression or from the rhetorical violence of the socialists. Politicians of the 1930s had learned this lesson.

Yet most "constitutionalist" leaders also seemed to prefer fascism to compromise with the left. Prime Minister Salandra said fascism was now "the salvation and the only valid garrison against subversion and anarchy. . . . It was necessary in my opinion to give a legal form to the inevitable advent of fascism without delay." Other ex-prime ministers, Facta and Giolitti himself, followed suit. They were not true "constitutionalists," committed to parliamentary institutions. Over two decades Giolitti had selectively repressed and manipulated. Office patronage had provided him a "guaranteed majority" and turned parliament into a market where negotiations for privileges were carried out and where they were paid for. Corruption had lessened the attractions of liberalism, encouraging dissidents on left (syndicalists) and right (Corradini, D'Annunzio, and fascists) to assert that legitimacy lay not in parliamentary institutions but directly in the "people" or "nation" – and in a minority volunteer movement that would represent the people "organically."

Liberal and conservative commitment to democracy remained contingent. They had failed to make the transition from notable to mass parties because they had become badly split. The war had brought divisive mass-mobilizing nationalism. Liberals and conservatives had been split down the middle, and there had been significant defections from both to D'Annunzio and then the fascists. Then the church changed its political stance from hostile neglect of politics (that at least had allowed the secular liberal and conservative notables of the north to dominate prewar parliamentary politics) to participation through its own mass mobilizing PPI. This weakened the old secular notables' hold on political power and divided them from the new religious centrists. Their weakened and assailed position made them very receptive to ideas such as those of Carl Schmitt, discussed in the previous chapter. Confronted by a young fascist movement, they also had the uneasy feeling that at least some of the fascist combination of nation-statism and paramilitarism might be the wave of the future, more effective in modern conditions of dealing with turbulence than their own somewhat corrupt and semi-authoritarian subterfuges. As Gentile (1996: 1–18) emphasizes, prewar elites, particularly those in the executive half of the state, had sought repeatedly but ineffectually to cultivate a more mobilizing patriotism. Their failure made them turn a favorable ear to more "modern" fascist methods. A problematic political transition had muddied party politics, corroded the state executive, and made more difficult liberal conciliation of class conflict.

Since there were no elections it is impossible to know how deep-rooted were these fears among their mass supporters. Many people of all classes presumably did fear disorder. Though we have seen that the "threat" from the left was exaggerated, these did seem dangerous times. The Bolshevik Revolution and revolutionary turbulence in other countries served to inflame the threat. Mass circulation newspapers exaggerated the threat so as to increase readership, sensationalizing violence and anarchy – just as their counterparts today alarm us about sex, drugs, and criminal violence. Newspapers, mostly rightist, were the main means of communication at the time (there were fewer than 100,000 radios in Italy). Such fears may have become quite deep-rooted. Yet there were no mass demonstrations (apart from the fascists themselves), and the March on Rome brought little popular response. The organization of complicity was almost entirely elitist. So the answer is, yes, the elites did think they were turning to fascism to defend "order," which certainly including defending themselves from socialism. Part of their motive was that a political crisis had undermined more moderate options for them. Yet this would still be an insufficient explanation. They also found fascist solutions to crisis attractive because they endorsed other fascist values, too.

As Mussolini's pamphlet had made clear, fascism focused on organic nationalism and a paramilitarism leading toward a highly statist and imperialist regime. Italian nationalism had tended to focus on foreign policy grievances against the peace settlements of 1918–19. Nationalists demanded bits of the Austrian Tyrol and Yugoslavia, and D'Annunzio's followers had seized Fiume (Ryeka) but then been stopped by the constitutionalist government wishing to respect the peace treaties. Mussolini made great play of this. The "plutocrat" nations, Britain and France, had dominated the peace treaties, with Italian liberals as their lackey. The "proletarian nation" must rise up to achieve equality and perhaps also to seize its natural territories. As Gregor (1979) has emphasized, Italian fascism had a pronounced "developmentalist" ideology. Italy would grow prosperous by collective mobilization of the resources of the nation. This was appealing rhetoric with a broad popular appeal.

It is not clear to which groups it especially appealed. Aggressive nationalism such as this is usually identified as "middle-class." Yet what relevance
did these issues have to the concerns of any major class? Fiume, poor African
colonies, or the arrogant British or French were a long way from Italians'
everyday concerns. New territories would contribute little to economic
development; another war was an appalling prospect. But smaller constituencies of support did exist. First, fascism attained easily its highest recruitment
rates in the northern border provinces. Nationalism here meant removing
the sense of vulnerability of border Italians by giving them privileges over
"second-class" Slavs and Germans. Second, the nationalists initially following D'Annunzio or fascism were mostly former *arditi* who had risked life
for nation. They felt humiliated by the postwar settlement. Third, much of
the state-centered "humanistic bourgeoisie" favored an expanding state –
and the military and civil servants had material interests in this. These three
groups seem to add up not to a class but to a smaller, more particular, and
"nation-statist" core constituency for paramilitary nationalism.

Mussolini sought to broaden this narrow constituency of nationalist support through a populism oriented to both past and future. He garbed his
movement in Roman imperial symbols, claimed descent from Garibaldi,
wove fascist rituals into the young nation's memorial days, and acquired
the sacred blessing of Italy's church. He called for the rebirth of Rome and
the fulfillment of Italy's thwarted drive for dignity and power. Personally,
he struck a quintessentially Italian pose as "the virile man, the passionate person, the poor man who shouts and shakes his fist at the nations
of the world . . . expropriating . . . the comic traditions of street theatre in
his grimaces and posturings" (Passerini 1987: 191–2). Yet this "proletarian
nation" was not very aggressive. Most Italians distrusted militarism. They
again proved poor soldiers – though very sensible human beings – in World
War II. Most Italians were too shrewd to favor aggression abroad, and
Mussolini sensed this. Though he initially joined in the clamor over the
Adriatic, he abandoned it in November 1920, when fleetingly offered the
chance to break with D'Annunzio and join Giolitti's coalition government.
Declaring that "Italy needs peace to recover," he denounced those "hypnotized by the sight of a few islands and beaches in the Adriatic" (Tasca 1976:
84–5). Though he probably desired glorious Roman imperial expansion,
he remained realistic at this stage about Italy's chances of achieving it.

So Mussolini's nationalism (like most fascists') initially centered on *domestic* rebirth. Murri, a convert from Christian democracy, saw fascism as the
organic solution to modern Italian history: "Today, as in the Risorgimento,
the aim is to make Italians into one Nation and one State . . . to seek and

firmly establish a vision of national unity . . . and an ethically valid State that would function in our very consciences" (Gentile 1996: 57). Thus fascist aggression was mainly directed at "internal enemies" whose "internationalism" supposedly weakened the nation. Socialists, described as foreign "Bolsheviks," had opposed the war and then imported "Russian" political practices. The PPI was denounced by more radical fascists as representing a cosmopolitan church, which had always been hostile to the Italian nation-state. The struggle between socialism and capitalism only divided the nation, while parliamentary institutions worsened divisions into "anarchy." A fascist sympathizer in the Florence prosecutor's office wrote in an official report of June 1921:

Sympathizers follow the fascist movement with satisfaction, and if they do not approve of it, they at least justify its violence, for they feel that in no other way would a scant minority of hardy souls have been able to wear down the preponderance of socialists, anarchists and populari who by virtue of government inaction would no doubt have driven Italy into a chaotic and bolshevik state as in Russia. (Maier 1975: 316)

At this time Russia was racked by civil war. Mussolini said that if Bolshevism had worked, fine. But "Bolshevism has ruined the economic life of Russia" (Delzell 1970: 8). Fascists would use paramilitaries and the state to suppress class conflict and to restore organic unity. They had been the only true patriots during 1914–18. They were entitled now to shout "Viva Italia" and label their enemies as "antinational." They denounced not "the working class" or "the proletariat," but rather "Marxists" and "Bolsheviks" who were labeled "the other Austrians," "traitors and denigrators of victory," and "traitors to the nation." Their early antibourgeois rhetoric was smothered by a barrage of nationalism and anti-Bolshevism, Prime Minister Bonomi observed (De Felice 1977: 117–18).

This was nearer to everyday Italian experience. It appealed less to the two contending class camps, more to those on the margins despairing of a solution – to the "humanistic bourgeoisie" outside the sphere of direct production, to some of the unorganized two-thirds of the proletariat, to small and medium farmers. It also appealed to the elites of a state that had lurched in a decade to manhood suffrage and formal parliamentary sovereignty. The military, the monarchy, the higher civil service, the regional prefects – plus the politically entrenched old regime (the church and local notables) – doubted the liberal constitution alone could keep social chaos at bay. They shared Carl Schmitt's second concern (discussed in the previous chapter): Italy needed a state "above" the fractious contention of a society dividing into armed camps. Could the old authoritarian part of the state suffice? Or would it need help from a new elite, as Schmitt had come to accept?

The fascist local bosses, the *ras*, perceived and exploited the state's dilemma. They saw that "two states" actually existed, one waveringly democratic, centered on the constitutional parties, the other more authoritarian, centered on its executive arm. They sought to widen this fissure and infiltrate both. In May 1922, Balbo organized a march of forty to fifty thousand laborers into the center of Ferrara to demand employment. He persuaded the police and troops to stay away from the mob, promising that the *squadristi* would keep order. The authorities were pleased to avoid a riot. Then he said he could not control the mob unless some of its demands were satisfied. He demanded the prefect promise a public works program within forty-eight hours – or violence would break loose. Frantic telephoning between the prefect and Rome secured the promise within the day. Who now ruled? many asked. Then Balbo moved on Bologna with 20,000 supporters. Bologna's prefect was one of the few genuine constitutionalists. Yet even he dared not to use the troops, many of whom were now fraternizing with the fascists. There was stalemate, solved when Mussolini persuaded the ministry to transfer the prefect. In Ravenna, Balbo warned the police chief that his men were intending to burn socialists' houses. But Balbo said he could prevent this if the police provided a fleet of trucks to take them out of the city. He did so but kept the trucks, which he then used to spread "a column of fire," burning socialist and communist headquarters throughout the provinces of Ravenna and Forlì.

These tactics were repeated in the March on Rome. A half-orderly paramilitary advance amid an immobilized army forced a divided government to yield. The unity and authority of the ostensibly democratic, in reality dual, state was destroyed. To preserve national unity and state order, its officials and politicians turned to fascism. A radical populist movement embodying considerable paramilitary violence had undermined elites' capacity to resist by appealing simultaneously to its class and to its nation-statist prejudices.

THE FASCISTS IN POWER

Italian fascism was not a unitary movement. It contained very diverse tendencies and factions – socialists, syndicalists, statists, conservative nationalists, radical *squadristi*, and agrarian reactionaries. Mussolini himself may have favored a socialist-flavored fascism, but his opportunistic antennae enabled him to seize power by playing off the various factions with policy zig-zags. In this respect he resembled Hitler. Yet major differences between them were revealed after they had seized their states. Mussolini lacked Hitler's radical racial transcendentalism, and his statism sought not to purge factional differences but to envelop them all in a loose corporatism. Once in power, he gave them all a piece of the action. Fascists had not conquered power. Rather, they had pushed close to it and then done deals with nonfascist elites. Attempting to satisfy all these powerful groups produced a dispersal of state sovereignty among a monarchy, a traditional bureaucracy, the Fascist Grand Council, the Ministry of Corporations, the Syndicates, the Party – and the Duce himself. At the local level the party secretary, the prefect, the syndical leaders, and the podesta all competed for authority. Fascist statism, militarism, syndicalism, and opportunism actually created a highly pluralist state. The kinds of conflict and compromise that liberal democracy institutionalized in parties and parliaments now came in more private forms within the fascist state.

Radicals were thwarted in their attempt to establish a syndicalist state, but were bought off with monopoly control over unions, just as the employers' associations were given similar powers over the other side of the bargaining process and in the ministry of corporations. After 1926 large material benefits were distributed to fascist militants through the syndicate dues, buying out their desire to make violent trouble (Riley 2002). Elsewhere, the regime conceded powers to nonfascist elites. This was noticeable at once in the countryside, as the landowners took over fascist organization during 1922. It took longer in the towns where radical *fascios* continued to generate turbulence throughout the 1920s. The fascist unions also became more middle-class, dominating the lower and middle ranks of the civil service and local government (Lyttleton 1987: 217–20, 278). After the coup the PNF had a declining worker and peasant presence, as many middle-class opportunists joined. Scattered data on local parties in 1927 reveal few worker members and a predominance of the public sector (Forgacs 1986: 50 n. 32; Revelli 1987: 25–34). Nonetheless, from about 1935 the syndicalists began to revive, and the growing popularity of Hitler's regime emboldened Mussolini to become more radical in both domestic and foreign policy. He was now able to use the energies of the fascist militants to reduce the power of some of the old elites (Sarti 1990; Dahl 1999).

Both the stabilization of his own power and the rise of Hitler allowed Mussolini a more aggressive foreign policy. He moved aggressively against the weaker Africans in Libya and Ethiopia (I deal with this in my forthcoming book). But, as Mallett (2000) shows, he had early realized that Britain and

France blocked Italy's access to real empire across the oceans. After Hitler's rise to power, he pursued an alliance with Germany to combat them. By the time of Italy's entry into World War II, he had begun a capital ship and submarine program that he thought might challenge Britain's dominance in the Mediterranean and Red Seas. The expansionist side revealed in his 1932 essay had come to disastrous fruition, despite his apparent awareness that it could have only two possible outcomes: either Italy would be defeated or it would become subservient to Germany (Ceva 2000).

By broadly satisfying its various factions and providing order and a sense of expansion, the regime also became quite popular. The elections of 1924 were not entirely free, but the unexpectedly large fascist majority seemed mostly genuine. There was widespread relief that order had been restored. Once firmly in power, after about 1926, the regime needed little further violence and seems to have achieved a broad if not very intense popularity. The introduction of special courts and secret police did not lead to terror: 80 percent of those tried of political offenses were acquitted, and most of those convicted were sentenced to less than three years' imprisonment. From 1927 to 1940 there were only nine political executions. Even the war brought only a further twenty-two. Significantly, most victims were Slovene nationalists. In the war the fascist regime condemned to death only ninety-two Italian soldiers, compared with the 4,000 death sentences handed out by its "liberal" predecessor in World War I – and to the 35,000 death sentences of its ally, the German Wehrmacht (Payne 1995: 117; Knox 1996: 128). All this indicated only a low level of repression. There were few signs of proletarian, peasant, or any other disaffection aside from discontented local party bosses.

De Felice (1974: chap. 2) said this showed that the regime had the active consent of Italians. The regime weathered the Great Depression (though not as well as it claimed). It asserted Italy's position as a Great Power – until it made the dreadful mistake of entering World War II. Passerini's (1987) interviews with old Italian people reveal more ambiguous views than simple "consent" or "dissent." Their jokes – about the regime, its songs and slogans, and about their own sometimes dubious compromises with it – indicated ambivalence toward fascism. Fascist trade unions and women's, youth, and leisure movements provided services and rituals for their many members. Berezin (1997) says that fascist rituals penetrated the practices of everyday life, appropriating and intensifying ordinary patriotism, harnessing Catholicism and the village priest to its projects. Even if fascism did not actually "resacralize" the Italian state and nation, it did implant itself as normal and Italian. World War II brought more radicalism and less popularity. Police reports indicate that from 1943 many Italians regarded the food shortages and the bombing as the consequences of a stupid war, forced on a weak regime by the more powerful Germans (Abse 1996). Italy then became deeply split, as many rose up against fascism and as the fascist rump radicalized. Yet before then, a few thousand old fascist fighters and more numerous opportunists seem to have ruled Italy without undue strain.

CONCLUSIONS

Fascists killed democracy and a few thousand Italians. The targets were political rather than ethnic, mainly because the country had secure territorial boundaries. Only the insecure northeast tempted local fascists into aggression against ethnically defined enemies. Ignoring Africa and the last year of the war (discussed in my forthcoming book), Italian fascism was the most benign fascist movement I discuss here. That is why self-proclaimed "neo-fascists" reemerged in Italy in recent years.

Fascists emerged as a response to a crisis of mass mobilization warfare. Italy was marginal in the Great Power system and Italians were divided by the war. It divided the political parties and created space for new ones. A few hundred fascists then became a mass movement as further crises of postwar Italian society exacerbated the class struggles of capitalism and energized a paramilitary youth movement. Paramilitarism became seen as the solution to class struggle. But to view Italian fascism merely as paramilitary organization applied to a capitalist goal would be to oversimplify. As elsewhere, the possessing classes turned to the gun "too early," when neither property defense nor profit were actually threatened. To explain this apparent overreaction, we must add a political and ideological crisis created by a dual state. Italy had not possessed a cohesive "old regime." The church was powerful but opposed the state. Liberal and conservative elites had run the prewar state without possessing deep social roots, and the state had not effectively mobilized nationalist sentiments. The parliamentary half of the state was making a rapid transition to masculine democracy, confronted by two new "mass armies," parties of radicalizing socialists, and incoherent Catholic populists. The executive half of the state possessed a monopoly of military power but had been corroded by dreams of a more mobilizing nationalism and statism. In a country where an old regime could not mobilize its own authoritarianism, fascism had early appeal. That is why the fascist repressive option was called in "too early." But the very close sequence of World War I, postwar class confrontation, the attempt by a weak state to deepen democracy, and the young fascist surge makes it difficult to establish the relative causal weights of these four crises.

Italian fascists offered plausible solutions to crisis. They claimed to transcend class struggle, especially attractive to those located outside the proletarian ghettos and outside the industrial/commercial core of the capitalist class. They claimed to achieve social development through nation-statism, attractive to those with stronger links to nation or state. The chosen means, paramilitary violence, appealed especially to the military–cum–macho values of demobilized young men. The militancy of these fascist thousands brought fascism close to power. But elites also came to favor fascist repression of class dissent, partly because the political crisis had narrowed the alternative options, but also because fascist nation-statism appealed to them. Their defection enabled the actual seizure of power. Each of these elements brought distinct core constituencies toward fascism – classes, sectors, regions, generations. The variety of this support may have finally required something like Mussolini's own acute opportunism to enable the seizure and holding of power. It is a story of thousands, not millions – the paramilitary striking force of thousands of fascists and the betrayal of thousands among Italy's varied elites. The socialists and *popolari* had the numbers to oppose them, but they did not have paramilitary force or an equal appeal to elites. The majority of Italians watched with mixed feelings. They seem not to have disapproved of a result that brought social peace and moderate progress. But they were largely irrelevant to the fascist surge into power.

My explanation has been more multifaceted than either the class or the fascist theories presented at the beginning of the chapter. I have invoked all four sources of social power – ideological, economic, military, and political – in order to explain the first fascist seizure of power. The complexity of this explanation would ideally require more precise and extensive data than I have been able to marshal. Let me finally admit what accounts of Italian fascism rarely do. All general interpretations of Italian fascism, including my own, rest on fairly flimsy evidence. Data on the fascists and their allies, their backgrounds, and their motivations do not permit very confident generalization. I turn to the much better-documented Nazis.

4

Nazis

Germany was the greatest power and the most developed country to go fascist. The Nazis were the world's largest fascist movement, with the largest paramilitaries and the largest vote. This was the most "radical" fascism, committing the greatest evil. Thus it is especially urgent to explain who the Nazis were, what they believed in, and how they seized power. Luckily, this is the best-documented case. Though there are always more questions to ask and more data to seek, this chapter and the next can come close to explaining the rise of the Nazis, solving some puzzles left by the sparse Italian database discussed in the previous chapter. And though fascist movements all differed, they shared enough for us to use the solidity of German data for broader, more comparative purposes.

Yet there were obvious differences from Italy. Unlike Italy, Germany had lost World War I. Germany also had a distinct postwar political history. A short period of revolutionary turbulence ushered in an advanced liberal democracy, the Weimar Republic, which conceded female suffrage and the most developed welfare state in the world. Germany also contained not one but two major Christian faiths, Protestantism and Catholicism. Since Hitler seized power only in 1933, the Nazi rise was also slower, affected by unfolding interwar events: an inflation crisis, disputes with the Entente Powers over borders, reparations, and armaments, the Great Depression, and the general surge of interwar authoritarianism. Far more than the Italian fascists, the Nazis seriously contested elections; far less, however, did they challenge the military power of the state. Finally, German fascism was far more racist than Italian fascism. All these differences mattered.

So did the long-term peculiarities of German history, often described as a *Sonderweg*, a unique path of historical development. This is usually seen in terms of class politics: Lacking a "bourgeois revolution," Germany became an advanced country while retaining a semi-authoritarian old regime state

139

that the bourgeoisie supported. Together, it is argued, the old regime and the bourgeoisie undermined Weimar democracy and drifted toward supporting fascism. Yet the German nation, as well as its classes, had its own special path. The German nation-state had two alternative possible boundaries: a *Klein* or a *Gross Deutschland* (small or big Germany). Sixty million Germans lived in the Weimar Republic, but almost twenty million lived outside it, mostly in adjacent territories. This gave the German "nation" a less state-centered and more ethnic and potentially more racist identity, and it gave a potential project of territorial expansion. The "small" German state (originally Prussia, now Weimar Germany) might unify the entire "great" German nation, mainly through expansion in the east. I consider the role of these distinct legacies of class, nation, and state.

I ask who supported Nazism and why. In this chapter I discuss Nazi members. In the next I discuss the two other main ingredients in the Nazi rise to power, Nazi voters and elite "co-conspirators." I also discuss how members, voters, and elites got mobilized together as the Nazis surged to power. These chapters take the story only up to 1933. The ensuing twelve-year Reich is discussed in my forthcoming volume. This chapter takes Nazis seriously. What did they believe in, who were they, and what was the nature of their activities?

OFFICIAL NAZI IDEOLOGY

Many observers and scholars have emphasized that Nazi ideology was incoherent. The Nazis, they say, were politically "semi-illiterate," wielding only "a ragbag of ideas," drawing on the "scrapheap of ideas current in this period" – ambiguous, contradictory, unprincipled, notable only for "the gripping effectiveness [of] popularized snippets of ideas and dogmas of salvation . . . a political myth for the masses" (Broszat 1987: 38, 186–90; cf. Peukert 1989: 39; Bracher 1971). Such views are part of the tradition of not taking fascism seriously. Part of the problem is that, since Nazism is generally thought of as a very ideological movement, many have had unreasonable expectations of its ideological sophistication. It was not like Marxist parties. No fascist party possessed the theoretical ballast (one might alternatively say doctrinal rigidity) that Marxism provided to some socialist parties. Rather like conservative and liberal parties, the Nazis had a looser orienting ideology – the German term *Weltanschauung* ("view of the world") is apposite – informing their policy proposals. As among all effective parties, this was also compromised by political opportunism and the fudging of internal disagreements. But there is a curious sense in which we might regard fascist opportunism as "principled." Since fascists worshipped power, elitism, and leadership, leaders were actually empowered by their followers to behave arbitrarily if this was likely to secure power. Fascism also privileged action over dogma. Many Nazis liked to affect that they were merely men of action. They would boast that they had never looked at the party program and say (though only in private) that they had never opened their copies of *Mein Kampf*. Eichmann said pointedly (while on trial for his life in Jerusalem), "The Party program did not matter, you knew what you were joining." I explore the "shared knowledge" to which Eichmann was alluding, more than any canonical dogma. At this level Nazis had more ideological cohesion than is conventionally argued.

Some of their shared knowledge might seem patently absurd to us and also to many contemporaries. The notion that Jews, 0.76 percent of the population (and rising to a peak of only 2 percent among Germany's bankers and stockbrokers, i.e., "Jewish finance capital"), constituted a major threat to Germany should have been laughable. It was surely also absurd of voters to support the very party that was committing most of the violence in Germany on the grounds that this was necessary to stop violence. But many parties offer bizarre yet somehow resonant "solutions" to a country's problems. Politics are about not truth but minimally plausible resonance. I have lived in countries whose elections have also been won by parties identifying a caricatured, almost imaginary main enemy: Neither the conservative and rather bumbling British trade unions nor the truly feeble domestic power of the U.S. federal government could in truth be held responsible for much of their countries' ills during the 1980s.[1] Nazi blaming of the Jews was even less plausible, but the real difference lay in its infinitely greater potentiality for evil.

I start with a classic Nazi text, the party program of 1920. Some scholars downplay this document, yet (with one exception) it is a clear summary of Nazism, and of a cleansing nation-statism. Its opening points were constantly repeated by Nazis: the "union of all Germans in a Greater Germany," revocation of the peace treaties, and "land and territories (colonies) to feed our people and to settle our surplus population." "Only those of German blood, whatever their creed, may be members of the nation. Accordingly, no Jew may be a member of the nation." Further clauses listed the educational, economic, legal, media, and health policies and the authoritarian corporate state such goals required. These domestic policy clauses were drenched in *völkisch* language: Non-Germans should be barred from influence in the media, religious freedom would be permitted only if it did not threaten the State or "offend the moral feelings of the German race." The penalty for non-Germans infringing these provisions is twice stated as deportation. In a speech of 1923 Hitler made perfectly clear how important "enemies" were to Nazism:

Nationalism is above all innoculation against a bacillus, and the anti-Semitic concept is the necessary defence, the antibody if you like against a pestilence which today has a grip on the whole world. . . . There is only one differentiation: one is either German or anti-German. The National Socialists spearhead the march of Germany, and we declare we will not sit down at a table with criminals who already once stabbed us in the back. (Sereny 1995: 58–9)

It is a Manichean vision of the world divided into Germans and their enemies. However, like the Italian fascists, the Nazis began more leftist than they later became. The party program included a sketch of Nazi "socialism": not the abolition of private property, economic democracy, or equality but "the primacy of the worker over the exploiter" – which was defined as big capital and high interest rates. This was vague but statist: The state was to provide a livelihood and welfare for its citizens, abolish incomes unearned by work, and take action against big finance and Jewish capital. There was also a radical land reform program that included expropriating landed property.

This early leftism appeared in even simpler form in countless early party handbills. Here is one of 1920:

NATIONAL SOCIALIST GERMAN WORKERS' PARTY

With untiring activity the agents of the Jewish international stock exchange and moneylenders are trying to make Germany ripe for collapse, so that they may hand over the state and the economy to the

INTERNATIONAL FINANCE TRUSTS

This requires the division and thereby the weakening of our people at home. Hence also the embittered struggle of the

MERCENARIES

of international high finance against a party which, unlike all the other parties, is not composed of

"BOURGEOIS" OR PROLETARIANS

but of the creative mental and manual workers of our people. They alone can and will be the supporters of the future Germany. (reproduced in Noakes and Pridham 1974: 37–41)

But in the streets Nazis confronted neither capitalists nor Jews. They were involved in street fighting against leftists proclaiming the virtues of internationalism and Russia. So the Nazi emphasis changed. Regional studies of Nazism reveal that right across Germany the voicing of anti-Semitism by Nazis declined during the late 1920s. Though anti-Semitism was not abandoned, from now on "Bolsheviks" or "Marxists" were viewed as the preeminent "anti-Germans" – in some areas they always had been (Heilbronner 1990). But the Nazis also claimed that violence against Bolsheviks and restraints on capitalists were essential to reach a positive goal. This was the creation of the *Volksgemeinschaft*, "an organic community of the people," whose role was to transcend class and other conflict.

Additions to the program were made as the movement grew. Some firmed up the fascism. Early rhetorical attacks on the "civilian" Republic developed into a more principled attack on democracy itself: The desired "strong" state became avowedly authoritarian. In the mid-1920s, after Hitler's release from prison, its centerpiece became the "Führer principle": unconditional loyalty to the leader, the personification of the German *Volk*. It helped that Hitler was charismatic, with a remarkable capacity to generate faith in his followers. He was a man who could express a "vision," lacking concrete specifics, expressed in rather simple black-and-white dichotomies, but seemingly blindingly clear and sincere (Kershaw 1998: 290–1). We tend nowadays to puzzle over the manic magnetism he displayed at the Nuremberg rallies. But his leadership qualities were more evident in private settings. Nazi memoirs also tell of men and women stifling doubts and criticisms after quiet but firm words from Hitler in private. After about 1927 Nazis seem to have given almost unconditional devotion to their leader, the personification of Germany, as is revealed by the most familiar Nazi slogan of all: *"Ein Volk! Ein Führer! Ein Reich!"* But compared with Italian fascists, Nazis downplayed blueprints of a future society. For them the "corporate state" was a foreign ideal, either Italian or Austrian. The shape of the future Reich was left to Hitler, and he was not too specific. Though "statism" was greatly emphasized, its exact contours remained a little vague.

The major backtracking was from "socialism." In 1928 the party abandoned its commitment to radical land reform. Its anticapitalism also wavered and became more contested within the movement. Under the influence of Feder, Hitler had distinguished "productive" from "unproductive" or "parasitical" capital, the former truly "German," the latter international or Jewish. But from 1930 he was seeking the approval of businessmen who did not understand the distinction. Nazi "socialism" was now downplayed, in favor of the constantly repeated and vaguer demand for "social justice." This was the major Nazi ambiguity. Nonetheless, the movement did keep some "socialistic" leanings. They were to influence the way political economy figured in Nazi electoral strategy after the Great Depression struck, as we see in the next chapter.

THE IDEOLOGY OF NAZI MEMBERS

Is it worth taking this general *Weltanschauung* seriously? The important question is, was it shared by Nazis in general? Obviously, we have only limited evidence on the hundreds of thousands of "ordinary" Nazis. Our richest source on the beliefs of Nazi militants are the 581 essays written for a competition advertised in a Nazi party journal on "Why I Became a Nazi." These were solicited in 1934 by the enterprising American sociologist Theodore Abel. The essays reported in his book of 1938 have been twice reworked by Peter Merkl (1975, 1980). The essayists were obviously not a random sample or a cross-section of Nazis. They provide us with a very literate, and so a rather middle-class, sample of "old fighters," more committed to fascism than the average member. But these Nazi militants did share the beliefs expressed above. The central ideological theme of 32 percent of the essays was a transcendent *Volksgemeinschaft*, 23 percent of the essays expressed "super patriotism" (pride in Germany plus hatred of foreigners), 18 percent identified with Hitler as the embodiment of the *Volk*, 14 percent centered on anti-Semitism, 6 percent centered on "blood-and-soil romanticism," and 5 percent advocated military recovery of the lost territories – quite a narrow ideological range.

These militants were also very strong on "enemies." Marxists/communists/socialists were seen as the main enemy in 63 percent of the essays, Jews in only 18 percent, liberals/capitalists in 8 percent, and Catholics in 5 percent. A third of the essays showed no evidence of anti-Semitism, half revealed some, and 13 percent seemed obsessed by it. Some 22 percent showed hatred for foreigners abroad, 15 percent for "foreigners" in Germany, and 5 percent referred to a conspiracy between both. Almost all said they hated the Weimar Republic, 30 percent because it was run by Jews or other "un-Germans," 19 percent because it was a multiparty system, 9 percent because it was Marxist, 3 percent because it was liberal capitalist, 23 percent because it was "liberal or capitalist" *and* "Marxist," 6 percent because it was "black" *and* "red." A slight majority believed their enemies could not be reached by reasoned argument. Some 21 percent used terms excluding enemies from human or moral status (such as "subhuman," "rodents," "murderers"). Some 40 percent advocated war, and 48 percent had engaged in violence "such as to imply sadism or masochism." But apart from the Fuhrer cult and militarism, there was much less statism expressed in the essays (Merkl 1975: 453–542). The main enemies had become Bolsheviks, though often linked to Jews and "the system" of Weimar. Biomedical racist language was frequent, while ethnic and political enemies seemed closely entwined. Violence would cleanse them from the Volksge-meinschaft. It would be redemptive, as Friedlaender (1997) has remarked of Nazi anti-Semitism, bringing great emotional attachment to Germany, to the movement, and to the Fuhrer. The Nazi "hard core" was endors-ing the transcendent, cleansing organic nationalism expressed in the party program and propaganda. But it involved more than mere instrumental rationality. It involved a leap of faith and commitment. Ideological power rarely depends on the sophistication of its message. At its strongest it in-volves simple but resonant appeals transcending mundane reality and giv-ing meaning to action. This gave the Nazis their distinctive fervor and drive.

What of other more "ordinary" Nazis who might not have been up to writing essays? Here the evidence is less systematic, but we can still find some.

We can reach down to very "ordinary" Nazis through the form required of applicants to the Sturm Abteilung ("Storm Section"), or SA. From 1930 they had to complete a "reasons for joining" question. Most responses were simple but to the point. An engineer declared:

I joined the SA to support my leader and Germany in the battle against communism and the SPD, those traitors to people and homeland, and to support the eradication of these parasites, to the very end, may it cost me my life!

Since by 1930 some 70 percent of new SA members were now workers, most of their answers were even simpler:

Work was out of the question because the Marxist government did not understand how to provide the people with work and bread.

To participate in that organization which guarantees the unity of the German people and provides the German worker with the means of reintegration within the productive process.

I am in the SA because I was brought up as a nationalist from childhood because my father [also a worker] had no time for the SPD or KPD.

The new movement, the Leader Principle, aroused my interest long ago, since I was convinced by our leader's National Idea.

I am nationally minded, love the Fatherland and have not previously belonged to any political party.

I have long since yearned for an ordered Germany, uninfested with Jews, and yearned for the day when the SPD's boss-rule would be abolished.

As an Aryan German it was beneath me to support this boss and Jew government.

They too were making a leap of faith, "to the very end," involving "love" and "yearning" for the goal of "reintegration." In more mundane form, they were also endorsing the party program and the Abel essays. They "knew what they were doing."

I do not here go into motivations drawn from my sample of Nazi war criminals, presented in my forthcoming volume (since they might be rather unusual people). But like all successful movements, Nazism attracted many adherents for vague or minimal reasons. SS officer Gerstein (who later risked his life to expose Nazi genocide) remembered that he had joined (just graduated with engineering and medical degrees) because of simple idealistic nationalism. The Nazis would revive Germany, he believed. Scheltes, a young architect in the office of Albert Speer (Hitler's architect and economic planner), felt he "had to make a choice . . . everything in Germany had become political . . . between left and right. . . . I chose right, which was the National Socialists." Hupfauer, eventually Speer's administrative assistant, was an ambitious lawyer, hoping to study abroad. But "friends persuaded me to stay. . . . The party was intending to change the whole concept of labour relations, based on the principle of co-determination and shared responsibility between management and workers. I knew it was Utopian, but I believed in it with all my heart. . . . Hitler's promises of a caring but disciplined socialism fell on very receptive ears" (Sereny 1995: 146, 180–1, 356). These two members of Speer's staff were also revealing a leap of faith, though as intellectuals they were also aware of the essential political and class ambiguity of Nazism: Was Nazism rightist or was it genuinely transcendent of class?

All the main tensions of the movement focused on this ambiguity. In 1932 and 1933 the SA became restive at Hitler's opportunistic dealings with elites and his apparent backtracking on Nazi "socialism." The usual contradiction had emerged between revolutionary and bureaucratizing tendencies of fascism (see Mann 1997). The SA evinced a proudly proletarian tone, as in this marching song:

> We are the swastika army,
> Raise the red flag high,
> We fight for German labour's freedom.

Though the SA leader Röhm was no theorist, he did support a state of "workers, peasants and soldiers," based on "Germany's front-line soldiers" (all the quotes derived from Fischer 1983: 55–6, 82–3, 149–59).

I am suggesting that this movement was stronger in its emotional commitment and no less cohesive in its beliefs and tendencies than most modern movements. Indeed, it contained the normal dynamics of political movements: tension among the three elements of the official ideology, a more radical rank-and-file, and more conservative leadership trimming. The ambiguity that resulted was of a form and at a level normal to political movements. In this case Hitler's undisputed authority succeeded in damping it down. These were the beliefs emotionally endorsed by the Nazis. But what kinds of people were they? Can we begin to identify the core Nazi constituencies?

NAZI CORE CONSTITUENCIES

Male and Female

As in other parties of the time, most Nazi activists and all the leaders were men. Women made up 5 to 10 percent of ordinary party members (and later of perpetrators of genocide). But there were far more women Nazis than this suggests. Some 90 percent of the women in the party were unmarried; on marriage the husband's membership was assumed to represent his whole family. Most women joined only women's auxiliary organizations. I do not know their numbers, but it is probable that adding them would bring Nazi women above the (varying through time) 10 to 23 percent of women in the socialist SPD and the 9 to 16 percent in the communist KPD. The center and right parties had fewer women members, but some also had auxiliary women's organizations.[2] Other parties' leaderships included 5 to 15 percent women, but these were rarely influential. The liberal DDP formed a women's committee to marginalize its feminists whom it considered vote-losers. Thus *all* parties in the Weimar Republic were masculine. Only at the leadership level did the Nazis take this to an extreme. In the town of Marburg, Nazi women outnumbered other parties' women in both absolute and relative terms. And whereas female leftists were mostly working-class and conservatives were middle-class, Nazi women came from all classes (Weber 1969: I; Bacheller 1976: 321; Kater 1983: 149–52; Wickham 1983: 324; Frye 1985: 95–6; Koshar 1986: 239; Boak 1990; Brustein 1996: Table 3.2).

But Nazi ideology was unique in formally subordinating women to patriarchal authority. Left and liberal parties claimed to be feminist. Even the conservatives claimed they wanted more women activists. Nazi ideology was decidedly "macho," insisting that women remain in the private sphere, to bear and to nurture the "master" race. Under the Nazis German female labor force participation remained lower than in other combatant countries until 1943. Yet according to their own lights, the Nazis cared for women.

They provided welfare subsidies to widows and mothers and denounced as decadent the "woman as sex object" culture of the liberal democracies. Their women's organizations were active in charitable and educational work and in sponsoring sports and physical exercise among girls. Hitler Youth leader von Schirach remarked, "It doesn't matter how high a girl jumps, or how far she puts the shot, but that her body develops properly, harmoniously" (Steinhoff et al. 1989: 20). The Nazis were concerned with the health and well-being of the bearers and nurturers of the race. Their concern with the latest medical, public health, and dietary knowledge, its diffusion through the latest mass communication media, and their sports, parades, and communal programs all indicate a rather modernist form of patriarchy – proclaimed more loudly than liberals or leftists proclaimed feminism. The Nazis kept some of their views relatively quiet but they were proud of their patriarchy.

This proved popular among women as well as men. Ecological analysis of voting (discussed more in the next chapter) suggests that women, less likely than men to vote Nazi in the 1920s, thereafter closed most of the gap. Indeed, Protestant women, the majority, eventually voted a little more Nazi than Protestant men did. Among Catholics, the Nazis could not compete with the Center Party, which drew 70 percent of Catholic women's votes, compared with 56 percent among Catholic men (Mayeur 1980: 133; Childers 1983: 260; Falter 1986, 1991: 136ff). Since the Center Party was also (more traditionally) patriarchal, few women seem to have been put off by ideologies excluding them from the public sphere. Nazi propaganda images of women are familiar to us – healthy, attractive (though not sexy), dressed in virginal white, scrubbed and smiling, playing ball games, admiring nature, presenting flowers to Hitler. These were effective images, part of the Nazi claim to represent the "clean, healthy and consciously German" *Volk*. Though few women were militants, many were loyal to Nazism. Some proved this by assisting in genocide (they are discussed in my forthcoming volume). Yet this was a decidedly masculinist movement, with consequences to be discussed later.

Youths and Military Veterans

We saw that Italian fascists had been mainly young military veterans. The Nazis were also young, though with fewer veterans. The average age of 1923 members was twenty-seven, rising to twenty-nine through the late 1920s. Militants were younger still. In a 1929–32 sample of very active SA members, 60 percent were under twenty-five, while "martyrs" killed in street fighting during 1923–3 averaged twenty-four. Half the party members and three-quarters of SA militants were unmarried. As in Italy, most fascists were free from family commitments, their "careers" at the disposal of the movement. Around 1930 Nazi leaders were a full decade younger than the leaders of all other Weimar parties except for the communist KPD. Socialist SPD militants were rather older than the German population. The "bourgeois" parties and the socialists personified the stagnant wisdom of the middle-aged, not the dynamism of youth, so the Nazis proclaimed, "Make way you old ones!" Eventually, of course, the Nazis began to age: New members averaged thirty-six in 1933 and forty-seven in 1939. By then Nazis were representative of the age-structure of Germans as a whole (Weber 1969: II, 26; Merkl 1975: 13, 1980: 98; Douglas 1977: 71; Kolb 1979: 101; Madden 1982a, 1982b: 50; Fischer 1983: 49–51; Kater 1983: 139–48; Peterson 1983: 216; Jamin 1984: 85; Brustein 1996: Chart 5.2b).

Abel's Nazi autobiographies reveal that the NSDAP and the SA were considered adult organizations, usually reached after an apprenticeship in a rightist youth movement. Nearly all these militants had been in a youth group, half in the Hitler Youth or rightist paramilitaries, another fifth in civilian rightist movements (Merkl 1980: 205–6). So most Nazi militants had begun extremist activities as young as Italian fascists, in their late teens or at the beginning of their twenties.

Thus many explain Nazism as a generational phenomenon, a "youth culture of revolt." World War I is said to have been experienced similarly by "The Generation of 1914," born 1890–1915, too young for much adult experience before the war. Within this age cohort are distinguished a "front generation," born 1890 to about 1901, fighting in the war, and a younger "home generation," experiencing war only as children. Both experiences alienated young men from Weimar and drove them rightward. Less attention has been paid to the war experiences of young women. The "front generation" had confronted death daily, developing intense, egalitarian, and masculine comradeship. But their sacrifice was "betrayed" by middle-aged civilian elites back home. Then "the home generation" joined in, experiencing material and paternal deprivation during the war, developing a voyeuristic militarism and nationalism. Their romance with war was then shattered by the surrender and the return of defeated father figures. In the prosaic and feeble civilian democracy, unemployment also fell mostly on the young. They longed for a more integrated community and a strong father-figure – and found them in *Volk* and Führer. Such is the generational story (Merkl 1975, 1980; Wohl 1979: 64–84; Madden 1982a; Loewenberg 1983; Ziegler 1989: 59–79).

This story contains both truth and problems. In the 1920s the Nazis were still a small minority, with smaller youth movements than their socialist, Catholic, and "bourgeois" rivals. Thus only a few of this generation became fervent Nazis. There were also many Nazis of other generations. The average Nazi member in 1920 had been born in 1887 and so was slightly older than the war generation. The age group eighteen to twenty-nine was only a little overrepresented in the Nazi party: The ratio of its percentage in the Nazi party compared with its percentage in the population was around 1.25, rising to 1.40 in 1927. No age cohort was much underrepresented. Only the ratio for the over sixties dipped below 0.90 (Kater 1983: 261, 269–73). Thus all age groups were quite well represented. Ecological studies of voting suggest that, if anything, by 1930 older voters were a little more Nazi than were younger ones (Falter 1991: 146ff). Of the twenty-four top leaders, nine were over twenty-four when war broke out in 1914. Though Hitler himself (born 1889) had barely any adult accomplishments before the war broke out, Ritter von Epp (age 46) was already a high-ranking officer, Schwarz and Hierl (both 39) were a respectable civil servant and a middle ranking officer, and Frick (37) was a higher civil servant with a doctorate in law. These mature men already embraced extreme rightism, from which their Nazism then developed.

A "youth culture" had also formed well before 1914. The universities were an important breeding ground for Nazism. Some argue that their postwar expansion created a distinctive generational experience (especially where parents had not attended university). Yet university expansion had been greater in the prewar era (Flora 1983–7: 808, 811). Conservative nationalism already dominated the universities by 1890. By 1918 it was decidedly *völkisch*. This important term literally means "popular" but denotes a racist and anti-Semitic–tinged organic populism. *Volkisch* politics emphasized the ethnic unity of Germans wherever they lived, endorsing geopolitical expansion in the East. Though Jews were picked on as the most obvious "enemy" of such an eastward-tilting project, Slavs were also included. Before 1918 students were loyal to the *Kaiserreich* and so remained conservative. But the collapse of that state in 1918 meant that racist-tinged nationalism could now flourish independently of conservative statism. It did until they joined it up with Nazi statism. In 1928 the journal of the university fraternities declared, "Not economics but race determines the fate of a *Volk*" (Mosse 1971: 141). By 1930 most students were probably Nazis. But this was the culmination of a long-term trend.

One important antecedent of postwar youth organizations was the *Wandervogel* movement, organizing hiking and work camp parties from around 1900. Its leaders were adults, encouraging young people to seek activities and ideas that would express the romantic, idealistic soul of the German *Volk*. From this emerged small political youth organizations that after 1918 expanded and became more *völkisch*, antidemocratic, and militaristic. Half a million mainly middle-class members drilled, wore uniforms, and sometimes carried weapons. They liked to describe themselves as a "third force" between capitalism and socialism. Nazis such as the Strasser brothers and many of the Abel sample first imbibed protofascist ideas there (Mosse 1971: 118ff; Stachura 1983a). Most of the organizations were controlled by adult parties and veterans' and *völkisch* associations. The Nazis grew up in the shadow of a larger paramilitary, the *Stahlhelm* ("Steel Helmet"), led by *völkisch* veterans. Its leader, Franz Seldte (later the DNVP party leader), declared: "We must fight to get the men into power who will call upon us to smash once and for all these damned revolutionary rats and choke them by sticking their heads into their own shit" (Ziegler 1989: 77). But the *Stahlhelm*'s real innovation was in the organization of civil society. Its paramilitary parades, its celebratory "German Days," brought many thousands of Germans, including many women, into the streets in great bursts of nationalist community activism – on which base the Nazis were to build (Fritzsche 1998: 134–6).

Thus though youth culture had been transformed by the war, so had adult culture. Nor was it youth revolt against adult culture. Half the Abel essays detail their father's politics. Only 14 percent of these fathers had supported conventional parties (from conservative to socialist), while 15 percent reported an apolitical home environment. No less than 68 percent of fathers had been extreme nationalist, militarist, or *völkisch*. And only 2 percent of respondents reported acute conflict with their fathers (Merkl 1975: 295). Most of these Nazis were not revolting but *amplifying* the political characteristics of home upbringings that had also been changed by the war. These families could hardly remain bastions of conservative, system-endorsing militarism and nationalism when that system had vanished.

Nazis were often military veterans. Even as late as 1933 one-third of party members were veterans. Some 84 percent of the Abel sample who were of draft age had served in the war (similar to the Italian fascist figure), somewhat overrepresented (Merkl 1980: 107–9). The SS came heavily from army family backgrounds (as we see later). Local studies find that once the Nazis became serious political contenders, they received much support from local veterans' associations. Among the 60 *Gauleiter* (regional leaders) and *Reichsleiter* (national leaders) who could have fought in the war, all but one did so (Goebbels, rejected for military service on medical grounds).[3] They were spread through the ranks: At least 27 had been officers (including one general, one colonel, and two majors); 29 were definitely other ranks. At least 34 had seen action at the front, only one was definitely stationed in the rear. At least 25 had been wounded, and none had deserted. Corporal Hitler had performed a lowly but dangerous role carrying messages between the trenches; Göring was a much-decorated fighter pilot. Naturally, the Nazis flourished their warrior credentials at election time. With these credentials, plus the traditional authoritarian rightist ethos of the German armed forces, the Nazis could obviously tug at the moral and political sentiments of the small peacetime army. Hitler's very first postwar agitations had been financed by army funds. He then marched next to General Ludendorf in postwar demonstrations. In contrast, the German left was antimilitarist. Some 57 communist KPD leaders could have fought in the war. But 16 had definitely been civilians, five had been officers, 34 other ranks. Eleven had definitely been at the front, four definitely at the rear. Only five had definitely been wounded, outnumbered by the six who had deserted or been court-martialed. Many had been active in the 1918 workers' councils that the right saw as betraying the armed forces (Weber 1969: II). Almost all the councils organized by leftist sailors and soldiers had occurred among reserve troops, among inactive garrisons, or among naval forces cooped inside German ports, not among troops at the front. The war was a formative experience for right and left. The right drew on the virtues of militarism and the "myth of the front"; the left drew on the exploitative conduct of the war.

As in Italy there are two main explanations for military veterans' fascism. One is economic: Germany was full of unemployable military veterans, trained only to fight, their discontent translated into radical rightism. But though the German army was the most reduced by the peace treaties, veterans were accorded preferential and (by the standards of the time) generous employment programs. Employers complained at being forced to hire them. Most unemployment was short-term (Bessel 1988; Geary 1990: 100–1). Veterans' organizations also played down material interests in favor of calls for a "national, social, military, and authoritarian" state, rejecting the values of a "defeated," civilian, and democratic republic (Diehl 1977). No doubt material discontents played a role, but not the major one. And why would they lead to extreme *rightism*?

The second explanation centers on the translation of military into paramilitary values. As the war ended, demobilized soldiers and a few students tried to defy the emerging Republic and the peace treaties, forming free-booting paramilitaries such as the *Freikorps* to fight "Bolsheviks" at home and Slavs across the disputed eastern borders. They, not the regular *Reichswehr*, had put down the early postwar leftist risings. The leaders of the Weimar Republic were embarrassingly indebted to them – Weimar politicians did not command a monopoly of military power in Germany. Some of the *Freikorps* were soon to constitute a first wave of Nazi recruits. Their campaigns were increasingly publicized through the 1920s in best-selling memoirs and novels containing chilling brutality:

We made the last push. Yes, we roused ourselves one last time and stormed ahead across the entire line. Once again we pulled the last man with us, taking him from his cover, and plunged into the forest. We ran over the fields of snow and came to another forest. We fired into the surprised enemy and raged and shot and beat and chased. We drove the Latvians like rabbits over the fields and threw fire into every house and pulverized every bridge into dust and broke every telegraph pole. We threw the bodies into wells and threw hand grenades in after them. We slew whatever fell into our hands; we burned whatever could be burned. We saw red; we had nothing more of human feelings in our hearts. Where we had lived, there the earth groaned under our annihilation. Where we had attacked, there lay, where once were houses, ruins, ashes, glowing beams, like suppurating wounds in the open fields. (Von Salomon, quoted by Hamilton 1982: 340)

The stories combined nationalism, brutality, adulation of comradeship, and disturbing male sexual fantasies, praising violence for its capacity to purify and liberate masculinity from the suffocation of conventional morality (Theleweit 1987, 1989). Though the *Freikorps* killed and raped with abandon, they had no developed theory of political or ethnic cleansing. The "enemy" was to be scared off, some killed, but his identity was straightforwardly geopolitical: He was usually a Pole or a Balt allowed by the 1918 Peace Treaties to seize German lands. There was anti-Slav racism, but the "Judeo-Bolshevik," later central to Nazi demonology, was rare. The nihilism pervasive in this literature was also common in postwar art. Leftist artists such as George Grosz depicted grotesque war scenes intended to turn us against all war; rightist artists produced stark images of dehumanized, armored power, dignifying the warrior as the efficient instrument of a modernist war machine.

Postwar paramilitarism might have died away but was boosted by the events of 1923, as French and Belgian troops occupied the Rhineland to enforce reparations demands. This yielded a second wave of Nazi recruits, teenagers of the "home generation," drawn especially from these occupied territories (i.e., "threatened border Nazis") and from the sons of civil servants and soldiers (i.e., "statists"), denouncing a Weimar unwilling to defend its reduced territories. They again encroached on the state's formal

monopoly of military power, donning uniforms, some shooting at the occupying troops, but most marching and beating up "collaborators." It was
not successful – the French remained – but it was defiance and it evoked
considerable sympathy among Germans. These two waves – of "threatened
border" and "statist" recruits – constituted almost half the Abel sample. A
third wave of recruits arrived at the end of the 1920s, mostly young workers,
disillusioned by Weimar political and economic stagnation. Most of them
were not rejecting but amplifying the values of their upbringing: more aggressive nationalism, increasing hostility to democracy and socialism (Merkl
1975: 68–89, 139; cf. Diehl 1977; Grill 1983). All three waves centered on
paramilitarism. Until the seizure of power most Nazi members were also in
one of the paramilitaries.

"The myth of the front" and the myths of "the stab in the back" and of
Weimar ingratitude escalated in the late 1920s. They were not true: Most
returning army units had actually been feted as heroes, says Bessel (1988).
It was probably the military feebleness of the republic that nourished the
myth. But the Abel essays show fascist veterans recalling the war fondly:
Egalitarian yet hierarchical military discipline had produced personal and
national fulfilment:

National Socialism was conceived in the experiences of the trenches. It can only
be understood in terms of these front-line experiences.

[T]he war had taught us one lesson, the great community of the front. All class
differences, staunchly entrenched before the war, disappeared under its spell. Out
there it was what a person *was*, not what he seemed to be, that counted. There was
only a people, no individuals. Common suffering and a common peril had welded
us together and hardened us; that was why we were able to defy a world for four
years.

My old world broke asunder in my experiences. The world of the trenches instead
opened itself to me. Had I once been a loner, here I found brothers. Germany's
sons stood shoulder to shoulder in heated battles aiming their rifles at the common
enemy. We lay together in the bunkers, exchanging our life stories, sharing our
possessions . . . we tied up each others' wounds. Who would ever question authentic
German-ness, or how much education you had, or whether you were a Protestant
or a Catholic? (Abel 1938: 142; Merkl 1980: 113).

Indeed, from 1916 the German army *had* been quite egalitarian and technocratic, with the highest proportion of fighting troops of any of the combatant
powers. Geyer (1990: 196–7) describes it as "Taylorism for the organization
of violence," a model able "to organize the nation at large" by dissolving "the
boundaries between military and civil society." Abel respondents claimed

only the Nazis maintained this spirit. In the *Stahlhelm* one had found "no spirit of comradeship [only] class distinctions" (Merkl 1980: 211). Paramilitarism could thus transform politics.

As in Italian fascism, therefore, Nazis were disproportionately single young males with military backgrounds – though Nazis got older, more married, and more civilian as the war receded. Successive male generations amplified the right-wing nationalism and statism of their home backgrounds – through prewar youth activism, then through the trenches, and finally through a decade-long paramilitary struggle against civilian leftism and foreign intervention. The real generational story is thus rather complex, not exactly a "revolt" and involving at least two generations. Nazism emerged as a paramilitary nation-statism enhanced especially for one broad generation by the war, then amplified by later events. Perhaps more significant was the perpetuation of the violent young male-dominated paramilitary into the government of a major power.

Religious and Regional Cores

Since Germany possessed two great churches, Evangelical Protestant and Catholic, the Nazis tried to appeal to both once they aspired to be a major party. The Party Constitution of 1920 advocated "positive Christianity," that is, deism, but since this only alienated both churches it was soon played down. Hitler was a lapsed Catholic, as were many of his early cronies. Yet Nazis were from disproportionately Protestant backgrounds. Only the pre-1933 *Gauleiter* differ: Their proportions are close to the national average of 62 percent Protestant, 37 percent Catholic (Rogowski 1977: 403). But of the thirty-three principal Nazi leaders, sixteen said they were Protestant, only three Catholic (the rest saying they had no religion, Knight 1952: 31). In the Abel essays, two-thirds do not mention their religious upbringing, 25 percent say Protestant, only 10 percent Catholic. Lacking information on the religion of ordinary party members, we rely on ecological data: Precoup Nazis from Catholic areas were substantially underrepresented (Brustein 1996: fig. 1.4). The paramilitaries did record religious background: Samples of officers and men in the SA and officers in the SS were between 3 to 1 and 5 to 1 Protestant, though SS rankers were only 2 to 1 Protestant (Merkl 1980; Jamin 1984: 90; Ziegler 1989: 87–9; Wegner 1990: 239–42). German Nazis were thus disproportionately from Protestant backgrounds. The next chapter shows Nazi voters were, too. My forthcoming volume shows that the core perpetrators of genocide were disproportionately from Catholic backgrounds. I explain this puzzle there.

We lack good data on regional backgrounds. Scholars have been obses-
sive about class while ignoring geography. The full title of Kater's major
book is *The Nazi Party: A Social Profile of Members and Leaders, 1919–1945*
(1983), yet "social" has for Kater a rather restricted meaning. Some 90 percent of the time he discusses occupational class, 10 percent age. Studies of
the paramilitaries tend to conclude that there were few regional variations,
yet the geographic classifications of the authors lack sophistication. Some
merely divide Germany into "north" and "south" and find no significant difference between them. Others divide it into provinces and find
only an overrepresentation of Bavarians – which is itself interesting, since
they would be mainly Catholics, who were underrepresented in the party
(jamin 1984: 92–3; Ziegler 1989: 83; Wegner 1990: 235–9). Yet "ethnic Germans" from abroad and men from the "lost territories" and the
"threatened border" areas adjacent to these formed 36 percent of the Abel
sample, an overrepresentation of between 2.0 and 3.0. Merkl stresses that
the French invasion of 1923 had produced fervent Nazis in the southwest (Merkl 1975: 105, 1980: 136–7). Some 12 percent of the top Nazis
but only 4 percent of Weimar Cabinet Ministers had been born abroad
(Knight 1952: 28; cf. Kater 1983: 188). Austrians and "ethnic Germans,"
mostly refugees from the east, were also overrepresented among SS officers
(Ziegler 1989). We encounter these groups below in more sinister circumstances. These samples are of hard-core Nazis, those with long-term career
commitment to Nazi organizations. Newman (1970: 291–6) believes "fron-
tiersmen" were generally overrepresented among interwar fascists. They
were certainly overrepresented in the Nazi hard core. I delay exploring
why Protestants were so Nazi until examining voting patterns in the next
chapter.

Working-Class Nazis

We now move into class, the obsession of almost all previous scholarship on
the Nazis. The data on the social class of Nazi party members are therefore
abundant. They are summarized in Tables 4.1 to 4.6 in the Appendix.[4] They
almost all detail Nazis *before* the seizure of power. Thereafter opportunism
and careerism obviously influenced joiners, especially for those in the public
sector. Many of these were "Bandwagon Nazis" rather than committed
ideological Nazis. I return to the Bandwagon when dealing with its possible
role in Nazi genocide.

I start with blue-collar manual workers. In the various local, regional,
and national samples of Table 4.1 workers form 28 to 52 percent of Nazi

members. The lowest figure is the earliest, deriving only from a single city, Munich, with little industry. In other data for the early period, workers were also underrepresented, petty bourgeois groups overrepresented – fitting the traditional stereotype (Douglas 1977; Madden 1982; Grill 1983: 81–8). This was when the party was of no significance, for Germany or for the world. Yet as it grew, its base broadened and its workers increased. In the table the remaining samples yield a range of 31 to 52 percent workers. From now on workers formed between a third and a half of Nazis.

Two rather different conclusions may follow from this. We may stress that many Nazis were workers, obviously with some impact on the party. Alternatively, we may stress that workers were slightly underrepresented in the party (this disappears later when we add the paramilitaries). Workers formed 55 percent of the German labor force in 1933, though just under 50 percent in most of the regions and towns cited in the table. Most worker ratios in these samples would be between 0.75 and 0.90, indicating slight underrepresentation (cf. Brustein 1996: chap. 4). The higher ratios in this range tend to be Mühlberger's regional figures, drawn from local party file cards; the lower ones are from the national party statistics. Mühlberger believes this reflects the party's difficulties in retaining workers: Some joined and left local parties too quickly for the central party to track them. Rapid turnover was an even worse problem for the mainly proletarian Communist Party.

What kinds of workers were Nazis? Skilled workers were slightly over-represented when compared with unskilled workers (Rosenhaft 1987; Mühlberger 1991; Fischer 1995: 115; Brustein 1996: fig. 4.4). This is not surprising: Skilled workers are more likely to join all kinds of voluntary association (since they have more social and organizational skills). Few Nazis were agricultural workers: 8 percent of the national labor force, less than 4 percent in the Nazi samples in my Appendix, 5 percent in Brustein (1996: fig. 3.1). But there weren't many socialists or communists among farm laborers, either. Most of these laborers lived and worked among their employers (unlike southern European farm laborers) and lacked the autonomy to join radical political movements. Again, this may be an organizational rather than an ideological disincentive. Farm workers, like unskilled workers, may have been sympathetic but found joining difficult.

Elsewhere, there were more Nazi workers. Discounting agriculture would push up worker ratios to around 0.90, nearly at parity. Workers were actually overrepresented in the Hitler Youth until after the seizure of power (Mühlberger 1987: 110–11; Stachura 1975: 58–62). The Nazis did better in small to medium towns than in the biggest cities. Nazi worker ratios must have been above 1.0 in many smaller towns, yet down near 0.5 in some big cities. Outside the big cities perhaps 40 to 55 percent of Nazi members were workers, in the big cities only 30 to 40 percent.

Most studies argue that the Nazis did worst in larger firms in heavy industry, since these were already locked up by the socialist unions and party. The most hospitable employers were in the public sector – transport, postal services, and public utilities – especially since the public sector took on long-service military veterans (who were often Nazis). Most scholars see the Nazis as also doing well in smaller workshops and in the service sector (construction and hotels being well represented), because these had little social distance between boss and workmen and a shared rightist perspective (Kratzenberg 1989: 175–95; Mason 1995). Workers in the Abel sample were mostly from the public sector, handicrafts, and artisanal trades. The few working in large-scale manufacturing often reported being victimized by their "Marxist" colleagues. Brustein presents detailed data on sectors (1996: figs. 4.2 and 4.3). His ratios do not vary that much: Nazis were slightly overrepresented, at 1.3, in the service sector, at 1.2 in handicrafts, and at 1.1 in "mixed branches." They were slightly underrepresented, at 0.9, in big industry. Only agriculture, with a ratio of 0.7, deviates much.

Brustein found greater differences between branches within sectors. In agriculture the results are clear: more Nazis in livestock rather than in grain or vegetable farming areas (once we control for the distorting effects of religion). He attributes this to rational responses to Nazi economic policy such as protectionism, support for impartible inheritance, and opposition to subsidies for eastern grain growers. Brustein's "rational economic actor" model of fascism, which he has applied also to Italy (see Chapter 3 above) and to the Belgian Rexist movement, works best for peasant farmers. They buy and sell directly on the market and their fortunes are directly and visibly affected by government economic policies. Yet for the vast majority, working in the industrial or service sectors, the political economy that would further their own economic interests is far muddier. Would it be redistribution or trickle-down economics, free trade or protectionism? How can we judge which would benefit most? All political movements argue with great confidence that their varied prescriptions would be beneficial. Much of the political game turns on the relative plausibility of rival appeals to people whose social position does not give them a clear view of their "rational" economic interest.

That said, here are Brustein's industrial branch results. Workers in metalwares were most overrepresented, with a ratio of 3.0, followed by woodworking, food products, and leather (all above 2.0). Ratios were lowest in mining and earth and stone (0.3), and in rubber, asbestos, chemicals, utilities, metal products, and textiles (all 0.1–0.2). These are big differences. He argues that workers in different branches had different economic interests and so responded differently to the Nazi economic program. He focuses on one issue: A domestic rather than an export orientation in an industry results in higher Nazi membership, since the Nazis favored autarchy. I am a little dubious. The proportion of Protestants and skilled workers in an industry are both good predictors in his data. Brustein believes skilled workers were angry at employer attacks on their privileges and liked Nazi encouragement of social mobility. Yet skilled workers tend to be "joiners" of all parties: The same result might well be found for SDP members. Of course, miners differ from textile workers in many respects. We need to know more about the characteristics of workers in each industrial branch to interpret these results properly.[5]

Some suggest that the experience of unemployment made workers Nazi (Kratzenberg 1987: 204–24, 245–63; Fischer 1991: 130–1; Stachura 1993: 706–10; Mason 1995). This is sometimes linked to the more general notion that fascism appealed especially to the deprived and the marginal. Yet Brustein (1996: fig. 1.2) finds no relationship between local unemployment rates and Nazi membership rates (membership was highest in communities with middling unemployment). Since the Nazis were young, and youths were more likely to be unemployed, we would actually expect Nazi unemployment to be higher than the national average. SA militants did have a higher unemployment rate during the Depression, but their unemployment could have been the effect rather than the cause of their time-absorbing militancy. This was so in the Abel sample. One-third had been made unemployed, bankrupted, or otherwise suffered severe damage from the Depression (probably close to the national average). Yet almost all had held fascist beliefs or were involved in Nazi or similar organizations well before the Depression (Merkl 1980: 191–4). The voting data presented in the next chapter suggest that the communist KPD, not the Nazi NSDAP, became the party of the unemployed. Nazi workers were probably not more materially deprived than other workers.

But equally relevant is whether the Nazis had more workers than other parties. Appendix Table 4.4 shows that the socialist SPD and the communist KPD really were "proletarian parties." Some 80 percent of KPD members in 1927 were workers or craftsmen. Adding most of the "housewives" (probably the wives of workers) would push this close to 90 percent. Yet since the KPD was much smaller than the Nazi Party, it actually mobilized fewer workers. The SPD remained the dominant proletarian force, mainly through

its massive unions. Workers and their wives still comprised 60 to 80 percent
of its interwar membership lists. Skilled workers were overrepresented in
the SPD, though probably not the KPD (Weber 1969: I: 27; Fischer 1991:
128–32; Lösche 1992: 14–17). Yet the Nazis were more proletarian than
the center or right parties. Appendix Table 4.4 reveals that only 1 percent of
the conservative DVP were workers. Appendix Table 4.1 details members
of the ultraconservative DNVP and Nazis in comparable local areas. Workers made up only 2 percent of the Osnabruck DNVP, but 39 percent of
Hanover Nazis. In the industrial Ruhr, workers formed 11 percent of the
Düsseldorf DNVP, 41 percent of South Westphalian Nazis, and 52 percent
of Western Ruhr Nazis. Appendix Table 4.5 details party activists in the
rather bourgeois town of Marburg: 16 percent of Nazis were workers, far
less than the 63 percent in the SPD and KPD, but more than the 3 percent
in the "bourgeois" and the 7 percent in the "special interest" parties.[6] The
left parties were "proletarian," the right were "bourgeois," the Nazis were
more multiclass.

Since Nazi leaders were much more bourgeois than ordinary members,
some have argued that Nazism became "embourgeoised." Yet workers diminish up the hierarchy of *any* party – this was part of Michels's famous
"Iron Law of Oligarchy," based on his knowledge of the German Socialist
Party. The vital question is: Were Nazi leaders more "embourgeoised" than
those of other parties? Appendix Table 4.5 compares the Reichstag deputies
of all parties. Here Nazi workers lagged well behind the SPD and KPD,
were rivaled by the Catholic Center Party, but were well ahead of the three
"bourgeois" parties. Appendix Table 4.2 shows that of Nazi Reichstag candidates, 16 percent were workers and 6 percent white-collar in 1929, and
18 percent were workers and 13 percent white-collar in 1930. These figures
dwarf the worker and white-collar representation among DNVP candidates
and provincial leaders. Appendix Tables 4.2 and 4.6 contain data on all levels of the Nazi hierarchy. At the top, the national *Reichsleiter* contained no
ex-workers unless we count Hitler himself (a painter forced to paint houses
and a corporal). The regional *Gauleiter* were 7 percent ex-workers; while
among the next 250 bureaucrats and local leaders, workers contributed 21
to 25 percent. In Frankfurt local elections, 48 percent of KPD, 42 percent
of SPD, and 32 percent of Nazi candidates lived in working-class neighborhoods (Wickham 1983).

The Nazis kept a substantial worker and white-collar presence at every
leadership level except the very top. Though not a proletarian party, they
remained broadly rooted.

Middle-Class Nazis

I turn now to the occupational groups labeled as lower middle-class, petty bourgeois, or *Mittelstand* – small farmers, white-collar workers in public and private employment, and "the classic petty bourgeoisie" (artisan masters and small businessmen and traders). Combined, these groups usually comprised 31 to 36 percent of the party – slightly overrepresented, with ratios of 1.20–1.30.

Small farmers became overrepresented only after 1928 – with big regional variations. I have already mentioned Brustein's economistic arguments in this regard. But farming districts were also more religiously segregated than were urban areas. Solidly Protestant farming areas produced many Nazis, solidly Catholic ones rather few. Finally, the anxiety of "frontier" regions seems to have brought the Nazis some farming recruits, though previous scholars have made this argument only to explain the high rate of Nazi membership in Schleswig-Holstein. All three of these explanations seem to have some weight.

White-collar workers in the private sector were usually somewhat over-represented, especially in the national samples in my Appendix (cf. Brustein 1996: fig. 3.6). The "classic petty bourgeoisie" was neither under- nor overrepresented. Within this group artisan masters were underrepresented (ratios of only 0.3 to 0.6), self-described "merchants" overrepresented (ratios around 1.3 in the national samples, greater in the regional samples). Mühlberger suggests the latter is an artefact: A young commercial clerk would describe himself as a *Kaufmann* (almost untranslatable, but literally "merchant"), in order to impress. White-collar workers may have thus been a little more overrepresented – they certainly tended to switch from leftist to rightist trade unions through the late Weimar period. Some white-collar fascism was caused by economic discontent. But rising unemployment af-fected manual workers more, while white-collar sectors moving rightward actually had lower unemployment rates than other sectors, said Speier (1986: 62ff, 104). Though in this period wages were falling, so were prices. The real incomes of private-sector salaried employees increased by 13 percent between 1929 and 1932. Small business was underrepresented among the Nazis yet was worse affected by the Depression. Speier (a Weimar sociol-ogist) suggested that clerks were angry at the erosion of privileges such as weekly salaries rather than hourly wage payments, insurance schemes, and the right to be called "*Herr*" in work. He noted that the mimicking of military command structures in German offices nurtured an authoritarian culture that might turn discontent rightward. Economic and "authoritarian" motivations may both have been present among white-collar fascists.

Two middling groups were even more likely to join: lower professionals and lower civil servants. From the late 1920s both joined the party in proportions almost identical to their seniors in the German census classifications, "academically qualified professionals" and "higher civil servants." Jarausch (1990) also finds no difference between the two levels of professionals in his study of individual professions. As in Italy this suggests a sectoral rather than a class effect. Thus I have classified both lower groups with their seniors in my Appendix tables.

The German census grouping of "elite occupations" enables us to identify the top 5 percent of the labor force, including entrepreneurs, professionals and higher managers, and civil servants. They were disproportionately Nazi. Ratios fluctuate (small numbers will tend to do this) but they are usually upward of 2.50, the largest found so far. This would seem to aid a "bourgeois" rather than a "petty bourgeois" interpretation of fascism. But we should pause a moment. Elites dominate most political parties, as they do voluntary associations (other than unions). Again, the vital question is: Were elites more dominant in Nazism than in other movements?

Appendix Tables 4.4 and 4.5 show that elites were few in the two left parties, but dominated the other parties. We should be wary of the SPD and KPD figures: Many of the originally working-class leaders had spent years as comfortably-off party or union functionaries. Things were transparent in the three "bourgeois" parties. Over half the ultraconservative DNVP leaders and candidates held elite status – mostly big landlords and businessmen, then retired officers, senior civil servants, and educated professionals. At the local level (in Düsseldorf and Osnabrück) the *Mittelstand*, mainly the classic petty bourgeoisie, predominated in the DNVP. In the conservative DVP 60 percent of activists were from elite occupations, mostly businessmen and top managers, followed by senior civil servants, with a smattering of classic petty bourgeoisie, very few white-collar workers, and no workers (cf. Fritzsche 1990: 94–100). Large merchants and businessmen, lawyers, and teachers dominated the top of the liberal DDP (Schneider 1978: 50–1; Frye 1985: 1–2). Even among Catholic Center deputies landed and industrial elites were much more numerous than among Nazi deputies (Morsey 1977: 35). In Marburg elites formed 41 percent of "bourgeois" party members, 18 percent of the special interest parties, 15 percent of Nazis, and only 1 percent of the combined SPD/KPD. Marburg women active in the "bourgeois" and special interest parties were mostly elite, while Nazi women were mainly nonelite. Except in the left and Nazi parties, *Mittelstand* members and activists were drawn disproportionately from small business and trade (Koshar 1986: 238–9). In a local East Prussian Nazi women's group 50 percent were workers' wives, followed by the wives of civil servants of all levels (Fischer 1995: 165).

Thus the Nazis were less elitist and less business-oriented than any except the two left parties. Landlords, industrialists, and higher executives dominated the "bourgeois" parties but were rare among the Nazis. Small business was overrepresented in the "bourgeois" and special interest parties compared with the Nazis. Instead, the Nazis most recruited civil servants and professionals from the elite, and lower civil servants followed by white-collar workers among the *Mittelstand*. This is beginning to look a little like what I suggested might be the Italian pattern: recruited from the "nation-statist" bourgeoisie, which was also somewhat removed from the sphere of direct production relations.

But figures for civil servants and state-employed teachers raise a methodological problem. They were banned from Nazi membership by various provincial and city governments from 1925, by Prussia from 1929 and in the whole of Germany from 1930. Thus declared Nazi membership among them was low. When the government applied pressure, Nazi members would ask the party for "withdrawal" papers showing (falsely) that they were no longer Nazis. Brustein (1996: 167–75) finds civil servants neither over- nor underrepresented before 1933, which (given the disincentives) he believes demonstrates impressive Nazi commitment. Contemporaries believed civil servants and teachers had covert Nazi sympathies, while the Nazis aimed more pamphlets at them than any other occupational group. Historians have instanced many local officials and schoolteachers semi-covertly assisting the Nazis (Childers 1983: 176, 238–43; Grill 1983: 203–5; Caplan 1986, 1988; Zofka 1986).

To control for the problem of deception we can examine the backgrounds of full-time Nazis and of Abel's 1933 sample of long-term militants, neither of whom needed concealment. In the Abel sample civil servants were easily the most overrepresented occupational group – four times as likely to be Nazis as Germans as a whole (Merkl 1975: 14). Among the fifty-four full-time Nazi *Gauleiter* up to 1928, 56 percent had previously worked as civil servants or as state-employed teachers, rising to over 60 percent thereafter – five times the representation of other persons of comparable social status. These years predate the Nazi coup, after which civil servants might benefit from joining the party. Among mid-level Nazis such as the *Kreisleiter* (sub-regional bosses) or local Nazi deputies in 1933, a quarter had been public employees. Local membership records were affected by clandestinity. But even here public employees made up 10 to 25 percent of members (Kater 1983). In 1933 only 5.7 percent of the labor force worked in the public sector. Some 10 percent of civil servants had joined the Nazis by 1933, 18.4 percent by 1935. These are high levels of mobilization. By 1932 some government departments were dominated by Nazis – so their chiefs warned (Mommsen 1991: 116). Jamin (1984: 258) also finds that civil servants were always "drastically over-represented" in her samples of the paramilitary SA.

Rightist penetration of the state was not new. Civil servants had domi- nated pre-1914 nationalist pressure groups (Mann 1993: 585–8). After 1918 this gradually amplified into Nazism. A quarter of the Abel respondents came from "military-civil service" family backgrounds (Merkl 1975: 50– 61). Wegner's (1990: 240–1) study of high-ranking SS officers reveals an enduring connection between militarism, education, and the state. Some 17 percent had previously been army officers, 15 percent police officials, 22 percent teachers, and 6 percent other civil servants. Half their fathers had been in the public sector. The German state sector was to contribute half of those who later became the managers of genocide.

But again we must pause. The vital question is the comparative one: Were civil servants more likely to belong to Nazism or to other movements? As in other countries, public officials and teachers were overrepresented in most parties. My Appendix Tables and other sources show that in Germany the entire right, Nazi or not, attracted them as members and local leaders, with the political center lagging and the left trailing way behind. Before 1933, but not afterward, there were fewer civil servants among the Marburg Nazis than in the "bourgeois" or special interest parties. In the Reichstag public employees were overrepresented in all parties. Before 1930 this was most pronounced in the bourgeois parties and the Catholic Center, then the *Völkische* bloc and the Nazis. After 1930 they were distinctly more Nazi (Stephan 1973: 308; Bacheller 1976: 365–6, 379, 453–62; Linz 1976: 63– 6; Morsey 1977: 34–5; Mühlberger 1987: 106–7; Sühl 1988: 203–5, 227; Lösche 1992: 14–16). Civil servants *became* disproportionately Nazi.

Weimar civil servants were ripe for the picking because they already pre- ferred the executive to the legislative part of the state: "The interests of state" were higher than "party political interests," they said. When democracy wa- vered, this "statism" waxed stronger, enabling civil servants to usurp the role of politicians in the post-1930 authoritarian governments of Brüning, Papen, and Schleicher and fomenting Nazi sympathies in the service (Mommsen 1991: 81–4; Caplan 1988). Was there also a material motive? This does not seem very likely. Higher civil servants were so privileged that neither unemployment nor poverty could have driven them rightward. In 1930 the first Brüning government did cut salaries, pension entitlements, and even jobs (Mommsen 1991: 79–118). Yet since prices were falling, the real incomes of civil servants between 1929 and 1932 actually rose slightly. Ecological data reveal that civil servants were slightly more prone to vote Nazi in the aftermath of the two economic crises of 1924 and 1929, though the relationship also endured during the good times (Childers 1983: 171–8). Nazi propaganda directed at them focused not on their economic interests but on a broader nation-statism – in which they would obviously play an important role (Caplan 1988). Their rightism probably blended a very broad sense of occupational self-interest with a more ideological nation-statism – as I also suggested in Italian fascism. I myself believe that investment in public education today is necessary to economic growth – but I am a professor in a public university. Can my self-interest and my economic theory be disentangled? My motives are probably mixed – and so were probably those of the Nazi civil servants.

Finally, university-trained professionals (i.e., "academic professionals") were overrepresented in the NSDAP and in the SA and SS officer corps – more than was the "business and managerial" group. They also dominated the ultraconservative DNVP. Jarausch (1990: esp. 78–111) attributes this to economic discontent. Yet his own data do not support his conclusion. He acknowledges that workers and white-collar workers suffered more. He shows that professions harder hit by the Depression were not more Nazi. His multivariate analysis of the backgrounds of schoolteachers shows that Protestantism was the best predictor of Nazism, followed by urbanism, youth, and masculinity. Rank and salary differences lagged far behind. The most Nazi professions – foresters, veterinarians, university-trained farmers, judges, and doctors – did not face most Jewish competition (though Jews hardly overwhelmed any German occupations, the highest figures being 16 percent among lawyers and 10 percent among doctors). The most Nazi professions seem attracted by *völkisch* and "blood and soil" nationalism plus statism. Nazi propaganda focused not on their economic deprivations but on political and ideological themes: antimaterialism, loyalty to the state rather than to the parties, nationalism, and a class-free modernism. A pamphlet aimed at engineers denounced "the suffocating Jewish-materialist embrace of our life elements" that held back advanced technology. The party claimed that its educational policy "never focused struggle on professional, bureaucratic, pay or hiring questions. Its will has always centered on the ideological penetration of German education, the fight for political power in the state and the cleansing of our cultural life from all Marxist destructive tendencies."

Jarausch's own data suggest that ideological predominated over personal material motivations in forming attitudes to Nazism. And like other Nazi strongholds, the professions were removed from the direct relations of production.

Of course, professionals, teachers, and civil servants were also highly educated. Perhaps this was the cause of their Nazism. The universities had turned against the republic from the first. The student fraternities were mostly *völkisch* and anti-Semitic. Perhaps half of the German students were Nazi sympathizers by 1930, with few differences between social backgrounds or academic disciplines – apart from far less support among Catholics. The Nazis won a majority in the national student elections of 1931. Remember that these dates precede the Nazi breakthrough in national politics: The Nazis captured the universities *before* other major institutions.

Did economic deprivation cause student fascism? Many students were poor (not unusual, of course). Yet in Marburg majors who had the worst job prospects, in medicine and the natural sciences, were less likely to be Nazis (Koshar 1986: 243). In any case, the universities had been rightist since the 1880s, when the originally liberal notion of *Bildung* (cultured education in the Enlightenment tradition) had become more nationalist and when nationalism had begun its biological and racist turn. Few professors were Nazis but most were conservative nation-statists. As higher civil servants with tenure and privileges, recent recipients of large salary increases, they were perhaps the most secure group in Germany – followed closely by other civil servants and members of the free professions (Weisbrod 1996: 31). Their nourishing of authoritarian racism could not have flowed from economic deprivation or insecurity. Secondary and primary teachers were also more likely to be Nazis and among the more secure members of the work force. Educational institutions had long been central to the German nation-statist tradition – they had moved toward *völkisch* sentiments, and they now radicalized to Nazism (Kater 1975, 1983: 44; Linz 1976: 67; Giles 1978, 1983; Marshall 1988).

One female student, born 1910, tells how her nationalism had been strengthened by the French occupation of her hometown, Düsseldorf. But then at the university, friends took her to a Nazi meeting:

The Nazis told us that Hitler had learned a great truth from his experiences in the war. The important thing was not whether someone had money or a title, but whether he contributed to the well-being of his people. Hitler said nationalism and socialism should be identical. The nationalist should be there for every one of his countrymen and socialism must be adapted to the nature of a people. Thus, National Socialism. For us it meant comradeship – solidarity. . . . We said, "This is the only possible answer to Bolshevism." And that's how I came to join the National Socialist German Students' League." (Steinhoff et al. 1989: xxviii)

Thus the Nazis attracted two generations of young people, mostly males. The first came through war experiences, the second was socialized later in German schools, universities, and youth movements. The more intellectually minded there discussed the latest ideas of the age and attempted to combine them with the romanticism, idealism, "spirituality," and racism of German culture. Many believed the liberal and bourgeois age had collapsed in the war and its aftermath. The socialist alternative seemed old, materialistic, and too proletarian to be hospitable to intellectuals (Mosse 1971: 144–51). Many preferred more organic visions of modernity in which a movement and state embodied the nation and so brought social and moral development. Fascism was capturing the young and educated males because it was the latest wisdom of half a continent. Its ideological resonance in its era – far more than the specific sufferings of an age cohort – was the main reason it was a generational movement.

THE NAZI PARAMILITARIES

All this has concerned the Nazi Party. But we must add the paramilitaries – the SS and especially the SA, which was ten times the size of the SS before the coup. By 1932, combined, they had more members than the party. Since only somewhere around half their members were also party members, the paramilitaries provided alternative channels of access to fascism. Appendix Table 4.3 assembles the relevant data, which are more complete for the SA than the SS. Only white-collar workers in the private sector seem to have been (slightly) overrepresented in the precoup SS. Workers were the largest group, slightly underrepresented before 1933, then at parity. In their occupations the SS seems broadly representative of German men. This was to change considerably during the mid-1930s as the SS became viewed as "the elite" of the Nazi regime, though it was to change in ways congruent with my argument in this chapter (very large overrepresentation of higher civil servants, academic professionals, and students, with contrasting underrepresentation of those in industry – see my forthcoming volume).

In contrast the SA was proletarian. Appendix Table 4.3 indicates that workers rose from comprising 60 percent of SA members before 1929 to 70 percent thereafter. The Depression increased the SA unemployment rate to a staggering 60 to 75 percent. But did workers join the SA because they were unemployed, or did SA activities disqualify them from employment?

Probably both. The Abel sample contains many SA men who committed their lives to the cause well before the Depression, whatever the economic consequences. SA files also indicate employers did not like hiring
SA men, since they were prone to answer back and to absent themselves to
go marching. On the other hand, some SA recruits gave unemployment as
their reason for joining. Overall it seems likely that the SA began as proletarian and as unemployed as the age group from which it was drawn, and
then became even more proletarian and unemployed under the pressure
of the Depression (Fischer 1983: 25–47).[7] Paramilitarism provided alternative full-time activity to work. Maybe this was the main material role of
Nazism.

We also have data on the street-fighting core of the paramilitaries. Among
300 Nazis killed in street fighting, 57 percent were workers (a ratio of
1.22) and 25 percent were "business, professions and students" (probably
mostly students, since they were young). All other groups were underrepresented (Merkl 1980: 98–9; cf. Stachura 1975: 59). These fascist fighters
were not as proletarian as their communist counterparts. Some 90 percent
of communists arrested for street fighting in Hamburg and Berlin, and about
70 percent of the party's "martyrs," were workers (Kater 1983: 253; Peterson
1983: 214; Rosenhaft 1983: 167–207). Nonetheless, as in other countries,
most dead fascists were workers or students.

Before 1933 the paramilitaries and the party combined contained half a
million workers, and they were roughly proportionate to their numbers in
the German population. Overall the Nazis were not especially petty bourgeois or bourgeois. They comprised a broad cross-section of the German
class structure. In this sense, they were what they claimed to be: a national
party, yet they were biased away from the urban-manufacturing sector and
toward the state and educational sectors.

SOCIAL MOBILITY AND SOCIAL MARGINALITY

Uniquely, Nazi samples enable us to assess social mobility and success. It is
often said that Nazis were downwardly mobile, taking out career frustrations
on the political system. Yet in the Abel autobiographies just under half had
experienced no significant mobility, a quarter had risen significantly above
their origins, and only a seventh showed signs of decline (Merkl 1975: 62–
76). Of Rogowski's (1977) *Gauleiter*, 64 percent had enjoyed secure jobs and
75 percent had occupational careers commensurate with their educational
qualifications. Some 40 percent had been upwardly mobile compared with
their fathers, only 21 percent downwardly mobile. Their upward mobility

was thus double that of all Germans. Groups with most upward mobility – army veterans, university graduates, and white-collar employees – also provided most Nazis. Kater (1983: 182–4, 375) concludes that Nazi functionaries "did not project the image of a group of losers living on the fringes of society." He tracked down more *Gauleiter* than Rogowski had and believes their upward mobility was not quite so high. Nonetheless, they "exceeded by a very significant margin the upward mobility standard set by the population at large" – though Kater adds that such upward mobility must have given them an "excruciating" fear of toppling down again. Are only the immobile secure? Kater adds that high party technocrats had more stable and conventional upper-middle-class backgrounds and education, with no indications of marginality.

Ziegler (1989: chap. 4) concludes that the SS was a genuine meritocracy. Its officers had already achieved modest educational and occupational success before joining, but this accelerated once they were in the SS. Many contrasted the SS favorably with the "status-ridden" occupational world of Weimar. A minority of Wegner's (1990: 251–62) sample of SS officers (no figures given) experienced postwar downward mobility, while some of the younger recruits had feared economic difficulties. Yet none of his individual case studies had been economically marginal – except for true "desperadoes" such as Theodor Eicke, whose frequent sackings and brushes with the police had resulted from his political extremism, not vice versa (see my forthcoming volume for more details of this terrible man). Both studies show that military and nationalist values played a much larger role than economic deprivation in attracting SS recruits.

Jamin (1984) deviates from this consensus. She says that the careers of SA officers demonstrated "social inconsistency." The officers lacked "a stable place in the social hierarchy" and experienced much downward mobility. Yet her actual data are not so clear-cut. Half of her main sample of SA leaders had experienced no significant intergenerational mobility and half no intragenerational mobility (as in the Abel sample).[8] Of the mobile SA officers, she says that twice as many had been downwardly as upwardly mobile. Yet this disproportion is contributed by her category "ambivalent downward mobility," measured (intergenerationally) by having a father as "self-employed, artisan or farmer" and self as "white-collar employee, skilled worker, professional soldier." This is dubious for three reasons: Most "artisans" were workers, not middle-class; the term "soldier" is too vague to denote social status in a world war; and outmigrating farmers' sons may have been escaping poverty rather than moving downward. If we accept her categories, 25 to 30 percent of SA leaders had experienced downward mobility; if we do not, 10 to 15 percent had. If we settle for 20 percent, this is hardly overwhelming. Against the other evidence reviewed here, this cannot sustain her conclusion that Nazism represented the "socially up-rooted and isolated" and so could not develop a "positive socio-political programme and rationally represent the real social interests of its members." But Nazism did represent "real social interests" – though not primarily class ones.

The notion of marginality has influenced many analyses of Nazism. Of course, Hitler himself fits the stereotype perfectly – failed painter, international migrant, discharged corporal, vegetarian in a meat-eating era, a man without real family life, probably sexually inactive. Yet his racialism had originated through the "normal" experiences of an Austrian anti-Slav Pan-German nationalist whose casual anti-Semitism became something much more dangerous as a result of his experiences in the revolutionary years following 1917 (Hamann 1999). "Mass society" theorists used to argue that "atomized" masses and "marginal" individuals, without strong social roots, turn to radical utopian movements and charismatic leaders. The theory has been recently updated in the notion that a healthy democracy rests atop a vibrant "civil society," dense networks of sociability among the citizens, centered on voluntary associations dominated by neither the state nor the economic market. Supposedly, the best guarantor of a free society and of democracy is a dense network of sociability centered on voluntary associations.

Unfortunately, the Germany that became Nazi was exactly this, a very dense "civil society" – and the Nazis were at its very heart. Germany had high levels of interest group and voluntary association membership, including dense white-collar as well as manual worker unionization. It was such evidence years ago that enabled Hagtvet (1980) effectively to demolish mass society theory of Nazism. There is now further evidence to support his argument. The voting studies discussed in the next chapter suggest that whole communities, not marginal individuals, swung round to the Nazis: In agriculture, for example, the most cohesive Protestant communities went Nazi. The Nazis were also very successful at organizing in, and often taking over, professional associations. They were also hyperactive in local community associations. In Marburg, Koshar (1986) demonstrates, Nazis were more active in other local social clubs than was any other political movement. The local party depended on and mobilized social networks provided by sharpshooting clubs, veterans' leagues, gymnastic and sports societies, singing societies, and student fraternities. It was partly this social activism that led the Nazis toward the elitist view of themselves as being the "consciously German" part of the population. This is similar to Fritzsche's (1998) argument that Nazi community activism had built on top of *Stahlhelm* innovations to provide the main source of their popularity: They did actually organize the German nation. Koshar concludes that the Nazi surge to power can be interpreted in one sense as a revolt by local community activism against the failures of the national political system. That is what Abel's Nazi militants and the SA recruits quoted earlier were saying: They were against "the system."

Germany was thus a very strong civil society, and Nazis were at its heart. Led by Nazis it became a strong but evil civil society. As we saw, Riley (2002) shows a similar association between civil society and fascism in Italy. My forthcoming book similarly reveals a general tendency for movements of ethnic cleansing to be more strongly rooted in the voluntary movements of "civil society" than were their liberal opponents. Civil society may not be very civil! Indeed, this is not very surprising. It is rare to find marginal losers among political elites – we look for losers in bars, jails, and morgues, not politics. Those who seek to change the world, and to court danger while doing it, are more likely to be confident, feeling empowered by social success. Most German fascists felt empowered by a mixture of personal military, educational, social, and career success, buttressed by a sense of being "good Germans" with an ideology that was the latest wisdom of the age.

CONCLUSIONS

Class and Sector

Since class theories have dominated approaches to the social bases of Nazism, it is worth summarizing my conclusions on the economic and class correlates of Nazism. Though Nazism started with a particular base among predominantly lower middle-class groups, by the time it became a mass movement after 1930, its contours differed.

(1) There was no overall correlation between class and German fascism, unlike in Italy. Almost all classes were well represented in Nazism.
(2) As in Italy, rural classes moved from under- to overrepresentation, though few German agricultural workers became fascist members.
(3) As in Italy, the educated "nation-statist" bourgeoisie was the most overrepresented, while the business bourgeoisie, large and small, was underrepresented. This also influenced the education of young people. State and Protestant (though not Catholic) education assisted the emergence of fascism as a generational movement.

(4) As in Italy, the Nazis found difficulty penetrating working-class communities in the urban-industrial economy. Yet since more workers lived and worked outside than inside these communities, the Nazis picked up plenty of workers from other social settings.

(5) As I suspected but could not prove for Italy, German fascists were neither social marginals nor economic losers. Where we have background data relevant to their motivation, these would not usually suggest economic or career frustration. If anything, they were more secure, protected from the vagaries that economic booms and slumps bring to groups more directly related to business activities. And socially they were at the heart of civil society. Though this was a very strong civil society, it was not a very nice one – unlike the almost universal portrayal of civil society in contemporary social science.

(6) As in Italy, fascists tended to be distant from the main arenas of modern class conflict: few businessmen, "classic petty bourgeoisie," private sector managers, or urban-industrial workers. Nazis were indirect, not direct, observers of the most pronounced class struggle – these people were, of course, responding to the Nazi claim to be able to "transcend" class conflict (a point I discuss further in the next chapter).

Of these six points only the last might have surprised the Nazi leaders. The lack of overall class bias was no surprise: They claimed they transcended class structure, as a *Volkspartei*, a people's party. We have seen the claim was plausible, though there was a religious gap in their "national" credentials. They had few Catholic supporters – which the next chapter discusses. Overall, however, the Nazis were the party most able to project themselves at their meetings as "classless." Their platforms would deliberately include speakers ranging from Prussian princes to railway clerks, retired generals to students and workers, speaking in varied accents – a public display of classlessness epitomized by Hitler, the little corporal with the derided accent of Austrian provincialism.

The Significance of Nazi Militancy

We have now seen something of the beliefs and social base of Nazi militants. But what did they actually do, and how did this help them to power? By the time of the coup the Nazis had over a million members. But what mattered was less their overall size than the activism of the core militants. As in all movements, there were many nominal and marginal members. As the party grew to great size it experienced difficulties with rapid turnover of members, especially working-class members (Mühlberger 1991). Nonetheless, the average Nazi member was far more active than the average member of any other movement. On almost every given occasion the local leadership could call out tens or hundreds of militants to march, to demonstrate, to pack halls, and, if necessary, to brawl, and the members would turn out, leaving their jobs (annoying employers considerably) and giving of their time and energy generously. The bourgeois parties were respectable notable parties lacking much sense of "militancy." They did not march and rarely demonstrated. Their meetings were formal, polite, depending heavily on routinized practices of deference to the platform and the social status of their speakers. If their meetings were disrupted by determined hecklers or by pushing and punching, they could not call on their supporters for a determined collective response. They were overwhelmed by the greater collective energy, enthusiasm, and violence of the Nazis. Even the socialists and communists, who had invented the notion of militant comradeship, were rocked back on their heels.

Rituals were key to Nazi mobilization of militants. Since we can listen to recordings of Hitler's speeches and watch newsreels of his mesmeric Nuremberg performances, we tend to view such grand rituals as the key. Yet Hamilton (1982: chap. 12) reminds us that Nuremberg-style mass meetings involved only a tiny minority of Germans, while Hitler could not dominate radio or newsreels until he seized power. Rather, the party mobilized through the local party cell, using telephones and trucks for physical communication and the typewriter and cyclostyle for written communication – all manned by activists willing to leave their jobs at a moment's notice to perform these roles. In "Northeim" (population 10,000) about sixty to seventy party and SA members plus seventy-five Hitler Youths generated more meetings, demonstrations, and marches than any other party. Their actions, energy, and enthusiasm were presented to onlookers on ritual occasions as microcosms of the new and future Germany. It did not seem particularly authoritarian, for it exhibited the "collective effervescence" that Durkheim regarded as the key to solidifying rituals. It is worth stressing that the Nazis thrived on liberal democracy – on freedom of assembly, demonstration, and duplication of the printed word. This was most intense at election time, but it carried on the whole time. They could not have done so well against an authoritarian regime. Apart from anything else, their own violence would have been promptly exposed by police and army units as mere amateur brawling, which as we see in Chapter 8 eventually happened to Romania's fascist "legionaries."

Local Nazi leaders enjoyed some legitimacy as people willing to put in time and energy for the work of the local community. They found members through the networks of local clubs, engaging in activities such as sports, singing, sharpshooting, which were formally apolitical but which had acquired nationalist coloration in the late nineteenth century. Nazi militancy then grew to generate quite a wide range of activities. The Hitler Youth and the women's movements were widely seen as worthy, attractive movements, encouraging healthy bodies and minds. Though the party and the paramilitaries half-overlapped, their activism can be partially distinguished. Party members tended to stand in small groups on street corners, leafleting, speechifying, and then packing into meetings. Some did this full-time but most did not.

The paramilitary SA had distinctive appeal and powers. Its members moved together in rather larger ritual displays. SA men were younger, more likely to be single. More were full-time, often living together in small barracks, their subsistence paid for out of party funds. Just like the Italian *squadristi*, they were caged into an enjoyable life of disciplined comradeship, drinking together, swaggering around in their uniforms, reveling in the Nazi elitism that made them special, "consciously German." Some units added homosexual solidarity to this. Most of the time their violence was largely symbolic. They would form guards of honor for speakers or would intimidate leftists and Jews just by their collective presence. Then they would eject hecklers, so that Nazi meetings created an impression of orderliness, in contrast to other parties' meetings that they were successfully disrupting. When violence came, they reveled in it, for they were an organized and armed gang of young males committed to radical means and goals by their movement. Most of their violence was aimed against the left (in eastern border areas it was against Poles), with much less against Jews or the "bourgeois" parties. The Nazis sought to legitimate their violence by proclaiming it "defensive." They claimed "Bolsheviks" had already taken over parts of Germany. SA tactics were based explicitly on provoking the enemy. The enemy was never the state. Nazi paramilitary power never took on the state's military or police powers. The enemy was other movements or Jews. It was far easier to appear defensive against the left, since Jews and the "bourgeois parties" were completely nonviolent. SA units were ordered into the strongest socialist and communist strongholds to march and to shout and to sing, and so to provoke attacks on them. Brawls would follow and wounds were then paraded to validate their claim that "there isn't a night in which SA men don't lie in the streets as victims of the Communist terror." Merkl comments: "[A] bogus enemy, the aggressive, brawling Communists or Socialists, was substituted for the real object, the conquest of state power."

But Nazi tactics were actually subtler than this. They did not intend to conquer the state by direct paramilitary power, since they knew they could never take on the German army. Nazi violence had three other goals: actually to solidify their own comradeship, emotionally "toughened by battle," to intimidate their opponents, and to demonstrate that the "Marxist threat" could be overcome by their own disciplined paramilitarism. Nazi propaganda and the biased press then transmitted this claim to millions who had never directly witnessed the violence (Abel 1938: 99–110; Allen 1965: 23–34, 73; Noakes 1971: 99, 142, 202–19; Hamilton 1982; Merkl 1982: 373; Bessel 1984: 26–32, 45–9, 75–96; 1986; Heilbronner 1990).

Nazi violence was thus effective, not so much in actually destroying the enemy (as fascist violence had in Italy), since German socialism was initially much better at defending its own communities, as in persuading its own members that they were a solidary, comradely elite, willing to take risks for radical goals, and in persuading many Germans and German elites that ritualized "orderly" violence was needed to solve the country's "anarchy." Once in power they would provide a state more committed to "order." Indeed, the second paramilitary, the SS, a rather small organization before the seizure of power, did blend the notions of violence and order. The SS was committed to the notion that paramilitary discipline could generate a new social, political, and racial elite. Thus, in contrast to the SA, it attracted many of Germany's young educational and professional elite (this is discussed more in my forthcoming volume). This range of militancy – from the worthy to the violent – made Nazism appeal to very diverse types of people. It also confused ordinary Germans' responses to Nazism, since it fused together what we normally think of as the legitimate and the illegitimate. This takes us toward the response of the two other vital ingredients in the Nazi surge to power: the electorate and elites.

5

German Sympathizers

The Nazis were able to seize power because a shrewd leadership was able to mobilize three essential power resources: the activism and violence of Nazi militants (discussed in the previous chapter), the votes of one-third of the German electorate, and the ambivalence of German elites concerning Weimar democracy. Unlike the Italian fascists, the Nazis seriously and successfully contested elections. Over a third of Germans voted for them, and this enabled them to reach the very brink of power by constitutional means. But, like the Italian fascists, the Nazis actually seized that power with help from the country's elites. I first consider the breadth and the motivations of the electoral support. For the sake of brevity, I focus on the main period of electoral success, after 1930. I consider the mass ideological power resources of the Nazis: what electoral message the Nazis tried to put across and how voters perceived it.

NAZI ELECTORAL STRATEGY

Some say that the Nazis would do anything for votes; not ideology but opportunism dominated their electioneering. This is part of the tradition of not taking fascists seriously. Childers (1990) says that leaflets and speeches were tactically aimed at specific interest groups, with policies opportunistically tailored to each. Indeed, Hitler's book *Mein Kampf* openly reveals contempt for the masses and explains how to manipulate them and their hatreds. As he once explained to his confidants: "Comprehension is a shaky platform for the masses. The only stable emotion is hate" (Kershaw 1991: 51). But at election times he instructed the movement to downplay warmongering and hatred for "enemies" such as Jews and Slavs. More than other German parties the Nazi leaders held repeated tactical meetings, trained their speakers, and instructed militants on whom to address, what to say, and what to avoid saying. The Nazi were innovators in political manipulation. Of course, compared with the political parties of today, they were amateurish in their techniques and bleedingly sincere in expressing their hatreds.

The message was actually fairly clear and consistent. Nazi propaganda centered, as we might expect, on strong nationalism. The electorate was told that Germans were racially and culturally superior, destined to rule over other nations. The party promised territorial expansion into a "Greater Germany" that would liberate millions of Germans living under foreign domination. It described the Russians as bestial but backward, unable to resist the power of modern Germany; while the French and British were "civilized" but "decadent," probably unwilling to fight. The harsh borders they had imposed on Germany was an international (sometimes a "Jewish") conspiracy. The Nazis had a strongly revisionist foreign policy, making simple demands for the restoration of lost territories and "German's rightful place." This was not very controversial. Almost all German parties argued thus, though many Nazi orators spoke in a more inflammatory way. But the Nazis had two advantages in making such foreign policy claims. First, as an out-of-power party, the Nazis had an edge, since most other parties participated in the Weimar coalition governments and could be accused of selling out to foreign powers. Hitler's consistent revisionism, his advocacy of rearmament, and the Nazi movement's own militarism boosted the appeal of Nazi foreign policy. These *were* harsh peace terms that most Germans felt were unjust. The stripping of German territory and industry boosted the electoral chances of a revisionist movement such as the Nazis. Of course, the geopolitical reality was that the foreign powers were committed to a timetable of withdrawal from the Rhineland and the ending of reparations. Thus Germans did not expect that wielding a big stick to get justice quicker – perhaps even to recover some lost territories – would lead to a major war. In geopolitics Hitler talked the way they talked, the way a Great Power such as Germany was entitled to talk. Thus Nazi foreign policy was popular: aggression but without war. For six years of his rule Hitler did indeed deliver this fine combination.

But that was not electorally decisive, since German voters (like most electorates) were concerned more with domestic issues. Yet the second Nazi advantage was the greater span of its nationalism. For Nazism also had a uniquely vigorous domestic message, which was at one both with its foreign policy and with the apparent classlessness of the party itself. One of the Abel respondents recalled first hearing a Nazi advocating transcendent nationalism:

I was swept along not only by his passionate speech, but also by his sincere commitment to the German people as a whole, whose greatest misfortune was being divided into so many parties and classes. Finally a practical proposal for the renewal of the people! Destroy the parties! Do away with classes! True *Volksgemeinschaft!* These were goals to which I could commit myself without reservation.... Thus I entered the Hitler Youth and found what I had sought: real comradeship. (Merkl 1980: 251)

A schoolteacher's diary describing hearing a Hitler speech given to a massive crowd imparted a rather concrete meaning to transcendence:

There was immaculate order and discipline ... for the man who had drawn 129,000 people of all classes and ages. There stood Hitler in a simple black coat.... Main theme: Out of parties shall grow a nation, the German nation. He censured "the system" ("I want to know what there is left to be ruined in this state!") ... he made no personal attacks, nor any promises, vague or definite.... How many look up to him with touching faith! as their helper, their saviour, their deliverer from unbearable distress – to him who rescues the Prussian prince, the scholar, the clergyman, the farmer, the worker, the unemployed, who rescues them from the parties back into the nation. (Noakes and Pridham 1974: 104)

Note how she specifies the classes. The last chapter established that the Nazi claim was not mere rhetoric – it mirrored the actual composition of the Nazi movement. Most Nazi speakers entwined the foreign and the domestic aspects of nationalism together, in classless and often rather aggressive rhetoric that was not so universally popular. Political enemies were denounced as foreign or alien. Leftists were (Slav) Bolsheviks or Jews; finance capital was foreign or Jewish; liberals and Catholics were internationalists. For the Nazis "enemies" always had a mixed ethnic and political identity, and this was persistently affected by border issues. The Nazis always advocated a policy of mixed ethnic and political cleansing. They would "do away with," "eliminate," "crush" "the Marxist-capitalist-Jewish extortion system," the "black-red internationalism" that kept the German nation divided. The Nazis promised to "knock all their heads together" to secure social peace. The "bourgeois" and special interest parties were portrayed as "splinter parties" of class or sectional interests, while appeals to class, *Stand* (status group), and *Beruf* (profession) divided the nation. When the upper-class leaders of the rightist DNVP party also urged suppressing class differences for the sake of German unity, hypocrisy was evident, especially to workers. The DNVP speakers, like those of the other "bourgeois" parties, were from the privileged classes. The socialists and communists were mainly working-class with an added sprinkling of Jews. The classless Nazis were different, seeming to be a more plausible instrument for a neutral but Germanic social justice. This claim to an organic nationalism pervaded all Nazi policy.

As well as somewhat appealing general rhetoric, the Nazis had more concrete policies. Amid a Depression, the Nazis could not ignore economic issues. Yet Hitler and most Nazis scorned narrow "economics" and subordinated them to politics. Their economic policies had solid roots in a German statism stretching back to Friedrich List, through Rathenau's autarchic "state socialism from above" during World War I, acquiring *völkisch* tinges during the 1920s (Barkai 1990). Distinctions between productive/creative and unproductive/Jewish capital were borrowings from this academic tradition.

This political economy was aimed at various interest groups. Autarchy (involving lower interest rates) was proclaimed especially to farmers, who might benefit from lower food imports and indebtedness. Many farmers voted Nazi for what they perceived as their material interests (as Brustein 1996 emphasizes). But these were not one-off policies, tailored specifically to farmers. Nazis set agricultural policies amid broader themes. In the *Official Statement on Farmers and Agriculture* "national self-determination" would reverse "bondage by debt to international high finance" and "international Jewish capital." Reparations placed burdens on agriculture and must be ended. So must be a parliamentary democracy that failed to protect farmers. The Nazis claimed these policies were more moral than economic. Farmers were "the main bearers of a healthy *völkisch* heredity, the fountains of the youth of the people, and the backbone of military power." But farmers' sectional interests must come second in the "political war of liberation": "[T]his war cannot be carried on from the standpoint of a single occupational group; it must be carried on from the standpoint of the entire people," represented by "the consciously German members of every occupation and rank" (Fischer 1995: 147–8). In rural Lower Saxony the overall ideology appealed more than specific policies (which in many ways resembled the policies of the rival rightist DNVP party), says Noakes (1971). Anti-Semitism figured in some rural campaigns: German "blood and soil" was exploited by Jewish moneylenders. In reality it was not. Jews were a useful alien symbol of the farmers' real resentments against a cosmopolitan urban world that they thought was grinding them down. But the Nazis always set specific material interests amid a broader ideology – as successful political movements do. That is how they sought to transcend (or perhaps to evade) the real-world multiplicity of interests.

They also promised to save the "essentially German" middle class, "crushed between international socialism and Jewish stock-market capital." Again, sectional interest was set amid a broader theory of alien exploitation, reinforced by an attack on liberal democracy that failed to protect the victims. But they spent twice as much organizing effort on workers (Brown 1989). They denounced Bolsheviks, but not the working class. They glorified the productive worker: Productive workers and productive capitalists alike were praised as being "consciously German," as opposed to exploiting capitalists who were "unproductive," "profiteering," or "usurious" – and Jewish or foreign. Thus the core of the Nazi *Weltanschauung* – Germans against aliens at home and abroad – was presented to the voters. And the voters responded.

The original party program promised work and welfare for all, though with little sense of how to achieve this. In the Depression the party began to firm this up. It first developed its own voluntary labor service, "Socialism of the Deed," in which it improbably boasted: "[A]ll do the same work: architects, engineers, merchants, office workers, salaried employees, craftsmen, students, skilled and unskilled workers. Here the *Volksgemeinschaft* manifests itself truly and honestly" (Kele 1972: 193). At this moment of the Depression the Brüning government was deflating the economy, which involved cutting vocational training, job-creation schemes, and remedial education programs. Many young people would be reluctant to cast their first votes for the conservative or liberal parties that this government represented – or even for the socialists who were still cooperating with it.

In a May 1932 speech in the Reichstag, Gregor Strasser moved further, proposing Nazi public works programs financed by "productive credit expansion." Behind this was a radical program proposed by the Nazi Economic Policy Section, including higher taxation on the rich. Hitler was reluctant to publicize this, fearing to alienate big business – that could wait until after the Nazis came to power, he assured the head of the Section (Turner 1984). Yet Strasser's promises were publicized in the next election campaigns, and they were popular. Indeed, once in power, much of the policy was implemented. The major Nazi goal was actually to finance rearmament, but the consequent investment in heavy industry did reduce unemployment. The electoral slogans "work and bread" and "the right to work" were also set amid nation-statist rhetoric: "national economic self-determination so that international capital can no longer decide whether or not Germans work and live" (Childers 1983: 148–53, 246–8). This was attractive rhetoric to many, but it was not just rhetoric.

German official statistics suggested that unemployment was slashed during the period of Nazi rule, and many have accepted this claim. Some economic historians look skeptically at the figures. Probably unemployment did fall, but not by all that much (Silverman 1988). Yet the figures were the only ones available, and because after 1933 workers could no longer organize autonomously of Nazi institutions, workers who were unemployed had little opportunity to discover how many they were. Many of them were also put very conspicuously to work on beautification projects smartening up Germany's towns. Thus "the ending of unemployment" *seemed* to be a major Nazi achievement. And in truth the Nazis did have more of a positive impact on the economy than almost any other contemporary government – at least until about 1938 when overheating became apparent. The Great Depression had stimulated the Nazis to give some substance to "productivist socialism." In contrast, most of the capitalist right and the Marxist left believed in "the laws of the capitalist economy" and so did nothing. The socialists were betraying their workers more thoroughly than the Nazis did theirs (some socialists also advocated Keynesian policies, but were squashed by their leaders). Since the Nazis rejected the primacy of material forces, they believed in no capitalist laws, and this enabled them to pioneer a kind of Keynesian-militarist nation-statism. The Depression did help the Nazis, but precisely because they were fascists, plausibly claiming to solve it.

Brustein (1996) especially emphasizes that workers appreciated the Nazi promise of jobs. Yet we saw that SA recruits' reasons for joining often embedded personal material interests amid a broader nationalism: They could feel their own job security was also part of a national reawakening. In speech after speech, Hitler hammered home the message that the Nazis were centrally concerned not with day-to-day policies but with a "gigantic new programme," a "vision," a "high ideal" that would overcome social divisions (Kershaw 1998: 330–2). Socialists in Germany, as elsewhere in the interwar period, often made the mistake of believing that class and national identity were alternatives. A good half of German workers disagreed. They were proud of being workers *and* Germans. And the Nazis trumpeted the dignity of both identities.

Of course, the Nazis could not really transcend class conflict, as they promised. Half the leadership wanted to delay any such goal until well after the seizure of power. Conservative Nazis such as Göring persuaded Hitler to seek power by conciliating capitalists and other reactionaries. They could settle accounts later. The "radical" Goebbels wavered. Though no socialist, he hated capitalism because he believed that Jews were at its core and that remedy would come through "the spirit of sacrifice, the berserker steadfastness of freedom that slumbers in the proletariat and will one day awaken." This spirit, he believed, could be used for national, not class ends. Hitler made his own views clear in his argument with Otto Strasser (the most leftist leading Nazi):

HITLER: [O]ur organization . . . is based on discipline. . . . Those who rule must know they have a right to rule because they belong to a superior race. They must maintain that right and ruthlessly consolidate it. . . .

STRASSER: Let us assume Herr Hitler, that you came into power tomorrow. What would you do about Krupp's? Would you leave it alone or not?

HITLER: Of course I should leave it alone. Do you think me so crazy as to want to ruin Germany's great industry. . . . There is only one economic system and that is responsibility and authority on the part of directors and executives. I ask Herr Amann [his office manager] to be responsible to me for the work of his subordinates and to exercise his authority over them. Herr Amann asks his office manager to be responsible for his typists and to exercise his authority over them; and so on to the lowest rung of the ladder. That is how it has been for thousands of years, and that is how it will always be. . . . A strong state will see that production is carried on in the national interests, and, if these interests are contravened, can proceed to expropriate the enterprise concerned and take over its administration. (Noakes & Pridham 1974: 99–100)

Otto Strasser now left the party claiming that Hitler had betrayed National Socialism by endorsing capitalism. Yet his brother Gregor, who stayed loyal, more correctly observed that Hitler had promised protection only to capitalists who served National Socialist interests. It was the authority principle that was at stake, and Otto, not Hitler, was betraying it, said Gregor (Kele 1972: 159).

As long as capitalists lent their authoritarian work organizations to Nazi goals, Hitler allowed them to reap profits. If they resisted, he smashed them. Capitalism as private property did not interest him. Capitalism as disciplined, authoritarian production did. This was the ideological source of the Nazi procapitalist bias – practically reinforced by their antisocialist street fighting. The Nazis did not transcend class struggle, but they muted it with full employment, repressed it with violence, and subordinated it to nation-statist goals. And after eight years all of Germany's social classes would begin to suffer catastrophically from Nazi rule.

The Nazis did not conceal their racism. Though extreme, it built on top of mundane sentiments of the time. The Weimar Constitution itself defined the German nation as a union of "tribes," and "German blood" defined citizenship (Brubaker 1992). Racial theory was influential in contemporary biomedical science in many countries, and common-sensical racial

assumptions were everywhere made. Germans and other nations were defined by blood, hereditarily, and to this was yoked a sense of national superiority common among Great Powers. Germans were regarded as racially
superior to nations around them, especially to the supposedly less civilized
nations to the east and to "Semites." Anti-Slav jokes, songs, and graffiti
were common through the east of the country, even in the SPD. Was this
very different from the "Polack" jokes of Americans or the Irish jokes of
the British? Ethnic and racial slurs were commonplace in the early twentieth century. "Casual" anti-Semitism was so widespread in Germany that at
elections the Nazis did not need to flog it. It was enough to invoke strong
German nationalism and a casual, loose-tongued anti-Semitism – such as
the endlessly bellowed marching slogan "Germany Awake! Jewry Croak!"
Was this to be taken more seriously than the chants of modern football
hooligans? Even Jews doubted it, since few feared more than economic
discrimination and discomfort under Hitler. Most Germans disliked Jews,
or rather they disliked the dominant cultural images of "the Jew." But this
was not a high priority in their lives. As we saw in the last chapter, casual
anti-Semitism figured in the essays of half the Abel sample, but dominated
only a small minority. Only a handful of Nazi leaders were originally drawn
to the movement by anti-Semitism, and many Nazis were deeply troubled
by SA violence and anti-Jewish laws during the 1930s (see my forthcoming
volume for more sustained discussion of these themes).

Of course, Hitler was different, as were the Nazi intellectuals drawn from
the "Vienna-Munich" axis of *völkisch* nationalism that had arisen in the late
nineteenth and early twentieth centuries. Hitler had apparently not been
particularly anti-Semitic in prewar Vienna (says Hamann 1999). Yet the war
and the revolutionary years at the end of it seem to have changed him.
His writings in Germany before *Mein Kampf* contained three times as many
passages about Jews as Bolsheviks (Friedlander 1986: 26). By the time of
Mein Kampf he asserts that the stateless Jews were a "bacillus," "disease,"
"plague," "parasite," "contagion," or "virus" in the host body of other
nations. German Marxists and capitalists had both been infected by "spiritual
Judaism." Marxism, the Russian Revolution, and capitalism were *all* Jewish
plots. The Jew must be "removed altogether," "eliminated" "by the most
severe methods of fighting." Yet it is unclear quite what he meant by this.
Hitler used hyperbolic prose all the time, and when he got worked up, he
used violent words indiscriminately. In a conversation with him, Chancellor
Brüning once received the full treatment. Hitler bawled at him that he was
going to "annihilate" (*vernichten*) the KPD, the SPD, "the reaction," and
France and Russia – he did not here mention Jews (Kershaw 1998: 339).

It was still unclear, even perhaps to Hitler himself, what all this ethnic and political cleansing might practically entail (Gordon 1984: chaps. 3 and 4).

Nonetheless, the Nazi leaders knew enough about the priorities of Germans to downplay anti-Semitism at election time, except as the routine and casual accompaniment of antiusurer or anti-Bolshevik rhetoric. It was also useful in papering over the contradiction between transcendent ideals and pragmatic capitalist bias. If the adjective "Jewish" were casually added to Marxism and finance capital, they seemed bedfellows whose heads must be knocked hard together. But anti-Semitic policies relating to real-life Jews were not vote-winners, especially in the cities, where almost all Jews lived. Though the image of the Jew was usually negative, most Germans perceived Jews as either mildly useful or too minor a problem to decide their vote. So the party kept anti-Semitism as loose-tongued slogans – until dictatorship, war, and the SS state allowed different options (Kele 1972: 77; Grill 1983; Gordon 1984; Zofka 1986; Schleunes 1990).

Hitler would not have reached 5 percent of the votes if he had promised either a second world war or the murder of millions of Jews and Slavs. Nor did he seem to have such goals directly in mind. But the leading Nazis did hide from the electorate the systematic depth of their hatred. Amid more contingent events, these would later lead them into war and genocide. With the enormous exception of this deception (which was partly self-deception), the Nazis came to offer a fairly coherent, often sincere and plausible, and sometimes innovative electoral program based on organic nation-statism.

When the Depression made the ruling parties unpopular, the electorate began to respond more. From only a 3 percent vote in 1928 the Nazis reached 18 percent in 1930 and 37 percent in July 1932, dropping slightly to 33 percent in November 1932 (the last free election). One-third of Germans came to vote for them. This fell short of a majority, though in many democracies this would have given them the government. The Nazis had a higher percentage of the total electorate, for example, than today's Democrats or Republicans get in the United States. In Germany this did allow them constitutionally, as the largest single party, to try to form the next government. A clear majority could be obtained with the support of the other authoritarian-leaning parties, and together they did form a government. This was important since it meant that the Nazis did not have to launch a risky full-scale coup. In 1933 they were able to manipulate the Constitution's Emergency Powers Provisions. They did not have to break the Constitution.

Why did they get so many votes? Voting is a minimal act, usually involving little commitment to a party ideology. Contemporaries believed the NSDAP drew many protest votes – not surprising in a party identifying so many "enemies." When the German economy was in such trouble, one did not need to be a convinced fascist to consider voting for the NSDAP. "I've tried the others, its time to give Hitler a chance" was the simple motivation of many. From 1930 first-time voters provided 20 percent of the Nazi vote, a mixture of previous nonvoters and young voters (Falter 1986). Their knowledge of Nazism was perhaps limited. However, other correlates of voting Nazi suggest more resonance of Nazi ideas. Let us try to identify the core Nazi constituencies.

NAZI VOTERS

Religion and Region

In the major national studies, easily the best predictor of Nazi voting is religion (Falter 1986, 1991; Childers 1983). Of all registered voters in July 1932 (including people who did not vote), about 38 percent of Protestants supported the Nazis, only 16 percent of Catholics – a big difference. The greater the percentage of Protestants in an area, the greater its Nazi vote. In solid Catholic areas the Nazi vote was commonly below 10 percent, in solid Protestant areas it was commonly above 60 percent. All but seven of the 124 constituencies with the highest Nazi vote in 1930 were majority Protestant (Falter and Bömermann 1989). Even in the big cities, where the two faiths lived among each other, the religious impact was as important as class (Hamilton 1982: 38–42, 371–3, 382–5). And in the small towns with a population of fewer than 25,000, where two-thirds of Germans lived, religion far exceeded class as a predictor of Nazi voting.

Thus the electoral surge of the Nazis was disproportionately a surge among Protestants. Conversely, the collapse of the liberal and conservative parties in the face of the Nazi electoral surge was only a Protestant collapse. The two Catholic parties (the Center Party and the Bavarian BVP) managed to hold up their vote, which was correlated around .90 with the percentage of Catholics in a constituency. Thus Catholics in the Catholic areas barely wavered. Yet the three so-called bourgeois parties – the liberal DDP, the conservative DVP and the ultraconservative DNVP – had depended on Protestants. From 1928 the Nazis began to mop up much of these. Even the two ostensibly secular socialist parties were actually mostly Protestant, and so were at risk. The trend was greater among women: Catholic women voted overwhelmingly for the Center/BVP, Protestant women mostly for "bourgeois" parties, then for the Nazis (Falter 1986: 163–70).

Thus *all* other correlations reported here were only partial ones: It was overwhelmingly *Protestant* classes, *Protestant* veterans, *Protestant* students, a *Protestant* generation, and so on, which were drawn particularly toward Nazism. Strong Catholic communities were insulated against the charms of Nazism – just as a similar number of Germans were insulated inside cohesive "proletarian ghettos." In the end neither "reds" nor "blacks" were untainted by authoritarianism. The Catholic parties supported reactionary authoritarianism after 1930, in order to head off what they believed to be the worse dual threats of fascism and Bolshevism. In 1932–3 they cooperated with Hitler. And the Communist Party made its crazed attack on the "social fascism" of the SPD, during which it often cooperated with the Nazis. In the end the KPD and SPD united to oppose the Nazis, but this was verbal resistance. They finally submitted without a fight. All this meant that most Catholics, socialists, and communists exhibited only frailty and foolishness, not something worse.

The importance of religion to Nazism has been recognized, but under-theorized. In general, scholars stress Catholic resistance to Nazism, but see Protestantism less as pro-Nazi than as "weaker" than the Catholic Church, less able to resist (e.g., Brooker 1991: chap. 7). There are also puzzles. The association between Nazism and Protestantism was not constant. Initially, the core Nazis, especially the core theorists, tended to be renegade Catholics (like Hitler) coming from the Vienna-Munich axis. And from the late 1930s renegade Catholics were to reassert themselves, being disproportionately involved in the worst excesses of Nazism (see my forthcoming volume). Nor was the relationship constant across Europe. As we saw in Chapter 2, the democratic northwest was mostly Protestant – and its democratic Nordic areas were mostly Lutheran, which was the Protestant denomination doctrinally the closest to German Protestants. So why at this particular stage did German Protestants support Nazism?

The causal link runs less through theology or church strength than through the churches' relation to the nation-state. The Catholic Church looked askance at the German state. Catholicism's heartlands were in southern provinces incorporated fairly unwillingly into the Prussian-dominated *Kaiserreich* in the nineteenth century. The German Catholic Church was controlled from abroad and favored transnationalism, not "nation-statism." This had moved the Center Party toward support for liberal democracy, to resist the authoritarian tendencies of the *Kaiserreich*. Catholics who were less tied to Rome had looked to Catholic Vienna, not Protestant Berlin, for political protection. Thus they had imbibed pan-German aspirations (the union of all Germans), not the *Kleindeutsch* (little German) strategy of

Prussia. The Protestant Church – strictly, the Evangelical Church – had been in a complicated way the Established Church of Prussian Germany, and so was "nation-statist" in an implicitly *Kleindeutsch* way. It was actually a federation of various provincial *Länder* churches belonging to three Protestant denominations, Lutheran (the majority), Reform, and United. From the Reformation these churches had been headed in each German mini-state by its local ruler. After national unification (1871) they were administered and financed by each provincial *Land* government. Their assemblies, pulpits, and publications supported the *Kaiserreich* and its official values of discipline, piety, order, and hierarchy. Weimar had removed the monarchy and most state controls, but not the government subsidies or the identification with the nation-state. Thus the Evangelical Church remained, in its traditions and expectations, rather "nation-statist." It looked to the state to provide social order, positive Christian-German and mainly conservative values, and an active national social policy.

But such a Christian-conservative state no longer existed, and conservatives and Evangelicals were now searching for a stronger state capable of embodying German culture and morality. Few initially supported the Nazis. More drifted through *völkisch* or conservative organizations toward the Nazis. From the mid-1920s the irreligious Nazi leaders were surprised by a spate of Protestant churchmen endorsing the party from the pulpit and party platforms. Nazis in the small town of "Northeim" studied by Allen (1965) responded by adding prayers and hymns to meetings, and they ran "Christian-National" candidates for school board elections. Protestant themes attracted votes to the Nazis from the "bourgeois" parties. The Nazis thus succeeded in splitting the Evangelical Church, as they could not the Catholic. The Evangelical "German Christian" Nazi front organization won a two-thirds' majority in the Evangelical Church election of July 1933. But it then overreached itself, proposing to expunge the whole of the (Jewish) Old Testament from the Bible! Nonetheless, over half the church remained "Nazi German Christian," the rump forced to form an independent "Confessing Church" (Helmreich 1979; Brooker 1991: chap. 10). The affinity between Nazism and the Evangelical Church, evident in both membership and voting data, had an obvious ideological core: their common nation-statism. Since it was Protestant civil servants, Protestant students, Protestant veterans, and so on who were becoming Nazis, this doubled their nation-statism.

But once an expansionist Reich was established, the Evangelical Church might not offer such ideological support. A powerful Austria no longer existed to block union of all Germans in a single *Grossdeutsch* state. The further expansion of a German state would be mainly among Catholic Germans, in Austria, Silesia, and Alsace-Lorraine, while pan-Germanism had not been associated strongly with the *Kleindeutsch* Evangelical Prussian/ German state. My forthcoming volume shows a religious shift in the core Nazi constituency, from Protestant to (ex-)Catholic, occurring in the late 1930s as Nazism "radicalized."

Protestantism also helps to explain much of the regional pattern of voting. In the early elections Nazi support, though low, seems to have come from both religious communities. In 1924 two of their four regional votes of over 10 percent were in Protestant Mecklenburg and Franconia, two were in Catholic Bavaria. Yet by July 1932 the highest Nazi-voting regions were overwhelmingly Protestant: most of the Protestant northeast (East Prussia, Pomerania, Mecklenburg, Brandenburg, Lower Silesia, and Thuringia), the whole of the Protestant northwest, and the more Protestant parts of Hesse and Bavaria (i.e., Franconia). A secondary cause was also visible. Rural and agrarian Germany was somewhat more Nazi. Thus Protestant areas that voted less for the Nazis tended to be dominated by urban-industrial workers – Berlin, Saxony, and Western Westphalia/Rhineland Ruhr. These remained quite faithful to the left parties (Milatz 1965; Passchier 1980). A third cause of regional variations still lay half-concealed. The heaviest-voting Nazi areas were Schleswig-Holstein and the northeastern areas that were cut in two by Poland (the only other area voting over 45% Nazi in 1931 was Hanover). These might be described as "threatened border" areas, next to territories that the Versailles Treaty confiscated from Germany. It may be countered that the allies also took away German control from much of the Saar and Ruhr in the southwest, yet this did not produce high Nazi voting – since these areas were both majority-Catholic and urban-industrial. Once Catholics and the industrial working class lost their insulation from Nazism – after the seizure of power – "threatened border" regions were to emerge as the bastion of radical Nazism. But before the seizure of power, the core Nazi voting constituencies were primarily Protestant and secondarily rural.

Class

Much attention has been paid to class voting. Since we lack exit polls, we rely on ecological studies of voting. Were those polling districts voting more Nazi also more middle-class, as one prominent theory of fascism asserts? The first major ecological study was Hamilton's (1982) of the big cities. He found there support for bourgeois class theory: The higher the social class of an area, the more it voted Nazi. Most mixed areas, where he deduces more of the lower middle class lived, gave support close to the national average. But later studies have considerably qualified this finding. Childers (1983, 1984, 1991) analyzed the whole country. He found that up to 1928 the Nazis did best in areas with many artisans, small shopkeepers, and civil servants. From 1928 small farming areas joined in. Thus, he says, the original Nazi nucleus was among the "old" lower middle class – the classic petty bourgeoisie plus lower civil servants – but not the "newer" middle class of white-collar workers and managers. Since Childers classified most "artisans" as petty bourgeois rather than working-class, he probably overstated classic petty bourgeois support for Nazism. Up until 1930, Nazism would fit partially into the mold provided by petty bourgeois class theory. Thereafter, however, Childers accepts that support widened and class correlations weakened, usually into insignificance. He interprets this (not quite taking them seriously) as the Nazis becoming a national "catch-all" party of protest, "a mile wide but an inch deep."

Falter's (1986, 1991, 1998) national data are the most recent and the fullest. They support Childers's post-1930 conclusion. Falter shows that the proportion of workers in a constituency made little difference to the Nazi vote. Overall, there was no class bias. But there were important sectoral differences. Agricultural workers were the most Nazi (despite there being few party members among agricultural workers), then workers in construction, services, and public employment. But in industrial working-class areas the Nazi vote was lower – except for areas with government-owned plants. Childers (1983: 255) also found a relationship between Nazism and handicrafts and small-scale manufacturing, especially after 1932. So by 1930 the Nazis drew about 30 percent, and by 1932 some 40 percent, of their votes from workers. By then about 50 percent of German workers voted socialist or communist, 30 percent voted Nazi, 10 percent voted for the Catholic parties, and 10 percent for the "bourgeois" parties. There was much switching in the three "radical" parties after 1930. The Nazis attracted three million votes from the SPD, half a million from the KPD, while a million and half a million flowed in the reverse directions (Falter 1991: 116). The SPD had flirted with some *Volksgemeinschaft* ideology in the early 1920s, aware that many workers saw themselves as *both* working-class and German nationalists (Fischer 1995: 115–16). But, notes Falter, the Nazis actually did create a "Volksgemeinschaft-type of movement" (1998: 123).

The voting data confirm the membership data presented in the previous chapter. Workers were no less attracted to Nazism than were other classes. Middle-class theories of fascism are wrong, in the case of Germany. But the core of proletarian fascism lay not in large-scale private manufacturing in big cities, but in the agricultural, service, and government sectors and in smaller plants scattered through smaller towns and the countryside. Fascist workers were plentiful, not at the heart of contemporary class struggle but at its margins.

Falter also shows that among middle-class voters the Protestant small farming areas became distinctly Nazi in 1932, while Catholic ones voted Nazi at about the national level. The self-employed (though not independent artisans) were slightly Nazi, as were communities with many retired persons and housewives (cf. Childers 1983). Most white-collar areas were a little less Nazi when the effects of other variables are partialed out, though Falter says that the Nazis tended to be from the "old middle class" – independent businessmen, artisans, and farmers. Correlations between Nazi voting and civil servant numbers are modestly positive, weaker than in Childers's more aggregate data. Only rarely do Falter's correlations between middle-class groups and the Nazi vote exceed .20. But he also shows that Nazi voting was lower in areas of high unemployment, especially during the Depression. Prosperous Catholic areas still voted for the Center but prosperous Protestant areas turned Nazi. Areas of high unemployment voted socialist or communist. Employed persons from all classes were more attracted to Nazism than were the unemployed (cf. Stachura 1986). Economic success thus helps to explain Nazism more than does deprivation, as we saw was also the case among Nazi members. In Chapter 1 we saw that middle-class theories of fascism were often yoked together with theories of economic deprivation. Neither will work when applied to German voting – once the Nazis had become a force to be reckoned with.

CLASS, THE ECONOMY, AND THE DECLINE OF THE DEMOCRATIC PARTIES

However, middle-class theories might still be partially rescued. The Nazi vote rose largely at the expense of votes for the so-called bourgeois parties, that is, the conservatives and liberals (the DNVP, the DDP, and the DVP) and the smaller "special interest parties," such as the Peasants League, the Tenants Party, or the Interest Alliance. Childers (1991: 320) argues that the "bourgeois" parties made little attempt to cross class, regional, or religious cleavages, especially ignoring workers, while special interest parties focused on specific bourgeois occupations. Both, he says, practiced the politics of status group and profession.

In fact all the older parties bore the legacy of the prewar semi-authoritarian *Kaiserreich*. Since the Reichstag had not controlled the executive, its parties had not been ultimately responsible for policy. They had little experience in compromising with each other in order to produce a policy outcome, since the Kaiser's ministers had made the necessary deals. Parties tended to represent only their own special interest constitutencies. In its early years the Weimar Republic had held together because the formerly antisystem parties, the socialists and Catholic Center, had joined with some of the bourgeois parties in a broad coalition. When the socialists left the coalition, had the bourgeois parties been genuinely "liberal" or "conservative" in the broadest sense, they might have widened their appeal. But instead they carried on representing their narrow support base (Jones 1988). When the Nazis began to offer a broader vision, after 1928, they were able to mop up their voters. Conversely, two votes held up, the Catholic and the left (in which the communists gained at the expense of the socialists). The left appealed mostly to the urban working class, the Catholic parties to Catholics of all classes. All this might reinforce a class interpretation of the Nazi rise: "Bourgeois" organization collapsed as middle-class voters moved to the Nazis (Kitchen 1976). Though the middle class may have been no more likely to vote for the Nazis after 1930, it could have been shifts in the middle-class vote that brought about their success.

Yet can parties be identified so simply with classes? Some of the special interest parties were actually more sector- than class-specific. To win elections, peasant parties had to recruit laborers and dwarf holders as well as independent farmers. Handicrafts parties had to recruit masters *and* men. The "Interest Alliance" that won a quarter of Marburg's votes in 1924 represented renters, apartment- and house-hunters, veterans, land reformers, white-collar workers, and big families. It stressed consumers' interests and trawled as widely as it could for votes (Koshar 1986: 84). These were not merely bourgeois parties. Nor even were the so-called bourgeois liberal and conservative parties. They appealed to the nation, or alternatively to a middle class that supposedly included workers (as in contemporary American usage of the "middle class"). In most countries around one-third of workers vote routinely for conservative parties, mobilized by patron-client networks, believing in conservative ideologies or the superior competence of conservative notables. Falter (1986: 167–9) shows that the overall percentage of workers in a locality did not make much difference to the vote for the "bourgeois" parties (though the formerly liberal DVP got slightly more votes in areas with more workers). They all picked up most votes in the primary sector and fewest in industrial areas. The Nazis probably swept up most of the working-class supporters of the "bourgeois" parties – especially in agriculture and services – just as they swept up their supporters from other classes. These parties were bourgeois in leadership and usually in policies, but *not* in mass support. They would never have been major parties if they could only attract bourgeois support. So the Nazis seem to have swept up and to some extent "radicalized" most conservative-minded Germans of all classes.

Why did the conservatives and center collapse? Was it related to the health of the economy? The vote of the so-called bourgeois parties remained static at 35 to 37 percent during the inflation and stabilization crisis of 1923–4. It began its slide during the economic boom years. By the economic high point of May 1928, the "bourgeois" parties had lost almost a third of their electorate – *before* the Great Depression started (Childers 1991: 326). Meanwhile the Nazis had also quietly mopped up the votes of the smallish *völkisch* movement to become the major party of the radical right (Grill 1983). The first big Nazi breakthrough, at the local elections of 1930, was also before the recession bit. Even the national breakthrough, in December 1930, occurred before it was clear this was a "great" depression. The Nazis now became the main *völkisch* party, able also to tug at nationalist, statist, and anti-Semitic sentiments in the "bourgeois" parties. As they had risen, therefore, the "bourgeois" parties had declined continuously, over a decade – though the smaller "special interest" parties collapsed suddenly, near the end.

As a response to their decline, these parties all thought they saw the trend of the times and sought to move rightward. The liberal DDP had been unequivocally committed to the democratic republic, and it declined first (down to 1% of the vote by 1932). Its response was to favor strengthening the state. The conservative DVP had favored a constitutional monarchy, but when it lost votes (down to below 2% by 1932), it embraced semi-authoritarianism. The most conservative of the three, the DNVP, had inherited the mantle of prewar semi-authoritarianism. Its vote held up better than its rivals, but it still declined, to 8.3 percent in November 1932. By then it was at the heart of the reactionary authoritarian government of the immediate pre-Nazi period.

Thus voters supporting the "bourgeois" parties turned steadily against democracy. They shifted to the less democratic of these parties until 1930, then they voted Nazi. All three parties perceived this shift and reacted by turning away from democracy. Though the leadership of the parties was "bourgeois," their fears were founded on very widespread sentiment across the country outside the two internationalist "red and black," Marxist and Catholic, camps. Only these two subcultures strongly resisted the Nazi allure. Industrial workers surrounded by other industrial workers continued to vote for the left. Catholics living and working among other Catholics voted for Catholic parties. Both provided networks of voluntary associations to reinforce the party line. The Center held onto its votes in districts with more active churchgoing and increased its votes where priests made voting a confessional issue (Kühr 1973: 277–95). While the SPD, the KPD, and the Center held on to most of their stronghold constituencies, the Nazis had stolen half the strongholds of the "bourgeois" parties (Falter and Bömermann 1989). Outside these two communities Germans were at risk, regardless of class – indeed, *most* of them may have voted Nazi in 1932. Unpalatable as it might be, most of the German nation that was neither "red" nor "black" turned steadily against liberal democracy, and then toward Nazism. The Nazis were a national party in two distinct senses. They did appeal broadly across the nation. But they also mobilized the nation in a more mythical sense, against two large and supposedly "antinational" communities within Germany, the "reds" and the "blacks." The Nazis did not appeal specifically to the bourgeoisie or the petty bourgeoisie, but they did specifically appeal to Protestants of all classes, and they radicalized them. That was the core of their mass constituency.

WEIMAR ELITES

We must now turn to upper-class theories of fascism. The Nazis did not attain an electoral majority. As in Italy, they came to power helped by backstairs plots among upper-class and elite groups. Elites began to gravitate toward authoritarianism from 1930, when coalition government began to creak under the strain of the Great Depression. Brüning's center-right government began to avoid the Reichstag, ruling by presidential decree under the Constitution's emergency powers. Then the semi-authoritarian regimes of von Papen and von Schleicher brought the first actual repression. Then in 1933 von Papen and Hindenburg invited Hitler, now the leader of the largest Reichstag party, to join the cabinet. This was a brief attempt at semi-reactionary authoritarianism. But Hitler was not much of a sharer. Helped by President Hindenburg's death, he quickly took over the entire government and established the Nazi dictatorship. Who were implicated in this drift of elites toward fascism, and what were their motivations?

Let us consider first the usual suspects in this type of theory – capitalists – and their likely motives. In the case of Germany the argument has to concern only one of the two "capitalist motives" I have been identifying, that is, the desire for profit rather than property defense. German capitalists might have reasonably shown some concern for basic property rights during the immediate postwar years – though actually the moderate Social Democrats had then been quite willing to bring in the troops and rightist paramilitaries to crush the few actual revolutionaries. But by the end of the 1920s the SPD was monolithically moderate and respectable, and though the communist KPD was growing, it tended to mobilize the least powerful groups of workers. There was no significant threat to property from the left. But through 1929 to 1933 capitalists might feel squeezed between Great Depression and the progressive taxation and welfare policies of the Weimar Republic and so seek repression wielded by an authoritarian regime as a solution to profitability.

Capitalist support for Weimar had been indeed lukewarm, born not of conviction but of aversion for the threat of postwar "revolution." Many were initially unhappy with the postwar social and labor reforms. Unemployment insurance, public housing, and municipal projects were paid for out of progressive taxation, including wealth and corporation taxes. Labor laws restricted the working day, forced employers to hire the disabled and veterans, prohibited unfair dismissal, and forced employers to recognize trade unions, to consult with factory councils, to submit to government arbitration, and to seek government approval if laying off more than fifty workers. Even before the Depression, employers were growing restive. Thus Ruhr iron and steel bosses launched a lockout in 1928 to resist a government-imposed wage settlement.

The Depression increased their unhappiness. Taxes were raised on them as government expenses rose but profits declined. Heavy industry suffered most, though political differences between sectors were not great (Geary 1990; Patton 1994). Most politically active capitalists approved the rightward drift of the "bourgeois" parties. They wanted deflation, more labor market flexibility, cuts in welfare, a break with the SPD, and government by presidential decree. Some economic historians argue that the Depression simply put too much pressure on Weimar democracy, which could not solve the structural economic weaknesses it exposed (Borchardt 1982; James 1990). Excessive wages and welfare payments plus labor market rigidities were protected by conciliatory Weimar institutions. A reflationary strategy was blocked since foreign loans would have carried unacceptable conditions and domestic loans would have led to inflation (and possibly breached Reichsbank rules). There was in any case a low rate of domestic savings. This economic theory of Weimar breakdown might be extended into explaining the repressive solution: The republic, it might be said, embodied too much worker power for the liking of many capitalists, so they turned first to semi-authoritarians, then to the Nazis, for repressive salvation. Indeed, many of the actors – even some of the Nazi leaders – believed that this is what was happening after 1930. I am inclined to agree that if there had been no Great Depression, there would have been no Nazi regime. For the Nazis to surge into power, Weimar breakdown was a necessary precondition. And it was the Great Depression that rocked the somewhat precarious republic. But did it happen through the agency of class conflict? This seems more dubious.

The first counterargument had been made by economists perceiving a viable alternative class scenario. Holtfrerich (1990) argues that the low rate of domestic savings could have been tackled by agreement among capital, labor, and a government diverting resources into popular savings schemes. Perhaps such policy solutions require a degree of Keynesian wisdom from contemporaries that was available only rather later. Yet the northwestern democracies facing Depression offered democratic solutions that did not involve great wisdom. Politicians muddled their way through day-to-day crises. British Conservatives waited for the governing Labour Party to split and then did a deflationary deal with its right wing. In the United States the New Deal offered a proindustrial counterdeflationary strategy, buying the support of moderate unions, "corporate liberals," and an internationally oriented fraction of capital. Scandinavians began to enter collective agreements among capital, labor, farmers, and government to restructure labor markets and mildly reflate. None of these solutions as yet made an enormous amount of economic difference. Nor did they claim to "transcend" class conflict. But they did deepen class conciliation. The democratic solution combined slight alleviation of suffering with making the parties and classes jointly responsible for the mess. This was no revolution – on balance in most countries most of the pain fell on the workers, in the shape of unemployment. German conservatives could have developed their own version. A few tried, but most did not – they preferred solutions escalating along the authoritarian continuum to fascism. Something more than mere economic pressure is required to explain this.

The second counterargument is that few capitalists figured among the Nazis or even in the plots of von Papen, von Schleicher, and the circle around President Hindenburg. Gregor Strasser aptly labeled Schleicher's proposed semi-reactionary authoritarian government "the cabinet of anti-capitalist longing." Even fewer capitalists turned to the Nazis. A meeting at Bad Harzburg in October 1931 has often been assumed to mark the first major cooperation between industrialists and Nazis. But Turner (1985) has shown that only one powerful industrialist was present, the others being smaller businessmen or relatively unimportant company executives. Indeed, most capitalists seem to have hoped that more conservative authoritarians would deflate the economy, abrogate labor reforms, *and* control Hitler.

The third counterargument is that most capitalists did not want a Nazi regime since they distrusted Nazi economics and feared Nazi radicals. Press and cinema newsreels barons seem to have been the closest to being Nazi sympathizers. Hugenberg, an extreme nationalist, controlled the largest media empire. Under his leadership the DNVP shifted to semi-reactionary authoritarianism. He made the world-historical mistake of giving favorable coverage of the Nazis, believing his fortunes and those of the Nazis would rise together. Most popular newspapers were rather apolitical, preferring to report personalities, scandals, and sports. They reported Nazi activities briefly, though usually without hostility. Most of the quality press supported the bourgeois parties, viewed as combating "the internationalist Marxist parties . . . who would destroy people and nation, family and German spirit" (as the *Hamburger Nachtrichten* put it). Nazi "socialism" equally turned them off. But as the bourgeois parties declined, some quality newspapers came to see the Nazis as just overenthusiastic patriots: "[S]harp and ruthless national fighters," said the *Rheinisch-Westfälische Zeitung*, endorsing them in 1932. The Nazis now received more favorable press coverage, which increased their vote (says Hamilton 1982: 125, 165). This was quite general across the early twentieth century: Media barons mobilized a populist nationalism that boosted audiences and moved politics rightward. In Britain the Northcliffes and Beaverbrooks boosted conservative imperialism; so did men such as Hearst in the United States; in Germany they moved conservatism back into authoritarianism. I have no good explanation of this, but it was of some political significance, given the ideological power of media barons.

Yet most of business distrusted the Nazis. Hitler kept assuring them he hated socialism, but they feared the Nazi radicals of the Economic Policy Section. Nazi violence worried them, but the Nazis did not attack property rights – they assaulted those who did. The Nazi "authority principle" was congenial. They would have greatly preferred other solutions. Yet the enemy of my enemy may be my friend. Many finally welcomed their accession to power, few had helped them, but even fewer had hindered them.[1] This is not massive capitalist culpability, unlike in Italy.

The fourth counterargument is that there was an absence of profound class struggle in Germany. The countryside was especially peaceful. Turbulence had peaked in 1918–20 and then declined. KPD growth after 1930 was a little worrying, since communists preached revolution. But this was a minority party, mainly recruiting the powerless unemployed. The socialist SPD and its unions were far larger. Since 1925 they had been formally committed to a "class struggle" line. But in reality the SPD was moderate, having run several *Länder* governments for over a decade. "Class struggle" rhetoric reappeared whenever the SPD felt the KPD was stealing its votes, but the SPD fought neither Brüning's deflationary strategy nor Hitler's half-coup. There was objectively no revolution in the offing – except the Nazi one. There was no need for capitalists to defend their property. No one was likely to expropriate it. If profit was all that concerned them, why were they not more pragmatic in their political economy?

But class arguments might make a riposte at this point. Perhaps capitalists were motivated by a more diffuse fear of violence, concerning supposed "anarchy" as much as class conflict. There were some major disturbances. Yet, as usual, socialists were more victims than perpetrators: 22 murders committed by leftists resulted in an average sentence of 15 years for 38 persons plus 10 death sentences; 354 murders committed by rightists resulted in average sentences of four months for 24 persons – and no death sentences. Though in 1927 the 22 rightist killers who were members of the "Black Reichswehr" conspiracy received six death sentences and six long prison sentences, the death sentences were commuted, and only two of the defendants were still in prison three years later. When the rightist paramilitary *Stahlheim* marched, police protection was arranged; when leftists marched, the police harassed them (Tilly 1975: 224–5, 229; Southern 1982: 339). The SPD "militia" remained defensive, and until 1928 so did the KPD. But then the Comintern instructed Communist parties that "the mass-struggle of the proletariat . . . [will] . . . burst the bounds of . . . trade-union legality." The communists became more violent. Yet by 1931, of 29 persons killed, 12 were communists, two socialists, six Nazis, one *Stahlheimer*, four policemen, and four of unknown affiliation – a ratio of two leftists to one rightist. Then the communists, afraid, drew back, saying that anything more than vigorous self-defense might alienate neutral workers and compromise party ideals (Newman 1970: 227–36; Merkl 1980: chap. 2; 1982: 377; Rosenhaft 1982: 343–52). The left's flirtation with violence had been brief and ineffective.

In contrast the Nazis embraced tactical paramilitary violence from the beginning. But it was small-scale. Unlike the Italian *squadristi*, they never launched full-scale military attacks, never besieged socialist headquarters nor drove them out of towns. Parades, uniforms, flags, and a sense of disciplined power were used to impress, to launch provocative demonstrations and marches, and to break up enemy rallies. It was aimed to provoke rival movements, not the state. It did not alienate state elites but it did cow the rival movements. In July 1932 it was not the Nazis but the semi-authoritarian von Papen who used executive powers to remove the socialist Prussian provincial government. Goebbels wrote in his diary, "You've only got to bare your teeth to the Reds and they lie down. The Social Democrats and the trade unions don't lift a finger. . . . The Reds have missed their chance. There won't be another." The next year the Nazis seized power. The SPD protested to the constitutional authorities, the communists "went underground" but did little. The right, not the left, committed almost all the German violence – and capitalists did not need fascists to defeat German socialism. Since they knew this, they did not at first favor them.

However, other elite groups were much more complicit. The army was crucial, since its military capacity could have overwhelmed the Nazi paramilitaries. The Nazi leadership was careful with the army, believing it would resist an out-and-out coup attempt. But while many older officers opposed Hitler, younger ones often sympathized. The armed forces wanted rearmament above all else, and this was exactly what the Nazis were consistently promising (Geyer 1990). In contrast, publicly declared the High Command, the Weimar Republic would not give it the resources to be able to defend Germany with "any chance of success." By 1932 its loyalty was more to the head of state, the renowned ex-general Hindenburg, than to the republic, while political generals such as Schleicher were players in the semi-authoritarian intrigues around the head of state. In truth the political leadership of the republic had never possessed a real monopoly of the means of military violence. The armed forces had retained much of their professional autonomy, sitting apart from political strife, grumbling yet nourishing their own sense of pride and honor. After 1930, however, both semi-authoritarians and Nazis were politicizing among the troops and the officer corps. Generals such as Blomberg and Reichenau admired Hitler and openly supported the Nazi constitutional maneuvers that avoided the necessity for a coup.

Thus in 1933 the army's loyalty was not actually tested. There was no "march on Berlin" against which a legitimate government might have sought to deploy it. Yet the army was clearly now split, no longer a separate coherent caste. While most of the High Command remained deeply professionally jealous of the SA, clearly a potential rival, some regional army groups were actually training SA units (Fischer 1995: 22, 132). Since Hitler had great plans for the German armed forces, once in power he needed to restore its unity and professionalism and ensure its commitment to his regime. He was able to sweep away most army opposition by murdering Röhm and the SA leadership in June 1934 – with army assistance. Within two months every German soldier was swearing a personal oath of loyalty to the Fuhrer. With the help of several purges of the High Command, the army was then lured into bed with the Nazis, implicated in their worst atrocities (see my forthcoming book).

There was no Nazi coup. The last legitimate governments of the Weimar Republic acquiesced in their own downfall. Leading civil servants, judges, and the leaders of the "bourgeois" and Catholic parties were especially complicit, though less in the Nazi coup than in ditching democracy. These were the old regime circles in which Carl Schmitt moved, and his ideas (discussed in Chapter 2) were very influential. Brüning, leader of the Catholic Center Party and Chancellor from 1930 to 1932, embraced Schmitt's notion that the state had to be "above" the contending "armies" encroaching on the state. He used the economic crisis to rule by decree "above" party political strife. Through 1932 parliament met on only fourteen days. Brüning saw the semi-authoritarian *Kaiserreich* of the pre-1918 period as his constitutional model (Mommsen 1991: 84–5). But von Papen, von Schleicher, and Hindenburg (and Schmitt) thought the monarchy obsolete. They engineered his dismissal. The DNVP and *Stahlhelm* leaders, plus generals and civil service chiefs, briefly became the leading players. Representing not modern capitalism but the last bastions of the old regime and old money still entrenched in the state, they foolishly believed they could either split the Nazis between Strasser and Hitler or bring the whole NSDAP into alliance with them. The transition to Nazi dictatorship was accomplished through the last flailings of old regime leaders, the law courts, and the higher civil service. In Hitler's first cabinet there were only four Nazis but five conservative aristocrats, Hugenberg the DNVP media magnate, the DNVP head of the *Stahlhelm*, and a Catholic rightist. For at least two years, these rightist nationalists had wanted authoritarian government but could not accomplish it themselves. Only the Nazis could provide the shock-troops for the elite. Since the Nazis also possessed the will to power, the game was up for the old regime.

Thus Germany differed from Italy, where most of the ruling class was involved in the fascist half-coup. Here ruling class aid was very uneven. In fact, elite support mirrored popular support. It was stronger outside the main bastions of modern capitalism. German industrial and financial leaders did not oppose Hitler but neither did they do much to help him. The main help came from the dying remnants of the old regime, somewhat removed from the heartlands of class conflict. They saw the crisis as the constitutional theorist Carl Schmitt had seen it. "Mass armies" of class and nationalism had invaded the liberal-conservative parliamentary debating space, as well as (through welfare programs) the ministries. There was no longer a higher, neutral state able to arbitrate their claims authoritatively. The Chancellor's Emergency Powers (for which the great sociologist Max Weber was partly responsible, and for which the renowned jurist Carl Schmitt now offered a vigorous legal defense) offered a breathing space. But – they again agreed with Schmitt – the required state really needed a new elite. Though some believed they were it, they were soon forced to recognize the superior claims of the Nazis.

THE CRISIS OF CLASS AND ECONOMIC THEORIES OF NAZISM

I have now presented four empirical objections to directly economic and class theories of the rise of Nazism.

(1) The decay of Weimar democracy had continued through both good and bad economic times, as the electorate and the "bourgeois" parties gradually withdrew their support. It had hastened with the Depression, and this was important. Nazism was already becoming significant within Germany, yet the Depression may well have been a necessary cause of its surge to power. That is probably the core truth of economic explanations of Nazism. Nonetheless, other causes besides economic crisis must also have been involved in the decay.

(2) The key Nazi constituencies, though alarmed by class confrontation, were not very directly involved in it and were among the least affected by economic crisis and deprivation.

(3) Capitalists were involved in the overstraining of democratic government, but they were not main players in its actual collapse, still less in the Nazi coup. On balance their contribution was not supportive of Weimar democracy but neither did they usually support the Nazis.

(4) The "crisis" and "class stalemate" period was too short and too lacking in political initiatives to explain an entire break with democracy – unless this was already groggy from other blows (as Kershaw 1990 also notes).

In fact, class theories of Nazism have been decaying for some years. Kele (1972), Mason (1995), Merkl (1980: 153), and Eley (1983) had years ago emphasized that there was considerable working-class support for Nazism. More recent writers have moved rather grudgingly away from class theory, accepting instead more of Nazism's view of itself. Stachura (1993) abandoned his former class interpretations (1975: 58; 1983b) to suggest that nationalism, widely shared by Germans of all classes, was the key to Nazi success. Falter (1991: 51ff., 169–93) sees Nazism as a broad national "popular party of protest." Mühlberger (1987: 96, 124; 1991: 202–9) and Childers agree that the Nazis were more a national than a class movement, though they argue that this made them relatively incoherent. Nazism, says Childers, was

a remarkable heterogeneous coalition of social forces. Yet, just as that support was remarkable broad, it was also remarkably shallow. . . . [T]he socially disparate elements of the National Socialist constituency formed a highly unstable political compound, and signs of its nascent decomposition were already evident in the November [1932] elections . . . [not] a movement of genuine social integration, a *Volksbewegung*, as its leaders maintained. Instead, the NSDAP was ultimately a highly volatile catch-all party of protest whose successes were built on economic crisis and whose constituency was tenuously held together by anger, frustration, and fear. (1984: 53; cf. 1991)

Eley (1983) suggests that Nazi ideology centered on "national populism" or "right-wing Jacobinism," defined as "activist, communitarian, antiplutocratic, and popular, but at the same time virulently antisocialist, anti-Semitic, intolerant of diversity, and aggressively nationalist." Fascism, he concludes, "becomes primarily a type of politics, involving radical authoritarianism, militarized activism, and the drive for a centrally repressive state." This is close to my own view. But to explain its popularity, Eley then returns us toward class analysis: Class confrontation produced the political stalemate that allowed the Nazis in. This seems overstated. Fischer goes a little further: The Nazi *Volksgemeinschaft* was a truly national ideology, shared by millions of Germans of all classes. He suggests it was recognizably of the same twentieth-century family as the notion of "citizenship," which privileges national integration over class confrontation (1995: 125–8). This is very close to my own position that Nazism offered a plausible transcendent nation-statism.

Yet none of these scholars goes the next step, to identify a nationalist constituency that gave structural coherence to the Nazi movement. Indeed, Baldwin (1990) goes to the other extreme. Since he accepts that class will not explain things, he believes all "social interpretations" are finished. He rejects all social structure in favor of a psychological interpretation. "Anomie" and "uprootedness," he argues, indicate the *absence* of social structure in the Nazi appeal. Like many others, he seems to believe that "economic" or "class" equals "social": If class explanations of Nazism do not work, then Nazism must have lacked all social structure. These historians could benefit from a little more sociology, to appreciate that there are other social structures besides classes and markets. Nazi coherence rested – just as Italian fascism probably did – in the social constituency of what I termed "transcendent paramilitary nation-statism."

CONCLUSION: MOBILIZING THE CONSTITUENCY OF TRANSCENDENT
PARAMILITARY NATION-STATISM

Let me finally assemble the overall core Nazi constituency, providing enough committed members and sympathizers to permit the Nazi seizure of power. Of course, Nazis came from across the country, across its social, age, and gender structures. I make no claim to have explained all the German support for them, only its disproportionate core sources. One of these was at this stage Protestant, because the Evangelical Church saw itself as the soul of the German nation-state. Nazism was also strongly rooted among ethnic German refugees and among Germans from border areas that could be plausibly regarded as "threatened." It was strongly rooted among public sector employees, especially among men who had experienced military discipline, but also among civil servants, state-employed teachers, and public sector manual workers. All these might especially look to a strong state as the solution to social problems, but believe the Weimar state to be divided and feeble. It was strongly rooted among the universities and in the most educated strata in the population, imbued with a *völkisch* nationalism. All of these groups shared "nation-statism," the belief that an activist state, embodying the culture of the *Volk*, could embody collective moral purposes.

These environments, already rightist nationalist before the war, then nourished the key carriers of fascism, two generations of young males launching paramilitary violence against "foreign" enemies at home and abroad. Members and militants from this core had stronger social roots to the nation-state than to modern industrial capitalism or class struggle. Their collective movement borrowed socialist notions of committed militancy and comradeship, adding a distinctive paramilitarism that heightened the caging of the youthful members. They were committed, "consciously German," and some were very idealistic, while others were very violent (and some were both). The overall combination confused onlookers who were not interpreting social reality through the prism of either socialist or Catholic communities.

As well as these key carriers – thousands marching and assaulting – the Nazis attracted more diffuse support from most classes and generations – millions voting or sympathizing. The most striking characteristic of this broader one-third of the German population was that it was somewhat removed from the front line of class struggle. It was mainly outside the big city industrial areas, outside the sphere of the organized industrial working class, outside the highest, most modern circles of capital, outside the economically fraught world of the independent petty bourgeoisie, outside the high unemployment areas of the Great Depression. This popular support was most likely to fall for the Nazi paramilitary tactic that Nazi violence was only defensive and required buttressing by a regime more thoroughly committed to order. Popular support was reinforced by the more secretive machinations of a military and a civilian old regime that was also somewhat removed from the main arenas of modern class struggle. The sympathizers were not marginal to society as a whole. They were not deprived or alienated. They were more from agriculture, the public sector, the professions, education, small workshops, and small towns. Thus class conflict resulting in a supposed "class stalemate" was an important cause of the rise of Nazism to power – not primarily because Nazism represented some classes in conflict with other classes (though it was not entirely neutral, either), but because it promised to transcend class conflict, and because this promise was minimally plausible in terms of policies offered and the social composition of those who offered them.

Most of these Germans were tired of class politics and German national weakness. Prewar conflict between the *Kaiserreich* old regime and the ostensibly Marxist proletariat had actually been rather ritualized, and so through it all Germany had remained united and strong. But the war had destabilized the rituals and weakened both the old regime and the nation as a whole. A crushing and unexpected war defeat could be plausibly blamed on either the reactionary elites in charge of the war effort or on the socialists who lacked patriotism and assumed governmental responsibility for the surrender. Germans then witnessed the turbulent class confrontations of the early postwar years, the loss of German territories, the burden of reparations, all enforced by foreign powers, enriching the French, the British, and the Slav populations of the east. Complicit in all these "internationalist" humiliations were the socialists and liberals who ran early Weimar and, perhaps less plausibly, the Jews. Germans then witnessed two international economic disasters – the inflation crisis and especially the Great Depression – which also brought a limited revival of class conflict. This one-third of Germans could be persuaded to curse foreigners and both class camps. Socialism offered only an utopian future and a chaotic present – as "Bolshevism" or "Judeo-Bolshevism" (as White Russian exiles and eastern ethnic Germans claimed) was doing just then in Russia. German socialists lacked the support and the resolve to overthrow capitalism. They brought no solution, only more problems. Nor could an industrial and financial capitalism, identified with internationalism, Judaism, liberalism, and Depression, overcome socialism and regenerate the economy. Nor did either great class camp seem willing to do much to remedy the laws of capitalist economics.

Hitler offered another solution, plausibly asserting that he would subordinate class conflict and capitalist "laws" to the common good of the nation – just as he would submit foreign powers and their domestic lackeys to resurgent German power. To this third of the German population, located where it was, there seemed two plausible tasks: for a transcendent "third force" to acquire state power to overcome class conflict by any means necessary and to achieve progress by mobilizing a German national solidarity against all forms of divisiveness and foreignness. These seemed good reasons for taking Nazis seriously and sympathetically – for giving them a chance.

To those of us living amid functioning democracies, a military and an economic crisis still do not seem enough to cry out for such an extreme solution. That the Nazis would abolish democracy if they came to power was quite well known. Germany was not in chaos; its depression was no worse than the American depression. Democracy can handle such level of crisis. Party politics operate, as Lipset famously noted, as "the democratic translation of the class struggle." Yet this is to ignore the political crisis of the German state. An advanced parliamentary democracy had not yet institutionalized its rules of the game as the only rules in town. The rapidity of the transition had left conservative parts of parliament and the executive with ambivalent feelings toward democracy. Elites still felt they had an alternative authoritarian option. Nor was the most pro-Nazi part of the German population strategically placed to initiate class and democratic compromise. Instead it was strategic and receptive to a "nation-statist" solution: an "autonomous" state standing "above" class conflict, pursuing the demands of the nation. Conservatives preferred a semi-authoritarian *Kaiserreich*. But that had been destroyed by catastrophic war defeat. Not only the monarchy but also the formerly ruling conservative and national-liberal parties of the prewar period had been destroyed. The civil service was largely intact, but the army was radically cut back, licking its wounds, reluctant to intervene. As in Italy, the armed forces were immobilized by both old regime disintegration and their own receptivity to the paramilitary and militarist leanings of fascism. In neither country did fascists merely triumph merely through public opinion or the ballot box. They also deployed paramilitary force entwined with electoralism and they could also count on some elite sympathy for their goals and their paramilitary means. The old regime had been immobilized. Any milder authoritarianism would have to depend on the successor conservative and centrist parties, all (except the Catholic party) in decline, and the civil service. From 1930 these did indeed attempt their own authoritarian rule, but lacking the capacity for social mobilization, they failed. The shrewd use of these three resources – highly committed militants, widespread voter sympathy, and elite ambivalence and weakness – allowed the Nazi leaders to seize power with a mixture of coercion, electoral contest, and constitution manipulation.

The Nazis were indeed a third force – but less a third-class force than a distinctive nation-statist force that promised a "cleansing" paramilitarism. In descending order of explicitness the nation was to be cleansed of Bolsheviks/Marxists, Jews, Slavs, divisive politicians, and internationalists. Exactly what was meant by terms such as "exclusion" or "elimination" was unclear, especially to the German electorate, whose attention span was as limited as most electorates'. Had more than a handful bothered to wade through *Mein Kampf*, Hitler's drift might have been clearer. But it needed other conditions, occurring after the seizure of power, to add mass murder to that drift – as my forthcoming volume shows.

6

Austro-Fascists, Austrian Nazis

During World War II the Allies proclaimed Austria "the first victim of Nazi aggression." To define the 1938 *Anschluss* as a German invasion was to depict Austrians as innocent victims and Austrian fascists as a clique of collaborators, not a national mass movement. This is a distinctive way of not taking them seriously. The youthful wartime activities of the U.N. Secretary-General Kurt Waldheim that were revealed in 1988 shocked the world because they seemed to put him into this terrible extremist clique. Yet the truth is more shocking. Waldheim was no deviant, just a young, ambitious Austrian officer "doing his duty" (he said), assigned in the Balkans to assist in what the regimental reports termed "cleansings" to be carried out "without pity or mercy," since "only a cold heart can command what needs to be commanded." The majority of the Austrian electorate may have also thought this normal Austrian behavior, since despite the revelations they then voted him in as President of Austria (Ashman and Wagman 1988: chap. 4; Sully 1989).

Indeed, Austria might seem the most fascist country in the interwar world, since it had two fascist movements, each with mass support, each able to seize power and to govern the country. Yet some of their success was due to Austria's position as a lesser Germanic power. The successes of Hitler were especially admired and emulated in Austria. Yet Austrians then contributed substantially to the German war effort and especially to the Final Solution, whose perpetrators were disproportionately Austrian (as we see in my forthcoming book). Austrian anti-Semitism was particularly brutal, sometimes shocking German SS officers administering deportations of Jews from the country (Botz 1987b; Bukey 1989, 1992; Ferenc 1989: 217; Parkinson 1989: 319–22; Stühlpfarrer 1989: 198–204). This chapter seeks to explain why fascism involving strong anti-Semitism was so popular in Austria. Though "the ordinary Austrian" was neither a fascist nor a murderer, the extent to which these acquired legitimacy, was nowhere greater than in Austria. So I ask who the Austrian fascists were, how they acquired legitimacy, and how they came to power.

TWO NATION-STATES, TWO FASCISMS

In 1918 the Austrian nation-state was brand-new. Until that year Austria had been the heartland of the multinational Austro-Hungarian monarchy, ruling over fifty million people spread across much of Eastern and Southeastern Europe. Now a rump republic covered only that smallish country we call Austria, with six and a half million people, of whom 94 percent were ethnically German. But if Austrian Germans were now to have a nation-state, which one would it be? There were two possible candidates: Austria itself – a second *Kleindeutsch* state – or *Anschluss*, union with neighboring Germany (the *Grossdeutsch* solution). The two rival fascisms became the more extreme versions of the two possible answers to this basic "national question." Their extremism had two basic sources: a positive valuation of statism derived from this having been the heartland of a great historic state, and a positive valuation of a revisionist nationalism in reaction against that "cosmopolitan" Empire and the Slav states that had displaced it. "Revisionism" was also double-edged. Austrians knew they could not restore empire themselves. Either Germans under the leadership of Germany could restore lost territories and dominion or they could recriminate against those "traitors" who had lost them.

The movement generally called "Austro-fascism" wavered around the option of an independent but recriminating Austria. Austro-fascism emerged out of paramilitaries formed in the aftermath of World War I, then consolidated into the *Heimwehr* ("Homeguard") rightist paramilitary of the late 1920s and early 1930s, and out of the conservative Christian Social Party, which won around 40 percent of the national vote in interwar elections and headed all the elected governments. The Christian Socials offered old regime continuation from the Habsburgs: No monarch, but a Catholic conservative nationalism with some authoritarian leanings. They were strongly rooted among the middle classes and across most of the countryside and provincial towns. But from 1930 their government depended on support in parliament from the more "radical" deputies of the *Heimwehr*. Most Christian Social leaders, including Chancellors Dollfüss and Schüschnigg, now drifted through corporatism toward fascism, though their fascism was more one of intentions than accomplished practices.

Austro-fascists drew heavily on the Catholic Church and the Habsburg legacy. The new Republic of Austria had been reduced down to the Empire's Catholic heartland, distinctively conservative, attached to hierarchy and order. Yet old regime conservatism was now widely considered insufficient. Fascism seemed to offer a more modern alternative. Mussolini offered a promising blend of nationalist mobilization and hierarchical corporatism, resonating here in Social Catholicism and in a romantic view of the supposedly corporate "estate" traditions of Austrian history. Conservatives might thus continue to rule by appropriating the more "top-down" elements of fascism. This was the main thrust of Austro-fascism. In its desire to modernize and mobilize while also relying on the power of traditional social hierarchies, it began semi-authoritarian and then moved to semi-reactionary authoritarianism and beyond. Though it drew some doctrines from Italian fascism, it most resembled the Franco and Salazar regimes: authoritarian, corporatist, traditionalist, a Catholic strain of fascist ideology lacking the turbulent, violent mass paramilitarism characteristic of German and Italian fascism. Its *Heimwehr* paramilitary did aim to fill this role, but had only limited success. The single party introduced in 1934, "The Fatherland Front," was (like its Spanish and Portuguese counterparts) a top-down organization, integrated into the traditional state. Its leaders wanted mass members the better to control them, and people joined in order to get on. Chancellor Schüschnigg, visiting an industrial town, is said to have asked a local party boss about local conditions:

"Well," came the reply, "there is a little handful of communists, perhaps two or three per cent. The Nazis, unfortunately, are fairly strong; lets say twenty per cent, perhaps twenty-five ... the 'Reds' were always well organized here. There is no doubt that sixty per cent remain with them and possibly even..." "My God!" interrupted Schüschnigg, "How many are in the Fatherland Front?" "Why everybody, Herr Chancellor – absolutely one hundred per cent." (Pauley 1981: 160)

The *Heimwehr* provided most of the radicalism. It began as a loose association of paramilitaries formed around 1918, fighting against "reds" and foreigners in border regions. After the territories were lost, nationalist recrimination took over their rhetoric. I leave anti-Semitism until later, but Austro-fascism expressed "Aryan" nationalism, with a strong sense of the "enemy," aiming to unify "the entire German *Volk*" to "fight against Marxism and bourgeois democracy, [for the] creation of an authoritarian state" and to "combine on a *völkisch* basis and eliminate the international Jewish rabble which is sucking the last drop of blood from our veins." It inherited the *völkisch* tradition of denouncing capitalism as "Jewish," but funding by employers undermined its claims to be a "third force" (Siegfried 1979). Nor could it agree on the form of its authoritarian state. The 1930 rambling Korneuburg Oath advocated seizing the state and remolding the economy: "[W]e repudiate western parliamentary democracy and the party state," desiring "government by the corporations (*Stände*)" and "fighting against the subversion of our *Volk* by Marxist class-struggle and liberal and capitalist economics"; corporatism "will overcome the class struggle" since "the state is the personification of the whole *Volk*." The enemy was "Bolshevism, Marxism and their handmaid, the democratic-parliamentarian party system, the causes of the existing corruption and the principal enemies of *völkisch* traits, Christian convictions, German ideology [and] . . . a Germanic racial consciousness." One leader declared that "only fascism could now save us (loud and enthusiastic applause)" (quotes from Carsten 1977: 44, 47, 172, 213–14; Jedlicka 1979: 226, 233–4). Though lacking an actual policy program, the slogans sounded fascist: Cleanse the nation from its ethnic/political enemies and establish authoritarian statism. But the claim to class transcendence was undercut by an evident capitalist bias. What "cleansing" might imply, moreover, was obscure. Most Christian Social politicians implied only discrimination and second-class citizenship for their enemies, but some *Heimwehr* activists seemed to imply a great deal more. Seeing their enemies in racial terms, they believed they could not be "converted" or persuaded to cooperate.

Estimates for 1928–30 put *Heimwehr* members at 200,000 and its armed paramilitaries at 120,000. This is probably exaggerated. It would have been greater than the Austrian army, reduced by the peace treaties to only 25,000 men plus the police and security forces of 14,000. *Heimwehr* units were never cohesive and their performance always fell far short of their boasting (Wiltschegg 1985: 292). The paramilitaries then declined to around 50,000 amid factionalism caused by the leadership turning to electoral politics. Its mediocre electoral results were just sufficient to end the absolute parliamentary majority of the Christian Socials. *Heimwehr* leaders were now invited to enter the cabinet, and their influence on the Christian Socials grew. They were obvious allies in the struggle against socialism and might be used to undercut the appeal of the more secular Nazis. But they also influenced the Christian Socials. In 1934 Dollfüss proclaimed his regime corporatist and formed his Fatherland Front. The *Heimwehr* helped to put down an attempted Nazi putsch later in the year, though Dollfüss was killed in the fray. His successor, Schüschnigg, merged the *Heimwehr* into the Fatherland Front in 1936. As the leaders of the *Heimwehr* became domesticated inside the regime, many of its more radical militants became disaffected and joined the

Nazis. One of them was Kaltenbruner, who rose to be Himmler's deputy in the SS. The drift was particularly evident in Styria. At least three of the future SS police chiefs of occupied Eastern Europe (Constantin Kammerhofer, August Meyszner, and Hans Rauter) began their life of illegal violence in the Styrian *Heimatschutz*.

The *Heimwehr* provided the turbulent bottom-up paramilitarism characteristic of fascism. But its ideology was woolly and varied: In Styria it was clearly fascist, in Lower Austria and the Tyrol probably only reactionary authoritarian. In government the movement was somewhat conservative and procapitalist. Its "estates" corporatism was proudly proclaimed, but not implemented. Its nationalism was racist and anti-Semitic, but which state should embody it? It had considered *Anschluss* with Germany, but since Germany was dominated first by socialists, then Nazis, Austro-fascists came to favor an independent Austria.

So some doubt whether Austro-fascists were truly "fascist" (Carsten 1977: 237, 244–5; Payne 1980: 109). Some call them "clerico-fascist" (Gulick 1948: II, part 7). Edmondson (1978, 1985) portrays them as violent "spoilers" for fascism rather than the real thing. Wiltschegg (1985: 270) aptly sums up with two Austrian colloquialisms, *Möchtegern* and *Maul* – loosely translated as "wannabee" and "gob" – fascism. Yet, unlike the Iberian cases, Austro-fascism combined corporatism, violent para-militaries, and cleansing anti-Semitic nationalism. It certainly aspired to be a violent and ruthless mass movement, even if it could not quite become such. After the *Anschluss* most of its activists participated enthusiastically in the National Socialist regime of the Greater German Reich. They were quite ready for fascism, even if they could not quite get there by their own efforts. Adding all these characteristics together yields a borderline fascism containing much tension between fascists, corporatists, and semi-reactionary authoritarians.

But the Austrian Nazi Party clearly was fascist. It could trace its ancestry back to 1903, well before the German Nazis. After 1918 its combination of racist nationalism and proletarian socialism brought growth in the border areas nurturing *völkisch* movements. The Nazis emerged mostly out of the constituency of the German Nationalist parties, which received around 20 percent of the early interwar vote, dominating border regions next to Yugoslavia, Czechoslovakia, and Germany. Their nationalism was more racist. But anticlericalism, disunity, and later subservience to Hitler led to stagnation. Up to the early 1930s its ideology and organization closely resembled German Nazism. There is no need here to repeat these details, though it is worth noting the Austrian party was probably more anti-Semitic. A Social Democrat wrote to his wife from prison: "The real plague are the National Socialist [prisoners]. . . . Most of them are terrible anti-semitic rowdies whose only argument is 'The Jew'" (Carsten 1977: 251). Hitler's successes in Germany turned the Austrian Nazis decisively to the *Anschluss* option and aided their growth. In the last free local elections between 1931 and 1933 the Nazis usually polled 15 to 24 percent of the vote (Kirk 1996: 35–9). They reached 41 percent in the very last election, in Innsbruck in 1933. The German National Party was collapsing and the Nazis were also capturing 10 to 20 percent of the Christian Social and Socialist votes. Some say the Nazis would have peaked at 25 to 30 percent of the national vote (e.g., Pauley 1981: 83, 86). Chancellor Dollfüss disagreed, since he risked no further elections and tried to suppress the Nazis. Yet the clandestine party continued to grow: 69,000 members in 1934, 164,000 by time of the *Anschluss*, and 688,000 by 1941 – 10 percent of the Austrian population. This "illegal period" was crucial in the training of a core of "radical" Austrian Nazi killers, who came into their own during the Final Solution (as we see in my forthcoming book).

These two authoritarian rightist camps were opposed by the Socialist Party of Austria, receiving just under 40 percent of the vote, dominating urban working-class districts, especially in Vienna. Since only Socialists resisted fascism to the end, Austria was the only country in which fascism was endorsed in free elections by parties representing the majority electorate. This success makes it urgent that we explain the rise of Austrian fascists.

WHO WERE THE FASCISTS?

Age, Gender, and Militarism

Fascists were again disproportionately young, male, and military. Both movements remained quite young, especially the Nazis. In the late 1920s *Heimwehr* members averaged twenty-seven years of age; in the early 1930s two national leadership groups averaged thirty-eight. In the late 1920s Nazi members averaged twenty-nine, while the SA averaged only twenty-three. The Nazi Party did not age much: In 1933 Nazis still averaged only thirty-three, in early 1938 only thirty-six, rising to thirty-nine during 1940–41, before a massive injection of new blood from the youth movement brought it down to twenty-three in 1942–4. Yet, as in other countries, extreme left activists were just as young. The Nazis rounded up in prison camps after 1934 were slightly younger than their communist-socialist and Austro-fascist counterparts (since more were under twenty), but slightly older than the leftists killed, wounded, or arrested during the disturbances of 1919 and 1927 (Botz 1983: 66, 155, 325–7).

As in Germany, it is usually asserted that Austrian fascism was dominated by two age cohorts: the "front generation" of younger ex-soldiers (born 1890–1900) and the "home generation" (born 1900–14), the schoolchildren of the war period, with some of both cohorts becoming the first postwar university students (Pauley 1981: 91–2; Wiltschegg 1985: 274; Botz 1987: 253–7). Age data for the Nazis show a ratio of only 0.20 for those born before 1878, rising to 0.75 for 1879–88, parity for 1889–93, and then overrepresentation increasing from 1.2 for the 1894–8 cohort to 1.5 for those born 1899–1903 and 1904–8, 1.8 for the 1909–13 cohort, and then back down to parity for the few born later. Thus the "front generation" was not nearly as prominent as the younger "home generation" that dominated the movement far more than in Germany. Nazis remained younger than Austro-fascists, as we might expect from a movement peaking later.

I have found no exact data on soldiers in either movement. Yet military veterans were obviously important, especially among the first wave of Austro-fascists, able to appropriate the military traditions of the old empire. The original core of the *Heimwehr* was the 50,000–strong "Association of Front Fighters." Initial postwar Nazi growth may have also depended on ex-soldiers, but its stagnation, followed by later growth, diminished their relative contribution. Since both movements remained quite young, and since Austria was allowed only a tiny interwar army, there would have been few war veterans in either movement by the mid-1930s. The lasting impact of militarism, as in other countries, was rather in the realm of paramilitary organization and ideology. The combination of discipline, comradeship, and hierarchy encouraged "organic" authoritarianism and the cult of the leader. But police, security forces, and army personnel also provided considerable aid, first to the *Heimwehr*, then later to the Nazis, especially younger officers and men (Carsten 1977: 330, 252). Austrian fascisms were capable of renewing themselves among young soldiers and civilians, as middle-aged veterans dropped out, presumably to spend time with their families. Thus, though first boosted by the wartime experience of a particular generation, fascism conquered Austria (as it did Germany) by its ability to socialize a second generation into paramilitary nation-statism through the interwar period. Fascism was the coming idea of the age, at least in this region of Europe.

For gender the data are sparse. There were no women members in the *Heimwehr*, though there was a large women's support group. I have found no information on gender and *Heimwehr* voters. But the Nazis had lots of women members. In 1919 women had comprised 15 percent of the party's candidates in the national election, as much as any party anywhere in this period. Then it masculinized, partly on Hitler's express orders: Women made up only 6 percent of new members during 1926–31. Thereafter they rose again, to 12 percent among 1933 new members, 28 percent in 1938, and remaining just below 20 percent during the war. But these many women were kept in subordinate roles, as they were in Austro-fascism. Uniquely, Austrian women voted separately from men, so we know how many women voted Nazi. Most voted quite similarly to men, probably as family blocs. Yet there were slight differences. Women contributed 46 percent of the Nazi vote in 1919, 42 percent in 1930, and 47 percent in 1932 in Vienna – very slight underrepresentation. The Communists got proportionately fewer women's votes than Nazis did, the Socialists slightly more, while the Christian Socials got the most, with women contributing a clear majority of its votes, presumably through women's greater religiosity (Pauley 1981: 101–2; 1989: 42). Women were probably supportive of the Dollfüss regime – though there were now no elections to test this. Women seemed at least as committed as were men to Nazism after the *Anschluss* and seemed to have a bigger impact on the new regime than they did in Germany. The regime operated less gender-segregated policies in Austria than in the Reich as a whole. For example, female labor force participation was much higher (Bukey 1992: 223–4).

Austrian fascism thus seems less gender-biased than most fascisms, or indeed than most political movements of the period. Though its paramilitaries resembled the adolescent male gangs of fascism elsewhere, it received almost majority approval (and substantial participation) from Austrian women. Many eyewitnesses describe women bystanders as being particularly unpleasant toward Jews during deportations. Fascism resonated amid "national" climates. Austro-fascism resonated in political traditions and in the Catholic Church, Nazism resonated in pan-German nationalism. Neither of these was distinctively masculine. Open demonstrations of anti-Semitism were considered more legitimate in Austria than in countries to the west or south, and so could be evinced by ordinary women and children, as well as by male militants. Austrian fascism and anti-Semitism was at the heart of national life, led by young men but abetted by much of the population.

Region and Religion

Since Austria was 96 percent German-speaking and 90 percent Catholic, the only significant ethnic/religious conflict was Christian versus Jew. Almost no Jews were Nazis, and few were Austro-fascists. Yet regional patterns of support for fascism reflected national and religious undertones as well as class and sectoral differences. Like Spain, the country had a politically riven capital. Vienna was the historic seat of a great empire, with strong military, civil service, and Catholic traditions, all of which fueled Austro-fascism. It also contained the bulk of the Jewish population, fueling both fascisms among some of their Christian neighbors. Yet Vienna also had large-scale industry and a well-organized proletariat that gave political control of the capital to socialism. Fascism increasingly dominated the provinces and the countryside. Here class mattered less in determining political loyalties than it did in the capital. Some provinces felt border tensions. Many Germans of all classes who lived adjacent to the new Slav states felt threatened. Both fascisms recruited disproportionately from Carinthia, Styria, and areas of Burgenland lost to Hungary. One small Burgenland village alternating between Hungarian and Austrian control produced dozens of Nazis and several SS men, the most notorious being the brutal Gestapo war criminal Alois Brunner. As small children this cohort of locals had imbibed anti-Slav and anti-Semitic sentiments from family and church, and they had nurtured German nationalism in school, where they had been forced to learn Magyar (Epelbaum 1990). Their border anxieties, more than their class composition, made them fervently nationalist, favoring a strong state to protect the nation.

Austria also had a half-buried religious history influencing regional recruitment into its two fascisms. The old Habsburg heartland was deeply Catholic and sustained the Christian Socials and Austro-fascism, whereas the westerly formerly Protestant provinces were a little more secular, and moving toward German Nationalism and Nazism. Nazi relations with the Catholic Church proved ambivalent. Though many Nazis were anticlerical, Nazi leaders knew unrestrained anticlericalism would mean political suicide and were ready to compromise with the church. Ambivalence was reciprocated by the clergy. Some priests were later imprisoned and a handful executed as opponents of the Nazi regime. But though initially Austro-fascist, the church hierarchy became collaborators. They preferred Nazism to democratic socialism. Thus they negotiated with − and then came to support − the regime except when it threatened the church's institutional interests. The 4 percent of the population who were Protestant seemed to have voted overwhelmingly Nazi, and their ministers were often alleged to be Nazis (Carsten 1977; Pauley 1981: 96, 99–100; Botz 1987: 262–3; Hanisch 1989; Bukey 1992: 226).

These religious and regional differences involved different views regarding the nation-state. Initially, the Catholic Church supported an independent

Austria (since that would be Catholic), while Protestants wanted to lean on Germany. Those in the regions bordering Germany felt more akin to Reich Germans than did those in the Habsburg heartlands. Those bordering Czechoslovakia and Yugoslavia looked to the stronger protection a pan-German state could provide. Though the different provinces had slightly different class structures, this paled beside their different visions of the nation-state. Yet by 1938 preferences were changing: It was now clear that Austria could not have its own nation-state but would be absorbed into the German Reich. Historic aspirations for a "Greater Reich" were being realized. Such a Reich would not be distinctively Protestant and it would tilt eastward, into the traditional Austrian sphere of influence. More Austrians could thus support it. Thus Austrian fascists of both types, of both religions, of most regions, and of most classes, could now serve it with some enthusiasm. Nazism became truly a national movement.

Class, Sector, and Economy

How much can be explained by class conflict and other economic power relations? Previous chapters have found that different fascist movements had somewhat different class compositions. Though both the Italian and German movements recruited members from all classes, the Italians were somewhat more petty bourgeois and bourgeois than were the Germans. The two Austrian fascisms, one more influenced by Mussolini, the other by Hitler, differed accordingly.

Yet opinions differ about the *Heimwehr*. Newman (1970: 261) says it got recruits from all but the urban-industrial working class. Edmondson (1978: 38–9, 59) says it was led by professional and reserve officers, disentitled aristocrats, white-collar workers, and "disillusioned youth," with the rank and file being "probably peasants and lower middle classes" – which he explains means tradesmen, lawyers, and bureaucrats. August Meyszner seems to fit this leadership stereotype perfectly. The son of an army lieutenant, he served in both the police and the army before World War I, was wounded and decorated in the war, and then – deprived of his minor title – farmed in his native village in Styria. He was a *Heimwehr* militia leader, then a Heimatblock parliamentary deputy before switching to the Nazis. He was imprisoned several times during the republic, and looked back proudly on his record of violence. Meyszner became a notorious wartime SS police chief, eventually hanged by the Yugoslavs in 1948 (Birn 1991).

But Edmondson also endorses the *New York Times*'s improbable estimation in 1927 that the *Heimwehr* was 70 percent peasant, 20 percent student, and 10 percent industrial worker. Carsten (1977: 93, 113, 120, 123) says that most of the Viennese branch were workers and public sector employees. But elsewhere (apart from Styria during the Depression), he believes it was mainly a rural "movement of protest against modernization and urbanization." He notes that both the *Heimwehr* and the Nazis recruited among *völkisch* community clubs, especially gymnastics clubs, and these were important for attracting students and young people. Botz (1987a: 257–63) believes that many *Heimwehr* leaders were aristocrats, military veterans, and students, and speculates that agricultural, especially forestry, workers on large estates were overrepresented among members. Most agree it was essentially rural.

Not all these views can be correct. The quantitative data, though limited, refute some of them. Though there were a few prominent aristocrats, Wiltschegg shows they represented under 2 percent of leaders. My Appendix Tables 6.1 and 6.2 show that *Heimwehr* leaders and activists were drawn quite broadly from across the class structure, somewhat biased toward the upper and middle classes, but less so than other nonsocialist parties of the period. There were many ex-army officers and NCOs. They were mostly provincial, though not rural. The *Heimwehr* (and the Christian Socials from whom they drew) were the only movements relying fairly equally on rural and urban activists. We also have small samples of militants. Among thirty-six mostly urban militants arrested by the police for political violence, the "classic petty bourgeoisie" and workers were both overrepresented, with ratios of 1.71 and 1.16, respectively (Botz 1980). Among forty-two Heimwehr "martyrs," 43 percent were workers, 21 percent were entrepreneurs (big or small?), and the rest were scattered through the class structure (Wiltschegg 1985: 278). Can we conclude that the most violent of the *Heimwehr* were disproportionately workers (as usual among fascists) and the classic petty bourgeoisie (very unusual)? With such small samples we cannot be sure.

The *Heimwehr* vote was not rural, but slightly urban. In 1930 there was a negative correlation (−.15) between its vote and the proportion employed in agriculture in each commune, and positive correlations between its vote and the degree of urbanization (.14) and the proportion employed in the tertiary sector (.15; Botz 1987a: 269). Since these are low correlations, Austro-fascism probably appealed quite broadly across the country. It also had workers' associations. Though much smaller than those of the Social Democrats, they totaled nearly 100,000 members, especially concentrated among white-collar and public sector workers, and their numbers were holding up better than were the socialist unions after 1930 (Wiltschegg 1985: 274–83; Kirk 1996: 33). The *Heimwehr* did well in a mining and heavy industrial area in Upper Styria, whose members were mainly workers

(Pauley 1981: 76). Its trade union outstripped the socialist union from 1928, and the area returned a *Heimwehr* MP from 1930. Lewis (1991) attributes this success to management repression of socialist unions and favored treatment given to the organization. Since socialists were weak in this area and most jobs were unskilled, management could fire leftists and replace them with the docile unemployed. But this cannot explain the electoral success here (in a secret ballot) of the *Heimwehr*. Workers seem to have turned more willingly toward fascism than Lewis will admit. The Styrian branch was the most violent in the *Heimwehr*, actually affiliating with the Nazis in 1933. Though probably skewed toward the bourgeoisie and petty bourgeoisie, Austro-fascism was fairly broadly based. While its conservatism encouraged a bourgeois and rural composition, its fascism encouraged countertrends.

We know more about the Nazis. Their 1930 vote was similar to the *Heimwehr*'s: a low negative correlation of $-.20$ with agricultural employment and low positive ones with urbanization (.15) and tertiary sector employment (.21). Originally urban, they were keen to expand among peasants, whom they referred to as "the backbone of Austria." Electoral success followed in the early 1930s in rural Styria and Carinthia as the *Heimwehr* stalled. The participation of peasants in the failed Nazi putsch of 1934 shocked conservatives. But the fairly low correlations may indicate that their support, though uneven, was quite broad. The Nazis also had one attraction only contingently connected to fascism: They favored *Anschluss* and after Hitler's coup they were the party most likely to accomplish it. Many supported the Nazis as the most likely way to achieve union with Germany – and economic prosperity. Anyone depending on tourism, an important industry, might acquire Nazi sympathies: *Anschluss* would open the borders and bring the tourists back. German-owned companies were also interested in free trade, whereas many Austrian ones favored Austrian protectionism. Electoral support need not indicate fascist beliefs, only materialism.

Yet the Nazi core was genuinely fascist. The small prewar DAP and the early postwar DNSAP were genuinely nationalist *and* socialist. Their members were mainly workers, especially railway workers (public sector workers yet again). Yet the early 1920s saw an influx of students, teachers, and professionals. A class-cum-generational conflict then weakened the party for most of the decade (Pauley 1981: 27–9, 40–1). Appendix Table 6.1 contains membership data from 1923. The ratio for workers during 1923–5 was 0.82 – slight underrepresentation – dropping to a very low 0.36 among the new members of 1926–32, rising again to 0.67 among new members of 1934–8. As in Germany, public sector workers were more fascist. But though the party always contained between a quarter and a third workers and artisans, it had become more middle-class than its German counter-part. This was essentially because Austrian socialism was better entrenched in the urban-industrial areas, especially in Vienna. Here the socialists dom-inated working-class districts. Appendix Table 6.1 shows that socialism was much more proletarian than Nazism. The Nazis offered serious competi-tion only among public sector workers, especially railroads, trams, and postal services, and in outlying mining areas and in German-owned companies in the provinces.

As in other countries, workers figured more prominently in the paramili-taries than in the parties. Appendix Table 6.1 shows that many workers were among those Nazis on police files and that workers comprised 52 percent and 39 percent of Botz's small samples of the SA and SS, respectivly – though this was well below the 82 percent worker membership in the milder so-cialist paramilitary, the *Schutzbund*. One SA leader described his worker recruits as being "the true believers," and during the Dollfüss repression the percentage of workers increased (Botz 1980: 196, 206, 221; Pauley 1981: 97–8).

Fascism appealed more to workers outside Vienna. "Red Vienna," where half the socialist members lived, was not typical of Austria. Provincial so-cialism was weaker, less Marxian, more fluid. As in Romania and Hungary, fascism and socialism could overlap, especially in German Nationalist areas where many socialists and Nazis shared anticlericalism, anticapitalism, and anti-Semitism. Though socialist leaders opposed anti-Semitism, they were reluctant to much publicize this since they believed many of their supporters hated Jews. Their preferred solution to the "Jewish problem" was assimila-tion of the Jews, not multiculturalism. Nor did all provincial socialists share the Viennese orthodoxy that socialism and Nazism were polar opposites. Both parties believed discontented militants were switching between them, the better to fight the real enemy, Austrian conservatism. After 1934 much of this movement went to the Nazis, though its extent is difficult to gauge (Kirk 1996: 44). A few socialist *Schutzbund* units defected en bloc, while two socialists who fled Linz after the failed uprising in 1934 returned in 1938 as SS officers (Bukey 1986: 136). The Nazis plausibly promised full employment. Since this had been achieved in Germany, this promise was influential among workers. The Gestapo reported during the *Anschluss* that "an enthusiasm existed among the workers for national Socialism such as no other government before had been able to sustain" (Bukey 1978: 317). For a while in 1938 the new regime kept its promises: Unemployment was slashed by 60 percent, benefits improved, and wages rose for at least a year. Thereafter the Nazi economy was in difficulties. Middle-class opportunists were now entering the Nazi Party in large numbers, while worker disillusionment grew. The limited wartime dissent found by Kirk (1996) – leaflets, graffiti, and barroom shouting matches – mainly came from workers (Bukey 1989: 155–6; 1992: 210–19; Konrad 1989). Workers had made more of a contribution to Nazism during the period that really mattered, 1934 to 1938. But this was a cross–class, not a proletarian, party, like its German counterpart.

Who were the middle–class members? Even more than in Germany, before 1934 they were disproportionately "academic professionals" – civil servants, qualified professionals, and students (the so–called Aryan intelligentsia). By 1918 the universities were suffused with authoritarian ideas, especially the Catholic corporatism of the sociologist Othmar Spann, whose ideas were a common jumping–off point for intellectual fascism. From 1930 Nazi student organizations captured student governments at several universities and became the largest national student movement. Teachers and professors became especially Nazi, followed, it is usually said, by lawyers, veterinarians, pharmacists, architects, and engineers – many apparently switching from the *Heimwehr* (Carsten 1977: 191, 198; Pauley 1981: 94; 1989: 41–2). Appendix Table 6.1 shows that public employees were the most overrepresented among the Nazis before 1933 and again between 1939 and 1941 (constituting 20 to 27% of members, with ratios of between 2.0 and 2.5). My forthcoming volume shows that war criminals were disproportionately drawn from the police force, the military, and lawyers in the public service. In the period of persecution, from 1934 to 1938, the "official" numbers of Nazi public sector workers obviously declined. Bukey (1978) estimates that half the Linz party had depended on state employment, many now being fired (some fled to Germany). Others concealed their membership.

In my sample of war criminals discussed in detail in my forthcoming volume, it is especially difficult to tell when some of the Austrians who were police officers or civil servants had actually joined the Nazis. Men such as Franz Stangl, commandant at Treblinka, on trial for his life, tried to put the date of joining as late as possible. However, men like him were already informally cooperating with the Nazis. The Nazi vote was almost always higher in those provincial capitals and county seats containing substantial public administrations (Pauley 1981: 95). Civil servants, judges, and other administrators were persistently biased toward both fascist movements, while the Vienna civil service helped to organize the *Anschluss* (Botz 1988).

We can directly compare different kinds of political activists in Linz. Bukey's (1986) data are given in Appendix Table 6.2. They indicate that the

Nazis had more professionals than any other party and were more proletarian and less petty bourgeois than any other except communists and socialists. Appendix Table 6.1, rows 8 and 9, detail Nazis and leftists on Vienna police files for violence. Some 82 percent of the leftists and 40 percent of the Nazis (a ratio of 0.75) were workers; there were more white-collar and student Nazis (ratios of 2.64 and 16.67). Rows 10 and 11 detail inmates of a prison camp after the failed socialist and Nazi uprisings of 1933–4 – a sample of the fighters of the two movements. But there is a problem: the numerous "artisans." In my table they are assigned (as they are by the author of the study) to the petty bourgeoisie. This yields only 38 percent of workers among the Nazis (a ratio of 0.71), 48 percent (0.90) among the socialists, and 53 percent (0.98) among the communists. It is unlikely that workers would be underrepresented among all three political groups. As in Germany, many of the "artisans" were probably workers. If we added half of them, workers would be equally represented at around parity (1.00) among Nazis and socialists and overrepresented among the communists (at about 1.20). This is probably closer to the truth. Nazi fighters would thus appear fairly proletarian – and included the most unskilled workers. Among the middle-class inmates, students (a massive ratio of 11.00) and private employees (ratio 1.70) were overrepresented among the Nazis, and professionals among all three groups (ratios just above 2.50). The SA also had more students and workers than did the party (Carsten 1977: 198). Thus Nazi fighters were mostly young workers and students, with a broad scattering of the middle class – and an absent "classic petty bourgeoisie."

So the Nazis were led by public employees (especially those concerned with public order) and by professionals, with a broad-ranging if slightly bourgeois and petty bourgeois membership, though depending on young workers (especially in the public sector), students, and white-collar workers to do the paramilitary dirty work. Probably underrepresented were the "classic petty bourgeoisie" and most groups in the private manufacturing and distributive sectors. Again, we see a constituency seemingly surveying class conflict from outside, probably responding to fascist claims to be able to transcend class conflict.

Can fascist support be explained in terms of the condition of the economy? Partially, yes, because of the distinctive way the Austrian economy related to the German one. The Great Depression certainly hurt Austria hard. Its 23 percent fall in GDP was the greatest in Europe, as Table 2.1 showed (though it was less than the fall in the United States and Canada). The peak year for unemployment proved to be 1933. Yet unemployment remained high until the *Anschluss*, partly because of Hitler's blockade of the Austrian economy. Fascist surges in Austria correlate quite well with economic recession. The *Heimwehr* and antiliberal, anticapitalist populism grew rapidly at the onset of the Depression; the Nazis grew as it peaked and endured. The Dollfüss/Schüschnigg governments certainly believed that economic distress lay behind political discontent. Fascists claimed that behind government economic failures lay national disunity fomented by Jews and Bolsheviks. National cleansing and corporatist reorganization could remedy this. Some Austrians accepted this argument, but more perceived that governments were not delivering the economic goods and that a union with Germany might, since it would bring integration with the successful economy next door. Economic crisis was a major factor in the collapse of the republic and especially in the Nazi seizure of power. The Nazis seemed to have the best policy solution: *Anschluss*. Nazism resonated strongly in the material experience of Austrian families, for more straightforward economic reasons than in any of the other countries.

But were the worst hit by economic difficulties also the most fascist? The fascist core identified above is often explained in terms of overcrowded universities and professions, unemployed former civil servants and army officers, and declining civil servant living standards. Fascists were "the groups which were the main victims of the great economic crisis" (says Carsten 1977: 206, 331–2; cf. Siegfried 1979). This is to explain fascism principally in terms of economic power relations. Yet the evidence is equivocal. Much of the Austrian public sector, armed forces and universities, previously the backbone of a Great Power, were "the ultimate losers" in the Hapsburg collapse (Bukey 1978: 325). "Losing" obviously did mean material loss, though it also meant losing position in society, social meaning, and purpose. Yet Botz (despite appearing to accept a materialist argument) shows that civil servant income levels and unemployment rates had not worsened in relation to those of workers. Newman (1970: 257) observes that though many civil servants and officers were unemployed, most had already been German nationalists for many years, and this was the decisive spur to their fascism. Moreover, the Nazi elite in Linz had seen more upward than downward mobility, with a relatively high level of education. Bukey (1978: 323–5) doubts they were "marginal men," especially after bourgeois Pan Germans began to swarm into the movement during the 1930s. Economic problems gave a general boost to Nazism but do not seem to have particularly attracted its militants.

Of course, since Austrian unemployment levels remained high right up to the *Anschluss*, many Nazis were unemployed. But in my sample of war criminals (a sample of more "radical" Nazis described in my forthcoming volume) it is usually difficult to tell which came first, extremism or unemployment. Vinzenz Nohel, a mechanic, was intermittently unemployed, but probably when already a Nazi member (his brother, an SA militant, certainly was). Josef Schwammberger, a shop assistant, ended fifteen months' unemployment by joining the SS, where he promptly became extremely active. But he had been forced to move at age six with his family from the Austrian Tyrol when the area was ceded to Italy in 1918, and seems to have had extreme views while quite young. He ended up an NCO guard in death camps, where a survivor said of him, "I couldn't call him a beast because I wouldn't want to embarrass the beast. He just killed because he wanted to kill." Herbert Andorfer, later commandant at Semlin camp, Belgrade, was forced by the Depression to leave the university without completing his degree. But he seems to have joined the Nazi Party a few months earlier. Dr. Irmfried Eberl, later briefly commandant at Treblinka death camp, could not find public medical employment in Austria, but this was apparently because he was already a known Nazi. Adolf Eichmann, not actually unemployed but not a success as a salesman, joined the Nazis on the advice of his more successful acquaintance, Kaltenbrunner. So far as we can tell (behind the lies he told during his trial), career frustrations were inextricably mixed up with his ideological discontents. Obviously, mass unemployment did play a substantial role in drawing Austrians toward Nazism – especially since Hitler seemed to offer a solution. But Nazism does not seem to have appealed disproportionately to those actually unemployed. Economic problems brought mass Nazi sympathizers, but not the core militants who actually secured victory.

Both Austrian fascisms were boosted by economic discontent, both had their class biases. Both probably underrepresented industrial workers in the party, though not in paramilitary activism. Both overrepresented public employees, the Nazis underrepresented farmers, the *Heimwehr* underrepresented private sector white-collar workers. Yet their electoral support was broader spread than their rivals'. The Socialist Party of Austria, with a massive negative correlation in 1930 of −.70 with agricultural employment and large positive ones of .60 with urbanization and .45 with tertiary sector employment, was trapped inside urban-industrial ghettos. Since in Austria these were large, the socialists did well. But not quite well enough actually to win national elections. The Christian Social Party reversed all three correlations (respectively, .45, −.40 and −.31), being relatively weak outside agriculture. The Austro-fascist social base then steadily narrowed. The Dollfüss regime, swimming against the pro-German tide, became distinctly upper-class and old regime, its group photographs filled with clerical and military uniforms and expensive suits. In contrast, the Nazis became more populist.

Botz concludes that they were two "heterogeneous catch-all-parties" or "asymmetrical people's parties" – a conclusion identical to the new orthodoxy on German Nazism. In this country, many turned to the Nazis because their main attraction or repulsion was felt for others. The Austrian Nazis rose on the coat-tails of Hitler and the economic and military strength of Germany – both increasingly attractive to Germans in neighboring countries. And in a three-way rivalry – between Social Christians, German Nationalists, and Socialists – each could appeal to the enemy of its enemy. In the late 1930s the Nazis recruited more workers and socialists by offering the only remaining "radical" alternative to the Austro-fascists, and they recruited Austro-fascists by offering the only viable nonsocialist nationalism. Yet nation-statist constituencies provided a solid basis of support. Once again, those in public institutions (army, civilian employment, and higher education, with an academic professional penumbra) plus those whose position made them believe in a strong, integral nation (especially border Austrians) provided the core. Once again, Austrian fascism also added on support from people lying outside the urban and industrial capitalist core of the class struggle. Having seen the republic stalemated by conflict between an urban-industrial socialism and a rural-provincial conservatism, many gravitated to a plausible fascist promise to "transcend" national division. But the unusually strong appeal of fascism here was probably due to the possibility that this ethnic German country could unite with the economically and geopolitically more successful Nazi Reich. All four sources of social power seem to have been involved in this appeal, though with macro-economic factors playing a larger role than elsewhere.

AUSTRIAN ANTI-SEMITISM

Austria's most significant contribution to European fascism was to heighten its political anti-Semitism. Though there had historically been fewer pogroms than in Poland or the Ukraine, Austria had been the pioneer in developing modern anti-Semitic political movements. From the 1850s Austrian politics had been permeated by a rhetoric that associated Jews with rapacious capitalism, political and religious radicalism, an antinational cosmopolitanism, and an eastern racial threat to "Western civilization." Pulzer (1993: 38) notes that though scholars like to distinguish among economic, political, and religious anti-Semitism, Austrian politicians thrived on blurring them into a single threat to the unity of the Austrian or German people.

Their rhetoric was paralleled by newspaper scare stories and exaggerated statistics about the number of Jewish banks, department stores, newspapers, cinemas, and so on. Anti-Semitism acquired deep popular resonance. From the 1880s Schonerer and Lueger made anti-Semitism the core of their mass nationalist parties. Schorske (1981: chap. 3) says that they developed "politics in a new key," sponsoring their own newspapers, sporting clubs, and mass and violent demonstrations. From such populism, fascism easily developed.

As the Habsburg Empire weakened, Austrian and German nationalism strengthened. By the first years of the twentieth century Jews were seen as cosmopolitan stooges of the Habsburg antinationalist and antidemocratic regime. As early as 1884 SPD leader Karl Kautsky warned: "The anti-Semites are . . . much more dangerous than in Germany because their appearance is oppositional and democratic, thus appealing to the workers' instincts" (Carsten 1977: 16). They remained more dangerous in a popular sense. From the late 1930s though committed German Nazis exhibited the most vicious anti-Semitism, more Austrians seem to have participated in riots, grabbing Jewish neighbors' property, and local deportations before the Final Solution (Botz 1987b; Bukey 1992: 214–19).

The strength of Austrian anti-Semitism is sometimes explained in predominantly materialist terms: The working class resented Jewish wealth, the middle class resented Jewish competition (Pauley 1981: 16–17). This could be plausible only in Vienna, where 91 percent of Jews lived. Elsewhere, Jews were largely absent from conspicuous consumption and competition. But in Vienna they comprised about 10 percent of the city's population, a noticeable and prosperous minority. By 1914 Viennese Jews were predominantly middle-class and well educated. Some 35 percent of students at the Vienna Gymnasium (the best high school) were Jews, as were 28 percent of the city's university students. They were highly cultured. Viennese Jews such as Freud and Mahler were among the greatest figures of European high culture. Jews provided 62 percent of the city's lawyers and dentists, 47 percent of doctors, 27 percent of university professors, and 18 percent of bank directors. Some 94 percent of advertising agencies were Jewish, 85 percent of furniture retailers, and 70 percent of those involved in the wine and textile trades (Pauley 1987: 154–5). These are formidable concentrations. Overall, about 200,000 Christians had Jewish employers, though Jews were far fewer in most manufacturing branches and in other towns. Unlike Germany we find plausible material roots for anti-Semitism, expressed through urban resentment of Jewish-dominated finance and service capitalism and in rural resentment of supposedly Jewish-dominated towns.

Yet with one main exception, Nazism and Austro-fascism were actually stronger where there were fewer Jews. Jews comprised under 2 percent of the population outside Vienna. Though some professions might have contained religious rivalry in Vienna, this was rare elsewhere. Few teachers were Jewish, Jews were a minuscule 0.25 percent of civil servants, and even fewer were in the army. Yet Nazism was entrenched inside state employment, outside Vienna – and especially in the border areas of Carinthia and Styria, where there were fewest Jews of all. While Austro-fascism did eventually become important in the Viennese middle class, its heartland lay in the provincial towns and countryside. Anti-Semitic fascism seems to have thrived on distance from Jews, not proximity. "The Jew" could be a convenient symbol for urban domination. But this would be a more plausible explanation for Austro-fascism than for Nazism, which was more urban.

The urban exceptions are a few professions and, more important, students. Students formed the most Nazi group in the entire population and the group most likely to encounter Jews. Their anti-Semitism often did focus on Jewish competition. Students vocally demanded a *numerus clausus* (maximum quota) for Jews entering university. Did material interests make them the principal ideological carriers of anti-Semitism to a more distant population? To some extent, yes. Yet student anti-Semitism had actually preceded the big Jewish immigration at the beginning of the century and had always been entwined with other rightist ideals, especially pan-German nationalism. The gradual turning of this toward fascism was a long-term process, seemingly unrelated to employment fluctuations (Whiteside 1966; Pauley 1981: 17–19, 93–4).

Ernst Kaltenbrunner, later head of Hitler's SD, led Viennese student attacks on Jews and "reds" in the 1920s. But he was only following a family tradition. In the 1890s his father had also led student attacks on Jews, describing them as an "alien body" in the nation. Both father and son then had successful careers as provincial lawyers, while maintaining their nationalist activities. Josef Fitzhum, later an SS police chief in the Balkans, claimed his career chances in Vienna had been blighted by Jews. Yet (leaving aside one job dismissal for embezzlement) already in 1918, as he was leaving the army, twenty-two years old, before his career had even begun, he was describing the republic as dominated by the "red rabble," "communist criminal gangs," and Jews. There seems more to Nazis' anti-Semitism than mere materialism, a something that was ideologically connected to their strong nationalism.

We are familiar with the materialist anti-Semitic stereotype of the Jew as Shylock, the dissembling, sharp-practiced, "shyster" moneylender, landlord, or small entrepreneur (in some cultures the lawyer is added). This stereotype was widespread in interwar Austria. But it coexisted with a second stereo-type, of Polish or Ukrainian Orthodox Jews from the Pale of Settlement, still living and dressing in the old style, a symbol for many Austrians (and others) of Eastern barbarism – the supposed antithesis of Austrian Habsburg Catholic civilization and the supposed antithesis in the interwar period of the civilized, Christian German nation. But by connecting the cultured Viennese doctor or tailor or salesman – or Sigmund Freud – to a distant, alien, but threatening "other," Hitler and other Austrians might justify ex-cluding them from the nation by force. This might allow neighbors and colleagues to seize their property and jobs – perhaps a satisfactory solution to any material resentments they might have felt. We must still explain this ideology of antithesis between the Jew and the civilized nation. But its causes look less material than its consequences.

Two further ideological connections seem to have been necessary. First, anti-Semitism was central to nationalist ideology in this region of Europe (as it was further east, as my forthcoming volume details). Parkinson (1989: 327) rather psychologizes this:

specifically Austrian ... anti-semitism, with its venom and greed, is explicable only in terms of the psychological condition in which Austrians found them-selves.... Cursed with a rankling inferiority complex toward both Germans and Jews but unable to vent their spleen on the former, the Austrian majority tried to cope by fawning on the Germans while savaging the Jews.

But we must also remember that in the prewar period the cosmopolitan Jews had been identified (not inaccurately) as supporters of the Habsburg ruling dynasty, who had also been antinationalist. As Kautsky noted, populist movements argued that Jews propped up the hated old regime. Before 1900 Schönerer's populist anti-Semitic movement had voiced such anti-Semitism. Then Mayor Lueger's Christian Social administration of Vienna had targeted a "Judeo-Magyar" enemy of Austria. Elsewhere in the Habsburg successor states Jews remained scapegoats for centuries of Habsburg oppression (Sugar 1971: 154), but in Austria itself Jews were scapegoats for the collapse of Aus-trian power. After 1918 they were the only nonnational reminder left of the disastrous "Habsburg multi-national experiment." We have already noted the importance of the more diffuse *völkisch* movement, carried through a Vienna-Munich nexus of intellectuals, in the formation of German Nazism. In Austria in the interwar period it permeated through much of the political spectrum, drifting from the right toward the left (Whiteside 1966; Carsten 1977: chaps. 1 and 5). Jews actually were enemies of the organic nationalism now being expressed by German nationalists.

Second, Nazi ideologists, as in Germany, insisted that Jews exacerbated class conflict: Were not most of the biggest, most exploitative capitalists *and* most of the leading "reds" Jewish? This was not without truth. Many (though not most) prominent socialists and capitalists *were* Jews. It is believed that 75 percent of Viennese Jews voted Socialist. The Nazis dichotomized between an idealized German nation and its "enemies" – "foreign" international/Jewish capitalism plus "barbarous" Eastern "Judeo-Bolsheviks." Austro-fascism substituted an Austro-German nation-state, but visualized a similar enemy (though hating the Jews as much for religious as racial reasons). An anticapitalist populism could attract many workers not insulated inside the core socialist communities (in the end it attracted many of them), while anti-Bolshevik nationalism attracted much of the middle class and the agrarian and provincial population. As in other countries, the notion of a strong state knocking together the heads of *both* classes in that urban-industrial sector attracted broad support. But here, as in other countries to the east, most of the targeted heads looked Semitic.

Jews were the tangible symbol of all these "aliens" and so became the main candidates, along with Bolsheviks, for national cleansing. Since in rump Austria there were no other significant ethnic or religious minorities, attacks on "aliens" focused on them. Jews had become entangled in popular consciousness with both nationalism and class conflict. Anti-Semitism was a general property of Western Christian civilization. But it moved up a gear during the interwar period, toward systematic "cleansing," where the removal of Jews might plausibly reduce class conflict and make the nation more integral. The problem with a materialist explanation of anti-Semitism, or indeed of fascism more generally, is not that economic interests and resentments were not important. It is that self-interest does not automatically lead to *any* particular political outcome. Between a sense of personal economic frustration and being anti-Semitic, conservative, or socialist is a realm of ideology and politics in which political movements seek to persuade us of who might be our enemy and who our friend. If these enemies and friends are as broad as "classes" or "nations," our actual material experience cannot possibly confirm their "truth," only their surface plausibility. So it is primarily the realm of politics and ideology, mediated by more complex and local social structures than just class or nation, that explanations of mass anti-Semitism must explore. This was especially so in Austria. Though Austrian fascism came to have a substantially economic component, this was far less true of its anti-Semitism – a key part of Austrian fascism and especially of its virulence and violence.

AN ELITE CONSPIRACY? CLASS MOTIVATIONS

Was there also an Austrian upper-class conspiracy, as in Italy and (to a lesser extent) in Germany? Did the ruling classes aid fascists as a way of repressing the lower classes, compromising the fascist claim to represent the nation and transcend class? With the Austro-fascists, the answer is very clearly yes. The *Heimwehr* had intimate relations with the clergy and officer corps and received large subsidies from politically minded capitalists (obviously a minority of all capitalists) once they perceived the republic had become insecure (the *Heimwehr* also took money from Mussolini). The Dollfüss regime was staffed by the old regime, with the support of modern capitalists. Big landowners and businessmen dominated its deflationary economic policy. After the Hitler regime promulgated the Nuremberg racial laws, even Jewish capitalists aided Austro-fascism, since they now lived in terror of its rival, Nazism. Some Austrian capitalists also feared the increased competition *Anschluss* would bring. Thus elites and capitalists led the undermining of the republic and its replacement by Austro-fascism. Elites were *central* to Austro-fascism, as they had not really been to either Italian or German fascism. In contrast, only a few German-owned businesses contributed to the Austrian Nazis. Most members of the upper classes were actually very suspicious of Nazi radical populism. Their direct responsibility for the Nazi takeover was small.

What was the motivation of the Austro-fascist elites? Was it a straightforward class motivation? They sometimes admitted it was, though (as in other countries) claiming self-defense – that is, defense of property rights and capitalist profit. They claimed their support was a justified response to the violence of the socialists. I go through the various parts of their argument. First, they said the socialists proclaimed "revolution," which clearly threatened property. Indeed, the socialists had proclaimed revolution in 1918–19, amid the collapse of the Habsburg Empire. But the socialists had themselves immediately defused the revolution by demobilizing workers' and soldiers' councils, advising demonstrators to return home, praising republican constitutionality, not even asking for civil service or army purges. Though in response to the rightist paramilitaries they formed their own paramilitary in 1923, the *Schutzbund*, this was a rather defensive organization. True, they refused to join a national coalition government, flourishing Marxian reasons: The Socialist Party was the party of the proletariat, other parties represented opposed classes, there could be no alliance between them. They also believed (not without reason) that the offer was a ploy to make them share responsibility for the mass unemployment of the Depression. Their intransigence was a tactical sop to the socialist left. Tactically, it worked: The left did not defect to the small Communist Party yet was unable to influence party policy. Yet it was a strategic disaster. It polarized Austria to a level where violence (more efficiently mobilized by the right) might seem a reasonable solution, and it made socialist soldiers and civil servants vulnerable to Christian Social purges. In 1933 the Socialist Party become desperate, changed tack, and offered compromise and coalition to The Christian Socials. But this was too late: the Christian Socials were now embarked on their journey through authoritarian solutions (Gulick 1948: II, 1266–78).

In practice the Socialist Party had long adhered to "bourgeois democracy" and reformism. The reformist drive was greatest in so-called Red Vienna, to whose regional government (controlled by the socialists) the constitution assigned considerable powers, including taxation. The scale of Red Vienna's housing, education, and welfare projects was not particularly large when placed in comparative perspective, but the method of financing them was: progressive taxes paid disproportionately by the middle and upper classes. If its massive public housing blocks were the symbol of interwar social democracy, redistributive taxes were its infrastructure (Gruber 1985; Marcuse 1985). This tended to squeeze the profits of the rich, as such programs do everywhere. The second class motivation of the propertied classes, capitalist profit, kicked in. In the short term this might be a justified fear. But in the long term such redistribution did not actually reduce profit. Such aggressive reformism was only the equivalent of what Swedish and Danish socialists undertook slightly later – and what indeed the Second Austrian Republic accomplished in more consensual fashion and achieving spectacular macro-economic results after World War II. Neither provoked fascist backlashes. And since most Austrians, and especially most Austrian fascists, did not live in Vienna, it is difficult to see the actual achievements of Austrian socialism as requiring a *fascist* response from the right.

Second, they claimed that the fascist backlash was a response to mass inflammatory strikes, rhetoric, and occasional street violence by the left. But the Austrian strike rate was not particularly high, and only occasional strikes were violent after 1920. Strikes peaked in 1931 and then declined to near-zero in 1934, as a result of the Great Depression and moderate levels of repression. Conservatives might conceivably claim that a semi-authoritarian regime should continue, but they could hardly justify either Austro-fascism or Nazism as a response to strikes.

Third, rightist criticisms of socialist rhetoric usually focused on a clause in the party's "Linz Programme" of 1926. This has been often taken to advocate "dictatorship of the proletariat." It is worth quoting this clause:

The Social Democratic Workers' Party must . . . maintain for the working class the possibility of destroying the class rule of the bourgeoisie by democratic methods. If, however, despite all these efforts of the Social Democratic Workers' Party, a counterrevolution of the bourgeoisie should succeed in shattering democracy, then the working class could only conquer the power of the state by civil war. . . . If, however, the bourgeoisie should resist the social revolutionary change, which will be the task of the state power of the working class, by planned constriction of economic life, by violent uprising, or by conspiracy with foreign counter-revolutionary powers, then the resistance of the working class would be compelled to break the resistance of the bourgeoisie by means of dictatorship.

The prose is tortuous, but all I (and Lowenberg 1985: 73–4) can read into it is the right of a legally constituted government or party to arm in self-defense, if attacked. Indeed, Austrian socialists actually demonstrated extraordinary, even suicidal restraint against rightist provocation (Stadler 1981). Its paramilitary, the *Schutzbund*, was about 80–90,000 strong but poorly armed and minimally trained. Its violence was almost always reactive, concerned only to defend the city's most proletarian areas. Unlike the two fascist paramilitaries it rarely paraded outside its ghettoes. It did not go in for the provocative tactics that were universal among fascist movements. Of course, on the ground, shouting and marching often turned into brawling that paid scant attention to distinctions between offense and defense. Yet larger actions were tightly reined in by the party leaders, fearful of "provocations" by their rank and file (Botz 1985). Socialists had had bad experiences. In 1927 two right-wing *Frontkämpfer* members who had unprovokedly shot two socialist workers were acquitted by a partisan court. A riot ensued, and the Palace of Justice was fired. Ignoring socialist leaders' pleas for restraint and cooperation in defusing the situation, the Christian Social government sent in armed police, who shot dead between eighty-five and ninety of the crowd. The headline of the official mass-circulation newspaper of the Christian Socials shouted "A just judgement." Christian Socials, German Nationals, *Heimwehr*, and Nazis all cried Bolshevism! Revolution! But though rank-and-file socialists were now inflamed, the socialist leaders calmed them down, defusing the situation with mere parliamentary protest.

Socialist restraint continued right into 1934, into the teeth of Dollfüss's repressive measures and violent *Heimwehr* demonstrations that were intended to turn into a "rolling putsch." Both sought to provoke the *Schutzbund* into resistance that the state would then crush (the *Heimwehr* were also trying to provoke the Nazis to rise). But the socialists now limply abandoned their proclaimed right to self-defense. Almost the entire party leadership submitted without a fight, to the end offering concessions to Austro-fascist leaders to permit their own survival. In March 1933, when Dollfüss prevented parliament from meeting, the *Schutzbund* was finally ordered to mobilize, though in defensive positions. Yet immediately the socialist leader Otto Bauer ordered it to stand down again, as a gesture of goodwill. The government responded by ordering its dissolution. At the end, in February 1934, Richard Bernaschek, the *Schutzbund* leader in the city of Linz, did start a local insurrection against a police raid. This spread immediately and spontaneously through socialist organizations in various parts of the country. But the rising was against the expressed orders of the party leadership, described contemptuously by Bernaschek as "the brakemen" of socialism. He had telephoned the signal "To Arms!" at the very moment the police were breaking down his door to arrest him. Leaderless, without coordination, untrained to attack troops or even to occupy strategic neutral space, the socialist militias could not survive the onslaught of regular troops, police, and *Heimwehr* formations. They had been successfully provoked into a belated, disorganized rising. And revealing the pacific nature of interwar socialism, this was the greatest proletarian resistance to fascism we find anywhere outside Spain.

Later, in exile, Bauer rued his mistake: In March 1933, he said, the Socialist Party should have ordered a general strike and offensive action – as the Linz program had proclaimed. "We were then still stupid enough to trust Dollfüss' promise.... It was an error, the most fatal of our errors." In Austria, as in all other countries, it was not the socialists but the two fascist movements who honored violence. The *Heimwehr* was proud of its paramilitary aggression, though leaders did sometimes recoil from rank-and-file excesses. The Nazis proudly proclaimed "storm troop terror" and "ruthless violence against bestial terror." And as we find in every country, the imbalance in commitment to violence was reflected in the casualties. Among the 859 dead or seriously wounded during the civil strife from 1918 to 1934 we find the usual 2 to 1 ratio of socialist to fascist victims (Botz 1982: 303; Bukey 1986: 120–37).

Quite contrary to the right's claims, Austrian socialists were basically democrats. In contrast, the two nationalist camps were at most only "accidental" democrats (to use the Spanish expression discussed in Chapter 9). They were democrats for only as long as they could stay in power by democratic means. But they would not yield power to socialists. Instead, they chose authoritarian and fascist options. Even in the 1920s there were many authoritarians in the Christian Social party and in the Catholic Church. From the mid-1920s Christian Social governments were encroaching on constitutional rights, purging socialists from the army and administration, engaging in selective repression, cooperating with the *Heimwehr*. The army's main function became suppressing strikes. Then Nazism in the army was purged. By the mid-1930s the army was a reliable arm of Austro-fascism – though from 1936 it was infiltrated again by Nazis (Stülpfarrer 1989: 194–5). As the Depression brought economic crisis and as the Christian Socials and the German Nationalists faced pressure from fascists, both broke with democracy. Some leaders and activists went directly into the two fascist movements, others pressured their own movements to the right.

They need not have done so. They might have sought a grand democratic alliance with the socialists. This would have involved concessions on the staffing and role of the armed forces and police, plus Keynesian concessions to alleviate the Great Depression. Or they might have turned their repression against the fascists and attempted to restore the quasi-democratic status quo of the mid-1920s. The police and army may not have consented to suppress the *Heimwehr* (they did half-suppress the Nazis in 1934, though they would have refused to do so in 1938). But since these were the Christian Socials' own repressive agencies, this reveals only how the regime had become permeated with authoritarian sentiments. Or they might simply have gone ahead with a minority government and be prepared for further elections. Pauley (1981: 80) cannot argue that the Nazis could attain only 25 percent of the vote and yet also argue that Dolfüss could move only further to the right (if no alliance with the socialists could be obtained). Some apologists for the Dollfüss and Schüschnigg regimes argue that they suppressed the socialists to introduce a "temporary authoritarianism," to give a breathing space to stand up to Nazism. This is unconvincing: It is bizarre to defend democracy by suppressing the largest group of democrats. No; men such as Dollfüss and Schüschnigg *preferred* authoritarianism, and in the crunch they preferred fascists to democratic socialists – that is why they themselves became fascist fellow-travelers and why they used the armed power of the state to repress democrats.

A study of the city of Linz, in Upper Austria, which was Hitler's hometown, reinforces this judgment. Through the 1920s Linz seemed a model of compromise democracy. This partly resulted from constitutional arrangements: The city had a socialist administration, yet got its revenue from the provincial government of Upper Austria, which was Christian Social. There has been undue focus on Vienna, whose city had the constitutional status of a province and so could raise its own taxes and avoid compromise with conservatives. But in Linz, as in other cities, to avoid complete breakdown the two administrations had to cooperate and compromise. Even into the first days of the Dollfüss regime a few Christian Social and even German National leaders resisted its encroaching authoritarianism. When the break came in Linz, it first came in the Catholic Church as the local bishop, a long-term authoritarian, banned political activity by his more conciliatory clergy. Then came the collapse of the main grassroots organization of the Social Christians, the Catholic People's Association, which was now torn apart by dispute and was somewhat redundant in an authoritarian regime. The Upper Austrian Christian Socials were brought into authoritarian line by the regime by the time Bernaschek launched his desperate resistance (Bukey 1986: esp. 39–74, 112–19). Some conservatives were committed to democratic conciliation, but for most this had been short-lived and "accidental" – not principled.

As in other countries, Austrian conservatives had embraced fascism and reached for their guns too early. A class theory of their unseemly haste would have to center on their desire to maintain capitalist profit, not property per se. They resisted reform rather than revolution, since they were threatened only with reform. They reacted with hostility to almost every demonstration, they distorted the "violence" of socialist programs, they themselves perpetrated far more violence and with far more enjoyment. Of course, they felt vulnerable and threatened. They had been the ruling elite of a major power until 1918. They had been scared by the insurrectionary movements of 1918, though had managed to regain power. They had views similar to their German counterparts (discussed in the previous chapter). They felt that the state must possess powers of public order over and above those of a parliament, which could captured by the "mass armies" of civil society. Viewing the failure of German conservatives, they tried to bolster their own power with a mass movement, Austro-fascism. They might have succeeded, as Franco and Salazar did. It was essentially Hitler's greater success next door that undermined them. Once again, democracy was not stably institutionalized. In a crisis the right had other options. They embraced them for substantially class reasons, as Marxists argue. They fully intended their corporatist state to repress the left and to augur a more "harmonious" capitalism. Austro-fascism was certainly capitalist-biased. Yet that is not all Austrian fascism was.

THE APPEAL OF NATION–STATISM

Entwined with its capitalist bias was a second motive, more dominant in the populist wing of Austro-fascism and dominating Austrian Nazism. Here the genuine preference for fascism over democracy had more nation–statist sources. These fascists preferred an authoritarian, mass-mobilized, one-party state embodying the "racially pure" nation, cleansed of "aliens" and "traitors." They were not greatly interested one way or the other in capitalism. They had nothing of importance to say about capitalism beyond the cleansing of alien elements from its two contending classes, "Bolsheviks" from the ranks of labor and "Jews" from capital. Indeed, these two were often fused into a singular composite enemy, "Judeo-Bolshevism." They proudly proclaimed the superiority of this brutal vision to the conciliation and compromise that is democracy's essence. They were predominantly young and well educated at a time when fascism was sweeping adjacent countries. Thus they believed extreme, cleansing, transcendent nation-statism was the coming idea of the age. They also inflected their nation-statism with the racial anti-Semitism that was growing in their region of Europe.

Both a procapitalist bias and a more populist nation-statism permeated both movements, though capitalist bias increasingly dominated the leadership of Austro-fascism and nation-statism always predominated in Nazism. Once Austro-fascism was in power, the tensions between the two motivations began to blow it apart. Once Mussolini could no longer protect Austria from Germany, and once Hitler applied economic pressure, the Nazis could exploit its frailty and even infiltrate the regime, stealing away most of its militants. By the time of the German "invasion" the Austrian administration was hopelessly divided and the army stood aside, evincing clear pro-Nazi sympathies, unwilling to put its formal monopoly of military power at the service of the state. Until about 1936 administration and army had moved to embrace Austro-fascism. When that decayed, so did they. Hitler was astonished by the warmth of his reception and by the ease with which the Austrian Nazis seized most provincial administrations before German troops arrived anywhere near them (Pauley 1981: 216–17). The Nazi seizure of power lessened the capitalist bias and increased cleansing nation-statism.

The macro-causes of Austrian fascism have proved to be quite similar to those operating in other cases discussed so far. A military crisis (here a catastrophic defeat plus postwar border skirmishes) coupled with continuing economic crisis (continuing recession and class conflict) made fascist ideology seem plausible and generated its political support base (paramilitaries plus constituencies supporting nation-statism and class transcendence). Two Austrian peculiarities then made this a very distinctive blend of fascism. First, since there were two different nation-state ideals (a small Austria and a big Germany), there were two rival fascisms. Austro-fascism was the small option, more corporatist and old regime, Nazism was the big option, more radical. Since the old regime had survived the disasters of 1918 in fairly good shape, it could merge into Austro-fascism to take control of the country. Indeed, it might have ruled as long as the Franco or Salazar regimes. But, second, the German Big Brother who lived next door ensured the triumph of big Germany and therefore of Nazism. This explanation combines ideological, economic, military, and political power relations, though in a distinctive overall configuration. In particular, paramilitarism played a different and lesser role here in the seizure of power. Both fascisms mobilized paramilitaries. But the Nazis mobilized them against the military power of the state in 1934 and were flattened; while the success of the two "coups," of Austro-fascists in 1934 and Nazis in 1938, was also guaranteed by the military power of a state.

Austrians were to commit many atrocities before losing the war. But this was not the final dénouement, since Allied myth making pardoned most of them. There were few Austrian war crimes trials. The wages of sin proved to be a life of ease in one of the wealthiest and seemingly most harmonious countries of the world. The close postwar cooperation between Socialists and Christian Socials owed something to the legacy of fascist corporatism. Perhaps it owed something else to a guilty shared secret – "if we do not hang together, we will surely hang separately."

7

The Hungarian Family of Authoritarians

INTRODUCTION TO EASTERN EUROPE

Most discussions of fascism concentrate on Italy and Germany (occasionally extended to include its Austrian *Ostmark*). Yet no analysis can be complete without Eastern Europe where fascism diffused widely – not only as a distinct movement, but also as a corrosive radical force within more conservative authoritarian regimes. For authoritarians here remained through the interwar period as a fractious family whose reactionary, corporatist, and fascist members struggled noisily for overall dominance. Here also economies were less developed and old regimes survived well. Here most states and nations also had problematic boundaries, encouraging rival versions of organic nationalism. How different were these Eastern families? Might we consider them as late economic development strategies, as resistance to exploitation by more advanced countries, or as the product of local ethnic rivalries? Would we here find the same core fascist constituencies? I answer these questions with chapters on Hungary and Romania, the countries with the most significant fascist movements.

Both movements were large. The Hungarian Arrow Cross movement[1] had around 250,000 members during 1939–40, 2.7 percent of the national population (Szöllösi-Janze 1989: 128–33). The Romanian Legion of the Archangel Saint Michael (sometimes called the Iron Guard) had 272,000 members in 1937 and 300,000 to 500,000 in 1941 – 1.5 to 2.8 percent of the Romanian population (Heinen 1986: 382, 454; Ioanid 1990: 72). These are higher percentages than the 1.3 percent attained by German Nazism and the 1.0 percent by the Italian PNF before their seizures of power. Both movements also achieved large votes in elections. The Romanian party was officially credited with 16 percent of the vote in 1937, despite government harassment and result fixing. The chief of police later confessed

237

its real vote was nearer 25 percent; while other extreme nationalist and anti-Semitic parties received almost another 25 percent (Ioanid 1990: 69). The Arrow Cross coalition did receive 25 percent in the fairly genuine Hungarian election of 1939, while other parties took the combined "radical rightist" vote well over 50 percent. Since only Hungarian men over age twenty-six and women over thirty could vote, and young people were more fascist, these percentages must understate their popular support. Both movements were thus large and they were clearly fascist in ideology and organization, deploying the usual fascist paramilitaries and ceremonials, forcing many of their rivals to don similar clothing.

Both fascist movements acquired brief governmental power only during the war, yet they also penetrated and influenced other interwar and wartime governments. Since fascists surged later in Eastern Europe, governing elites could learn from Italian and German experience how to keep fascists at bay by alternately repressing them and stealing their ideas – a strategy they explained to British diplomats (whose reports to London have been edited by Vago 1975). This helped to contain self-proclaimed fascism, yet it meant that from the mid-1930s these countries' regimes were pervaded by fascist ideas and practices, blended into more conservative authoritarianism. It also meant that "true" fascists here never learned much opportunism since old regimes were not as keen to enter into conspiracies with them. Instead, fascists largely remained outside power, as "radical" uncompromising fascists.

The two countries thus become crucial to any general understanding of fascism. They differed from each other in three important respects. First, Hungary was (along with Austria) the biggest loser from World War I, ceding 68 percent of its territories and 59 percent of its population. Romania, the main acquirer of those territories and people (plus gains from other losers, Austria, Russia, and Bulgaria), was easily the biggest winner. Second, their rural class structures differed greatly. The Hungarian "gentry" class kept its political power after World War I, and so land reform was minimal. Yet Romania had few large estates, and fewer still after postwar land reforms directed mainly against ethnic minorities. Hungary had a powerful landlord class, Romania a potentially powerful peasant class. Third, Hungary had hitherto been one of the more tolerant countries toward Jews, who had supposedly enjoyed a prewar "Golden Age," while Romania had been the most anti-Semitic country in Europe, the only one still denying Jews citizenship in 1918. This should restrain us from making any simple generalizations concerning the impact of world war, reactionary landlords (both discussed in Chapter 2), or traditional anti-Semitism on fascism. But the two countries were similar in some other important respects. They were neighbors, less developed countries, and lesser powers. They enable us to broaden our understanding of fascism.

Yet these two fascisms have not been taken seriously. Their history was poorly recorded, then distorted over forty years of communist historiography that dismissed fascists as "criminal," "depraved," "lumpen," and "petty bourgeois," marginal to the country, supposedly its only significant source of anti-Semitism (e.g., Lackó 1969; Ránki 1980). The fall of communism has not yet produced a blossoming of local research. Hungarians and Romanians remain understandably reluctant to confront the possibility that fascists and anti-Semites had been close to the mainstream of national life during their countries' last experiment with democracy. So explaining these fascisms is not easy. The scarcity of good data seems to have persuaded some historians of Hungary to take the easiest explanatory route, embracing traditional class theory. Hungarian fascism, they say, is essentially petty bourgeois. This has not been quite so true of Romania, where Eugene Weber (1966a) long ago demonstrated its cross-class support. And even in Hungary we find dissenters. The English businessman John Keyser reported to the British Foreign Office in 1939 that the Arrow Cross was

First, a national movement to regain lost territory . . . secondly, a middle class movement which aims at occupying the positions held by the capitalists; and, thirdly, a movement of the masses – both urban and rural – which seeks to destroy capitalism. Both the second and the third are, of course, included in the first and share an expression of their aims in a common anti-semitism.

He added that the fascists' popularity had led the government to borrow from their program, a strategy he considered "somewhat dangerous, for it may play straight into their hands" (Vago 1975: 354). The research now available confirms Keyser more than it does petty bourgeois theory. Berend (1998: 142–3) summarizes it. He does not quite abandon all the traditional class theory I discussed in Chapter 1, for he notes the presence in East European fascism of "lumpen intelligentsia and uprooted people from whatever social strata." But he does also perceive that the fascist parties of Hungary and Romania (and also Croatia and Slovakia) "manifested a highly populist, peasant and working class character." Szöllösi-Janze (1989) has concluded not dissimilarly. He wields the available Hungarian data to conclude that Hungarian fascism was a popular movement of the oppressed masses led by excluded elites. This is correct as far as it goes. But we must also go beyond class, to note the way that the state, sectoral, and ethnic conflicts entwined with class to generate the core constituencies of Hungarian and Romanian fascism.

THE HUNGARIAN NARRATIVE

Hopes for stable liberal democracy in the new rump state of Hungary were shattered quickly, in 1919–20. An insurgent communist-socialist government led by Bela Kun had attempted to recover some of the territories lost through war and to defy the Entente's desire to impose harsh peace terms. But the leftists were defeated by Romanian and other foreign troops and finished off by Hungarian rightist "White" militias declaiming what they called the "Szeged Idea" from their base, the frontier town of Szeged. The Szeged Idea advocated violence directed against a "Judeo-Bolshevik" enemy, a notion borrowed from the White forces of the Russian Civil War and here given plausibility by the fact that twenty of Kun's twenty-six ministers and vice-ministers were Jews. The Whites promptly massacred large numbers of leftists and Jews and drafted others into coercive "labor service units" to build roads (these units were revived to maltreat Jews during World War II). But the Szeged ideal was vague in its positive ideals. It embodied an organic nationalism (Hungary was neither east nor west, and so promised a "Third Way," but for Magyars alone) and an unspecific call for a "strong" state. The combination was potentially fascist, and some of its adherents borrowed in the 1920s from Italian models to develop what was called a "gentleman's fascism," organic nationalism and a top-down, nonmobilizing populism and limited corporatism.

The core of these protofascist movements lay among the "Heroes Association," a movement of military veterans and refugees from the "lost territories" taken from Hungary by the Entente under the 1920 Treaty of Trianon. It is said that the refugees were mainly displaced army and civil service personnel who now formed the core of an "imperial revisionist" movement seeking to recover the lost territories. Refugees formed 5 percent of the Hungarian population but supposedly over half of the counterrevolutionary paramilitaries. Between a third and a half are said to have been former army officers, mostly young. But some detachments were formed from students (especially medical students) of whom it is said about a third were refugees. These statements do not seem to rest on much data. Bela Kun's defeat then emasculated the left, leading to an emigration of thousands of left and liberal intellectuals, especially Jewish ones. The old regime could demilitarize and institute a semi-parliamentary regime. We have a few data for the parliamentary deputies who then inherited the rightist leadership. Refugees were overrepresented among all parties, but most so in the far rightist party (the KNEP) – with a ratio of 6.9 (almost seven times overrepresented), double the ratio of 3.3 among centrist deputies. Refugee deputies were also younger and better educated (Braham 1981: chap. 1; Mócsy 1983: 126–9, 137–8, 146, 172–4).

The rightist victory in the civil war enabled the old regime to recover most of the power lost in 1918 and to refresh itself with a more radical rightist generation of young military veterans and refugees. Hungary remained a monarchy, though without a monarch, since there was no viable claimant to the throne. Executive powers were exercised by a regent, Admiral Horthy (an admiral without a navy, since the much-reduced rump state was landlocked!). The executive parts of the state remained largely in place. This was a semi-authoritarian regime, in the sense defined in Chapter 1, since an elected parliament and Horthy and his executive both possessed autonomous powers. But only a minority had the vote, and in the countryside balloting was open and subject to corruption and strong-arm tactics, wielded especially by old regime landlords. The communist party was banned and there was considerable censorship. A *numerus clausus* (maximum quota) was introduced in 1920 that restricted the number of Jews who could attend university to 6 percent of the student population – the first anti-Semitic legislation in postwar Europe. Horthy himself was essentially a conservative wobbling rightward with the times. But he did formally endorse the Szeged Idea and British diplomats reported that his conversation was dominated by hatred of Jews, communists, and the peace treaties (Vago 1975: 174). Yet he was no mobilizer of the masses and his policies were cautious. During the 1920s he and Prime Minister Bethlen professed their desire to move toward western democracy – lamenting only that the country was not yet ready for it. They did make some attempts to move toward the center, and from 1926 the radical Szeged rightists were marginalized. In 1928 the *numerus clausus* provisions applying to universities were modified, though the numbers of Jews who could be enrolled as students remained limited (Sakmyster 1994; Ságvári 1997: 406; Berend 1998: 140–2).

But old regime strength also prevented genuine land reform. The power of reactionary landlords remained intact and agrarian populism remained muted. There was no equivalent here to the large Romanian National Peasant Party, and socialism was also weak. Thus there seemed little chance that Hungary's parliament might become genuinely independent of the executive and the old regime. The radical right also benefited from the popularity of imperial revisionism. Though since 1867 Hungary had in effect been an imperial nation, ruling over half the Habsburg Empire, this domination had been short-lived, and so Hungarian nationalism still embodied a romanticized liberation struggle credo, the product of a long battle against the Turks and the Habsburgs. As in Serbia this history had produced a nationalism that we might think was actually rather imperialist – after all, they were dominating other ethnic groups – but which for the locals seemed a kind of liberation theology. The imperium now lost, Magyars (like Serbs later) claimed they wanted not Empire but "freedom." Every day, Hungarian schoolchildren chanted their version of the Pledge of Allegiance, the Magyar Creed:

> I believe in one God,
> I believe in one Fatherland,
> I believe in one divine eternal Truth,
> I believe in the Resurrection of Hungary.
> Hungary dismembered is no country.
> Hungary united is Heaven. Amen.

Rightist pressures, exacerbated by the onset of the Great Depression, led Horthy to restrict the suffrage, to limit civil liberties, to purge leftists and Jews from the public sector, and (to buy off the refugees) to expand university places and civil service jobs. His regime moved right in the early 1930s to become close to what I termed in Chapter 2 as "semi-reactionary authoritarian," dominated by landowners and the upper civil service and military, alternating clientelism, patronage, and repression to keep the masses passive (Szöllosi-Janze 1989: 101; Sakmyster 1994). The drift rightward was to continue through the interwar period.

Defeat and Trianon had also brought massive economic disruption. Living standards plummeted. Horthy and centrists pinned their hopes on the steady, if unspectacular improvement in the economy during the 1920s: By 1929 GNP per capita was 14 percent higher than it had been in 1913 (Bairoch 1976: 297). As elsewhere in an Eastern Europe being influenced by theories of later development, the methods chosen were mildly nationalist. Tariffs were enacted in 1925 and the first attempts were made at import-substitution policies. But then the Great Depression struck, exacerbating discontent. Since the socialist left was so weak, solutions to the Depression took a rightist autarchic and nationalist direction, as happened elsewhere in Eastern Europe. Import substitution was furthered, protecting domestic industry at the expense of agriculture and creating a state-industry alliance that prevented structural economic change and reinforced archaic practices benefiting old regime classes under a thin veneer of corporatism (Aldcroft and Morewood 1995: 58–95; Berend 1998: 234–65). For a time this increased the influence of Italian fascism on the right.

The heavy burden of Hungarian foreign debt was eased by a French loan. But this came with the much resented condition that the regime abandon all attempts to revise the peace treaties. The treaties involved guarantees for the rights of minorities, which in rump Hungary largely meant Jews. Aggrieved persons could petition the League of Nations in Geneva for redress against their government. Since petitioning was intermittently occurring through Eastern Europe, the issue of ethnic, especially Jewish, rights became a live issue, headlined in newspapers and politicians' speeches. Interpreted by nationalists as "foreign interference," it further politicized anti-Jewish sentiment: The Jews seemed allied to foreign powers imposing their terms on poor, weak Hungary. Since these Powers were also "capitalist," populists could add a class gloss to the blame: Hungary was being exploited by foreign – western and Jewish – capital. Thus imperial revisionism fused into a "proletarian" sense of the Magyar nation. Populist protest began to take radical rightist and anti-Semitic forms, led (it is said; there are no data) by lower civil servants, teachers, and the military, with refugees again prominent. This made some also susceptible to Nazism. In this drift rightward economic, geopolitical, and more diffuse nationalist and statist currents are not easy to disentangle.

In 1932 many feared social unrest, especially in the countryside, which was suffering disastrously from the Depression. Horthy, under pressure, moved further to the right by appointing as premier General Gömbös, an old friend, the key Szeged man and organizer of "White Terror," and noted anti-Semite. He moved steadily toward fascism. He declared violence to be "an acceptable means of statecraft . . . to shape the course of history, not in the interest of a narrow clique, but of an entire nation." He now embraced corporatist solutions to national unity and moved closer to Mussolini. After Hitler's coup, he promised Göring he would introduce totalitarianism and he wrote to Hitler describing himself as "a fellow racist." He declared that his government would "secure our own national civilization based on our own special racial peculiarities and upon Christian moral principles." Yet his conception of fascism was mainly top-down corporatism – "the Hitlerism of the better classes," said the British ambassador. He and his allies feared genuine fascists stirring up the masses from below and this fear bound them to Horthy and the old regime. Szollösi-Janze characterizes his government as "radical new right," centered on a radicalized bureaucracy and army, wielding a top-down single party, basing formal legitimacy on the masses but careful not actually to mobilize them. His sudden death in 1936 thwarted a likely coup abolishing parliament altogether (Berend 1998: 308–11). The regime remained mostly semi-reactionary authoritarian. Parliament endured, but more power was shifting into a radicalizing executive.

By then the Depression was receding. Yet the economy grew only slowly through the 1930s, while agriculture stagnated. The recovery was then led by rising military expenditures, which was as in Germany a boost to an authoritarian Keynesian approach to the economy. Hungary was also being drawn into the expanding German sphere of influence by the offer of what were initially very favorable terms of trade. The liberal powers and Jews were blamed for Hungarian backwardness, Nazi Germany praised as Hungary's friend. Economics and geopolitics remained closely entwined. In 1938 the *Anschluss* brought the Nazis into Austria next door, while the humbling of Czechoslovakia enabled Hitler to restore to Hungary its former territories in Slovakia. Revisionists saw they had a German ally. As Nazi influence mounted, parliament kept going but the executive half of the state split. Horthy's semi-reactionary authoritarians controlled the police and the interior and agriculture ministries, but pro-Nazi corporatists colonized finance, industry, and defense (Szöllösi-Janze 1989: 97). Under German influence, anti-Semitism was growing, and in 1938 the far-rightists secured discriminatory laws against Jews (Mendelsohn 1983: chap. 2). When Major Ferenc Szálasi managed to unite most of the small fascist parties, many radical officers and civil servants joined him. The executive state was now split three ways, among semi-reactionary authoritarians, corporatists, and fascists. A succession of more "moderate" premiers (the term is a relative one) periodically banned the fascists. Szálasi himself was arrested three times. Without the war, the outcome of such rivalries was far from clear. A peacetime dialectic between fascism and more conservative forms of authoritarianism might have had alternative outcomes.

The war greatly changed the resonance of the various political options. Yet even during the war the regime did not simply radicalize into fascism. Horthy was induced by geography, Hitler's willingness to see Hungary's territories restored, and his own fierce anticommunism into joining the Axis Powers. He accommodated to German hegemony while preserving some freedom of action. His main bargaining card with Hitler was that the Germans preferred his more orderly regime to the local, unruly fascists. In return for the alliance, Hitler returned most of the "lost territories" in 1940 (which also brought back more minorities into the realm). While the Arrow Cross languished, intermittently persecuted by the regime, other radical elements in the government introduced laws banning Jews from elite occupations and property ownership. Many thousands were deported in labor battalions abroad, not to return. Most of the Holocaust in Hungary was the work of Hungarian radical rightists. Yet Horthy resisted German demands to implement fully the Final Solution until March 1944, when German troops took over the country. In October the SS and Szálasi engineered a coup, leading to a brief fascist Arrow Cross regime. The Red Army arrived in January 1945, overwhelming and then executing Szálasi and his colleagues. Wartime events are discussed more fully in my forthcoming volume.

This brief narrative permits us to perceive five broad interwar trends.

(1) Economic discontent generated populist protest movements, including radical rightism. Yet the rightist drift persisted through both bad times and good, and so cannot be simply attributed to the state of the economy.

(2) After the civil war Hungary lacked much of a left and instead had a radicalizing old regime. Popular protest against exploitation was increasingly expressed by radical rightists, including fascists. But since the left was so weak, it would be implausible to attribute the continuing surge rightward to a desire by capitalists or others to repress the left. It already had been emasculated.

(3) Statist ideals of development surged through the period, yet statists remained split between alternative rightist ideals. The regime eventually stole fascist clothes while repressing actual fascists. Yet the fascists were gathering strength.

(4) Organic nationalism was rather distinctive, focused overwhelmingly on Jews, the only significant, supposedly "hostile" minority left in the country. Hungary had been formerly thought of as "good for the Jews," without pogroms. Many Jews were killed in the explosion of 1919–20, as fear of "Judeo-Bolshevism" swept the right. Anti-Semitism then continued to bubble, though it exploded again only in the late 1930s. It seems unrelated to the general state of the economy.

(5) Geopolitics pressured Hungarian governments toward allying with other revisionist powers against the liberal powers that had imposed Trianon. Hitler's successes meant that Hungarian revisionists came to favor a German alliance, and some of them were thus seduced into Nazism.

The conjunction of these trends boosted fascism, but unevenly. Though there was an enduring political crisis and a persistent drift toward more authoritarian solutions in the interwar period, the fascist outcome was more contingent, and so needs detailed explanation. Let us turn first to the fascist movement itself. What did fascists believe in, and who were they?

THE IDEOLOGY OF THE ARROW CROSS MOVEMENT

Szálasi was unfortunately given to turgid homilies rather than punchy slogans. It is not easy to make the next paragraphs readable. Fascism, he said, would "turn together the moral, spiritual and material interest of the I and the Us." The moral principle, he said, was Christian, the spiritual was "Hungarism," that is, nationalism, and the material principle was National Socialism. Szalasi argued that each was necessary, yet any single idea or principle had to be restrained from excesses. Thus if nationalism was not restrained by socialism, it led to chauvinism, imperialism, and war. If socialism was not restrained by nationalism, it led to unending class conflict or "state capitalism" on the Soviet model. National Socialism could transcend such conflict, its "organic" state and its party elite providing "a third factor of production" – adding to capital and labor a collective "intelligence" or "planning." Szálasi's "socialism" was distinctly productivist. It combined defense of "the worker as the builder of the nation," with attacks on finance capital and state planning to abolish unemployment. "Work was the basis of material life," unemployment was "material death." The new order would be corporatist, militarist, and statist: "all aspects of social life subordinated to the government . . . an active, and brutally realistic etatism." There was considerable Italian influence here, though there was also a distinctive Hungarian emphasis on the army, the "messiah which could force the country on the true road."

The third, spiritual principle of "Hungarism" expressed "the most perfect totality of the nation." Magyars, "the only Turanian people of occidental culture," could uniquely mediate between eastern and western civilizations. Along with the Germans and Japanese, they were destined to be one of the three "ruling peoples" of the world. Their "armed nation" would bring a "Pax Hungarica" to the Danube basin and a "workpeace" to the "working classes" (defined oddly as peasants, workers, intelligentsia, soldiers, women, and youth). But Hungary must recover, by force if necessary, the lost territories. There had been earlier attempts at "total social organization" made by the military, the church, and capitalism. Hungarian fascism would complete the totalizing work they had begun. The military would now support Hungarism – since its values were quite similar. But the church and capitalism could be expected to oppose it.

Szálasi denied being an intolerant nationalist, claiming that Hungarism implied "conationalism." But this was undercut by his liking for racial theories and his anti-Semitism. He encouraged his followers to collect skulls to confirm the biological superiority of the Turanian race. Though he insisted he was "a-Semitic," not anti-Semitic, this meant that he believed in a Hungary "free of Jews." He also argued that Magyars were economically exploited by Jews, who must be expropriated and encouraged to emigrate. Though Szálasi did not talk of "elimination" (the code word for mass murder), he said the Jewish question was the "only concrete question" facing the movement. And like Hitler, he equated Judaism with all his main enemies: "communism" or "Marxism," "freemasonry," "finance capital" or "bankocracy" or "plutocracy" or "the gold standard," and "liberalism" or "the liberal democracies" or "parliamentarism." Considering himself a good Catholic, he argued that the Old Testament showed "how God despised the Jews," while the New Testament was "the sanctification of God's contempt" (quotations from Weber 1964: 157–64; Szöllösi-Janze 1989: 220–250; Janos 1982: 272–6; Karsai 1998: 103–4).

Szálasi's fascists built on ideas that were fairly conventional on the Hungarian right – organic "liberationist" nationalism, "the third way," and Christian/nationalist anti-Semitism. They fused these with ideas drawn from both Mussolini and Hitler. From Italy they adapted corporatism plus Corradini's notion of a "proletarian nationalism" dedicated to throwing off the yoke of foreign exploitation. From Nazism they worked up Magyar populism into a more developed *Volksgemeinschaft*, made anti-Semitism more racial and blended it into anti-Bolshevism. Szalasi's own respect for the armed forces made for less of a conflict between Arrow Cross paramilitarism and the military power of the state, and he seemed sometimes more saccharine, sometimes more pragmatic than many fascist leaders. Some of his followers were more menacing, yet paramilitarism was not as important in Hungary as in the other four main fascist countries. The Arrow Cross demonstrated, marched, and sometimes brawled, but they seem to have gone no further until the war years. This seems to have been the main deviation from the normal blend of elements we have come to recognize as fascist.

This was the formal movement ideology. It would be nice to know how much of it was accepted by the ordinary rank-and-file fascist, but the data seem wholly lacking. I am compelled to turn straightaway to what kinds of people fascists were. And even on this, we don't know very much.

WHO WERE THE FASCISTS?

Our data are not as good as for other countries studied so far, forcing us to rely more on the qualitative judgments of contemporaries. But fascists were certainly youthful. British diplomatic reports continually emphasized this while fascism appeared first in the universities and among young soldiers. Though the movement aged, its leaders remained younger than other political elites (Janos 1982: 282–4). More than one generation was involved. For Szálasi and most of the early radical rightists, combat in the war and civil war was *the* formative experience, reinforced by the university environment of the early 1920s. The early core thus combined "front" and "home" generations. But after stagnation there was rapid expansion in the late 1930s among young men lacking any experience of war. Again, fascism was more the ideology of a period than of a single generation.

Observers and historians of Hungarian fascism have neglected gender. I have found no good data on Arrow Cross women, though this does not mean they were absent, except as leaders. There were female auxiliary groups and supporters, though I have found no data on who they were.

The data on class are also very limited. In the light of this, many have fallen back on the conventional wisdom of "petty bourgeois" theory (Nagy-Talavera 1970: 152–4, 287; Janos 1982: 270–1; Vago 1987: 308–15). Yet the one purportedly authoritative source does not confirm this view. Deak (1966) writes that a former Arrow Cross minister gave him details of all members in 1937 and 1940. According to this source, in 1937 some 50 percent of members were industrial workers (a ratio of 1.86), in 1940 some 41 percent (1.50), a substantial overrepresentation of workers.[2] Peasants and farm workers combined provided only 8 percent (0.27) and 13 percent of the party (0.44) – decided underrepresentation. The civilian middle class was also underrepresented, providing 12 and 19 percent of the two samples (ratios of around 0.40 and 0.60, respectively), while army officers comprised a very large 17 percent of the 1937 members (phenomenally overrepresented; 1940 figure not given). This would indicate an urban proletarian-military fascism – different from fascist movements we have seen in other countries so far. But we need more data before we accept what may be a source of dubious provenance.

We have no more data on ordinary fascist members, but a little on fascist leaders, presented in Appendix Table 7.1. Row 1 of this table details the leadership in 101 small rural communities. Almost half were small-holding peasants, seemingly rather poor. Most of the other leaders were small traders, artisans, and workers, in descending order of importance. Given that most leaders were literate, and most landless peasants were not, the rural parties may have been quite popularly based. Fascism may have attracted peasants for economic reasons. Governments had failed to do much to alleviate the Depression's collapse in farm prices. Since the German Nazis seemed to have successfully combated the Depression, many peasants believed fascism might also work in Hungary – so reported British diplomats. But there was more to it than that.

Row 2 of the table details middling-level leaders in larger towns and cities. These were predictably from more urban and bourgeois backgrounds. Almost half were independent professionals. Those from the biggest cities were overwhelmingly professionals plus government employees. The main professions were medicine, then the law. Szöllösi-Janze issues a familiar caution: Since public sector employees and the military were banned from being officials of fascist parties, their real level of covert participation in the Arrow Cross must have been higher. Most scholars would add civil servants, officers, and students (too urban to be in the first sample, too young to be in the others) to the groups overrepresented in these samples.

We have data on the national parliamentary deputies of various parties. Hungary had been an imperial country, junior partner to Austria, effectively running half the Habsburg Empire. In the early 1920s most politicians were still very much drawn from the old regime – landlords, establishment professionals, and bureaucrats who were members of the gentry estate. They were local notables delivering the votes of their dependents – typical patron-client "conservative" and "liberal" regime parties of the period. Yet this old regime had been destabilized by defeat in war, by a 50 percent reduction in territories that made the country more urban and less controllable by notables and by enraged refugees. Several would-be mass parties emerged – small socialist and peasant parties, plus rightist "National Radicals" drifting toward fascism. If we combine the National Radical and fascist parliamentary candidates and ministers of the interwar period, we find that they were 68 to 76 percent commoners, compared with only 19 percent commoners among the government parties. As Appendix Table 7.1 shows, the latter remained dominated by landowners, civil servants, and professionals (mainly lawyers), with only a handful of small-holding peasants and no one from industry at all. In contrast half the fascists were in the public sector or professionals (doctors, lawyers, army officers, and teachers), while the other half were drawn quite widely, from peasants, petty bourgeoisie, and a few workers (Batkay 1982: 42–5, 51–3, 64; Janos 1982: 282–4).

But we face a complication. As across most of Eastern Europe, class and ethnicity were entwined. In Hungary this most affected the middle class and Jews and Germans (of whom there were nearly two million). Whereas civil servants, landowners, and professionals were overwhelmingly Magyar or German, commerce and industry were dominated by other foreigners, especially by Jews. Only by understanding the links between Jews, ethnic Germans, and Magyars can we understand Hungarian fascism.

The Germans were mostly descendants of "Swabians," plus a few *Ungarndeutsche*, or "Zipser" refugees from Slovakia (which Trianon transferred from Hungary to the new state of Czechoslovakia). They had been originally encouraged to settle in the country centuries ago so as to develop agriculture, commerce, and industry. During the nineteenth century many had shifted over to the higher-status professions and to the public sector, especially the army. They had become largely Magyarized. Yet the rise of the German Empire had rekindled their German ethnic pride, especially among those trained in German or Austrian universities or military academies (Szelenyi 1998: part 3). The rise of modern Germany had increased the influence of Germany over Hungary, with Swabians at the helm (Janos 1970: 220–4; 1982: 282–4; Rothschild 1974: 308; Mendelsohn 1983: 113; Szöllösi-Janze 1989: 130–1, 159–63). The Swabians were now rather proud to be Hungarians *and* Germans. Many admired Hitler's successes and saw him as assisting the modernization of Central Europe. They became ambivalent about which state they wanted to serve, Hungary or Germany. Many Germans solved the dilemma by joining the Nazi-leaning radical right, where they became prominent. In interwar Hungarian cabinets only 30 percent of radical rightists – including some Arrow Cross men – had names indicating Magyar lineage, compared with 88 percent among liberal and conservative ministers. Almost all the remaining names were German. The Arrow Cross seems to have become concerned with this, since it doubled its proportion of Magyar-named candidates at the 1939 election. But its National Council, ruling the country in 1944–5, reverted to being only 30 percent Magyar-named. Both Szálasi and Gömbös were part German. Some interpret this as part of a broader tendency for fascist leaders to be of peripheral ethnicity. Hitler was an Austrian, the Romanian leader Corneliu Codreanu was the son of immigrants (the father probably of Polish origin, the mother from a German family from Bukovina), and the Slovak leaders Jozef Tiso and Vojtech Tuka had first spoken Magyar. I am skeptical. In Hungary there were more direct reasons for Swabian fascism.

Before World War I Hungarians had not seemed particularly anti-Semitic. The notion that this was a "Golden Age" for Jews is somewhat undercut by the fact that casual anti-Semitism was, as elsewhere else in Europe, buttressed by Christianity. But the newer European current of political anti-Semitism was weak. Hungarians had acquired political control over half the Habsburg Empire only in 1867. Aware of their minority numbers in that half, Magyar nationalists had not gone the organic route. They had espoused the doctrine of "ethnic balance," needing all the support they could get from other minorities who were not associated with rival states. They also seemed content to rule the state – there were plenty of pickings from their new dominion – and to let others dominate capitalism. Jews were allies in both regards (Karady 1993). This meant that Jews were offered an "assimilationist contract." Jews would be integrated into citizenship and protected from persecution. In return they would assimilate, Magyarize, and put their economic resources in the service of the Hungarian state. If they went further and baptized, they could even work in the state sector. But by and large the effect was to create a "dual market system": Jews were entrepreneurs, Magyars staffed the state. And in the census of 1910, 76 percent of Jews said Magyar was their mother tongue, many had Magyarized their names, and some were in the forefront of attacks against "ethnic aliens" (such as Romanians or Serbs). Assimilation was well under way (Karady 1997).

This was threatened by the settlement of 1918. Magyars so dominated their new rump state that they had no need of cosmopolitan allies. This was their organic state, yet it was also greatly threatened from outside. The supposed triad of the Bela Kun regime – the Soviet Union, domestic Bolsheviks, and Jews – produced the atrocities of 1919. In possession of only a weak state, Magyars needed to strengthen it with strategies of economic development. Yet the economy was controlled by cosmopolitan Jews, not Magyars. Jews became the main enemy. Nationalists now reversed their former tolerant policy, aiming for "dissimilation," separating the Jews from the nation. The 1920s saw a flood of anti-Jewish invective, permeating the literary elite as well as the pamphleteers (Ozsvath 1997). In this switch we see the importance of geopolitics to nationalism. One geopolitical configuration had generated the notion of an ethnically balanced state; another generated the notion of a state committed to cleansing nationalism.

By 1930 there were only just over half a million Jews, 5.1 percent of the national population and declining. But they were highly concentrated. Some 20 percent were in Budapest, and 40 percent of those were in Budapest's trade, commerce, and finance. An extraordinary 80 percent of owners (and 44% of white-collar workers) in the financial sector were Jewish. So were 53 percent of owners and 48 percent of white-collar workers in trade. Jews comprised 38 percent of mine owners (and 21% of mining white-collar workers) and 12 percent of manufacturing owners (and 39% of white-collar workers in industry). Jews made up 62 percent of all employers in commerce with more than twenty workers, and 47 percent of such industrial employers. These are extraordinary figures. Half the entire realm of capitalism in Hungary – big and small – was Jewish. Finance capital was astonishingly four-fifths Jewish. Some of the most privileged professions were also fairly Jewish. Of doctors, 60 percent were Jewish, lawyers 51 percent, journalists 34 percent, engineers 30 percent. Jews were only slightly overrepresented in the universities as a whole, since only 2 percent of the public sector was Jewish. But Jews comprised only 7 percent of industrial workers, 2.5 percent of transport workers, and 0.3 percent of the agricultural population (figures from Szöllösi-Janze 1989: 58–60). As Mendelsohn (1983: 92) observes: "The Jews, for better or worse, were totally identified with capitalist, bourgeois,

Westernized, urban Hungary. And they did not win the admiration of the many enemies of capitalism and of the city."

Such divisions led to mixed ethnic-class tensions, exploitable by populists inveighing against "foreign," that is, Jewish "exploitation." The divisions also generated differing views of modern economic development: Magyars and Germans were more statist, since it was *their* state. Jews and other capitalists were more market- and internationally oriented – for this was their own social experience. These two contrasts, involving nation and state, set the stage for the growth of fascism among Magyars and Germans seeking a strong nation-statism to defend them against "alien exploitation."

But let us turn more directly to the question of the class composition of fascism. Explanations here often start off in straightforward materialist terms. Fascism is explained as resulting from "middle class proletarianization" and "academic overproduction" (Janos 1970: 210–11; Nagy-Talavera 1970: 69; Rothschild 1974: 178, 308; Vago 1975: 320; 1987: 286). It is argued that employment prospects could not keep up with university expansion. Thus students and overcrowded professions exploded in protest. Since most were from middle-class homes, the protest was rightist, not leftist. The large numbers and better prospects of Jewish students turned student protest toward anti-Semitic fascism, said the British diplomats (Vago 1975). Jewish dominance over better jobs turned the middle class anti-Semitic, says Rothschild (1974: 196). Was this true?

"Overproduction" is most plausible immediately after the war, when Magyar civil servants, officers, and students came flooding back as refugees to the reduced prospects of the rump state; it might also be plausible in the Great Depression. Yet overproduction could not explain the period of fascism's greatest growth, in the late 1930s, when the economy was recovering (Barany 1971). However, the recovery was boosted by Nazi Germany, now the main customer for Hungarian agricultural produce. Fascists argued that the Nazis had saved Hungary from the "parasitical tyranny of Jewish finance capitalism." Thus though economic collapse may have early fueled Hungarian fascism, it was economic growth, more than depression, that helped to generate fascism as a mass movement.

Does the "overproduction" thesis explain the growth of extreme organic nationalism aimed against Jews? For the most part, no. As in Austria – and again with the exception of students and some professions – fascists came from occupations and sectors with fewest Jews. Middle-class fascists were most likely to come from the civil service and the army, where there were almost no Jews. In fact, Horthy had quite early placated rightists by purging liberal and Jewish civil servants and teachers, expanding the universities and schools, and maintaining a bloated civil service largely barred to Jews. Public sector economic discontent had grown as budgetary pressures tightened during the Depression, but then they eased. Yet extreme rightists were always grossly overrepresented in the public sector, while the schools and universities increasingly taught ultranationalism and so generated young fascists. Short-term economic motives do not seem to have dominated this fascism.

Army veterans had been the vanguard of early fascist tendencies, and the army remained the most important source of Hungarian fascism. Contemporaries suggested that 40 to 50 percent of the army was profascist by the late 1930s (John Keyser went as high as 80 to 90%). Sometimes they referred to "officers," sometimes they implied that the ordinary soldiers were also fascist. They always reported that younger officers or soldiers were the most attracted. Regular army personnel may have been supplemented by "Lumpenguardists," irregular rightist paramilitary formations of former soldiers who turned toward fascism. I have found no details of these, however. There was little Jewish competition nor serious economic deprivation in the military, which was expanding throughout the 1930s. Other influences must have nourished military fascism. In Hungary the normal resonance of rather orderly, disciplined, top-down far rightism among the armed forces seems to have been greater than elsewhere. The officer corps was also recruited disproportionately from the usual nation-statist constituency: from civil servants and the free professions, not industry or commerce. And it had a high proportion of Swabian Germans, including twenty-one out of the twenty-seven generals in 1941 (Janos 1982: 253). Thus the army became a *Mitteleuropa* wedge, blending German, Austrian, and Magyar traditions with a more modern Nazi-German militarism. During the war the army remained pro-Nazi, anticommunist and strongly anti-Semitic. Though Horthy wished to emulate the Romanian government and to switch to the Allied side in 1944, he believed the army would not countenance this. In the end the Hungarian army drew short of complete complicity in the Holocaust, yet in the war it proved to be Hitler's "last satellite" (Gosztony 1985; Szöllösi-Janze 1989: 194–201; Ránki 1971: 69).

Anti-Semitism in the areas of fascist strength was thus directed not inward against Jewish competition but outward against Jewish domination of finance and trade – against both Budapest monied interests and small-scale rural trading and money lending. This was buttressed by anticapitalism among workers and poor peasants. To this stereotype was once again paradoxically added its apparent opposite: the Jew as socialist. Though socialism was relatively weak, it had attracted much of a generation of young bourgeois Jews at the beginning of the century. Socialist leaders had been more Jewish than in any other country. Some 40 to 77 percent of various samples of Hungarian socialist leaders, from Bela Kun's regime onward, were Jewish (Janos 1982: 177; Mendelsohn 1983: 95). The bourgeoisie hated the memory of Bela Kun for class reasons; many younger workers, little exposed to socialism, may have thought of Kun as just an alien Jew.

As in Austria, there were exceptions. The universities and some professions had many Jews and fascists. The universities were hotbeds of anti-Semitism. Students rioted several times, demanding quotas on Jewish entrants. Under their pressure the government had imposed quotas in 1920 and then lifted them in 1928. In any case, 13 percent Jews in the universities was not exactly a "swamping" level, destroying Christians' job prospects. And whereas the Magyar and German students came from and were later going to the state/professional/landowning sectors, the Jews were predominantly commercial in origins and destinations. They were more on different career trajectories than direct economic rivals. It was probably more their cultures that differed, making coexistence difficult.

But what about those few jobs where the different ethnic groups did intersect, among some of the liberal professions? Was fascism here a response to overproduction, proletarianization, and a Jewish material "threat"? Kovács (1991) suggests not: Engineers and medics were in prospering professions; they were not an academic proletariat. In the early years of the century they had been drawn leftward, where "modern" ideas were assumed to lie. But after the Kun debacle their professional associations turned toward the vision of modernity offered by the extreme right. In 1937 *all* the twenty-three engineers elected to parliament represented fascist parties. Kovács sees fascism as flowing from their "technocratic" (engineers) and "biomedical" (doctors) professional ideologies. The former linked scientific progress to the state, the latter to the race-nation. In contrast, she says, most lawyers continued to support the regime parties because their practices depended on capitalism (and, I might add, on the old regime). Though there were fascist lawyers, they constituted a far smaller proportion of their profession than the fascist medics and engineers did of theirs. And though there were many Jewish doctors, Kovács argues that medical fascists were interested less in economic competition than in inserting anti-Semitism into a broader nation-statist ideology.

Thus "overproduction," direct Jewish occupational rivalry, and other forms of economic deprivation played some part in the rise of fascism, while the Great Depression played a large part in one particular period. But in any case materialist motivations came heavily entwined with ethnicity.

Fascism appeared to be more the product of a sectoral conflict between Magyar/German nation-statism and a supposedly international and Jewish capitalism. To this was added a class/ethnic conflict that ranged Magyar workers and peasants against "alien" capitalists. The first conflict helped form the whole of the Hungarian radical right, the second was more specific to fascism.

FASCIST VOTERS

The 1939 electoral data enable us to get closer to worker and peasant support (results in Lackó 1969; Ránki 1980; Vago 1987: 306–10; Szöllösi-Janze 1989: 153–65). The Arrow Cross coalition drew 25 percent of the national vote. But it did best in the "red belt" industrial suburbs outside Budapest. Allied with a small quasi-fascist party, there it received 42 percent of the vote. It also did well in mining communities and poorer agricultural areas. Budapest city districts with more workers gave more votes to the fascists. The rise in their Arrow Cross vote was also proportionate to the decline in the Socialist vote: Fascism was stealing socialist voters. Indeed, the banned Communist Party instructed its members to vote for the Arrow Cross, which it declared to be the most proworker party. The Socialist vote remained highest in the older proletarian ghettos. Newer working-class areas were more vulnerable. Szöllösi-Janze suggests that younger workers were more receptive, though there is no direct evidence on age and voting. Deak (1966: 396–7) observes that the socialist unions recruited relatively privileged and skilled workers in well-established industries, their sectionalism alienating other workers who could then be recruited by populist, anti-Semitic movements.

Indeed, the Arrow Cross was in many ways genuinely leftist. Its claim to transcend class politics was not undermined by capitalist biases found further west. It maintained a stronger antifeudal, anticapitalist stance than any fascist party we have yet analyzed (Janos 1982: 287). True, it rarely attacked capitalism head-on, preferring to denounce "adjectival capitalisms": that is, "foreign," "finance," and (especially) "Jewish" capitalism. But these attacks included demands for redistribution of property. A League of Nations financial adviser reported in 1938 that the fascist program was

to put the conduct of affairs into the hands of men who are uncorrupted by wealth or by the political game ... to take finance and industry out of the hands of the Jews, thus providing jobs for the educated unemployed, split up the big estates and give land to the landless peasant, and make rearmament the cardinal point in the Government's programme.

This representative of fiscal orthodoxy did not add that the fascists portrayed rearmament in quasi-Keynesian terms, as economy-boosting and job-creating, developing a rival nation-statist view of economic development. Observers sometimes claimed that the Arrow Cross became the final resting place of ex-communists. The British ambassador improbably reported that 60 percent of its followers had earlier followed Bela Kun (Vago 1975: 320–1, 265, 308, 215). But the Arrow Cross sat on the left in the chamber and organized strikes, most prominently a large miners' strike in 1940. Remember that the socialists and communists had been crushed in 1919 and remained weak. Horthy had allowed socialists to organize in the towns if they remained moderate and stayed out of the countryside. In fact, there were socialist deputies in parliament throughout the war, even when the Nazis were controlling much of Hungary. At the same time Horthy had ruthlessly repressed the communist party. As he intended, this dual policy factionalized the left. One radical faction joined the Arrow Cross en masse, advocating populist violence plus syndicalist planning (Wessely 1991). Yet it may be that a substantial organized working-class presence among Hungary's fascists made it more like an "ordinary" mass party, increasing electoral at the expense of paramilitary organization.

Within the middle class, areas with many civil servants also had a higher fascist vote, in contrast to areas with most traders and independent artisans (these were also the most Jewish areas). Districts with more ethnic Germans were more fascist. The socialist and liberal vote held up best in the more Jewish areas, suggesting that Jews supported the traditional left. The government party did best in the most bourgeois areas and those with most civil servants.

Region also figured somewhat. Though the Arrow Cross vote spread across most of the core provinces of the country, it was lower in the far north and in the southwest. This may have been because these borders were less "threatened," since neither Austria nor Czechoslovakia were perceived as the real obstacles to imperial revisionism. But there were certainly fewer Magyar refugees and fewer Jews in these regions around which extreme nationalism might mobilize.

Though such electoral data are not so detailed as in the German studies, they indicate that Hungarian fascism appealed most to industrial workers, then to poorer peasants. Fascism was also fiercely competing with other rightists for the public sector. Hungarian fascism seems to have had a nation-statist bourgeois leadership mobilizing a proletarian electoral base against "foreign exploiters."

CONCLUSIONS

Fascists seized power in Hungary only when it was too late, in October 1944. Other members of the authoritarian family kept them at bay, though only by stealing so many fascist clothes that it becomes difficult to distinguish who was truly a fascist. Thanks to the civil war, the old regime was able to reacquire power but with a radical wing. The civil war also ended the power of the left and serious, overt class conflict. Old regime conservatives here were not panicked into an alliance with fascists. Radical rightism, including strains of fascism, appealed for more nation-statist reasons that initially combined territorial revisionism with late development statism. But as organic nationalist and Nazi influence grew, an alien enemy was also identified within Hungary. Radical nationalists including fascists focused on Jews, who they plausibly connected to cosmopolitan capitalism and (less plausibly) to international Bolshevism. Thus much of the agenda of a rather Nazi-leaning fascism was eventually adopted by a large part of the entire Hungarian family of authoritarians.

Since I found only limited evidence on the fascists, no judgment on them can be definitive. The better-evidenced Romanian case clarifies some of these issues. Yet three broad Magyar trends have emerged. Two were as in other countries: Fascism was a movement of two separate generations of young men, and it was led by a variant of the usual bourgeois "nation-statist" core constituency. This time, however, it had a stronger military and a weaker paramilitary component. This was mainly because the old regime survived so well. This was from early on a rather "official" and "statist" fascism, with a greater respect for existing authority structures than other fascist movements. I need not detail once again my explanation of these two core constituencies of support – that fascism was the coming idea of this age of crisis in countries where democracy was not securely institutionalized, appealing most to the young, the highly educated, and those with close ties to the nation and/or the state. Of course, "true" fascists never attained majority support in Hungary nor did they come into power in any viable way. Yet boosted by late development statism, imperial revisionism turned into a more "proletarian" sense of foreign exploitation. Influenced greatly in the 1930s by Nazi Germany, Hungarian authoritarian rightists were busy stealing fascist clothes while repressing self-declared fascists. Organic nationalism had also emerged in the postwar period, aimed at a singular Jewish enemy, turning the Hungarian right toward Nazism. Hitler's expansion had then reinforced this. By wartime nation-statist elites were fascist fellow-travelers.

Yet the third characteristic of Hungarian fascism differed from Italian fascism or Nazism: Its mass support was rather proletarian. The Arrow Cross did more than appeal to workers outside the core "proletarian ghettos" (as other successful fascisms managed to do). It also penetrated *inside* the proletarian ghetto, in the capital and in some rural areas. This owed much to the weakness of socialism. Devastated by its revolutionary overambition in 1918, then by repression and Horthy's clever tactics, socialists and communists could not offer plausible leadership to the oppressed. Fascists filled the gap. They attacked the corruption and wealth of the old regime and they attacked exploitation by finance, foreign, and Jewish capital. They praised productive workers, supported some of their struggles, and demanded full employment – all amid a modernism alternative to that offered by socialists. This was linked to a "proletarian" foreign policy: Poor, dependent Hungary was being exploited by the plutocratic finance-capitalist liberal powers. And since the ruling class spent much time imprisoning them, fascists were forced willy-nilly toward a proletarian rather than a capitalist bias. Theories attributing fascism to the desire of the propertied classes to repress labor by "reaching for the gun" simply do not apply to Hungary. But then, Hungarian fascism, with less of a paramilitary presence than other fascisms, also offered fewer guns.

Nonetheless, there must have been some tension between "top-down" elitism, statism, and militarism and "bottom-up" proletarianism. This was eased by a more specific cement binding together nation-statists and the proletariat into a more Nazi-like fascism: anti-Semitism. As in Austria and (we see below) Romania, Jews could be plausibly labeled as the enemies of both the nation-state and the proletariat. To the fascists Jews seemed an important ally of the old regime and foreign and finance capitalism. Ethnic conflict was thus reinforced by a sectoral conflict: Statism opposed industrial and finance capitalism supposedly oriented to foreign and Jewish, rather than national, goals. This capitalism had recently brought enormous sufferings to the people; relief was now being brought by National Socialism, as could be seen in Germany. Jews did not loom quite so large for workers. Yet Jewish dominance over credit and trade encouraged a materially motivated anti-Semitism among poor peasants and (probably less frequently) among urban renters and consumers. Direct class conflict could be identified between many miners and industrial workers and their Jewish employers. And it was in anti-Semitism that Magyar organic nationalism took off into murderous ethnic-political cleansing, as we see in my forthcoming volume.

Socialist theories of class conflict have appealed to far more workers than have fascist ones. Yet in the absence of effective socialism, the three-pronged fascist theory of class conflict – that *finance, foreign,* and *Jewish* capital exploited workers – seemed plausible in some interwar countries. And in politics, minimal but resonant plausibility – never some higher standard of truth – rules.

8

The Romanian Family of Authoritarians

INTRODUCTION: BACKGROUND

I delineated the overall contours of Romanian fascism in my introduction to the previous chapter. Here I introduce Romania the country, the most economically backward and the politically newest country I analyze in this book. Modern Romania had emerged only in 1861 as a union between Moldavia and Wallachia (itself composed of the provinces of Oltenia and Muntenia), just wrested from the retreating Ottoman Empire. World War I then brought an extraordinary bonanza to this small country, as can be seen in Map 8.1.

Tempted by territorial bribes from the Entente, Romania had declared war on the Central Powers in 1915. The payoff in the Peace Treaties was immense: the province of Bukovina gained from Austria, Transylvania and parts of the Crisana-Banat from Hungary, Bessarabia from Russia, and Dobruja from Bulgaria. This more than doubled Romania's territories and population, while non-Romanians rose to 30 percent of total population (despite large-scale emigration of minorities back to their "homelands"). Ethnicity was now more politically relevant and more entwined with class, since the lower and rural classes of the new territories tended to be Romanian, while the upper and urban classes were mostly drawn from formerly ruling nationalities (especially Magyars and Germans) plus Jews. Non-Romanians – mainly Jews, Hungarians, and Germans – owned the majority of manufacturing and commercial enterprises, and a large majority of the bigger ones. Jews alone, 4 percent of the total population, owned 40 percent of the commerce and credit and 28 percent of the industrial-artisanal sector. They were a quarter of the only liberal professions open to them, physicians, pharmacists, and veterinarians. The Romanian middle class dominated only the public sector and the nonscientific professions

261

Map 8.1. Romania.

(Ianciu 1996: 65–76). This made it understandable that an organic form of nationalism should appear among the state-dependent and "humanistic" middle class, proclaiming Romania a "proletarian nation," "exploited" by foreigners (especially Jews) at home, "threatened" by revisionist powers along its borders.

But would anyone listen to them? The army and the state, composed of monarchy and notable politicians, had eventually emerged triumphant from a difficult war. The Orthodox Church was loyal. Only the foreign landlords were now gone. We cannot quite call this an "old regime," since it had ruled only for half a century. But the ruling elite was quite well entrenched, mobilizing a mild nationalism that they hoped to continue controlling from above. In this backward country nationalism was mostly an urban affair. Few of the peasant masses at first identified with the nation. Their concerns were more parochial and subsistence-minded. They did hope the postwar state would materially improve their lives and they welcomed the initial land reforms. Yet the Romanian economy needed greater agricultural productivity through increased investment. Land reform made this less likely, since it proliferated small peasant holdings. This also increased the birthrate beyond what the agricultural practices of family farming could sustain. Many poor peasants were forced to turn from wheat, the main export crop, to maize, a labor-intensive subsistence crop. Poverty, disease, and subsistence remained the lot of most Romanian families. GNP per capita grew a paltry 7 percent between 1913 and 1938 (Bairoch 1976: 297). The infant mortality rate – a good indicator of rural poverty – slightly worsened after 1930, though average life expectancy had improved from prewar levels. No longer controlled by landlords in most areas, peasants might begin to listen to radical political solutions to remedy their dire straits.

Romania was formally a liberal democracy. Under Entente pressure, Romania had conferred the suffrage on all adults, including Jews, becoming the last European state to grant Jews citizen rights. Yet alongside parliament, the king retained considerable executive powers, including the right to choose ministers and to control the police and army. Thus he and notable politicians, conservatives, and liberals ruled through the 1920s with the usual semi-authoritarian blend of elections, patronage, corruption, and selective repression of extremists (including fascists). This was cynically called "government by rotation," seen as corrupt and ineffective. With liberalism ineffective and socialism seen as foreign, the way was open for the fascist "third way." Yet the government did offer a nationalist economic policy, "by ourselves alone," a mildly statist strategy of late development, centering on protective tariffs, described by their main architect, the economist Manoilescu, as the "wonder weapon" of economic nationalism. This was coupled with an attempt at forcible assimilation of minorities and "Romanianizing" public institutions, especially education, street signs, and business advertising. Since this involved taking away rights from hitherto privileged minorities, protest and some imperialist revisionism appeared among them, provoking organicist backlashes among Romanians. Thus were dozens of Magyars killed when troops fired on their protest meeting in Transylvania in 1919. Even Romanian conservatives and liberals were pursuing mildly nation-statist goals in the early interwar period.

Being urban modernizers, the government also favored industrial more than agricultural development, and they used oil revenues (the country's one great economic asset) to boost industrial development and to restrain imports. The revenues also fueled corruption. When agriculture stagnated, the peasants gave the National Peasant Party, an "out" party not as yet involved in corruption, a landslide victory in 1928. The NPP was committed to freer trade, social protection for peasants and workers, and more democracy, less corruption. Its best-known leaders also called for ethnic and religious toleration, though anti-Semitism was not absent from the party. It represented the main chance for harnessing the majority peasants to a progressive liberal democracy, one that might even have encouraged ethnic toleration. The king, however, was deeply suspicious of the reformist tendencies of his new government. And 1928 was a bad year. The Great Depression destroyed the credibility of the NPP government (as happened to many governments during the Depression), and it never fully recovered. Since industry produced mainly for the domestic market, and the main export industry was oil, industry was not too badly hit by the Depression. By 1933 production levels had returned to those of 1929. Agriculture was worse hit. Peasant incomes declined about 58 percent during this period. Fearing unrest, the state restructured peasant debts – the last major pro-peasant act performed by interwar governments. But Romanian politicians drew the lesson from the Great Depression that industrial protection worked (oil apart). They strengthened import substitution policies with an explicitly anti-imperialist and "proletarian" cast: Western exploitation kept Romania poor, therefore bar western imports. By 1938 Romania was 80 percent self-sufficient in industrial products. Though its major foreign customer became Germany, it was not so subjected to German economic dominance as Hungary, being farther away. Employment and power utilized in industry had risen about 50 percent since 1929 – well above the growth of the world economy. This had been achieved by increasing the state sector, restraining consumption, and starving agriculture of investment (Berend and Ranki 1974; Chirot 1978; Verdery 1983: 278–86; Ronnas 1984: 37, 116–122, 241; Aldcroft and Morewood 1995: chaps. 3 and 4; Berend 1998).

Government was now by increasingly authoritarian coalitions among notables and nationalists, supported and manipulated by King Carol. "I do not care for elections," he bluntly told a British journalist. He had to put up with them through the 1930s, though, acquiring more powers for the executive, which acquired tinges of semi-reactionary authoritarianism, and then of Italian corporatism. From the late 1930s Carol and then his successor the dictator General Antonescu also felt compelled to steal more of the clothes of Romania's own fascist movement (Zach and Zach 1998: 809–15). The entrenched political power of the executive part of the state, plus the economic pressures of the Great Depression, provided most of Romania's initial drift toward authoritarianism.

Thus in the interwar period it was the mainly non-Romanian industrial and commercial bourgeoisie, plus the Romanian state sector, that were doing best, followed by industrial workers, with peasants lagging. We might thus expect "normal class conflict," exacerbated by the Great Depression, to set peasants and perhaps workers against a bourgeoisie protected by the state and the king. But ethnic-political conflict intervened to restructure collective senses of exploitation. It is relevant that the greatest interwar success story was in education, a key infrastructure of ideological power. Interwar literacy rates doubled. This had the effect of increasing ethnic consciousness, since shared literacy in the Romanian language heightened national identity and receptivity to nationalist ideology. This was especially likely since, as in most other countries, the teachers, journalists, and the compilers of dictionaries and grammarbooks tended to be nationalists. Social movements claiming Romanians were a "proletarian nation" exploited by foreigners attracted more followers, especially from the young and newly educated.

THE IDEOLOGY OF THE LEGION OF THE ARCHANGEL MICHAEL

The Romanian variant of fascism was essentially homegrown, though it borrowed a little from both Nazism and Italian fascism. Its leader or "captain" was Corneliu Codreanu, born in 1899 in a small Moldavian border town to a German mother and a teacher father who, although originally Polish, became an active Romanian nationalist. Codreanu was educated at military academy and Jassy University and qualified for the law. At Jassy he came under the influence of the famous nationalist professor, A. C. Cuza, the founder of a far rightist movement renamed in 1925 as the League of National Christian Defense (the LANC). Cuza espoused an extreme anti-Semitism deduced from organic nationalism. The nation must be one, purged of all non-Romanian elements. The Jews were the greatest danger – they were "dangerous parasites," a "bastard nation, degenerate, sterile, without land, who cannot form a complete and productive social organism." They must be "eliminated," a word of unclear meaning, but certainly including mass deportations abroad, expropriation of their property, and banning their participation in public life. In the early 1920s this was as extreme as what anyone was saying in Europe. But Cuza was a traditionalist. Though he adopted the swastika as his symbol before Hitler did, its four corners were emblazoned with words adding up to a traditionalist slogan: "One country, one law, one people, one king" (Ianciu 1996: 186–96).

But Cuza was a professor, not a man of action. It was this that bothered the young Codreanu, who broke from Cuza in 1927 to create his own movement, the Legion of the Archangel Michael (which he had initially formed within the LANC as its youth movement). In turn this generated the Iron Guard (open to all ages) in 1930. From then on the two organizations were virtually synonymous. I simplify by referring to them both as "the Legion." Codreanu's main disagreement with Cuza was over tactics. Codreanu wished to engage in a planned campaign of violence, directed initially against Jews. Anti-Semitism utterly dominates the autobiography he addressed to his legionaries in 1936 (Codreanu 1990). But his anti-Semitism was of a particular kind. He *always* denounced Jews as rich exploiters – they were parasites, leeches, and so on, dominating industry, banking, and trade, "squeezing" the Romanians into abject poverty and dependency. Even in Bessarabia, where he also denounced Jews as "communists" (this had been a Russian province before 1918), he also denounced them as Shylocks. His seems to be almost entirely a "proletarian" type of anti-Semitism – though he does not use the term – in which Romanians are the oppressed proletariat, Jews the capitalists. His desire for more "action" than Cuza would countenance came from his discovery that provocative demonstrations against rich Jews, plus consequent "defensive" violence against the police chiefs and administrators who protected Jews and repressed local discontent, brought considerable support from the local population. Indeed, juries acquitted him of murder and intimidation during the 1920s because they also hated corrupt politicians and brutal police chiefs. Bad experience with the authorities made him see politicians as mere lackeys of the Jews – being literally "bought" by their bribes – again a view more normally associated with "proletarian" leftist movements than rightist ones. This led him to the revolutionary view that the entire political system must be overthrown – except for the monarchy (for which institution he retained a reverence conditioned by his view of its historic role in liberating the nation). But in the climate of the early 1920s, and with the aid of the military values inculcated by his cadet school background, such actions and views led him to provocative paramilitarism against the state as well as enemies in civil society – and this led to fascism.

His autobiography includes his principal political pronouncements. His first major political statement, his "Creed of National Christian Socialism" of 1920, began and ended thus:

I believe in one and undivided Romanian State . . . the holder of all Romanians and only of Romanians, lover of work, honor and in fear of God . . . giver of equal rights, both civil and political, to men and women; protector of the family . . . supporter of social harmony through minimizing of class differences, nationalizing factories (the property of all workers) and distributing the land among all the ploughmen. by restricting class divisions. . . . I await the resurrection of national conscience even in the most humble shepherd and the descent of the educated into the midst of the tired, to strengthen and help them in true brotherhood, the foundation of Romania of tomorrow. Amen.

The creed also included details of economic redistribution between the classes, plus support for the monarchy and Orthodox Church. It was a somewhat statist, very leftist, and deeply religious form of organic nationalism. The individual was subject to the nation and the nation was subordinate only to God. Many of Codreanu's later pronouncements appear less political. The 1927 Program of the Legion paradoxically declared itself not a "political" or "party" program at all but "a program for a new man." The wrongs of politicians and the "infection" of Judaic influence require new men. For "man's reform . . . the Legion will be more a *school* and an *army* than a political party," to create the "spiritual and moral atmosphere" amid which a "hero in the warlike sense" can be molded from the Romanian character. He then listed the qualities of this hero, making the legion sound more like a militant religious sect than a political party. He also laid down eight "ethical norms of legionary life," proceeding from such generalities as "moral purity" and "enthusiasm" to such fascist-sounding values as "faith, work, order, hierarchy, discipline," and "deeds not words." The legion, he averred, was not only a "logical system . . . it is a living faith." But this faith was also militaristic: "[I]t will be a constant call to battle, the appeal to bravery, the stirring up of the warlike qualities of our race." Like Hitler, Codreanu did not much elaborate his statism beyond the leadership principle. This he deduced from his organic nationalism. A united nation can have one single will, or "state of spirit," and its leader can perfectly express this. Indeed, he claims, this cannot be "dictatorship," where the dictator imposes his will over the people. Where the people and chief have a single will, the state is no more than an "elevated *national conscience*." The leader will select an elite chosen by their fitness to rule. He opposed democracy, therefore, as dividing and ruining the nation – do soldiers elect their best generals? he asked. Democracy also permitted Jews equality and becomes enslaved to bankers (Codreanu 1990: 15–17, 219–22, 226, 231, 242–3, 304–10; cf. Ianciu 1996: 199–200).

Though unfortunately there is little evidence available on the beliefs of ordinary militants and members, the legion was well organized to socialize its members in such values. It consisted of a network of "nests" garbed in paramilitary trappings. Nest leaders had to cultivate an "aristocracy of virtue" in their militants, following six golden rules: disciplined loyalty, work, silence, self-education, mutual aid, and honor. These would prepare legionaries for self-defense, sacrifice, and martyrdom – "the blood of all us must flow" in a struggle between good and evil. The "New Man" must "overcome the evil within himself and within his men" and then "defeat the powers of evil and crush the clique of evil-doers." He must "do battle and win over the enemies of our Fatherland, his battle and victory having to extend even beyond the material world into the realm of invisible enemies, the powers of evil." He must separate "good" Romanians from the "chaff," to whom no mercy must be shown.

The emphasis was more on moral activism than violence or weapons training. This was a distinctive paramilitary that for a long time wielded little organized violence. Codreanu's charismatic authority kept serious violence within tight political limits. Individual acts of public provocation were all that was required. This would draw forth repression from the local authorities, exposing the ties between rich Jews, bankers, and politicians and bringing mass support. Up to his own murder in 1938, the legion was reported as having killed only eleven persons, almost all prominent politicians and policemen, while taking losses of 501 at the hands of the police. The notion of "defensive violence," which we saw the Nazi SA trying to put about in Chapter 4, was here rather more genuine – though still a deliberate tactic. And this violence, unlike that of other fascist movements, was also aimed at the state – though usually by individual fascists at individual officials. And not violence but the uniformed, singing procession was the most common sighting most Romanians had of the legionaries until quite late in the legion's development. From the very beginning the legionaries also labored hard on their own collective construction projects, building first their own headquarters, then rural development projects. The legion was very effective in caging its members through such everyday practices that were hard, time-consuming, and socially solidifying. Whatever the legion lacked in numbers, it thus made up in commitment. It was especially effective in winning elections, when its members could flood into a single constituency, without funds, behaving quite unlike any other party by sleeping rough among the amazed peasantry whose votes they were cultivating. This was populism in practice. It was also committing the Legion primarily to an electoral route to power. But until rather later they were less effective at a national election, when their resources were more stretched.

Legionary propaganda usually left vague the future form of the state. The legion considered itself a liberator, a cleanser, bringing a new man and nation more than a new state form. In this respect it resembled Nazism more than Italian fascism. Yet its religiosity and its peasantism was distinctively Romanian. Codreanu believed the Romanian "soul" was rooted in the "cosmic singularity" of a nation who were "the only orthodox Latins, the only Latin orthodox," embodying true "Christian purity" (this was mainly taken from Cuza and other nationalists). The real soul lay not among cosmopolitan elites but in the peasantry, who for centuries had practiced an uncorrupted form of direct democracy in local village assemblies. Peasant soil and peasant culture were primary to the nation, blood and race were secondary (until Nazi and SS influence was felt during the war). Thus Codreanu was quite happy to admit into the legion those he described as "Macedonian-Romanians," living in the newly acquired southeast. For they, too, had been oppressed for centuries and could now be peacefully assimilated into the nation. Style, rhetoric, and cultic practices were profoundly religious – for example, the wearing of bags of soil around the neck to symbolize the earth of the forefathers. The legion made little reference to the doctrines of Orthodox christianity, yet its rituals drew heavily on Orthodox ones. The legion's religious title derived from an icon Codreanu had acquired of the patron saint of Romania, St. Michael, vanquishing Lucifer. In iconography and songs the legion *was* St. Michael, while Lucifer combined communism, capitalism, and Judaism. Legionaries wore a white cross on their green uniforms; some also wore swastikas. Other fascist movements gave themselves religious titles – the Arrow Cross Movement and the Belgian Christus Rex (which was disowned by the Catholic Church). All claimed religious credentials, but only the legion really resembled a church. In rural areas it even deployed "miracles" as part of its appeal.

The legion argued that foreign oppressors had degraded the pure Romanian peasant soul, and that Jews continued to do so. Many Romanians readily accepted this. Casual anti-Semitism was not specific to the legion but a general characteristic of the country. The political right specialized in it, but the center and even liberals were also influenced. Though they sometimes denounced violent anti-Semitism, their goal of "Romanianizing" the economy involved displacing foreigners from dominance of the private sector. The doctrine of "by ourselves alone" involved legislation as early as 1934 introducing quotas and bans aimed at minorities. The law of 1934 obliged all enterprises to employ 80 percent Romanians and have at least 50 percent Romanians on their boards. The chairman must also be Romanian. Though this law applied to all minorities, implementing it proved very difficult among the Germans and Magyars. In the areas where they lived, there were few Romanians to fill such positions. From 1937 the antiminority legislation increased rapidly, justified by the slogan "Romania for the Romanians." Jews continued to feel its main thrust. And though the rise of Hitler and the expansion of Nazi Germany did influence this development, its main and initial thrust was Romanian (Mendelsohn 1983: chap. 4; Ancel 1993: 215; Ianciu 1996: 76–7, 280–306).

The diary of Emil Dorian, a Jewish doctor, records many instances of Romanians taking out life's frustrations on the "Kikes." Many bizarre rumors circulated about Jews, and even the government pandered to them. A legislative ban on Jews hiring young maids, he says, derived from a rumor

that Jews were organizing a white-slave trade. Here Dorian extracts humor
from one incident:

A scene on the streetcar. A Jew stands up and offers his seat to an old man.
    "I'm not going to take a seat that has been occupied by a kike," the old man
announces fiercely.
    Another Gentile, standing near the old man, asks him: "You don't want to sit
down?"
    "I certainly don't."
    The second Gentile takes the seat offered by the Jew. After two minutes he gets
up again. "There, you can sit down now," he addresses the old man, "the seat has
been Romanianized." (Dorian 1982: 289–90)

The content of anti-Semitism varied a little between provinces. Kaftan-
wearing Orthodox Jews played economic pariah roles in Northern
Moldavia and Bessarabia and were denounced as "alien" exploiters of the
peasants. Bessarabian Jews were also suspected of having Bolshevik sentiments. "Judeo-Bolsheviks" were the ostensible targets of pogroms from
1919 onward. Indeed, the small Romanian Communist Party was substantially foreign and Jewish. Of the twenty-four leading party delegates in
1931, only nine were ethnic Romanians. Six were Jews, and there were four
Hungarians, three Ukrainians, and two Bulgarians (Treptow et al. 1996:
422). Most southern Jews resided in the capital, almost all the rest in
southern Moldavia, and they were resented for their dominance of the
private sector – they were "capitalist exploiters." The highly Magyarized
Transylvanian Jews were resented economically and identified as collaborators with the Magyar enemy (which had sparked off the first student
anti-Semitic riots of the 1920s). The common fear of these apparently contradictory labels was that Jews were essentially antinational in two senses.
First, they sided with foreign enemies of Romania. Second, as either capitalists or Bolsheviks they fomented class conflict, thus dividing the nation. There were also more traditional sources of anti-Semitism, especially
Christian ones, but the Romanian right also linked these to nationalism.
The Jews were "the killers of Christ" and so "the enemies of the Christian
nation." As Ianciu (1996: 318) puts it, "Anti-semitism in Romania was
above all a primordial component of nationalism, and in nationalist milieux
the Jews were perceived as a foreign entity, menacing the homogeneity and
even the existence of the Romanian people." The more Romanians espoused nationalism, the more their marked casual anti-Semitism became
politically charged, usable by fascism.

All that really distinguished legionary anti-Semitism amid this rising tide
was that it was inserted into a more general fascist-Christian vision of the

state that legitimated paramilitary provocative violence and eventual rebellion. Crainic, a prominent legionary theorist, offered an "ethnocratic state" founded on "Romanian soil, blood, soul and faith." This state was superior to "the democratic state," which was a mere "registration office" counting population numbers "without racial or religious distinction." He singled out Jews as "a permanent danger for every national state" but added, that "any unassimilated member of a minority, active in the organism of the state, is an element of dissolution and ruin . . . it is a vital necessity for Romania to be an exclusively ethnocratic state." Thus he called for the "purification" of Romanian society by the "elimination" of foreign elements. Another legionary intellectual, Banea, added, "The Jews . . . cannot be persecuted on a racial or religious basis – only on the basis of the danger they represent to the state." Codreanu himself demanded "desperate defense" against Jewish "invasion" and "infiltration." "A dirty Jewish nest" dominated the cities, spreading "an infection of Judaic culture caricature." Defense involved spreading "death *and* mercy" to the "Jewish wasp nests." The language was often violent, involving demands for cleansing, especially of deportation: "the Jews to Palestine." During World War II the Vichy Embassy in Bucharest reported back to Paris that legionary anti-Semitism was wilder and more cruel than that of the Nazis themselves and that Codreanu had favored a mixture of extermination and expulsion. However, it was really only after World War II began (after Codreanu's death) that this mixture became the actual policy of the legion, rather than rhetorical flourish. This moral descent is discussed in my forthcoming volume (for the above, my principal sources are the autobiographies of the two legionary leaders, Sima 1967 and Codreanu 1990; see also Weber 1964: 165–8; Webster 1986; Fischer-Galati 1989; Veiga 1989: 128–38; Ioanid 1990: 60, 116–31; Volovici 1991: 93–6; Niessen 1995: 275; Ianciu 1996: 201–5; 1998: 14–17, 72).

These were legionary variations on standard themes of Central and Eastern European fascism: cleansing nationalism and anti-Semitism, a claim to transcend class and party conflict, a paramilitary elitism, and authoritarian statism. But Romanian fascism also had three distinctive traits. First, its foreign policy was pacific, since Romania had all the territories it could cope with. This is one reason why it was not all that statist. Second, it was religious, preoccupied with personal moral reform, very contemptuous of materialism. We find it difficult to make sense of its antirationalism, its denunciation of political programs, its celebration of "the Romanian soul," its imprecise slogans and excessive use of song, its "doctrine of the act," combining moralism and violence. Its resonant rituals gave legionaries a high degree of emotional comradeship, tenacity, and often even willingness to accept martyrdom. Third, it evinced strong "proletarian nationalism," identifying the enemy as class exploiters allied to revisionist powers, whose fifth column was headed by Jews. How did such ideas take a hold in Romania? I first consider the legionaries themselves, then their broader appeal.

WHO WERE THE LEGIONARIES?

As always, these fascists were young and predominantly male. British diplomats confirmed what the fascists said themselves – that the movement "swept" the country's young men. Weber describes it as "a crusade of adolescents" (Weber 1966b: 514, 519; Sturdza 1968: 102; Vago 1975, 1987: 286–97). First surfacing in the universities, the legion continued to recruit many students and schoolchildren. Codreanu says that in the legionary "excursions," those who rode on horseback around their leader were mostly aged twenty-five to thirty, while the "foot soldiers" were largely students. Young soldiers were present, though far less prominent than in Hungary. Legionary leaders remained younger than other political elites, and militants remained younger still. Legionary average age in both 1927 and 1942 was twenty-seven to twenty-eight. The Vichy Embassy reported that by wartime the legion was "composed almost exclusively of young people" and was never rich in experienced politicians (Ianciu 1998: 72). Repression had contributed to this since many experienced older leaders were murdered, jailed, or exiled by the authorities, while a few fought and died for Franco in the Spanish Civil War.

Legionaries were so young that there were soon not very many military veterans. Codreanu managed to join in one World War I battle before being discovered and packed off to military school as too young for the front. For him, as for his first followers, the war was extraordinarily significant: the first great feat of arms by modern Romanians. The nationalist euphoria of the age cohort then infected the universities of the early 1920s where the "front" and "home" generations eagerly discussed nation-statist remedies to social problems. Then a lull during the rise of the National Peasant Party, then rapid legionary expansion through the 1930s, first in the countryside, then the towns, again mostly among the young, born after the world war was over. Men around the age of thirty, then rising to forty, were through the 1930s teaching the young the virtues of a somewhat naive form of fascism, lacking the hard edge of real military or armed paramilitary violence.

But the legion also organized women. Three of the thirty-four party cells of 1933 were women's groups, called "citadels," and women constituted 8 percent of members at this time. They formed 10 percent of the

842 members attending a party work camp in 1936 (the males are analyzed in Appendix Table 8.1, row 2); "children" added a further 6 percent, through day care arrangements. The women divided about equally into housewives and students, with one hairdresser (Heinen 1986: 385–7). There were no major women leaders, yet photos of the legionaries' 1941 insurrection show that the armed insurgents included a smattering of young women and children (Veiga 1989: 265; Ioanid 1990: 72). That women and children should actually fight appears unique among fascist movements. Work camps and ideology also combined family and feminist themes in an unusual way for the period. Codreanu's creed had proclaimed a kind of fascist feminism: The movement was the "giver of equal rights . . . to men and women" and the "protector of the family." This was the first element in Romanian fascism that might be considered "progressive." There are others. It is not clear why this was a less-gendered movement than most, though this was a new nation without great traditional baggage and a movement without much military experience, whose mysticism probably restrained machismo.

The legion began in the cities, where it was first led by ex-officers and university students – making it very middle-class, though some detect artisans as well. It quickly attracted a circle of intellectuals and then spread down into the secondary schools. This milieu generated romantic peasantism:

On the one hand, the modern Rumania of the cities, of comfort and well-being, of material civilization, of the West, of industry and the machine, of the opposition between bourgeois and proletarian, is at bottom a foreign Rumania. On the other hand, the Rumania of the villages, the Rumania of the Rumanians, the Rumania of the spiritual, autochthonous configuration that has preserved this nation on this earth in forms that have remained almost unchanged from the time of Darius . . . No! The real opposition of the social tendencies in this generation is not the opposition between dictatorship and democracy . . . nor the opposition between bourgeoisie and proletariat, because the bourgeoisie as well as the proletariat are not for the most part Rumanian. The real opposition . . . [is] between the two Rumanias. (Quoted by Ioanid 1990: 149–50)

Several legionary leaders were the sons of leading prefects and policemen and often had the experience of being maltreated by their fathers' colleagues. Others were the sons of peasants or of priests and teachers in rural areas (Weber 1966b: 569; Heinen 1986: 383; Veiga 1989: chap. 4). Verdery (1983) suggests from oral histories that middling Transylvanian peasants saw higher education leading to professional or public employment as the route to the advancement of their elder sons. This might enable the father to leave the farm intact to the second son. The elder son tended to imbibe nation-statism as he advanced through this career, while idealizing the peasantry and the soil from which he had sprung. Of course, in Romanian universities a claim to peasant origins may have had the same social cachet as working-class origins had among student radicals in the 1960s. Some students may have fabricated their peasant origins. But it was a milieu likely to generate a peasantist fascism.

Though many of these early fascists seem upwardly mobile, materialist "overproduction" explanations of early fascism are nonetheless common. The war is said to have produced unemployable ex-soldiers and swelled student numbers who could not be absorbed into middle-class occupations. There was little point in graduating, and few did so – supposedly only 8 percent during the period 1921–32 (I find this hard to believe). Rootless displaced persons, denied upward mobility, chronically dissatisfied, were the fascist recruits (say, Weber 1966b: 514; Barbu 1980; and Vago 1987: 286). I am very skeptical of all this. Romania had its territories doubled by the peace treaties. Magyar, Austro-German, Russian, and Bulgarian civil servants and officers had fled the country. Opportunities for educated Romanians in the public sector were greater than in any other European country. If students left the university before graduation, perhaps they could find employment without it (as Vago 1987: 287, suggests). Things became difficult in the inflated public sector during the Great Depression, when wage cuts and casualization were introduced. But there was recovery from 1935, when the great fascist surge began. Observers referred to the legionaries as the "best" of their generation, not as a lumpenbourgeoisie. The Polish vice-consul, lamenting the effects of the ferocious 1938 persecution of the legion, wrote, "The movement is no longer dominated by the university and other idealistic youth or by an intellectual elite" (Watts 1993: 186).

It should be disconcerting to the "overproduction" thesis that Hungary probably had the worst middle-class job prospects, Romania the best – yet both produced fascism among those most affected, students and public sector workers. This must shake the notion that fascism was a response to middle-class deprivation. Instead, it seems a response of the highly educated and the public sector, *whatever* their prospects. Fascism was now the coming ideology, supposed capable of solving the problems of modern society. Since it argued that salvation would come from a strong nation-state, it especially appealed to those located at the heart of the nation-state. Since in Romania only the peasantry could constitute the body of the nation, and at least some of its leaders were upwardly mobile from peasant milieux, fascism would also probably be peasantist. Fascism made apparent sense of this generation's sustained social experience, not just of recent slump (or boom).

Nor were the officers deprived. Romania had demobilized less of its army than most countries (since it was surrounded by countries wanting their territories back). There were no contemporary references to hordes of rootless soldiers (unlike postwar Germany or Hungary). Ex-officers figured in fascism's first phase. By the 1930s the military had settled down and few soldiers were legionaries. Yet as war approached and as King Carol became unpopular, with Russian, Hungarian, and German pressure on the borders, there was a second military drift rightward. Few soldiers were formal members of the Legion, yet wartime governments doubted the loyalty of officers and conscripts, permeated (they believed) by legionary sympathies (Vago 1987: 300; Watts 1993: 242, 284, 296). When the legion joined Carol's government in 1940, its cabinet members included two generals. Fascism resonated among soldiers and militarism resonated in fascism. Codreanu modeled his legion (and its name) on a romanticized version of his own military training: "The order, the discipline, the hierarchy inculcated into my blood at a tender age, constituted, alongside the feeling of soldierly dignity, the guideline for my whole existence." Another legionary wrote: "Yes, military dictatorship. That is, a dictatorship of authentically Rumanian blood, a dictatorship of the soldier's discipline and morale, a dictatorship of heroic spirituality" (Ioanid 1990: 134, 114). As usual it was not a materially deprived military that leaned toward fascism, just the military.

We have details of several leadership cadres during the 1930s. Half the leaders mentioned in one 1937 list were reserve or ex-officers (serving officers could not hold such an open position), with the remainder spread around diverse middle-class occupations. This is the only list containing any capitalists – one industrialist and one bank director. In other years, most leaders were teachers and professors, Romanian Orthodox priests, and lawyers. The Iron Guard parliamentary candidates of 1937 were 98 percent professional, led by priests (33%) and teachers (31%). Other parties retained more traditional notable leadership: 40 percent of all members of parliament were lawyers and 18 percent were large landowners (Ioanid 1990: 39, 70–2). The first row of Appendix Table 8.1 analyzes a list of urban legionary leaders put on trial in 1934 for the assassination of a former prime minister. Over a third were students, a quarter were in public employment (half being teachers) and a quarter were professionals (mostly journalists, priests, and officers).

This is middle-class leadership, but of a distinctive type. There were many Orthodox clergy attracted by the legion's religiosity (Nagy-Talavera 1970: 287). Priests figure in almost all lists of legionaries, especially in rural areas.

The Orthodox Church was now the "established" church of the country, but in the nineteenth century it had come to symbolize the oppressed nation and was now sympathetic to proletarian nationalism – including anti-Semitism, expressed here by the patriarch himself:

most of the Jews . . . lived in easy circumstances, monopolizing all the riches of the country, commerce, houses, towns, etc. With the acme of refinement they insti-gated and cultivated the germ of social corruption and other ills; and had acquired the monopoly of the press which, with obviously foreign aid carried out a sinister campaign against the very soul of Roumania. . . . Large number of Jews . . . came over like a flood during the war and after it, and had thus begun to endanger the very existence of all Roumanians and Christians. . . . The fate of the poor Roumanian people from which the Jews squeezed out even the marrow from the bones made one weep with pity. To defend oneself was a national and patriotic duty and was not anti-semitism.

He suggested coercive deportation, resettling Jews in Africa, Australia, Asia, or "some other island" (Vago 1975: 235ff.).

Codreanu says that initially most priests were hostile, but from the mid-1930s many welcomed the legion into their villages and agreed to consecrate its banners and parades (Vago 1975: 209; Veiga 1989: 264; Ioanid 1990: 71, 139–48). Lawyers were also overrepresented among some lists of leaders. The legal profession was bloated – which might conceivably be remedied by the expulsion of Jewish lawyers (as the legion proposed). But up to half of the fascist lawyers were actually government officials – bringing us to the most overrepresented middle-class group, public employees. As elsewhere, public employees were banned from fascist membership, though here it seems not to have been a deterrent. A network of "secret militancy" assisted the legion in town halls and police stations through the country. The state was deeply split (Veiga 1989: 125–6) – yet another dual state. The British embassy reported that the judiciary and the police favored the legion throughout the 1930s (Vago 1975: 181, 191, 209). Something more than just hard times was driving public employees toward fascism.

Heinen (1986: 458) says that the legionary core was "the state-oriented middle strata." Sugar (1971: 150–3) stresses the importance of soldiers, civil servants, teachers, university professors, and the clergy in all Habsburg "suc-cessor state" fascisms. He says this indicated strong links across the whole region between fascism and "overbloated" bureaucratic states, ultranation-alist schools, "corporative-Christian" churches, and military veterans. We have observed the same core constituency in all European fascisms, though Romania does seem to have been its peak. Adding together civil servants, state-employed teachers, and half the lawyers would account for between

25 and 50 percent of the persons in all of the legionary lists, except for the rather proletarian insurrectionaries of 1941 (see below). Public employees made up under 10 percent of Romania's labor force. By contrast, the legion contained few from the productive bourgeoisie or petty bourgeoisie: entrepreneurs, managers and private sector white-collar workers, and petty traders (though artisans occasionally appear). Once again we see a fascism that was deeply statist in its core constituency.

The legion was also receiving widespread support among intellectuals. There was already much racial anti-Semitism among the country's intelligentsia, who often saw the Jew and the Romanian nation as diametrically opposed. The distinction between the Romanian "productive classes" and the "dirty business world," dominated by "usurious," "banking," "vagabond" Jewish capital was common, as was the solution – a Romania "disburdened" or "disinfected" of Jews. The legion borrowed all this, but gave anti-Semitism a place in a broader national struggle against Soviet communism and western exploitation. As in other countries, fascists were quick to exploit modern propaganda techniques. In legionary iconography the symbols of Judaism were carefully chosen: "first came the *rabbi*, the occult force, next the *banker* and then the *journalist*" (Volovici 1991: 66).

As fascism spread, more prominent intellectuals were attracted. Mihai Manoilescu was one of the most famous economists of the century. The scion of a wealthy family, he was director of the Central Bank and Minister of Industry in several interwar cabinets. Originally a liberal, he developed Romania's tariff and import-substitution policies, as explained in his book *The Theory of Protection and International Trade* (1931). He founded a political party, the National Corporatist League, in 1933 and explained its philosophy in *The Century of Corporatism* (1934). There he famously proclaimed, "The twentieth century will be the century of corporatism just as the nineteenth was the century of liberalism." "The nineteenth century knew the economic solidarity of *class*. The twentieth will know the economic solidarity of *nations*" (a rather simplified sentiment that many contemporary sociologists now seem to be repeating). Drawing on German and Italian rightists, Manoilescu argued that the poorer nations of the European periphery could achieve freedom and development by a state-directed "pure and integral" corporatism, a "planned work of engineering," authoritatively regulating all social conflict. This would inaugurate what he called "the socialism of the nations." "Artificial and temporary" nineteenth-century class conflicts would be transcended by a nationalist transformation of "the scales of moral and social values." Corporatism would eventually integrate "all the spiritual, moral and material forces of the nation."

Manoilescu continued to move rightward, as did his small party. His 1936 book *The Single Party* abandoned this rather innocent view of corporatism. Now corporatism "must be held in tutelage ... [by] the single party" since "the biological necessity which orders every people to organize its life in its entirety implies the idea of singularity in the political body of supreme power." His main references now were to Alfred Rosenberg and Carl Schmitt (by now a Nazi), and he also quoted Mussolini, Hitler, Goebbels, and Salazar. It is unclear whether Manoilescu actually joined the legion, but all now saw him as its supporter. In 1940 he expounded a "new traditionalism" and a "return to ancestral truths": "[H]ierarchy, union and love among brothers of the same blood and creed" would lead to a new era of "totalitarian nationalism." He proposed the "Romanization" of capital against "Jewish power" and "foreign capital" (Volovici 1991: 159–62; Heinen 1986: 180–2).[1] He was now a fascist. For a time he had an uncertain relationship to the legion itself, since he was the Foreign Minister who bore the odium of having signed the 1940 treaty by which Hitler stripped Romania of most of its territorial gains of 1918. Yet in early 1941 he was appointed to head the legionary government's new "Economic General Staff" (Ianciu 1998: 108).

The most prominent Romanian literary intellectual was Mircea Eliade, the theorist of comparative religion (who later had a distinguished career in the United States). In 1934 he was endorsing "Romanianism," "the desire to have an organic, unitary, ethnic and equitable state." By 1936 he was markedly less equitable: "[W]e are waiting for a nationalist Romania, frenzied and chauvinistic, armed and rigorous, pitiless and vengeful." The next year he published "Why I Believe in the Victory of the Legionary Movement":

While the aim of all contemporary revolutions is *the winning of power* by a social class or by a person, the supreme target of the Legionary revolution, is, as the Captain has said, *the salvation of the people*, the reconciliation of the Romanian people with God. That is why the sense of the Legionary movement will lead not only to the restoration of the virtues of our people, to a valorous, dignified and powerful Romania; it will also create a *new man* attuned to a new *type of life* in Europe. (Volovici 1991: 85; Eliade's own emphasis).

After the 1939 German invasion of Poland, a friend remarked in his diary, "Mircea more Germanophile, more anti-French and antisemitic than ever. He says of Romania 'Better a German protectorate than a Romania invaded by the Yids'" (Ianciu 1998: 17). Eliade's many admirers in the west have tactfully ignored his fascism.

Emil Cioran, also a very prominent Romanian writer, was more extreme in his views. Much influenced by Nazism, he announced:

Hostility to foreigners is so characteristic of Romanian national feeling that the two will always be inseparable. The first national reaction of the Romanian is not pride in the destiny of Romania, or a sentiment of glory . . . [as in] French patriotism, but revolt against foreigners, often aired as a swear word, and sometimes crystallized in a durable hatred. . . . We have lived under foreigners for 1,000 years; not to hate them and not to eliminate them would demonstrate an absence of national instinct.

What was needed was a "national revolution," whose violent cleansing mission Cioran spelled out with relish:

An unfettering of irrational forces, of fanaticism and violence, the imperialist fulfillment of the national destiny. All means are legitimate when a people opens a road for itself in the world. Terror, crime, bestiality and perfidy are base and immoral only in decadence, when they defend a vacuum of content; if, on the other hand, they help in the ascension of a people, they are virtues. All triumphs are moral. . . . Romania needs exaltation reaching fanaticism. . . . The fanaticization of Romania is the transfiguration of Romania. (Volovici 1991: 128)

Fascism seems to have attracted more intellectuals in Romania than anywhere else. It acquired much of "The Generation of 1922," a group of literary students who became prominent men of letters. Eliade and Cioran became the best-known fascists among them. Two of the group did not join and have left descriptions of the others' conversion. Sebastien did not join because he was a Jew. He spoke of his erstwhile friends joining as "a religious conversion." Eugen Ionesco did not join because he was culturally more French than Romanian. Later he wrote a great play about his friends, though without ever mentioning fascism or Romania. In *Rhinoceros* (1960) the inhabitants of an apparently French small town turn absurdly into rhinoceroses. This surrealist change is willed by the mutants themselves, simply because they wish to conform to the herd. Their only explanation for their decision is through banalities such as, "We must move with the times!" In 1970 Ionescu confirmed that his satire had been aimed at his former friends in Romania: "the professors, the students, the intellectuals became Nazis, Iron Guardists, one after the other . . . To begin with, they were not Nazis . . . one of our friends would say 'I don't agree with them, though on certain points, I recognize what they say, like, for example, the Jews' etc. And that, that was the signal. Three weeks later, or two months later, this man became a Nazi. He engaged gear, he admitted all, he became a rhinoceros." (Ianciu 1998: 14–17). Vacuous slogans of modernity still dominate politics, of course, but they now tend to be centrist – Bill Clinton's "bridge to the twenty-first century," Tony Blair's "new" everything. Fascists ran well with such banalities in the interwar period.

During the period 1934–7 the legion was also maturing into respectability, beginning to attract society figures such as the diplomat Prince Michel Sturdza and the general Gheorghe Cantacuzino-Granicerul. Governments were beginning to steal its clothes and attempting to "Romanianize" the economy by setting quotas for the employment of Jews and other foreigners in all branches of the economy. Negotiations were even opened between the Legion and the National Peasant Party to seek a common socially progressive political program. Its leader, Iuliu Maniu, was a defense witness in Codreanu's trial in 1938. Its influence among the intelligentsia gave fascism a powerful subterranean influence among the governing class as a whole. Such governments became increasingly drawn toward fascist ideas, even while repressing actual fascists.

Yet the legion also became increasingly populist. Its activism centered on the so-called Excursions among the People shown in Map 8.2. Codreanu's successor, Horia Sima, a professor of literature from the border Banat province, describes these in his memoirs (1967: 33, 199–205). The first excursions were mostly into the rural heart of the country. No one was allowed any official rank in the movement until he had participated in excursions. Some of the legion's "nests" became work camps sponsoring rural development projects. Youth labor camps emerged sporadically through Central Europe during the 1930s. Idealistic urban young people would go out to repair rural roads, schools, and churches. The legionaries turned such idealism toward the politics of practical fascism. Their camps were staffed by students and persons with middle-class and artisanal skills – the first postwar student cohort grown up. One church-building project involved 636 people, of whom 69 percent were local peasants, 11 percent were workers, 8 percent artisans, 5 percent students, and 4 percent professionals and civil servants.[2] The nonlocals in another camp were fairly equally divided between students, professionals, and workers. Appendix Table 8.1, row 2, gives details of nonlocals in a larger work camp. Here a third were students, a quarter were in public employment, and there were clusters of professionals, workers, and peasants. Peasants contrasted government projects run by corrupt notables with the idealism of these young men and women. What seems like romantic rhetoric had a practical presence. These fascists were do-gooders, to their own evident self-satisfaction. They took themselves seriously.

The second excursionary phase occurred in 1936–7, under the slogan "Let us go down among the workers," shifting the focus to the urban working class. Romanian socialism was weak, reaching its electoral peak of 6 percent in 1931 and then declining. It was stunted by being associated with Jews and with the Comintern – which supported Russian claims to Bessarabia. Fascism was able to steal much of its constituency. As in Hungary, socialism ceded even some working class "ghettos" to fascism (though here the data are more patchy). In 1938 the Bucharest Legionary Workers' Corps had 8,000 members, with a "death squad" of 3,000. It has been suggested (though I have seen no actual evidence) that these members were especially recruited from the armaments industry and transport (especially taxis, public tramways, and railways) and that most were newly urbanized peasants (Weber 1966a: 548–9; Heinen 1986: 395–6; Vago 1987: 309; Ioanid 1990: 71, 169).

This proletarian fascism had a strong sense of its enemy as "foreign" and "Jewish." Dorian (1982: 126) believed it might soon be disappointed:

The workers and the peasantry rallied round it in the belief that their complaints would be redressed when capitalism disappeared, unaware that when the Iron Guard spoke of "exploiters" they merely meant . . . the Jews.

Some communist historians have claimed that the legion depended on subsidies from capitalists, but this is improbable. Most capitalists were Jews or foreigners. The legion received some money from Germany (less than its anti-Semitic and protofascist rival, the LANC) and some from pro-German capitalists. Other regime groups, including King Carol on one occasion, helped out when attempting to use the legion for their own purposes. But funding was overwhelmingly by the party faithful (Heinen 1986: 337–41; Watts 1993). The legion's corporatist slogans of harmony between the pro-ducing classes might have been attractive to capitalists had they been more threatened by socialism, but the rest of the upper class favored more con-servative authoritarianism. Throughout its short and bloody life the legion was alternately used and suppressed by ruling elites who had learned lessons from Mussolini's and Hitler's coups.

LEGIONARY VOTERS: NATION–STATIST CONSTITUENCIES

The legion formed a front party, "All for the Country" (TPT), to con-test the election of 1937. It formed a tactical alliance with the liberal and communist parties, all out of power. Together they attacked regime "cor-ruption," conveniently personified by King Carol's own moral laxity. His close relations with a wealthy court *camarilla* and a Jewish mistress were pub-lic knowledge. Sima said that Codreanu had identified three exploiters of the masses – first the communist, then the Jew, finally the "dirty politician"

(1967: 44). The legion was adept at modern electoral propaganda, specializing in lurid cartoons depicting communists, Jews, and politicians as dragons, monsters, devils, or spiders, engaged in battle with the Archangel Michael, usually drawn with Codreanu's handsome features. As legionaries marched through the country, they sang:

> The country calls on us, O Christian brothers,
> To fight and free it from the many leeches,
> Perversions that are sprawling in palaces,
> The yids who're robbing us of our riches.
> (Volovici 1991: 174–5)

Note the connection between religion and class-cum-ethnic exploitation.

Such techniques paid off. Sturdza (1968: 103) attributes his party's success at the polls of 1937 to legionary idealism and its promise to cleanse the country's "corruptions and impurities":

They entered the villages in orderly formations, assembled before the local churches, knelt down and prayed, then rose and sang. The peasants looked with love and admiration at these young men who did not pester them with the bombastic speeches of the professional politicians but contented themselves with fervent prayers and songs of faith and heroism that everybody understood and approved.

Though Sturdza lays it on a bit thick, such self-presentation probably did have some effect. They did live simply and were not corrupt, they were being beaten by the police, one half of their message was one of piety and progress, while the other half was hatred for alien oppressors. The main reasons for not voting for them were probably their naivete and lack of political experience and influence. The legion was not a part of influential patronage networks. Corruption had its political payoff.

Most interpretations of who voted for the legion have relied on Weber's (1966a) analysis of the votes cast in most of Romania's counties (e.g., Barbu 1980; Veiga 1989: 105–21; Ioanid 1990: 64). Weber noted that the legion had first "gone to the people" in poor areas with historic "free villages" where peasants were relatively free to organize. This is where he believes the legionary vote was concentrated – in the poorest, most backward counties of the country. Yet, using fuller data, Heinen (1986: 403–14) demonstrates the reverse: positive ecological correlations between the legionary vote and literacy ($r = .27$) and radio ownership ($r = .22$), and a negative correlation with the infant mortality rate ($r = -.19$). He also notes that eleven of the twenty-two most industrialized counties were legionary strongholds, as were ten of the twenty most forested counties, in which large-scale lumber industries operated. On balance he believes the legion attracted votes from

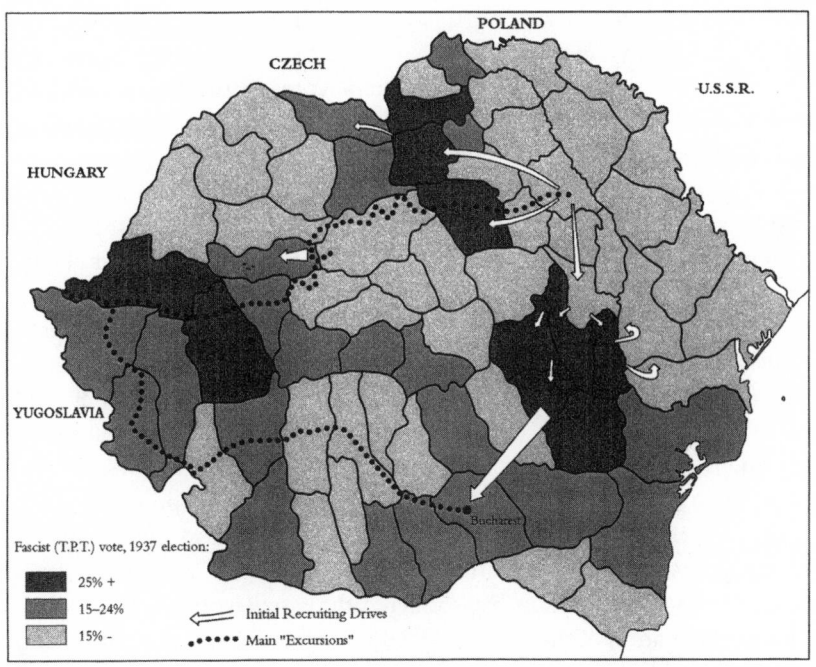

Map 8.2. Romania: counties of fascist strength.

more socially and economically developed areas. It was the legion's main rival on the right, the PNC (authoritarian nationalist and anti-Semitic, but not fascist), that did better in backward peasant regions. The legion had first grown by taking votes in more advanced rural areas from the PNC's predecessors, the LANC and other anti-Semitic parties. Yet Heinen finds no relationship between the fascist vote and the density of the population or the road network. The relationship between fascism and level of development is positive but weak.

To better understand the social base of the fascist vote we must return to Map 8.2. We see that the legionary vote came in three regional clusters. The first was in the center-north: The province of Bukovina (next to Poland) voted disproportionately for the legion, as did adjacent counties on all three sides in Northern Moldavia, Transylvania, and Maramures. This had been the area of strength for the LANC while Codreanu was still within it. All of its ten parliamentary deputies elected in 1926 (including Codreanu's father) came from the center-north. The second cluster was in the center-west, encompassing much of the Banat and Crisana-Maramures and the westerly part of Transylvania. The third cluster was in the southeast, straddling southeastern Moldavia and northeastern Muntenia, including the capital city, Bucharest (which voted 22% for the legion). Northern parts of this cluster had also seen the highest legionary votes in the legion's first elections, in 1931 and 1932 (Codreanu 1990: 299, 321). There were no isolated legionary counties. They came in clusters.

The clustering followed historic provincial boundaries, and so this somewhat depresses linear correlations with indices of development, such as those of Heinen (we see the same depressing effect in Spain in the next chapter). The vote of two provinces plus the capital can actually account for Heinen's economic correlations. The legion's highest provincial vote, 24 percent, was in fairly prosperous Bukovina, while Bucharest was the most prosperous of all. One very poor province, Bessarabia, voted only 5 percent fascist. Take away these three and the correlation between fascism and economic development disappears altogether. Over the remaining fifty-seven counties fascist voting was unrelated to per capita sugar consumption, radios per capita, electricity consumption per capita, the infant mortality rate, and percentage working in agriculture. Level of development does not explain much. Other variables must have affected the fascist vote.

One explanation of the clustering might be legionary organization. Since the legion had little access to radio or major newspapers, it could not reach the whole country at once. It had to rely on networks of nests, marches, "excursions," work camps, and the local word of mouth and leafleting that accompanied them. When a nest exceeded its limit of sixteen persons, it formed another nest, and then another, so that nests gradually spread along lines of communication. Or a work camp set up by immigrant legionaries would recruit locals to form their own nests. Map 8.2 shows a relation between earlier proselytizing and the fascist vote. Most of the regional vote clusters, outside the far southeast, had been early centers of legionary activity. Most of the southern swath deviated, having seen few excursions. Of course, the legion chose where to proselytize according to where it thought it would find a receptive audience.

Two different types of receptivity seem revealed by the map: areas of distinctive ethnic mixes and fairly industrialized areas (ethnic and economic data from Institul Central de Statistica 1939–40). The confusing effects of ethnicity prove to be the main factor depressing the correlation of the fascist vote with economic development. Fascism was supported by ethnic Romanians, rather than by the minorities – Germans, Magyars, Ukrainians, Bulgarians, Szeklers, gypsies, or Jews. Where there were few Romanians, we find few fascist voters. In only two of the nineteen counties where Romanians were under 50 percent of the population did the legion get a (slightly) above average vote, and overall in these nineteen they averaged less that half the average national vote. Nonetheless, the ten legionary strongholds (i.e. receiving 25% or more of the vote) had an average of only 62 percent Romanians, compared with a national average of 72 percent. Thus the legion tended to get most votes in counties where there were sizable numbers of *both* Romanians and minority ethnicities whom Romanian nationalists thought "threatened" them.

Heinen found no significant correlation between the fascist vote and local Jewish numbers. Jews lived mostly in the north plus Bucharest. They comprised 4 percent of the national population, only 3 percent in Transylvania, 2 percent in Muntenia, under 1 percent in Oltenia and Dobrogea. But they were 12 percent in Bucharest, 11 percent in Bukovina, and 7 percent in Bessarabia. In these areas they were also urban: 14 percent of the population of Romanian cities, 30 percent of Bukovinan cities, 27 percent of Bessarabian, 23 percent of Moldovian (mostly in northern Moldavia), 12 percent in Bucharest, and 10 percent in Transylvanian cities (mostly in the north). They dominated credit and commerce – 70 to 80 percent of this sector in Bukovina, Bessarabia, and some cities in northern Moldavia and Mamures. Yet fascism was not mostly northern. And in the north, the provinces with the most Jews – Bukovina, Bessarabia, and most of northern Moldavia – represented the two extremes of fascist support: high in Bukovina, low in the other two. These areas shared long traditions of anti-Semitism, including pogroms. They also had many Romanians (and nonfascist Bessarabia had more Romanians). Why was fascism strong in Bukovina but weak in Bessarabia and northern Moldavia? Fascism could not have simply pitted Romanians against Jews.

Though Romanian fascists did see Jews as a "threat," fascists mostly thrived in areas where there was also a second ethnic enemy associated with a formerly ruling power: Magyars in formerly Hungarian provinces and Germans in areas formerly part of the Austro-Hungarian Empire. The "Austro-Germans" mainly inhabited the cities of Eastern Bukovina, of Arad in the Banat, and of Nasaud in northeastern Transylvania. These cities had Germans, substantial Jewish communities, and Romanian nationalists mobilizing the nearby peasants. The result was a relatively high fascist vote.

Livezeanu (1995: chaps. 2 and 3) shows that from 1918 Bukovinan anti-Semitism fused with a newer Romanian nationalism directed against the former Austro-German rulers, who had imposed their language on the state. As the Austrian armies surrendered, nationalists seized local government institutions, demanding that Romania refuse to insert minority rights in the Constitution (as the Allies were demanding). The nationalists failed in this goal, but they did secure control of local administration and they ended German and Jewish domination of public education. Professionals, the army, and Orthodox priests now launched a drive to teach and use the Romanian language in public institutions. This was the usual nation-statist core constituency of fascism ranged against former "oppressors," Jews and Germans. Historic anti-semitism thus fused with a new nation-statism, encouraging fascism. Indeed, local anti-Semitic (LANC and PNC) movements began to don fascist trappings in order to compete with the legion (Vago 1975: 167).

But not all the German speakers of Romania were perceived as enemies. The largely non fascist east of Transylvania contained "Saxons," mostly rural communities who had migrated from Germany centuries ago. Near them resided another long-settled and "unthreatening" rural minority, the Szeklers, an ethnic group of unknown origins. Since neither had been linked in the past to an oppressor state, their relations with Romanian nationalists were now quite cordial. Neither minority endorsed irredentism, neither was felt to be exploiting Romanians. Romanian nationalists said Szeklers were "submerged" former Romanians and were potentially assimilable to the nation. Romanians and Saxons had compromised on the grant of some local communal autonomy within an uncontested Romanian state. Local Romanian farmers also attributed their prosperity partly to Saxon farmers teaching them more advanced farming techniques (Verdery 1983; Ronnas 1984: 127). In these areas Romanian nationalists were moderates, few becoming fascists. Szekler counties were extremely unlikely to vote for the legion. Saxons did eventually become a little more receptive to German Nazi influences as war approached, propelling some toward the legion, and during the war into the SS.

The other main ethnic "threat" came from the formerly ruling Magyars. In western Transylvania, Maramures, and the Crisana-Banat, Romanians had been serfs to Magyar landowners for centuries. Here many Magyars supported the revisionist border claims of Hungary. Thus local nationalists urged aggressive Romanization of the schools and a unitary nation-state (Livezeanu 1995: chap. 4). This conflict went back to the eighteenth century. The center of Romanian resistance to the Habsburg attempt to impose the "Uniate Church" on Transylvania had then been in the counties of Hunedora, Alba, and Sibiu (Verdery 1983: 118).[3] Map 8.2 shows that these counties were now disproportionately fascist. Heinen found a negative correlation across Transylvania between the fascist vote and the size of the local Uniate congregation ($r = -.38$) – a fascinating historical residue. Maramures had witnessed early legionary and anti-Semitic disturbances, its capital containing the largest proportion of Yiddish-speakers in Transylvania

(Livezeanu 1995: 290–5). It also had as many Hungarians as Romanians. Note the low fascist vote in two Hungarian border counties, Salaj and Satu Mare. Neither had many Jews, while Romanians formed less than 25 percent of their urban populations.

Thus the legion thrived on direct confrontation between a large Romanian population and *two* predominantly urban ethnic "enemies," one Jewish, the other a formerly ruling nationality. There it could blend nationalism and anti-Semitism into fascism. So Bessarabia was not fertile fascist soil. It lacked not Jews or anti-Semitism (it had both in abundance) but other ethnic enemies. True, this had been a Russian province before the war, almost declared again for the Soviets in 1918 and which fell again to the Soviets in 1940, provoking Romanian nationalist outrage. But here the local Romanian bourgeoisie was not very nationalist. Most of it spoke Russian and associated the Romanian language with the local "backward" peasantry. It now preferred Romania to the Soviet Union, though for obvious class rather than nationalist reasons. Since the few communists were disproportionately Jewish, this fueled anti-Semitism. But the local Romanian bourgeoisie actually wanted more provincial autonomy and stronger ties with the neighboring province of Moldavia (the two shared a common history) rather than with the whole Romanian nation-state. Thus nation-statism remained stunted among Bessarabia's Romanians. They supported the anti-Semitic LANC and PNC but not fascism (Shapiro 1974: map 1). This was also true in northern Moldavia. The LANC/PNC vote across Romania *was* correlated to the proportion of Jews in the population ($r = 0.23$; it had been 0.46 in 1933). In both of these areas bourgeois fears of the Soviet Union also made them suspicious of the "revolutionary" legion – which communists were rumored to be infiltrating. It was the broader fascist ideology of the legion that attracted or deterred, and its anti-Semitism was connected to a broader conception of the proletarian nation-state.

But this argument works only for the two fascist clusters in the north and the west. The southeast cluster was more solidly Romanian: Here only Covurlui had many Jews (almost 10%), and none had significant other minorities. Tulcea had Russians and Bulgarians but few Jews; while the capital had many Jews, but few of other minorities. A second theme, statism, was probably more important in the capital and the industrial regions. The most advanced industry was clustered in Bucharest and Brasov and most of the oil industry was in Prahova, both benefiting from import-substitution policies and favoring statist doctrine (Ronnas 1984: 118–20). Weber (1966a: 110–11) says that two rural fascist-leaning counties (Putna and Covurlui) contained many of the historic "free villages," able in the 1930s to organize local resistance against forestry and lumber companies (though two other such counties he names did not offer the legion much support). These were among the poorer legionary counties – as were the southern Wallachian counties, Dolj, Teleorman, and Vlasca, which he says had old traditions of peasant socialism. There were few Jews in any of these southern counties. Here the legion emphasized a third theme, a class struggle between poor peasants and distant "alien" capital – a variant form of proletarian nationalism.

It may seem a little ad hoc to identify three distinct regionally specific reasons for voting fascist. Additionally, these data do not permit certainty. Romanian counties were large, some containing varied economic and ethnic conditions. The legion nowhere officially got more than 36 percent of a county's vote. It is hazardous to guess which local subgroups voted for it, but probable that it "swept" no large subgroup anywhere. Nonetheless, my analysis tends to suggest that some parts of the country might support fascism as extreme nationalism. Where local Romanian nationalists faced the "threats" of Jews plus a ruling national minority, many looked favorably on fascism. In other parts of the country many supported fascism more as defense of the peasant proletariat, as extreme statism, or as the defense required for a "proletarian" nation to withstand foreign exploitation. Class was very important in Romanian fascism, but filtered through the legion's proletarian nation-statism.

FASCIST END-GAME

The electoral results were bad news both for democracy and for King Carol (Shapiro 1974). The shift toward fascism was unmistakable – indeed, it continued the drift rightward under way since 1929. The National Peasants retained 20 percent of the vote, but they were not as prodemocratic or as multicultural as they once had been. The other quasi-democratic and ethnic minority parties could muster only another 10 percent. Carol's own semi-authoritarian government bloc got 36 percent, the largest political bloc but still too small to form a new ministry. What happened next was not inevitable. Carol *could* have moved back in the direction of a more liberal democracy and formed a coalition between these groupings. But he was no democrat and had no wish to. Thus he had to bend to the right – though there he had to face the hostility of the legion. After complex secret negotiations (including an apparent attempt to assume command of the legion!), he invited the rival far-rightist and anti-Semitic National Christian Party (with only 9% of the vote) to lead the government. He hoped that it could govern with the support of the former regime parties and a few others, without too many changes. However, the National Christians had been borrowing legionary clothes, and the new government declared for a pro-German foreign policy, corporatism, and "Romania for the Romanians." It now extended previous legislation to completely ban Jewish and other minority participation in public and professional life. Romanians were moving toward organicist solutions but not very violent ones.

Yet the new government parties lacked authority and sought to do a deal with the legion. Carol was alarmed, fearing their joint power might be turned against himself. He dissolved parliament, assumed total power, and turned violently against the legion. There was no immediate paramilitary resistance. Fourteen leaders, including Codreanu, were arrested, given long prison sentences for sedition, and then summarily strangled in November 1938 – with the incredible cover story that they had died while attempting to escape. The paramilitary weakness of this movement had been exposed. While individual fascists had been put up to assassinate Jews and officials, the assumption was that other fascists could carry on organizing openly and electorally. Now that the regime was thoroughly authoritarian, however, it could change the rules of the game and wipe out the fascist leadership at a stroke. It did not wipe out fascism, however. Indeed, Codreanu now became the Christian/fascist martyr, influential even after his death. The legion went underground, assassinating the prime minister responsible for the killings in September 1939 (the fourth serving or former prime minister it had murdered). Around 400 leading legionaries and their families were summarily executed in retaliation, many of their bodies being strung up in the streets on lampposts. We have data on many of these leaders: They were professionals (especially lawyers), priests, teachers, and other public employees. Other urban militants fled to Germany and were interned. Students formed the largest group of the internees, followed by the usual professionals and public employees, though with some workers as well (rows 2 and 4 of Appendix Table 8.1). It was in response to this second repression that the underground legion adopted real organized, collective, violent paramilitarism.

Carol had erected a semi-reactionary authoritarian regime with some corporatist pretensions, but he attempted to maintain a neutral foreign policy. By 1940 he was under considerable German pressure. With revisionist powers for neighbors (one of them the communist USSR), Romania needed an alliance with either Germany or the liberal powers. France was no more, Britain might not survive much longer. Carol became willy-nilly Hitler's ally, the Romanian economy was reoriented toward supplying Germany, and the numerous Germans now working in Romania increased the influence of fascism. Carol became more corporatist. He formed a one-party regime, the "Party of the Nation," drew the legion into it, and intensified anti-Jewish legislation (this and the ensuing policies of deportation and liquidation are discussed in my forthcoming volume).

But Hitler double-crossed him. The treaty between Hitler and Stalin, plus Hitler's pro-Hungarian policy, resulted in Romania losing northern Bukovina and Bessarabia to the USSR and northern Transylvania to Hungary. With the king's policies in ruins, General Antonescu forced his abdication and established himself as dictator. He was no lover of Germany but believed that Germany would win the war and hoped Hitler would eventually give him back Transylvania. Since Antonescu had little track record, Hitler did not yet know whether to trust him. So for a while the shrewd general ruled jointly with the fascists. The new leader of the legion, Horia Sima (a friend of Himmler), became vice-president of the council, and legionaries held five ministries, most of the directorships of the ministries, and forty-five of the forty-six regional prefectures (indicative of their strength in the public sector throughout the country). We know the prior occupations of forty of these legionary prefects. Nineteen had been lawyer civil servants, twelve had been professors, six had been army officers, and the remaining three were other professionals (Ioanid 1990: 201–2). The legion also continued to attract young and educated militants: Over 18,000 secondary school students and over 1,100 teachers were active in it in 1941. The legion showed special interest in trade-school students and apprentices. With the suppression of the Communist Party, the legion also monopolized workers' organization. The Legionary Worker Corps was active in most enterprises, and it organized at least one major mining strike (Ioanid 1990: 72; Hitchins 1994: 461).

General Antonescu is sometimes described as a fascist. His prior record had revealed only an effective soldier, honest but repressive and fiercely anticommunist. Though now formally endorsing a corporatist authoritarianism, his ultimate loyalty was to existing institutions, not a new fascist order (Watts 1993: 275). He was essentially a semi-reactionary authoritarian, stealing some corporatist and fascist clothes so as to appear to move with the times. His main substantial link to the fascists was his primitive nationalism, revealed when he addressed his Council of Ministers in April 1941:

We have to inspire Romanians with hatred against the enemies of the nation. This is how I grew up, with hatred against the Turks, the kikes and the Hungarians. This sentiment of hatred against the enemies of the nation must be pushed to the ultimate extremes. I take responsibility for this. (Braham 1998: 15)

But this was not a harmonious family of fascists. Antonescu became alarmed by the radicalism and new collective violence of his legionary allies, and by the rumored movement of communists into the legion. In November 1940 he was enraged when legionaries murdered sixty-five politicians being held in prison. The reports of the Vichy Embassy in Bucharest give ample testimony of the struggle under way between Antonescu and his vice-premier Sima. Antonescu would call for "calm and order," Sima for further "deeds of prowess." Sima was infiltrating the ministries, the universities, the hospitals, and especially the "Commission on Romanianization" with legionary "committees of surveillance," and he was adding legionary auxiliary police to the police forces in order forcibly to "purify" the nation. Antonescu was trying to subordinate all these legionaries to men loyal to himself. Yet Antonescu was yielding ground on policy, promulgating measures of proletarian nationalism, encouraging equality of wages and salaries, attacking capitalist "speculators," and, especially, cleansing the country of its Jews. The French diplomats perceived a "revolutionary" situation leading to a complete stagnation and anarchy of government. This, they said, alarmed respectable politicians and churchmen, encouraging "communistic" legionaries, the mass of whose members they believed were now recruited from "the lowest classes," keen for plunder from Jews and other rich "traitors" (Ianciu 1998: 73–84, 91–2).

It could not last. An attempted legionary coup followed in January 1941. Himmler sympathized but Hitler supported Antonescu, believing he could better control the country and so ensure the safe flow of Romania's oil to the German war machine. Legionaries briefly held most public buildings in Bucharest. They attempted unsuccessfully to assassinate Antonescu. The British legation sent home a long list of army units reported to have defected, but the French Embassy was more skeptical and accurate in its observations. Antonescu had summoned the legionary prefects to Bucharest and took over their regional administrations in their absence. He was a respected general and he had ensured the loyalty of key army units around the capital. Had King Carol still ruled, the outcome might have been different. But this army, despite some disunity, stood and fought. In such circumstances military power can almost always defeat paramilitary power – especially one with only recent familiarity with military tactics as the legion. After some delay, Antonescu deployed loyal army units to overwhelm the insurgents – delaying until the legionaries' violence had discredited them in the eyes of the Germans. The new German envoy Manfred von Killinger clearly brought with him orders from Hitler to suppress the revolt, and German troops paraded a show of force to intimidate the legionaries (Ancel 1993: 228–31; Ianciu 1998: 111–20). Some 250 legionaries were killed, 9,000 arrested. Students had led the demonstrations that began the insurrection, though those arrested were predominantly proletarian, with the remainder scattered among the usual nation-statist middle class (row 4 of Appendix Table 8.1).

The legionaries had learned the same bitter lesson as the Arrow Cross: The Nazi regime preferred orderly semi-reactionary and corporatist authoritarians to unruly fascists. The legion hung on through further persecution, managing to infiltrate many government agencies until allowed to reappear and to participate openly in the Final Solution. As the fortunes of war shifted, so did Antonescu, eventually becoming an ally of the invading Soviets. The legion rebeled again, seizing control of the western part of the country, committing its own little Final Solution until overwhelmed by the Red Army. The legionary life of violence – by them, against them – seemed over.

The postwar communist government proved surprisingly sparing. Antonescu and some fascist collaborators were executed, but the Ceausescu regime later used many ex-legionaries and exhibited pronounced legionary symptoms: extreme ethnic nationalism, forcible eugenicism, and peasant worship. Student fascism briefly reappeared in the aftermath of communist collapse, in the early 1990s. But the strong state is for the moment discredited and there are virtually no Jews left in the country. Only the presence of a substantial Magyar minority causes concern of a revival of organic Romanian nationalism. But perhaps at long last Romanian fascism may now be finished.

CONCLUSION

We have witnessed a broadly familiar story in interwar Romania: surging authoritarian statism and organic nationalism. Yet those responsible were a little different. Here ruling elites were not old, but they had survived the war intact. By radicalizing a little in nationalist and statist directions they could remain in power. State military power (narrowly) held firm against fascist paramilitary power. A king and a general sawed off the fascist threat from below. Though I identified elements of the usual "ruling-class conspiracy" against democracy, this one sought to evade not only democracy but also fascism. And though I identified fascists as the core of this surge, Romanian fascists were distinctive. There were actually two main fascist core constituencies. The first was the usual "nation-statist" ideology and constituency of leaders and militants – though here adding many priests. But the legion also had a rather proletarian ideology and base, among poor peasants and industrial workers – though not across all regions of the country. Thus Romanian fascism was not a movement of the bourgeoisie in general or of the petty bourgeoisie in particular. Had they not suffered disabling repression, fascists might have won majority support from the electorate. Their tactics were more electoral than paramilitary, since until very late the legion's violence was rather individual and primarily intended to provoke limited repression from the state, which would then generate more popular support.

Yet the legion's base seems an odd alliance between disparate groups. What brought them together? The legion first profited and then suffered from political elites' failure to solve the country's pressing problems. In 1918 Romanians had got vast new territories and the promise of a modern democracy. Yet the reality was that it was a desperately poor country and a ramshackle collection of provincial institutions. Political cement was provided by a governing old regime, strengthened by war victory, of patron-client "notable parties" and a monarchy, dispensing state offices and development projects to their clients. In the interwar period such semi-authoritarian methods were showing signs of strain everywhere, undermined by increasing density of communication, assailed by modernizing ideologies, especially fascism. The Great Depression revealed these regimes' incapacity to alleviate distress, especially in agriculture. And as in some other countries, resentment took ethnic as well as class forms.

The king and most of the notables consistently preferred a less rather than a more democratic solution to Romania's problems. They were thus complicit in the drift toward nation-statist authoritarianism – as similar groupings were in just about every interwar country of Eastern and Southern Europe. Yet they did not assist fascists into power. Instead, they themselves embraced some of the fascist vision, partly as a sincere attempt to become more "modern" but partly opportunistically, in order to preserve their own rule by greater force. Though fascists themselves were manipulated and purged, fascism then partially triumphed as King Carol and Marshal Antonescu borrowed corporatist and fascist trappings to become, in effect, "fascist fellow-travelers."

The central fascist message was for a new, clean, modern beginning by an organic nation-state. This embodied a bit of the usual message of class transcendence: "Knock their heads together" with paramilitary violence and then use corporatist institutions to achieve national harmony. But the class emphasis here differed from more westerly Europe. "Bolsheviks" were too weak to much threaten national harmony – except in the form of Russian imperialism in Bessarabia. Domestically, the greater threat seemed to be "foreign" capitalist exploitation of the nation. Exploitation seemed centered on a foreign economic elite, especially Jews – and Carol, a "German" monarch with a Jewish mistress and a "foreign" court *camarilla*, could not eventually avoid being identified with it. The conjoining of "foreignness," "corruption," and "exploitation" was the weakness of this regime, allowing fascism to almost overcome it. But fascism chose more of an electoral than a paramilitary route to power, until too late. Since the regime retained its military power predominance, it survived by force.

The towns, the ostensibly democratic institutions, and the capital thus had an ambiguous position in the new nation-state: supposedly representing the modern future of the nation, yet also its foreign, its cosmopolitan, its corrupting antithesis. Livezeanu (1990; cf. Nagy-Talavera 1970: 258–60) argues that an essentially rural nationalism, articulated by students from rural backgrounds, was now directed against the capital, its monarch, its elites, its productive bourgeoisie, and its Jews. Peasants and the sons of peasants would destroy their power and make Romania into an organic nation-state. This seems exaggerated. More peasants remained loyal to parties that were more democratic than the legion, though the legion did acquire considerable rural support. Yet fascism was not exclusively rural. It resonated in the state sector and the army and also became popular among industrial workers. Socialism was weak and "foreign." But capitalism was Jewish, German, Magyar, and Greek, borrowing French capital. Romanian workers, especially those around the capital, had benefited from statist policies. They supported the nation-state but not capitalism. Capitalists were alien Jews. As it took over from the socialists, the legion became the only viable collective organization open to workers. Workers imbibed fascism as part of collective bargaining.

Into all this we can fit the distinctive strength of anti-Semitism in Romania. Nationalists could harness a radical populism to anti-Semitism. But only the legion was at first adding a broader, supposedly progressive, and modernizing vision: a fuller sense of nationhood, to be wrested from the totality of its exploiting enemies, based on a vision of the potentiality of the Romanian soul rooted in the past but combined with a fascist vision of the future. Thus, as we saw in the voting data, fascist support depended on the *combined* presence of local nation-statists plus ethnic aliens connected to exploitative foreign powers. Jewish "exploitation" inspired anti-Semitism, but was insufficient to generate fascism. This depended on the plausibility of a more total vision, of a proletarian nation "threatened" by exploiting ethnicities and nations.

For all the disparate class groupings – nation-statist middle class, workers, and peasants – anti-Semitism played a large role in generating support for

Romanian fascism, for reasons that are more materialistic and "proletarian" than in the case of German Nazism. Jews were believed to be exploiting the Romanian nation. Thus fascist anti-Semitism resonated among those who considered themselves to be the exploited core of the Romanian nation-state. The legion spoke for Romania as a "proletarian nation." But its oppressors, though supposedly "foreign," were not primarily abroad. Fascists' mission was at home: Cleanse the alien oppressors, strengthen the borders, and so achieve national purity, integration, and progress. My forthcoming volume on ethnic cleansing shows just how far Romanian fascists and fellow-travelers went.

9

The Spanish Family of Authoritarians

Spain differed from the countries discussed above, though not from some of the other countries of the center, east, and south of Europe. The whole family of Spanish authoritarians – semi-authoritarians, semi-reactionaries, corporatists, and fascists – stood united against democrats and leftists. But uniquely in Europe the latter did not cave in but stood and fought. Their bloody three-year civil war ended in massive political (rather than ethnic) cleansing by the victors and then in the longest-lived rightist authoritarian regime in Europe, enduring until General Franco died in his bed in 1975. Thus Spain saw a broader-based and longer-lived authoritarianism, coming to power after both authoritarians and democrats had chosen sides, not only in elections, but also on the battlefield. As a result, we perceive certain things more clearly in Spain.

From the 1880s until 1923 Spain had been "semi-authoritarian," as defined in Chapter 2, with both parliamentary and executive autonomous powers coexisting side by side. There were elections under a restricted franchise but the king could remove ministers, initiate legislation, and declare martial law. Despite its multiethnicity, the country was also highly centralized. The system of *el turno pacifico* ("peaceful change") gave the monarch distinctive powers to alternate Conservative and Liberal ministries at will. When he decided on a change, the local political bosses (the *caciques*) were told that executive patronage would shift to the opposition. This undermined the democratic half of the state, since the *caciques*, eager to continue swilling at the trough, duly switched their allegiance, ensuring the opposition's victory – usually with a low turnout and a third of seats uncontested (Tusell Gómez 1976). But *el turno* was eventually undermined in the more advanced regions by expanding industrialization, literacy, and suffrage, all encouraging political mobilization independently of the *caciques*. Socialism and anarcho-syndicalism stirred the proletariat; regional autonomy movements appeared among Catalans and Basques; modernizing centrist ideologies stirred the middle class. From about 1910 onward some politicians on right, center, and left alike were offering genuine principles and programs, inching toward real liberal democracy.

Yet twice movement toward democracy was stifled. In 1923 General Primo de Rivera marched in his troops and began a corporatist-leaning dictatorship. He fell in 1930 and next year a democratic republic was inaugurated, with liberal and social democratic objectives, granting significant regional autonomies. But the republic lasted only five years before a military rebellion led into the civil war. By its end 300,000 to 400,000 Spaniards lay dead, almost half of them murdered in cold blood, the victims of the last and most violent of the interwar struggles between liberal democracy and authoritarian rightism. The subsequent Franco regime (though it changed through time) can be broadly labeled as a mixture of semi-reactionary and corporatist authoritarian, highly repressive and keeping its numerous fascists leashed yet apparently contented. It faltered only when Franco himself faltered, in old age. But Spanish democracy was safely secured only in 1981 after another attempted army coup fizzled out.

This chapter pursues two main sets of questions. Who in 1923 and especially in 1936 killed off the moves toward democracy, and why? And why did Spain move along the rightist continuum identified in Chapter 2 – but only to an authoritarianism that was able to domesticate its fascists?

BACKGROUND: CAPITALISM AND THE NATION–STATE IN SPAIN

We must begin with the economic and political background. Economically, Spain (along with Portugal) was the most backward country in Western Europe. Industry lagged and few Spanish goods could compete internationally. Neutrality in World War I allowed some export-led growth, but this ended in postwar recession followed by very slow growth. With little foreign trade, Spain did not suffer all that much in the Great Depression. Things got much worse in the small export sectors, especially Asturian coal and Valencian agricultural produce, and in backward agriculture, still employing 45 percent of the labor force. Employers in these sectors sought lower labor costs, intensifying conflict. Continued slow growth frustrated hopes for modernization. Spaniards expected life to improve, yet this occurred painfully slowly and not at all in many agricultural areas. Class tensions increased. As we see below, class conflict was very important in the failure of Spanish democracy.

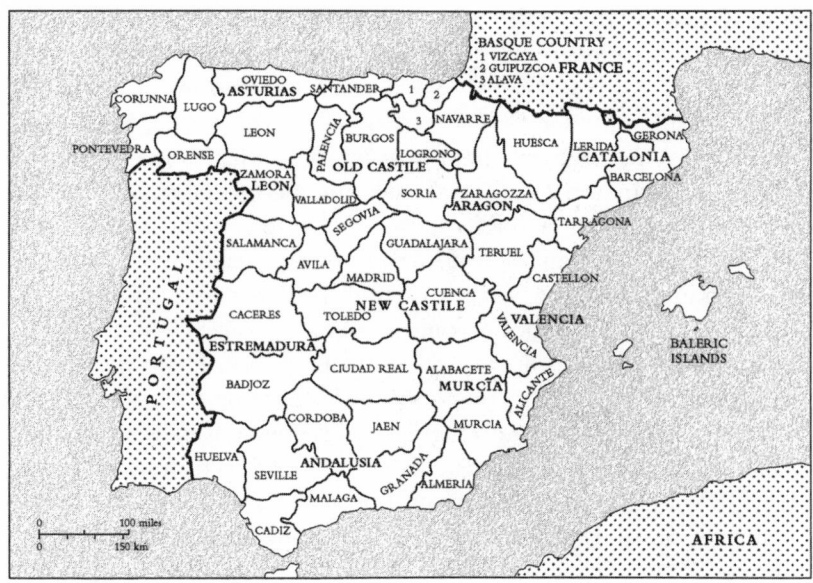

Map 9.1. Regions and provinces of Spain.

But in Spain (see Map 9.1) economic and class tensions always came entwined with regional–national ones. The economy varied greatly by region, probably more so than in any other country considered here. In agriculture most farms in the north were run by small independent or lease-holding peasants. Running in an arc across the north, these were very poor in Galicia in the northeast, just making out across the Castillian center, and more prosperous along the Catalan and Valencien Mediterranean littoral. Peasant owners and leaseholders tended to favor centrist politics, while dwarf-holders and laborers could be more radical. Yet all could be pushed rightward where the Catholic Church was strong (in the center), leftward where it was weaker (along the Mediterranean). But in the south, in Andalucia and Extramadura and in parts of Castile west of Madrid, 40 percent of land belonged to large (250+ hectares) latifundio estates. Two-thirds of the population were completely landless and in desperate economic circumstances. Some 40 percent of all landless farm workers depended on harvest-time contracts for their very survival (though some sailed annually to Cuba to participate in a second harvesting, on sugar cane plantations). Most southern landlords were absentee owners living in the towns.

Absent intransigent landlords, transparent economic exploitation and laborer control of the everyday life of the village are precisely the sociological conditions ensuring that there would be violent, community-reinforced class conflict across the south – as strong as anywhere in Europe. Thus, amid many local and regional variations (too complex to enumerate here), we can perceive a north–south divide – peasant centrism in the north, class insurrectionism in the south.

Region also mattered greatly in industry, which had come late and unevenly to Spain. Industry had mostly grown in peripheral regions that possessed distinct regional cultures resisting the historic political domination of Castile and its capital Madrid. There were textiles in Catalonia and Valencia, mining in the Asturias, iron and steel and some banking in the Basque country. Though not overall a very industrialized country, Spanish industry was highly concentrated, fostering intense local "proletarian ghettos" and class struggles. In certain parts of Spain arose a threatening, even seemingly a revolutionary working-class movement, as extreme as any in Europe. Here perhaps upper classes had good reasons to fear and perhaps to lash out with their own extremism. But such confrontation was regional more than national. Development in these regions had also brought a large, more modern contingent of the middle class, not usually leftist but often liberal and secular, concerned to throw off the old regime yoke. This combination of progressives lay behind what Map 9.2 reveals below: Southern agriculture, Catalonia, and the Asturias were the main republican regions in elections.

Regionalism was not sufficiently strong to persuade many workers to support autonomy movements (which tended to be rather bourgeois). Class ideologies had diffused among workers before the great growth of regional sentiments. But there were strong indirect effects of region on class politics. Much of the core industrial proletariat gravitated (as in other countries) toward socialism. Yet Catalan workers and southern agricultural laborers felt oppressed by a distant state and could conceive of life without it. Indeed, the Spanish state was mainly a repressive presence for the lower classes, especially in these regions and sectors. Workers here became more attracted by the anarcho-syndicalist vision of a general strike, ignoring the state, that would eventually destroy both capitalism and the state. Until the 1930s anarcho-syndicalism also attracted numerous unskilled workers, especially outside heavy industry. Thus though Spanish economic structure nurtured intense agrarian and industrial class struggle, the labor movement was divided between socialists and anarcho-syndicalists, each with distinct regional bases, neither a truly national movement. This was to weaken the Spanish left – and the Second Republic.

In contrast to its late capitalism, Spain had a very old state, though it was also regionally uneven. The *cacique*-ridden parliamentary side I have mentioned already. The executive part of the state rested on three pillars: the Catholic Church, the army, and the Bourbon monarchy. Catholicism was in practice the state religion. Had not this church and state together "Christianized half the world"? El Escorial, outside Madrid, symbolizes their relationship: The great palace of Philip II is wrapped around the dome of a massive church, the altar clearly visible from his bed. The church remained deeply embedded across the more agrarian parts of Spain, especially among the peasants and middle class of Castile and Léon. In some other areas it was weakly implanted, except among old regime elements. There peasant insurrections had included intermittent killings of priests. The church's uneven implantation and bitter experience tended to make it rather reactionary, suspicious of modernity, of "Social Catholicism," of trade unions, and of democracy (Lannon 1987: 55–65, 183–94). The old regime could mobilize considerable ideological power through the church, but varying by region and at the political cost of provoking an opposing alliance between traditional anticlericalism and more modern secularism.

The army was large and important but also somewhat regional. Most officers were from the somewhat poor provincial bourgeoisie of Castile, Léon, and the south. More than any other European army, it recruited the sons of its own officers and noncommissioned officers, bringing them young into military academies, with barely any teenage, let alone adult, experience. Franco entered at age fourteen. It was a caste, though one with a class bias that was now growing. Though its nineteenth-century roots had been liberal, its broad martial law powers were increasingly deployed in defense of the propertied classes (Ballbé 1983; Alpert 1989: 51–2). Since the governments of this poor country could not adequately maintain the large armed forces conferred by its imperial history, military disasters ensued. In 1898–9 Spain's global empire disintegrated after a brief one-sided war with the United States, and in 1921 in the last remaining colony a Spanish army was cut to pieces by Moroccan tribesmen at the battle of Anual. On both occasions the army and politicians traded the blame, opening up a split between the civilian and military state. The officer "generation of 1898" began to abandon traditional liberalism and conservatism to flirt with modern statist ideologies (Busquets 1984: 94–111, 155–7; Ben-Ami 1983: 66–72; Gomez-Navarro 1991: 313–20). Deprived of its empire, the army became a garrison army in Spain itself, plus Morocco. But this was a professional army, and Spain stayed out of World War I. Thus Spain had few discharged young male veterans and the paramilitary ideals they espoused. Military statism remained conservative, top-down even when modernized, unaffected by popular paramilitarism or fascism.

The Bourbon monarchy was the weakest of the three executive pillars. Alfonso XIII was widely blamed for the defeat at Anual. He was sidelined by General Primo de Rivera and exiled in 1931. The monarchy had been persistently challenged, and not only by liberals and democrats. The most monarchist province, Navarre, actually supported the rival "Carlist" dynasty, thus splitting Spanish monarchists. Spanish statism would not take a very monarchist track.

Since the core of all three pillars lay in the backward regions and institutions, the state was not modern. In some ways it resembled the typical premodern European state: a court, an army, and a church, with very little in the way of permanent administration. Its tax base was primitive, its educational, health, and communications infrastructures rudimentary. It could repress and it was considered reasonably legitimate, but it could not get things done – that is, its infrastructural power was weak. Ideologically, it looked backward, to the Golden Age of Philip II for its nationalist myth of *Hispanidad*, Spain's historic mission to the world. Indeed, it often confronted more modern enemies – bourgeois-centered autonomy movements in the advanced provinces and the international ideologies of liberalism, socialism, and anarchism. Nonetheless, the old regime did receive some more modern support from Catalan industrialists and Basque bankers, threatened by aggressive local proletariats and so also favoring organic (always in Spain called "integral") unity against regionalism.

Though this old state was decaying and divisions were opening within it, its decline was very gradual. It had stabilized in the 1880s after a period of regime changes and Carlist dynastic wars. Military disasters were far away and Spain remained neutral during World War I. Unlike all the other states considered so far, there was no external threat to the country, the regime was very old, and there was no sudden loss of legitimacy. A more conservative and infrastructurally weak form of twentieth-century statism than in the countries examined so far might survive the crises of the period. Indeed, most scholars have noted that the durability of the old regime was the most important reason that genuine fascism was relatively weak in Spain.

Spanish "nationalism" was even more distinctive.[1] As a very old state Spain had no contested borders with other countries, except in Africa. There were no territorial revisionists, no enraged refugees (unless we count the *Africanistas* we encounter later). Relations with France and Portugal were entirely peaceful (a characteristic of neighbors in the European northwest, not the center, east, and south), and Spain kept clear of the Great War. Thus many have said that nationalism was weak because the country faced little foreign threat. Payne (1962: 1), for example, argues that Spanish fascists (like those elsewhere) would have thrived on international conflict yet could stir little up. This is where I disagree. It is true that most Spaniards had the good sense to accept their geopolitical decline, and nationalists (including fascists) showed little aggression toward other nations. Nonetheless, Spain faced considerable internal divisions, and as we have seen in other countries organic nationalism tended to thrive as much on these as on foreign conflict. Thus the Spanish right – as in other countries – did come to mobilize a mass "integral" (organic) nationalism against supposed internationalist and separatist "enemies" within. Spanish nationalism was strong, but it was domestically not internationally oriented. It was also resolutely political and cultural rather than ethnic. Indeed, it was regional separatists who stressed ethnicity. Organic nationalists would come to support political rather than ethnic cleansing, since they saw their enemies as presenting an essentially political (separatist and leftist) threat.

Thus a quick tour of the country has revealed pronounced but regionally varied lower class insurgence confronting a conservative, regionally rooted three-pillared state and old regime, still intact, if infrastructurally weak, beginning to decay, and generating a domestically oriented nationalism. Thus the Spanish right lacked not modern nationalism but a modern version of statism – and so it eventually got a more reactionary state than fascism, committed to violent political but not ethnic cleansing. But only a little of this had surfaced at the time of Spain's first twentieth-century encounter with authoritarianism.

THE RISE AND FALL OF GENERAL PRIMO DE RIVERA

The background to the coup of General Primo de Rivera lay in the "Bolshevik Triennium," three years of class conflict (1918–20) involving mass strikes and occupations similar in those occurring in many European countries at this time. However, here the conflict was infused with the distinctive fondness of Spanish insurgents for small arms and homemade bombs. The most aggressive were anarcho-syndicalist CNT union *pistoleros*, gunning down about fifty Barcelona employers, officials, and moderate trade unionists in 1920 alone (Morego 1922). Since the army was ineffective against individual killings, employers also helped to organize volunteer militias and violent rightist unions, the most important of which were known as the Sindicatos Libres (free unions).

The Libres were in a sense the first stirrings of Spanish fascism. These unions were led by Catholic, conservative, and Carlist (Navarre was nearby) workers, fed up with anarchism, anticlericalism, and unproductive leftist "maximalism." They became more violent and more like "yellow unions," as they received employer subsidies to break strikes. For several years they matched the CNT in assaults and assassinations. They recruited most effectively outside the "proletarian ghettos" of heavy industry and large textiles – among groups such as those who specialized in textile trades; railroad, gas, and electricity employees; barbers; carters; cafe, bar, and kitchen workers; bakers; milkmen; masons; carpenters; leather workers; graphic artists; and glass workers. A list of twenty-three Libres "martyrs" killed in the 1920s reveals three metallurgists, three glaziers, three typesetters, two cooks, two bank employees, one baker, one trucker, and eight from the textile dyers' union (Winston 1985: 178–87). In their violence and roots among workers outside the core proletarian ghettos, the Libres resembled fascist worker movements of the period, though their ideology was not so developed or coherent.

And 1920 proved to be their high point. Most of the CNT terrorists were killed, swinging power in the CNT to moderates, especially in Barcelona itself. The reformist socialist UGT unions also began to expand at the CNT's expense. The number of days lost in strikes dropped in 1921 and remained under half the 1920 level in the next three years, the last ones of the semi-parliamentary regime. More strikes concerned wages and working conditions, and more were won by employers (Payne 1970: 44–61; Ben-Ami 1983: 8–14, 34–40; Carmona 1989: 467–8, 495–6; Martin 1990: 226–30). Barcelona was, after all, a modern industrial city in which the power of a legitimate state remained firm. Most workers realized that guerrilla action against it was futile. The violence of the Libres was no longer needed and they declined. The economy recovered and real wages rose. The parliament (the Cortes), though factionalized and corrupt, also showed signs of liberalism. In late 1922 the cabinet announced a program of electoral reform, compulsory arbitration and profit-sharing in industry, army reform, and an end to the Moroccan War. Genuine democracy seemed around a couple of corners.

Yet this seemed to alarm many conservatives. The *caciques* opposed electoral reform, the employers opposed labor conciliation, and the army felt its own corporate interests threatened (Boyd 1979: 276). They resorted to military power and Primo marched in his troops. The church was not involved, the king dithered, but there was financial support from big business. The coup was greeted with enthusiasm by well-dressed crowds and the stock market rose. This was predominantly a class-based coup, though actually accomplished through an army pursuing its own corporate interests. Together those elites possessing economic and military power killed off the first attempt at democracy.

Some scholars advance an even stronger class explanation, saying that the coup was *necessary* to protect class interests. "A revolution from above to avoid one from below," says Ben-Ami (1983: 45–7, 77–87, 401). Gomez-Navarro (1991: 487–90) argues that late economic development had desta-bilized the old regime, "requiring" a more modern authoritarianism based on the two most efficient institutions, the army and state bureaucracy. But the trouble with this functionlist class explanation is that Primo's coup had occurred not when revolution threatened but when reform was being cau-tiously aired by bourgeois liberals. Though rightists claimed that they were averting social chaos, violence and strikes were actually diminishing. Once again in interwar Europe, rightists were reaching for the gun too early, with a touch of hysteria – "panic-stricken" (Boyd 1979: 116–40) with an "obses-sive fear of revolution" (Gonzalez Hernandez 1990: 129). Even Ben-Ami (1983: 8–14) agrees, quoting a contemporary jibe:

... the muse of fear, the diligent companion of the conservative classes, [generates] ... madrigals and ballads in tribute to social order. Social order before anything else! Everything should be sacrificed on the altar of social order.

So there does remain the puzzle with which we have become familiar in this book. Why were conservatives so fearful, reaching for the gun so early? Were they irrational or playing safe rather than sorry? Were they really opposing not revolution but reformist democracy of the Northwestern European variety? Since conservatives displayed similar fears during the much better-documented republic, I delay my answer.

For a while Primo satisfied his supporters. He abolished the Cortes and replaced civil governors with military captains-general. He repressed re-gionalists and the CNT and rejected agrarian reform. But he had an unex-pected side. As a military modernizer he was drawn toward fascism. He told Mussolini that "your figure is not only Italian, but global. You are the apostle of the campaign that Europe has embarked upon against disintegration and anarchy." Primo acted on his fascist sympathies. He replaced the Cortes with a corporatist assembly in which sat a single tame party, the Unión Patriotica. He embarked on autarchic economic development programs. A more radi-cal influence from fascism was syndicalism, and he offered the socialist UGT unions an equal role in compulsory labor arbitration (while he repressed the CNT). The socialists accepted, and by 1929 the scheme covered almost half the industrial work force, and the labor courts were finding more often against employers than workers. Strikes fell. Primo's finance minister was Calvo Sotelo, widely read, attracted by fascist notions of the corporate state, even attempting to tax the rich to finance welfare programs (Ben–Ami 1983; Rial 1986). He was seeking to increase the state's infrastructural capacity and to redistribute power resources minimally among classes who would allow themselves to be incorporated into the regime. All this amounted not to fascism but to an idiosyncratic blend of semi-reactionary and corporatist authoritarianism.

Top-down corporatism weakened the chances for fascism from below. Since Primo had repressed the anarcho-syndicalists and tamed the socialists, the Libres were irrelevant and they declined terminally. But his own UP party and his tame National Assembly were also top-down organizations, unable to actually mobilize the peasants and middle class whom they mostly "represented" (see Appendix Table 9.2, row 6, and Gomez-Navarro 1991: 207–304, 499–506). Lack of mobilized support was unfortunate for Primo, since his quirky policies had multiplied his enemies. The church and capitalists had come to oppose most of his innovations. He mishandled a fiscal crisis and had to seek military economies, which alienated his own soldiers. His erstwhile allies forced his resignation. But it was hastily done – as coups against generals who have command of troops tend to be. There was no agreement about what regime would replace him. Many of the power brokers refused to have back the unpopular king, and they couldn't agree on an alternative authoritarian regime. Massive popular demonstrations erupted in the power vacuum, and in response a democratic republic was proclaimed by centrist politicians. The army could not move against such insurgence led by such moderates. Primo had made the old regime unexpectedly split apart, making a new one possible. The second democratic experiment, bolder and more radical than the first, began.

THE SECOND REPUBLIC: THE OVERALL POLITICAL PROBLEM

The republic began with high hopes, yet has received the worst form of historical censure – the judgment that it was doomed from beginning to end. The memoirs of the conservative politician José Maria Gil Robles (1968) assert that the republic remained trapped between the inexorable extremism of left and right, with democracy becoming unviable and authoritarianism inevitable. The historians Thomas (1977), Robinson (1970), Seco (1971), Juliá (1984), and Payne (1993) tend to agree. Linz (1978) accuses all the parties of valuing their own ends over democratic means. These writers distribute blame fairly even-handedly, though some blame the left more (e.g., Payne and Robinson), others the right (Jackson 1965; Montero 1977; Preston 1978). Who is correct?

Historical and comparative sociology would suggest one preliminary point. The movement for democracy has never been merely "procedural," seeking only a particular method of government. It has also had a substantive purpose. Popular movements became interested in parliaments only in order to make substantive gains from old regimes. In the seventeenth, eighteenth, and early nineteenth centuries, they had fought against taxes and military conscription. In the late nineteenth century, they had added demands for education, welfare, and rights for workers. A redistribution of power and resources from dominant to middling and lower classes, from despotic central states to the provinces and regions, and from men to women has been the whole *point* of "rule by the people" in the modern era. Liberal democracy thus also concerns shifts in real power resources, which constitutions then guarantee.

Thus if liberal institutions failed to deliver *any* redistribution of power and resources, in no country would popular movements have continued to support them. In the countries of the northwest, when pressed hard, old regimes had conceded both democratic institutions and some redistribution of resources. Most Spaniards expected the brand-new republic to deliver reforms. But the Spanish old regime was neither shaken by crisis nor yet greatly pressured or reformed. Its previous political ruler had unexpectedly fallen. Yet when the mass demonstrations died away, most of the executive half remained controlled by the same "old regime" as before, and many *caciques* remained in the parliamentary half. Popular movements, centrist politicians, and the old regime executive differed in their expectations. Republican legislators found that the executive (backed by the right) did not implement their laws, and this pushed reformists leftward; other centrists then became alarmed by the threat that popular pressures posed to social order. Centrists – who provided the key swing voters – became ambivalent, wanting reform *and* stability. If a center-right alliance gained control of both executive and legislature and refused reforms, the left might then revolt. If a center-left alliance gained control of "both states," the right might revolt. If each side controlled part of the state, chaos might ensue. Unfortunately, the republic oscillated through all three scenarios.

Whatever the failings of the republic, to be chronicled later, it had one great success. In Catalonia class conflict declined, employers accepted conciliation, and the church accepted compromise with secular modernity. The Catalan regional assembly, unlike the Madrid Cortes, did not polarize. From 1933 the broadly based center-left Esquerra Party formed the regional government, while the conservative Lliga acted rather like a "loyal opposition" (Molas 1973: 344–8; Barrull Pelegrí 1986: 342–5). Here the center held, hammering out an autonomy deal with Madrid that faltered only when a centralizing rightist *integralismo* government appeared in Madrid in 1934. Anarchist numbers halved. True, landlords appealed to Madrid against rural tenancy reforms enacted by the Esquerra, while its industrialists and the church favored Franco in 1936. But, left to itself, and with goodwill in Madrid, Catalonia compromised. The most advanced region of Spain, hitherto racked by class confrontation, was embracing liberal democratic practices. So was the Basque region, whose church was also quite liberal and whose dominant conservative party, the PNV, declared for the republic in 1936. Both regions saw that a center-left alliance in Madrid would grant more regional rights than would the *integralismo* right. So this is the first asymmetry – the left certainly favored more regional democracy than the right did. And the consequence was to defuse further the possibility that ethnic tensions might escalate into something worse.

There were three different governments during the republic. During 1931–33 Spain was governed by a center-left coalition. Then electoral gains brought a center-right coalition, until the election of February 1936 brought in the center-left "Popular Front." This lasted only until July, when a military revolt ushered in civil war. All three governments had to be coalitions because there were dozens of parties. Though these were varied and changeable, they tended to group around five broad political tendencies. Somewhere close to 10 percent of Spaniards supported the anarcho-syndicalist left – and so rarely voted at all. About 20 percent supported the socialist (and communist) left, 20 percent the left Republicans, 30 percent the right Republicans, and 20 percent the antirepublican right – these last two percentages being reversed from 1933 onward. But included across most of this spectrum were close to 10 percent (mostly from Catalonia and the Basque country) who were primarily interested not in "left–right" politics but in greater regional autonomy. Though these broad tendencies had a fairly stable overall voting strength, the electoral system did not accurately reflect this. Small shifts in voting led to big changes in seats in the Cortes, as we see in Table 9.1.[2]

We see that the Cortes shifted substantially to the right in 1933 and to the left in 1936. Yet no single tendency could dominate for long: The republic required compromise between many of its parties and it failed when this collapsed.

What social constituencies were mobilized by the parties? There were, first, striking regional patterns of voting, as we see in Map 9.2.

We see that the republican/socialist vote was concentrated heavily in the south, Catalonia, and the Asturias, the main areas of class confrontation in agriculture and industry. The Levante, Galicia, and the Basque seaboard were evenly divided. Castile and Leon were heavily rightist, though the city of Madrid was republican/socialist. We see the dual effects of regions with

Table 9.1. *National Elections in the Second Spanish Republic, Number of Seats Won by Main Political Groupings*

Party grouping	1931	1933	1936
Socialists/Communists	118	63	119
Left Republicans	110	36	125
Catalan and Basque regionalists	53	56	58
Right Republicans	164	113	30
Antirepublican right	25	180	142

Note: No political classification of the many Spanish parties can be wholly authoritative. I have omitted five to ten deputies in each Cortes who were especially difficult to classify.
Sources: Varela Díaz 1978: 33, 69–74; Irwin 1991: 269; Tusell Gómez et al. 1993: II; supplemented by Montero 1988 for help in grouping the parties.

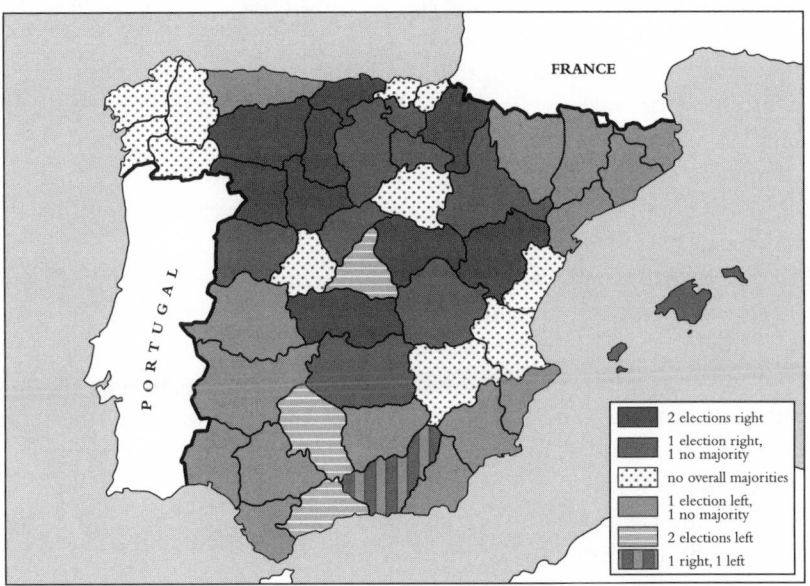

Map 9.2. How the Spanish provinces voted in the elections of 1933 and 1936.

differing levels of class conflict and regions with varying political distance from the old Castilian church and state. There were no "threatened border" areas turning rightist, only peripheral center-opposing regions turning left-ist, sometimes cross-cutting, sometimes reinforcing the class composition of those regions.

But we lack national ecological studies of voting comparable to those of the Weimar Republic. We must fall back on an assortment of local ecological studies. The main ones are of Madrid (Tusell Gómez 1970), Alicante (García Andreu 1985), Aragon province (Germán Zubero 1984), Zaragoza (Germán Zubero et al. 1980), Logroño (Bermejo Martin 1984), Lleida, in Catalonia (Mir 1985; Barrull Pelegrí 1986), and Catalonia as a whole (Vilanova 1986). These studies show that social class was usually strongly related to voting. Almost all districts dominated by urban workers, rural laborers, and poorer farmers voted more leftist. Many of them also had the distinctive patterns of low turnout that indicated the presence of substantial support for anarcho-syndicalism. Yet "left" in this context did not merely mean socialist or anarcho-syndicalist. Outside the main urban-industrial and latifundio "proletarian ghettos," working-class neighborhoods were as likely to vote for the middle-class–led left Republicans as for the socialists. And especially in the backward *cacique* areas, between one-quarter and one-half of working-class people voted for the right. Working-class women, especially if working themselves (most often as servants, influenced by their conservative employers), voted more rightist, as did workers in more religious districts, and as did older workers. People in the service sector and in the so-called liberal professions also voted more rightist.

Thus, on the one hand, Spain contained straightforward class politics. There was here no significant fascist or populist movement confusing this relationship by providing core constituencies that transcended class across the country as a whole. On the other hand, economic sector, religion, gender, age, and especially region and religion also had effects that in some places might rival class effects and that, if added together, were nationally as important as class. Political movements had to try to appeal to all, or at least most, of these sources of social identity. I now move across the political spectrum, from left to right, discussing groups' bases of support, their policies, their violence, and their responsibility for the fall of the republic. Then, for the rightists (who are my main concern in this book), I address their roles on the front lines of the civil war.

ANARCHO-SYNDICALISM

Spain's two labor movements hated capitalism, but they also hated each other. Since anarcho-syndicalists wanted to abolish the state, they also hated the republic. Lacking a political party, their main organization was the CNT union federation. This was highly decentralized, able to intensively mobilize many local communities but with a weak national presence. Its membership was fluid and difficult to estimate, but by the mid-1930s it was probably just over a million – 13 percent of the labor force, about the same as the socialist UGT (with Catholic and Communist unions organizing a further 2% each). Catalonia provided 30 percent of its members, Andalucia and Valencia 15 percent each. Support centered on rural laborers in Andalucia, Catalan, and Valencian textiles and construction, and peasant dwarf-holders around Zaragoza. Heavy industry was underrepresented. Only 5 percent of members were white-collar workers and 5 percent were women – though the latter is misleading since far more women were active in its communal activities. This was therefore an overwhelmingly proletarian movement, and most of the leading militants were workers. We glimpse this, for example, in a police roundup of Logroño activists – a painter-decorator, a garage mechanic, a lathe operator, a caretaker, a cobbler, a barber, two metal workers, a bricklayer, a day laborer, a blacksmith, and a salesman (Bermejo Martin 1984: 253).

Yet the movement was split between more moderate syndicalist trade unionists and younger, more urban, and more violent anarchists led by a distinct organization, the FAI. In 1933 the FAI took control of the CNT when the syndicalists split over whether to collaborate with the republic. But their coup was poorly timed. The incoming rightist government promptly imprisoned or exiled them. Their 1936 pardon by the Popular Front government gave the two CNT factions just enough time for a reconciliation before the military rising struck (Tuñón de Lara 1972: 718–19, 785–9, 873–81; Guinea 1978: 96ff.; Bar 1981; Vega 1987; Kelsey 1991; Fraser 1994: 542–52). So during the republic the movement was rather disorganized – perhaps as anarchists should be!

But the CNT did call repeatedly for a revolutionary general strike. The rhetoric of FAI pamphlets was especially inflammatory, advocating "revolutionary gymnastics," violent uprisings to train workers for the eventual revolution, sung in the language of violent political cleansing:

Death to the police! Death to the soldiers, sons of our class, who have taken up arms against us! Death to the sly bourgeois gentlemen of feudal capitalism! Death to the wretched spongers, to the priests, to the politicians of all stripes! If today you do not rise up strong and pitilessly, tomorrow they will kill you without forgiveness or quarter! Harden your hearts in the moment of combat, take up arms. Overthrow the churches, convents, barracks, fortresses, prisons, town halls and slums! (Ramírez Jiménez 1969: 106)

Such rhetoric must have seemed terrifying – especially to clerics, the one exposed, defenseless group among the "enemies" named above. In Spanish history clerics had long been victims in popular insurrections. But the CNT's enemies exaggerated the reality behind the rhetoric. The authorities routinely claimed to have discovered plots and arms caches, and the press would print highly exaggerated alarmist stories. These "plots" were then used to justify repression.

Let us examine what the CNT actually did. It declared three "general strikes" during the republic: in January 1932, January 1933, and December 1933, yet these had ambiguous aims, revolutionary intent entwining with more limited protest demonstrations. Most militants were content to occupy factories or land and to demonstrate noisily in the streets. However, a few went much further, cutting communications, occupying public buildings, destroying government records, or even firing at civil guards barracks or bombing the odd building. The few deaths resulted more by accident than design. The rhetoric of the movement as a whole tended to be the opposite of murderous. Indeed, it was often naively idealistic – as in one village's revolution:

All citizens are informed that the regime of libertarian communism is hereby established and, as a result, the use of money is abolished. The revolutionary committee announces that everybody can obtain all the products which they need from the shops but that they should take good care not to remove a greater quantity than that necessary for their normal daily requirements. (Kelsey 1991: 96)

All three insurrections were pitiful failures. Scattered CNT bands rose up, usually in more remote villages or in workers' districts of towns, occupied them for a day or so, and ran away when attacked by the police. These were not revolutions, though some intended them as such.

Most other CNT actions began as ordinary labor disputes. But since employers were hostile and the CNT devalued collective bargaining, negotiations were often perfunctory. Then the CNT would attempt coercion, mobilizing hostile crowds and blocking roads. Sometimes this worked. If it didn't, vandalism and occasional acts of arson or explosions would occur. If the police or Civil Guard intervened, barricades and handguns might appear. Workers in some industries could acquire dynamite, and that might produce deaths. Yet the violence had limits. The militants cared little about property, but violence against persons was rarely premeditated (despite anarchist rhetoric). They were also badly armed. The CNT did not form paramilitaries, did not train, uniform, or build arms depots. These were agitators. True, most had done military service and some had access to old rifles and pistols. But these were better for shooting rabbits than Civil Guards, and when they fired, most of these shots were into the air. What the newspapers reported as "continuous firing" for an hour or more would oddly bring no casualties.

Let us try to estimate the deaths. Linz (1978), using data collected by Malefakis, began the attempt to quantify deaths in political conflicts during the republic. He reached a grand total of just under 2,000, which he acknowledged was "an approximation, subject to revision, probably upward." My own calculation, based only on the secondary sources listed for this chapter, reached 2,500 – probably still an underestimate. Some 1,500 of these were killed in a single event, the 1934 insurrection in the Asturias (discussed below, when I come to the socialists). The remaining 1,000 were killed in about 100 separate incidents scattered across Spain. But I attempted this rather crude data collection because previous research using primary sources did not attempt to establish one vital fact: who killed whom. I cannot be sure of this in all cases and for all persons. But I can usually distinguish among "leftists," "rightists," and the police or military authorities – though "leftist" (and to a lesser extent "rightist") victims must have often included people who were actually marginal to the dispute (such as children). I have also attempted to distinguish between the anarcho-syndicalists and the socialists/communists (sometimes measured rather crudely by whether the incident took place in a socialist or anarchist stronghold). As the "fascists" became prominent, I also distinguish them, as well as other rightist civilians. I was unable to identify either the victims or perpetrators of about 150 killings, and I have removed twenty-nine bystanders and a handful of centrist politicians from the calculations of the dead. Data on the remaining 812 political murders are given in Table 9.2.

Perhaps the first point to make concerns what is absent from this table: ethnic actors. There were only a handful of Catalans, Basques, or Carlists killing or being killed by their "Spanish" opponents. This was overwhelmingly political cleansing, along orthodox left/right lines, even if this was sometimes exacerbated by regional conflicts.

Table 9.2. *Perpetrators and Victims of Political Murders during the Second Republic*

	Victims					
Perpetrators	Anarcho-syndicalists	Socialists/Communists	Rightists	Fascists	Military/Police	Total
Anarcho-syndicalists	1	4	20	18	70	113
Socialists/Communists	2	0	42	56	61	171
Rightists	4	19	0	0	0	23
Fascists	10	75	0	0	0	85
Military/Police	252	177	0	1	0	430
Total	269	275	62	75	131	812

The table shows that most deadly violence occurred between the police/military and the left. Fascists got in on the act in 1935 and early 1936, when there were also some other rightist victims and a handful of other rightist perpetrators (almost all Carlists). But the police and military were not really neutrals. They were the core of the old regime state, part of the Spanish right – as their participation in the 1936 rising was to demonstrate. And they were more far deadly than the left: They were 3.3 times more likely to be killers than killed, whereas the socialists and communists were 1.6 times and the anarcho-syndicalists were 2.4 times more likely to be victims. Violence was not evenhanded: Far more was aimed at the left than by the left, and most of it was by state agencies, not by more "popular" forces. Thus I reject some previous interpretations of murderous violence during the republic. Linz gives an "evenhanded" account. Payne (1993: 360–4) puts most of the blame on the left because of the upsurge in killings that occurred during late 1934 and more particularly in 1936, under the Popular Front government. But it was leftists who were disproportionately killed. Blaming the victim seems a little tough.

The CNT were the most victimized. When they frontally attacked employers and the state, the retaliation was far more lethal. Thus by 1935 anarcho-syndicalism was in trouble, many militants dead, most leaders in jail, the rest arguing acrimoniously. Objectively, they did not now imperil the social order. Talk of a "revolutionary threat" from them was now unreasonable. The CNT may have done more to undermine the republic by refusing to help along its reforms. It did not participate in labor conciliation, land reform, or elections because as one militant later reminisced,

Those of us who didn't believe in politics simply laughed. We knew that politics was nothing more than that – politics. Under the republic, under any political system, we workers would remain slaves of our bit of earth, of our work. (Fraser 1994: 97)

In 1933 CNT abstention may have given the result to the center-right. But in 1936 the frightened CNT leaders abandoned abstention, and enough anarcho-syndicalists voted for the Popular Front to tip over a closely contested election (Cancela 1987: 144–5, 194–7, 260–75). CNT militants were now also cooperating with socialists and communists (Balcells 1971; Forner Muñoz 1982). But it was too late. CNT hostility was a major cause of the republic's failure. Indeed, some anarcho-syndicalists welcomed that failure: It would allow them to begin "the revolution."

Above all, anarcho-syndicalism was counterproductive. Uncoordinated local risings without paramilitary organization inevitably brought defeat, unless the police and army would refuse to fire. So did the belief that taking on everyone else at once would bring victory. Their violence, and especially their rhetorical violence, seemed to vindicate rightist horror-stories, alienating the bourgeoisie, middle peasantry, and many workers – especially women, the elderly, or the more religious. Anarcho-syndicalist tactics might, from their own perspective, have been justified if they could have actually made a revolution. But amid a divided labor movement, their main effect was to increase the strength, extremism, and moral fervor of authoritarian rightism. Beside that accomplishment must pall all our sympathy with their sufferings, all our admiration for their bravery and irrepressible optimism.

SOCIALISM

Since Spain had only a small communist party (until the civil war), the major leftist party (then as now) was the socialist PSOE. The PSOE had 60,000 to 80,000 members, its core being skilled industrial workers enlarged by a recent influx of agricultural workers. Socialism was thus also a predominantly proletarian movement – though most of its leaders were drawn from the 15 to 25 percent of the movement who were nonmanual workers. Most of its Cortes deputies were teachers and writers, though there were more workers than among other parties' deputies (Appendix Table 9.1, row 9). Party leaders in the Seville party were employed persons of all classes, mostly white-collar workers (Appendix Table 9.2). Its youth movement became large and ultraleftist – and socialist voters were younger than those of other parties. Fewer women than men voted for the party, and women's sections provided only 10 percent of members (Contreras 1981: 84–112; Aubert 1987: 181–2; Palomares Ibáñez 1988). The socialist unions were federated into the much larger UGT, which surged to a million members in 1932, over 80 percent being manual workers (Guinea 1978: 38, 96, 401; Contreras 1981: 108–9). Socialists also organized *casas del pueblo* across Spain: local social, educational, and mutual benefit societies important in solidifying the "proletarian ghettos" of the more advanced regions.

Socialist leaders mixed reformism with evolutionary Marxism, adding a distinctive Spanish dose of "moral" socialism. Most started with positive expectations of reform from the republic. The 1931 election made the PSOE the largest single party in the Cortes, and its three ministers in the center-left government – Largo Caballero, Indalecio Prieto, and Fernando De Los Ríos – proved effective reformers. Even the party's orthodox Marxist faction argued that the party should cooperate, for the bourgeois revolution must be completed before the proletarian one could begin. Like some other socialist parties of the period, the party did not rate "bourgeois democracy" highly as a goal and was formally committed to "revolution" – though apparently one without much violence. The first two years of the republic saw co-operation between Republican and Socialist leaders. The new labor conciliation committees, the Jurados Mixtos, spread in areas of socialist strength, while labor reforms added to UGT membership (Carmona 1989: 408; Bosch 1993).

Yet two problems rapidly became evident. First, the government's reforming decrees and laws encouraged workers and poor peasants to demand yet more, exacerbating tendencies toward direct action. The balance of local political and military power seemed to be shifting, with the apparent weakening of *caciquismo* and repression. Strikes and land occupations grew. These relied on weight of numbers rather than highly organized violence and were aimed usually not at "revolution" but at reforms that would secure basic material adequacy (Bosch 1993). But they were breaches of public order. Second, the Republican-Socialist coalition did not even control the entire state, let alone the country. The crucial Ministry of the Interior – the heart of the old regime executive in domestic affairs – was staffed by conservative republicans. This was not accidental. As in many democratizing regimes care was taken to make appointments here that would keep the army and police happy. But (as is also normal) they also tended to appoint conservative provincial administrators – in Spain the civil governors – willing to marshal emergency powers against leftists. Calvo Sotelo observed in 1935 that the republic had ruled for only twenty-three days without any emergency powers (this, for him, was an argument in favor of its abolition). Labor legislation was especially patchily implemented. The infrastructural weakness of the Spanish state was worsened by its internal political divisions. In areas controlled by landlords and the church, leftists were aptly taunted "Go Eat Republic!" For in such regions the republic was just talk. A few local socialist administrations were able to ensure reform (Collier 1987), but leftists complained that legislation was not being implemented over much of the country.

The year 1933 was a bad one for the republic.[3] It began with CNT risings, climaxing in the terrible massacre of villagers in Casas Viejas, Andalucia. The whole cabinet (including the Socialist ministers) at first expressed satisfaction that a seemingly violent insurrection had been suppressed. As information spread that the Casas Viejas bloodshed had actually been perpetrated by the Civil Guard on orders from the provincial administration, leftists denounced their leaders' participation in "state terrorism." The socialist agricultural union led southern land occupations that Juliá (1989: 25) says began a "trade union invasion of the political sphere," too attuned to the turbulent rhythms of mass strikes to allow the formation of responsible politics. As the center-left coalition weakened, the republic ceased to deliver reform. In the summer employers' associations stopped cooperating with the government and demanded the repeal of recent reforms. Caballero, the Minister of Labor, was already receiving delegations of workers protesting that reforms were not being implemented. In August his rhetoric lurched leftward: If reform was impossible, he declared, socialists must abandon bourgeois democracy.

Events in Germany, Portugal, and especially in Catholic Austria (much publicized in Spain) were influencing socialists. To protect reform, said some socialists, the "fascism" taking over the Spanish right must be met with force. This was a kind of mirror-image of the reactions we saw in the last two chapters in the cases of Hungary and Romania. There it was the right that felt that it had to head off fascism with force. Of course, the Spanish right was not fascist. But nor had been Salazar, nor Dollfüss when first in power, nor the German governments during 1930–2. Spaniards could perceive a European-wide pattern, beginning with reactionary authoritarianism, ending in fascism. They were already experiencing coercion from landowners, employers, and civil governors – loudly supported by rightists in the Cortes. Thus it seemed plausible that Spain was also drifting toward fascism. Indeed, when the center-right won the November election (for reasons given below), the new government veered further right, repealing some reforms, watering down others. Not all its actions were regressive. But from May 1934 the government began dismantling the agrarian reform and its hard-line Interior Minister and civil governors began dissolving leftist local administrations and associations. In June a strike by the socialist agricultural union was met with 7,000 arrests and many prison sentences. The right now controlled both states, blocking reform – some said the right was even poised for the abolition of democracy, though this was probably not so.

Caballero now argued that if the republic was undoing even his mild reforms, revolution and the dictatorship of the proletariat was the answer. Juliá (1983) sees the Caballero "revolutionaries" as merely frustrated corporatists, seeking and now denied influence within the state for labor unions. Yet genuine revolutionaries were now appearing on Caballero's left, especially in the youth movement. The killings perpetrated by socialists (as we see in Table 9.2) now escalated, involving small clandestine organization among leftist army and police personnel, though still not trained paramilitaries. Though reformists maintained their majorities on the PSOE executive, they could not carry the UGT or the youth movement. Socialist debates were saturated with Marxist rhetoric of class struggle in which the moral high ground was occupied by the left. In this rhetoric each class was assigned its own political party. The "party of the proletariat" should not ally with "bourgeois parties." Yet in many parts of Spain the supposedly "bourgeois" left Republicans attracted as many workers' votes as did the socialists (many workers also voted for the right). But appeals to other classes, or to nonclass identities such as region, religion, or gender, were denounced as "opportunist deviation." With only 20 percent of Spaniards voting socialist, such appeals were actually essential (as Tuñón de Lara 1985: 151 observes). The left Republican leader Azaña drily reminded his socialist allies: "The country will not second an insurrection, because four-fifths of it is not socialist."

Probably most socialist supporters remained reformist. UGT members continued their involvement in the Jurados Mixtos; socialists cheered loudly at Azaña's mass meetings when he would fervently ask for utter respect for the Constitution; and moderate socialists usually got more votes than extremists (moderate candidates also got more votes on the right). Yet the party was badly split, and the actions of the new center-right government assisted the far left. In September 1934 the whole left (socialist, communist, and small Trotskyist parties) declared unacceptable the rumored entry of the antidemocratic CEDA party into the center-right cabinet. Socialist ranks closed around this demand. The reformist Prieto was even asked by the party to organize a future rising. He was supposed to contact sympathetic soldiers, though it seems he did not. He did acquire some arms already procured by the Azaña government to help Portuguese rebels. This could have been the first step toward organized paramilitarism. But his goal seems to have been merely tactical: to use threats to dissuade the president from admitting CEDA to the cabinet. It didn't work: In October CEDA ministers did join the cabinet.

The UGT responded by declaring a general strike. Many thought this the prelude to revolution. As we observed in other countries, however, leftists *talked* a good revolution, but did not actually *do* it. UGT leaders had obligingly given the government twenty-four hours' notice of the strike, to encourage conciliation. Instead, it gave the government time to imprison them. Most of those remaining free spent their efforts trying to restrain a rank-and-file whose expectations their rhetoric had brought onto the streets (Juliá 1984). The weakened agricultural union could contribute little in the countryside. Some Catalan workers rose, though they were not supported by the CNT or UGT, and the main rising was launched by the regionalist Esquerra government, appalled at the entry of the *integralismo* CEDA to the government. Perhaps seeking to forestall moves from the Catalan left (which was allegedly now drilling worker detachments), the Esquerra declared Catalan independence. Some have argued this was merely a bargaining counter in the agrarian dispute still raging with Madrid, others that it was an invitation to Madrid to bring in the troops. At any rate the Esquerra surrendered soon after sighting army detachments. Fifty people had been killed in Catalonia.

Only the northern Asturias region saw a determined insurrection, the first in Western Europe since the Paris Commune of 1871. It was launched and coordinated by miners, and must be understood in terms of the spatial defensive control that miners can secure over their own isolated occupational communities. Their unions had supported legislation on mine safety, accident compensation, working conditions, and pensions. Yet the employers had blocked this on the grounds of costs. The Depression pressured employers into layoffs, lockouts, and looser safety standards – emboldened by the shift in government. Since the CNT and communists were recruiting among the angry miners, the UGT radicalized to compete. A common front was set up between them – one of the few genuine "Popular Fronts" in Spain during these years. The insurgents seized the mines, factories, and some public buildings, acquiring weapons from surrendering police and munitions factories. They controlled the mining valleys but failed to take the main buildings of Oviedo, the provincial capital. Like leftists right across Europe, they lacked the planning and the drilling that is necessary for offensive warfare, even of this rudimentary type. They despised and neglected military power. They were able to doggedly defend their territory against police and regional troops, but the arrival of 26,000 soldiers, many experienced in Moroccan counterinsurgency, brought overwhelming odds (Aguado Sanchez 1972; Preston 1978: 127–8; Shubert 1987).

After two weeks the rising collapsed. Some 1,500 people lay dead. The authorities had killed about 1,200, just over half in the fighting, the rest in a wave of retribution at the end. The insurgents killed 281 police and soldiers and about 40 civilians, including 29 priests, murdered in cold blood. The center-right government made the repression national, focusing on the CNT, whose role had actually been marginal, egged on by press exaggerations of the events. However, the legal forms of martial law were observed and there were few murders. Some 20,000 leftists and regionalists were imprisoned, including most of the CNT, UGT, and PSOE executives. The *casas del pueblo* and local unions were closed. Over 10 percent of Spain's mayors were replaced by executive decree. Even Azaña was charged with complicity, though the Cortes would not proceed with the charges. Had the right been determinedly authoritarian, it could now have dissolved the republic. Had it contained much "radical" populism or fascism, the retribution might have been more murderous. But the main goal was to overturn reform – in an orderly, legal way. Control over both states and a defeated left gave it the ability to do this within republican institutions.

The October uprising was not a revolution. It lacked leadership and coordination except in the Asturias. Elsewhere youthful militants, misled by their own naivetey and Caballero's rhetoric, had launched themselves into the streets, lacking organization, arms, or mass support, to be quickly rounded up – much like a CNT "revolution." The Asturias differed, but even there workers lacked offensive military power. Its end was inevitable if unsupported elsewhere. Prieto admitted that "we are going to deserve a catastrophe because of our stupidity," and leftists now urged restraint. The number of violent strikes was decreasing, and CNT, UGT, and communist unions began to cooperate (Balcells 1971; Forner Muñoz 1982). Calvo Sotelo confided days before the military rising that the chances of a leftist insurrection had plummeted over the past year (Payne 1993: 352).

Violence remained in the youth movement and in a small-scale street war now beginning with the fascist Falange and the Carlists. This accounts for most of the killings perpetrated by socialists and communists, detailed in Table 9.2. By the end of 1935 small groups of socialists, communists, and anarcho-syndicalists were beginning to form ad hoc armed groups. But these remained rudimentary. The socialist movement was not remotely prepared for the revolutionary resistance it would soon be required to mount. The UGT response to the military rising was only a call for a general strike. Military power would supposedly be combated by withholding economic power.

So socialist responsibility for the collapse of the republic was threefold. First, its class- and revolution-saturated ideology hindered perception of a political reality in which class consciousness was only one among several important sources of social identity. Thus it alienated the uncommitted. Marxism told the socialist party it alone represented the proletariat, and the party avoided principled political alliances and appeals to other groups, which was actually necessary to defend the republic. Individual reformists did tradeoffs with "bourgeois" republicans but could not carry the party with them or flourish political principles to compete with the dominant high-minded Marxism. This was not a peculiar weakness of Spanish socialists, since many socialist movements of the time falsely believed they had the only key to modernity. In fact, high-minded Marxism probably also prevented the left from organizing any real paramilitary violence. Second, the party was badly split after 1933, preventing any coherent strategy vis-à-vis the republic or the Depression, as well as the ability to discipline its own supporters (Preston 1978; Juliá 1989; Macarro Vera 1989). It also prevented its reformists from formally joining the "Popular Front" government in 1936. Third, an ultraleftist minority, occupying crucial party power positions, turned anti-Republican, alienating many centrists. In 1936 the reformists were regaining control but too late. These socialist weaknesses helped to foment an ongoing military conspiracy.

Yet I doubt that the party was as devoted to socialist ends over democratic means as Linz, Payne, or Robinson suggest. The reformist wing remained willing to compromise to keep a centrist government alive; Besteiro's Marxist faction supported the "bourgeois phase" of revolution. The Caballerist, ultraleft, and youth movements bear more direct responsibility, of a type we have witnessed throughout Europe. They helped to undermine the republic by rhetorical insurrectionism, but they did not actually threaten it. Many knew this, on the right and in the army. Rightist leaders repeatedly discussed military intervention with the generals, who told them that neither the army nor the public would be very supportive. Their solution might be to provoke a leftist uprising that would fail. The CEDA leader, Gil Robles, was later candid:

I asked myself this question: "I can give Spain three months of tranquillity if I do not enter the government. If we enter will the revolution break out? Better that it does so before it is well repaired, before it defeats us." This is what we did, we precipitated the movement, met it and implacably smashed it from within the government.

Since real politics (especially in a crisis) are messy, emotional, and unpredictable, I doubt that the right was actually as cleverly Machiavellian as Gil Robles is here implying. Yet rightist plots were more organized than leftist ones. And they involved the determined mobilization of military power. The responsibility was not symmetrically distributed – as we see clearly below when we deal with the right.

THE REPUBLICAN CENTER

The Republican parties of the center had to be the fulcrum of any democratic compromise, and their maneuverings did cause both changes of government. They were indeed moderates – no movement of the center contributed to the political killings outlined in Table 9.2, nor did they organize any serious violence, nor did they contribute much to the military insurrection. When the time came, much of the center did stand by the republic.

What was unique to Spain (among the cases discussed in this book) was that most "bourgeois" centrists did not defect from democracy. They stood and fought for it.

This was often termed the "Bourgeois Republic" or sometimes "The Republic of the Intellectuals," since these seemed to dominate the republican parties. The most prominent writers of the age participated – Miguel de Unamuno, José Ortega y Gasset, and Salvador de Madariaga. The main center-left party, Azaña's Acción Republicana, had 140 original sponsors, of whom 112 were writers or professors. Journals, clubs, and masonic lodges emerged to claim their republic – just as in the French Revolution (Espín 1980: 39, 288–92; Aubert 1987; Marco 1988: 171–5; Alvarez Rey 1993). Indeed, the tradition of militant secular liberalism begun by American and French revolutionaries lived on in the democratic zeal of these intellectuals. In this country, most intellectuals – in reaction against the church and the old regime – went more for a reforming democracy than for authoritarianism, let alone fascism. Galvanized by the disasters of 1898, which they often encountered while students, they believed in rescuing Spain by "Europeanizing" it (Marco 1988: 100–2).

Data on the social backgrounds of party leaders are given in rows 4–6 and 8 of Appendix Table 9.1 and in rows 7–9 of Appendix Table 9.2 (cf. the local studies of Tusell Gómez 1970; Bermejo Martin 1984; Germán Zubero 1984; and Cancela 1987). Apart from left republicans in rural areas, the center parties were dominated by professionals, followed by public employees and property owners. Seville leaders (detailed in Appendix Table 9.2) spread right across the middle class: Professionals were best represented, then commercial personnel, with businessmen represented in the center-right, white-collar workers in the center-left. The major professions contributed distinctive politics. Schoolteachers spread across the whole left, but were most important among the socialists and the left Republicans (the Radical-Socialists, as in France). Doctors and veterinarians spread right across the center, lawyers across this spectrum and the antirepublican right as well. We also know that most lawyers voted center-right in the Supreme Court election of 1933 (in which they could vote). Officers were mostly rightists, agronomists and priests wholehearted rightists. University professors and journalists provided leaders in all parties.

In these details we catch glimpses of "two" states. One was civilian and service-oriented. It tended to be secular and center-left. The other was military, clerical, and order-oriented. It tended to be old regime and rightist. There were very few workers among any of these party leaders, and only left republican leaders included many white-collar workers. Big businessmen were few, small businessmen participated locally. Though these were mostly "bourgeois notable" parties, their secularism, modernizing stance, and moderation on class issues also brought them votes in the more secular middle- and working-class areas.

But for much of the center-left, class issues mattered less than anticlericalism and antimilitarism (Espín 1980: 106–12, 293–6; Farré 1985). This seems to have been the main reason why such activists would not defect to the right, as in other countries. Any potential class solidarity between "bourgeois" liberals and conservatives was undermined by their fundamental disagreements on military and religious matters. Yet it had the consequence of pushing more traditional military and religious conservatives rightward. In Spain the chasm opened up right across the center, rather than pushing most of the center to the right. But in the Cortes Unamuno accurately predicted the consequences:

In this chamber there are too many professors. Whenever the army has transgressed, they form an anti-militarist party; whenever the clergy has transgressed, they form an anti-clerical party. Our children, our grandchildren, will encounter an anti-academic party in Spain. (Aubert 1987: 186)

Some blame the left republicans for provoking the church into attacking democracy (e.g., Payne 1970). Yet this seems exaggerated. The church was already reactionary, and the republic's laws were no more extreme than those already passed in other Catholic countries (Jackson 1965: 48). As elsewhere, the republicans were separating church and state, proclaiming religious toleration and declaring that the state had no official religion. The state would cease financing the secular clergy after two years, and the religious orders would have to register their property, keeping only what was necessary for their functions. The Constitution forced the expulsion of the Jesuits (as in other countries) unless they forswore their unconditional oath of obedience to the Pope (which they would not do). More provocative was banning the orders from teaching except to train priests. But the main problem was that the legislation was presented rapidly and aggressively against a reactionary church, which saw republicans as being in alliance with the more violent anticlericalism of the far left.

The Pope was no problem. He sought compromise and forced the resignation of the intransigent primate, Cardinal Segura. Yet the Spanish hierarchy followed its primate's lead and told lay pressure groups to intensify opposition to the republic. Their provocations were mirrored by Azaña, who seemed to delight in the conflict, proclaiming in the Cortes that "Spain has ceased to be Catholic," adding – like a Robespierre or a St. Just – "Let no one say to me that this is contrary to liberty, for it is a question of public health." He certainly failed to appreciate the effect of his rhetoric on ordinary devout Catholics of all classes (Payne 1970: 92, 1993: 82–3). It drove them (especially women and the elderly) and the center-right parties further to the right. As we see below, the church provided the soul of Spanish authoritarian rightism.

The main factions in the center-left coalitions tended to focus on different policy areas. On class issues, the socialists were more extreme yet also more responsible, at least in the industrial sector, since these issues mattered enormously to it. But though the center favored class conciliation, it lacked real interest and would back down if faced with employer opposition. On agrarian issues neither was much interested, since neither had grown up in the countryside or was used to representing it (Heywood 1990: 139–43). On religion some socialists lacked real interest. Thus policy was rarely supported wholeheartedly by the whole coalition if opposition was encountered in the Cortes or inside the state administration. The failure to prosecute policy, more than a lack of belief in democracy, proved the Achilles heel of the center-left alliance.[4]

The center-right had a different weakness. Inheriting the traditions of *el turno*, its main concern was office and patronage. The largest group was the Radical Party, staffed by notable lawyers rather than intellectuals, with middling farmer and industrial and commercial middle-class activists. It initially drew broad support, including some organized workers. Unlike the PSOE and the CEDA, it lacked a solid regional base of support. Originally liberal and anticlerical, it had drifted rightward to embrace a populism strong on rhetoric, vague on policy. Its leaders appealed for reforms for *todos los españoles* and *el pueblo* (their populist use of "the people" was borrowed by republicans and socialists during the civil war) but offered no formula by which class and regional differences might be settled. Though it had attracted support from all classes, it became more bourgeois. The Radicals now drifted rightward again, partly pushed by an influx of moderate monarchists, conservative on class issues. The party's most liberal faction now quit and joined Azaña (Manjón 1976: 192–201, 252ff., 403–8, 589–600, 611–14, 681; Bermejo Martin 1984: 453–4; Townson 1988: 65–7).

The Radicals' consequent move out of the center-left coalition precipitated the 1933 election. The result made them the leading party in the new center-right government, seeking to revise the Constitution to better protect order and property. The repressive Interior Minister during 1934 was a Radical. But the Radicals were also opportunists, believing (like many modern parties) that access to power and influence is more important than declaiming abstract principles. In a republic of too many principles such pragmatism might help democracy, since this center party would compromise with almost anyone who would offer it cabinet posts. But corruption is the temptation of such a party and scandals surfaced in 1934 to break it. Its support began hemorrhaging in late 1934; it was decimated in the 1936 election. This was important in the coming to power of the Popular Front.

The Radicals differed from the right parties, among whom "principles" – property, order, hierarchy, religion, the integrity of Spain – were overabundant. Yet the two could unite in casualness over democracy itself. Access to power and conservative principles could both be elevated over democracy. This Achilles heel of the center-right led it to endorse appeals to the army during 1936. The center-left may have been ineffectual in pursuing reforms and defending the republic, but it tended to believe in the republic and it kept its popular support. The center-right was losing votes rightward and became ambivalent about the republic. Its more rightist factions joined in the appeals to the military to destroy the republic.[5] A more limited hollowing-out of the center-right than in the Weimar Republic helped to undermine the Spanish Republic.

THE RIGHT

Yet the major political partner of the military rising was Spanish conservatism. Ambivalent about the popular new republic, conservatives had done badly in the first elections. *El Debate*, the major conservative newspaper, then urged: "We must all defend Spain and ourselves and our material and spiritual goods, our convictions . . . the conservation of property, hierarchy in society and in work." It thus advocated what became known as "accidentalism": Any constitution was less important than ("accidental to") these political goals. Democracy would be accepted as "the lesser evil" *if* it pursued conservatism. Yet conservatives realized that they had no immediate alternative to join the electoral process with greater vigor, attempting mass mobilization through modern political parties. A few were flirting with fascism or nurturing military conspiracies, but most knew that for the moment electoralism was the only game in town (Preston 1978: chap. 2; 1986: 111–26; Alvarez Rey 1993: 448).

Let us go through the various components of Spanish conservatism. The Spanish capitalist class was one of its bastions, and much of it bore some responsibility for the fall of the republic. Outside agriculture, employers faced demands for reform, not revolution, but they nonetheless strongly resisted, believing reform threatened their property rights. Their statements were stamped by a "reactionary provincialism" that Cabrera believes reflects an "agrarianization of the Spanish bourgeoisie." Faced with labor discontent, many were content to rely on legal repression by bringing in the civil governors, the police, the Civil Guard, and the army. This was how about a third of the killings recorded in Table 9.2 occurred. Pressured by the Depression, employers then collaborated from 1933 with the center-right government to weaken the Jurados Mixtos. These were brought back inside the Interior Ministry, where they found more often for the employers. Employer intransigence was stiffened in 1936 by the Popular Front's election victory, by its incoherent economic policy, and by a strike wave to raise wages and reduce hours. Many now believed they could not afford the republic (Cabrera 1983: 251–86; Carmona 1989: part 3; Macarro Vera 1989; Tusell Gómez et al. 1993).

But few industrialists or financiers were political activists. Though this makes it difficult to judge most capitalists' views, they would probably have preferred a semi-authoritarian "law and order" republic (such as the pre-Primo regimes or the regime of 1934 and 1935) to a military dictatorship. Businessmen were more common in the center-right parties than in the antirepublican right (Appendix Table 9.2). Some capitalists did bankroll the "accidentalist" CEDA and the traditionalist and overtly authoritarian Acción Española and Renovación Española (Montero 1977; Cabrera 1983: 307–12; Morodo 1985: 48–52; Preston 1986). Yet subsidies to the fascist Falange declined once its radicalism became evident, though they increased again in the months immediately before the military rising. Though many eventually supported military intervention, few were privy to the conspiracy (Payne 1962: 61–2; Preston 1978: chap. 7). Industrialists and financiers did not themselves kill the republic, though their contribution was negative.

Latifundistas were more obvious accessories. Rentiers residing in Seville were most active in far-right antirepublican parties (Appendix Table 9.2, rows 1 and 2). Almost everywhere landowners opposed unions, the Jurados Mixtos, and indeed all Republican reforms. If pushed hard in the more prosperous or small peasant areas, most hirers of labor would yield (Bosch 1993). But bigger landlords, especially in the south, were more intransigent. Their associations encouraged them to refuse to work their lands (to starve the workers into submission) rather than agree to higher wages or limitations on hiring freedoms. About a third of the killings in Table 9.2 resulted from their calling in the authorities to repress unrest. Much of southern agriculture was in ferment. Land seizures were endemic, and many politicians realized that only major land reform could stop them. But this was not easy. Neither the state nor the church possessed lands that could be redistributed. Since the southern bourgeoisie had bought into land in the late nineteenth century, the problem could not be blamed simply on "reactionary feudalism." It concerned thoroughly contemporary class relations. The state, small and underfinanced, could not compensate landlords. Southern conflict could be solved only by a strong state – either by repression of the laborers or by land reform forced on landowners.

The republic had started with good intentions. Caballero extended legislation on accidents, inspection, and conciliation to the agrarian sector and banned the import of scabs from other districts. Wages rose while the Depression was reducing prices, which tended to alienate even small farmers hiring labor. Leasehold reform was also contemplated, though only Catalonia possessed a large tenant organization capable of pressuring this. But the south dominated the agrarian question (Malefakis 1970; Tuñón de Lara 1985: 210–218). The first center-left government promised radical reform and floated reports and bills to achieve it. But rightists and farmers opposed them so strongly that centrists wavered. Nor was it easy to draft proposals geared mainly to the south that would also work in other regions. Unfortunately, center-left attention focused elsewhere, the Republicans on anticlericalism, the Socialists on urban-industrial class conflict. Of 470 deputies, only 189 participated in the crucial agrarian vote. Then the rise of the FNTT, the socialist agricultural union, put pressure on the socialists for action. But the most interested groups were the reactionary Agrarian Party and the anarcho-syndicalists – both hostile to the republic.

Thus the first agrarian reform was botched. It allowed confiscations from over 80,000 small to middling farmers as well as *latifundistas*. In order of priority, those receiving land would be the genuinely landless, two-year members of agrarian workers' societies (mainly UGT), owners with less than ten hectares, and finally renters or sharecroppers farming under ten hectares (though small six-year tenants could acquire their land). This created many inequities. Neither left Republicans nor socialists seriously worked at detaching the small peasants from the landowners or the church. The law was then patchily implemented, often by hostile civil governors and local administrations. Most 1933 strikes and land seizures protested failure to implement the legislation.

The election of 1933 brought in the center-right government led by the Radicals, supported by CEDA and the Agrarians (the landlord party).

Landlords were now inside the government, neutralizing reform pressures coming from CEDA's small Social Christian wing. The Radicals seemed uninterested and most CEDA deputies joined the Agrarians in blocking all proposals made by the Social Christian Agriculture Minister. The Socialist Party was under pressure from the FNTT to declare for agrarian revolution, not reform. The Agrarian Law was scrapped and southern ferment intensified.

The 1936 victory of the Popular Front meant that agrarian reform was pushed energetically forward. Azaña and socialists both realized this was the only way to stave off social chaos. Five percent of all Spanish croplands were redistributed amid popular pressure for more. Landowners realized that the government would not send in troops to repress further land occupations (in which socialist mayors were participating). They now lacked legitimate military power. If I were an Andalucian absentee landowner seeking to preserve my fine and civilized way of life, I might indeed have turned to the generals at this point. But the problem (as we also found with Italian landowners) is how these landowners persuaded others to fight for their interests. Were others "agrarianized," and why?

It is not easy to test whether Spanish conservatism was agrarianized. It had been traditionally tied to the three state pillars – monarchy, army, and church – and these all had their roots in the countryside plus the older administrative towns. But monarchy split them into different parties supporting different dynasties. The army was sympathetic, and concerns about order and security clearly had a last resort – a military coup. But the army was something of a separate caste, at arm's length, politically burned by Primo's coup and then by later abortive coup plots, now wary of more. The Catholic Church was to be the active unifier, mass mobilizer, and provider of moral fervor. Conservatives were Christianized more than agrarianized.

The church was deeply antirepublican, fearing anticlerical reforms, with nightmares of a revival of nineteenth-century priest killing that the anarchists seemed to encourage (unfortunately, its own intransigence helped to guarantee this). Its influence permeated the right. Most conservative notables emphasized their Christian identity and were also involved in Catholic pressure groups – of fathers, mothers, women's and youth organizations, associations of publicists, educators, health workers, and so on. In Valladolid, for example, organizations located in the leftist Casa Del Pueblo had 6,000 members, under half the numbers organized from the Casa Social Católica. The Catholic consumer coops and educational and medical benefit societies were much larger than their socialist rivals (Palomares Ibáñez 1988: 58–77,

123). Nationally, the Catholic unions grew to 10 percent of the combined socialist and anarcho-syndicalist unions, not massive but a mobilizable force.

Let us consider the conservative parties, beginning with the more mainstream ones. Among the most important early ones was Acción Popular (AP), which was socially surprisingly diverse. Seville members in 1932 (detailed in Appendix Table 9.2, row 3) were drawn right across the class structure, though overrepresenting all middling groups. In Zamora, 26 percent of AP members were workers, artisans, or servants, 8 percent were peasants, 16 percent were white-collar, 13 percent were professionals, 18 percent were priests, and 19 percent were entrepreneurs and traders. Of two rural locals, one was 70 percent farmer and 20 percent worker (mostly farm workers), the other was more diverse, with entrepreneurs and workers the largest groups. The church was central to recruiting lower- and middling-class members – as it was in the large women's section (Mateos Rodríguez 1993). It was the church that most fundamentally secured cross-class support for Spanish conservatism.

In early 1933 most of the conservative parties coalesced into the CEDA (Spanish Confederation of Autonomous Rightists). This soon claimed 735,000 members, which (if true) made it easily the biggest party in Spain. It was also (unofficially) the most influential party in the 1936 military coup. CEDA national and regional leaders were professionals and substantial property owners, with bankers and clerics prominent in some regions. Lower down, their composition broadened out among the middle classes: Of seventy-seven local committee members throughout Spain, 33 percent were professionals, 20 percent public employees, 13 percent businessmen, 9 percent white-collar, 9 percent landlords/farmers, and 12 percent were workers (Appendix Table 9.1, row 4). The large CEDA youth movement, the JAP, is said to have been dominated by middle-class students, though there are no actual figures.

As significant as class, however, were religion, gender, and farming. The Madrid branch said that its members were 45 percent women, unparalleled among contemporary parties (Payne 1993: 168), while in most provinces farming families provides the bulk of members. The church was very important in mobilizing both women and farmers, both highly involved in church attendance or organization. CEDA stressed the restoration of church privileges above all else. Many CEDA locals were avowedly confessional, emerging out of Catholic lay organizations – with more members than the local labor unions (for Murcia, see Moreno Fernandez 1987; for Salamanca,

Vincent 1989: 83). The Catholic farmers' association was the largest CEDA affiliate, centered in Castile. Its organizers sought to recruit respected community worthies of all classes, focusing on those active in religious and charitable affairs (Castillo 1979).

CEDA did not neglect material interests. It emphasized the common landlord and capitalist and petty bourgeois commitment to property rights. In its peasant core it emphasized the common sectoral interest peasants, and landowners shared in high food prices and cheap wages (Montero 1977: 419–49). But class and sectoral interests were interpreted within a broader moral order, centered on an ideology of integral nationalism, guaranteeing order and security, which claimed to "transcend and suppress" class and regional conflict and disorder. Its Social Christian wing's social concern for the poor was ideologically important in election appeals, though its practical influence on CEDA policy was not great. Care was taken with social labels. The terms *"labrador"* (technically, ploughman) and *"agricultor"* (husbandman or farmer), often concealing an absentee rentier, conveyed a dual sense of someone of worth and substance who also got his hands dirty. In CEDA records these terms make it difficult to identify activists' exact class location – as was the intention. Though CEDA branches were often dominated by the old regime, in more religious areas of the countryside and older administrative towns of the Castillian center, it attracted votes from all classes. Thus the party could mobilize broadly outside the "proletarian ghettos," the secular bourgeoisie, and regional autonomy movements.

CEDA remained ideologically "accidentalist" about democracy. This was partly to avoid constitutional argument between its disparate main factions – Christian Democrats, *caciques*, and authoritarians (Tusell Gómez 1974). CEDA discussed constitutions more in terms of "tactical possibilities" than principles, with democracy often seen merely as "the lesser evil" (Montero 1988: 17; Preston 1986: 111–26). The constitution was less important than ("accidental to") the goals it served – a belief shared by many on the left, of course. CEDA insisted that the republic revise its constitution regarding church–state relations, then it broadened the conditions. Provided the republic secured order, property, church rights, class harmony, and the integrity of Spain, then CEDA would accept democracy. If not, it was not spelt out, but most understood it meant a regime installed by the military. Yet CEDA was patient, prepared to wait at least until the republic's fourth anniversary (December 1935), after which a simple Cortes majority would be sufficient to amend the constitution. The CEDA leader Gil Robles preferred a constitutional outcome since he had staked his leadership on the parliamentary route. Yet even he hedged his bets. In December 1933 he declaimed:

today I will facilitate the formation of center governments; tomorrow when the time comes, I will demand power and I will carry out a reform of the Constitution. If we do not receive power, if events show that a right-wing evolution of politics is not possible, the Republic will pay the consequences. This is not a threat but a warning.

By October 1935, his "warning" was tinged by fascism:

We must found a new state, purge the fatherland of judaising freemasons. . . . We must proceed to a new state and this imposes duties and sacrifices. What does it matter if we have to shed blood! . . . We need full power and this is what we demand. . . . To realise this ideal we are not going to waste time with archaic forms. Democracy is not an end but a means to the conquest of the new state. When the time comes, either parliament submits or we will eliminate it. (Preston 1978: 98, 48)

Except for a distinctive Catholic obsession with freemasonry, this could be a speech of Hitler or Mussolini.

Thus republicans and socialists began to call CEDA "fascist," declaring unacceptable its entry into coalition governments. CEDA was not fascist. It supported traditional state institutions and specifically rejected paramilitarism. CEDA was actually as varied as the Socialist Party, but with a difference – this church-centered party was more disciplined. Republicans tried to split CEDA by luring its "left" into a coalition government – which would have been an excellent solution for the survival of a democratic republic. But their efforts failed: CEDA "leftists" believed that they could not survive on their own, outside the protective mantle of a party whose core was not fascist but reactionary authoritarian Catholicism. But for socialists, republicans, and regional autonomists the difference between fascism and reactionary authoritarianism was insignificant. They knew that CEDA would reverse republican reforms, repress their movements, and imprison them. They were less interested in the motive – fascist or merely Catholic reactionary – than the likely deed. "Fascist" became the standard word used by the European left and center-left for authoritarians who wished to imprison them. In other countries such people often did become real fascists – and laggard Spain was aware of this. As a card-carrying sociologist, committed to terminological precision, I do not call CEDA "fascist," but its opponents were (in a very personal sense) perhaps entitled to do so.

Once in control of the two states, in late 1934, CEDA revealed semi-authoritarian leanings, for it spearheaded the legal repression after the October rising. Yet this backfired, alienating uncommitted centrists (Montero 1977: II, 124ff.). When the scandal-ridden Radicals began to collapse, the CEDA leader Gil Robles assumed that (as leader of the largest party in the governing coalition) he would be asked to form the next government. But fear of CEDA "fascism" was so widespread that President Zamora refused, declaring an election instead. CEDA, still confident, mounted an aggressive election campaign denouncing its opponents as immoral traitors to the nation. This alienated some conservative republican and regional parties, who revoked their alliance with CEDA. In the election this brought the Popular Front an extra 5 percent of votes. Frightened anarcho-syndicalists, voting for the first time, probably brought more. Combined, their weight cost CEDA the election. In the near future it could not attain its goals through democracy or legal means.

Compromise was difficult for CEDA, the ultraright, and the church because of their tendency to demonize their opponents. Their newspapers, pamphlets, and speeches persistently invoked a *reconquista*. This resonant word refers back to the historic wresting back of medieval Spain from Islam. Now modern Spain was to be forcibly wrested back from what CEDA termed the "*Anti-España*" of atheistic socialists, anarchists, and republicans, alien to the integral (i.e., organic) nation. The republic had brought divisions, deaths, and anarchy. CEDA election posters declared, "To vote for the Republic is to vote for Civil War." Spain must be saved from "Marxists, Masons and Separatists [occasionally also Jews], serving the interests of international foreigners. They are not Spaniards!" The church weighed in, labeling this a "moral" not a political struggle, between "construction and destruction; between the Spain of ancient traditions, religious principles and the conservation of society and the anti-Spain of demolition, church burning and . . . revolution." Its "Crusade of Prayer and Penance" urged prayers, offerings, and penance for the defeat of "those against Christ [who] have unfurled the banner of destruction and hatred . . . the enemies, apostates of their religion and of their birthplace." In the 1936 election the Catholic press for the first time denounced conservative Republicans as un-Christian (Vincent 1989: 80–6; Montero 1977; Bermejo Martin 1984; Lannon 1984; cf. Alvarez Chillida 1992; Alvarez Rey 1993: 334–6). This was a decisive moment, the throwing of the weight of the church behind an exclusionary organic nationalism, prefiguring its description of the military rising as a "crusade against anti-Spain." Amid such powerful ideological pressure, it was difficult for many Spaniards to relate the rival party programs to their own private interests in a calculated way. It was also difficult for capitalists outside southern agriculture to relate them to their interests in retaining their property or generating profits. Ideological power was being mobilized to considerable effect, turning more intransigent Catholics' sense of economic power and interest. True, the purpose of all this rhetoric was to win a democratic election. But what if they lost it? Could they consent to being governed by people they had just described as alien enemies and traitors?

Rightist nationalism was thus much more coherent and more dangerous in its combination of hate and morality than was its statism. Its statism was truly "accidentalist," since the right did not know what kind of authoritarian state it wanted. A few CEDA militants were drawn toward a somewhat fascist mixture of repression and the transcendent "third way" of order, hierarchy, and harmony. Its youth movement, the JAP, adopted fascist trappings, including mass mobilization, street violence, and adulation of "The Leader" (Montero 1977: I, 621ff., II, 81ff. and 248ff.; Preston 1986: 63–8). But no single tendency dominated everywhere. In the Seville party there was less fascism than a return to *caciquismo* (Alvarez Rey 1993). The JAP adopted an appropriately half-baked fascist salute – raising the right arm halfway and bending it at the elbow back across the chest. Try it – it feels too wimpish to be fascist, a fascism of the closet, ashamed to quite come out. Nor were there yet many rightist paramilitaries. Some JAP groups called for them, but the CEDA leadership did not permit this. Except for the Carlist levies and the small Falange, the right looked to the army for force. CEDA did not need a blueprint for a future society; a military *pronunciamento* would suffice. CEDA accidentalism finally applied even to itself. Once the army rose, CEDA disappeared: The time for parties was over. CEDA personnel simply moved over into the new regime. They had been the main political destroyer of Spanish democracy. Their "accidentalist" trajectory toward this was far more damaging than the supposedly "revolutionary" trajectory of the anarcho-syndicalists or socialists.

To their right, and overlapping with CEDA's own right wing, were those styling themselves as "traditionalist" parties, who openly rejected the republic and democracy – the Agrarians and most of the Alfonsine and Carlist monarchists. However, through the republic they increasingly embraced more modern authoritarian corporatist ideas that the pressure group Renovación Española was advocating. On the far right the lines separating the authoritarian family members were blurring. They had distinct regional and religious cores. Their leaders were usually landowners, lawyers, priests, and officers, but they could mobilize local cross-class communities of the faithful, whom they appealed to as "persons of moral reliability, profoundly Catholic, in love with patriotic traditions." Sympathetic workers were styled "Catholic, worthy and honorable." The high moral tone of these ultras was one of their attractions, appealing especially to students (Alvarez Rey 1993: 307–11). The Carlists offered a somewhat uneasy combination of populist local democracy and top-down monarchist corporatism. They dominated Navarre, with only pockets of support elsewhere. Since they recognized the legitimacy of neither Republic nor its main alternative, a Bourbon monarchy, they had no inhibitions against organizing their own armed violence. They formed Carlist paramilitaries, arming and drilling for an eventual uprising. By 1936 they alone, of all political movements, could firmly secure military control of their heartlands. Their contribution in terms of military power to the collapse of the republic was thus as great as their limited numbers would allow.

FASCISTS

There were not many true fascists in Spain – until the civil war began. The existing authoritarian institutions of the Spanish old regime were too powerful to leave much space for a movement with a new theory of authoritarianism. Instead, new theories were blended into the old institutions. But not all were absorbed.

The dominant fascist group was the Falange, spouting a rather Italianate type of fascism. But it had an unusual and charismatic young leader, José Antonio Primo de Rivera (the ex-dictator's son), who was killed by republicans in the first days of the civil war. His poetic and sentimental style, squeamishness, and political innocence typified the kind of "moral fascist" who rarely survived at the top of fascist movements. The Falange did not reach 2 percent of the national vote and before 1936 had fewer than 10,000 members. Since no sudden crisis had engulfed the state, reactionary authoritarianism remained entrenched, borrowing corporatist ideas, cramping the space for populist fascism. Conservatives could rely on the army and Civil Guard rather than unreliable street fighters. Things changed somewhat in 1936 as the Falange grew rapidly to 20,000 to 25,000 members by the outbreak of the civil war, partly because the military conspirators wanted civilian allies to increase their legitimacy. By October the Falange provided 43,000 of the 65,000 volunteer militiamen to the Nationalist cause – the Carlists providing most of the rest (Casas de Vega 1974). Political polarization had heightened the allure of paramilitary fascism, especially for the young.

Though we have little data on the fascists, it is generally assumed they were "petty bourgeois" (as were many of the smaller fascist parties of Europe). Their vote was largest in the most affluent and rightist districts, but since they almost never received 5 percent of the vote, we cannot close in on actual fascist voters through ecological studies. Suarez Cortina (1981: 157) has limited data for the Asturias indicating leaders who were teachers, lawyers, businessmen, and petty traders but able to mobilize student and Catholic worker support. He guesses their vote was highest in petty bourgeois districts. Details on 1,103 members in Madrid province survive. As everywhere, these fascists were young, 60 to 70 percent being under twenty-one. A surprising 55 percent were workers, which may be misleading, since there were probably another 1,000 to 2,000 local fascist students not recorded on this list (students could not officially join any party if under twenty-one). And the Falange was usually at its strongest in university cities (Payne 1965: 45, 63, 68–70, 81–3, 225–6; 1980: 423–6). In Cádiz the newly formed Falange immediately recruited twenty students and eighty workers, disillusioned with the performance of all the republic's parties (Cancela 1987: 222). In Seville, students formed the core, aided by skilled workers then by hotel sector workers and some service sector white-collar workers (Alvarez Rey 1993: 385–92). Since the Catholic-authoritarian right already mobilized the mass support that in countries such as Germany and Italy went to fascism, the Falange may have mobilized only those who usually provided the hard-core paramilitary fascists – younger hotheads, with students and workers from outside the proletarian ghettos prominent.

These fascists were not at first very effective. Until spring 1934 the Falange was in an unusual situation for a fascist party: Though advocating violence, it was inflicting less killing than it suffered. Over the next two years its own *pistoleros* evened things up (see Table 9.2). During 1936 it concentrated its violence in the major cities, especially Madrid – doing damage to the republic out of all proportion to its size, augmenting the fear that public order had collapsed.

But the Popular Front electoral victory of 1936 led to desperate measures on the right. As conservatives conspired with generals, and as CEDA militants began defecting from their pragmatic leaders, the Falange expanded greatly. It is said (on the basis of little actual data) that this was among the educated middle classes of towns in Castile and Léon, then among small farmers and the entire middle classes (Blinkhorn 1987: 335–9). CEDA leaders claimed that 15,000 of its JAP youth members joined the Falange during the spring, and most of the Nationalist militants interviewed in old age by

Fraser were recent converts from CEDA and JAP. They were socially rather varied – several small farmers, a print worker, a lawyer, a student – but they were all from strongly Catholic backgrounds, despairing of CEDA "cowardice" in the face of the "disorder" and "anti-Christian" goals of the republic. They tended to describe their enemies as "Bolsheviks." Some, like this farmer, espoused radical social-Christianity:

It meant redistributing part of the wealth of the country in a new, more just manner; it meant that everyone would have to work – but work in harmony together; it was pure evangelism, the doctrine of Jesus Christ that everyone should live better, not that some should be well-off and others poor. (Fraser 1994: 87)

The petty bourgeois stereotype of the Falange seems oversimplified, mainly because region and religion also mattered. The Falange was rather ambivalent about religion, yet it was in the more rightist and religious provinces – Castile, Léon, and Navarre, especially – that the attractions of authoritarianism and fascism increased among all social groups who were not insulated by strong leftist organization (and relatively few were in these regions). That is surely how we must interpret the mass response in these core regions to the voluntary enlistment program of the Falangist and Nationalist militias only months later. Some regions allowed fascism to recruit more broadly among the classes, but this was not a fascist movement that could plausibly claim to transcend class on its own merits. What mattered above all almost throughout the Spanish political spectrum was the entwined triad of class, region, and religion.

MILITARY POWER, MILITARY FRONT LINES

But Franco never depended on votes, parties, or mass movements. Nor had Primo before him. They led army revolts. Thus we must analyze the specific organization of the military to ask how the state lost its monopoly of military power. As noted earlier, the officer corps was ingrown, half its recruits the sons of officers, half from the genteel but rather poor provincial middle class – both mostly from Castile and Léon. Thus the officers were attracted to modernized conservatism in the form of integral nationalism. Officers' corporate caste interests also tended to turn them against the republic. There were too many of them for the reduced military needs of the country, bringing conflict with civilian governments seeking to keep salaries low, to retard promotion, and to stint modernization. The army thus contrasted military virtue with civilian vice. A rebel general summed this up in his memoirs:

The army . . . had developed a distinctive psychological state: believing itself alone in an immense desert, the sole possessor of truth amid thousands of erring compatriots; the only source of justice and honor, the only patriot; and this exaltation of a particular egoism logically led it to impose its opinions on others by all means, despotically, dictatorially, declaring war on the state. (Kindelan n.d.: 188)

The center-left governments worsened the conflict, cutting budgets and creating a state paramilitary, the Republican Assault Guard, controlled by civilian authorities, to replace the army's public order role. This was the only paramilitary force on which republicans could rely in 1936. Center-left governments then tried to protect themselves from a coup by promoting officers loyal to the republic, which was obviously a deviation from strict meritocracy. This carried the short-term downside of completing the transformation of corporate caste interests into principled ideology – authoritarian technocratic modernity versus corrupt civilian democracy (Boyd 1979: 19–43, 276; Espín 1980: 183–201; Busquets 1984; Alpert 1989; Gomez-Navarro 1991: 313–20). But until the church demanded the moral support and the intolerance of all true Spaniards, army ideology remained a little caste-like, discontented, hostile to republicanism, but fearing that it was isolated. It remained reluctantly "loyal." The army then rebelled as its own interests became entwined with statist and corporatist political principles and Christian and nationalist morality.

These values had also acquired a harder edge during Spain's dirty Moroccan war, when it was defending sacred España against a "barbarous" anti-Christian foe. Franco played a major role in developing the more modern and murderous tactics that produced eventual victory in Morocco for the Army of Africa. He was then summoned by the center-right government in 1934 to more counterinsurgency, leading units of the Army of Africa in the suppression of the Asturias insurrection. He described this action in half-Moroccan terms, declaring: "[T]his is a frontier war against socialism, communism and whatever attacks civilization in order to replace it with barbarism" (Preston 1993: 105). He was to prove equally ruthless during the civil war. Very noticeable in July 1936, in the first days of the rising, was the more ruthless determination of rebel officers compared with Republican loyalist officers. The rebels were much more likely to shoot immediately or to have executed their superior officers if they sensed opposition. *Africanistas*, officers who had served for long periods in Morocco, were prominent among them. I have tried to quantify this in Table 9.3.

Table 9.3. *Africanistas among the Military Elite of the Civil War*

	African service			
Civil war allegiance	−5 years	5 years + (Africanistas)	Unclear	Total
Republican	13	5	1	19
Nationalist	5	39	2	46
Total	18	44	3	65

Note: The sample is of general officers listed by Suero Roca (1975, 1981) or indexed in Thomas (1977) whose service records were clear from the sources used in this chapter. Of my sample, sixty saw their main service in the army, three in the navy, and two in the air force. Almost all served at least briefly in Africa. This research could be greatly strengthened by utilizing the actual service files of the officer corps.

The table shows clearly the overrepresentation of *Africanistas* among the nationalist rebels: 87 percent of rebel generals were *Africanistas*, compared with only 26 percent of Republican generals. To some extent this was because the Republic had sought to "exile" rightist generals to Morocco and the Canary Isles. But the experience in Africa had also fueled their sense of moral hatred of alien enemies, outside and inside Spain.

As soon as the Popular Front won the election of 1936, preparations for a military rising began. During 1931–3 the right had conducted its campaign within the Cortes and state administration. From 1934 legal repression within parliamentary forms had sufficed. Now it turned to its other, military option. Before even leaving office Gil Robles asked the president to declare martial law and the generals to intervene. Though Franco showed some interest, the president refused and most senior officers said the army was not ready. From March there were consultations between generals, monarchists, and CEDA politicians. Gil Robles felt it proper to keep in the background. Yet he admits he collaborated "with moral stimulus, with secret orders for collaboration, and even with economic assistance, taken in appreciable quantities from the party's electoral funds." He tried to mediate the conspirators' disagreements over a postcoup constitution and he instructed CEDA members to be prepared to join the army rather than form paramilitaries (1968: 719, 728–30, 798–802). But he played no part in the civil war or the Franco regime.

In April 1936 the conspirators recognized General Mola as the clandestine commander of the coming uprising, though Franco was seen as the most effective rebel general. Mola and Franco tried hard to avoid Primo's error: They knew that the political goals of the coup should be clarified beforehand. Yet this proved impossible. Only some of the conspirators were monarchists (and they were divided between Alfonsines and Carlists); some wanted a corporatist dictatorship and some wanted only a semi-authoritarian republic. They could agree only to proclaim a military rising to rescue Spain from its "enemies," making no mention of any constitution. Its form was truly "accidental" to the real, substantive goal: to overthrow democracy by authoritarianism, any authoritarianism, and to cleanse the land of political enemies. Franco was quick to fashion a corporatist dictatorship once the fortuitous deaths of Mola and others left him in command. He then used fascists in his regime, and sometimes spouted fascism, insofar as his political needs dictated. But the rising knew more about the anti-España it was attacking than about the political constitution of the true España.

Mass preparation came from a semi-secret military society, the UME, claiming 3,436 officers (one-fourth of the active officer corps), plus 1,843 retired officers and 2,131 NCOs. Its Republican counterpart, the UMRA, had only about 200 officers, more NCOs and Assault Guard police, mostly in Madrid. Their main deed was the assassination in early July of the Renovación Española leader (and former minister of Primo de Rivera) Calvo de Sotelo, a much-respected figure on the right. For some rightists this was a genuine last straw, for others it was the pretext – for the plot had actually been maturing for some months. The military rising began. In the event one-quarter of the officer corps remained loyal to the republic, while two-thirds declared for the rising. The Civil Guard divided similarly, but most of the small new Republican Assault Guard stayed loyal to the republic.

Map 9.3 reveals the initial front lines of the civil war, in which patterns of military and political logistics were entwined. The initial division into two Spains, Nationalist (i.e., rebel) and Republican, partly reflects prior areas of leftist or rightist political strength, partly areas of army strength. The republic predictably held Catalonia, Valencia, and Madrid itself, plus radical rural areas in the center-north. They recruited most of their socialist and anarchist militias from these areas. The Nationalist political heartland was in the rest of Castile and Léon, which contributed more than their share of army recruits, though fewer Falangist volunteers. Madrid was split, since it included a disproportionate share of both the rich and the working class. It was also the seat of the old state and the new republic. It declared for the republic, with the considerable aid of the main units of the Republican Assault Guard. Catalan cultural ideology and industrialism had reinforced one another to generate leftism among workers and liberal republicanism among the middle classes, both suspicious of rightist centralization. Barcelona became a revolutionary bastion during the civil war. Down the coast the secular, moderate autonomy sentiments of Valencia converted into moderate republicanism.

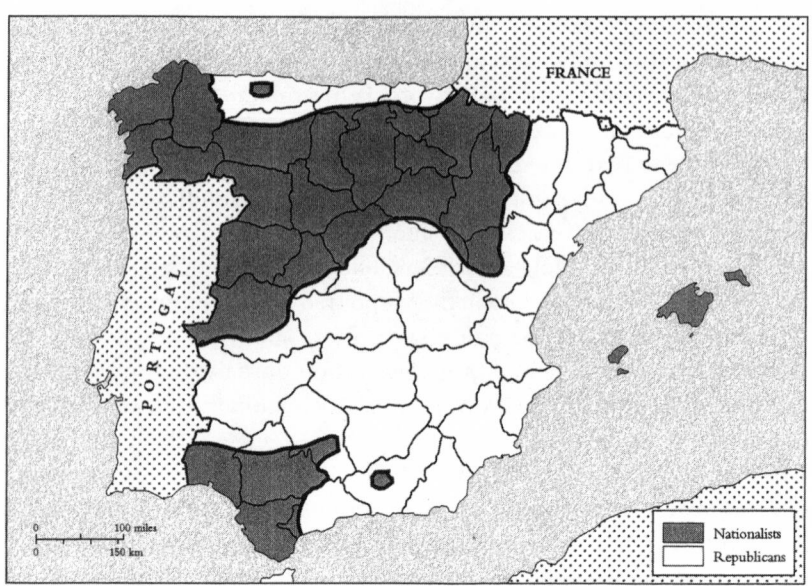

Map 9.3. Civil war: initial areas of control, July 1936.

In Andalucia the leftists were predictably far more numerous, but they were swiftly defeated by Franco's invading Army of Africa. The region provided less than its share of Nationalist volunteers and very few Falangists.[6] Up the west, where Extramadura meets Old Castile, Catholicism and Francoism strengthened. In the northwest, in Galicia, Catholicism and *caciques* were undercut by mild regionalism to produce moderate support for Franco. It provided many Nationalist army recruits but few Falangist volunteers. In the Asturias, badly scarred by 1934, sides seem to have been mainly chosen by class: Most workers opted for the republic, the bourgeoisie for the Nationalists. Basque elites wavered. They distrusted the left, yet since the republic offered regional autonomy most supported it. Yet in neighboring Navarre regionalism went rightist, since it was Catholic and Carlist and had secured regional concessions from the Nationalists. It raised proportionately the most Falangist volunteers, as well as most of the Carlist militias (Blinkhorn 1975; Payne 1980: 427–8).

Consider in particular the variations we find in a single but very large class fraction, small peasant proprietors. In general, their collective economic associations saw republican and socialist parties as favoring laborers and urban consumers at their expense. In Castile, Léon, and some other areas the church had also been able to implant some of the economic infrastructures of "Social Catholicism" – credit banks, coops to provide machinery and marketing services, and professional and social organizations. Increasingly, the church and its lay notables provided leadership for all social initiatives. Thus schools, women's increasing religiosity, newspapers, and local political parties steered Catholic peasants into hostility to secular republicanism and socialism (Montero 1977; Castillo 1979; Perez Diaz 1991: 47–9, 96–100, 177). These peasants had made up much of the mass membership of the dictator Primo de Rivera's tame party. In the 1930s they were the backbone of the CEDA. In 1936 they fatefully swung behind Franco – providing the single greatest refutation that the Nationalist side was simply a front for the bourgeoisie. Yet similar poor-to-middling peasant proprietors in the Levante drifted toward different politics. Here economic class interests and social Catholicism were undermined by anticlericalism and anti-Castillian regional sentiments. These peasants had mostly voted Republican and now they declared for the republic. Neither region's peasants were extremists within their camp, but they were in different camps. So too were the agrarian classes of Catalonia and the Basque country (Republican) versus those of Navarre (Carlist, then Nationalist). In these cases regional-religious conflicts, more than agrarian relations of production, determined the side chosen (see the essays by Blinkhorn, Fusi, and Jones in Preston 1984). Conservative Catholics were crucial to Primo and Franco. Primo's failure had pushed many into flirting with corporatist and fascist ideas. Then Franco's ability to claim a "holy crusade" was critical not only to winning the civil war, but also to the subsequent stability of his regime (Lannon 1984: 35–58; 1987: 203–34; Morodo 1985: 21–39, 52–7).

The army was not sufficiently caste-like to be uninfluenced by any of this. Officers and especially the rank and file were affected by the sentiments of the areas in which they were stationed. In the more solidly conservative areas, when the officers rose up, their troops obeyed them, and the few army loyalists and Republican street fighters were quickly suppressed. The cities of Zaragoza and Oviedo were exceptional. There a core of determined military rebels seized control before large popular forces could mobilize. But where the rebels quickly faced hostile, armed local crowds, many officers and men (and whole units of the Assault Guard) declared for the republic rather than attack the crowds. But the stance of the soldiers, and especially the officer corps, also mattered. Without the loyalist military minority supporting the republic, the rising would have been a mere coup, successfully taking over the government within days. But without the backing of most of the officer corps, the coup would have fizzled out just as rapidly. Across the south local army and Civil Guard detachments grimly defended their barracks against the majority leftist sentiment, spearheaded by enthusiastic but untrained Republican armed crowds, secure in the knowledge that Franco's Army of Africa, easily the most effective fighting force, would soon arrive to support them. This army then swiftly conquered the south.

Though Falangist, Carlist, and other popular levies quickly added half-trained numbers to the Nationalist side (as anarchist and socialist militias did to the republic), the initial rebellion half-succeeded only because of its military core – and it half-failed only because the republic had its own troops (Fraser 1994: 106–13). The military was now the epicenter of Spanish authoritarian rightism. Its superior military organization (aided by fascist Italy and Germany, outweighing the Soviet contribution to the republic) was decisive in eventually winning the war. Though the republic's territories were more advanced and so contained a much larger population and resource base, its ability to organize this into a concentrated military striking force was inferior. The rebels had an army, equipped, supplied, and with a unified command structure – precisely the resources of military power that the republic now lacked. Wars, even civil wars, are won by superior military power.

THE SCALE OF POLITICAL CLEANSING

Once the military rising was under way, both sides sought to cleanse their zones of political opposition. Both developed ideologies legitimating this. The Nationalists proclaimed a Crusade "to cleanse" (*limpiar*) España of atheistic, communist, "foreign" anti-España. The Republicans developed a leftist exclusionary organic nationalism, depriving the enemy from true membership of the *pueblo* – the word meaning both people and village, from which the upper classes were absent. Many priests were killed amid massive church desecrations.

We cannot know the exact numbers killed by each side. Estimates have varied considerably. Estimates of total killings by Republicans vary from 20,000 to 75,000, though the lower half of this spectrum seems more plausible. Nationalist killings are generally estimated between 50,000 and 200,000. However, a recent spate of detailed studies of individual provinces enables us to generate a rough estimate. These have documented 75,000 killings by Nationalists across twenty-four provinces and 38,000 by Republicans across twenty-two provinces. Between them they cover most of the killing in most of Spain's fifty provinces (Juliá 1999: tables 1 and 3). Increase both figures by a third and we might reach very rough approximations of the total killings of both sides across Spain. Of course, more Republicans probably died during forced labor and were not counted, and about 165,000 Republicans fled into foreign exile, fearing a similar fate. Nationalists probably exacted two to three times the vengeance over unarmed persons that Republicans did. Of course, they won, and so were in a position to do so.

On the Republican side the civil war began with a terrible burst of priest killing. Over 6,000 clerics were murdered, mostly in the first weeks of the war, mainly in areas controlled by anarchist militias (Moreno 1961: 758–68; de la Cueva 1998). This alone was significant in turning a military rising into a holy crusade. Nationalist atrocities bunched in two periods, varying somewhat by region. First, as their forces advanced, came the initial "liberation" of a district from the republic, followed by systematic killing of captured leftists surrounded by a penumbra of less discriminating butchery and rape. This killing tended to diminish in scale through the war, since leftists increasingly fled as defeat loomed. In Granada rightists murdered an estimated 5,000 persons, in batches over several months, virtually all in cold blood, driven to the cemetery at night and shot, without trial – including the poet Federico García Lorca. The leading executioner in Granada, Ruiz Alonso, is generally portrayed as a downwardly mobile psychopath with a private vendetta against the republic. Yet this is probably to misunderstand him. His vendetta sprang originally from principle: A printer, he had refused to join a leftist union. From this political stance flowed his downward mobility, since he was blacklisted from employment by the union. This led him to activism in rightist unions and eventually to murderous political cleansing (Gibson 1979). Lacking biographical details of other perpetrators, we can only guess whether his combination of ideological zeal and savage hatred of the enemy was typical.

Second came the long reprisals after the war, mass shootings, forced labor under appalling conditions, systematic maltreatment, and malnutrition of Republican prisoners. Under Franco's "Law of Responsibilities" in February 1939, mere support for the republic expressed after 1934, membership of Republican organizations or masonic lodges, and even "serious passivity" became crimes. Republicans, leftists, Catalan autonomists, and others could expect only a cursory trial and arbitrary justice. Some 23,000 Republicans were officially executed by the Franco regime after the war ended. Franco had to sign all the death sentences and almost invariably did so. In March 1943 the Minister of the Interior admitted to there still being 75,000 political prisoners, not including forced labor battalions and those in military prisons. Some 45 percent of the state budget of 1946 was devoted to the police, the Civil Guard, and the army. Such a budget was required by a regime engaged in half-paranoid, half-vengeful overkill. No other regime in Europe – not even Hitler's – killed as high a proportion of its political (nonethnic) enemies.

We know something of the motivation of the man ultimately responsible. Franco's faith in hierarchy and authority was absolute, his anticommunism was paranoid, his methods were permeated by his experiences in savage colonial warfare. He believed, against all the evidence, that the 1934 rising had been planned and executed in detail by Soviet agents. Thereafter he believed the Republican left was awash with Soviet gold and money stolen from the propertied classes in 1934. In 1937 he declared to a French journalist: "[O]ur war is not a civil war. . . . but a Crusade. . . . Yes, our war is a religious war. We . . . are soldiers of God and we are not fighting against men but against atheism and materialism." This was denying basic humanity to his political enemies. He reneged on deals made through foreign negotiators to exchange prisoners of war, instead handing over common criminals. As the Republican resistance collapsed in 1939 Franco told advisers that a negotiated peace was out of the question "because the criminals and their victims cannot live side-by-side." Those who shared Franco's obsession with "enemies" – such as the Prime Ministers Carrero Blanco and the butcher of Malaga, Arias Navarro – also favored continuing the repression (Preston 1995: 16, 104–5, 114, 146, 225–7, 290, 315–6, 436, 527, 549). Franco was committed to more extreme political cleansing than were Mussolini or Himmler because his politics incorporated religious and quasi-racial elements. They could view "Bolsheviks" as compatriots – if they recanted. But Franco's España was purer politically. By 1940 few Spaniards wanted to restart the civil war. The republic had lost. Franco could have been much more conciliatory; indeed, this would have helped the recovery of the country. But he saw good against evil, and evil must die.

Some Nationalists objected to the scale and savagery of the killings. Opposition was especially voiced by traditionalist officers. General Kinderlán believed the repression was destroying the prestige of the army. Colonel Yagüe, who defended the savagery of his own troops during the civil war, afterward argued for conciliation. Opposition was unexpectedly voiced by Heinrich Himmler, visiting Spain in 1940. Taken aback by the executions and overflowing prisons, he commented that it made more sense to incorporate working-class militants into the new order rather than to annihilate them (Preston 1993: 392, 449). He did not seem to realize that working-class militants were to Franco what Jews were to himself. Franco was to refuse Hitler's and Himmler's repeated requests to hand over Spanish Jews, but toward leftists he was merciless. This is the difference between political and ethnic cleansing.

THE FRANCO REGIME

Historians and sociologists of Spain have long argued over how to label the Franco regime and how much power Franco and the various regime "families" possessed (e.g., Miguel 1975; Giner 1977; Jerez Mir 1982; Chueca 1983; Fusi 1985; Preston 1990: chaps. 4–6; 1993). But broad brush strokes will suffice here. By September 1936 the sudden deaths of his main rivals left Franco as undisputed head of state, Generalissimo and Caudillo,[7] of the Nationalist forces. Running a three-year war followed by sustained repression of the losers gave him institutionalized infrastructures of personal rule lacked by most other interwar dictators. Stability was maintained by staying out of World War II – perhaps a result of his own good sense, more probably due to Hitler's refusal to pay the price in French North African territories he demanded for his alliance (see Preston 1993: chap. 15). His regime never had a formal constitution, which allowed Franco to rule for over three decades as an arbitrary absolutist ruler, dividing and ruling among the diverse "families" who had won the civil war. He never allowed any one of them complete power, dismissed ministers who argued with each other, allowed compliant ministers administrative autonomy and longevity, and kept Council of Ministers' meetings to administrative rather than to political agendas. His own style appeared lazy, distrustful of change, without vision. The regime could drift without goals beyond keeping its families in power and its enemies repressed. Since the families also shared many values, including the desire to keep on swilling at the trough, the balancing act was not all that difficult.

It is usual to distinguish three main "families": the army, the Falange and Catholics – some scholars subdivide the last family into the church, traditionalists/Carlists, and/or monarchists. Franco recognized that he depended on the army for military power and on the church for ideological power. The ministries of state were dominated by generals and colonels, the education ministry was dominated by Catholics, the labor ministry was shared between Catholics and the Falange, and the Carlists got control over Navarre plus the national Justice Ministry until 1973. The High Command collectively discussed only military, not political matters, and Franco kept it on a shoestring budget. In 1939 Franco incorporated Falange and Carlist volunteers into the officer corps to weaken its solidarity and as a specific counterweight to monarchist officers. He dangled before monarchists the possibility that a king might eventually succeed himself (which did indeed happen), but indefinitely postponed making any actual succession arrangements. The church did have a strong collective life, but it did not usually interfere directly in the state. Instead, its influence was more diffuse, expressed through the strong religiosity of many conservatives.

He felt less at ease with some of the Falangists. They had been necessary during the war and shortly thereafter, providing much-needed popular mobilization. They provided him with most of his regime trappings from 1937, when the Falange was fused with the Carlists into a single party with an incredibly long and uninformative title. Abbreviated F.E.T. y de las Jons, it was popularly referred to as just the Movimiento – a "movement" whose character could not be defined. While the tide of war was turning toward Hitler and Mussolini, Falange ideology was prominent, accepted by Franco as the rhetoric of the future. Nonetheless, Franco ruthlessly repressed the more populist falangists and from about 1947 falangists were relegated to visible but subordinate positions, running unions without power, welfare programs without money, and an agricultural ministry without power. The binding together of the families was through shared interests, overlapping values, and top-down corporatist structures headed by a decidedly reactionary despot. Thus I label this regime as a mixture of two of the categories presented in Chapter 2 – as semi-reactionary and corporatist authoritarian.

The regime was also profoundly class-based. It was recruited disproportionately from the upper classes and the most highly educated, and it severely repressed all independent lower class organization. Yet curiously, not industrialists, bankers, nor even landowners played much collective role in the regime. And their goals smacked more of reactionary rentiers than profit-seeking capitalists. Their property rights were oversecured by ferocious repression of labor. Then they mildly and ineffectually opposed the subsequent policy of integrating workers into the corporate state through Falange unions. They seemed satisfied to draw rent from their property and from state office and patronage rather than pursue rational profit-seeking capitalism. This suited Franco, who was interested in capitalism as order, not capitalism as economic development. Spain stagnated under his policies of "barracks autarchy," its people remained poverty-stricken, its bourgeois officers, fascists, and other regime favorites given sinecures on the boards of public and private companies. Capitalist technocrats remained ignored until the rise of the Catholic Opus Dei organization in the 1960s. Spain eventually modernized more because it was in Western Europe than because of any efforts by the regime. The European Economic Community and Vatican II were eventually great liberalizing influences. As the church backed away from Franco, the regime lost its soul. The officer corps and the Falange remained loyal until after his death, preventing insurrection – which much of the country dreaded anyway, fearing another civil war. But in the Western

Europe of 1975 most Spanish elites of right and left alike knew that a modern regime had to be a liberal democracy. The cautious way into this was through a restored but constitutional Bourbon monarchy. King Juan Carlos, confronted in 1981 by a military coup carried out in his name, dithered for some hours. He is reputed to have called Valerie Giscard d'Estaing, the French president, for advice. Giscard is supposed to have asked him whether he wanted to be the last of the Bourbon kings of Europe. If not, choose democracy, he said. Juan Carlos repudiated the coup, which quickly collapsed.

CONCLUSION

This chapter asked two main pairs of questions. The first was: Who killed Spanish democracy, and why? We saw that a controversy has raged over whether there was a joint extremism of left and right that doomed the republic. The answer must be "yes" in southern agriculture and at an important moment in Asturias. Southern landlord intransigence was mirrored by insurrectionist, land-hungry laborers. For both, possession of the land mattered more than any constitution. Compromise land reform was possible only if imposed from outside. Since the landlords controlled the regional state, they could sit tight. Since the laborers controlled the villages, they could seize the land if no state repression followed. This indeed became the situation under the Popular Front in early 1936. Similarly, in 1934 Asturian miners had briefly believed they also had the local power to seize their region. These were quasi-revolutionary situations in which class conflict was becoming unmanageable by only local police forces. The south needed sustained deployment of the Civil Guards, plus strategic garrisons of regular army units; the Asturias needed divisions of regular troops. Had this constituted the whole of Spain, we could conclude that attempted revolution, civil war, and massive political cleansing were all mainly escalations of class struggle. Economic power relations would have ultimately determined political outcomes.

But elsewhere in the country class intransigence was neither symmetrical nor unbridgeable. Neither most industrial capitalists nor unions, landlords, peasants, and rural laborers in other regions were hell-bent on class victory at any cost. Most employers favored "law and order" Republicanism, only semi-authoritarian at most. The majority of organized workers supported reformist varieties of Republicanism, socialism, and syndicalism. Compromises among these class forces did occur, in the Jurados Mixtos, in land reform, and in national and local coalition government. Thus economic class conflict across Spain as a whole – though somewhat destabilizing – did not dictate the fall of the republic, still less the mass killings that followed.

Indeed, the gravediggers of the republic did not have the symmetry conferred by the dialectic of class struggle. The left remained more deeply split on means and constitutions. Most of its leaders were reformists, but there were also influential revolutionaries. Most militant workers and peasants (even perhaps in the south) appeared to want reform. They greeted the republic by disproportionately joining unions with reformist leaders. Most of their strikes and occupations with political goals were aimed at securing the implementation and completion of Republican reforms. And only a handful on the left were so despairing of democratic institutions that they turned to paramilitarism before the civil war began. As among the left throughout Europe, their violence was more that of rhetoric, plus demonstrations and marching crowds with a fringe ready to break windows and noses. The Republican center also favored reform and it more uniformly supported parliamentarism.

These groups, with the grudging consent of most employers and union members, might have forced through a substantive reform program that would have assuaged popular discontent and saved the republic. That they failed was partly their own fault. The left was divided and irresponsible, encouraging wild rhetoric and some violence among its rank and file. In the divisions ideological power played a key role. Marxism and anarcho-syndicalism appeared powerful theories of modernity, coming with great intellectual authority, making pragmatists seem less principled, more "corrupt." Yet these theories were inappropriate in the ways they were applied to Spanish class relations and counterproductive for those who espoused them. The center-left may have been too zealous and imprudent in pursuing its ideological goals of a secular state and a civilian-controlled military – though these were (in comparative terms) normal modernizing goals. Left and center-left also had different priorities, failing to support each other adequately against opposition entrenched especially in the executive "half" of the state. On the center-right clientelist traditions of *el turno* lessened commitment to liberal democracy, bringing the stench of corruption and its own collapse. All of these ghastly mistakes were not accidental but deeply rooted in these leftist and centrist political movements. But they were still mistakes, since few of those involved deliberately aimed at killing democracy.

Things differed on the right. Traditionalist and corporatist rightists and the few fascists persistently sought executive powers incompatible with republican democracy. The much more numerous CEDA "accidentalists" had no such clear-cut goal, being deeply divided on constitutional issues. But these diverse factions were more respectful of hierarchy and more determined to retain the privileges of the old order. Thus accidentalists and ultras joined forces to oppose the republic's substantive reforms, using their control over state executive agencies to block implementation of legislation. Finally, faced with the Popular Front government plus direct action from workers and peasants, they sought to destroy the republic by military might and replace it with an authoritarian one.

In this class economic interests were important. They first sought to defend property relations with mildly semi-authoritarian "law and order" measures, including enhanced executive powers and the routine deployment of state paramilitaries. But they were also deeply entwined with ideological, political, and military power. The right was enormously assisted by a reactionary church, which had its own material and ideal interests and whose ideological power was the greatest source of the right's mass popularity. This increased their sense of moral outrage and helped to persuade them that there were higher-order goals than constitutions or political pragmatism. They also used the political power of the state's executive arm through predominant old regime control of the police, interior ministry, and prefects. They then escalated further, turning toward their "last resort" of a decidedly nondemocratic alliance with a military caste. This caste was authoritarian, favoring repression of class and regional discontents and with its own vested interests. Thus the majority of conservatives eventually invoked a military power that shared many of their values.

Those who "evenhandedly" blame left and right ignore the obvious disparity in military power between the two sides. Assuming that political bias is not the explanation for this, it must be part of the general neglect in the human sciences of military power relations. We must understand that there are very different levels of "violence" involved in power struggles. The republic contained the normal strife and struggle of democracies faced with severe crisis: turbulent elections, crowds, and demonstrations; the pressure of strikes, occupations, and lockouts accompanied by some physical intimidation; and backstage pressure to deploy police, strike-breakers, and goon squads (on both sides). The main contending parties tried these techniques and on occasion they all bent the rules of democratic and constitutional procedures. This was symmetrical struggle by left and right alike, intermittently turning into physical violence, mainly directed at class purposes. But none of this destroyed the republic. It tended to reinforce the morale of one's own core support but alienate enough moderates to tip elections to the other side. This level of violence was electorally counterproductive – which is how democracies are supposed to operate.

The republic fell before a qualitatively different level of violence. It fell in over one-half of Spain at the hands of a military revolt, and it was driven out of the rest of the country by a better organized, more professional army, aided by the armed forces of the two major fascist powers. Leftist talk of comradeship, struggle, force, and revolution paled beside rightist military organization. I find it bizarre that Payne (1993: 383–4) spends the last pages of his book, which sum up the overall causes of the fall of the republic, detailing the verbal aggression of its main defender, Manuel Azaña. Can he not distinguish between political rhetoric and artillery barrages as forms of violence? In the last instance, which actually arrived during 1936–9, rightist military power prevailed, overthrowing a democratic republic (more turbulent than most, but indubitably a democracy), bringing mass murder, and installing a repressive thirty-year dictatorship.

My second pair of questions concerned the victorious regime. Why did it take the form of a fairly harmonious collaboration between reactionary and corporatist authoritarians, and why were the fascists so well domesticated by Franco? Much of the answer is not hard to find and has been given many times before. The Spanish old regime suffered very little dislocation in the twentieth century. Though its three pillars – church, army, and monarchy – were in some decline, and the monarchy was decidedly shaky, the national territories were not remotely threatened, governments stayed out of European wars, and even the Depression was not really a "great" one. A move against liberal democracy would probably take conservative, even reactionary forms. There was insufficient crisis to open up space for a radical right capable of attracting popular forces for a mass-mobilizing fascism. When fascism did suddenly expand greatly in 1936, its principal adherents came from the conservative right. There were very few socialists-turned-fascists in Spain. But this meant that the right had little mass mobilizing power (except on Sundays and holy days). To overthrow democracy thus required the army, which itself also favored more conservative, orderly, and top-down methods of rule than fascism.

This alliance was then welded further together, and acquired a little more "bottom-up" fascist mobilization, by the decision to fight a war against the republican-leftist government. We see the importance of the right's common commitment to order and hierarchy in the fact that they stayed much more united than did the Republican side. There was virtually no fratricide among the Nationalists during the civil war, unlike on the Republican side. After the war, the institutions of Franco's undisputed authority were already in place, and he took care to let the various regime "families" share at the trough. Again, the regime kept neutral in the 1940s and experienced no severe crises, though there was persistent stagnation. There was nowhere else for the fascists to go, except out of power and then perhaps to prison. They were domesticated by military and political power and economic inducement – and by the fact that their ideologies overlapped considerably, anyway. Thus the Spanish right developed a largely reactionary and limited, not a modern and ambitious, "statism" as the solution to social crisis. But its organic nationalism was quite as fierce as any we have witnessed, save in the area of anti-Semitism. It came to endorse large-scale political cleansing. It is sobering to realize that had not other old regimes been weakened by the crises surrounding World War I, and had not their successor authoritarian regimes not been first dislocated by the economic crises and the advance of the Axis Powers during the 1930s and then destroyed by World War II, then Franco-type regimes might have dragged on comfortably, disastrously, and repressively for decades through much of Europe.

One major puzzle remains. It is the usual one, given a different twist in Spain because this was such a "successful" authoritarian regime, one that survived for almost forty years. This was a country of very pronounced class conflict, one in which the resort to authoritarianism had particularly overt class motives on the part of the propertied classes. Yet from the point of view of rational capitalist profit taking, this was disastrous. The combination of Franco's reaction, repression, and corporatism spelled economic and social decline over a long period. We would have to be very pessimistic indeed about the Second Republic to suppose that its survival beyond 1936 would have had a worse outcome for the bourgeoisie than Franco's regime brought. If anyone actually benefited from Franco's regime, it was his family and personal networks (and later the Bourbon family and connections) and some in the church, the military, the Falange, and the landowning class. But the beneficiaries did not include Spanish capitalists or the middle class in general. Instead of preserving western civilization, the regime effectively excluded Spain from it for over a generation, except for the sight of sun-baked Europeans lying on its beaches. Perhaps the sight proved too much for the regime. In Franco's last years his regime abandoned all vestiges of fascism and waited for him to die. This was, in Payne's (1998) words, "defascification from within."

Though I do not claim to be certain of my answer to the puzzle, the special circumstances of Spanish agriculture, riven by class conflict and with landowners well entrenched in the old regime state, did partially "agrarianize" Spanish capitalism. Thus the Spanish bourgeoisie exaggerated the threat to their property and elevated this fear above the calculative pursuit of profit. But they were more substantially encouraged in their overreaction by a minority of the country's leftists and by the powers exercised by two of the three pillars of the old regime state. For the church and the army had better founded fears concerning their own privileges. The combination was an ideological power movement able to convince very many capitalists – and indeed persons of all social classes fearing disorder and insecurity – to define opponents as enemies and traitors and to see salvation as coming through a military power able to impose a transcendent organic nationalism. Once again, it was a gigantic mistake that rightists made, this time letting in not fascism but a reactionary corporatist dictator who greatly harmed their material interests. Nor was it only a "mistake," since it led many of them to the commission of great evil. But that is what humans do when they are confronted by complex, entwined, imploding crises concerning several sources of social power at once – as the twentieth century so amply demonstrates.

10

Conclusion

Fascists, Dead and Alive

I first summarize my explanation of the rise of fascism. Then I ask whether fascism is just history or whether it may return to haunt the world again. Are all the fascists dead ones?

DEAD FASCISTS

I offered a two-part explanation of the rise of fascism. The first part concerns the forward surge of a broader family of authoritarian rightists who swept into power across one-half of interwar Europe, plus a few swaths in the rest of the world. In Europe the surge carried regimes further across the spectrum I identified in Chapter 2, from semi-authoritarianism to semi-reactionary and thence to corporatist. A few then went further, to fascism.

Authoritarian rightism was a response to both general problems of modernity and particular social crises left by World War I. Modernization was consciously pursued by most authoritarians: industrial growth and restructuring, more science and economic planning, more national integration, a more ambitious state, and more political mobilization of the masses. After some initial hesitation, most rightists embraced most of the modernist package while rejecting democratic mass mobilization. However, their embrace was also pressured by a series of crises – economic, military, political, and ideological – brought on or exacerbated by the war. Without these crises, and without the war itself, there would have been no major authoritarian surge, and fascism would have remained a series of sects and coteries rather than a mass movement.

Serious economic crises came at war's end and then again as the Great Depression struck in 1929. In between, in the mid-1920s, came lesser inflation crises. Yet few interwar economies were ever very buoyant. Since governments were now expected to have economic policies to ameliorate hardship, economic crises destabilized governments. "Old regimes" also feared the secular economic trend of the period, since many members lived as rentiers from the profits of the least modern parts of the economy. Modernity and crisis-induced restructuring might be their nemesis. Ruling regimes, especially "old" ones, felt they had to do something.

The war produced military crisis, defeat for some, and dislocation plus sudden demobilization for all. Crisis was felt more severely in the center and east of the continent, which contained most of the defeated powers. But military crisis also endured where "revisionists" continued to challenge the terms of the peace treaties and to seek restoration of "lost territories." Embittered refugees and aggressive nationalist movements kept the pot stirred. Would revisionists triumph in Austria, Germany, and Hungary, would the many new successor regimes of the vanquished multinational empires survive, would France or Romania keep their territorial gains, would Serbia keep its Yugoslav dominance? Then military crisis became more general, as a second world war loomed and as the threat and influence of revisionist Nazi Germany grew.

The political crisis was distinct to the center, east, and south of the continent. The northwest had already stabilized liberal regimes before 1914. Its governments and electorates confronted the economic and military crises with orderly changes of government leaving unchanged the basic constitution of liberal democracy. Yet the center, east, and south were at this very time attempting a transition toward liberal democratic parliaments while leaving many old regime state powers intact. There crisis was confronted by dual states, half liberal democratic, half authoritarian. Since old regime conservatives usually controlled the executive part of the state, including its military and police, they had the option of using repression to solve crisis – reducing or overturning the power of the state's parliamentary half. Indeed, the war had enhanced the resonance of militarism, while a short postwar burst of class conflict had normalized the deployment of troops in civil strife. Yet most of the right felt that repression was no longer sufficient to maintain rule in the modern era. It was also necessary to undercut democracy with alternative ways of mobilizing the masses. Conservatives responded differently in the two halves of Europe. In the northwest the dominance of liberal institutions pushed conservatives toward building more populist political parties playing according to the rules of electoral democracy. But in the center, east, and south, conservatives launched coups by their executive half of the state linked to more mobilizing authoritarian movements. Let me emphasize: Fascism was not a crisis of liberalism, since institutionalized liberalism weathered all these crises without serious destabilization. Fascism was a product of a sudden, half-baked attempt at liberalization amid social crises.

These crises were exacerbated by an ideological crisis. On the right, though only in one half of Europe, this became a sense that modernity was desirable but dangerous, that liberalism was corrupt or disorderly, that socialism meant chaos, that secularism threatened moral absolutes – and so cumulatively that civilization needed rescuing before modernization could proceed further. So there emerged a more authoritarian rightist view of modernity, emphasizing a more top-down populist nationalism, developmental statism, order, and hierarchy. Such values began to circulate widely, especially among young moralists – middle-class youth in high schools, universities, and military academies, as well as in "established" churches that leaned toward nationalism or statism anyway. So across one-half of the more developed world occurred a conservative political offensive by the propertied classes, led by an old regime wielding state repression while sponsoring mass political parties with nationalist and statist ideologies. This insurgent authoritarian rightism was not purely reactionary (as Mayer 1981 suggests), since it wielded novel visions of modernity.

Nor was it merely a class strategy, explicable in straightforwardly functional Marxian terms. It was not even the most economically rational strategy available to the possessing classes. These had two alternative economic motives: "property defense" and "profit maximization." The early postwar burst of class struggle might threaten private property, so might some later Spanish revolutionaries, so might too close a proximity to the Soviet Union. But there was no general fundamental threat to property looming across Europe after about 1921. The revolutionary left had been defeated. Most of the rightist offensive thus occurred *after* any serious revolutionary threat from below had died away. During the relevant period no determined property defense was necessary. "Profit maximization" is more likely a motive, though it is also more complex. It is less zero-sum, since it is not necessarily the case that for one side to gain, the other must lose. It is also more difficult to calculate alternative profits. Some leftist governments and the pressures of the Great Depression led to a squeeze on profits, and it might make some short-term sense for capitalists to redress the balance by forcing labor bear more of the costs – thus to repress labor. But political elites in the countries of the northwest and beyond were devising much better strategies of profit maximization – corporate liberalism in the United States, social democratic compromise in Scandinavia, splitting the Labour Party in Britain. The first of these policies may have benefited both sides in the class war, the second certainly did, while the third probably benefited only capitalists. These were effective democratic strategies to protect the survival and profitability of capitalism – and this was the primary goal of the northwest's leading economist, Keynes.

Why were the possessing classes so hypersensitive to opposition from the left that they reached for the authoritarian gun so quickly, when neither property nor profits were much threatened? I found five reasons for their overreactions, ranging over all the sources of social power.

(1) The last decades had revealed that revolution was a real possibility in modern societies. The prospect appeared now to be receding, but property owners could not be certain of this. One version of the "security dilemma" stressed by recent political scientists suggests that people may overreact to a threat that is "life-threatening" even if the threat has a low probability of being realized. The chance of a Bolshevik Revolution occurring in Germany after 1922 might be low, but German capitalists might overreact to leftists on the principle "better safe than sorry." For the political right, "certainty," "safety," and "order" were linked values.

(2) A particular class fraction had greater reason to fear. The property rights of agrarian landlords *were* more vulnerable. Land reform was considered desirable through much of interwar Europe; there was also some direct threat to them from below in several countries; and their hold on old regime states would probably not last much longer. For the moment, however, they still possessed unusual executive political power, especially through officer corps and ministries of the interior. *Cacique* patronage systems also still conferred on them a certain parliamentary strength in relatively backward areas. For them "certainty" of possession could be ensured through a combination of repression and disproportionate political power within the propertied classes as a whole. Why risk uncertainty when property preservation could be *guaranteed* through authoritarian rightism? Note, however, that whereas the old regime's own motivation was economically rational, that of their allies among the possessing classes was probably not. They were being led by the nose by the political and military power of the old regime, especially agrarian landlords.

(3) Some military officer corps reasoned similarly. Their caste-like autonomy, linked to the old regime, was threatened by demands for civilian control over the military by liberals and the left. Their budgets were threatened. Some officer corps were used to staging coups, others were not, but the appearance of more military-minded rightist movements seemed to offer them succor.

(4) Some churches reasoned similarly. They faced leftist secularism threatening their own property and wealth, plus their control over education,

marriage, and other social practices. They were also part of the old regime and their stress on "order" and "hierarchy" also carried a more diffuse ideological power among the community of the faithful, especially in more rural areas. These possessors of ideological power favored authoritarian rightism to protect their own material and moral interests.

(5) "Order" and "threat" were not merely problems of domestic class relations but also of geopolitics. These made some ethnic, religious, or political minorities seem especially threatening because linked to foreign powers. The right characteristically fused together supposed domestic and foreign "enemies" – leftists were seen as (Russian) "Bolsheviks" and "Judeo-Bolsheviks"; foreign, finance, and Jewish capital and liberal separatists and so on were all seen as both domestic and foreign threats.

Combined, these fears worsened the overall sense of threat. As threats became more diffuse, they seemed more vaguely threatening, so the response was to "root them out," "stifle them at source." So goals were displaced away from a narrow instrumental rationality calculating about economic interest to a broader "value rationality" in the sense of Max Weber's use of the term. Order, safety, security, hierarchy, the sacred rather than the secular, national rather than class interest become the primary slogans, while the enemy was demeaned, even demonized, as the antithesis of all these values, unworthy of democratic or (in extreme cases) of humane treatment. What might have begun as the economically motivated behaviour of propertied classes was displaced through the mediation of others' sense of threat onto far more diffuse goals of nationalism and statism. Thus the propertied classes (even perhaps agrarian landlords) did not pursue the most instrumentally rational course of action. The ensuing authoritarian rightism then developed its own economic rationality by pioneering statist economic policies useful both for late development and for combating depression. But the search for order, hierarchy, and risk avoidance made most rightists lower their sights below what countries in the northwest were beginning to accomplish with increased capacity for democratic mobilization.

So though class struggle played a substantial part in the surge of the authoritarian rightist family, we must also link it in our explanation to political, military, and ideological power relations. When multiple crises generate multiple goals among collective actors who overlap and intersect in complex ways, ensuing actions rarely follow narrow interest group rationality. This led authoritarian rightist regimes into dangerous areas that threatened their own survival. Relying on a more militarized and more sacred nation-state "threatened" by domestic-foreign enemies had dangerous consequences. It made war more likely, and modern total warfare produces far more losers than winners. Some of these regimes provoked wars with the potential to destroy them all. This actually happened in 1945. Endorsing rightist authoritarian values also made them vulnerable to being outflanked by more radical rightists.

Enter the fascists. We reach the second part of the explanation as fascists piggy-backed on top of all this. They would not have grown large without war-induced crises faced by dual states and panicking old regimes and possessing classes generating nation-statist values. Fascists did not grow large where crises came without dual states and panicking old regimes, in the northwest of the continent. Fascists were nurtured among the authoritarian rightists and continued to have close family relations with them. As in all families, their relationships could involve love or hatred. Thus the second part of the explanation involves explaining which occurred, and where.

I have emphasized that fascists were distinctive. Neither their organization nor their values allowed them to be simply a vehicle for class interests. Organizationally, they were unlike other authoritarians, for they were a "bottom-up" movement, not a top-down one. And they were driven in "radical" directions by their own core values: They believed in a paramilitary, transcendent, and cleansing nation-statism. Fascism was not committed to the existing state nor to its military arm but sought to revolutionize them, "knock class heads together," cleanse the nation of its enemies, and so transcend class and political conflict. Since they saw themselves as a "popular" movement, they were not averse to elections as a strategy of coming to power. Most fought elections vigorously, pioneering mass electoral techniques of ideological manipulation. Only in Italy, where they came very rapidly to power, was electioneering not a central part of fascist activity. Unlike the more conservative authoritarian rightists, fascists could not use the power of the state to manipulate and fix elections (until after they came to power). Though fascists did not believe in democracy, it was vital to their success.

But electoralism sat alongside a second form of popular struggle. Their activist core consisted of voluntary paramilitary formations committed to organized street violence. This had three purposes. It was "provocative," intended to produce a violent reaction from its political rivals. This would enable fascists to declare that their own violence was "self-defense." Second, it would repress enemies, since fascist paramilitarism conferred logistical superiority in street warfare, enabling them to bring "order" to the streets. It was hoped that both "self-defense" and "success" would bring more support and legitimacy to the notion that fascist "orderly violence" could end social chaos. This was then further exploited electorally. Third, paramilitarism could in the last resort launch a coup – provided the army was also immobilized (since most fascists knew that their paramilitarism was inferior to the military power of the state).

Such paramilitary activism brought distinctive recruits and distinctive values to the movement. The first cohort of recruits, without whom fascism would never have got off the ground, consisted largely of young military veterans transmitting wartime values of comradeship, hierarchy, and violence into a peacetime political movement. In this respect fascism as a mass movement would never have surged beyond being a coterie of intellectuals without World War I. Indeed, fascist activists remained cross-class gangs of young men for whom the combination of demonstrating, marching, and brawling had a special attraction. Hence they were disproportionately students, cadets, athletes, and young working-class roughnecks (who are also well represented among the perpetrators of atrocities in my forthcoming volume on ethnic cleansing). Fascism also reflected modernization impacts on young people: the liberation of young males from family discipline, and of young females from much of the burden of childbirth, the growth of organized sports, and the growth of professions requiring extensive further or higher education, especially the profession of war. Scholars of fascism (or indeed of the twentieth century in general) have paid insufficient attention to these age-cohort effects that contributed to the emergence of a general feature of the twentieth century, the cult of youth. Fascism was the first great political manifestation of this cult.

Bottom-up nationalism and statism were fascist values everywhere, drawing distinctive core constituencies of popular support. Fascism resonated especially among embittered refugees, "threatened border" regions, state employees (especially including armed forces), state-owned or state-protected industries, and churches that saw themselves as "the soul of the nation" or "the morality of the state." As class theorists have observed, fascism would not have surged without the prior surge in class conflict, and not surged so much without the Bolshevik Revolution. But it does not follow – as class theorists have argued – that fascists represented only one side in this class struggle or indeed any single class at all. Their core constituencies reflected the appeal of the goal of transcending that struggle. Fascism tended to appeal neither to the organized working class nor to persons from the middle or upper classes who were directly confronted by organized labor. Instead, it appealed more to those on the margins of such conflict, persons of all classes and various sectors, in smaller or newer industries and the service sector, persons likely to cry "a plague on both your houses." The fascist core, especially fascist militants, rested preponderantly on macho youth receptive to paramilitarism and on social environments receptive to the message of either extreme nation-statism or class transcendence.

Nonetheless, fascist regimes did not succeed in transcending class. Since they were not actually anticapitalist, they could come to terms with the capitalist class; since they were promilitarist, they could come to terms with the armed forces; and since most of them cared little about religion, they were willing to sign concordats with powerful churches. Thus in practice, and once they neared power, fascist movements became biased on questions of class struggle. They tilted toward the capitalist class, the propertied classes more generally, and the old regime in particular. Yet, of the main fascist values, class transcendence was the one that varied most among the various national movements. Italian fascism was rather conservative and bourgeois in outcome, Romanian became decidedly proletarian.

Since big fascist movements were varied and emerged in rather varied circumstances, it is not so easy to generalize about their rise as it was for the whole family of authoritarian rightists. I first summarize their variations case by case, then move to their overall similarities.

Italian fascism rose and seized power early, in the immediate postwar years when class conflict was only just beginning to decline (and was still raging in agriculture). Thus it had a more direct class component than the other cases. There was an obvious fascist/propertied class alliance, and so Italian fascism can be partially explained in functional Marxist terms: The upper classes turned to fascists to rescue them from class revolution. But the closeness of World War I also made for a more direct military/paramilitary contribution to fascism through young male military veterans. One might almost say that paramilitarism was the means and agrarian-led class repression was the goal of Italian fascism. This would be to oversimplify, however, since paramilitarism also brought distinctive recruits and goals. Though not geared to electoralism, Italian fascism's combination of "self-defense" and success (it did destroy socialist and *populari* power) increased fascism's popularity among those valuing social order. Fascism's broader nation-statist goals were also popular and undermined the will to resist of the old regime and state executive. Geopolitical and political power relations also mattered. Since Italy had largely uncontested borders and was unthreatened from abroad, its nationalism contained little external aggression or racism inside Europe (Africa was a different story).

The Italian state was also dual, and both halves of the state were in weakened condition. This made it vulnerable to a coup. Liberal parliamentarism was not directly challenged by fascism, since fascism's sudden rise occurred between elections. But parliament had been weakened by the traditional hostility of the church and the rapidity of the transition toward full democracy. Socialists, Catholic *populari*, liberals, and conservatives were not yet socialized into the rules of the parliamentary game and failed to form the coalitions that would have best served them and democracy. But since the church had hitherto stood aside from politics and since Italy was characterized by uneven economic development, the country also lacked a homogenous old regime. Landowners, big capitalists, the army, and the church could not subvert the transition to democracy with their own conservative authoritarianism. Some were quickly driven toward the fascists (who were often their own sons). There were thus three causes of the triumph of Italian fascism: intense class struggle, postwar paramilitarism, and a weakened old regime.

German Nazism rose later, after a sustained attempt to make Weimar democracy work. Again, the condition of the old regime was extremely important. War defeat had unseated the monarchy and its loyal conservative and national liberal parties, and it had greatly shrunk the armed forces. The old regime could not now rule. As democracy faltered from 1930, conservative authoritarianism had little support outside the state executive itself.

Second, paramilitarism was again important, though its role differed from the case in Italy. Military veterans were important to the first cohort of Nazis and other populist extremists, but they needed reinforcing by later cohorts of Germans who had not fought in the war. From 1928 the Nazis were thriving on the electoral process of the republic, quite unlike Italy. This meant that their paramilitarism was more geared to gaining electoral support and rolling over its enemies in street brawling than to seizing the state.

Third, class conflict, though relevant, was not dominant. It grew during the Great Depression, but was much less severe than in the immediate postwar period and was insufficient to threaten capitalist property rights. However, there was a squeeze on profits, and one solution would be to repress labor. There was thus some complicity in the Nazi coup by the propertied classes, though much less than in Italy.

Fourth, Nazism was also a popular electoral movement, unlike Italian fascism, making two main mass appeals to the voters. The apparent "class stalemate" during the Depression made Nazi claims to class transcendence appealing, especially since the Nazi movement was the most classless in Germany. Second, its populist nation-statism thrived on Germany's geopolitical and ethnic bitterness. A Great Power resenting its loss of territories, sucked into the Central European (formerly Habsburg-centered) tensions of Germanic, Jewish, and Slav peoples, Germany had refugees, "threatened

borders," and ethnic "enemies" at home and abroad. Organic cleansing nationalism had quite broad appeal. Nazism's statism was limited to Führer
worship and militarism. But its nationalism was more intense and racist.
Thus Nazi transcendent nation-statism was sufficiently popular to bring it
to the brink of power. Its own paramilitarism and the weakness (sometimes
the complicity) of the old regime took it over the top. This is a broad
explanation entwining ideological, economic, military, and political power
relations.

Austrian fascism was divided between two rival fascist movements. Though
the monarchy and empire were gone, there was much continuity from prewar times in the institutions of parliament, the state executive, and the
Catholic Church, and the old regime lived on in Christian Social governments. "Austro-fascism" and the Austrian Nazi movement both emerged
as rivals out of postwar revisionist paramilitaries and continued to thrive
on discontents expressed through the electoral process. Both movements
exploited the intensity of Austro-German antipathy toward Slavs and Jews.
Austro-fascism was the less populist and radical of the two movements,
being more top-down and more procapitalist. It strengthened as the mild
semi-authoritarianism of the Christian Socials seemed unable to overcome
Austria's class stalemate, which the Depression helped perpetuate. But the
rise of Hitler next door in Germany was the decisive factor. This intensified
the appeal of fascism, undermined Austro-fascism, and gave the prize to the
Austrian Nazis. The paramilitaries of both parties attempted coups but got
into power only with help from the military power of a state (respectively,
Austria and Germany). The final result was *Anschluss* between two Nazi
movements, though they had got to power in different ways, and one was
vastly more powerful than the other.

Hungarian and Romanian fascisms differed substantially from the others. The
two countries had fought on opposite sides in the war, Hungary emerging as
a big loser, Romania as a great victor. Yet the contrast was weakened by the
ensuing civil war in Hungary, which resulted in the crushing of the Hungarian left and allowed the Hungarian old regime to reemerge, if in embittered
and radicalized form. Rule was by a dual state composed of the traditional
executive and bureaucracy and a parliament dominated by the gentry. Yet
the old regime now contained many younger radical rightists, making more
populist, revisionist (i.e., demanding the return of "lost territories"), and
modern appeals to the country. Romania differed somewhat. Its (mainly
foreign) landed gentry had been dispossessed, but this and the great war
victory allowed the monarch, bureaucracy, and army to reemerge, as a more
nationalist though still corrupt regime. Thus the old regimes survived quite

well in both countries, if somewhat radicalized and then destabilized by further radicals emerging within and around them. The political competition on the right was especially fierce within the universities and military schools and through the electoral process. Large fascist movements only emerged in the mid-1930s, well after the threat from the left had subsided. Thus fascists had no capitalist bias; indeed, they became rather proletarian in their composition. In both cases paramilitarism was used more as an electoral tool than to repress rivals or to seize power. An unequal dance of death ensued, in which military triumphed over paramilitary power, and radicalizing regime authoritarians triumphed over fascists. Only the chaos of the last war years allowed the fascists a brief, doomed victory.

Spanish fascism was different again. Neutral in World War I, Spain's old regime experienced the least disruption among all my case studies, and so conservative authoritarians, not fascists, dominated. Indeed, this, and not fascism, was the most common outcome across the center, east, and south of the continent. Portugal, Bulgaria, Greece, and the Serb core of Yugoslavia resembled Spain in this respect. The new successor states of the collapsed empires – the three Baltic republics, Poland, and Albania – also moved in crisis only to reactionary or corporatist authoritarianism. Though their political regimes were not "old" but brand new, they had the power and legitimacy of being "national liberators." They, not fascists, developed veterans associations and populist parties.

The Spanish old regime did have one weak element, an unpopular monarch, and this let in the military regime of General Primo de Rivera. His failure led to the democratic Third Republic, the breakup of which did eventually produce a sizable fascist movement, complete with hastily formed paramilitaries. But these remained subordinate to the Nationalist army in the civil war and were marginalized under Franco's regime. His main props were the army, the church, and the "old" propertied classes. His regime is largely explicable in terms of my earlier general explanation of the surge of the authoritarian rightist family.

All these cases differed. To explain them required analysis attuned to local histories and social structures. Nonetheless, through the variety I perceive common forces determining the power of fascists. One potential cause actually played relatively little role: the threat from the working-class movement. This was not correlated with fascist strength. The threat was probably greatest in Spain, where there was not much fascism. The threat may have seemed substantial (though it had already peaked) in Italy; it seemed substantial though was actually more formal than real in Austria; Germany had a large but mostly moderate labor movement; Romania and Hungary had negligible lefts by the time fascism loomed – indeed, fascism itself provided their main labor movements. Fascism was to a limited and variable degree supported by the propertied classes to save themselves from labor, but this is not a very powerful general explanation of fascism.

The main attraction of fascism was the intensity of its message. This always brought committed support from mainly young people, willing to give more of their time and energy than were activists in any other political movement. Fascist militancy, always with a paramilitary component, was necessary to fascist success. By their energy and violence, the thousands could hope to both attract and defeat the millions. This militancy centered on the ability to trap young single men within comradely, hierarchical, and violent "cages." Fascist parties and paramilitaries were almost "total institutions." Fascism also attracted substantial (though not majority) electoral support, attracted by varying combinations of statism, nationalism, and class transcendence, though less by paramilitarism and cleansing. As we have seen, the first three of my five fascist characteristics had much greater plausibility in the countries that generated large fascist movements.

But the popularity of fascism was also greatly affected by the political strength and stability of old regime conservatism, which (more than liberal or social democracy) was fascism's main rival. Only weakened and factionalized old regimes let in large fascist movements. United old regimes repressed or subordinated them, weaker ones enabled fascists to find military and political organizing space. World War I provided the space for legitimate paramilitarism, initially provided by discontented war veterans. Their values were then transmitted to two further generations of recruits drawn predominantly from among young students, cadets, and workers. Democratic elections provided the second space. Fascists thrived on a three-way electoral struggle, pitting the left against a conservative/liberal center and radicalizing conservatives. Fascists could then swallow up part or all of the radical right while the center was hollowed out and the left repressed. That was how the fascists achieved electoral success.

As they said themselves, fascists were not mere "reactionaries" nor "stooges" of capitalism or anyone else. They offered solutions to the four economic, military, political, and ideological crises of early twentieth-century modernity. They propounded plausible solutions to modern capitalism's class struggles and economic crises. They transmitted the values of mass citizen warfare into paramilitarism and aggressive nationalism. They were a product of the transition of dual states toward "rule by the people," proposing a less liberal and more "organic" version of this rule. Finally, they bridged the ideological schism of modernity. On the one hand lay the tradition of the Enlightenment, "the party of humanity," that would steadily widen the sphere of reason, freedom, democratic citizenship, and rational planning in human society. On the other hand lay the modernist renewal of Romanticism: the perception that human beings also possessed sentiments, emotions, souls, and an unconscious and that modern forms of organization – crowds, mass movements, total war, mass media – might encourage these quite as much as it encouraged reason. Fascists claimed to have fused these two aspects of human and mass behavior. We may not like any of their four solutions, but we must take them seriously. Fascists were and remain part of the dark side of modernity.

So fascists were generated in large numbers by postwar crises in ideological, economic, military, and political power relations to which a transcendent nation-statist ideology spearheaded by "popular" paramilitaries offered a plausible solution. Fascism occurred only where rule was by dual states containing weakening "old regime" executives and vibrant but only half-institutionalized democratic parliaments. Dual states with more stable old regimes produced more conservative forms of authoritarianism. Fascism resulted from the process of *democratization* amid profound war-induced crises. Fascism provided a distinctly statist and militarist version of "rule by the people," the dominant political ideal of our times. Fully parliamentary regimes (in the northwest) survived all four crises with their institutions intact and fascists as small minorities.

LIVE FASCISTS?

Are there fascists still among us, poised to revive and dominate once more? Will we find such preconditions and consequence again? Or was fascism "European epochal" rather than "generic"? Clearly, some of the causes I identified were not merely conditions specific to the interwar period but remain perennial possibilities of modern societies. Having identified five characteristics as key to fascism – nationalism, statism, transcendence, cleansing, and paramilitarism – we will obviously find some of them scattered around the world, probably in varied combinations. Movements can be more or less fascist. Yet it is doubtful whether comparable movements appearing in the future will call themselves fascist. As a word in usage today, it appears largely as the exclamation "Fascist!" – a term of imprecise abuse hurled at people we do not like. Only a few crackpots and thugs call themselves fascists or Nazis. Since a few Italians and Romanians carry a somewhat romantic view of Mussolini and Codreanu as well-meaning victims, they have styled themselves "neofascists." But labels are not necessarily reality. There are currently movements in the world with more than a passing resemblance to fascism, on which I will spend a few final moments.

Yet there are few in fascism's original heartland, Europe. Fascism was defeated, its top leaders executed or imprisoned, and many others purged. Liberal democracy and communism triumphed and imposed their orders on Europe. There were no mass veterans' movements, no politics of territorial revisionism after 1945. There was prolonged economic growth in Western Europe and the institutionalization of quite effective communist authoritarianism in the East. In the West there was stable democratic competition between broad-based "catch-all" parties of the center-left and center-right. Since the present was clearly superior to the past, fascism withered. For the vast majority of Europeans, fascism still evokes images of evil. In Spain and Portugal corporatist regimes were decaying from within and were gone by 1975, unlamented. From 1989 authoritarianism began departing from the East. Fascism seemed finished.

From the 1970s, however, there seemed to be a bit of a revival in Western Europe. First, on the outer fringes many small but violent self-styled neo-fascist and especially neo-Nazi small groups achieved some prominence. They are historical revisionists (denying the Holocaust) and imitate the style and rituals of traditional fascism. They proclaim allegiance to fascist doctrines: hypernationalism grounded in biological racism, cleansing of alien foreigners, antidemocratic statism, the "third position" (though stated none too convincingly), and violence disguised as a call for "action" rather than words. Most of these small groups meet to some extent four of my five criteria of fascism, though open paramilitarism has not yet emerged. But they are tiny and likely to remain so. They mirror small groups of the far left: highly splintered, without popular support, thriving mainly off each other. They provide sensational copy for journalists and loom larger in the virtual reality of the Internet than in the reality of the street, still less the hustings.

More menacing has been a series of uneven upsurges of new radical rightist parties, usually followed by declines, but on a slightly upward secular curve. At their peaks these parties have so far received between 10 and 27 percent of the electoral votes in a number of countries. Following Ignazi (1997), I distinguish two main types. The first consists of those who style themselves neofascist. They do display some though not all of the five fascist attributes. Yet only two of these neofascist parties have ever achieved electoral significance, the Italian MSI and the German NDP, which inherited the two major national traditions of fascism. Other neofascist movements, such as the British BNP and the Dutch CP'86, have remained tiny. But only the MSI reached up to even 10 percent of the vote, and the peak of these neofascist parties was in the 1970s and 1980s (Taggart 1995). The MSI drew disproportionate support (as had interwar Italian fascists), from the service and public sectors and from the more marginal working class (Ferraresi 1998; Weinberg 1998). But both declined during the 1990s. The German NDP declined in the face of the nonfascist Republikaner, and in 1994 Gianfranco Fini renamed the MSI as the National Alliance and declared it not neofascist but postfascist. Under his leadership the party has grown into a major conservative "system" party, though some party stalwarts are unhappy with this makeover. A rump neofascist MSI splinter group remains, but it has shriveled. During the 1990s neofascism retreated to the margins of European politics and is currently insignificant.

Now dominating the extreme right are parties normally termed "populist" or "radical populist." Taggart (1995) says they emerged at "the end of the post-war settlement," responding to problems associated with globalization and postindustrialism. Ignazi sees them as "postindustrial": Globalization, the end of the Cold War, and the decline of the far left and of class conflict created new problems for the populist right to mobilize on. But it is rising immigration into Western Europe that offers the greatest opportunity to such parties during recent decades. The main parties in this group have been Le Pen's Front National in France, the German Republikaners, the Austrian Freedom Party of Haider, and the Flemish Volksunie and Vlaams Blok. Even more recent has been the rise of radical populist movements in Denmark (the DPP) and Norway (the FrP), receiving 12 to 15 percent of recent votes, and the late Pim Fortuyn's anti-immigration List in the Netherlands. As yet only Ireland, Portugal, and Spain appear to be entirely immune from such parties. They are now a persistent minority feature of Western European politics.[1]

Yet on three of the key characteristics of fascism they remain ambiguous. They denounce in very general terms "the system" and "the establishment," as well as the "sham" of a liberal democracy dominated by establishment parties that they say have lost touch with the real lives of ordinary citizens. But they rarely denounce democracy itself, and their goals are strictly electoral. They even sit united as a small bloc in the European Parliament. They are also ambivalent over the state. Since they tend to represent some of the most vulnerable citizens, they want state protection for them, sometimes including welfare state support. They always demand that the state enforces law, order, and traditional morality more toughly – because, they claim, immigrants dominate crime, prostitution, and drug pushing. Yet they resent a state controlled by the big parties, big business, and big unions, and so often say they want the state off their backs. Some even endorse neoliberal policies. In Austria Haider says he wants business radically deregulated, a flat tax rate of 23 percent, and the Austrian civil service cut by two-thirds.

On balance, this sounds closer to the state-hating Republican right in the United States than state-worshiping fascism. Thirdly, their *ninisme* – neither right nor left – sometimes influenced by the "third position" of neofascism, is rather vague and falls far short of the class transcendence offered by interwar fascists. But the main problem here is that the steam has been taken out of such principles by the decline in salience in class struggle. Liberal democracies have successfully institutionalized it. These three ambiguities and weaknesses of principle and policy also make for instability, as either extremists or moderates seek to enforce a more consistent line that then results in splits and expulsions, such as the makeover of the Italian MSI and the disintegration of the German Republikaner in the mid-1990s.

Though the most enduring of these parties do have a full complement of policies, their main attribute is a xenophobic and exclusionary nationalism derived from a single issue: the desire to end recent immigration into Europe (though this is less true of Italy). The enemy is nonwhite, non-Christian or East European, and asylum-seeking immigrants, the mixture varying by country. This does meet my nationalist and cleansing criteria of fascism. It also enables them to connect up to a number of other issues – law and order, moral decline, unemployment, and housing – supposedly posed by immigrants. But their nationalist xenophobia is unlike that of fascists or neofascists, since it rarely derives from a general hierarchical theory of collective will, culture, or race identity. Wieviorka (1994) has described this as a shift within racism from a "logic of [hierarchical] inferiorisation" to a "logic of differentiation." All that is claimed is that immigrants are incompatible with the culture and traditions of France, Germany, Austria, Denmark, and so on, and so should get out or be deported. Some even claim they are the true multiculturalists: All cultures and ethnicities should be free to develop as they choose, but separately. There is no desire to rule over them, or indeed over any foreigners. They do not support territorial revisionism or aggression toward other nations, as was the case with interwar fascism. In fact, they also claim allegiance to "European civilization," threatened by a flood of immigrants. Their international *bête noire* is American imperialism. They themselves are a long way from militarism.

Finally, there are no genuine paramilitaries organized by any of these Western European parties. Shocking though sporadic violence is committed by quite small fringe groups, very loosely organized, composed mainly of poorly educated and unemployed youths, the so-called skinheads, fueled by alcohol, their violence almost entirely aimed at immigrants. The vast majority of those committing offenses against public order are not affiliated with any far-right party or neo-Nazi group. The party leaderships are also unhappy about their violence, considering it a vote-loser. More people show some sympathy for their violence, but these tend to be poorly educated and mostly elderly (Willems 1995; Gress 1998: 238–50).

Surveys show that the rightist populist parties' core constituency lies among persons seeing themselves betrayed as citizens, supposedly fully enfranchised in their own states but in reality being pushed down by elites, big business, and immigrant newcomers. They tend to be the less educated, less skilled, middle-aged to elderly, small town working-class, small business, and small farming males – different from the core constituencies of classic fascism. So their xenophobia is not merely a response to direct job or housing competition from immigrants, nor indeed of any "objective" cultural incompatibility, nor merely of the prevalence of racism in the society at large. All these are mediated by a sense of betrayal of citizen rights that is especially strong among more disadvantaged citizens (Betz 1994; Wimmer 1997). As Eatwell (2001) notes, their support is more sectoral than class, since they seem to attract the sectors within each class that are most economically threatened today (though "globalization" is too trite a label for the diverse sources of current threats). The Austrian Freedom Party deviates somewhat, having broader-based support deriving from the third great fascist tradition that was not totally destroyed in 1945 (Bailer-Galanda 1998).

But the biggest electoral successes of these parties come when they can enlarge on their limited core constituencies by capturing broader discontent with the traditional governing parties. Such "protest voting" appears greatest where there are distinct regional grievances against the capital, as for the Flemish and Austrian parties – and, if we count it, the Italian Northern League. That such protest voting goes to the right and not to the left probably results (outside countries with strong fascist traditions) from the race issue, which leftist parties avoid (sometimes despite the sentiments of their supporters). However, their support does fluctuate considerably, between both districts and points in time. They can achieve very large votes in quite particular places, from Burnley to Antwerp to Carinthia (Eatwell 2001). This is probably a consequence of their dependence on a broad but not deep protest vote that they have the militants to mobilize in only a few places.

Yet their problems mount with success. Their ideological and policy vacuity (outside immigration) then becomes more closely scrutinized and criticized. If they are successful enough to share in coalition governments (as in Austria) or rule local districts (as in Belgium), their performance in office also comes under critical scrutiny. So far, the major system parties have then made a comeback. Austria's conservative party scored a major electoral success at the expense of the Freedom Party in 2002. The up and down cycles continue, which lead me to doubt whether they can continue on an upward trajectory. Indeed, if the major parties responded to the upsurge in xenophobia by severely restricting immigration, then support for radical-right parties would probably collapse. This is what happened in the first postwar European case, Britain in the 1960s. Tacit agreement between the Conservative and Labour Parties to restrict further nonwhite immigration ended the electoral threat from the radical right.

The rightist populist parties are nationalist and they support ethnic cleansing in the relative mild form of orderly and either voluntary or compulsory deportations. But they are not statist; they are only in the vaguest sense making claims to "transcend" class conflict – and this is no longer a burning issue in Europe – and they have no paramilitaries. Above all, the salience of their major issue, immigration, tends to undercut any general *Weltanschauung*, whether fascist or other. For these reasons they are not seriously fascist under the terms of my definition nor in terms of the definitions I quoted from Nolte, Payne, Eatwell, or Griffin.

I have argued in this book that institutionalized liberal democracy is proof against fascism. Postwar Western Europe has entrenched liberal democracy far too strongly for much support to be offered to neofascists or rightist populists on grounds more general than the immigration issue. Western Europe has successfully institutionalized the class conflict that helped to generate classic fascism. It is capable of institutionalizing most forms of conflict, just as it did in northwestern Europe in the interwar period. Only immigration raises a potentially intractable issue, for capitalism encourages immigration while liberal democratic or social democratic citizenship can be easily turned toward privileging native-born citizens. This contradiction enables rightist populism to flourish. It can make life unpleasant for immigrants but is unlikely to generate either fascism or any other totalizing ideology. These radical populist parties may be disturbing, but provided that European "system parties" adapt themselves to the changing macro-environment, remaining responsive to citizen demands, European fascism is defeated, dead and buried.[2] After their terrible twentieth century, Europeans can at least take comfort from this.

The ex-communist zone of Greater Europe has its own distinct problems. There liberal democracy has existed for only just over a decade and remains fragile. Authoritarianism lingers on among former communist regimes, and some pockets of ethnic conflict entwine with conflict between states. As we saw, Romania had the biggest interwar fascist movement. Predictably, it has the biggest neofascist movement. The Greater Romanian Party, nationalist and rather statist, tracing back its lineage to the Iron Guard, is neofascist and obtained nearly 30 percent of the vote in 2000. However, this is rare in the region. Hungary, closer to the European Union, does not seem set to recreate its interwar trajectory. Authoritarianism is not openly proclaimed in Eastern Europe; it is denied. Nor is it likely to be openly proclaimed as long as regimes desire entry into the EU or NATO or as long as they desire resources from the EU, the United States, or international financial institutions. Around the fringes of the continent, the EU requirement of democracy for entry has remained influential. Though in a sense we once again have "two Europes," the western part is now larger, it combines Social, Christian, *and* liberal democracy, and it is now dominant over the other Europe of dual states.

It is possible to envisage (e.g., in Russia) a future radical rightist movement that would combine elements of nationalism and communism to proudly proclaim extreme nation-statism. This would be much closer to fascism – though almost certainly without the name. Fascism did terrible damage to the region and then took fifty years of abuse from communist regimes. Few will endorse it now.

Across parts of the south of the world statism and nationalism are often more important than in the north. Though dented somewhat by recent neoliberalism, most southern countries accept that states must play a substantial role in promoting their social and economic development. In some of them mass-mobilizing nationalism, usually ethno-nationalism directed at internal minorities assisted by a "homeland" state next door, is reinforced by territorial revisionism and military aggression. Many of these states also have the dual destabilizing form we observed in the interwar period, combining parliamentary institutions and a strong executive power. Militaries play an especially important role across much of the South. Where states weaken and factionalize, paramilitaries also often emerge, especially in Africa.

But these various elements, which all contributed to fascism, are almost never found together. The statism of countries such as Argentina, Brazil, and Mexico did originate in corporatist regimes highly influenced by fascism. Yet even in the heyday of Peron, Vargas, and the PRI they never added paramilitarism or aggressive nationalism, and they sought to incorporate and pacify the masses, not mobilize them. Today their statism has become conservative, a remnant of past import substitution polices plus institution-alized provision of job and business opportunities for clients, tinged in some cases (as in other countries, such as India) by Keynesianism. Many statist regimes are conservative and procapitalist, such as South Korea or Singapore. Military regimes tend to on domestic repression, ethno-nationalists on monopolizing state resources for their own ethnic group. Few military or ethno-nationalist regimes have serious macro-economic programs. A few do weave statism and populism into developmental rhetoric, but this generates more leftist than rightist populism, as in present-day Latin America (exemplified by Hugo Chavez in Venezuela). The whole fascist package of statism, nationalism, and paramilitarism is absent, as is any ambitious current theory of society and progress. There is no utopian Third Way, no transcendence.[3]

Perhaps fascism has come closest to resurrection in surprising, religious garb. *Theodemocracy* was the term used by the Islamic fundamentalist scholar Madoudi to indicate rule not by priests (which would be theocracy) but by the whole community of the faithful following the precepts of their religion.[4] Such populism often has fascist strains, especially in Islamic and Hindu political movements. Some of these strains were historically contingent, a product of which Great Powers supported their independence struggles. Arabs and Indians struggled against British and French domination. They did imbibe liberal and socialist anticolonial ideologies from their own oppressors. But they could extend socialism into communism with help from the Soviet Union and China. These were all secular ideologies, hostile or indifferent to Islam and Hinduism.

But the fascist powers, Germany and Italy, were also willing to support their liberation struggles, in order to weaken the liberal empires. But Nazis, fascists, Muslims, and Hindus were also struck by the compatibility of some of their ideas. Middle Eastern and Indian nationalists studied in Berlin and Rome during the interwar period, and some pronounced that their own movements could adapt fascism to their needs. Nazi theorists respected Hinduism as a pure Aryan religion, and the Hindu *varna* (classical caste) hierarchy also fitted well with fascist elitism. All these movements believed that the state should express the spiritual essence of the people, and all stressed the martial history and spirit of their people. Hindu nationalist theorists emphasize *hindu rastra* (Hindu nation) and *Hindutva* (Hinduness), both rather *völkisch* ideas. Muslim and Hindu nationalists of the 1930s also explicitly adapted fascist organizations, emphasizing hierarchy, discipline, paramilitarism, and segregation of male and female activists. The leaders of the large Hindu nationalist paramilitary, the RSS, often praised fascism and Nazism. Its most prominent theorist, Savarkar Gowalkar, noted of Hitler's "purging" of the Jews in 1939, "Race pride at its highest has been manifested here ... a good lesson for us in Hindustan to learn and profit by." Fascist tendencies were most obvious in the Indian military formations: the Indian Legion in Germany and the Indian army of national liberation, the INA, organized by the Japanese, both fighting the British in World War II.

But they backed the losing side and were destroyed. India was liberated not by them or by fascist-leaning Islamists but by moderate secular Indian and Pakistani movements. In any case, the similarities cannot be pressed too far. These movements found Italian statism exaggerated and were uneasy with Nazi racism, preferring to regard the Hindu nation as a "society" into which others could be assimilated. But in India, Hinduism, the religion of the overwhelming majority, has been bent toward a nation-statism that rivals the secular Indian nationalism proclaimed by the Congress, Socialist, and Communist Parties. Of course, since the Hindu Nationalist BJP party came to power in India in the 1980s, it has imbibed some of the secular moderation of previous governments, while the BJP also advocates neoliberal economic policies. Its opposition to the statism of the Congress Party partly derives from the fact that state patron–client networks favored Congress supporters. Overall, Hindu nationalism offers no distinctive role for the state in secular matters, and it offers only spiritual, not secular transcendence. There is no Third Way in the fascist sense. The paramilitaries remain active, though in recent years the RSS has been outflanked by more radical but less ideological local Hindu paramilitaries. Hindu nationalism does spawn off some fascist tendencies, but it is not really fascism.

The term "Islamic fascism" has recently become widespread, especially among Americans and Israels denouncing the Islamist *jihad* launched against them. The label is not without foundation. The new *jihadis* (popularly called "fundamentalists") do seek to create a monocratic, authoritarian regime that will enforce a utopian Koranic ideal. This regime will create a new form of state and a new man (and woman). Its predominant organization is the paramilitary, taking various but always dominant forms – guerrilla international brigades in the war against the Soviets in Afghanistan, armed bands of terrorizing enforcers under the Taliban and Iranian Islamists (rather like the SA or SS), and clandestine terrorist networks elsewhere. All this is decidedly fascist.

However, there are also some major deviations. Islamism is not nationalist. Islam is much wider than any single state or its people – there are currently fifty-four member states of the Islamic Conference. Thus Islamists oppose nationalists and see them as among their deadliest enemies – leaders such as Saddam Hussein and Hosnei Mubarak. In principle, Islamists aim for one giant Muslim state, the caliphate, and that would constitute a kind of pan-nation-state. But almost all acknowledge that this may be an impossible ideal. Nor do they have any role for the state except to enforce their conception of the sharia. We have three actual Islamist regimes as examples. The Taliban was ferocious on cultural matters such as burqas or videos, but had no policies on the economy, health, or education. Afghanistan degenerated materially under their stewardship. The Sudanese Islamists at their peak in the 1990s offered some development projects, together with attacks on Christians and pagans and therefore endless civil war, which also degraded the country. The Iranian ayatollahs were not as destructive, but their economic policies seemed largely unconnected to their policies on moral purity. Al Qaeda has said nothing whatever about economic policies. Jihadis have no principled role for the state or for its people in their doctrine, outside the sacred realm.[5] Once again, we do not find the complete fascist package.

It is clear that the term "Islamic fascism" is really just a particular instance of the word "Fascist!" – a term of abuse for our enemies. It is the most powerful term of abuse in the world today – much stronger than "Communist!" – and so it is understandable that Americans and Israelis, reeling under the impact of terrorism, should deploy it. But neither Islamism nor Hindu nationalism is really fascist. This is for a simple reason: Unlike fascism, they really *are* political religions. They offer a sacred, but not a secular ideology. They most resemble fascism in deploying the means of moral murder, but the transcendence, the state, the nation, and the new man they seek are not this-worldly. We might call this "sacred fascism," of course, though perhaps it is better to recognize that the human capacity for ferocious violence, cleansing, and totalitarian goals can have diverse sources and forms, to which we should give different labels – fascist, communist, imperialist, religious, ethno-nationalist, and so on.

So it does not seem that fascism, as I and other scholars have defined it, is flourishing in the world today. Fascism was generated by a world-historical moment when mass citizen warfare surfaced alongside mass transitions toward democracy amid a global capitalist crisis. Fascism made a not implausible claim to solve these worldly problems in a brave new world in which the nation, the state and even war might be seen as the bearers of progress. That moment has passed. War is now widely reviled (outside the United States and parts of the south of the world) as bringing social regress. Capitalism will always generate crises, while the transition to democracy remains difficult. But compromise blends of capitalism, democracy, and socialism are generally seen as bringing solutions and progress. Major crises will recur. In an increasingly global world, it is less likely that a combination of transcendent, cleansing, paramilitary nation-statism will be seen as providing the best solution.

However, fascist-leaning movements are most likely to recur in the south of the world if the north, led by the United States, continues besmirching the attractions of mild and democratic nation-statism to the south through their capitalist exploitation, American military imperialism, and widening north-south inequality. Then our descendants may have to cope with new social movements bearing more than a passing resemblance to fascism, mixed in with socialist tinges and with whatever local ideological sources of resistance they can also mobilize – as Islamism provides today. But for now fascists are dead and their resurrection is not imminent. Until now interwar fascism has been not generic but "European epochal" fascism. Its legacy currently lives on mainly in a different type of social movement: ethno-nationalists seeking murderous cleansing. In more recent years it is ethnic, religious, and more single-mindedly nationalist versions of "rule by the people" that have supplanted the more statist and militarist versions offered by fascism. But that story is for another book.

Appendix

Appendix Table 3.1: *Occupational Backgrounds of Italian Fascists (%)*

Sample	Landlords	Peasants	Agricultural laborers	Businessmen	Professionals	Public employees	White-collar	Petty bourgeois	Workers	Students	N
Italian labor force	–	31	22	1	1	2	1	12	26	1	151,644
PNF (Fascist Party), Italy, 1921	1	12	24	3	7	6	10	9	16	13	539
PNF, Udine, 1922	–	3	–	3	8	c18	c12	10	25	16	265
PNF, Reggio Emilia, 1922	5	7	3	–	13	c8	c8	33	18+	2	381
Squadristi, Bologna and Florence, cities, 1921–22	4	0	0	3	10	11	13	6	5	46	281
Squadristi, Bologna Province, 1922	2	13	c25	5	2	5	8	5	c22	10	
Fascist "Martyrs," Italy	?	8	–	9	1	19	5	5	27	27	145
MVSN paramilitaries, 1923–33	3	11	–	0	1	29	6	17	18	12	374
PNF deputies, 1924	4	1	5	6	68	17	2	1	0	0	313
Catholic PPI party deputies, 1921	3	3	6	5	60	21	3	3	3	0	117

Sources: Row 1: Sylos Labini, 1978: 61, Weiss, 1988: 33; Rows 2 and 6: Revelli 1987. In row 5 public sector includes 18 percent military, and self-employed are almost entirely artisans. Row 3: Preziosi 1980: appendix 1. "Clerks" distributed 50 percent public, 50 percent private sector. Row 4: Cavandoli 1972: 132–4. Public and private white-collar workers not separated in source. I have divided them into 50 percent public, 50 percent private. The worker figure is probably an underestimate; see text. Row 5: Suzzi Valli 2000: 136–7. "Baker," "mechanic," and so on divided 50 percent petty bourgeois, 50 percent workers. Rows 6 and 7: Reichardt 2002: 279–81, 306–7, 344. Workers in agriculture and industry cannot always be distinguished, while for the martyrs the "upper classes" are distinguished. Rows 8 and 9: Linz 1976: 57–8.

Appendix Table 4.1: *Occupational Backgrounds of German Nazi Members (%)*

District	Farmers	Agricultural laborers	Businessmen	Professionals	Public employees	White-collar	Petty bourgeois	Workers	Others	N
Munich, 1921	1	−1	2	12	14	14	20	28	11	2,222
Western Ruhr, 1925–6	−1	–	1	5	6	23	9	52	4	698
South Westphalia, 1925–8	1	–	1	7	8	16	25	41	1	672
Hanover, 1925–32	3	–	3	6	5	12	23	39	2	427
Hanover-Brunswick, 1925–33	8	4	2	8	11	12	18	34	2	2,241
Württemberg, 1928–30	5	2	2	6	6	9	26	43	3	4,099
Hesse-Nassau, 1929–31	7	1	2	7	5	12	22	41	2	9,773
Mainly Bavaria, 1923	8	2	2	7	8	13	20	36	5	4,450
Germany, 1925	4	0	1+	4+	13	21−	19	37	5	23,000
Germany, 1927	6	–	1+	2+	5	19−	17	46	3	15,900
Germany, 1929	18	–	1	2	6	15	19	37	3	61,000
Germany, 1930–2	13	–	2	7	6	11	22	36	3	1,954
Germany, 1933	9	–	5	7	15	11	22	31	2	3,316
Germany, 1937	7	–	3	6	18	17	14	35	1	3,997

Sources: Rows 1 and 8: Mühlberger 1987: 55, 66, 131; Douglas 1977; and Madden 1982b: 42. In row 1 "others" are students. Rows 2 and 4–7: Mühlberger 1991: 34, 77; rows 3 and 9–14: Kater 1983: 248–53. All agrarian occupations are combined in these rows. In rows 9 and 10 lower professionals and higher managers are classified as white-collar.

Appendix Table 4.2: *Occupational Backgrounds of German Nazi Leaders (%)*

Level of leadership	Farmers	Businessmen	Professionals	Public employees	White-collar	Petty bourgeois	Workers	N
Reichsleiter	8	12	16	50	4	4	0	24
Gauleiter, 1925–30	0	15	18	45	9	8	7	92
Top functionaries, 1929	7	5	7	19	16	21	23	246
Branch leaders, 1923–31	23	2	7	8	12	26	21	285
Reich Candidates, 1928	21	4	13	30	6	8	16	126
Reich Candidates, 1930	15	6	14	18	13	14	18	380
SA officers, 1930–4	8	1	8	11	12	11	47	75
SA officers, 1935	7	6	2	16	41	13	13	951
SS officers, 1938	6	1	15	10	31	1	25	1,895

Sources: Rows 1–3: Kater 1983; Rows 4–6: Mühlberger 1987: 98–101, 106. Row 4 is the aggregate of eight local branches scattered through Germany. Note that half of these branch leaders come from two fairly rural branches. Row 7: Mühlberger 1991: 171; Row 8: Jamin 1984: 194–5. It seems that the very large category "white-collar" includes both professionals and managers. Row 9: Ziegler 1989: 104–5. These are averages of his three samples of officers. "Others" are students.

379

Appendix Table 4.3: *Occupational Backgrounds of German SA and SS Rank and File (%)*

Sample	Farmers	Agricultural laborers	Businessmen	Professionals	Public employees	White-collar	Petty bourgeois	Workers	Others	N
SS, pre-1933	8	2	1	7	5	15	14	41	4	496
SS, 1933	4	2	1	5	4	16	12	53	3	802
SA Berlin, 1931	0	0	0	8	3	27	2	54	7	1,824
SA, 1929–32	3	0	0	3	7	17	3	58	9	1,306
SA, 1933–4	2	0	0	3	7	15	2	68	3	3,925
SA, 1931–4	6	2	1	4	7	7	11	55	7	924

Sources: Rows 1, 2, and 6: Mühlberger 1991: 189, 178. "Others" are students; Row 3: Bessel and Jamin 1979: 113; rows 4 and 5: Fischer 1978: 138–9. In row 4, some 5 percent "salaried manual" classified as public employees, in row 5, some 4 percent.

Appendix Table 4.4: *Occupational Backgrounds of Members and Leaders of Other German Political Parties* (%)

	Landlords	Farmers	Agricultural laborers	Businessmen	Professionals	Public employees	White-collar	Petty bourgeois	Workers	Others	N
DNVP leaders, 1927	17	1	1	14	12	34	8	3	3	9	106
DNVP candidates, 1924		13		7	15	38	c7	17	c4	0	418
DNVP, Düsseldorf, 1928	0	1	0	14	9	31	12	21	11	0	178
DNVP, Osnabruck, 1928	0	1	0	4	14	39	7	32	2	0	202
DVP members, 1919–33		4		7	7	25	1	19	1	5	3,298
SPD national executive, 1890–1933	0	0	0	4	8	4	16	0	63	8	27
SPD members, 1930		1		0	1	3	9	4	66	17	70,000
KPD central committee, 1924–9	0	0	1	1	4	9	11	1	68	4	91
KPD leadership cadres, 1924–9	0	0	1	2	0	12	11	4	63	6	504
KPD prisoners and martyrs, 1933–45	0	0	1	0	5	2	7	16	67	1	612

Sources: Rows 1, 3, and 4: Bacheller 1976: 321–3, 365–80, 453–67. Women are excluded from rows 3 and 4. Row 2: Liebe 1956: 77. White-collar and manual workers, totaling 11 percent, not separated in source. Row 5: Döhn 1970: 79. National sample of members. Some double-counting of jobs held by one person. Nine percent "wholesalers" counted as businessmen (as suggested by Mühlberger). "Others" are party officials. Rows 6 and 7: Guttsman 1981: 160; Hunt 1964: 103. "Others" are women or housewives, and women formed 25 percent of SPD membership. Rows 8 and 9: Weber 1969: 38, 27. All public employees are teachers, "others" are "professional revolutionaries." Row 10: Kater 1983: 253. In row 9, "others" are students.

Appendix Table 4.5: *Occupational Backgrounds of Political Activists in Marburg (%)*

Parties	Businessmen	Professionals	Public employees	White-collar	Petty bourgeois	Workers	Others	N	% women
Nazis, pre-1933	1	5	16	22	22	16	17	246	18
Bourgeois parties	6	7	36	6	35	3	6	155	16
Special interest parties	3	5	21	11	41	7	12	225	11
Socialist parties:									
SPD, USPD, KPD	0	0	10	20	4	63	3	70	7
Marburg labor force	0	0	13	23	4	30	20		

Source: Koshar 1986: 238–9. "Others" are either retired or housewives.
Students excluded from Koshar's table, but formed 55 percent of the local Nazi Party.

Appendix Table 4.6: *Occupational Backgrounds of German Reichstag Deputies (%)*

Parties	Farmers	Businessmen	Professionals	Public employees	White-collar	Petty bourgeois	Workers	N
Nazis, 1930–March 1933	14	8	22	18	9	14	15	727
Nazis, November 1933	14	6	17	28	11	15	13	547
DNVP, 1919–32	32	10	15	30	5	1	5	–
Catholic Center, 1919–32	14	10	26	28	9	4	15	176

Sources: Rows 1 and 2: Mühlberger 1987: 106–7. Those with unclear status and full-time party officials are excluded. Rows 3 and 4: Linz 1976: 63–6 and Morsey 1977: 35. Most "workers" are officials of Christian Unions.

Appendix Table 6.1: *Occupational Backgrounds of Austrian Political Activists* (%)

Parties	Farmers	Business managers	Professionals	Public employees	White-collar	Petty bourgeois	Workers	Others	N
Nazi members, 1923–5	0	–	2	11	26	8	44	9	167
New Nazi members, 1926–32	10	0	5	27	18	18	19	4	158
New Nazi members, 1934–8	11	0	1	14	13	22	35	1	438
Nazi candidates, 1930	4	1	6	53	17	8	14	0	80
Heimwehr (Austro-Fascist) candidates, 1930	26	10	7	19	7	20	17	0	90
Heimwehr leaders, 1930–4	23	22	7	30	–	–	15	2	324
Heimwehr militants, 1930–1	28	–	5	21	3	22	21	1	58
Militant Nazis	0	0	2	10	29	9	40	10	150
Militant Marxists	0	0	0	11	5	2	82	0	66
Militant Nazis, 1934	3	0	3	7	19	23–	38+	7	301
Militant socialists, 1934	1	0	3	19	14	14–	48+	0	457
Socialist members, 1929	–	–	–	9	12	6	51	23	416,170
Vienna Socialists, 1927	0	2	1	~10	~10	3	74	2	274
Vienna Socialists, 1934	–	–	–	16	10	4	48	21	122
Vienna Nazis, 1938	1	–	5	19	22	9	25	20	260
Austrian labor force, 1934	11	0	1	11	11	12	54		

Sources: Row 1: Bukey 1978: 305. "Others" are students. Rows 2–5 and 16: Botz 1987a: 258. Rows 4 and 5 = Candidates for Upper and Lower Austria. Note that students comprised 0.6 percent of the national labor force. Row 6: Wiltschegg 1985: 277–8. Aggregate of Heimwehr committees and candidates. White-collar workers are combined with civil servants, and self-employed with businessmen. Farmers are 20 percent peasants, 3 percent landowners. Leaders do not overlap with those contained in previous row. Row 7: Bukey 1986: 81, from two Heimwehr lists for Upper Austria. Rows 8 and 9: Botz 1980a. Nazis, socialists, and communists on police files for violence. "Others" are mostly students. Rows 10 and 11: Jagschitz 1975: 150–1. Militants imprisoned by Dollfüss government in Wöllersdorf concentration camp. Some skilled, employed workers may be wrongly classified as self-employed (see text). "Others" are students. Rows 12–14: Botz 1983: 156–7, 254. Row 12 is national membership of Socialist Party. "Others" include women. Row 13 is arrested, wounded, and killed demonstrators, July 1927. Public and private employees not separated, distributed 50–50. Row 14 is those arrested after the Socialist uprising of February 12, 1934. Row 15: Botz 1988: 218. "Others" included housewives (7%), students (4%), and pensioners (4%).

383

Appendix Table 6.2: *Occupational Backgrounds of Political Activists in Linz (%)*

Activists	Farmers	Professionals	Public employees	White-collar	Petty bourgeois	Workers	Others	N
Nazis, 1923–33	0	11	37	24	5	18	3	212
Nazis, 1933–8	1	16	23	14	14	28	4	74
Christian Socials, 1918–34	20	6	34	5	22	10	5	107
German Nationalists, 1918–34	0	13	31	16	21	4	9	102
Socialists, 1918–34	0	4	32	12	9	35	9	130
Communists, 1929–33	0	0	2	8	5	81	5	62
Heimwehr, 1927–31	5	5	41	14	19	11	6	81
Dollfüss fascists, 1934–8	2	3	31	19	15	27	4	126
Linz labor force	3	5	13	20	8	50		

Source: Bukey 1986. Bukey does not separate big or small agriculture or business. Labor force percentages are only approximate: I have estimated them from Bukey's partial data on occupations and sectors. "Others" are housewives, retirees, students, and persons inadequately described.

Appendix Table 7.1: *Occupational Backgrounds of Hungarian Political Activists (%)*

Sample	Landlords	Peasants	Business-men	Professionals	Public employees	White-collar	Petty bourgeois	Workers	N
Fascist village leaders, 1940–1	0	46	2	6	2	2	19	21	150
Fascist city leaders, 1940–1	4	3	4	18	4	5	3	2	43
Fascist candidates, 1939	12	16		32	16	0	16	8	75
Government party candidates, 1939	22	0		20	52	0	0	0	–
Fascist leaders, 1939–45	–	14		24	36	6	12	8	157
Government Liberal–Conservative deputies, 1921–32	–	29		26	35	1	6	0	314
Government National-Radical deputies 1935–9	–	30		22	35	6	6	–1	348

Sources: Rows 1 and 2: Szöllösi-Janze 1989: 136–47. "Fascists" throughout this table refers to members of the Arrow Cross Movement. "Master artisans" are placed in petty bourgeoisie, other artisans in workers. Where size of peasants' landholdings are indicated, these are normally very small. "Workers" in row 1 include two employed gamekeepers. Rows 3 and 4: Janos 1970: table 6.6. Big and small businessmen are not separated in original. Rows 5–7: Janos 1982: 280–5. Fascist leaders are Arrow Cross candidates and deputies of 1940 and National Socialist Ministers and National Council members of 1944–5. Rows 6 and 7 give details of the "government machine" in the House of Representatives, first in the "Liberal–Conservative" period, then in the "National-Radical" period. Since Janos does not give totals for these two periods separately, my percentages are averages of those for three years in the first period and for two years in the second. Big and small agricultural proprietors were not separated, nor were big and small business. The category "journalists and teachers" is split equally between professionals and public employment.

Appendix Table 8.1: *Occupational Backgrounds of Romanian Fascists* (%)

Legionary group	Landlords	Peasants	Businessmen	Professionals	Public employees	White-collar	Petty bourgeois	Workers	Students	N
Arrested, 1934	1	3	0	25	24	5	2	3	37	73
Workcamp activists, 1936	0	9	2	10	25	8	8	5	33	630
Surrendering or shot, 1939	0	2	0	48	20	2	7	5	15	383
Insurrectionists, 1941	0	22	0	4	8	6	13	44	2	2,143
Interned in Germany, 1942	0	3	–1	20	24	8	7	11	27	249

Sources: Rows 1 and 2 from Heinen 1986: 386–9. Row 1 details those arrested in connection with Duca assassination. Row 2 details male activists in Carmen-Sylva work camp. In all Romanian data I have assigned "graduates" (of high schools or universities) without stated profession half to white-collar, half to civil service. Rows 3 and 4 from Veiga 1989: 263–5. Row 3: Legionaries, mainly urban, surrendering to or shot by the government in 1939. Tailors, carpenters, and so on assigned to self-employed. Professionals include 13 percent priests. Row 4: Legionaries imprisoned after their failed insurrection of 1941. Row 5: Heinen 1986: 457. Weber 1966a: 108 gives a slightly different, less detailed version of the same list.

Appendix Table 9.1: *Occupational Backgrounds of Spanish Political Activists (%)*

Parties	Farmers	Businessmen	Professionals	Public employees	White-collar	Petty bourgeois	Workers	Others	N
Madrid Fascists (Falange), 1936	0	0	10	2	29	2	55	3	1,103
Basque Nationalists (PNV), 1931–6	20	–	5	5+	11	17–	36	4	1,700
Rightist (CEDA) committees, 1931–5	9	6	34	19	9	10	12	0	77
CEDA committees Murcia, 1931–3	17	11	23	12	10	19	5	4	151
Center-right (Radical) national delegates, 1932	0	18	44	14	5	13	5	1	474
Center-left (Republican) urban committees, 1930–6	2	–	48	–	15	29–	5	2	–
Republican rural committees, 1930–6	41	–	13	–	7	24	13	2	–
CEDA deputies, 1933, 1936	5	3	64	19	2	4	2	0	186
Center deputies, 1933, 1936	1	2	68	20	1	6	3	0	542
Socialist deputies, 1933, 1936	1	0	33	23	11	2	28	0	111

Sources: Row 1: Payne 1962: 82. "Others" are students. Row 2: de Pablo 1995. Given imprecise totals, I assume "more than 200" is 210, and that Vitoria and the rest of Alava contributed equally to their combined total. Some 16 percent of farmers were small proprietors or tenants, and 4 percent were laborers. Big businessmen are included within petty bourgeois, higher administrators within professionals. Rows 3 and 8–10: Montero 1977: 449. Row 3 is members of nine local committees. Row 4: Moreno Fernandez 1987: 156. Some 50 percent of farmers are small proprietors; "others" are students. Row 5: Partido Republicano Radical 1932: 48–59; Manjón 1976: 594. Rows 6 and 7: Farré 1985: 343. Given incomplete totals and Ns, I have calculated the average of the urban and rural parties. There are no separate figures for big or small business or civil servants.

Appendix Table 9.2: *Occupational backgrounds of Seville (Spain) Party Activists* (%)

Parties	Landlords	Businessmen	Professionals	Petty bourgeois	White-collar	Artisans and workers	Others	N
Antirepublican far right (CT, RE) leaders, 1931–6	48	1	38	7	5	1	0	128
"Accidentalist" conservative (AP, CEDA) leaders, 1931–6	37	6	43	10	1	3	0	78
AP conservative members, 1932	12	12	?	25	22	15	13	2,585
Center parties (PC, PL, CD), 1914–23	41	2	46	9	2	0	0	283
Primo de Rivera's regime party (UP) leaders, 1929	25	11	27	25	11	2	0	334
Center-right Republican leaders, 1931–6	16	19	34	21	10	0	1	101
Center-right Radical leaders, 1931–6	8	14	43	16	11	4	4	139
Center-left Republican leaders, 1931–6	6	5	28	17	33	7	4	174
Socialist (PSOE) leaders, 1931–6	0	12	22	17	34	12	2	54

Sources: Alvarez Rey 1993. Row 1: Professionals are mostly lawyers and army officers; row 2: professionals are mostly lawyers; row 3: the quality of this data source is questionable. Professionals are presumably classified elsewhere. Others are *dependientes*.

Notes

CHAPTER I

1. The notion that the twentieth century has seen the rise and fall of the state as the bearer of a moral project is the main theme of Perez-Diaz (1993).
2. The reader wishing to know more of my general theory could start with the introductory chapters of the two published volumes of my history of power in society (Mann 1986, 1993).
3. Note that Eatwell (2001) renounces the concept of "rebirth," which he had earlier used, abusing it as "philosophically banal." I deal with the rival primordial, perennial, and modern conceptions of the nation in my forthcoming book, chap. 2.
4. I write "large" movements because fascist movements often *began* among groups who *were* middle-class (especially students and junior officers). As fascist movements grew larger, they tended to broaden their base. Thus in Northwestern Europe where fascist movements remained small, fascism remained disproportionately middle-class. In France, where it eventually grew quite large, it broadened as it grew.
5. Homosexuality did intermittently accompany such intense male comradeship, though this remains a poorly documented aspect of fascism. It is well known that the Nazi leaders turned strongly against homosexuals in the Roehm purge of 1934. SS personnel records would sometimes note evidence of homosexuality, implying that the organization could use the member's sense of vulnerability to get him to undertake "hard" (i.e., murderous) tasks.

CHAPTER 2

1. Gregor anticipates the obvious riposte to this – "what about Germany?" (developed but fascist) – with the bizarre suggestion that "traumatic experiences" of the war and its aftermath meant that Germany "identified herself with the up-and-coming revolutionary countries."
2. Some fascists did have democratic aspirations, wishing their party to allow rank-and-file representation (Linz 1976: 21). The leader should embody the

389

"general will" of the movement. But such quasi-democrats lost out within all fascist movements.

3. The distinction was clearly influenced by U.S. foreign policy of the late Cold War period, which distinguished between friendly "authoritarian" governments (some of which were actually extremely nasty) and enemy "totalitarian" communist governments (some of which were milder than some of the "authoritarian" ones). The decisive criterion was not in reality their degree of authoritarianism, but whether the U.S. government (and U.S. big business) defined them as capitalist or communist, and therefore as friend or foe.

4. Payne's (1980, 1995: 15) distinction between "conservative rightist," "radical rightist," and "fascist" resembles mine, his middle category lumping together most of my two intermediate types. Yet he calls "conservative" some who I place in intermediate categories (e.g., Salazar, Smetona, King Carol of Romania).

5. The Baltic states do not fit perfectly into this typology. Since they had no states before 1918 and no monarchs after, their authoritarians were not strictly "reactionaries." Nonetheless, the three came to share other attributes of reactionary regimes. Pats was probably the most moderate. His regime probably straddled the borderline between semi- and reactionary authoritarianism.

6. By now there were few urban-rural differences in mortality rates (unlike the nineteenth century).

7. I have not attempted to measure *degrees* of democratization or authoritarianism. Measures based on elections and constitutions cope poorly with the often sham institutions of interwar regimes, while most of the east and south did not remain in one position along the continuum.

8. Taking infant mortality rates would narrow the range of historical comparison. The northwestern countries mentioned reached the 1930 rates of Spain and Italy only between 1890 and 1920. Obviously, their party democracies were even more entrenched by then. My other two indices would give intermediate historical ranges (except that the comparable date for agricultural employment in Britain would be pushed back to the 1820s – when there was mass, successful agitation for suffrage extension).

9. Using this term broadly to include presidents elected in the same competitive way as the members of parliament.

10. By this term I mean that the early northwestern property franchises had rarely distinguished between ethnicities. English, Welsh, and Scottish men of property were considered active citizens, and they rarely organized along ethnic lines (see my forthcoming volume).

11. The next three paragraphs are indebted to Balakrishnan (2000). The main works of Schmitt I paraphrase are *The Crisis of Parliamentary Democracy* (1923) and *The Concept of the Political* (1927). I also acknowledge the help of Dylan Riley in discussions of the crisis of parliamentary liberalism.

12. Spain did not fit this model, since the universities were more divided, influenced by older liberal and sometimes secular traditions, as well as by conservative statism (see Chapter 9).

CHAPTER 3

1. I have excluded the very large number of "others" from the labor force. They may be schoolchildren (since the census is of those age ten or more). I also exclude the military from both sides of the equation. Friuli was a border province housing large armed forces drawn from outside the province.
2. A large group in the labor force cannot reach as high or as low a ratio as a smaller one. Since manual workers generally formed around half of the labor force, even in an *entirely* proletarian party their ratio could not much exceed 2.0. Yet the ratio of a small group – such as students – might exceed 20.0. I could have added a standardizing correction factor into these ratios, but the resulting statistic would lack immediate, intuitive meaning. No single statistic can reveal all.
3. This assumes that the category "lavatori dell'industria" also includes service sector manual workers (though seamen are listed separately). If it does not, then the party membership figures would understate the worker contribution.
4. In almost all countries labels such as "artisan" or "craftsman" are ambiguous. Is this person an employed skilled worker or an independent small master, perhaps employing others? Studies of Nazism used to classify *Handwerker* mainly as the latter, that is, as classic petty bourgeois (e.g., Kater 1983), aiding a lower middle-class theory of fascism. Recent writers (e.g., Mühlberger 1987, 1991) classify most as working-class, aiding a relatively classless theory. The data remain the same; the interpretation changes.

CHAPTER 4

1. The one area of truly awesome U.S. federal government power, its military, was the only part exempted from the Republican attack. In a third country's election I witnessed, in 1993, Spain's ruling Socialist Party probably at the last minute managed to cling to power by ringing popular alarm bells that its rather harmless conservative opponent, the PP, secretly nursed Francoite authoritarian intentions. The PP is now the respectable government of democratic Spain, having won the following election.
2. This accounts for the extraordinarily high estimates of female membership in the "bourgeois" parties sometimes given in the literature. Women supposedly constituted 25 percent of the liberal DDP, 47 percent of the ultraconservative DNVP, and 35 to 60 percent of the center-right DVP (Boak 1990). By including the Nazi auxiliary organizations we would also reach large numbers.
3. I thank Ron Rogowski for his generosity in showing me his files on which he constructed his 1977 article on the *Gauleiter*.
4. My main worry about the representativeness of the samples is that Mühlberger's (1991) regional samples (perhaps the best data on the NSDAP) do not include any from the east of the country, from either rural Prussia or industrial Saxony.
5. I also share part of Hamilton's skepticism (1997: 333) regarding Brustein's methods. His source data are Nazi member file cards. They often record occupations in a desultory way. Of those I have seen for my war criminals sample, I would confidently classify "industrial branch" in only just over half the cases. I am

puzzled from such source data how Brustein managed to separate workers in "metalwares" (the most Nazi group) from workers in "metal products" (the least Nazi group). To proceed from that classification to the assumption that the person's conception of their own occupational interest would be dominated by the issue of free trade or protectionism also seems quite a leap.

6. Remember, however, that Koshar (1986) has excluded students (who would be predominantly nonproletarian) from his tables, and he tells us that students formed 55 percent of the local Nazi party.

7. Two SA units in rural East Prussia, analyzed by Bessel (1984), differ, dominated by "farmers, young farmers and agricultural supervisors" (35% and 45% of the two units) and "artisans and artisans' apprentices" (29% and 33%). "Workers" comprised only 12 percent and 8 percent. This encourages Bessel and Jamin (1979) to polemicize against a proletarian interpretation of the SA. But Fischer and Hicks (1980) and Mühlberger (1991: 164–5) have observed that in this easterly region many farm laborers were Slavs, not Germans, unlikely to join the racist SA. Moreover, some "artisans and apprentices" were probably workers. Obviously, there were differences among SA units, since local economies differed. But allowing for both corrections would bring the class composition of the East Prussian SA closer to the SA elsewhere.

8. Jamin's second sample, of SA leaders who had been purged, had a very low response rate on matters of mobility. Those for whom she was able to collect data did have higher downward mobility. These may have been the real ruffians of the movement – alternatively, perhaps they provided just a biased sample.

CHAPTER 5

1. This is a controversial matter in which I have adopted a middle position between viewing capitalists as either "guilty" or "innocent." In rough descending order of "guilt," see Mason 1972; Geary 1983, 1990; Hamilton 1982: 393–419, 428–33; Neebe 1981; and Turner 1985.

CHAPTER 7

1. Hungarian fascism comprised several small parties and groups whose disunity hindered their development. In the late 1930s the Arrow Cross managed to unite most of them under the leadership of Ferenc Szálasi, though small independent "National Socialist" groups survived into the war period. For the sake of simplicity I refer to the multiple factions of Hungarian fascism as "The Arrow Cross."

2. If his informant was including tertiary sector workers in this figure, the ratios would decrease to just above parity.

CHAPTER 8

1. Schmitter (1974: 117–23) relies heavily on Manoilescu in his brilliant review of theories of corporatism – his title is borrowed from Manoilescu. But he tactfully downplays Manoilescu's fascist and anti-Semitic leanings.

2. Unless otherwise stated, data on legionary groups derive from Heinen 1986: 384–9 and Veiga 1989: 165–6, 262–6. At present no English-language source offers such data.

3. In Romania this church is found only in Transylvania, the residue of a Habsburg attempt during the eighteenth century to increase Austrian control over Transylvania by merging Catholic and Orthodox doctrines.

CHAPTER 9

I would like to thank the Fundación Juan March for its generosity in supporting a year's stay at the Instituto Juan March in Madrid, which made possible the research underlying this chapter.

1. The Spanish normally reserve the term "nationalism" for the regional autonomy aspirations, based on a claim to a distinct ethnicity, found especially among Catalans and Basques, but also among some Galicians, Valencians, and others.

2. This resulted from an attempt to avoid single-member constituencies (which might be controlled by *caciques*) yet to ensure workable governmental majorities. The Constitution provided large multimember constituencies covering a whole province or its capital. A party winning a simple majority in the province or capital got 67 to 80 percent of its seats, while minority lists were guaranteed the remaining ones. Most parties thus tried to form electoral pacts, combining lists of candidates who could thus capture most of the seats. The right accomplished such a pact better in 1933, the left in 1936. Thus both had Cortes majorities greater than any real shift in popular support. A different electoral system might have induced more compromise between the two blocs, strengthening the center. The republic was probably not helped by its electoral laws.

3. My account of the ensuing tragedy on the left depends mostly on balancing the diverging accounts of Juliá 1977; Preston 1978: chaps. 4, 5, and 7; Heywood 1990; and Payne 1993: 189–223.

4. True, the left Republicans and the Socialists reacted badly to their defeat in 1933 and asked the president to call new elections (Payne 1993: 181–2). But this was pique of the moment, soon subsiding. The left Republicans never actually organized against democracy.

5. Payne (1993: 208, 255–6, 381–4) claims that the Radicals and other "centrist liberals" were the only true constitutional democrats. He produces no evidence beyond Azaña's short-lived negotiations with the president in October 1934 and one statement by its youth movement ("[we are] leftists, democrats and parliamentarians in that order") to support his exclusion of the left Republicans, while many of his "centrist liberals" favored severe repression of the left. Payne's account is also soft on CEDA and hard on the socialists (the inverse of Preston's).

6. Once freed of Francoism, this region returned to its preferred politics. Now the bastions of the Socialist Party (the PSOE) reach down south from Madrid to dominate Andalucia and Extremadura.

7. Usually translated as leader, military leader, or head of state, but also seeking to connect Franco to sacred historical figures such as El Cid and the medieval Kings of Asturias – Christian heroes and martyrs.

CHAPTER 10

1. Italy's Northern League is sometimes classified along with these, but it is really extreme only in its anti-immigrant stance. See Diamanti 1996.
2. So also say Larsen 1998 and Linz 1998. Eatwell seems to disagree, since he concluded a recent book with the claim that "fascism is on the march again" (1995: 286) – though his own evidence seemed to suggest otherwise.
3. And this is the general conclusion of the various essays contained in Larsen 2001.
4. I treat theodemocracy and India more fully in my forthcoming book. See also Jaffrelot 1996: 53–62; Gold 1991; Prayer 1991; and Larsen 2001: 749–58.
5. I discuss Islamism and *jihadis* in my book *Incoherent Empire* (2003), chaps. 4 and 5; see also the major studies of Roy 1994 and Kepel 2002.

Bibliography

Abel, T. 1938. *Why Hitler Came to Power*. New York: Prentice-Hall.

Abse, T. 1986. "The rise of Fascism in an industrial city: The case of Livorno 1918–1922." In D. Forgacs (ed.), *Rethinking Italian Fascism*. London: Lawrence & Wishart.

———. 1996. "Italian workers and Italian Fascism." In Bessel (ed.), *Fascist Italy and Nazi Germany.*

Aguado Sanchez, F. 1972. *La revolución de octubre 1934*. Madrid: San Martin.

Aldcroft, D., and S. Morewood 1995. *Economic Change in Eastern Europe since 1918*. Aldershot, Hants: Edward Elgar.

Alexander, M. S., and H. Graham (eds.) 1989. *The French and Spanish Popular Fronts*. Cambridge: Cambridge University Press.

Allen, M. 1995. "Engineers and modern managers in the SS: The business administration main office." Ph.D. dissertation, University of Pennsylvania.

———. 2002. *The Business of Genocide: The SS, Slave Labor, and the Concentration Camps*. Chapel Hill: University of North Carolina Press.

Allen, W. S. 1965. *The Nazi Seizure of Power: The Experience of a Single German Town, 1930–1935*. Chicago: Quadrangle.

Alpert, M. 1989. "The Spanish army and the Popular Front." In Alexander and Graham (eds.), *French and Spanish Popular Fronts.*

Alvarez Chillida, G. 1992. "Nación, tradición e imperio en la extrema derecha española durante la decada de 1930." *Hispania* 52/3.

Alvarez Rey, L. 1993. *La derecha en la II república: Sevilla, 1931–1936*. Seville: Secretariado de Publicaciones de la Universidad de Sevilla.

Ancel, J. 1993. "Antonescu and the Jews." *Yad Vashem Studies* 23.

Ashman, C., and R. Wagman 1988. *The Nazi Hunters*. New York: Pharos.

Aubert, P. 1987. "Los intelectuales en el poder (1931–1933): Del constitucionalismo a la Constitución." In M. Tuñón de Lara (ed.), *La segunda república España: El primer bienio.* Madrid: Siglo XXI.

Augustinos, G. 1977. *Conciousness and History: Nationalist Critics of Greek Society, 1897–1914*. Boulder, Colo.: East European Quarterly and Columbia University Press.

Bacheller, C. 1976. "Class and conservatism: The changing social structure of the German right, 1900–1928." Ph.D. thesis, University of Wisconsin-Madison.

Bailer-Galanda, B. 1998. "Old or new right? Juridical denazification and right-wing extremism in Austria since 1945." In Larsen and Hagtvet (eds.), *Modern Europe after Fascism.*

Bairoch, P. 1976. "Europe's gross national product: 1800–1975." *Journal of European Economic History* 5.

Balakrishnan, G. 2000. *The Enemy: An Intellectual Portrait of Carl Schmitt.* London: Verso.

Balcells, A. 1971. *Crisis económica y agitación social en Cataluña de 1930 a 1936.* Barcelona.

Ballbé, M. 1983. *Orden público y militarismo en la España constitucional.* Madrid: Alianza.

Bar, A. 1975. "La Confederación Nacional del Trabajo frente a la II República." In M. Ramírez (ed.), *Estudios sobre la II republica española.* Madrid: Technos.

———. 1981. *La CNT en los años rojos.* Madrid: Akal.

Baldwin, P. 1990, "Social interpretations of Nazism: Renewing a tradition." *Journal of Contemporary History* 25.

Barany, G. 1971. "The dragon's teeth: The roots of Hungarian fascism." In Sugar (ed.), *Native Fascism.*

Barbagli, M. 1982. *Educating for Unemployment: Politics, Labour Markets and the School System – Italy, 1859–1923.* New York: Columbia University Press.

Barbu, Z. 1980. "Psycho-historical and sociological perspectives on the Iron Guard, the fascist movement in Romania." In Larsen et al. (eds.), *Who Were the Fascists?*

Barkai, A. 1990. *Nazi Economics.* Oxford: Berg.

Barrull Pelegrí, J. 1986. *Les comarques de Lleida durant la segona república (1930–1936).* Barcelona: L'Avenç.

Ben-Ami, S. 1983. *Fascism from Above: The Dictatorship of Primo de Rivera in Spain, 1923–1930.* Oxford: Clarendon.

Batkay W. 1982. *Authoritarian Politics in a Transitional State: Istvan Bethlen and the Unified Party in Hungary, 1919–26.* New York: Columbia University Press.

Berend, I. 1998. *Decades of Crisis: Central and Eastern Europe before World War II.* Berkeley and Los Angeles: University of California Press.

Berend, I., and G. Ránki. 1979. *Economic Development in East-Central Europe in the 19th and 20th Centuries.* New York: Columbia University Press.

Berezin, M. 1997. *Making the Fascist Self.* Ithaca, N.Y.: Cornell University Press.

Bermejo Martin, F. 1984. *La IIa república en Logroño: Elecciones y contexto politico.* Logroño: Communidad Autónoma de la Rioja.

Bernardini, G. 1989. "The origins and development of racial anti-semitism in fascist Italy." In M. Marrus (ed.), *The Nazi Holocaust,* vol. 4: *"The Final Solution" Outside Germany* Westport, Conn.: Meckler.

Bessel, R. 1984. *Political Violence and the Rise of Nazism.* New Haven: Yale Universsity Press.

———. 1986. "Violence as propaganda: The role of the stormtroopers in the rise of National Socialism." In Childers (ed.), *The Formation of the Nazi Constituency.*

———. 1988. "The Great War in German memory: The soldiers of the First World War, demobilization, and Weimar political culture." *German History* 6.

Bessel, R. (ed.). 1996. *Fascist Italy and Nazi Germany: Comparisons and Contrasts.* Cambridge: Cambridge University Press.

Bessel, R., and M. Jamin. 1979. "Nazis, workers and the uses of quantitative evidence." *Social History* 4.

Betz, H.-G. 1994. *Radical Right-Wing Populism in Western Europe.* London: Macmillan.

Binchy, D. A. 1941. *Church and State in Fascist Italy.* London: Oxford University Press.

Birn, R. 1991. "Austrian higher SS and police leaders and their participation in the Holocaust in the Balkans." *Holocaust and Genocide Studies* 6.

Blinkhorn, M. 1975. *Carlism and Crisis in Spain 1931–1939*. Cambridge: Cambridge University Press.

———. 1987. "The Iberian States." In D. Mühlberger (ed.), *The Social Basis of European Fascist Movements*. London: CroomHelm.

———. 1990. *Fascists and Conservatives*. London: Unwin Hyman.

Boak, H. 1990. "Women in Weimar Politics." *European History Quarterly* 20.

Borchardt, K. 1982. *Wachstum, Krisen, Handlungsspielraume der Wirtschaftspolitik*. Göttingen: Vandenkoeck & Ruprecht.

Bosch, A. 1993. "Sindicalismo, conflictividad y política." In Bosch et al. (eds.), *Estudios sobre la segunda república*. Valencia: Edicions Alfons el Magnànim.

Botz, G. 1980. "Introduction" and "The changing patterns of social support for Austrian National Socialism (1918–1945)." In Larsen et al. (eds.), *Who Were the Fascists?*

———. 1982. "Political violence, its forms and strategies in the First Austrian Republic." In W. Mommsen and G. Hirschfeld (eds.), *Social Protest, Violence and Terror in Nineteenth- and Twentieth-Century Europe*. New York: St. Martin's Press.

———. 1983. *Gewalt in der Politik*, 2nd ed. Munich: Fink.

———. 1985. "Strategies of political violence: Chance events and structural effects as causal factors in the February rising of the Austrian Social Democrats." In Rabinbach (ed.), *Austrian Socialist Experiment*.

———. 1987a. "Austria." In D. Mühlberger (ed.), *The Social Basis of European Fascist Movements*. London: CroomHelm.

———. 1987b. "The Jews of Vienna from the Anschluss to the Holocaust." In Oxaal et al. (eds.), *Jews, Antisemitism and Culture*.

———. 1988. *Nationalsozialismus in Wien*. Wien: DVO.

Boyd, C. 1979. *Praetorian Politics in Liberal Spain*. Chapel Hill: University of North Carolina Press.

Bracher, K. D. 1971. *The German Dictatorship*. Harmondsworth: Penguin.

Brademas, J. 1974. *Anarcosyndicalismo y revolución en España (1930–1937)*. Barcelona: Ariel.

Braham, R. 1981. *The Politics of Genocide: The Holocaust in Hungary*, 2 vols. New York: Columbia University Press.

———. 1998. *Romanian Nationalists and the Holocaust: The Political Exploitation of Unfounded Rescue Attempts*. New York: Columbia University Press.

Brooker, P. 1991. *The Faces of Fraternalism*. Oxford: Clarendon.

Broszat, M. 1981. *The Hitler State*. London: Longman.

———. 1987. *Hitler and the Collapse of Weimar Germany*. Leamington Spa: Berg.

Brown, J. 1989. "The Berlin NSDAP in the *Kampfzeit*." *German History* 7.

Brubaker, R. 1992. *Citizenship and Nationhood in France and Germany*. Cambridge, Mass.: Harvard University Press.

Brustein, W. 1988. "The political geography of Belgian fascism: The case of rexism." *American Journal of Sociology* 53: 69–70.

———. 1991. "The 'Red Menace' and the rise of Italian Fascism." *American Sociological Review* 56.

———. 1996. *The Logic of Evil: The Social Origins of the Nazi Party, 1925–1933*. New Haven, Conn.: Yale University Press.

Bukey, E. 1978. "The Nazi Party in Linz, Austria, 1931–1939: A sociological perspective." *German Studies Review* 1.

———. 1986. *Hitler's Hometown: Linz, Austria 1908–1945*. Bloomington: University of Indiana Press.

———. 1989. "Popular opinion in Vienna after the Anschluss." In Parkinson (ed.), *Conquering the Past*.

———. 1992. "Nazi rule in Austria." *Austria History Yearbook* 23.

Burleigh, M. 2000. *The Third Reich*. New York: Hill & Wang.

Busquets, J. 1984. *El militar de carrera en España*. Barcelona: Ariel.

Cabrera, M. 1983. *La patronal ante la II república: Organizaciones y etrategia (1931–1936)*. Madrid: Siglo Veintuino Editores.

Caldwell, L. 1986. "Reproducers of the Nation: Women and the family in Fascist policy." In Forgacs (ed.), *Rethinking Italian Fascism*.

Campbell, A. 1998. "The invisible welfare state: Class struggles, the American Legion and the development of veteran's benefits in the 20th century United States." Ph.D. dissertation, University of California, Los Angeles.

Campbell, B. 1998. *The SA Generals and the Rise of Nazism*. Lexington: University of Kentucky Press.

Campos, M. 1986. *El socialismo espanol y la cuestión agrario (1890–1936)*. Madrid: Ministerio de Trabajo y Seguridad Social.

Cancela, D. 1987. *La segunda república en Cadiz: Elecciones y partidos politicos*. Cadiz: Diputación Provincial.

Caplan, J. 1986. "Speaking the right language: The Nazi party and the civil service vote in the Weimar Republic." In Childers (ed.), *The Formation of the Nazi Constituency*.

———. 1988. *Government Without Administration: State and Civil Service in Weimar and Nazi Germany*. Oxford: Clarendon.

Cardoza, A. 1982. *Agrarian Elites and Italian Fascism: The Province of Bologna, 1901–1926*. Princeton, N.J.: Princeton University Press.

Carmona, Á. 1989. *El trabajo industrial en la España contemporánea (1874–1936)*. Barcelona: Anthropos.

Carsten, F. 1976. "Interpretations of fascism." In W. Laqueur (ed.), *Fascism: A Reader's Guide*. Berkeley and Los Angeles: University of California Press.

———. 1977. *Fascist Movements in Austria*. London: Sage.

———. 1980. *The Rise of Fascism*. Berkeley and Los Angeles: University of California Press.

Casas de Vega, R. 1974. *Los milicias nacionales en la guerra de España*. Madrid: Editora Nacional.

Castillo, J. J. 1979. *Proprietarios muy pobres: Sobre la subordinación politica del pequeño campesino*. Madrid: Ministerio del Agricultura.

Cavandoli, R. 1972. *Le origini del fascismo a Reggio Emilia*. Roma: Editori Riuniti.

Ceva, L. 2000. "The Strategy of Fascist Italy: A Premise." *Totalitarian Movements and Political Religions*, issue 2.3.

Childers, T. 1983. *The Nazi Voter*. Chapel Hill: University of North Carolina Press.

———. 1984. "Who, indeed, did vote for Hitler?" *Central European History* 17: 45–53.

———. 1990. "The social language of politics in Germany: The sociology of political discourse in the Weimar Republic." *American Historical Review* 95.

———. 1991. "The middle classes and National Socialism." In D. Blackbourn and R. Evans (eds.), *The German Bourgeoisie*. London: Routledge.

Childers, T. (ed.) 1986. *The Formation of the Nazi Constituency, 1919–1933*. London: CroomHelm.

Chirot, D. 1978. "Neoliberal and social-democratic theories of development: The Zel_{etin-}
Voinea debate concerning Romania's prospects in the 1920s and its contemporary importance." In K. Jowitt (ed.), *Social Change in Romania, 1860–1940*. Berkeley: Institute
of International Studies, University of California.

Chueca, R. 1983. *El fascismo en los comienzos del regimen de Franco*. Madrid: C.I.S.

Clark, M. 1988. "Italian squadrismo and contemporary vigilantism." *European History Quarterly* 18.

Close, D. H. 1984. "The police in the Fourth-of-August Regime." *Journal of the Hellenic
Diaspora* 13.

Close, D. 1990. "Conservatism, authoritarianism and fascism in Greece, 1915–1945." In
M. Blinkhorn (ed.), *Fascists and Conservatives: The Radical Right and the Establishment in
Twentieth-Century Europe*. London: Unwin Hyman.

Codreanu, C. 1990. *For My Legionaries*, 2nd ed. Reedy, W.V.: Liberty Bell.

Collier, G. 1987. *Socialists of Rural Andalusia*. Stanford, Calif.: Stanford University Press.

Collins, R. 1998. *The Sociology of Philosophies: A Global Theory of Intellectual Change*.
Cambridge, Mass.: Harvard University Press.

Contreras, M. 1981. *El PSOE en la II república*. Madrid: Centro de Investigaciones Sociologicas.

Corner, P. 1975. *Fascism in Ferrara, 1915–1925*. London: Oxford University Press.

Craig, G. 1994. "The true believer." *New York Review of Books*, March 24.

Cruz, R. 1984. "La organización del PCE (1920–1934)." *Estudios de Historia Social* 31.

_____. 1987. *El partido communista de España en la II república*. Madrid: Alianza.

Dahl, O. 1999. *Syndicalism, Fascism and Post-Fascism in Italy 1900–1950*. Oslo: Solum Forlag.

Dahl, R. 1977. *Polyarchy*. New Haven, Conn.: Yale University Press.

Deak, I. 1966. "Hungary." In H. Rogger and E. Weber (eds.), *The European Right: A Historical
Profile*. Berkeley: University of California Press.

_____. 1992. "Survivors." *New York Review of Books*, March 5.

De Felice, R. 1966. *Mussolini il fascista: La conquista del potere 1921–25*. Turin: Einaudi.

_____. 1974. *Mussolini il Duce: Gli anni del consenso 1929–1936*. Turin: Einaudi.

_____. 1977. *Interpretations of Fascism*. Cambridge, Mass.: Harvard University Press.

_____. 1980. "Italian Fascism and the middle classes." In Larsen et al. (eds.), *Who Were the
Fascists?*

_____. 1995. *Mussolini il rivoluzionario 1883–1920*, 2nd ed. Turin: Einaudi.

De Grand, A. 1978. *The Italian Nationalist Association and the Rise of Fascism in Italy*. Lincoln:
University of Nebraska Press.

De Grazia, V. 1992. *How Fascism Ruled Women: Italy 1922–1945*. Berkeley and Los Angeles:
University of California Press.

de la Cueva, J. 1998. "Religious persecution, anti-clerical tradition and revolution: Atrocities
against the clergy during the Spanish Civil War." *Journal of Contemporary History* 33.

Del Boca, A. 1969. *The Ethiopian War 1935–1941*. Chicago: University of Chicago Press.

Delzell, C. 1970. *Mediterranean Fascism 1919–1945: A Documentary History*. London:
Macmillan.

De Pablo, Santiago. 1995. *Historia del nacionalismo vasco*. Vitoria-Gasteiz: Fundacion Sancho
el Sabio.

Diamanti, I. 1996. "The Northern League: From regional party to party of government."
In S. Gundle and S. Parker (eds.), *The New Italian Republic*. London: Routledge.

Diehl, J. 1977. *Paramilitary Politics in Weimar Germany.* Bloomington: University of Indiana Press.

Döhn, L. 1970. *Politik und Interesse: Die Interessenstruktur der Deutschen Volkspartei.* Meisenheim am Glan: Anton Hain.

Dorian, E. 1982. *The Quality of Witness: A Romanian Diary 1937–1944.* Philadelphia: Jewish Publication Society of America.

Douglas, D. M. 1977. "The parent cell: Some computer notes on the composition of the first Nazi Party group in Munich, 1919–21." *Central European History* 10.

Downing, B. 1992. *The Military Revolution and Political Change: Origins of Democracy and Autocracy in Early Modern Europe.* Princeton, N.J.: Princeton University Press.

Dunnage, J. 1997. *The Italian Police and the Rise of Fascism.* London: Praeger.

Eatwell, R. 1995. *Fascism, a History.* London: Chatto & Windus.

———. 1996. "On defining the fascist minimum: The centrality of ideology." *Journal of Political Ideologies* 1.

———. 2001. "Universal fascism? Approaches and definitions." In S. U. Larsen (ed.), *Fascism outside Europe.* New York: Columbia University Press.

Edmondson, C. E. 1978. *The Heimwehr and Austrian Politics, 1918–36.* Athens: University of Georgia Press.

———. 1985. "The Heimwehr and February 1934: Reflections and questions." In Rabinbach (ed.), *Austrian Socialist Experiment.*

Elazar, D. 1993. "The making of Italian Fascism: The seizure of power, 1919–1922." Ph.D. thesis, University of California at Los Angeles.

Eley, G. 1980. *Rethinking the German Right.* New Haven, Conn.: Yale University Press.

———. 1983. "What produces fascism: Pre-industrial traditions or a crisis of the capitalist state?" *Politics and Society* 12.

———. 1986. *From Unification to Nazism: Reinterpreting the German Past.* London: Routledge.

Epelbaum, D. 1990. *Alois Brunner: La Haine Irreductible.* Paris: Calmann-Levy.

Espín, E. 1980. *Azaña en el poder: El partido de Acción Republicana.* Madrid: Centro de Investigaciones Sociologicas.

Falter, J. 1986. *Wahlen und Abstimmungen in der Weimarer Republik.* Munich: Beck.

———. 1991. *Hitlers Wähler.* Munich: Beck.

———. 1993. "Die Jungmitglieder der NSDAP zwischen 1925 und 1933. Ein demographisches und soziales Profil." In W. Krabbe (ed.), *Politische Jugend in der Weimarer Republik.* Bochum: Universitatsverlag.

———. 1998. "Recurring patterns of West German voting behaviour: Continuities and discontinuities 1928 to 1953." In S. U. Larsen and B. Hagtvet (eds.), *Modern Europe after Fascism, 1943–1980s.* New York: Columbia University Press.

Falter, J., and H. Bömermann. 1989. "Die Entwicklung der Weimarer Parteien in ihren Hochburgen und die Wahlerfolge der NSDAP." In H. Best (ed.), *Politik und Milieu.* St. Katharinen: Scripta Mercaturae.

Fargion, L. 1989. "The anti-Jewish policy of the Italian Social Republic (1943–1945)." In Marrus (ed.), *The Nazi Holocaust,* vol. 4.

Farré, J. 1985. *La Izquierda Burguesa en la II república.* Madrid: Espas-Calpe.

Ferenc 1988. "The Austrians and Slovenia during the Second World War." In Parkinson (ed.), *Conquering the Past.*

Ferrari 1998. "The radical right in postwar Italy." In Larsen and Hagtvet (eds.), *Modern Europe after Fascism.*

Fischer, C. 1978. "The occupational background of the SA's rank and file membership during the Depression years, 1929 to mid-1934." In P. Stachura (ed.), *The Shaping of the Nazi State*. London: CroomHelm.

_____. 1983. *Stormtroopers*. London: Allen & Unwin.

_____. 1991. *The German Communists and the Rise of Nazism*. New York: St. Martin's Press.

_____. 1995. *The Rise of the Nazis*. Manchester: Manchester University Press.

Fischer, C. and C. Hicks. 1980. "Statistics and the historian: The occupational profile of the SA of the NSDAP." *Social History* 5.

Fischer-Galati, S. 1971. "Fascism in Romania." In Sugar (ed.), *Native Fascism*.

_____. 1989. "Fascism, communism and the Jewish question in Romania." In M. Marrus (ed.), *The Nazi Holocaust*, vol. 4: "*The Final Solution" Outside Germany*. Westport, Conn.: Meckler.

Flora, P. 1983–87. *State, Economy and Society in Western Europe, 1815–1975*. Chicago: St. James Press.

Fogarty, M. 1957. *Christian Democracy in Western Europe, 1820–1953*. London: Routledge.

Forgacs, D. 1986. "The Left and Fascism: Problems of definition and strategy." In Forgacs (ed.), *Rethinking Italian Fascism*.

Forner Muñoz, S. 1982. *Industrialización y movimiento obrero: Alicante 1923–1936*. Valencia: Institución Alfonso el Magnánimo.

Francini, M. 1976. *Primo dopoguerra a origini del fascismo a Pistoia*. Milan: Feltrinelli.

Franco Rubio, G. A. 1982. "La contribución de la mujer española a la política contemporanea: De la Restauración a la Guerra Civil (1876–1939)." In R. M. Capel Martinez (ed.), *Mujer y sociedad en España 1700–1975*. Madrid: Ministerio de Cultura.

Franzosi, R. 1996. "Mobilization and counter-mobilization processes: From the 'red years' (1919–20) to the 'black years' (1921–22) in Italy. A new methodological approach to the study of narrative-data." Unpublished paper, Trinity College, Oxford.

Fraser, R. 1994. *Blood of Spain*, 2nd ed. London: Pimlico.

Friedlaender, S. 1986. "Nazism: Fascism or Totalitarianism?" In C. S. Maier et al. (eds.), *The Rise of the Nazi Regime. Historical Re-assessments*. Boulder, Colo.: Westview.

_____. 1997. *Nazi Germany and the Jews*, vol. 1: *The Years of Persecution, 1933–1939*. New York: HarperCollins.

Fritzsche, P. 1990. *Rehearsals for Fascism: Populism and Political Mobilization in Weimar*. Oxford: Oxford University Press.

_____. 1998. *Germans into Nazis*. Cambridge, Mass.: Harvard University Press.

Frye, B. 1985. *Liberal Democrats in the Weimar Republic*. Carbondale: Southern Illinois University Press.

Fusi, J. P. 1985. *Franco: Autoritarismo y poder personal*. Madrid: El Pais.

Gaillard, J. 1990. "The attractions of Fascism for the Church of Rome." In J. Milfull (ed.), *The Attractions of Fascism*. Oxford: Berg.

Gallagher, T. 1990. "Conservatism, dictatorship and fascism in Portugal, 1914–45." In M. Blinkhorn (ed.), *Fascists and Conservatives: The Radical Right and the Establishment in Twentieth-Century Europe*. London: Unwin Hyman.

Gao, Bai. 1997. *Economic Ideology and Japanese Industrial Policy*. Cambridge: Cambridge University Press.

García Andreu, M. 1985. *Alicante en las elecciones republicanas 1931–1936*. Alicante: Universidad de Alicante.

Geary, D. 1983. "The industrial elite and the Nazis in the Weimar Republic." In P. Stachura (ed.), *The Nazi Machtegreifung*. London: Allen & Unwin.

———. 1990. "Employers, workers and the collapse of the Weimar Republic." In I. Kershaw (ed.), *Weimar: Why Did German Democracy Fail?* New York: St. Martin's Press.

Gentile, E. 1989. *Storia del Partito Fascista, 1919–1922*. Roma: Laterza.

———. 1990. "Fascism as political religion." *Journal of Contemporary History*

———. 1996. *The Sacralization of Politics in Fascist Italy*. Cambridge, Mass: Harvard University Press.

———. 2000. Fascismo e antifascismo: I partito italiani fra le due guerre. Florence: Le Monnier.

Germán, L., et al. 1980. *Elecciones en Zaragoza-Capital durante la II república*. Zaragoza: Diputacion Provincial.

Germán Zubero, L. 1984. *Aragon en la II república*. Zaragoza: Institucion Fernando El Catolico.

Geyer, M. 1990. "The past as future: The German officer corps as profession." In G. Cocks and K. Jarausch (eds.), *German Professions, 1800–1950*. New York: Oxford University Press.

Gibson, I. 1979. *The Assassination of Federico García Lorca*, 2nd ed. London: W. H. Allen.

Gil Robles, J. M. 1968. *No fue posible la paz*. Barcelona: Ariel.

Giles, G. 1978. "The rise of the National Socialist Students' Association and the failure of political education in the Third Reich." In P. D. Stachura (ed.), *The Shaping of the Nazi State*. London: CroomHelm.

———. 1983. "National Socialism and the educated elite in the Weimar Republic." In Stachura (ed.), *The Nazi Machtergreifung*.

Giner, S. 1977. "Sociologia del franquismo." Barcelona, papers, no. 6.

Giolitti, G. 1923. *Memoirs of My Life*. London: Chapman & Dodd.

Gold, D. 1991. "Organized Hinduisms: From Vedic truth to Hindu nation." In M. Marty and R. Appleby (eds.), *Fundamentalisms Observed*. Chicago: University of Chicago Press.

Gomez-Navarro, J. L. 1991. *El Regimen de Primo de Rivera*. Madrid: Catedra.

Gonzalez-Hernández, M. 1990. *Ciudadanía y acción: El conservadurismo maurista, 1907–23*. Madrid: Siglo XXI.

Gordon, S. 1984. *Hitler, Germs and the Jewish Question*. Princeton, N.J.: Princeton University Press.

Gosztony, P. 1985. "Annual Statistic al Romaniei." Bucharest: Institut Central de Statistica, 1939–40.

Gramsci, A. 1971. *Selections from the Prison Notebooks*. New York: International.

Gregor, A. J. 1979. *Italian Fascism and Developmental Dictatorship*. Princeton, N.J.: Princeton University Press.

Gregor, J. 1969. *The Ideology of Fascism: The Rationale of Totalitarianism*. New York: Free Press.

———. 2000. "Fascism, Marxism and some considerations concerning classification." *Totalitarian Movements and Political Religions*, issue 3.2.

Gress, F. 1998. "Right-wing extremism in the history of the Federal Republic of Germany." In Larsen and Hagtvet (eds.), *Modern Europe after Fascism*.

Griffin, R. 1991. *The Nature of Fascism*. London: Routledge.

———. 1995. *Fascism*. Oxford: Oxford University Press.

———. 2001. "Caught in its own net: Post-war fascism outside Europe." In Larsen (ed.), *Fascism outside Europe*.

———. 2002. "The primacy of culture: The current growth (or manufacture) of consensus within fascist studies." *Journal of Contemporary History* 37.

Grill, J. 1983. *The Nazi Movement in Baden, 1920–1945*. Chapel Hill: University of North Carolina Press.

Gruber, H. 1985. "Socialist Party culture and the realities of working class life in Red Vienna." In Rabinbach (ed.), *Austrian Socialist Experiment*.

Guinea, J. 1978. *Los movimientos obreros y sindicales en España: De 1833 a 1978*. Madrid: Iberico Europea de Ediciones.

Gulick, C. 1948. *Austria from Habsburg to Hitler*, vol. 2: *Fascism: Subversion of Democracy*. Berkeley and Los Angeles: University of California Press.

Guttsman, W. L. 1981. *The German Social Democratic Party, 1875–1933*. London: Allen & Unwin,

Hagtvet, B. 1980. "The theory of mass society and Weimar." In Larsen et al. (eds.), *Who Were the Fascists?*

Hamann, B. 1999. *Hitler's Vienna: A Dictator's Apprenticeship*. New York: Oxford University Press.

Hamilton, R. 1982. *Who Voted for Hitler?* Princeton, N.J.: Princeton University Press.

———. 1997. "Review of *The Logic of Evil* by W. Brustein." *Contemporary Sociology* 26.

Hanisch, E. 1989. "Austrian Catholicism: Between accommodation and resistance." In Parkinson (ed.), *Conquering the Past*.

Heberle, R. 1964. *From Democracy to Nazis*. Baton Rouge: University of Louisiana Press.

Heilbronner, O. 1990. "The role of Nazi antisemitism in the Nazi Party's activity and propaganda. A regional historiographical study." *Leo Baeck Institute Yearbook* 38.

Heinen, A. 1986. *Die Legion "Erzengel Michael" in Rumänien: Soziale Bewegung und politische Organisation*. Munich: Oldenbourg.

Helmreich, E. C. 1979. *The German Churches under Hitler*. Detroit, Mich.: Wayne State University Press.

Herf, J. 1984. *Reactionary Modernism*. New York: Cambridge University Press.

Hesse, S. 1990. "Fascism and the hypertrophy of male adolescence." In J. Milfull (ed.), *The Attractions of Fascism*. Oxford: Berg.

Heywood, P. 1990. *Marxism and the Failure of Organised Socialism in Spain, 1879–1936*. Cambridge: Cambridge University Press.

Hitchins, K. 1994. *Rumania 1866–1947*. Oxford: Clarendon.

Hitler, A. 1940. *Mein Kampf* New York: Reynal & Hitchcock.

Hobsbawm, E. 1994. *The Age of Extremes: A History of the World, 1914–1991*. New York: Pantheon.

Holtfrerich, C.-L. 1990. "Economic policy options and the end of the Weimar Republic." In Kershaw (ed.), *Weimar*.

Hughes, H. S. 1967. *Consciousness and Society: The Reorientation of European Social Thought*. London: Macgibbon & Kee.

Hunt, R. N. 1964. *German Social Democracy, 1918–33*. Chicago: Quadrangle Books.

Huntington, S. P. 1991. *The Third Wave: Democratization in the Late Twentieth Century*. Norman: University of Oklahoma Press.

Ianciu C. 1996. *Les juifs en Roumanie (1919–1938): De l'emancipation a la marginalisation*. Paris/Louvain: Peeters.

———. 1998. *La Shoah en Roumanie*. Montpellier: Université Paul-Valéry.

Ignazi, P. 1997. "The extreme right in Europe: A survey." In P. Merkl and L. Weinberg (eds.), *The Revival of Right-Wing Extremism in the 1990s*. London: Frank Cass.

Ioanid, R. 1990. *The Sword of the Archangel*. New York: Columbia University Press.

Ionesco, E. 1960. *Rhinoceros*. New York: S. French.

Institutul Central de Statistica. 1939–40. *Anuarul Statistic Al Românei*. Bucharest: author.

Irwin, W. 1991. *The 1933 Cortes Elections*. New York: Garland.

Jackson, G. 1965. *The Spanish Republic and the Civil War 1931–1939*. Princeton, N.J.: Princeton University Press.

Jaffrelot, C. 1996. *The Hindu Nationalist Movement in India*. New York: Columbia University Press.

Jagschitz, G. 1975. *Vom Justizpalast zum Heldenplatz*. Wien: DVO.

James, H. 1990. "Economic reasons for the collapse of the Weimar Republic." In Kershaw (ed.), *Weimar*.

Jamin, M. 1984. *Zwischen den Klassen: Zur Sozialstruktur der SA-Fuhrerschaft*. Wuppertal: Peter Hammer.

Jarausch, K. 1990. *The Unfree Professions: German Lawyers, Teachers and Engineers, 1900–1950*. Oxford: Oxford University Press.

Janos, A. 1970. "The one-party state and social mobilization: East Europe between the Wars." In S. Huntington and C. Moore (eds.), *Authoritarian Politics in Modern Society*. New York: Basic.

————. 1982. *The Politics of Backwardness in Hungary, 1825–1945*. Princeton, N.J.: Princeton University Press.

————. 1989. "The politics of backwardness in Continental Europe, 1780–1945." *World Politics* 61.

Jedlicka, L. 1979. "The Austrian Heimwehr." In G. Mosse (ed.), *International Fascism: New Thoughts and New Approaches*, 2nd ed. London: Sage.

Jerez Mir, M. 1982. *Elites politicas y centros de extracción en España, 1938–1957*. Madrid: C.I.S.

Jones, L. 1988. *German Liberalism and the Dissolution of the German Party System, 1918–1933*. Chapel Hill: University of North Carolina Press.

Jowitt, K. 1971. *Revolutionary Breakthroughs and National Development: The Case of Romania, 1944–1965*. Berkeley and Los Angeles: University of California Press.

Juliá, S. 1977. *La izquierda del PSOE (1935–1936)*. Madrid: Siglo XXI.

————. 1979. *Origenes del frente popular en Espana (1934–1936)*. Madrid: Siglo XX.

————. 1983. "Corporativistas obreros y reformadores políticos: Crisis y escisión del PSOE en la II República." *Studia Histórica* 1.

————. 1984. *Madrid, 1931–1934: De la fiesta popular a la lucha de clases*. Madrid: Siglo XXI.

————. 1989. "The origins and nature of the Spanish Popular Front." In Alexander and Graham (eds.), *French and Spanish Popular Fronts*.

————. 1990. "Guerra civil como guerra social." In *La iglesia católica y la guerra civil española*. Madrid: Fundación Friedrich Ebert.

Juliá, S., et al. 1999. *Victimas de la guerra civil*. Madrid: Temas de Hoy Historia.

Karady, V. 1993. "Antisemitism in twentieth-century Hungary: A socio-historical overview." *Patterns of Prejudice* 27.

————. 1997. "Identity strategies under duress before and after the Holocaust." In R. Braham and A. Pok (eds.), *The Holocaust in Hungary: Fifty Years Later*. New York: Columbia University Press.

Kallis, A. 2000. "The 'regime-model' of fascism: A typology." *European History Quarterly* 30.

Karsai, L. 1998. "The last phase of the Hungarian Holocaust: The Szalasi Regime and the Jews." In R. Braham and S. Miller (eds.), *The Nazis' Last Victims: The Holocaust in Hungary*. Detroit, Mich.: Wayne State University Press.

Kater, M. 1975. *Studentenschaft und Rechtsradikalismus in Deutschland 1918–1933*. Hamburg: Hoffmann & Kampe.

———. 1983. *The Nazi Party*. Cambridge, Mass.: Harvard University Press.

Kele, M. 1972. *Nazis and Workers*. Chapel Hill: University of North Carolina Press.

Kelikian, A. 1986. *Town and Country under Fascism: The Transformation of Brescia, 1915–1926*. Oxford: Clarendon.

Kelsey, G. 1991. *Anarchosyndicalism, Libertarian Communism and the State: The CNT in Zaragoza and Aragon, 1930–1937*. Amsterdam: Kluwer.

Kepel, G. 2002. *Jihad: The Trail of Political Islam*. Cambridge, Mass.: Harvard University Press.

Kershaw, I. 1990. "Introduction: Perspectives of Weimar's Failure." In Kershaw (ed.), *Weimar*.

———. 1991. *Hitler*. London: Longman.

———. 1998. *Hitler. 1889–1936: Hubris*. New York: Norton.

———. 2000. *The Nazi Dictatorship*, 4th ed. London: Edward Arnold.

Kershaw I. (ed.) 1990. *Weimar: Why did Weimar Democracy Fail?* New York: St. Martin's Press.

Kindelan, A. (Teniente General). n.d. *Ejercito y politica*. Madrid: Aguilar.

Kirk, T. 1996. *Nazism and the Working Class in Austria*. Cambridge: Cambridge University Press.

Kitchen, M. 1976. *Fascism*. London: Macmillan.

Kluge, U. 1984. *Der Österreichische Ständestaat 1934–1938*. Vienna:

Knight, M. 1952. *The German Executive 1890–1933*. Stanford, Calif.: Stanford University Press.

Knox, M. 1996. "Expansionist zeal, fighting power and staying power in the Italian and German dictatorships." In Bessel (ed.), Fascist Italy and Nazi Germany.

Kofas, J. 1983. *Authoritarianism in Greece: The Melaxas Regime*. New York: Columbia University Press.

Kolb, E. 1979. "Zur Sozialbiographie einer Führungsgruppe der SPD am Anfang der Weimarer Republik." In *Herkunft und Mandat: Beitrage zur Föhrungsproblematik in der Arbeiterbewegung*. Frankfurt and Cologne: Europaische Verlagsanstalt.

Konrad, H. 1989. "Social democracy's drift toward nazism before 1938." In Parkinson (ed.), *Conquering the Past*.

Koshar, R. 1986. *Social Life, Local Politics, and Nazism. Marburg, 1880–1935*. Chapel Hill: University of North Carolina Press.

Kovács, M. 1991 "The ideology of illiberalism in the professions: Leftist and rightist radicalism among Hungarian doctors, lawyers and engineers, 1918–45." *European History Quarterly* 21.

Kratzenberg, V. 1989. *Arbeiter auf dem Weg zu Hitler?* Frankfurt/Main: Peter Lang.

Kühr, H. 1973. *Partien und Wahlen im Stadt- und Landkreis Essen in der Zeit der Weimarer Republik*. Düsseldorf: Droste.

Lackó, M. 1969. *Arrow-Cross Men, National Socialists. 1935–1944*. Budapest: Akademiai Kiado.

Lannon, F. 1984. "The church's crusade against the republic." In P. Preston (ed.), *Revolution and War in Spain*. London: Methuen.

———. 1987. *Privilegio, persecución y profecía: La iglesia católica en España. 1875–1975*. Madrid: Alianza.

Laqueur, W. (ed.) 1976. *Fascism: A Reader's Guide*. Berkeley: University of California Press.

Larsen, S. U. 1998. "Overcoming the past when shaping the future." In Larsen and Hagtvet, *Modern Europe after Fascism.*

———. 2001. "Was there Fascism outside Europe? Diffusion from Europe and domestic impulses." In Larsen (ed.), *Fascism outside Europe.*

Larsen, S. U. (ed.). 2001. *Fascism outside Europe*. New York: Columbia University Press.

Larsen, S. U., and B. Hagtvet (eds.). 1998. *Modern Europe after Fascism 1943–1980s*. New York: Columbia University Press.

Larsen, S., et al. (eds.). 1980. *Who Were the Fascists? Social Roots of European Fascism*. Oslo: Universitetsforlaget.

Ledeen M. 1977. *The First Duce: D'Annunzio at Fiume*. Baltimore, Md.: Johns Hopkins University Press.

———. 1989. "The evolution of Italian fascist anti-semitism." In Marrus (ed.), *The Nazi Holocaust*, vol. 4.

Lee, S. 1987. *The European Dictatorships, 1918–1945*. London: Methuen.

Lewis, J. 1991. *Fascism and the Working Class in Austria, 1918–34*. Oxford: Berg.

Liebe, W. 1956. *Die Deutschnationale Volkspartei, 1918–1924*. Dusseldorf: Droste.

Lindstrom, U. 1985. *Fascism in Scandinavia, 1920–1940*. Stockholm: Almquist & Wiksell.

Linz, J. 1976. "Some notes toward a comparative study of fascism in sociological historical perspective." In W. Laqueur (ed.), *Fascisim: A Reader's Guide*. Berkeley: University of California Press.

———. 1978. "From great hopes to civil war: The breakdown of democracy in Spain." In Linz and A. Stepan (eds.), *The Breakdown of Democratic Regimes: Europe*. Baltimore, Md.: Johns Hopkins University Press.

———. 1980. "Political space and fascism as a late-comer." In S. U. Larsen et al. (eds.), *Who Were the Fascists?* Bergen: Universitetsforlaget.

———. 1998. "Fascism is dead. What legacy did it leave?" In Larsen and Hagtvet (eds.), *Modern Europe after Fascism.*

Lipset, S. M. 1963. *Political Man*. London: Heinemann.

Luebbert, G. 1991. *Liberalism, Fascism or Social Democracy: Social Classes and the Political Origins of Regimes in Interwar Europe*. New York: Oxford University. Press.

Livezeanu, I. 1990. "Fascists and conservatives in Romania: Two generations of nationalists." In M. Blinkhorn (ed.), *Fascists and Conservatives*. London: Unwin Hyman.

———. 1995. *Cultural Politics in Greater Romania*. Ithaca, N.Y.: Cornell University Press.

Loewenberg, P. 1983. "The psychohistorical origins of the Nazi youth cohort." In Loewenberg, *Decoding the Past*. New York: Knopf.

———. 1985. "Otto Bauer as an ambivalent party leader." In Rabinbach (ed.), *The Austrian Social Experiment.*

Lösche, P. 1992. *Die SPD: Klassenpartei – Volkspartei – Quotenpartei*. Darmstadt: Wiss. Buchges.

Lyttleton, A. 1982. "Fascism and violence in post-war Italy: Political strategy and social conflict." In Mommsen and Hirschfeld (eds.), *Social Protest, Violence and Terror.*

———. 1987. *The Seizure of Power: Fascism in Italy, 1919–1929*. London: Weidenfeld & Nicolson.

———. 1996. "The 'crisis of bourgeois society' and the origins of Fascism." In Bessel (ed.), *Fascist Italy and Nazi Germany.*

Macarro Vera, J. M. 1989. "Social and economic policies of the Spanish left in theory and in practice." In Alexander and Graham (eds.), *French and Spanish Popular Fronts*.

Madden, P. 1982a. "Generational aspects of National Socialism, 1919–1933." *Social Science Quarterly* 63.

———. 1982b. "Some social characteristics of early Nazi Party members, 1919–23." *Central European History* 15.

Maddison, A. 1982. *Phases of Capitalist Development*. Oxford: Oxford University Press.

Maier, C. 1975. *Recasting Bourgeois Europe*. Princeton, N.J.: Princeton University Press.

Malefakis, E. 1970. *Agrarian Reform and Peasant Revolution in Spain*. New Haven, Conn.: Yale University Press.

Mallett, R. 2000. *The Italian Navy and Fascist Expansionism, 1935–1940*. London: Frank Cass.

Manjón, O. 1976. *El partido republicano radical 1908–1936*. Madrid: Tebas.

Mann, M. 1986. *The Sources of Social Power*, vol. 1: *A History from the Beginning to 1760 AD*. New York: Cambridge University Press.

———. 1988. "The autonomous power of the state: Its origins, mechanisms and results." In M. Mann (ed.), *States, War and Capitalism*. New York: Basil Blackwell.

———. 1993. *The Sources of Social Power*, vol. 2: *The Rise of Classes and Nation-States, 1760–1914*. New York: Cambridge University Press.

———. 1995. "Sources of variation in working-class movements in twentieth-century Europe." *New Left Review*, no. 212.

———. 1997. "The contradictions of continuous revolution." In I. Kershaw and M. Lewin (eds.), *Stalinism and Nazism: Dictatorship in Comparison*. Cambridge: Cambridge University Press.

———. 2003. *Incoherent Empire*. London: Verso.

———. Forthcoming. *The Darkside of Democracy: Explaining Ethnic Cleansing.*.

Manoilescu, M. 1937. *Le Parti Unique*, 2nd ed. Paris: Alcan.

———. 1938. *Le Siècle du corporatisme: Doctrine du corporatisme integral et pur*, 2nd ed. Paris: Alcan.

Maravall, J. M. 1997. *Regimes, Politics, and Markets: Democratization and Economic Change in Southern and Eastern Europe*. Oxford: Oxford University Press.

Marco, J. M. 1988. *La inteligencia republicana: Manuel Azaña 1897–1930*. Madrid: Biblioteca Nueva.

Marcuse, P. 1985. "The housing policy of social democracy: Determinants and consequences." In Rabinbach (ed.), *Austrian Socialist Experiment*.

Marshall, B. 1988. "Politics in academe: Gottingen University and the growing impact of political issues, 1918–33." *European History Quarterly* 18.

Martin, B. 1990. *The Agony of Modernization: Labor and Industrialization in Spain*. Ithaca, N.Y.: Cornell University Press.

Mason, T. 1972. "The primacy of politics – politics and economics in Nationalist Socialist Germany." In H. A. Turner (ed.), *Nazism and the Third Reich*. New York: Quadrangle.

———. 1993. *Social Policy in the Third Reich*. Oxford: Berg.

———. 1995. *Nazism, Fascism and the Working Class*. ed. Jane Caplan. Cambridge and New York: Cambridge University Press.

Mateos, Rodríguez. 1993. "Formación y desarrollo de la derecha católica an la provincia de Zamora durante la Segunda República." In J. Tusell et al. (eds.), *Estudios sobre la derecha española contemporanea*. Madrid: Unea.

Mayer, A. 1981. *The Persistence of the Old Regime*. London: CroomHelm.

Mayeur J.-M. 1980. *Des partis catholiques a la democratie chrétienne, XIXe–XXe siecles*. Paris: Colin.

Meaker, G. 1988. "A civil war of words: The ideological impact of the First World War on Spain, 1914–18." In H. Schmitt (ed.), *Neutral Europe between War and Revolution, 1917–19*. Charlottesville: University of Virginia Press.

Melograni, P. 1965. "Confindustria e fascismo tra il 1919 e il 1925." *Il Nuevo Osservatore* 6 (Nov.): 834–73.

———. 1972. *Gli industriali e Mussolini: Rapporti fra Confindustria e fascismo del 1919 al 1929*. Milan: Longanesi.

Mendelsohn, E. 1983. *The Jews of East Central Europe between the World Wars*. Bloomington: University of Indiana Press.

Merkl, P. 1975. *Political Violence under the Swastika*. Princeton, N.J.: Princeton University Press.

———. 1980. *The Making of a Stormtrooper*. Princeton, N.J.: Princeton University Press.

Michaelis, M. 1995. "The current debate over fascist racial policy." In Wistrich and DellaPergola (eds.), *Fascist Antisemitism*.

Miguel, A. de 1975. *Sociologia del franquismo*. Barcelona: Euros.

Milatz, A. 1965. *Walher und Walhen in der Weimarer Republik*. Bonn: Bundeszentrale fur Politische Bildung.

Mintz, J. 1982. *The Anarchists of Casas Viejas*. Chicago: University of Chicago Press.

Mir, C. 1985. *Lleida (1890–1936): Caciquisme polític i lluita electoral*. Montserrat: l'Abadia de Montserrat.

Misefari, E., and A. Marzotti. 1980. *L'Avvento del Fascismo in Calabria*. Cosenza: Pellegrini.

Mitchell, B. 1993. *International Historical Statistics: The Americas 1750–1993*. New York: Grove.

———. 1995. *International Historical Statistics: Africa, Asia, and Oceania 1750–1993* New York: Grove.

———. 1998. *International Historical Statistics: Europe 1750–1993*. New York: Grove.

Mócsy, I. 1983. *The Effects of World War I. The Uprooted: Hungarian Refugees and Their Impact on Hungary's Domestic Politics, 1918–1921*. New York: Columbia University Press.

Molas, I. 1973. *Lliga Catalana: Un estudi d'estasiologia*, 2nd ed. Barcelona: Edicions 62.

Molony, J. 1977. *The Emergence of Political Catholicism in Italy*. London: CroomHelm.

Mommsen, H. 1991. "Hitler's position in the Nazi system." In Mommsen, *From Weimar to Auschwitz*. Princeton, N.J.: Princeton University Press.

Mommsen, W. 1990. "The varieties of the nation state in modern history: Liberal imperialist, fascist and contemporary notions of nation and nationality." In M. Mann (ed.), *The Rise and Decline of the Nation State*. Cambridge: Basil Blackwell.

Mommsen, W. J., and G. Hirschfield (eds.) 1982. *Social Protest, Violence and Terror in Nineteenth and Twentieth-Century Europe*. New York: St. Martin's Press.

Montero, J. R. 1977 *La CEDA: El catolicismo social y politico en la II república*, 2 vols. Madrid: Ediciones de la Revista de Trabajo.

———. 1988. "Las derechas en el sistema de partidos del segundo bienio republicano: Algunos datos introductorios." In Túñon de Lara (ed.), *La II república española*.

Moore, B. 1966. *Social Origins of Dictatorship and Democracy*. Harmondsworth: Penguin.

Morego, J. M. F. 1922. *Los atendados sociales en España, las teorias, los hechos, estadisticas*. Madrid: Casa Faure.

Moreno, A. M. 1961. *Historía de la persecución en España*. Madrid: Biblioteca de Autores Cristianos.

Moreno Fernandez, L. 1987. *Accion popular murciana: La derecha confessional en Murcia durante la II república*. Murcia: Universidad de Murcia.

Morodo, R. 1985. *Los origines ideologicos del franquismo: Acción Española*. Madrid: Alianza.

Morsey, R. 1977. *Der Untergang des Politischen Katholicizismus*. Stuttgart: Belser.

Mosse, G. 1964. *The Crisis of German Ideology: The Intellectual Origins of the Third Reich*. New York: H. Testig.

———. 1966. "The genesis of fascism." *Journal of Contemporary History* 1.

———. 1970. *Germans and Jews: The Right, the Left and the Search for a Third Force in Pre-Nazi Germany*. New York: H. Testig.

———. 1999. *The Fascist Revolution*. New York: Howard Fertig.

Mühlberger, D. (ed.). 1987. *The Social Basis of European Fascist Movement*. London: CroomHelm.

———. 1991. *Hitler's Followers*. London: Routledge.

Mussolini, B. 1976. *The Political and Social Doctrine of Fascism*. New York: Gordon Press. Originally published 1932.

Myklebust, J. and B. Hagtvet. 1980. "Regional contrasts in the membership base of the Nosjonal Samling." In S. Larsen et al. (eds.), *Who Were the Fascists? Social Roots of European Fascism*. Oslo: Universitets Farlager.

Nagy-Talavera, N. 1970. *The Green Shirts and the Others: A History of Fascism in Hungary and Romania*. Stanford, Calif.: Hoover Institute Press.

Neebe, R. 1981. *Grossindustrie, Staat und NSDAP 1930–1933*. Gottingen: Vanenhoeck and Rupricht.

Newman, K. 1970. *European Democracy between the Wars*. London: George Allen & Unwin.

Niessen, J. 1995. "Romanian nationalism: An ideology of integration and mobilization." In P. Sugar (ed.), *Eastern European Nationalism in the Twentieth Century*. Washington: American University Press.

Noakes, J. 1971. *The Nazi Party in Lower Saxony, 1921–1933*. Oxford: Oxford University Press.

Noakes, J., and G. Pridham. 1974. *Documents on Nazism, 1919–1945*. London: Cape.

Nolte, E. 1965. *Three Faces of Fascism*. London: Weidenfeld & Nicolson.

O'Sullivan, N. 1983. *Fascism*. London: Dent.

Oxaal, I., et al. (eds.). 1987. *Jews, Antisemitism and Culture in Vienna*. London: Routledge.

Ozsvath, Z. 1997. "Can words kill? Anti-semitic texts and their impact on the Hungarian Jewish catastrophe." In Randolph. Braham and Attila Pók (eds.), *The Holocaust in Hungary* (New York: East European Managraphs, 1997).

Palomares Ibáñez, J. M. 1988. *El socialismo en Castilla*. Valladolid: Universidad.

Parkinson 1989. "Epilogue." In Parkinson (ed.), *Conquering the Past*.

Parkinson, F. (ed.). 1989. *Conquering the Past: Austrian Nazism Yesterday and Today*. Detroit, Mich.: Wayne State University Press.

Parming, T. 1975. *The Collapse of Liberal Democracy and the Rise of Authoritarianism in Estonia*. Beverly Hills, Calif.: Sage.

Partido Republicano Radical. 1932. *Asemblea nacional extraordinaria*. Madrid: Imprenta Zolia Ascasibar.

Passchier, N. 1980. "The electoral geography of the Nazi landslide." In Larsen et al. (eds.), *Who Were the Fascists?*

Passerini, L. 1987. *Fascism in Popular Memory: The Cultural Experience of the Turin Working Class.* Cambridge: Cambridge University Press.

Patton, C. 1994. "The myth of moderation: German chemical employer responses to labour conflict, 1914–24." *European History Quarterly* 24.

Pauley, B. 1980. "Nazis and Heimwehr Fascists: The struggle for supremacy in Austria, 1918–1938." In Larsen et al. (eds.), *Who Were the Fascists?*

———. 1981. *Hitler and the Forgotten Nazis.* Chapel Hill: University of North Carolina Press.

———. 1987. "Political antisemitism in interwar Vienna." In Oxaal et al. (eds.), *Jews, Antisemitism and Culture.*

———. 1989. "The Austrian Nazi Party before 1938: Some recent revelations." In Parkinson (ed.), *Conquering the Past.*

Paxton, R. 1994. "Radicals." *New York Review of Books*, June 23.

———. 1996. "The uses of fascism." *New York Review of Books*, November 28.

———. 1998. "The five stages of fascism." *Journal of Modern History* 70.

Payne, S. 1962. *Falange: A History of Spanish Fascism.* London: Oxford University Press.

———. 1970. *The Spanish Revolution.* New York: Norton.

———. 1980a. *Fascism: Comparison and Definition.* Madison: University of Wisconsin Press.

———. 1980b. "Social Composition and Regional Strength of the Spanish Falange." In S. V. Larsen et al. (eds.), *Who Were the Fascists? Social Roots of European Fascism.* Bergen: Universitetsforlaget.

———. 1993. *Spain's First Democracy: The Second Republic, 1931–1936.* Madison: University of Wisconsin Press.

———. 1995. *A History of Fascism, 1914–1945.* Madison: University of Wisconsin Press.

Peirats, J. 1971. *La CNT en la revolución española*, 2nd ed., 3 vols. Paris: Ediciones CNT.

Perez Diaz, V. 1991. *Structure and Change of Castilian Peasant Communities.* New York: Garland.

———. 1993. *The Return of Civil Society.* Cambridge, Mass.: Harvard University Press.

Petersen, J. 1975. "Elettorato e base sociale del fascismo Italiano negli anni venti." *Studi Storici*, anno 16.

———. 1982. "Violence in Italian fascism, 1919–25." In Mommsen and Hirschfeld (eds.), *Social Protest, Violence and Terror.*

Peterson, L. 1983. "A social analysis of KPD supporters: The Hamburg insurrectionaries of October 1923." *International Review of Social History* 28.

Peukert, D. 1989. *Inside Nazi Germany: Conformity, Opposition, and Racism in Everyday Life.* Trans. R. Deveson. London: Penguin.

Polonsky, A. 1975. *The Little Dictators: The History of Eastern Europe since 1918.* London: Routledge.

Prayer, M. 1991. "Italian fascist regime and nationalist India 1921–1945." *International Studies* 28.

Preston, P. 1978. *The Coming of the Spanish Civil War: Reform, Reaction and Revolution in the Second Republic.* London: Routledge.

———. 1986. *Las derechas españolas en el siglo XX: Autoritismo fascismo y golpismo.* Madrid: Sustema.

———. 1990. *The Politics of Revenge.* London: Unwin Hyman.

———. 1995. *Franco: A Biography.* London: Fontana.

Preston, P., ed. 1984. *Revolution and War in Spain, 1931–1939.* London: Methuen.

Preti, L. 1968. "Fascist imperialism and racism." In R. Sarti (ed.), *The Ax Within: Italian Fascism in Action*. New York: New Viewpoints.

Preziosi, A. M. 1980. *Borghesia e fascismo in Friuli negli anni 1920–1922*. Roma: Bonacci.

Pridham, G. 1973. *Hitler's Rise to Power: The Nazi Movement in Bavaria, 1929–33*. London: Hart-Davies, McGibbon.

Poulantzas, N. 1974. *Fascism and Dictatorship*. London: New Left Books.

Pulzer, P. 1993. "The tradition of Austrian Antisemitism in the nineteenth and twentieth centuries." *Patterns of Prejudice* 27.

Rabinbach, A. (ed.). 1985. *The Austrian Socialist Experiment: Social Democracy and Austromarxism, 1918–1934*. Boulder, Colo.: Westview.

Ramírez Jiménez, M. 1969. *Los grupos de presión en la segunda república española*. Madrid: Technos.

Ránki, G. 1971. "The Problem of Fascism in Hungary." In Sugar (ed.), *Native Fascism*.

———. 1980. "The fascist vote in Budapest in 1939." In Larsen et al., (eds.), *Who Were the Fascists?*

Rath. J, and C. Schum. 1980. "The Dollfuss-Schusnigg Regime: Fascist or Authoritarian?" In Larsen et al. (eds.), *Who Were the Fascists?*

Reichardt, S. 2002. *Faschistische Kampfbünde*. Köln: Böhlau Verlag.

Renton, D. 2000. *Fascism: Theory and Practice*. London: Pluto.

Revelli, M. 1987. "Italy." In D. Mühlberger (ed.), *The Social Basis of European Fascist Movements*. London: CroomHelm.

Rial, J. 1986. *Revolution from Above: The Primo de Rivera Dictatorship in Spain, 1923–1930*. Fairfax, Va.: George Mason University Press.

Riley, D. 2002. "Hegemony and domination: civil society and regime variation in inter-war Europe." Ph.D. dissertation, University of California at Los Angeles.

Roberts, D. 1980. "Petty bourgeois Fascism in Italy: Form and content." In Larsen et al. (eds.), *Who Were the Fascists?*

Robinson, R. 1970. *The Origins of Franco's Spain: The Right, the Republic and Revolution, 1931–1936*. Newton Abbot: David & Charles.

Rogowski, R. 1977. "The *Gauleiter* and the social origins of Fascism." *Comparative Studies in Society and History* 19.

Rokkan, S. 1970. *Citizens, Elections, Parties: Approaches to the Comparative Study of the Process of Development*. Oslo: Scandinavian University Books.

Ronnas, P. 1984. *Urbanization in Romania*. Stockholm: Economic Research Institute, Stockholm School of Economics.

Rosenhaft, E. 1982. "The KPD in the Weimar Republic and the problem of terror during the 'Third Period,' 1929–33." In Mommsen and Hirschfeld (eds.), *Social Protest, Violence and Terror*.

———. 1983. *Beating the Fascists? The German Communists and Political Violence 1929–33*. Cambridge: Cambridge University Press.

———. 1987. "The unemployed in the neighbourhood: Social dislocation and political mobilisation in Germany 1929–1933." In R. Evans and D. Geary (eds.), *The German Unemployed: Experiences and Consequences of Mass Unemployment from the Weimar Republic to the Third Reich*. London: CroomHelm.

Rothschild, J. 1974. *East Central Europe between the Two World Wars*. Seattle: University of Washington Press.

Roy, O. 1994. *The Failure of Political Islam*. Cambridge, Mass.: Harvard University Press.

Rueschemeyer, D., E. Stephens, and J. Stephens 1992. *Capitalist Development and Democracy.* Chicago: University of Chicago Press.

Ságvári, A. 1997. "Did they do it under orders?" In R. Braham and A Pók (eds.), *The Holocaust in Hungary: Fifty Years Later.* New York: Columbia University Press.

Sakmyster, T. 1994. *Hungary's Admiral on Horseback: Miklos Horthy 1918–1944.* Boulder, Colo.: Colombia University Press.

Saladino, S. 1966. "Italy." In H. Rogger and E. Weber (eds.), *The European Right: A Historical Profile.* Berkeley: University of California Press.

Salvatorelli, L. 1923. *Nazional-fascismo.* Turin: Gobetti.

Salvemini, G. 1973. *The Origins of Fascism in Italy.* New York: Harper & Row.

Santacreu Soler, J. M., et al. 1986. "El anarchosindicalismo Alicantino durante la Segunda República." In Instituto de Estudios Juan Gil-Albert (ed.), *El anarquismo en Alicante (1868– 1945).* Alicante: Diputación Provincial.

Sarti, R. 1971. *Fascism and the Industrial Leadership in Italy, 1919–1940.* Berkeley and Los Angeles: University of California Press.

———. 1990. "Italian fascism: Radical politics and conservative goals." in M. Blinkhorn (ed.), *Fascists and Conservatives.* London: Unwin Hyman.

Schleunes, K. 1990. *The Twisted Road to Auschwitz: Nazi Policy toward German Jews, 1933– 1939,* 2nd ed. Urbana, Ill.: University of Illinois Press.

Schmidt-Hartmann, E. 1988. "People's democracy: The emergence of a Czech political concept in the late nineteenth century." In S. J. Kirschbaum (ed.), *East European History.* Columbus, Ohio: Slavica.

Schmitt, H. (ed.). 1988. *Neutral Europe between War and Revolution, 1917–1923.* Charlottesville: University of Virginia Press.

Schmitter, P. 1974. "Still the century of corporatism?" *Review of Politics.*

Schneider, W. 1978. *Die Deutsche Demokratische Partei in der Weimarer Republik 1924–1930.* Munich: Wilhelm Fink.

Schorske, C. 1981. *Fin-de-Siècle Vienna: Politics and Culture.* New York: Vintage.

Schwartz, R. 1989. "Nazi wooing of Austrian Social Democracy between Anschluss and war." In Parkinson (ed.), *Conquering the Past.*

Seco, C. 1971. "Introduction" to Gil Robles, *Discursos parlamentarios.* Madrid: Taurus.

Segrè, C. 1987. *Italo Balbo: A Fascist Life.* Berkeley and Los Angeles: University of California Press.

Sereny, G. 1995. *Albert Speer: His Battle with Truth.* London: Macmillan.

Seton-Watson, C. 1967. *Italy from Liberalism to Fascism.* London: Methuen.

Seton-Watson, H. 1967. *Eastern Europe between the Wars, 1918–1941.* New York: Harper.

Shapiro, P. 1974. "Prelude to dictatorship in Romania: The National Christian Party in power, December 1937–February 1938." *Canadian-American Slavic Studies* 8.

Shubert, A. 1987. *The Road to Revolution in Spain.* Urbana: University of Illinois Press.

Siegfried, K. J. 1979. *Klerikalfaschismus: Zur Entstehung und Sozialen Funktion des Dollfussregimes in Österreich.* Frankfurt: Lang.

Silverman, D. 1988. "National Socialist Economics: The *Wirtschaftswunder* Reconsidered." In B. Eichengreen and T. Hatton (eds.), *Interwar Unemployment in International Perspective.* Dordrecht: Kluwer.

Silvestri, C. 1969. "Storia del fascismo di Trieste dalle origini alla conquista del potere (1919–1922)." In *Fascismo, guerra, resistenza, lotte politiche e sociali nel Fruili-Venezia Guilia 1918–1943.* Udine: Del Bianco. '

Sima, H. 1967. *Histoire du mouvement légionnaire*. Rio de Janeiro: Editora Dacia.

Snowden, F. 1972. "On the social origins of agrarian fascism in Italy." *European Journal of Sociology* 13.

———. 1989. *The Fascist Revolution in Tuscany, 1919–1922*. Cambridge: Cambridge University Press.

Soucy, R. 1991. "French fascism and the Croix de Feu: A dissenting interpretation." *Journal of Contemporary History* 26, no. 1: 159–88.

Southern, D. 1982. "Anti-democratic terror in the Weimar Republic: The Black *Reichswehr* and the *Feme*-murders." In Mommsen and Hirschfeld (eds.), *Social Protest, Violence and Terror*.

Speier, H. 1986. *German White-Collar Workers and the Rise of Hitler*. New Haven, Conn.: Yale University Press.

Stachura, P. 1975. *Nazi Youth in the Weimar Republic*. Santa Barbara, Calif.: Clio Books.

———. 1983a. "German youth, the youth movement and national socialism in the Weimar Republic." In Stachura (ed.), *The Nazi Machtergreifung*.

———. 1983b. "The Nazis, the bourgeoisie and the workers during the *Kampfzeit*." In Stachura (ed.), *The Nazi Machtergreifung*.

———. 1993. "National Socialism and the German proletariat, 1925–1935: Old myths and new perspectives." *Historical Journal* 36.

Stachura P. (ed.) 1993c. *The Nazi Machtergreifung*. London: Allen & Unwin.

———. (ed.). 1986. *Unemployment and the Great Depression in Weimar Germany*. London: Macmillan.

Stadler, K. 1981. "Austria." In S. Woolf (ed.), *European Fascism*, 2nd ed. London: Weidenfeld & Nicolson.

Steinberg, J. 1986. "Fascism in the Italian South: The case of Calabria." In Forgacs (ed.), *Rethinking Italian Fascism*.

Steinhoff, J., et al. 1989. *Voices from the Third Reich: An Oral History*. New York: De Capo.

Stephan, W. 1973. *Aufstieg und Verfall des Linksliberalismus 1918–1933*. Göttingen: Vandenhoeck & Ruprecht.

Stephens, J. D. 1989. "Democratic transition and breakdown in Western Europe, 1870–1939: A test of the Moore thesis." *American Journal of Sociology* 94.

Sternhell, Z. 1976. "Fascist ideology." In Laqueur (ed.), *Fascism: A Reader's Guide*.

———. 1986. *Neither Right nor Left: Fascist Ideology in France*. Berkeley and Los Angeles: University of California Press.

———. 1994. *The Birth of Fascist Ideology*. Princeton, N.J.: Princeton University Press.

Stühlpfarrer, K. 1989. "Nazism, the Austrians and the military." In Parkinson (ed.), *Conquering the Past*.

Sturdza, P. 1968. *The Suicide of Europe: Memoirs of Prince Michel Sturdza, Former Foreign Minister of Rumania*. Belmont, Mass.: Western Islands.

Suarez Cortina, M. 1981. *El fascismo en Asturias (1931–1937)*. Madrid: Biblioteca Julia Somoza.

Suero Roca, T. 1975. *Los generales de Franco*. Barcelona: Bruguera.

———. 1981. *Militares republicanos de la guerra de España*. Barcelona: Peninsula.

Sugar, P. 1971a. "Conclusion." In Sugar (ed.), *Native Fascism*.

Sugar, P. (ed.). 1971b. *Native Fascism in the Successor States, 1918–1945*. Santa Barbara, Calif.: Clio Press.

Sühl, K. 1988. *SPD und öffentlicher Dienst in der Weimarer Republik*. Opladen: Westdeutscher.

Sully, M. 1989. "The Waldheim connection." In Parkinson (ed.), *Conquering the Past.*

Suzzi, Valli R. 2000. "The myth of squadrismo in the fascist regime." *Journal of Contemporary History* 35.

Sylos Labini, P. 1978. "Sviluppo economico e classi sociali." In M. Paci (ed.), *Capitalismo e classi sociali in Italia.* Bologna: Il Mulino.

Szelenyi, B. 1998. "German Burghers in Sixteenth-Nineteenth Century Hungary." Ph.D. dissertation, University of California, Los Angeles.

Sznajder, M. 1995. "The fascist regime, anti-semitism and the racial laws in Italy." In Wistrich and DellaPergola (eds.), *Fascist Antisemitism.*

Szöllösi-Janze, M. 1989. *Die Pfeilkreuzlerbewegung in Ungarn.* Munich: Oldenbourg.

Szymanski, A. 1973. "Fascism, industrialism and socialism: The case of Italy." *Comparative Studies in Society and History,* 15.

Taggart, P. 1995. "New populist parties in western Europe." *West European Politics* 18.

Tapia, A. R. 1990. "La justificacion ideologica del 'Alzamiento.' " In Tapia, *Violencia y terror: Estudios sobre la guerra civil española.* Torrejon de Ardoz: Akal.

Tasca, A. 1976. *The Rise of Italian Fascism, 1919–1922.* New York: Gordon Press. Originally published 1938. This edition, a reprint, was published under the pseudonym A. Rossi.

Therborn, G. 1977. "The rule of capital and the rise of democracy." *New Left Review,* no. 103.

Theweleit, K. 1987, 1989. *Male Fantasies,* 2 vols. Minneapolis: University of Minnesota Press.

Thomas, H. 1977. *The Spanish Civil War.* London: Eyre & Spottiswoode.

Tilly, C. 1975. *The Formation of National States in Western Europe.* Princeton, N.J.: Princeton University Press.

———. 1990. *Coercion, Capital and European States.* Oxford: Blackwell.

Townson, N. 1988. "Algunas consideraciones sobre el proyecto 'republicano' del Partido Radical." In Túñon de Lara (ed.), *La II república española.*

Treptow, K., et al. 1996. *A History of Romania.* New York: Columbia University Press.

Tuñón de Lara, M. 1972. *El movimiento obrero en la historia de España.* Madrid: Taurus.

———. 1978. *Luchas obreras y campesinas del siglo XX: Jaén (1917–1920), Sevilla (1930–1932).* Madrid: Siglo XXI.

———. 1985. *Tres claves de la segunda república.* Madrid: Alianza.

Tuñon de Lara, M. (ed.). 1988. *La II república española: Bienio rectificador y frente popular, 1934–1936.* Madrid: Siglo XXI.

Turner, H. A. 1985. *German Big Business and the Rise of Hitler.* New York: Oxford University Press.

Turner, H. A. (ed.). 1984. *Hitler – Memoir of a Confidant.* New Haven, Conn.: Yale University Press.

Tusell Gómez, J. 1970. *La segunda república en Madrid: Elecciones y partidos politicos.* Madrid: Technos.

———. 1971. *Las elecciones del frente popular en España.* Madrid: Cuadernos para el Dialogo.

———. 1974. *Historia de la democracia cristiana en España.* Madrid:

———. 1976. *Oligarquía y caciquismo en Andalucia (1890–1923).* Barcelona: Editorial Planeta.

Tusell Gómez, J., et al. 1993. *Estudios sobre la derechas espanola contemporanea.* Madrid: UNED.

Vago, R. 1987. "Eastern Europe." In D. Mühlberger, (ed.), *The Social Basis of European Fascist Movements.* London: CroomHelm.

Vago, R. (ed.) 1975. *The Shadow of the Swastika*. London: Saxon House.

Varela, Díaz, S. 1978. *Partidos y parlamento en la II república española*. Madrid: Fundación Juan March.

Vega, E. 1987. *Anarquistas y sindicalistas 1931–1936*. Valencia: Edicions Alfons el Magnánim.

Veiga, F. 1989. *La Mistica del Ultranacionalismo*. Barcelona: Universitat Autonomia de Barcelona.

Verdery, K. 1983. *Transylvanian Villagers: Three Centuries of Political, Economic and Ethnic Change*. Berkeley and Los Angeles: University of California Press.

Vilanova, M. 1986. *Atlas electoral de Catalunya durant la segona república*. Barcelona: Magrana.

Vincent, M. 1989. "The Spanish church and the Popular Front: The experience of Salamanca province." In Alexander and Graham (eds.), *French and Spanish Popular Fronts*.

Volovici, L. 1991. *Nationalist Ideology and Anti-Semitism: The Case of Romanian Intellectuals in the 1930s*. Oxford: Pergamon.

Watts, L. 1993. *Romanian Cassandra: Ion Antonescu and the Struggle for Reform, 1916–1941*. New York: Columbia University Press.

Weber, E. 1964. *Varieties of Fascism*. Princeton, N.J.: Van Nostrand.

———. 1966a. "The Men of the Archangel." *Journal of Contemporary History* 1.

———. 1966b. "Romania." In H. Rogger and E Weber (eds.), *The European Right: A Historical Profile*. London: Weidenfeld & Nicholson.

———. 1976. "Revolution? Counterrevolution? What revolution?" In W. Laqueur (ed.), *Fascism: A Reader's Guide*.

Weber, H. 1969. *Die Wandlung der deutschen Kommunismus*, 2 vols. Frankfurt: Europaische Verlagsanstalt.

Webster, A. 1986. "The Romanian Legionary Movement." *Carl Beck Papers, Center for Russian and East European Sudies, University of Pittsburgh*, no. 502.

Wegner, B. 1990. *The Waffen-SS*. Oxford: Blackwell.

Weinberg, L. 1998. "The MSI and the fascist heritage in Italy: The persistence of a neo-fascist party in the post fascist context." In Larsen and Hagtvet (eds.), *Modern Europe after Fascism*.

Weiss, L. 1988. *Creating Capitalism*. Oxford: Blackwell.

Weisbrod, B. 1996. "The crisis of bourgeois society in interwar Germany." In R. Bessel (ed.), *Fascist Italy and Nazi Germany: Comparisons and Contrasts*. Cambridge: Cambridge University Press.

Wessely, A. 1991. "From the labour movement to the Fascist Government: The End of the Road by Lajos Kassák." In S. Larsen et al. (eds.), *Fascism and European Literature*. Bern: Peter Lang.

Whiteside, A. 1966. "Austria." In H. Rogger and E. Weber (eds.), *The European Right: A Historical Profile*. Berkeley and Los Angeles: University of California Press.

Wickham, J. 1983. "Working-class movement and working-class life: Frankfurt am Main during the Weimar Republic." *Social History* 8.

Wieviorka, M. 1994. *Racisme et xénophobie en europe: Une comparaison internationale*. Paris: La Dévouverte.

Willems, H. 1995. "Right-wing extremism, race or youth violence? Explaining violence against foreigners in Germany." *New Community* 21:501–23.

Willson, P. 1996. "Women in Fascist Italy." In Bessel (ed.), *Fascist Italy and Nazi Germany*.

Wiltschegg, W. 1985. *Die Heimwehr*. Munich: Oldenbourg.

Wimmer, A. 1997. "Explaining racism and xenophobia: A critical review of current research approaches." *Ethnic and Racial Studies* 20:17–41.

Winston, C. 1985. *Workers and the Right in Spain, 1900–1936*. Princeton, N.J.: Princeton University Press.

Wistrich, R., and S. DellaPergola (eds.). 1995. *Fascist Antisemitism and the Italian Jews*. Jerusalem: Vidal Sassoon International Center.

Wohl, R. 1979. *The Generation of 1914*. Cambridge, Mass.: Harvard University Press.

Yavetz, Z. 1991. "An eyewitness note: Reflections on the Rumanian Iron Guard." *Journal of Contemporary History* 26.

Zach, K., and C. Zach. 1998. "Romanian fascism and communist take-over." In S. U. Larsen and B. Hagtvet (eds.), *Modern Europe after Fascism 1943–1980s*. New York: Columbia University Press.

Zamagni, V. 1979–80. "Distribuzione del reddito e classi sociali nell'Italia fra le due guerre." *Annali della Fondazione Giagiacomo Feltrinelli* 20.

Ziegler, H. 1989. *Nazi Germany's New Aristocracy. The SS Leadership, 1925–39*. Princeton, N.J.: Princeton University Press.

Zofka, Z. 1986. "Between Bauernbund and National Socialism: The political orientation of the peasants in the final phase of the Weimar Republic." In Childers (ed.), *The Formation of the Nazi Constituency*.

Zuccotti, S. 1987. *The Italians and the Holocaust*. New York: Basic Books.

Index

417